tURLOCK W9-CFH-441

YOUR Window TO History

Reading
like a Historian

Historians use paintings, like this detail of a Japanese folding screen from the 1700s, to help understand the past. As you study world history, you too will learn how to use different historical sources to **Read like a Historian.**

To find out more about reading like a historian and the historical sources that follow, visit

go.hrw.com
More Online
KEYWORD: HISTORIAN

By Frances Marie Gipson
Secondary Literacy Coordinator
Los Angeles Unified School District, Los Angeles, California

What Does It Mean to Read like a Historian?

In your history class you will be doing a lot of reading, thinking, and problem-solving. Much of your reading and thinking will center on different types of texts or materials. Since you are in a history class reading all sorts of things, a question to consider is, "What does it mean to think, read, and solve problems like a historian?"

Historians work with different types of sources to understand and learn from history. Two categories of sources are **primary** and **secondary** sources.

Primary Sources are historical documents, written accounts by a firsthand witness, or objects that have survived from the past. A study of primary sources might include letters, government documents, diaries, photographs, art objects, stamps, coins, and even clothing.

Secondary Sources are accounts of past events created by people some time after the events happened. This textbook and other books written about historical events are examples of secondary sources.

As you learn more about your work as a historian, you will begin to ask questions and analyze historical materials. You will be working as a detective, digging into history to create a richer understanding of the mysteries of the past.

How to Analyze an Artifact

Artifacts, such as this mask of an Aztec god, take many forms. They might be coins, stone tools, pieces of clothing, or even items found in your backpack. As you study artifacts in this textbook, ask yourself questions like the ones below.

- Why was this object created?

- When and where would it have been used?

- Who used the artifact?

- What does the artifact tell me about the technology available at the time it was created?

- What can it tell me about the life and times of the people who used it?

- How does the artifact help to make sense of the time period?

How to Analyze Written Sources

Magna Carta

"[17] Ordinary lawsuits shall not follow the royal court around, but shall be held in a fixed place . . .

[20] For a trivial offense, a free man shall be fined only in proportion to the degree of his offense, and for a serious offense correspondingly, but not so heavily as to deprive him of his livelihood . . .

[28] No constable or other royal official shall take corn or other movable goods from any man without immediate payment, unless the seller voluntarily offers postponement of this . . . "

– Magna Carta, 1215

Asking questions can help you determine the relevance and importance of primary sources such as Magna Carta, a document signed by King John of England in 1215 that limited the king's power. As you read the primary source above and the primary and secondary sources included in this textbook, ask yourself questions like the ones below.

- Who created the source and why?
- Did the writer have firsthand knowledge of the event, or report what others saw or heard?
- Was the writer a neutral party, or did the author have opinions or interests that might have influenced what was recorded?
- Did the writer wish to inform or persuade others?
- Was the information recorded during the event, immediately after the event, or after some lapse of time?

Timbuktu

ì Well placed for the caravan trade, it was badly situated to defend itself from the Tuareg raiders of the Sahara. These restless nomads were repeatedly hammering at the gates of Timbuktu, and often enough, they burst them open with disastrous results for the inhabitants. Life here was never quite safe enough to recommend it as the centre [center] of a big state.î

–Basil Davidson, from *A History of West Africa*

When reading secondary sources, such as the description of Timbuktu above, historians ask additional questions to seek understanding. They try to source the text, build evidence, and interpret the message that is being conveyed. For historians, reading is a quest to find evidence to answer or challenge a historical problem. As you study secondary sources, ask questions like the ones below.

Who is the author? What do I know about this author?

Did the author have firsthand information? What is the authorís relationship to the event?

What might be the authorís motivation in writing this piece?

What type of evidence did the author look at?

Are any assumptions or bias present?

How does this document fit into the larger context of the events I am studying?

What kind of source is it?

Is the source an original?

Is the content probable or reasonable?

What does the date tell me about the event?

What do I already know about this topic that will help me understand more of what I am reading?

How to Analyze a Historical Map

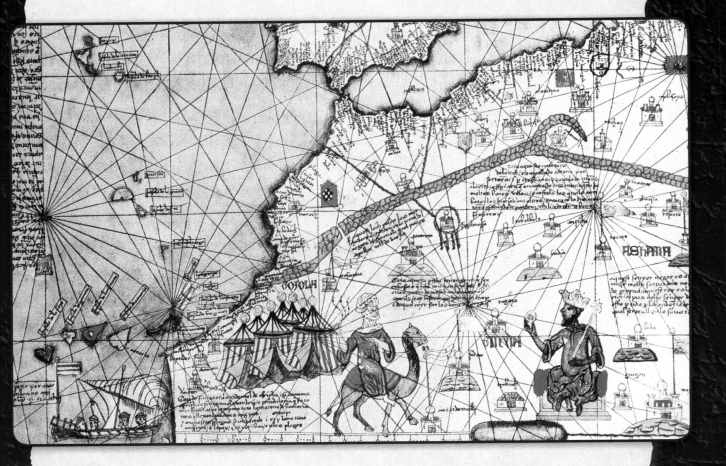

Maps are symbolic representations of places shown in relation to one another. The map above was created around 1375 in Spain and shows part of North Africa. All maps necessarily include some details and leave out others. As you study maps in this textbook, ask questions like the ones below.

- When and where was the map produced?

- What details has the mapmaker chosen to include (or exclude) on this map?

- Why was the map drawn?

- How can I determine if the map is accurate?

- How are maps used to analyze the past, present, and future?

How to Analyze Art

Art, like the tapestry above, which was created in the 1500s in France, is another important source for historians. One way to study a piece of art is to write down everything that you think is important about it. Then divide the image into four sections and describe the important elements from each section. As you study art in this textbook, ask questions like the ones below.

- What is the setting for the art?
- When and where in the past was the art created?
- What is the subject of the art?
- What other details can I observe?
- What does the art reveal about its subject?
- How can I describe the artist's point of view?

How to Analyze an Infographic

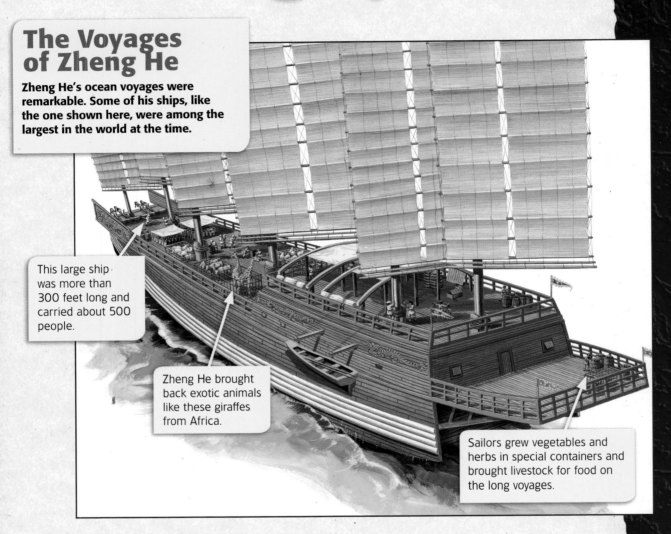

The Voyages of Zheng He

Zheng He's ocean voyages were remarkable. Some of his ships, like the one shown here, were among the largest in the world at the time.

This large ship was more than 300 feet long and carried about 500 people.

Zheng He brought back exotic animals like these giraffes from Africa.

Sailors grew vegetables and herbs in special containers and brought livestock for food on the long voyages.

Infographics give you information in a visual format, using captions and call-out boxes to help explain the intent of the drawing. As you study infographics in this textbook, use the helpful tips and questions below.

- List the parts of the drawing and the importance of each part.
- Describe the focus or significance of the drawing.
- Do the captions and call-out boxes clarify the drawing's purpose?
- Does the drawing help me understand the information that I am studying in my textbook better?

HOLT

CALIFORNIA SOCIAL STUDIES

WORLD HISTORY

Medieval
to Early Modern Times

Stanley M. Burstein

Richard Shek

HOLT, RINEHART AND WINSTON

A Harcourt Education Company

Orlando • Austin • New York • San Diego • Toronto • London

Authors

Dr. Stanley M. Burstein

Dr. Stanley M. Burstein is Professor Emeritus of Ancient History and former Chair of the Department of History at California State University, Los Angeles. Dr. Burstein received his B.A., M.A., and Ph.D. degrees from the University of California at Los Angeles and is the author of more than 100 books, articles, and chapters on ancient history. His specialties include ancient Greece, Greek and Roman Egypt, and Kush. Dr. Burstein has served as President of the Association of Ancient Historians and as a member of the California History–Social Science Standards/Course Models Project, the California Content Review Panel for History–Social Science, and the Content Review Panel for the California STAR test in history.

Dr. Richard Shek

Dr. Richard Shek is Professor of Humanities and Religious Studies at California State University, Sacramento. A native of China, Dr. Shek did his undergraduate work in Tokyo, Japan, and received his Ph.D. in history from the University of California at Berkeley. His specialties are East Asian cultural and religious history, and he has numerous publications on Confucianism, Daoism, Buddhism, and popular religion in China and Japan. Dr. Shek has served as a member of the California Content Review Panel for History–Social Science and is currently a member of the Content Review Panel for the California STAR test in history.

Copyright © 2006 by Holt, Rinehart and Winston

All rights reserved. No part of this publication may be reproduced or transmitted in any form or by any means, electronic or mechanical, including photocopy, recording, or any information storage and retrieval system, without permission in writing from the publisher.

Requests for permission to make copies of any part of the work should be mailed to the following address: Permissions Department, Holt, Rinehart and Winston, 10801 N. MoPac Expressway, Building 3, Austin, Texas 78759.

For acknowledgments, see page R81, which is an extension of the copyright page.

HOLT and the "Owl Design" are trademarks licensed to Holt, Rinehart and Winston, registered in the United States of America and/or other jurisdictions.

Printed in the United States of America

If you have received these materials as examination copies free of charge, Holt, Rinehart and Winston retains title to the materials and they may not be resold. Resale of examination copies is strictly prohibited.

Possession of this publication in print format does not entitle users to convert this publication, or any portion of it, into electronic format.

ISBN 0-03-073399-5

4 5 6 7 8 9 032 11 10 09 08 07 06

Program Consultants

Contributing Author

Kylene Beers, Ed.D.
Senior Reading Researcher
School Development Program
Yale University
New Haven, Connecticut

General Editor

Frances Marie Gipson
Secondary Literacy
Los Angeles Unified School
  District
Los Angeles, California

Senior Literature and Writing Specialist

Carol Jago
English Department Chairperson
Santa Monica High School
Santa Monica, California

Consultants

John Ferguson, M.T.S., J.D.
Senior Religion Consultant
Assistant Professor
Political Science/Criminal Justice
Howard Payne University
Brownwood, Texas

Rabbi Gary M. Bretton-Granatoor
Religion Consultant
Director of Interfaith Affairs
Anti-Defamation League
New York, New York

J. Frank Malaret
Senior Consultant
Dean, Downtown and West
  Sacramento Outreach Centers
Sacramento City College
Sacramento, California

Kimberly A. Plummer, M.A.
Senior Consultant
History-Social Science Educator/
  Advisor
Holt, Rinehart and Winston
California Consultant Manager

Andrés Reséndez, Ph.D.
Senior Consultant
Assistant Professor
Department of History
University of California at Davis
Davis, California

California Specialists

Ann Cerny, M.A.
Middle School History Teacher
San Dieguito Union High School
  District
Solana Beach, California

Julie Chan, Ed.D.
Director, Literacy Instruction
Newport-Mesa Unified School
  District
Costa Mesa, California

Gary F. DeiRossi, Ed.D.
Assistant Superintendent
San Joaquin County Office of
  Education
Stockton, California

Fern M. Sheldon, M.Ed.
Curriculum Specialist
Rowland Unified School District
Rowland Heights, California

California Program Advisors

The California program consultants and reviewers included on these pages provided guidance throughout the development of Holt California Social Studies: *World History: Medieval to Early Modern Times.* As the map below demonstrates, their valuable contributions represent the viewpoints of teachers throughout California.

Educational Reviewers

Anne Bjornson
A.P. Giannini Middle School
San Francisco, California

Michael Bloom
Ross School
Ross, California

Anthony Braxton
Herbert H. Cruickshank
   Middle School
Merced, California

Ann Cerny, M.A.
Middle School History Teacher
San Dieguito Union High School
   District
Solana Beach, California

Julie Chan, Ed.D.
Director, Literacy Instruction
Newport-Mesa Unified School
   District
Costa Mesa, California

Mary Demetrion
Patrick Henry Middle School
Los Angeles, California

Charlyn Earp
Mesa Verde Middle School
San Diego, California

Carla Freel
Hoover Middle School
Merced, California

Tim Gearhart
Daniel Lewis Middle School
Paso Robles, California

Frances Marie Gipson
Secondary Literacy
Los Angeles Unified School
   District
Los Angeles, California

Carol Jago
English Department Chairperson
Santa Monica High School
Santa Monica, California

Wendy Larson
La Loma Jr. High
Modesto, California

J. Frank Malaret
Senior Consultant
Dean, Downtown and West
   Sacramento Outreach Centers
Sacramento City College
Sacramento, California

Vicki Matthews
Elsinore Middle School
Lake Elsinore, California

Kimberly A. Plummer, M.A.
Senior Consultant
History-Social Science Educator/
   Advisor
Holt, Rinehart & Winston
California Consultant Manager

Andrés Reséndez, Ph.D.
Senior Consultant
Assistant Professor
Department of History
University of California at Davis
Davis, California

Sacramento
Fairfield   Elk Grove
Ross   Davis
San Francisco
Modesto
Merced
Paso Robles
Los Angeles   Rowland Heights
Santa Monica   Corona
Torrance   Lake Elsinore
Laguna Niguel   Costa Mesa
Solana Beach   La Mesa
San Diego

Fern M. Sheldon, M.Ed.
Curriculum Specialist
Rowland Unified School District
Rowland Heights, California

Joseph Snedeker
Niguel Hills Middle School
Laguna Niguel, California

Heidi Wajda
Raney Intermediate
Corona, California

Field Test Teachers

Debby Bonner
Dover Middle School
Fairfield, California

Tom Funk
Toby Johnson Middle School
Elk Grove, California

Ann Larkin
La Mesa Middle School
La Mesa, California

Sherry Marchant
Toby Johnson Middle School
Elk Grove, California

Gary Moore
Casimir Middle School
Torrance, California

Academic Reviewers

Jonathan Beecher, Ph.D.
Department of History
University of California, Santa Cruz

Jerry H. Bentley, Ph.D.
Department of History
University of Hawaii

Elizabeth Brumfiel, Ph.D.
Department of Anthropology
Northwestern University
Evanston, Illinois

Eugene Cruz-Uribe, Ph.D.
Department of History
Northern Arizona University

Toyin Falola, Ph.D.
Department of History
University of Texas

Sandy Freitag, Ph.D.
Director, Monterey Bay History
   and Cultures Project
Division of Social Sciences
University of California, Santa Cruz

Yasuhide Kawashima, Ph.D.
Department of History
University of Texas at El Paso

Robert J. Meier, Ph.D.
Department of Anthropology
Indiana University

Marc Van De Mieroop, Ph.D.
Department of History
Columbia University
New York, New York

M. Gwyn Morgan, Ph.D.
Department of History
University of Texas

Robert Schoch, Ph.D.
CGS Division of Natural Science
Boston University

David Shoenbrun, Ph.D.
Department of History
Northwestern University
Evanston, Illinois

Meet the Sikhs is a video that discusses the Sikh community in northern California. Starting with an annual Sikh celebration, the video provides an overview of the Sikh community, including the foundation of its religious beliefs and attire, immigration patterns, and the accomplishments of community members. The video can be downloaded for educational purposes only, and admission cannot be charged for any viewing of the piece. This video is available in QuickTime format at the KVIE Web site at http://www.kvie.org/education/outreachservices/.

Contents

UNIT 1 Connecting with Past Learnings 1

CHAPTER 1 Studying the Ancient World 2

California Standards

Analysis Skills
HI 5 Recognize that interpretations of history are subject to change as new information is uncovered.

History's Impact Video Series
The Impact of Archaeology

 California Standards

History–Social Science
7.1 Students analyze the causes and effects of the vast expansion and ultimate disintegration of the Roman Empire.

Analysis Skills
HI 4 Recognize the role of chance, oversight, and error in history.

 History's Impact Video Series
The Impact of Ancient Rome on the World Today

 California Standards

History–Social Science
7.4 Students analyze the geographic, political, economic, religious, and social structures of the sub-Saharan civilizations of Ghana and Mali in Medieval Africa.

 History's Impact Video Series
The Impact of the Salt Trade

 California Standards

History–Social Science

7.4 Students analyze the geographic, political, economic, religious, and social structures of the sub-Saharan civilizations of Ghana and Mali in Medieval Africa.

Analysis Skills

CS 3 Use a variety of maps to explain the expansion and disintegration of empires.

HR 2 Distinguish fact from opinion.

History's Impact Video Series
The Impact of the Salt Trade

 California Standards

History–Social Science

7.6 Students analyze the geographic, political, economic, religious, and social structures of the civilizations of Medieval Europe.

Analysis Skills

HR 4 Analyze primary and secondary sources.

 History's Impact Video Series
The Impact of the Feudal System in Europe

 California Standards

History–Social Science
7.8 Students analyze the origins, accomplishments, and geographic diffusion of the Renaissance.

Analysis Skills
CS 3 Use maps to identify the migration of people and the growth of economic systems.

 History's Impact Video Series
The Impact of the Renaissance and Reformation

 California Standards

History–Social Science
7.7 Students compare and contrast the geographic, political, economic, religious, and social structures of the Meso-American and Andean civilizations.

Analysis Skills
HR 3 Distinguish relevant from irrelevant, essential from incidental, and verifiable from unverifiable information.

 History's Impact Video Series
The Impact of Mayan Achievements on Math and Astronomy

 CHAPTER 15 **The Aztec and Inca Empires** 406

California Standards

History–Social Science

7.7 Students compare and contrast the geographic, political, economic, religious, and social structures of the Meso-American and Andean civilizations.

Analysis Skills

CS 3 Use maps to identify cultural features of neighborhoods, cities, states, and countries.

 History's Impact Video Series
The Impact of Mayan Achievements on Math and Astronomy

UNIT 8 The Early Modern World 440

 California Standards

History–Social Science
7.11 Students analyze political and economic change in the sixteenth, seventeenth, and eighteenth centuries (the Age of Exploration, the Enlightenment, and the Age of Reason).

Analysis Skills
HI 1 Explain central issues and problems from the past.

 History's Impact Video Series
The Impact of the Columbian Exchange on Europe and America

CHAPTER 17 **Enlightenment and Revolution** **470**

THE GRANGER COLLECTION, NEW YORK

 California Standards

History–Social Science

7.11 Students analyze political and economic change in the sixteenth, seventeenth, and eighteenth centuries (the Age of Exploration, the Enlightenment, and the Age of Reason).

Analysis Skills

HR 5 Detect different historical points of view on historical events.

HI 3 Explain the sources of historical continuity and how the combination of ideas and events explains the emergence of new patterns.

History's Impact Video Series
The Impact of the Declaration of Independence on America Today

Features

History and Geography

Explore the relationships between history and geography around the world.

Literature in History

Learn about people who lived in other times and places in excerpts from literature.

Charlemagne

BIOGRAPHIES

Meet the people who have influenced history and learn about their lives.

Charts, Graphics, and Time Lines

Analyze information presented visually to learn more about history.

Priests led religious ceremonies from the tops of temples.

QUICK FACTS

Examine key facts and concepts quickly and easily with graphics.

History Close-up

See how people lived and how places looked in the past by taking a close-up view of history.

LINKING TO TODAY

Link people and cultures from the past to the world around you today.

Points of View

See how different people have interpreted historical issues in different ways.

Historic Documents

Examine key documents that have shaped world history.

Social Studies Skills

Learn, practice, and apply the skills you need to study and analyze history.

Reading Social Studies

Learn and practice skills that will help you read your social studies lessons.

Writing Workshop

Learn to write about history.

FOCUS ON WRITING

Use writing to study and reflect on the events and people who made history.

FOCUS ON SPEAKING

Use speaking skills to study and reflect on the events and people who made history.

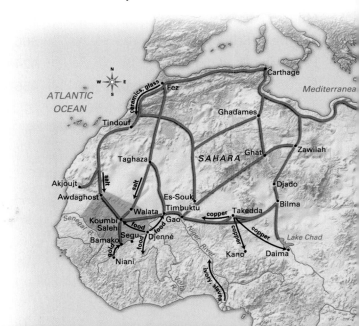

Maps

Interpret maps to see where important events happened and analyze how geography has influenced history.

Primary Sources

Relive history through eyewitness accounts, literature, and documents.

Mapping the Earth

A **globe** is a scale model of the earth. It is useful for showing the entire earth or studying large areas of the earth's surface.

A pattern of lines circles the globe in east-west and north-south directions. It is called a **grid**. The intersection of these imaginary lines helps us find places on the earth.

The east-west lines in the grid are lines of **latitude**. Lines of latitude are called **parallels** because they are always parallel to each other. These imaginary lines measure distance north and south of the **equator**. The equator is an imaginary line that circles the globe halfway between the North and South Poles. Parallels measure distance from the equator in **degrees**. The symbol for degrees is °. Degrees are further divided into **minutes**. The symbol for minutes is ´. There are 60 minutes in a degree. Parallels north of the equator are labeled with an N. Those south of the equator are labeled with an S.

The north-south lines are lines of **longitude**. Lines of longitude are called **meridians**. These imaginary lines pass through the Poles. They measure distance east and west of the **prime meridian**. The prime meridian is an imaginary line that runs through Greenwich, England. It represents 0° longitude.

Lines of latitude range from 0°, for locations on the equator, to 90°N or 90°S, for locations at the Poles. Lines of longitude range from 0° on the prime meridian to 180° on a meridian in the mid-Pacific Ocean. Meridians west of the prime meridian to 180° are labeled with a W. Those east of the prime meridian to 180° are labeled with an E.

Lines of Latitude

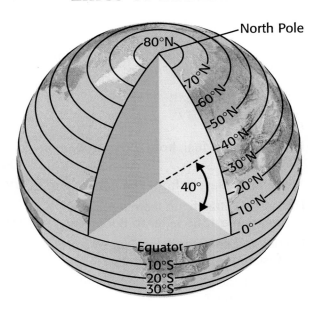

Lines of Longitude

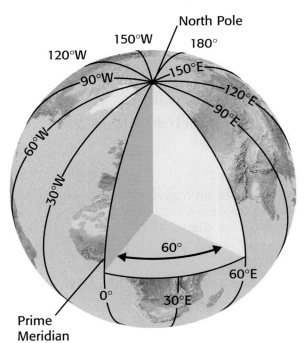

The equator divides the globe into two halves, called **hemispheres**. The half north of the equator is the Northern Hemisphere. The southern half is the Southern Hemisphere. The prime meridian and the 180° meridian divide the world into the Eastern Hemisphere and the Western Hemisphere. However, the prime meridian runs right through Europe and Africa. To avoid dividing these continents between two hemispheres, some mapmakers divide the Eastern and Western hemispheres at 20°W. This places all of Europe and Africa in the Eastern Hemisphere.

Our planet's land surface is divided into seven large landmasses, called **continents**. They are identified in the maps on this page. Landmasses smaller than continents and completely surrounded by water are called **islands**.

Geographers also organize Earth's water surface into parts. The largest is the world ocean. Geographers divide the world ocean into the Pacific Ocean, the Atlantic Ocean, the Indian Ocean, and the Arctic Ocean. Lakes and seas are smaller bodies of water.

Northern Hemisphere

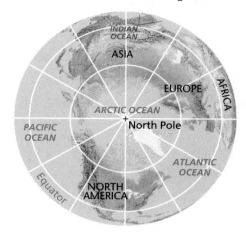

Southern Hemisphere

Western Hemisphere

Eastern Hemisphere

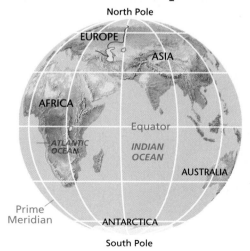

Mapmaking

A **map** is a flat diagram of all or part of the earth's surface. Mapmakers have created different ways of showing our round planet on flat maps. These different ways are called **map projections**. Because the earth is round, there is no way to show it accurately in a flat map. All flat maps are distorted in some way. Mapmakers must choose the type of map projection that is best for their purposes. Many map projections are one of three kinds: cylindrical, conic, or flat-plane.

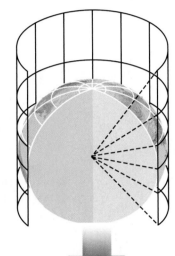

Paper cylinder

Cylindrical Projections

Cylindrical projections are based on a cylinder wrapped around the globe. The cylinder touches the globe only at the equator. The meridians are pulled apart and are parallel to each other instead of meeting at the Poles. This causes landmasses near the Poles to appear larger than they really are. The map below is a Mercator projection, one type of cylindrical projection. The Mercator projection is useful for navigators because it shows true direction and shape. However, it distorts the size of land areas near the Poles.

Mercator projection

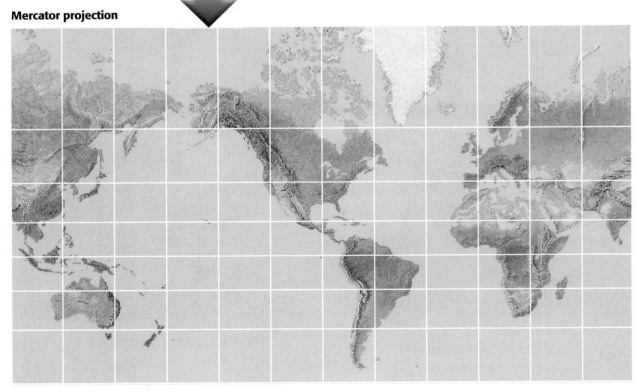

❷ Compass Rose

A directional indicator shows which way north, south, east, and west lie on the map. Some mapmakers use a "north arrow," which points toward the North Pole. Remember, "north" is not always at the top of a map. The way a map is drawn and the location of directions on that map depend on the perspective of the mapmaker. Most maps in this textbook indicate direction by using a compass rose. A **compass rose** has arrows that point to all four principal directions, as shown.

❸ Scale

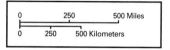

Mapmakers use scales to represent the distances between points on a map. Scales may appear on maps in several different forms. The maps in this textbook provide a bar **scale**. Scales give distances in miles and kilometers.

To find the distance between two points on the map, place a piece of paper so that the edge connects the two points. Mark the location of each point on the paper with a line or dot. Then, compare the distance between the two dots with the map's bar scale. The number on the top of the scale gives the distance in miles. The number on the bottom gives the distance in kilometers. Because the distances are given in large intervals, you may have to approximate the actual distance on the scale.

❹ Legend

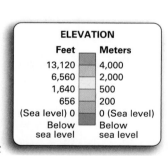

The **legend**, or key, explains what the symbols on the map represent. Point symbols are used to specify the location of things, such as cities, that do not take up much space on the map. Some legends, such as the one shown here, show colors that represent certain elevations. Other maps might have legends with symbols or colors that represent things such as roads. Legends can also show economic resources, land use, population density, and climate.

❺ Locator Map

A locator map shows where in the world the area on the map is located. The area shown on the main map is shown in red on the locator map. The locator map also shows surrounding areas so the map reader can see how the information on the map relates to neighboring lands.

Working with Maps

The Atlas at the back of this textbook includes both physical and political maps. Physical maps, like the one you just saw, show the major physical features in a region. These features include things like mountain ranges, rivers, oceans, islands, deserts, and plains. Political maps show the major political features of a region, such as countries and their borders, capitals, and other important cities.

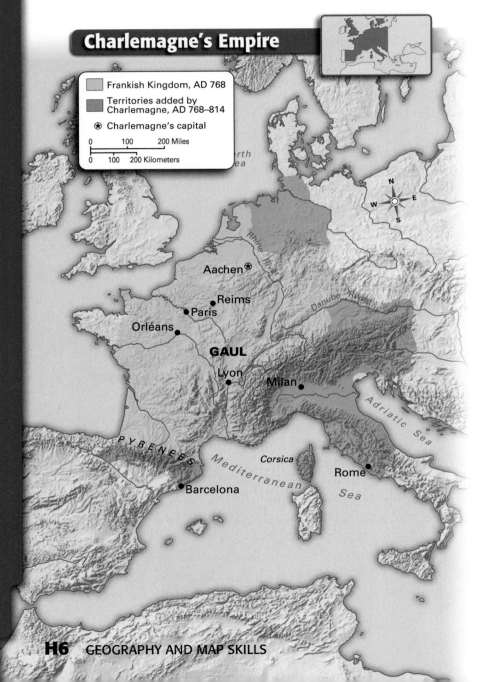

Charlemagne's Empire

Frankish Kingdom, AD 768

Territories added by Charlemagne, AD 768–814

⊛ Charlemagne's capital

0   100   200 Miles
0   100   200 Kilometers

North Sea

Rhine River

Aachen ⊛

Reims
Paris
Orléans

GAUL

Lyon

Milan

Danube River

Adriatic Sea

PYRENEES
Mediterranean
Corsica
Rome
Barcelona
Sea

Historical Map

In this textbook, most of the maps you will study are historical maps. Historical maps, such as this one, are maps that show information about the past. This information might be which lands an empire controlled, where a certain group of people lived, what large cities were located in a region, or how a place changed over time. Often colors are used to indicate the different things on the map. Be sure to look at the map title and map legend first to see what the map is showing. What does this map show?

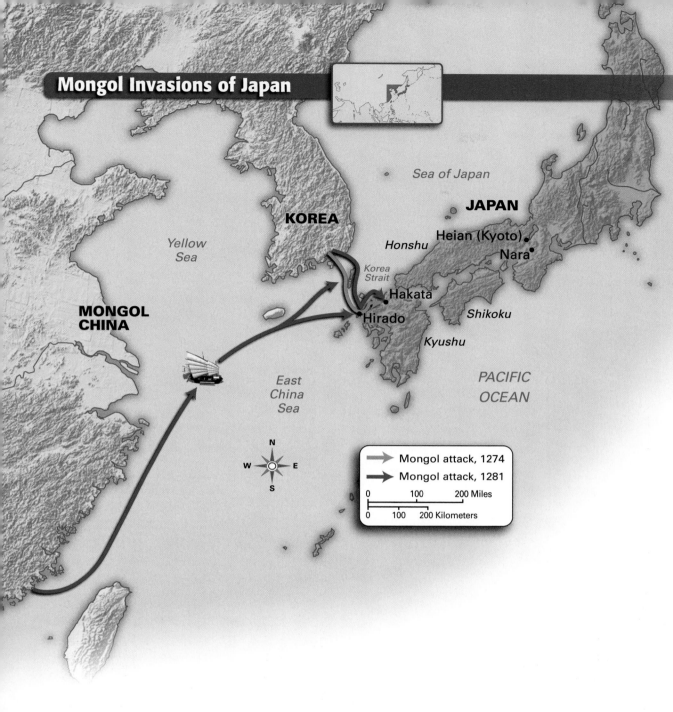

Mongol Invasions of Japan

KOREA

Sea of Japan

JAPAN

Honshu

Heian (Kyoto)

Nara

Yellow
Sea

Korea
Strait

Hakata

MONGOL
CHINA

Hirado

Shikoku

Kyushu

East
China
Sea

PACIFIC
OCEAN

N
W—◯—E
S

Mongol attack, 1274
Mongol attack, 1281

0   100   200 Miles
0   100   200 Kilometers

Route Map

One special type of historical map is called a route map. A route map, like the one above, shows the route, or path, that someone or something followed. Route maps can show things like trade routes, invasion routes, or the journeys and travels of people. The routes on the map are usually shown with an arrow. If more than one route is shown, several arrows of different colors may be used. What does this route map show?

The maps in this textbook will help you study and understand history. By working with these maps, you will see where important events happened, where empires rose and fell, and where people moved. In studying these maps, you will learn how geography has influenced history.

Geographic Dictionary

OCEAN
a large body of water

CORAL REEF
an ocean ridge made up of skeletal remains of tiny sea animals

GULF
a large part of the ocean that extends into land

PENINSULA
an area of land that sticks out into a lake or ocean

ISTHMUS
a narrow piece of land connecting two larger land areas

BAY
part of a large body of water that is smaller than a gulf

ISLAND
an area of land surrounded entirely by water

DELTA
an area where a river deposits soil into the ocean

STRAIT
a narrow body of water connecting two larger bodies of water

SINKHOLE
a circular depression formed when the roof of a cave collapses

WETLAND
an area of land covered by shallow water

RIVER
a natural flow of water that runs through the land

LAKE
an inland body of water

FOREST
an area of densely wooded land

COAST
an area of land
near the ocean

MOUNTAIN
an area of rugged
land that generally
rises higher than
2,000 feet

VALLEY
an area of low
land between
hills or mountains

GLACIER
a large area of
slow-moving ice

VOLCANO
an opening in Earth's crust
where lava, ash, and gases erupt

CANYON
a deep, narrow valley
with steep walls

HILL
a rounded, elevated
area of land smaller
than a mountain

PLAIN
a nearly
flat area

DUNE
a hill of sand
shaped by wind

OASIS
an area in the
desert with a
water source

DESERT
an extremely dry area with
little water and few plants

PLATEAU
a large, flat,
elevated
area of land

The Five Themes of Geography

Geography is the study of the world's people and places. As you can imagine, studying the entire world is a big job. To make the job easier, geographers have created the Five Themes of Geography. They are: **Location, Place, Human-Environment Interaction, Movement,** and **Region**. You can think of the Five Themes as five windows you can look through to study a place. If you looked at the same place through five different windows, you would have five different perspectives, or viewpoints, of the place. Using the Five Themes in this way will help you better understand the world's people and places.

1 Location The first thing to study about a place is its location. Where is it? Every place has an absolute location—its exact location on Earth. A place also has a relative location—its location in relation to other places. Use the theme of location to ask questions like, "Where is this place located, and how has its location affected it?"

2 Place Every place in the world is unique and has its own personality and character. Some things that can make a place unique include its weather, plants and animals, history, and the people that live there. Use the theme of place to ask questions like, "What are the unique features of this place, and how are they important?"

3 Human-Environment Interaction
People interact with their environment in many ways. They use land to grow food and local materials to build houses. At the same time, a place's environment influences how people live. For example, if the weather is cold, people wear warm clothes. Use the theme of human-environment interaction to ask questions like, "What is this place's environment like, and how does it affect the people who live there?"

4 Movement The world is constantly changing, and places are affected by the movement of people, goods, ideas, and physical forces. For example, people come and go, new businesses begin, and rivers change their course. Use the theme of movement to ask questions like, "How is this place changing, and why?"

5 Region A region is an area that has one or more features that make it different from surrounding areas. A desert, a country, and a coastal area are all regions. Geographers use regions to break the world into smaller pieces that are easier to study. Use the theme of region to ask questions like "What common features does this area share, and how is it different from other areas?"

Canada

LOCATION
Most of the United States is located in the Western Hemisphere, north of Mexico and south of Canada. This location has good farmland, many resources, and many different natural environments.

United States

Mexico

PLACE
New York City is one of the most powerful cities in the world. The people of New York also make the city one of the most ethnically diverse places in the world.

HUMAN-ENVIRONMENT INTERACTION
People near Las Vegas, Nevada, transform the desert landscape by building new neighborhoods. Americans modify their environment in many other ways—by controlling rivers, building roads, and creating farmland.

REGION
The United States is a political region with one government. At the same time, smaller regions can be found inside the country, such as the Badlands in South Dakota.

MOVEMENT
People, goods, and ideas are constantly moving to and from places such as Seattle, Washington. As some places grow, others get smaller, but every place is always changing.

Become an Active Reader

by Dr. Kylene Beers

Did you ever think you would begin reading your social studies book by reading about reading? Actually, it makes better sense than you might think. You would probably make sure you learned some soccer skills and strategies before playing in a game. Similarly, you need to learn some reading skills and strategies before reading your social studies book. In other words, you need to make sure you know whatever you need to know in order to read this book successfully..

Tip #1
Use the Reading Social Studies Pages

Take advantage of the two pages on reading at the beginning of every chapter. Those pages introduce the chapter themes; explain a reading skill or strategy; and identify key terms, people, and academic vocabulary.

Themes

Why are themes important? They help our minds organize facts and information. For example, when we talk about baseball, we may talk about types of pitches. When we talk about movies, we may discuss animation.

Historians are no different. When they discuss history or social studies, they tend to think about some common themes: Economics, Geography, Religion, Politics, Society and Culture, and Science and Technology.

Reading Skill or Strategy

Good readers use a number of skills and strategies to make sure they understand what they are reading. These lessons will give you the tools you need to read and understand social studies.

Key Terms, People, and Academic Vocabulary

Before you read the chapter, review these words and think about them. Have you heard the word before? What do you already know about the people? Then watch for these words and their meanings as you read the chapter.

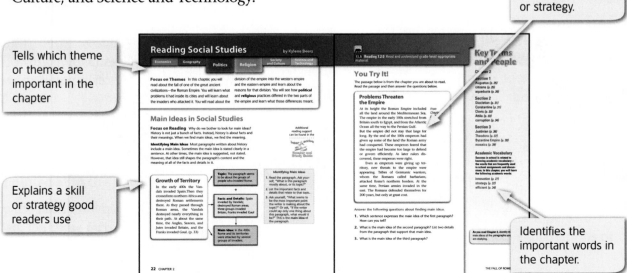

Tells which theme or themes are important in the chapter

Explains a skill or strategy good readers use

Gives you practice in the reading skill or strategy.

Identifies the important words in the chapter.

Read like a Skilled Reader

You will never get better at reading your social studies book—or any book for that matter—unless you spend some time thinking about how to be a better reader.

Skilled readers do the following:

- They preview what they are supposed to read before they actually begin reading. They look for vocabulary words, titles of sections, information in the margin, or maps or charts they should study.

- They divide their notebook paper into two columns. They title one column "Notes from the Chapter" and the other column "Questions or Comments I Have."

- They take notes in both columns as they read.

- They read like **active readers**. The Active Reading list below shows you what that means.

- They use clues in the text to help them figure out where the text is going. The best clues are called signal words.

  Chronological Order Signal Words: *first, second, third, before, after, later, next, following that, earlier, finally*

  Cause and Effect Signal Words: *because of, due to, as a result of, the reason for, therefore, consequently*

  Comparison/Contrast Signal Words: *likewise, also, as well as, similarly, on the other hand*

Active Reading

Successful readers are **active readers**. These readers know that it is up to them to figure out what the text means. Here are some steps you can take to become an active, and successful, reader.

Predict what will happen next based on what has already happened. When your predictions don't match what happens in the text, re-read the confusing parts.

Question what is happening as you read. Constantly ask yourself why things have happened, what things mean, and what caused certain events.

Summarize what you are reading frequently. Do not try to summarize the entire chapter! Read a bit and then summarize it. Then read on.

Connect what is happening in the part you're reading to what you have already read.

Clarify your understanding. Stop occasionally to ask yourself whether you are confused by anything. You may need to re-read to clarify, or you may need to read further and collect more information before you can understand.

Visualize what is happening in the text. Try to see the events or places in your mind by drawing maps, making charts, or jotting down notes about what you are reading.

Tip #3

Pay Attention to Vocabulary

It is no fun to read something when you don't know what the words mean, but you can't learn new words if you only use or read the words you already know. In this book, we know we have probably used some words you don't know. But, we have followed a pattern as we have used more difficult words.

Key Terms and People

At the beginning of each section you will find a list of key terms or people that you will need to know. Be on the lookout for those words as you read through the section.

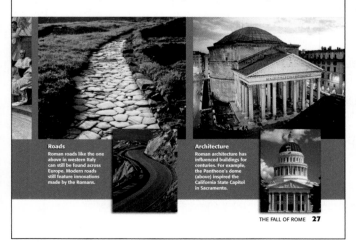

The Enlightenment's Roots

The main ideas of the Enlightenment had their roots in other eras. Enlightenment thinkers looked back to the Greeks, Romans, and the history of Christianity. The Renaissance, Reformation, and Scientific Revolution provided ideas also.

Greek and Roman Philosophers

Enlightenment thinkers used ideas from the ancient Greeks and Romans. Greek philosophers had observed an order and regularity in the natural world. Aristotle, for example, taught that people could use logic to discover new truths. Building on Greek ideas, Roman thinkers developed the concept of natural law, the idea that a law governed how the world operated.

With Greek and Roman beliefs as guidelines, Enlightenment thinkers began studying the world in a new way. They applied these beliefs not just to the natural world but also to the human world of society and government.

Christianity

The history of Christianity in Europe provides other clues about ideas that emerged in the Enlightenment. One theologian, Thomas Aquinas, had taught in the Middle Ages that faith paired with reason could explain the world. Although it was indebted to Aquinas, the Enlightenment was mostly a **secular**, or non-religious, movement. Enlightenment thinkers disliked its intolerance toward non-Christian beliefs.

The Renaissance and Reformation

Other reactions to the Christian Church in Europe also influenced the ideas of the Enlightenment. For example, some Renaissance thinkers used Greek and Roman ideas to raise questions about established religious beliefs. These Renaissance thinkers were known as humanists.

Although most humanists were religious, they focused on human value and achievement rather than the glory of God.

The use of reason advanced science and technology, which in turn influenced the Enlightenment. Here, the Italian scientist Alessandro Volta explains a new invention, the battery.

475

...o Aquinas, the Enlightenme... a **secular**, or non-religious, ... Enlightenment thinkers disag...

The skill of ancient Roman engineers inspired many later people to copy their techniques. For example, some builders still design stadiums in much the same way Roman engineers did. In fact, many techniques engineers and architects use today were directly inspired by the Roman engineers of 2,000 years ago.

Architecture

Architecture, the art of designing buildings, is closely related to engineering. Roman architects and engineers used many of the same ideas. They constantly sought ways to make larger, stronger buildings.

In addition to being large and strong, however, Roman architects wanted their buildings to be beautiful. Because they admired the beauty of ancient Greek

structures, they borrowed Greek ideas. For example, like the Greeks, the Romans used columns and open spaces to make their buildings look elegant and majestic. But the Romans added an **innovation** of their own. They used their engineering skills to make buildings larger and grander than anything the Greeks had built.

Later civilizations greatly admired the Roman architectural style, copying many elements of Roman design in their own buildings. Elements of Roman design are seen in many public buildings even today.

Art

Architecture was not the only field in which the Romans were inspired by the Greeks. Roman works of art also borrowed heavily from earlier Greek examples.

ACADEMIC VOCABULARY
innovation
(i-nuh-vr-shuhn) a new idea or way of doing something

Roads
Roman roads like the one above in western Italy can still be found across Europe. Modern roads still feature innovations made by the Romans.

Architecture
Roman architecture has influenced buildings for centuries. For example, the Pantheon's dome (above) inspired the California State Capitol in Sacramento.

THE FALL OF ROME 27

ACADEMIC VOCABULARY

innovation
(i-nuh-VAY-shuhn) a new idea or way of doing something

Academic Vocabulary

When we use a word that is important in all classes, not just social studies, we define it in the margin under the heading Academic Vocabulary. You will run into these academic words in other textbooks, so you should learn what they mean while reading this book.

Social Studies Vocabulary

We know that some words are special to this particular topic of social studies, world history. As you read this book, you will be more successful if you know the meaning of the words in the following list.

Social Studies Words to Know

Time

AD	refers to dates after Jesus's birth
BC	refers to dates before the birth of Jesus of Nazareth
BCE	refers to "Before Common Era," dates before the birth of Jesus of Nazareth
CE	refers to "Common Era," dates after Jesus's birth
century	a period of 100 years
decade	a period of 10 years
era	a period of time

The Earth and Its Resources

climate	the weather conditions in a certain area over a long period of time
geography	the study of the earth's physical and cultural features
landforms	the natural features of the land's surface
physical features	the features on the land's surface, such as mountains and rivers
region	an area with one or more features that make it different from surrounding areas
resources	materials found on the earth that people need and value

People and the Way They Live

civilization	the culture of a particular time or place
culture	the knowledge, beliefs, customs, and values of a group of people
custom	a repeated practice; tradition
economy	the system in which people make and exchange goods and services
politics	government
ritual	the regular form for a ceremony or observance
scholar	a person who has completed advanced study
society	a group of people who share common traditions
trade	the exchange of goods or services

Academic Words

If only . . .

If only reading in school were like reading a letter from your best friend.

If only reading in History were like reading *Harry Potter.*

It can be . . .if you learn the language!

There is a reason that you might feel uncomfortable with reading academic textbooks. Common words in these books account for less than 2% of the words in your favorite novels. No wonder reading in school seems so different from reading for fun!

Academic vocabulary refers to words that are used in most of your school subjects. The Holt Social Studies program has identified Academic Words that will be highlighted throughout this textbook. The Holt program provides structured practice to help support and improve your knowledge of this specialized vocabulary.

ACADEMIC WORDS

Grade 6 Academic Words

acquire	to get
agreement	a decision reached by two or more people or groups
aspects	parts
authority	power, right to rule
cause	the reason something happens
classical	referring to the cultures of ancient Greece or Rome
contract	a binding legal agreement
development	creation
distribute	to divide among a group of people
effect	the results of an action or decision
establish	to set up or create
ideal	ideas or goals that people try to live up to
impact	effect, result
method	a way of doing something
neutral	unbiased, not favoring either side in a conflict
primary	main, most important
principle	basic belief, rule, or law
process	a series of steps by which a task is accomplished
purpose	the reason something is done
rebel	to fight against authority
role	a part or function
strategy	a plan for fighting a battle or war
vary	to be different

Grade 7 Academic Words

affect	to change or influence
aspects	parts
authority	power, right to rule
classical	referring to the cultures of ancient Greece or Rome
development	the process of growing or improving
efficient/ efficiency	productive and not wasteful
element	part
establish	to set up or create
features	characteristics
impact	effect, result
influence	change, or have an effect on
innovation	a new idea or way of doing something
logical	reasoned, well thought out
policy	rule, course of action
principle	basic belief, rule, or law
procedure	a series of steps taken to accomplish a task
process	a series of steps by which a task is accomplished
rebel	to fight against authority
role	assigned behavior
strategy	a plan for fighting a battle or war
structure	the way something is set up or organized
traditional	customary, time-honored
values	ideas that people hold dear and try to live by
various	of many types

Grade 8 Academic Words

abstract	expressing a quality or idea without reference to an actual thing
acquire	to get
advocate	to plead in favor of
agreement	a decision reached by two or more people or groups
aspects	parts
authority	power, right to rule
circumstances	surrounding situation
complex	difficult, not simple
concrete	specific, real
consequences	the effects of a particular event or events
contemporary	existing at the same time
criteria	rules for defining
develop/ development	the process of growing or improving
distinct	separate
efficient/ efficiency	productive and not wasteful
element	part
establish	to set up or create
execute	to perform, carry out
explicit	fully revealed without vagueness
facilitate	to bring about
factor	cause
function	use or purpose
implement	to put in place
implications	effects of a decision
implicit	understood though not clearly put into words
incentive	something that leads people to follow a certain course of action
influence	change, or have an effect on
innovation	a new idea or way of doing something
method	a way of doing something
motive	a reason for doing something
neutral	unbiased, not favoring either side in a conflict
policy	rule, course of action
primary	main, most important
principle	basic belief, rule, or law
procedure	a series of steps taken to accomplish a task
process	a series of steps by which a task is accomplished
reaction	a response
role	assigned behavior
strategy	a plan for fighting a battle or war
vary/various	of many types

History–Social Science Content Standards

Students in grade seven study the social, cultural, and technological changes that occurred in Europe, Africa, and Asia in the years AD 500–1789. After reviewing the ancient world and the ways in which archaeologists and historians uncover the past, students study the history and geography of great civilizations that were developing concurrently throughout the world during medieval and early modern times. They examine the growing economic interaction among civilizations as well as the exchange of ideas, beliefs, technologies, and commodities. They learn about the resulting growth of Enlightenment philosophy and the new examination of the concepts of reason and authority, the natural rights of human beings and the divine right of kings, experimentalism in science, and the dogma of belief. Finally, students assess the political forces let loose by the Enlightenment, particularly the rise of democratic ideas, and they learn about the continuing influence of these ideas in the world today.

7.1 Students analyze the causes and effects of the vast expansion and ultimate disintegration of the Roman Empire.

1. Study the early strengths and lasting contributions of Rome (e.g., significance of Roman citizenship; rights under Roman law; Roman art, architecture, engineering, and philosophy; preservation and transmission of Christianity) and its ultimate internal weaknesses (e.g., rise of autonomous military powers within the empire, undermining of citizenship by the growth of corruption and slavery, lack of education, and distribution of news).

2. Discuss the geographic borders of the empire at its height and the factors that threatened its territorial cohesion.

3. Describe the establishment by Constantine of the new capital in Constantinople and the development of the Byzantine Empire, with an emphasis on the consequences of the development of two distinct European civilizations, Eastern Orthodox and Roman Catholic, and their two distinct views on church-state relations.

7.2 Students analyze the geographic, political, economic, religious, and social structures of the civilizations of Islam in the Middle Ages.

1. Identify the physical features and describe the climate of the Arabian peninsula, its relationship to surrounding bodies of land and water, and nomadic and sedentary ways of life.

2. Trace the origins of Islam and the life and teachings of Muhammad, including Islamic teachings on the connection with Judaism and Christianity.

3. Explain the significance of the Qur'an and the Sunnah as the primary sources of Islamic beliefs, practice, and law, and their influence in Muslims' daily life.

HISTORY–SOCIAL SCIENCE CONTENT STANDARDS

4. Discuss the expansion of Muslim rule through military conquests and treaties, emphasizing the cultural blending within Muslim civilization and the spread and acceptance of Islam and the Arabic language.

5. Describe the growth of cities and the establishment of trade routes among Asia, Africa, and Europe, the products and inventions that traveled along these routes (e.g., spices, textiles, paper, steel, new crops), and the role of merchants in Arab society.

6. Understand the intellectual exchanges among Muslim scholars of Eurasia and Africa and the contributions Muslim scholars made to later civilizations in the areas of science, geography, mathematics, philosophy, medicine, art, and literature.

7.3 Students analyze the geographic, political, economic, religious, and social structures of the civilizations of China in the Middle Ages.

1. Describe the reunification of China under the Tang Dynasty and reasons for the spread of Buddhism in Tang China, Korea, and Japan.

2. Describe agricultural, technological, and commercial developments during the Tang and Song periods.

3. Analyze the influences of Confucianism and changes in Confucian thought during the Song and Mongol periods.

4. Understand the importance of both overland trade and maritime expeditions between China and other civilizations in the Mongol Ascendancy and Ming Dynasty.

5. Trace the historic influence of such discoveries as tea, the manufacture of paper, wood-block printing, the compass, and gunpowder.

6. Describe the development of the imperial state and the scholar-official class.

7.4 Students analyze the geographic, political, economic, religious, and social structures of the sub-Saharan civilizations of Ghana and Mali in Medieval Africa.

1. Study the Niger River and the relationship of vegetation zones of forest, savannah, and desert to trade in gold, salt, food, and slaves; and the growth of the Ghana and Mali empires.

2. Analyze the importance of family, labor specialization, and regional commerce in the development of states and cities in West Africa.

3. Describe the role of the trans-Saharan caravan trade in the changing religious and cultural characteristics of West Africa and the influence of Islamic beliefs, ethics, and law.

4. Trace the growth of the Arabic language in government, trade, and Islamic scholarship in West Africa.

5. Describe the importance of written and oral traditions in the transmission of African history and culture.

7.5 Students analyze the geographic, political, economic, religious, and social structures of the civilizations of Medieval Japan.

1. Describe the significance of Japan's proximity to China and Korea and the intellectual, linguistic, religious, and philosophical influence of those countries on Japan.

2. Discuss the reign of Prince Shotoku of Japan and the characteristics of Japanese society and family life during his reign.

3. Describe the values, social customs, and traditions prescribed by the lord-vassal system consisting of *shogun*, *daimyo*, and *samurai* and the lasting influence of the warrior code throughout the twentieth century.

4. Trace the development of distinctive forms of Japanese Buddhism.

5. Study the ninth and tenth centuries' golden age of literature, art, and drama and its lasting effects on culture today, including Murasaki Shikibu's *Tale of Genji*.

6. Analyze the rise of a military society in the late twelfth century and the role of the samurai in that society.

7.6 Students analyze the geographic, political, economic, religious, and social structures of the civilizations of Medieval Europe.

1. Study the geography of Europe and the Eurasian land mass, including their location, topography, waterways, vegetation, and climate and their relationship to ways of life in Medieval Europe.

2. Describe the spread of Christianity north of the Alps and the roles played by the early church and by monasteries in its diffusion after the fall of the western half of the Roman Empire.

3. Understand the development of feudalism, its role in the medieval European economy, the way in which it was influenced by physical geography (the role of the manor and the growth of towns), and how feudal relationships provided the foundation of political order.

4. Demonstrate an understanding of the conflict and cooperation between the Papacy and European monarchs (e.g., Charlemagne, Gregory VII, Emperor Henry IV).

5. Know the significance of developments in medieval English legal and constitutional practices and their importance in the rise of modern democratic thought and representative institutions (e.g., Magna Carta, parliament, development of habeas corpus, an independent judiciary in England).

6. Discuss the causes and course of the religious Crusades and their effects on the Christian, Muslim, and Jewish populations in Europe, with emphasis on the increasing contact by Europeans with cultures of the Eastern Mediterranean world.

7. Map the spread of the bubonic plague from Central Asia to China, the Middle East, and Europe and describe its impact on global population.

8. Understand the importance of the Catholic church as a political, intellectual, and aesthetic institution (e.g., founding of universities, political and spiritual roles of the clergy, creation of monastic and mendicant religious orders, preservation of the Latin language and religious texts, St. Thomas Aquinas's synthesis of classical philosophy with Christian theology, and the concept of "natural law").

9. Know the history of the decline of Muslim rule in the Iberian Peninsula that culminated in the Reconquista and the rise of Spanish and Portuguese kingdoms.

7.7 Students compare and contrast the geographic, political, economic, religious, and social structures of the Meso-American and Andean civilizations.

1. Study the locations, landforms, and climates of Mexico, Central America, and South America and their effects on Mayan, Aztec, and Incan economies, trade, and development of urban societies.

2. Study the roles of people in each society, including class structures, family life, warfare, religious beliefs and practices, and slavery.

3. Explain how and where each empire arose and how the Aztec and Incan empires were defeated by the Spanish.

4. Describe the artistic and oral traditions and architecture in the three civilizations.

5. Describe the Meso-American achievements in astronomy and mathematics, including the development of the calendar and the Meso-American knowledge of seasonal changes to the civilizations' agricultural systems.

7.8 Students analyze the origins, accomplishments, and geographic diffusion of the Renaissance.

1. Describe the way in which the revival of classical learning and the arts fostered a new interest in humanism (i.e., a balance between intellect and religious faith).

2. Explain the importance of Florence in the early stages of the Renaissance and the growth of independent trading cities (e.g., Venice), with emphasis on the cities' importance in the spread of Renaissance ideas.

3. Understand the effects of the reopening of the ancient "Silk Road" between Europe and China, including Marco Polo's travels and the location of his routes.

4. Describe the growth and effects of new ways of disseminating information (e.g., the ability to manufacture paper, translation of the Bible into the vernacular, printing).

5. Detail advances made in literature, the arts, science, mathematics, cartography, engineering, and the understanding of human anatomy and astronomy (e.g., by Dante Alighieri, Leonardo da Vinci, Michelangelo di Buonarroti Simoni, Johann Gutenberg, William Shakespeare).

7.9 Students analyze the historical developments of the Reformation.

1. List the causes for the internal turmoil in and weakening of the Catholic church (e.g., tax policies, selling of indulgences).

2. Describe the theological, political, and economic ideas of the major figures during the Reformation (e.g., Desiderius Erasmus, Martin Luther, John Calvin, William Tyndale).

3. Explain Protestants' new practices of church self-government and the influence of those practices on the development of democratic practices and ideas of federalism.

4. Identify and locate the European regions that remained Catholic and those that became Protestant and explain how the division affected the distribution of religions in the New World.

5. Analyze how the Counter Reformation revitalized the Catholic church and the forces that fostered the movement (e.g., St. Ignatius of Loyola and the Jesuits, the Council of Trent).

6. Understand the institution and impact of missionaries on Christianity and the diffusion of Christianity from Europe to other parts of the world in the medieval and early modern periods; locate missions on a world map.

7. Describe the Golden Age of cooperation between Jews and Muslims in medieval Spain that promoted creativity in art, literature, and science, including how that cooperation was terminated by the religious persecution of individuals and groups (e.g., the Spanish Inquisition and the expulsion of Jews and Muslims from Spain in 1492).

7.10 Students analyze the historical developments of the Scientific Revolution and its lasting effect on religious, political, and cultural institutions.

1. Discuss the roots of the Scientific Revolution (e.g., Greek rationalism; Jewish, Christian, and Muslim science; Renaissance humanism; new knowledge from global exploration).

2. Understand the significance of the new scientific theories (e.g., those of Copernicus, Galileo, Kepler, Newton) and the significance of new inventions (e.g., the telescope, microscope, thermometer, barometer).

3. Understand the scientific method advanced by Bacon and Descartes, the influence of new scientific rationalism on the growth of democratic ideas, and the coexistence of science with traditional religious beliefs.

7.11 Students analyze political and economic change in the sixteenth, seventeenth, and eighteenth centuries (the Age of Exploration, the Enlightenment, and the Age of Reason).

1. Know the great voyages of discovery, the locations of the routes, and the influence of cartography in the development of a new European worldview.

2. Discuss the exchanges of plants, animals, technology, culture, and ideas among Europe, Africa, Asia, and the Americas in the fifteenth and sixteenth centuries and the major economic and social effects on each continent.

3. Examine the origins of modern capitalism; the influence of mercantilism and cottage industry; the elements and importance of a market economy in seventeenth-century Europe; the changing international trading and marketing patterns, including their locations on a world map; and the influence of explorers and map makers.

4. Explain how the main ideas of the Enlightenment can be traced back to such movements as the Renaissance, the Reformation, and the Scientific Revolution and to the Greeks, Romans, and Christianity.

5. Describe how democratic thought and institutions were influenced by Enlightenment thinkers (e.g., John Locke, Charles-Louis Montesquieu, American founders).

6. Discuss how the principles in the Magna Carta were embodied in such documents as the English Bill of Rights and the American Declaration of Independence.

Historical and Social Sciences Analysis Skills

The intellectual skills noted below are to be learned through, and applied to, the content standards for grades six through eight. They are to be assessed *only in conjunction* with the content standards in grades six through eight.

In addition to the standards for grades six through eight, students demonstrate the following intellectual reasoning, reflection, and research skills:

Chronological and Spatial Thinking

1. Students explain how major events are related to one another in time.

2. Students construct various time lines of key events, people, and periods of the historical era they are studying.

3. Students use a variety of maps and documents to identify physical and cultural features of neighborhoods, cities, states, and countries and to explain the historical migration of people, expansion and disintegration of empires, and the growth of economic systems.

Research, Evidence, and Point of View

1. Students frame questions that can be answered by historical study and research.

2. Students distinguish fact from opinion in historical narratives and stories.

3. Students distinguish relevant from irrelevant information, essential from incidental information, and verifiable from unverifiable information in historical narratives and stories.

4. Students assess the credibility of primary and secondary sources and draw sound conclusions from them.

5. Students detect the different historical points of view on historical events and determine the context in which the historical statements were made (the questions asked, sources used, author's perspectives).

Historical Interpretation

1. Students explain the central issues and problems from the past, placing people and events in a matrix of time and place.

2. Students understand and distinguish cause, effect, sequence, and correlation in historical events, including the long- and short-term causal relations.

3. Students explain the sources of historical continuity and how the combination of ideas and events explains the emergence of new patterns.

4. Students recognize the role of chance, oversight, and error in history.

5. Students recognize that interpretations of history are subject to change as new information is uncovered.

6. Students interpret basic indicators of economic performance and conduct cost-benefit analyses of economic and political issues.

How to Make This Book Work for You

Studying history will be easy for you using this textbook. Take a few minutes to become familiar with the easy-to-use structure and special features of this history book. See how this textbook will make history come alive for you!

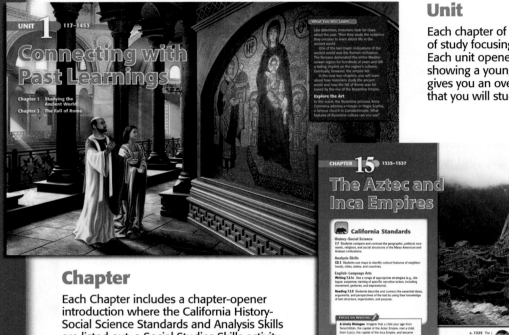

Unit

Each chapter of this textbook is part of a Unit of study focusing on a particular time period. Each unit opener provides an illustration showing a young person of the period and gives you an overview of the exciting topics that you will study in the unit.

Chapter

Each Chapter includes a chapter-opener introduction where the California History-Social Science Standards and Analysis Skills are listed out, a Social Studies Skills activity, Standards Review pages, and a Standards Assessment page.

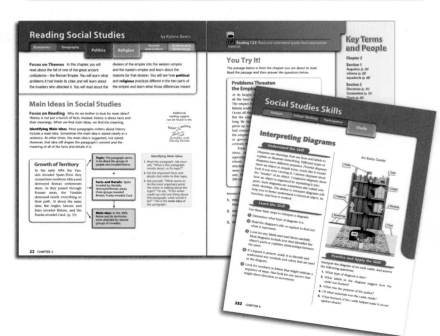

Reading Social Studies These chapter level reading lessons give you skills and practice that you can use to help you read the textbook. Within each chapter there is a Focus on Reading note in the margin on the page where the reading skill is covered. There are also questions in the Standards Review activity to make sure that you understand the reading skill.

Social Studies Skills The Social Studies Skills lessons give you an opportunity to learn and use a skill that you will most likely use again. You will also be given a chance to make sure that you understand each skill by answering related questions in the Standards Review activity.

Section

The Section opener pages include Main Idea statements, an overarching big idea statement, and Key Terms and People. In addition, each section includes the following special features.

If You Were There . . . introductions begin each section with a situation for you to respond to, placing you in the time period and in a situation related to the content that you will be studying in the section.

Building Background sections connect what will be covered in this section with what you studied in the previous section.

Short sections of content organize the information in each section into small chunks of text that you shouldn't find too overwhelming.

The California History-Social Science Standards for 7th grade that are covered in each section are listed on the first page of each section of the textbook.

SECTION 3

Growth of a Military Society

What You Will Learn...

Main Ideas
1. Samurai and shoguns took over Japan as emperors lost influence.
2. Samurai warriors lived honorably.
3. Order broke down when the power of the shoguns was challenged by invaders and rebellions.
4. Strong leaders took over and reunified Japan.

The Big Idea
Japan developed a military society led by generals called shoguns.

Key Terms and People
daimyo, p. 212
samurai, p. 212
figurehead, p. 213
shogun, p. 213
Bushido, p. 214

HSS 7.5.3 Describe the values, social customs, and traditions prescribed by the lord-vassal system consisting of *shogun, daimyo,* and *samurai* and the lasting influence of the warrior code throughout the twentieth century.

7.5.6 Analyze the rise of a military society in the late twelfth century and the role of the samurai in that society.

212 CHAPTER 8

If YOU were there...

You are a Japanese warrior, proud of your fighting skills. For many years you've been honored by most of society, but you face an awful dilemma. When you became a warrior, you swore to protect and fight for both your lord and your emperor. Now your lord has gone to war against the emperor, and both sides have called for you to join them.

How will you decide whom to fight for?

BUILDING BACKGROUND Wars between lords and emperors were not uncommon in Japan after 1100. Closed off from society at Heian, emperors had lost touch with the rest of Japan. As a result, order broke down throughout the islands.

Samurai and Shoguns Take Over Japan

By the late 1100s, Heian was the great center of Japanese art and literature. But in the rest of Japan, life was very different. Powerful nobles fought each other over land. Rebels fought against imperial officials. This fighting destroyed land, which made it difficult for peasants to grow food. Some poor people became bandits or thieves. Meanwhile, Japan's rulers were so focused on courtly life, they didn't notice the many problems growing in their country.

The Rise of the Samurai

With the emperor distracted by life in his court, Japan's large landowners, or **daimyo** (DY-mee-oh), decided that they needed to protect their own lands. They hired **samurai** (SA-muh-ry), or trained professional warriors, to defend them and their property. The samurai wore light armor and fought with swords and bows. Most samurai came from noble families and inherited their positions from their fathers.

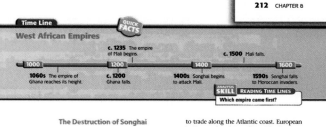

Time Line

West African Empires

- **1000**
- **1060s** The empire of Ghana reaches its height.
- **1200**
- **c. 1200** Ghana falls.
- **c. 1235** The empire of Mali begins.
- **1400**
- **1400s** Songhai begins to attack Mali.
- **c. 1500** Mali falls.
- **1600**
- **1590s** Songhai falls to Moroccan invaders.

ANALYSIS SKILL **READING TIME LINES**
Which empire came first?

The Destruction of Songhai

The Moroccans' guns and cannons brought disaster to Songhai. The swords, spears, and bows carried by Songhai's warriors were no match for firearms.

The Moroccans attacked Timbuktu and Gao, looting and taking over both cities. The Moroccans didn't push farther into Songhai, but the damage was done. Songhai never recovered from the loss of these cities and the income they produced.

Changes in trade patterns completed Songhai's fall. Overland trade declined as port cities north and south of the old empire became more important. For example, people who lived south of Songhai began

to trade along the Atlantic coast. European traders preferred to sail to Atlantic ports than to deal with Muslim traders. Slowly, the period of great West African empires came to an end.

READING CHECK **Predicting** What do you think happened to the people of West Africa after the empire of Songhai was defeated?

SUMMARY AND PREVIEW The empire of Songhai was known for its wealth, culture, and learning. In the next section you will read more about the major West African cultures and how we know about them.

Reading Check questions end each section of content so that you can test whether or not you understand what you have just studied.

Summary and Preview To connect what you have just studied in the section to what you will study in the next section, we include the Summary and Preview.

Section Assessments The section assessment boxes provide an opportunity for you to make sure that you understand the main ideas of the section. We also provide assessment practice online!

Section 3 Assessment

Reviewing Ideas, Terms, and People **HSS** 7.4.3
1. **a.** Identify In what part of West Africa did Songhai begin?
   b. Summarize What did **Sunni Ali** accomplish?
2. **a.** Identify What religion gained influence in Songhai under **Askia the Great**?
   b. Analyze How did contact with other cultures change Songhai's government?
3. **a.** Identify Which group of people invaded the Songhai Empire in the 1590s?
   b. Predict How might West Africa's history have been different if the invaders who conquered Songhai had not had firearms?

Critical Thinking
4. **Analyzing** Copy the graphic organizer on the right. In each oval, describe an important development in Songhai during the rule of Askia the Great.

[diagram: Askia the Great]

FOCUS ON SPEAKING
5. **Evaluating** Add information to your notes for Songhai's leaders. What were their achievements? Compare the Songhai achievements with those of Ghana and Mali.

go.hrw.com
Online Quiz
KEYWORD: SQ7 HP6

146 CHAPTER 6

Places You Will Study

As you study world history, you will learn about many places around the world. You will discover the places where civilizations developed, how geography influenced cultures, and how these cultures have helped shape the world today.

The maps that you see here show some of the main places you will study in this textbook. These are key places where empires began, new ways of thinking developed, religions spread, and cultures flourished. You will learn much more about these places and the people who lived in them as you study world history.

Mesoamerica
Mesoamerica was an early center of culture in the Americas and home to the Maya and Aztec civilizations.

South America
One of the most advanced American cultures, the Incas, developed in the Andes Mountains.

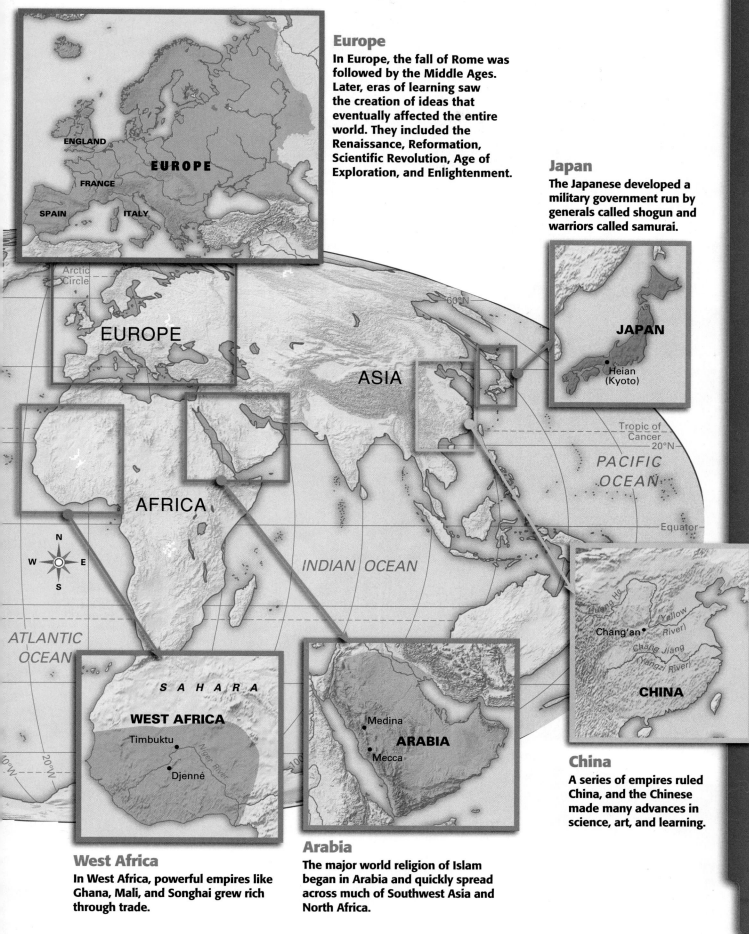

Europe

In Europe, the fall of Rome was followed by the Middle Ages. Later, eras of learning saw the creation of ideas that eventually affected the entire world. They included the Renaissance, Reformation, Scientific Revolution, Age of Exploration, and Enlightenment.

ENGLAND

EUROPE

FRANCE

SPAIN ITALY

Japan

The Japanese developed a military government run by generals called shogun and warriors called samurai.

JAPAN

Heian
(Kyoto)

Arctic
Circle

60°N

EUROPE

ASIA

Tropic of
Cancer
20°N

PACIFIC
OCEAN

AFRICA

Equator

N
W E
S

INDIAN OCEAN

Huang He

Chang'an

(Yellow
River)

Chang Jiang
(Yangzi River)

ATLANTIC
OCEAN

CHINA

S A H A R A

WEST AFRICA

Timbuktu

Niger River

Djenné

Medina

ARABIA

Mecca

China

A series of empires ruled China, and the Chinese made many advances in science, art, and learning.

West Africa

In West Africa, powerful empires like Ghana, Mali, and Songhai grew rich through trade.

Arabia

The major world religion of Islam began in Arabia and quickly spread across much of Southwest Asia and North Africa.

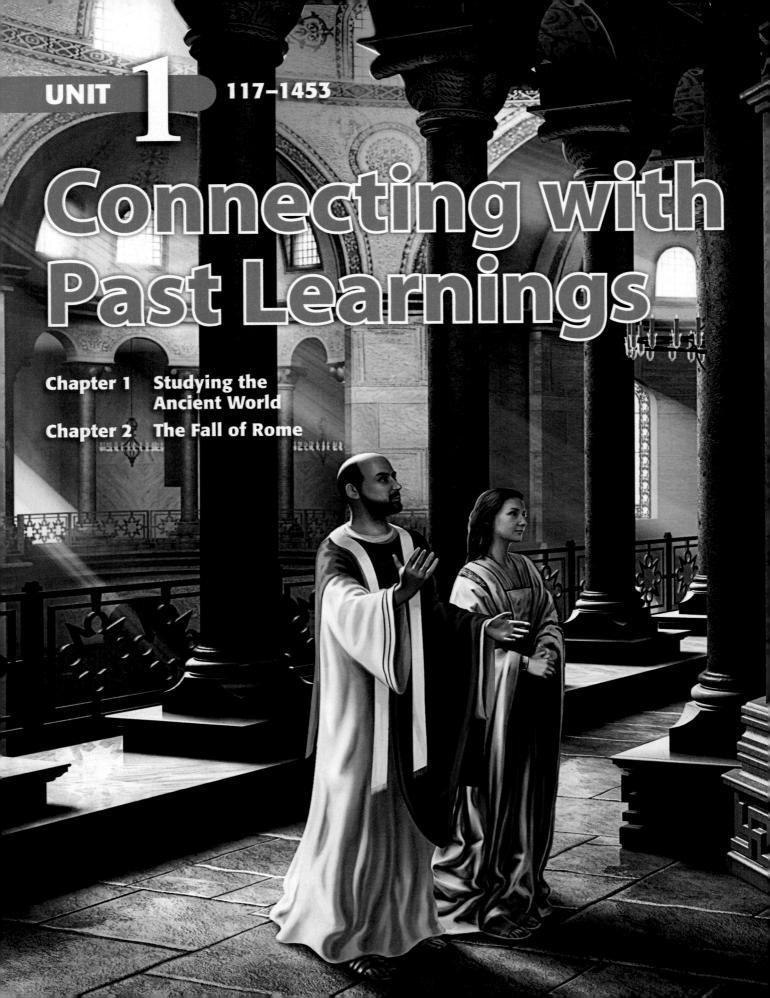

Connecting with Past Learnings

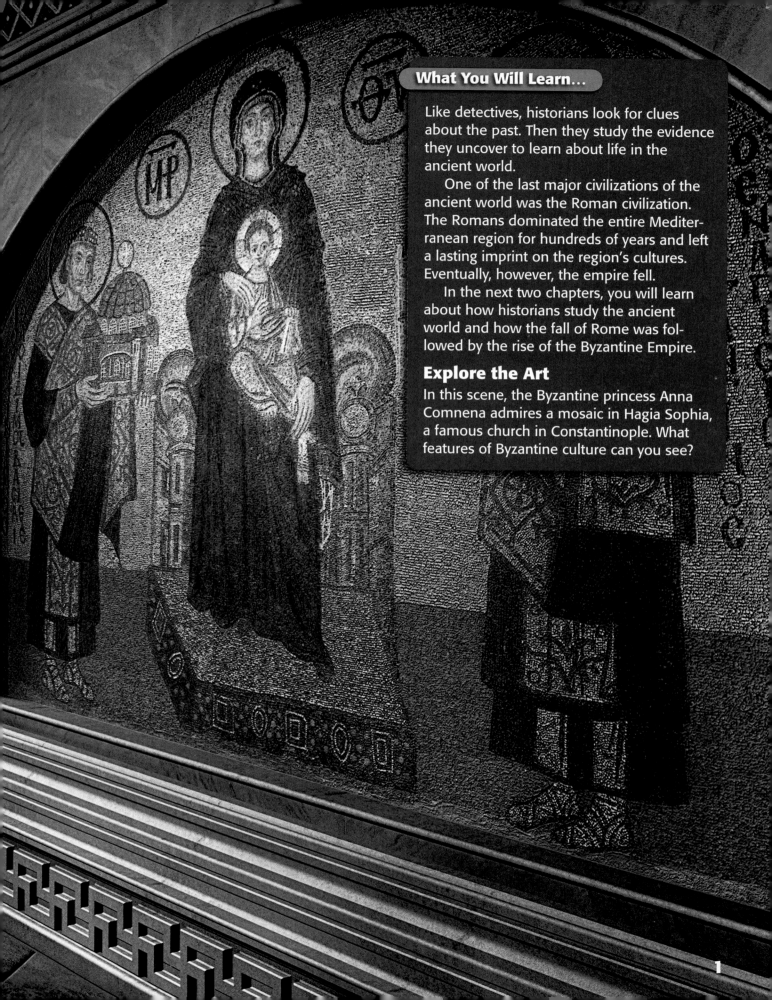

What You Will Learn...

Like detectives, historians look for clues about the past. Then they study the evidence they uncover to learn about life in the ancient world.

One of the last major civilizations of the ancient world was the Roman civilization. The Romans dominated the entire Mediterranean region for hundreds of years and left a lasting imprint on the region's cultures. Eventually, however, the empire fell.

In the next two chapters, you will learn about how historians study the ancient world and how the fall of Rome was followed by the rise of the Byzantine Empire.

Explore the Art

In this scene, the Byzantine princess Anna Comnena admires a mosaic in Hagia Sophia, a famous church in Constantinople. What features of Byzantine culture can you see?

Studying the Ancient World

California Standards

Analysis Skills

HI 5 Students recognize that interpretations of history are subject to change as new information is uncovered.

English–Language Arts

Writing 7.2.4 Write Persuasive Compositions

Reading 7.1.0 Students use their knowledge of word origins and word relationships, as well as historical and literary context clues, to determine the meaning of specialized vocabulary and to understand the precise meaning of grade-level-appropriate words.

FOCUS ON WRITING

A Persuasive Composition In this chapter, you will read about how scholars study the past by piecing clues together. You will pretend to be an archaeologist who has discovered ruins of a big building. In a letter, you will put together your own set of clues and try to convince the reader about the meaning of these mysterious ruins.

HOLT

History's Impact

▶ **video series**
Watch the video to understand the impact of archaeology on what we have learned about the past.

What You Will Learn...

In this chapter you will learn how historians study the ancient world to unlock the mysteries of the past. In this photo a diver examines an ancient jar off the coast of Israel.

Reading Social Studies

by Kylene Beers

Economics	Geography	Politics	Religion	Society and Culture	Science and Technology

Focus on Themes To learn about history, you must learn what historians do as they study the past. As you read this chapter, you will learn vocabulary that historians use and discover how they use written and unwritten clues from the past to learn about many topics, including **religion** and **society and culture**. You will learn the difference between primary and secondary sources and see how our understanding of history changes as new sources of each type are discovered..

Specialized Vocabulary of History

Focus on Reading Suppose you turned on the TV just in time to hear, "Depressed economic patterns indicate a downturn in consumer spending." Would you know that people are spending less money?

Specialized Vocabulary The sentence in the previous paragraph uses specialized vocabulary, words used in only one field, economics. History has its own specialized vocabulary. The chart below lists some terms often used in the study of history.

Additional reading support can be found in the

Inter active

Reader and Study Guide

Terms used with dates	
circa or c.	a word used to show that historians are not sure of an exact date; it means "about"
BC	a term used to identify dates that occurred long ago, before the birth of Jesus Christ, the founder of Christianity; it means "before Christ." BC dates get smaller as time passes, so the larger the number the earlier the date.
AD	a term used to identify dates that occurred after Jesus's birth; it comes from a Latin phrase that means "in the year of our Lord." Unlike BC dates, AD dates get larger as time passes, so the larger the number the later the date.
BCE	another way to refer to BC dates; it stands for "before the common era"
CE	another way to refer to AD dates; it stands for "common era"

Because historians deal with so many dates, they have created many ways to refer to events in the past. For example, the time line below shows that the 100s can also be called the second century. What do you notice about the names given to a century and the first number of the dates in it?

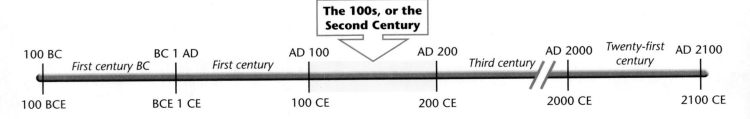

The 100s, or the Second Century

100 BC — First century BC — BC 1 AD — First century — AD 100 — AD 200 — Third century — AD 2000 — Twenty-first century — AD 2100

100 BCE — BCE 1 CE — 100 CE — 200 CE — 2000 CE — 2100 CE

ELA Reading **7.1.0** Use word relationships and historical context clues to determine the meaning of specialized vocabulary.

You Try It!

As you read this textbook, you will find many specialized vocabulary terms that historians use. Some of these terms will be highlighted in the text and defined for you as key terms. Others may not be highlighted, but they will still be defined. You may find a few words, however, that you do not know and that are not defined. In many cases, you will be able to figure out what these words mean from clues in the text around them. For an example, read the passages below and answer the questions that follow.

Vocabulary in Context

1. Artifacts also offer clues. These items can tell us about economic systems. Archaeologists may find Roman coins in China and Chinese coins in Rome. If the coins are from the same time period, we can conclude that the Romans and Chinese were doing business at a certain time.

2. Wrecks of Roman ships were recently found far off the Mediterranean coast. Scholars had thought that the early Roman traders sailed their ships close to the coast. The new finding suggests that sailors could navigate the open waters earlier than experts had thought.

From Chapter 1, pages 11, 13–14

Answer the following questions.

1. If you didn't know what *economic* meant, what clues in the first passage above might help you figure it out?

2. What clues could help you guess the meaning of *navigate* in the second passage?

3. In what century were you born? What is another name for it?

4. Put the following dates in order: AD 2000, the third century, 44 BC, the 1600s, CE 1215, 3100 BCE

Key Terms and People

Chapter 1

Section 1
history *(p. 6)*
primary source *(p. 7)*
secondary source *(p. 7)*
archaeology *(p. 8)*
fossil *(p. 8)*
artifacts *(p. 8)*

Section 2
society *(p. 10)*
social structure *(p. 13)*

Academic Vocabulary

Success in school is related to knowing academic vocabulary— the words that are frequently used in school assignments and discussions. In this chapter, you will learn the following academic words:

cause *(p. 7)*
effect *(p. 7)*
purpose *(p. 13)*

As you read Chapter 1, keep a list in your notebook of specialized vocabulary words that you learn.

Clues from the Past

What You Will Learn...

Main Ideas

1. Historians and archaeologists look for clues in written records and artifacts.
2. Other sources of clues include legends and luck.

The Big Idea

Historians and archaeologists study fossils, artifacts, and written records to learn about the past.

Key Terms

history, *p. 6*
primary source, *p. 7*
secondary source, *p. 7*
archaeology, *p. 8*
fossil, *p. 8*
artifacts, *p. 8*

If YOU were there...

You are spending your summer helping scholars search for the tomb of a great king. Local legends tell that the tomb lies under a nearby hill, guarded by traps that will harm anyone who disturbs the king's resting place. A single coin bearing the king's name has been found at the hill. However, an ancient scroll says that the king's body rests at the bottom of a deep lake, never to be found.

Should you continue to search for the tomb?

BUILDING BACKGROUND The story of the past comes to us from many directions. What we hear, find, and read make up the pieces of a very big and fascinating puzzle.

Looking for Clues

The task before you seems simple. You must fit together the pieces of a jigsaw puzzle to create a picture. But what if most of the puzzle pieces are missing, and you don't even know what the finished picture is supposed to look like?

This is the task that we may face when we try to learn about the past. To help us learn and to complete the picture, scholars from two basic fields work together like detectives.

What Historians Do

The main field that leads the investigation is **history**—the study of the past. History isn't just about events that no one alive remembers. It is both the distant and recent past. A battle that happened 5,000 years ago and an election that happened yesterday are both part of history.

Historians are people who study history. Historians are very curious about the past. They want to know who did what. They want to know how, when, where, and why people did what they did.

Evidence of the Past

Artifacts
The objects that people created and used, like this Maya mask, can tell historians about their culture, technology, and beliefs.

Fossils
The remains of early hominids can give us clues about their lifestyle. This skull from Africa is about 1.8 million years old.

Written Records
Written records, like this Japanese writing from the 1000s, are a valuable source of information about the past.

Historians are interested in the way individuals lived. How did they work, fight, and worship? What did they do in their free time? Scholars also look at what groups of people have done. What may **cause** a nation to become powerful and then to fade away? Why did a new religion spread? What was the **effect** of an invasion?

To study the past, historians mainly use written works. In the 5,000 or so years that people have been writing, they have recorded laws, poems, speeches, battle plans, letters, contracts, and many other things. In these written sources, historians have found details about every aspect of human life. In addition, people have not been limited to paper and pens. They have carved messages onto stone pillars, stamped them into clay tablets, scribbled them on turtle shells, and typed them on computers.

Historical sources are of two types. A **primary source** is an account of an event created by someone who took part in or witnessed the event. Treaties, court records, and laws are primary sources. Diaries and letters are, too. An audio or video recording of an event is also a primary source.

A **secondary source** is information gathered by someone who did not take part in or witness an event. Examples include textbooks and encyclopedias. The book you are reading right now is a secondary source. The historians who wrote it did not take part in the events described. Instead, they gathered information about these events from different sources. However, if a historian writes an opinion about something, that opinion is a primary source. The opinion is a record of how a historian at a certain time viewed history and the world.

ACADEMIC VOCABULARY
cause to make something happen
effect the result of an action or decision

What Archaeologists Do

Another field that contributes information about the past is archaeology (ahr-kee-AH-luh-jee). **Archaeology** is the study of the past based on materials that people have left behind. Archaeologists explore places where people once lived, worked, fought, hunted, or pursued other activities. In many cases, objects that people left behind at these places provide the only clues we have about their lives.

For information on the very first humans, archaeologists examine fossil remains. A **fossil** is a part or imprint of something that was once alive. Ancient bones and footprints preserved in rock are examples of fossils.

As human beings learned to make things, they also happened to create more sources of information for us. They made what we call **artifacts**, objects created and used by humans. Among the many types of artifacts are arrowheads, coins, tools, toys, jewelry, and pottery.

Although individual artifacts can give us useful clues, more useful are groups of artifacts from the same area and time period.

Archaeologists refer to these collections of related artifacts as a group's material culture. Just as important as the artifacts themselves are the places where they are found. For example, Viking coins and swords found in Russia can show that the Vikings traded and fought there.

READING CHECK **Comparing** How are the fields of history and archaeology similar?

Other Sources of Clues

Historians and archaeologists work together. Archaeologists use written sources to help them find sites where they will find artifacts. Similarly, historians examine material culture to help them understand what they read. Sometimes these scholars also get help from sources that may surprise you.

Legends

Stories and legends can point scholars toward discoveries. For example, you have probably read stories about King Arthur. Historians know that no such king really lived during the Middle Ages. However,

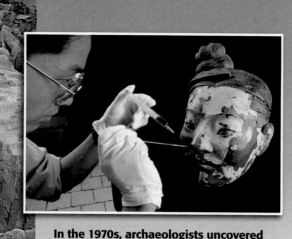

In the 1970s, archaeologists uncovered thousands of clay soldiers built to protect the tomb of a Chinese emperor. Scientists are still studying the site's artifacts, such as this warrior's head.

Khan, a mighty conqueror and ruler, to search for his tomb in his homeland of Mongolia. Archaeologists have found artifacts that suggest they are close to a major discovery, but so far Genghis Khan's tomb has not been found.

Luck

Sometimes luck can play a major part in uncovering history. In 1974 Chinese farmers were digging a well. When their shovels hit hard clay instead of dirt, they were amazed to find the first of the clay soldiers you see on these pages.

One day, perhaps you will make an amazing discovery or uncover new information that will explain what happened long ago. Perhaps you will even solve one of history's mysteries.

READING CHECK **Evaluating** Do you think that legends and luck are reliable sources of clues? Why or why not?

SUMMARY AND PREVIEW Historians and archaeologists use clues from many sources to learn about the past. Next, you will learn about some of the things they can discover by using these clues.

legends about Arthur encouraged historians to search ancient documents for information about England's distant past. In these sources historians found a warrior who lived in about AD 500. This man may have inspired the legends. Archaeologists, too, used the stories about Arthur as guides to make important discoveries.

Legends are still providing exciting clues that may lead to astonishing finds. For example, researchers in many fields are using legends about the burial of Genghis

---

Section 1 Assessment

go.hrw.com
Online Quiz
KEYWORD: SQ7 HP1

Reviewing Ideas, Terms, and People

1. **a. Define** What is **history**?
   b. Contrast How is a **primary source** different from a **secondary source**?
   c. Predict What kinds of things will future archaeologists study to learn about how we lived?
2. **a. Describe** How do legends help historians?
   b. Explain Why would archaeologists study written sources and historians study **artifacts**?
   c. Rank List the ways in which scholars look for clues, ranking the methods from what you think would be the most useful to the least useful.

Critical Thinking

3. **Categorize** Copy the diagram. In the empty circles, list the types of clues that historians and archaeologists use.

Historians and Archaeologists

WRITING JOURNAL

4. **Finding Your Ruins** Choose a large, familiar building that you will "discover" as an archaeologist, such as your school, a place of worship, or a shopping mall. Write down or draw pictures of what your building could look like 3,000 years from now.

Putting the Pieces Together

What You Will Learn...

Main Ideas

1. Using the evidence they have gathered allows historians to draw conclusions about societies in the past.
2. Views of the past change because of new discoveries and new interpretations.

The Big Idea

Historians and archaeologists put written and unwritten clues together to learn about the past and sometimes to revise their ideas about the past.

Key Terms

society, *p. 10*
social structure, *p. 10*

If YOU were there...

You are an expert on an ancient Asian language. For years you have worked at translating a long poem from that language into English. Now it is finally finished! The poem seems to be just a group of fairy tales, but you suspect that you can find some real facts within the fantastic stories. You want to know about the people who told the tales as they sat around their campfires.

What else can you learn from these tales?

BUILDING BACKGROUND The people who wrote down these stories didn't know that they were telling later generations about themselves. Yet that is just what they did. These unknown people were creating evidence that we can use to understand the past.

Using the Evidence

Archaeologists, historians, and other experts ask questions about the past. Then they gather clues and put them together to reveal information about past societies. A **society** is a community of people who share a common culture.

Social Structure and Family Life

Families are an important part of a culture's **social structure**—the way a society is organized. We often learn about family life and social structure in sources that are more about something else. For example, you may remember a work of literature called the *Rig Veda* from last year's study of ancient India. This work of literature is mainly about religion. It also tells, however, that Indian society was strictly divided into classes. Another text from India, the *Ramayana*, tells us about marriage in early Indian society. In this story, Rama and his wife Sita face many dangers. In Sita's constant loyalty, we see what the Indians considered to be a perfect wife.

The carving on the left from a Maya king's coffin is a clue to Maya beliefs about the afterlife. The carving has been redrawn below by scholars trying to unlock its meaning.

What can scholars learn from the carving?

Above the king is the Tree of Life, and atop the tree is a bird that symbolizes heaven.

The king is falling from the Tree of Life and being swallowed by the earth monster, symbolizing his journey into the underworld and afterlife.

Art can tell us about social structure and families, too. For example, Egyptian tomb paintings show the pharaoh at the top of Egyptian society and the other classes below him. Other paintings show the pharaoh at home with his wife and children. In these scenes we see the importance of family to the Egyptians.

Politics and Economic Systems

Ancient sources also inform historians about political and economic systems. Written sources can be especially useful for learning about politics, or government. For example, many speeches of politicians from ancient Athens have survived in written form. Today, we can read those speeches and see that the Athenians valued democracy and that politicians worked hard to protect people's freedoms.

Some written sources are useful for answering questions about a society's economic situation—the value of its goods and services. Many cultures left behind business records showing the value of different products. Other lists tell us how much workers were paid for various tasks.

Artifacts also offer clues. These items can tell us about economic systems. Archaeologists may find Roman coins in China and Chinese coins in Rome. If the coins are from the same time period, we can conclude that the Romans and Chinese were doing business at a certain time.

We may also find the actual items that people traded. Ancient North America provides an example. Centuries ago, people used a rock called obsidian (uhb-SI-dee-uhn) for making weapons. But few sources of obsidian existed. Archaeologists have found obsidian weapons hundreds of miles from the stone's sources. Using this information, experts can calculate how far trade in the valuable rock extended.

FOCUS ON READING
What words give you clues to the meaning of *politicians*?

This bronze container from China's Shang dynasty shows the incredible metalworking skills of the ancient Chinese.

Language

Learning about ancient languages can be especially difficult for historians. When scholars find a document in an unknown language, they don't find a dictionary for that language right next to it!

Sometimes historians can use clues from known languages to understand old ones. The most famous example is the Rosetta Stone. Created in ancient Egypt, the Rosetta Stone shows the same message in Greek and in two types of Egyptian writing. Because scholars could read Greek, they were able to translate the Egyptian writing also. Since the early 1800s, when its secrets were unlocked, the Rosetta Stone has helped historians read many Egyptian texts. Some ancient languages, however, are still complete mysteries.

Art and Architecture

Looking at a society's art can tell us more about a society than just what its people liked to draw or paint. One thing art may show us is religious beliefs. For example, you probably remember that archaeologists have found Egyptian tombs full of beautifully crafted furniture, jewelry, toys, and other everyday items. The fact that the Egyptians placed these goods in tombs shows they believed the person buried there would need them. From this evidence, we can conclude that the Egyptians believed in life after death.

Art can also give us clues about a society's level of technology. Do you remember the Shang dynasty of China? Although there are gaps in our knowledge of that long-ago time, we have found beautiful bronze objects that are amazing for their detail. These art objects show us that the Shang had incredible metalworking skill.

Architecture provides more evidence about societies. Clues come from the number and types of buildings. For example, if archaeologists find many temples in the ruins of a small town, they can assume that religion was very important there. Or, if none of the houses in a place were fancier than others, they may figure that no one was much richer than anyone else.

The structure of the buildings themselves can reveal clues, too. If an ancient castle had thick stone walls, perhaps war was a problem, and the people needed walls as protection from enemies. The beautiful temples that the Greeks built show the importance of the Greek gods. Similarly, buildings made with rounded arches show us the Romans' engineering talents.

Beliefs and Values

Finally, historians and archaeologists use many sources to interpret the beliefs and values of a society. Written sources like the teachings of Confucius tell us about the importance of the family to Chinese society. The Code of Hammurabi tells us that the Babylonian ruler of long ago valued justice. Written speeches show that the early Romans thought highly of citizens who served the republic.

Unwritten sources also provide information. Greek statues of athletes and images of athletes on vases show the value that the Greeks placed on sports. Unwritten sources can be harder to interpret, however. Sometimes archaeologists find artifacts whose **purpose** is unclear. Often, experts think these unidentified objects are related to religious beliefs. Other experts disagree. To understand the cultures that created these mysterious objects, we must find more information.

READING CHECK **Generalizing** What types of information can evidence reveal about past societies?

Views of the Past

Although we have evidence from many sources, our understanding of history changes. Archaeologists may find new clues that change what experts think about a society. In addition, changes in our own society may alter our ideas about history.

New Discoveries

New historical evidence can change our understanding of when events happened. In recent years, archaeologists have found extremely old human bones in Africa and the Americas. These remains may require the time lines of human development to be completely rewritten.

Another example comes from the bottom of the Mediterranean Sea. Wrecks of Roman trading ships were recently found far off the Mediterranean coast. Scholars had thought that early Roman traders sailed their ships close to the coast.

ACADEMIC VOCABULARY

purpose use or function

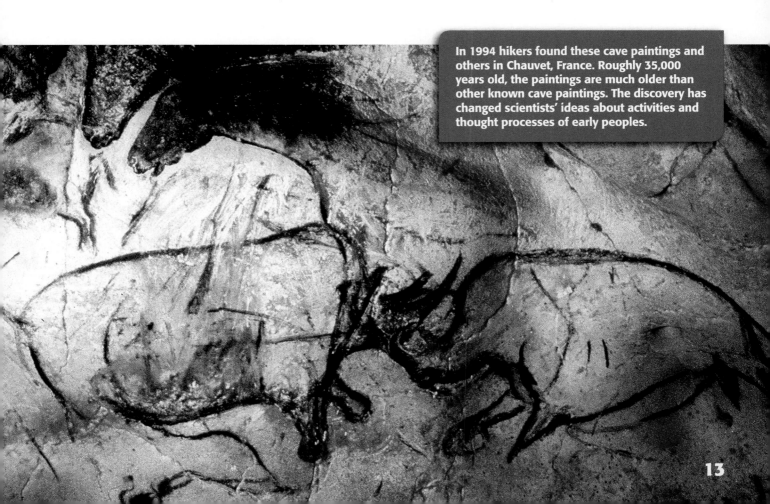

In 1994 hikers found these cave paintings and others in Chauvet, France. Roughly 35,000 years old, the paintings are much older than other known cave paintings. The discovery has changed scientists' ideas about activities and thought processes of early peoples.

The Legend of Troy

The work of the German archaeologist Heinrich Schliemann helped prove that Troy was not just a legend but a real place. Schliemann excavated a hill in Turkey and found the remains of an ancient city that most modern scholars believe was the legendary Troy.

GREECE Troy **TURKEY**

THE IMPACT TODAY

The site of Troy is a popular tourist attraction for Turkey.

The new finding suggests that sailors could navigate the open waters earlier than experts had thought.

How we view a society can also change with new archaeological finds. Not long ago, historians thought the Maya of Central America were a peaceful people interested mainly in studying the stars and making art. When scholars figured out how to read more Maya writing, however, they found that Maya rulers often made war on their neighbors. Scholars also learned that Maya religion included cruel, bloody rituals.

New evidence can even shed new light on old stories. Heinrich Schliemann (SHLEE-mahn) and his search for the city of Troy serve as a good example. For centuries, people had read Homer's tales about the Trojan War in the *Iliad* and the *Odyssey*. Most people assumed they were just stories. Schliemann, however, thought they described real events in a real place. After years of searching and digging, Schliemann found a whole civilization that no one knew had existed. He also found the site of Troy.

New Interpretations

Views of history also change depending on the time, place, and cultures within which historians live. The growth of democracy, the civil rights movement, and women's movements have affected how we study history. In the United States, for example, we now realize that women played key roles

As you study world history, think critically about what you learn, and be ready for change! Because new evidence can appear, and because our own culture shifts, a historian must keep an open mind. Consider new evidence carefully, and be prepared to revise your understanding of history.

READING CHECK **Analyzing** Why do views of history change?

SUMMARY AND PREVIEW Artifacts and written evidence help archaeologists and historians study and reconsider many aspects of past societies. In the next chapter you will study what historians and other scholars have learned about the fall of the Roman Empire.

go.hrw.com
Online Quiz
KEYWORD: SQ7 HP1

Section 2 Assessment

Reviewing Ideas, Terms, and People

1. **a. Define** What is a **society**?
   b. Explain What could price lists and lists of workers' wages tell us about a people's economic system?
   c. Evaluate What type of evidence do you think would be the most difficult to interpret? Why?
2. **a. Identify** What are two ways interpretations of history have changed?
   b. Explain Why should historians watch out for personal biases?

Critical Thinking

3. **Identifying Cause and Effect** Copy the graphic organizer. Use it to describe what we may learn about a culture after a historian figures out how to read an ancient language.

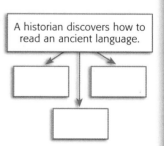

A historian discovers how to read an ancient language.

FOCUS ON WRITING

4. **Analyzing the Evidence** What can you learn about the past from the ruins you have found? What can various parts of the building tell you? What can you learn from the materials and arrangement of the building? Draw a map of your building and label important "clues."

in history. In the past their contributions received little attention, but today many historians study women in history—both as a large group and as individuals.

The attention historians have paid to rich and powerful people versus ordinary or poor people is another example of changing views. Once rich and powerful people got almost all of the attention in history books. Now historians also look at how ordinary people lived.

Personal opinions of historians can also affect their views of the past. Political opinions, for example, can make historians see past times in certain ways. Historians must always be careful not to let their personal biases affect their work.

Social Studies Skills

Analysis | Critical Thinking | Participation | Study

Understanding Historical Interpretation

Understand the Skill

Historical interpretations are ways of explaining the past. They are based on what is known about the people, ideas, and events that make up history.

Two historians can look at the same set of facts about a historical topic and see things in different ways. For example, historians decide which facts are the most important in explaining what happened and why. One person may believe certain facts are important, while someone else may believe other facts are more important. The amount of attention paid to different facts can lead historians to come up with different explanations of what happened in the past and why it happened.

The result of focusing on different facts is different interpretations of history. In addition, if new facts are uncovered about a topic, they may cause historians to reconsider their ideas, and still more historical interpretations may result. Being able to recognize and evaluate different historical interpretations is a valuable skill in the study of history.

Learn the Skill

Use the following guidelines to better understand and evaluate differing historical interpretations of people and events.

❶ Identify the main idea in how the topic is explained. What conclusions are reached? Conclusions may not be directly stated. They may only be hinted at in the information provided.

❷ Identify the facts on which the writer or speaker has relied. Do these facts seem to support his or her explanation and conclusions?

❸ Determine if the writer or speaker has ignored important information about the topic. If so, the interpretation may be inaccurate or deliberately slanted to prove a particular point of view.

Just because interpretations differ, one is not necessarily "right" and others "wrong." As long as a person considers all the evidence, and draws conclusions based on a fair evaluation of that evidence, his or her interpretation is probably acceptable.

Remember, however, that trained historians let the facts *lead* them to conclusions. People who *start* with a conclusion, select only facts that support it, and ignore opposing evidence produce interpretations that have little value for understanding history.

Practice and Apply the Skill

Reread the "If you were there" scenario in Section 1. Suppose that Historian A believes the king's body is in the hill, and Historian B believes it is at the bottom of the lake. Answer the following questions to evaluate their explanations of what happened to the king.

1. Is the coin strong evidence to support Historian A's interpretation? Explain why or why not.

2. Should Historian B ignore the local legend? If so, why? If not, how should he or she handle it?

3. Suppose each historian asks you to be part of their expedition to find the king's body. Which historian's group would you join? Explain why.

4. Suppose one day the group digging in the hill finds pieces of pottery like those that were usually put in the grave of an important person. How might this discovery affect explanations of what happened to the king?

Standards Review

Visual Summary

Use the visual summary below to help you review the main ideas of the chapter.

QUICK FACTS

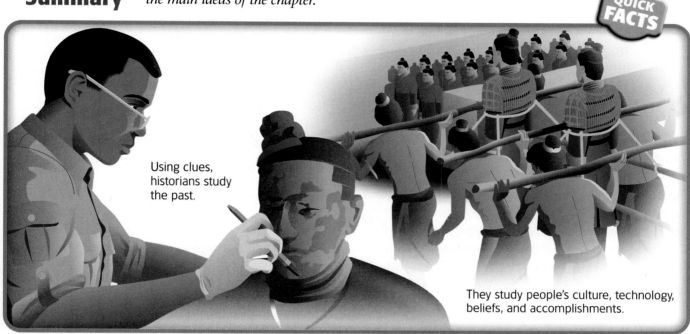

Using clues, historians study the past.

They study people's culture, technology, beliefs, and accomplishments.

Reviewing Vocabulary, Terms, and People

Choose the letter of the answer that best completes each statement below.

1. _____ is the study of the past.
  a. Archaeology   **c.** Societal structure
  b. Literature   **d.** History

2. A magazine article about an event that happened 100 years ago would be considered a(n)
  a. elementary source.   **c.** primary source.
  b. secondary source.   **d.** artifactual source.

3. A tooth from an ancient human skeleton is a(n)
  a. fossil.   **c.** artifact.
  b. remnant.   **d.** document.

4. The study of the past based on materials that people have left behind is
  a. history.   **c.** biology.
  b. archaeology.   **d.** geography.

5. An example of a primary source is a(n)
  a. textbook.   **c.** journal entry.
  b. encyclopedia.   **d.** dictionary.

6. Jewelry, tools, toys, clothing, and broken dishes may be examples of
  a. fossils.   **c.** social objects.
  b. primary sources.   **d.** artifacts.

7. If a historian studies how two events are connected, he may be studying the _____ that one event had on the other.
  a. effect   **c.** purpose
  b. cause   **d.** change

8. A community of people who share a common culture is a
  a. town.   **c.** society.
  b. country.   **d.** social group.

Comprehension and Critical Thinking

SECTION 1 *(Pages 6–9)*

9. a. Identify What two types of scholars gather clues to study the past?

b. Analyze What more could an archaeologist learn from studying a group's material culture than from just studying an artifact?

c. Evaluate Do archaeologists or historians have a more difficult job? Why?

SECTION 2 *(Pages 10–15)*

10. a. Describe What do scholars need to be able to interpret old languages?

b. Analyze Why do changing perceptions about our society today affect history?

c. Elaborate What may an archaeologist conclude about a society if the weapons she found in a ruined city were well made but the farm tools were poorly made? What might cause her to change her conclusion?

Reviewing Themes

11. Society and Culture Why might different historians draw different conclusions about a culture's social structure?

12. Religion What kinds of primary and secondary sources could provide clues about a society's religious beliefs?

Social Studies Skills

Understanding Historical Interpretation *Read the passage here and then answer the questions that follow.*

> "If such a thing as a 'purely objective' historian could exist, his work would be unreadable—like eating sawdust. Bias is only misleading when it is concealed."
>
> –Barbara W. Tuchman, from *Practicing History*

13. What role does the writer think bias, or personal opinion, plays in historical interpretation?

14. Why is it not possible for a "purely objective" historian to exist?

Using the Internet

go.hrw.com

KEYWORD SQ7 WH1

15. Activity: Researching Changing Views of History Recent archaeological finds can change interpretations of history. Enter the activity keyword to explore recent discoveries. Choose an archaeological site that interests you and write a paragraph to summarize what was found there. Then conduct research to find how the discoveries at the site have changed historians' views of that place or culture.

Reading Skills

Understanding Specialized Vocabulary *Read the following passages from the text and answer the questions after each one.*

16.
> "Some written sources are useful for answering questions about a society's economic situation—the value of its goods and services."

Where can you find the definition of "economic situation"? What is the definition?

17.
> "These items can tell us about economic systems. Archaeologists may find Roman coins in China and Chinese coins in Rome."

Notice that "economic systems" is not defined. How can you figure out what that term means? What does "economic system" mean?

FOCUS ON WRITING

18. Writing Your Composition Now you are ready to evaluate your building as if you were an archaeologist. Think about what will have changed in 3,000 years. Many features of your building will no longer be meaningful. For example, an archaeologist of the future probably could not read department store signs that say "Furniture" or "Ladies' Shoes." How can you gather information from unwritten clues? Could you interpret something incorrectly?

After considering these issues, draw your conclusions about the building's meaning and use. Then write a letter to another scholar in which you try to convince him or her of your conclusions.

Standards Assessment

DIRECTIONS: Read each question, and write the letter of the best response.

1

The tablet with ancient writing that is shown in this photo is a

A secondary source.

B secondary source and an artifact.

C primary source and a fossil.

D primary source.

2 A community of people who share a common culture is called a

A class.

B society.

C religion.

D country.

3 Can views of history change?

A Yes, if new evidence is found

B No, because history happened in the past and is over

C Yes, because people keep creating new primary sources

D No, because the people who did the things are dead

4 The source that would be *least* likely to provide information about a group's religious beliefs is

A an artifact found in a tomb.

B their sacred texts.

C their farming tools.

D their art.

5 Which statement *best* describes the relationship of legends to history?

A Legends prove that historians' theories about events are correct.

B Legends can sometimes guide historians to new discoveries.

C Legends never provide useful information.

D Legends are the most useful sources of clues that historians can find.

Connecting with Past Learnings

6 In your study of ancient history last year, you read from many different sources. All of the following were primary sources *except*

A the Code of Hammurabi.

B a chapter in your textbook.

C a quote from Homer's poem the *Odyssey.*

D the writing of a Greek philosopher.

7 Which of the following from your study of humans' earliest times in Grade 6 is an example of a fossil?

A a stone used for grinding seeds

B the remains of a 10,000-year-old hut

C the bone of a prehistoric animal

D an arrowhead found in an animal bone

The Fall of Rome

California Standards

History–Social Science

7.1 Students analyze the causes and effects of the vast expansion and ultimate disintegration of the Roman Empire.

Analysis Skills

HI 4 Recognize the role of chance, oversight, and error in history.

English–Language Arts

Speaking 7.1.6 Use speaking techniques, including voice modulation, inflection, tempo, enunciation, and eye contact, for effective presentations.

Reading 7.2.0 Students read and understand grade-level-appropriate material.

FOCUS ON SPEAKING

A Narrative Poem How do people remember great historical events like the fall of Rome? Sometimes it's because a poet created a poem to tell the story. As you read this chapter, you'll learn what happened to Rome as it became weak and lost its power. Then you'll write and present a short poem—8 to 10 lines—about this fascinating story.

117
Under Trajan, the Roman Empire reaches its greatest size.

CHAPTER EVENTS

100

WORLD EVENTS

c. 200
The Kushite civilization begins to collapse.

What You Will Learn...

In this chapter you will learn about the height of the Roman Empire, its lasting contributions, and its fall. This photo shows Roman ruins in what is now Syria.

220
The Han dynasty ends in China.

225

350

410
The Goths sack the city of Rome.

476
The last western Roman emperor is overthrown.

475

c. 570
Muhammad, the founder of Islam, is born in Mecca.

527
Justinian and Theodora come to power in Constantinople.

587
The first Buddhist monastery in Japan is established.

600

1453 The Byzantine Empire is defeated.

1450

THE FALL OF ROME **21**

Reading Social Studies

by Kylene Beers

| Economics | Geography | Politics | Religion | Society and Culture | Science and Technology |

Focus on Themes In this chapter, you will read about the fall of one of the great ancient civilizations—the Roman Empire. You will learn what problems it had inside its cities and will learn about the invaders who attacked it. You will read about the division of the empire into the western empire and the eastern empire and learn about the reasons for that division. You will see how **political** and **religious** practices differed in the two parts of the empire and learn what those differences meant.

Main Ideas in Social Studies

Focus on Reading Why do we bother to look for main ideas? History is not just a bunch of facts. Instead, history is about facts and their meanings. When we find main ideas, we find the meaning.

Identifying Main Ideas Most paragraphs written about history include a main idea. Sometimes the main idea is stated clearly in a sentence. At other times, the main idea is suggested, not stated. However, that idea still shapes the paragraph's content and the meaning of all of the facts and details in it.

Additional reading support can be found in the

Inter active
Reader and
Study Guide

Growth of Territory

In the early 400s the Vandals invaded Spain. Then they crossed into northern Africa and destroyed Roman settlements there. As they passed through Roman areas, the Vandals destroyed nearly everything in their path. At about the same time, the Angles, Saxons, and Jutes invaded Britain, and the Franks invaded Gaul. (p. 33)

Topic: The paragraph seems to be about the groups of people who invaded Rome.

+

Facts and Details: Spain invaded by Vandals; destroyed Roman areas; three groups invaded Britain; Franks invaded Gaul

Main Idea: In the 400s Rome and its territories were attacked by several groups of invaders.

Identifying Main Ideas

1. Read the paragraph. Ask yourself, "What is this paragraph mostly about, or its topic?"

2. List the important facts and details that relate to that topic.

3. Ask yourself, "What seems to be the most important point the writer is making about the topic?" Or ask, "If the writer could say only one thing about this paragraph, what would it be?" This is the **main idea** of the paragraph.

ELA **Reading 7.2.0** Read and understand grade-level-appropriate material.

You Try It!

The passage below is from the chapter you are about to read. Read the passage and then answer the questions below.

Problems Threaten the Empire

At its height the Roman Empire included all the land around the Mediterranean Sea. The empire in the early 100s stretched from Britain south to Egypt, and from the Atlantic Ocean all the way to the Persian Gulf.

From Chapter 2, p. 30

But the empire did not stay that large for long. By the end of the 100s emperors had given up some of the land the Roman army had conquered. These emperors feared that the empire had become too large to defend or govern efficiently. As later rulers discovered, these emperors were right.

Even as emperors were giving up territory, new threats to the empire were appearing. Tribes of Germanic warriors, whom the Romans called barbarians, attacked Rome's northern borders. At the same time, Persian armies invaded in the east. The Romans defended themselves for 200 years, but only at great cost.

Answer the following questions about finding main ideas.

1. Which sentence expresses the main idea of the first paragraph? How can you tell?

2. What is the main idea of the second paragraph? List two details from the paragraph that support that main idea.

3. What is the main idea of the third paragraph?

Key Terms and People

Chapter 2

Section 1
Augustus *(p. 25)*
citizens *(p. 25)*
aqueducts *(p. 26)*

Section 2
Diocletian *(p. 31)*
Constantine *(p. 31)*
Clovis *(p. 33)*
Attila *(p. 33)*
corruption *(p. 34)*

Section 3
Justinian *(p. 36)*
Theodora *(p. 37)*
Byzantine Empire *(p. 38)*
mosaics *(p. 39)*

Academic Vocabulary

Success in school is related to knowing academic vocabulary— the words that are frequently used in school assignments and discussions. In this chapter, you will learn the following academic words:

innovation *(p. 27)*
strategy *(p. 32)*
efficient *(p. 34)*

As you read Chapter 2, identify the main ideas of the paragraphs you are studying.

The Roman Empire

What You Will Learn...

Main Ideas

1. Leadership and laws helped the Romans in building the empire.
2. Roman advancements in engineering, architecture, art, and philosophy helped shape later civilizations.
3. Christianity spread quickly throughout the Roman world.

The Big Idea

The Romans made great advances in many fields that helped keep their empire strong.

Key Terms and People

Augustus, *p. 25*
citizens, *p. 25*
aqueducts, *p. 26*

HSS 7.1.1 Study the early strengths and lasting contributions of Rome (e.g., significance of Roman citizenship; rights under Roman law; Roman art, architecture, engineering, and philosophy; preservation and transmission of Christianity) and its ultimate internal weaknesses (e.g., the rise of autonomous military powers within the empire, undermining of citizenship by the growth of corruption and slavery, lack of education, and distribution of news).

If **YOU** were there...

You live in a distant province of the Roman Empire in about 200. Life is pleasant here, because your town has a theater and an arena. Of course, you have public baths and a marketplace. All Roman towns do! At school you learn Latin. Recently the emperor has given citizenship to nearly all free people in the empire. At last you can say, "*Civis romanus sum*—I am a Roman citizen!"

What new duties might you have as a citizen?

BUILDING BACKGROUND The citizens of the Roman Empire were both practical and inventive. Their ideas and accomplishments have influenced civilizations all over the world for more than 2,000 years. Some of the Romans' accomplishments, especially the creations of artists and engineers, are still admired.

Building the Empire

Between the 700s BC and the AD 100s, Rome grew from a tiny village to a huge city. As the city grew, so did its population, until Rome became home to more than a million people. Millions more lived in territories that the Romans controlled. Together, these territories surrounded the Mediterranean Sea, forming one of the largest states the world had ever seen.

As Rome gained more territory, its government changed. Originally ruled by kings, Rome turned into a republic run by elected leaders. For hundreds of years these leaders helped Rome become larger, richer, and more powerful.

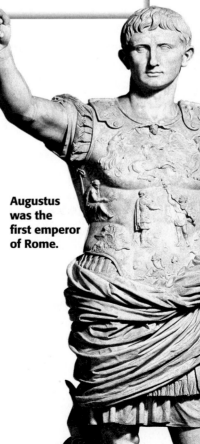

Augustus was the first emperor of Rome.

In time the republic broke down, however, and disorder spread in Rome. To restore order, the Romans again changed their government. They put control of the government in the hands of individuals who had great power. In other words, Rome became an empire.

Rome's Emperors

Rome's first emperor, **Augustus**, set many of the powers that later emperors would have. The emperor had the power to

- declare war
- raise taxes
- punish lawbreakers
- nominate public officials
- influence meetings of the Senate, the elected council that had once ruled Rome
- lead religious festivals

Later emperors benefited from the powers Augustus gained. Some used their powers well, expanding the empire and protecting its citizens. Others abused their power, seeking only to make themselves happy. Despite the selfish emperors, the empire survived for hundreds of years.

Laws and Citizenship

The empire survived, at least in part, because of its laws. Rome's laws were written down and kept on public display. These written laws were supposed to help protect Romans from unfair treatment. Because everyone knew the laws, officials had to treat everyone the same.

Rome's laws protected the rights of the city's **citizens**, the people who could participate in the government. Only citizens could hold public offices or vote.

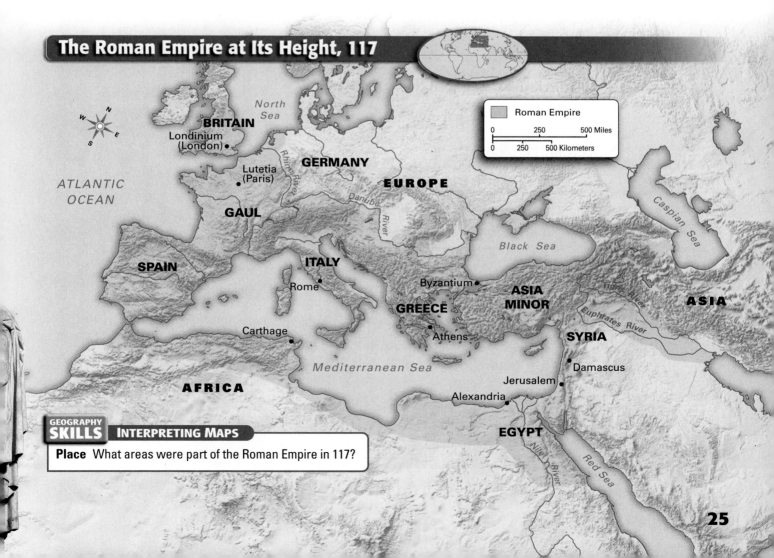

The Roman Empire at Its Height, 117

- North Sea
- BRITAIN
- Londinium (London)
- ATLANTIC OCEAN
- Lutetia (Paris)
- GERMANY
- EUROPE
- Rhine River
- Danube River
- GAUL
- SPAIN
- ITALY
- Rome
- Carthage
- Mediterranean Sea
- AFRICA
- Black Sea
- Byzantium
- GREECE
- Athens
- ASIA MINOR
- Caspian Sea
- ASIA
- Tigris River
- Euphrates River
- SYRIA
- Damascus
- Jerusalem
- Alexandria
- EGYPT
- Nile River
- Red Sea

Roman Empire

0   250   500 Miles
0   250   500 Kilometers

GEOGRAPHY SKILLS **INTERPRETING MAPS**

Place What areas were part of the Roman Empire in 117?

In addition to the rights to vote and hold office, however, all citizens had duties to perform. For example, citizens had to pay taxes, and male citizens had to serve in the army when needed.

Most Romans were very proud of their citizenship. They thought it was an honor to be a citizen of Rome. Roman citizenship was valued so much that many people the Romans conquered also wanted to become citizens. From time to time, Rome's emperors gave citizenship to groups the Romans had conquered. This act usually made the conquered people feel grateful to the emperor. As a result, they remained loyal to Rome and helped keep the empire strong.

READING CHECK **Categorizing** What rights did Roman citizens have?

Roman Advancements

While Rome's emperors and army worked to make the empire stronger, other Romans tried to improve life for its people. Engineers, architects, artists, and philosophers tried to make life more pleasant for their fellow citizens. In the process they created works of lasting strength and beauty.

Engineering

Roman engineers designed and built many structures to improve life in the empire. They built durable roads that have lasted for centuries and strong bridges that spanned raging rivers. They also built **aqueducts** (A-kwuh-duhkts), human-made channels that carried water from distant mountain ranges into Rome or other cities.

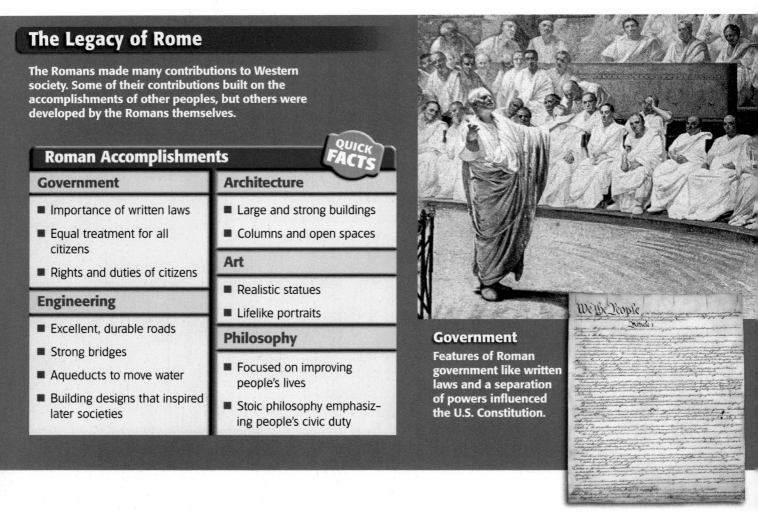

The Legacy of Rome

The Romans made many contributions to Western society. Some of their contributions built on the accomplishments of other peoples, but others were developed by the Romans themselves.

Roman Accomplishments

QUICK FACTS

Government
- Importance of written laws
- Equal treatment for all citizens
- Rights and duties of citizens

Engineering
- Excellent, durable roads
- Strong bridges
- Aqueducts to move water
- Building designs that inspired later societies

Architecture
- Large and strong buildings
- Columns and open spaces

Art
- Realistic statues
- Lifelike portraits

Philosophy
- Focused on improving people's lives
- Stoic philosophy emphasizing people's civic duty

Government
Features of Roman government like written laws and a separation of powers influenced the U.S. Constitution.

The skill of ancient Roman engineers inspired many later people to copy their techniques. For example, some builders still design stadiums in much the same way Roman engineers did. In fact, many techniques engineers and architects use today were directly inspired by the Roman engineers of 2,000 years ago.

Architecture

Architecture, the art of designing buildings, is closely related to engineering. Roman architects and engineers used many of the same ideas. They constantly sought ways to make larger, stronger buildings.

In addition to being large and strong, however, Roman architects wanted their buildings to be beautiful. Because they admired the beauty of ancient Greek structures, they borrowed Greek ideas. For example, like the Greeks, the Romans used columns and open spaces to make their buildings look elegant and majestic. But the Romans added an **innovation** of their own. They used their engineering skills to make buildings larger and grander than anything the Greeks had built.

Later civilizations greatly admired the Roman architectural style, copying many elements of Roman design in their own buildings. Elements of Roman design are seen in many public buildings even today.

Art

Architecture was not the only field in which the Romans were inspired by the Greeks. Roman works of art also borrowed heavily from earlier Greek examples.

ACADEMIC VOCABULARY
innovation
(i-nuh-VAY-shuhn) a new idea or way of doing something

Roads
Roman roads like the one above in western Italy can still be found across Europe. Modern roads still feature innovations made by the Romans.

Architecture
Roman architecture has influenced buildings for centuries. For example, the Pantheon's dome (above) inspired the California State Capitol in Sacramento.

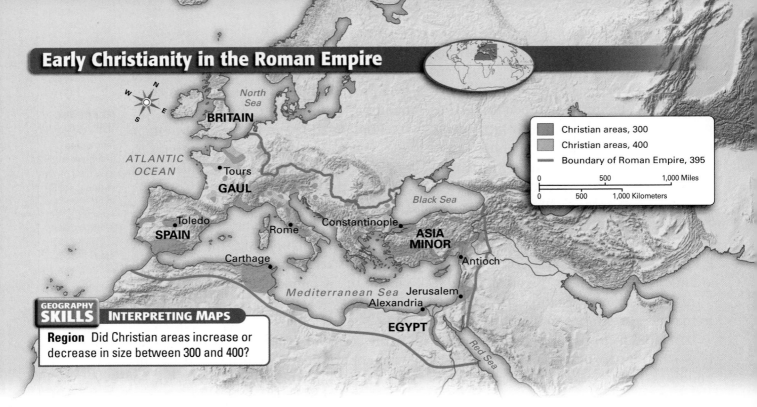

Early Christianity in the Roman Empire

North Sea

BRITAIN

ATLANTIC OCEAN

Tours

GAUL

Toledo

SPAIN

Rome

Carthage

Constantinople

Black Sea

ASIA MINOR

Antioch

Mediterranean Sea

Jerusalem
Alexandria

EGYPT

Red Sea

Christian areas, 300
Christian areas, 400
Boundary of Roman Empire, 395

0   500   1,000 Miles
0   500   1,000 Kilometers

GEOGRAPHY SKILLS | **INTERPRETING MAPS**

Region Did Christian areas increase or decrease in size between 300 and 400?

Like the Greeks, Roman artists tried to make their art incredibly realistic. They wanted their statues and paintings to look like they could come alive. Roman artists particularly excelled in creating portraits. Some Roman portraits are so lifelike that viewers can even tell what the subject's personality was like. For centuries, artists have studied Roman works to learn how to make their own works more realistic.

Philosophy

FOCUS ON READING

What is the main idea of this paragraph? How can you tell?

Like Roman artists, Roman philosophers, or thinkers, wanted to show the world as it really was. They disagreed with earlier Greek philosophers who spent their time thinking about ideal worlds. Instead the Romans focused on how their ideas could improve people's lives.

For example, Roman philosophers advised people on how they should behave in order to be happy. One large group of philosophers called the Stoics (STOH-iks) taught that people shouldn't be concerned with possessions. Instead, they should focus on living a virtuous life.

Stoic ideas influenced the Roman idea of civic duty. Inspired by the Stoics, Romans felt that they should act for the good of the city, not for personal gain. This notion of civic duty was passed on to later cultures, like our own in the United States.

READING CHECK **Comparing** How did the Romans improve on Greek architecture?

Christianity Spreads

Early in the first century AD a new religion, Christianity, appeared in Rome. At first the Romans saw the Christians as a branch of an older religion, Judaism. They didn't anticipate that Christianity would become a major force in the empire.

Christianity grew, though, spreading quickly through Rome. Worried by this growth, some officials tried to stop Christianity from spreading. It couldn't be stopped. Then in the 300s, a Roman emperor became Christian. Later emperors increased their support for Christianity until it became the official religion of the empire.

This Roman carving was created in the 300s. It shows scenes from the life of Jesus.

These two scenes show Jesus carrying the cross and being mocked by a Roman soldier.

This symbol, called a Chi-Rho, represents Jesus Christ. It is based on the first two letters of the word "Christ" in Greek.

During the period of the Roman Empire, Christianity spread from its birthplace in Southwest Asia into other parts of the world. Some historians estimate that, by the 300s, most of Rome's population was Christian.

As the church grew, the influence of church leaders grew as well. Soon the heads of the church became major figures in Roman society. The most influential of these leaders was the pope, the bishop of Rome. The influence of the pope and other church leaders helped unify Rome as a single Christian society.

READING CHECK Drawing Conclusions How did the Romans help spread Christianity?

SUMMARY AND PREVIEW The Romans made many great advances and created a great culture in their empire. By the 200s, though, Roman society had begun to weaken. Threats from both outside and inside the empire seemed likely to tear the empire apart.

go.hrw.com
Online Quiz
KEYWORD: SQ7 CH2

Section 1 Assessment

Reviewing Ideas, Terms, and People **HSS** 7.1.1

1. a. **Identify** What rights and duties did Roman **citizens** have?
   b. **Explain** How did **Augustus** influence the later development of the Roman government?
2. a. **Recall** What group of Roman philosophers taught that people should not be concerned with possessions?
   b. **Rate** What do you think was the Romans' greatest engineering accomplishment? Why?
3. a. **Identify** Whose conversion to Christianity helped make Christianity acceptable in Rome?
   b. **Make Generalizations** What role did church leaders play in the spread of Christianity?

Critical Thinking

4. **Categorizing** Draw a chart like the one below. In each column list one contribution the ancient Romans made.

Law	Engineering	Architecture	Art	Philosophy

FOCUS ON SPEAKING

5. **Choosing the Right Words** Poets use just a few carefully chosen words to tell a story. In your notebook draw a large circle. In the circle write words or phrases you might use in your poem—words like *empire, stoic,* and *weaken.* If necessary, write a brief description of each word.

Fall of the Western Roman Empire

What You Will Learn...

Main Ideas

1. Many problems threatened the Roman Empire, leading one emperor to divide it in half.
2. Barbarians invaded Rome in the 300s and 400s.
3. Many factors contributed to Rome's fall.

The Big Idea

Problems from both inside and outside caused the Roman Empire to split and the western half to collapse.

Key Terms and People

Diocletian, *p. 31*
Constantine, *p. 31*
Clovis, *p. 33*
Attila, *p. 33*
corruption, *p. 34*

HSS 7.1.2 Discuss the geographic borders of the empire at its height and the factors that threatened its territorial cohesion.

If YOU were there...

You are a former Roman soldier who has settled on lands in Gaul. In the last few months, groups of barbarians have been raiding local towns and burning farms. The commander of the local army garrison is an old friend, but he says he is short of loyal soldiers. Many troops have been called back to Rome. You don't know when the next raid will come.

How will you defend your lands?

BUILDING BACKGROUND Though the Roman Empire remained large and powerful, it faced serious threats from both outside and inside. Beyond the borders of the empire, many different groups of people were on the move. They threatened the peace in Rome's provinces—and eventually attacked the heart of the empire itself.

Problems Threaten the Empire

At its height the Roman Empire included all the land around the Mediterranean Sea. The empire in the early 100s stretched from Britain south to Egypt, and from the Atlantic Ocean all the way to the Persian Gulf.

But the empire did not stay that large for long. By the end of the 100s emperors had given up some of the land the Roman army had conquered. These emperors feared that the empire had become too large to defend or govern efficiently. As later rulers discovered, these emperors were right.

Problems in the Empire

Even as emperors were giving up territory, new threats to the empire were appearing. Tribes of Germanic warriors, whom the Romans called barbarians, attacked Rome's northern borders. At the same time, Persian armies invaded in the east. The Romans defended themselves for 200 years, but only at great cost.

The Romans struggled with problems within the empire as well. Because so many Romans were needed in the army, not enough people were left to farm. To grow enough food, the Romans invited Germanic farmers to grow crops on Roman lands. These farmers often came from the same tribes that threatened Rome's borders. Over time, whole German communities had moved into the empire. They chose their own leaders and largely ignored the emperors, which caused problems for the Romans.

Other internal problems also threatened Rome's survival. Disease swept through the empire, killing many people. The government increased taxes to pay for the defense of the empire. Desperate, the Romans looked for a strong emperor to solve their problems.

Division of the Empire

The emperor the Romans were looking for was **Diocletian** (dy-uh-KLEE-shuhn), who took power in the late 200s. Convinced that the empire was too big for one person to rule, Diocletian divided the empire. He ruled the eastern half of the empire and named a co-emperor to rule the west.

Not long after Diocletian left power, Emperor **Constantine** (KAHN-stuhn-teen) reunited the two halves of the Roman Empire for a short time. Constantine also moved the empire's capital to the east into what is now Turkey. He built a grand new capital city there. The new capital was called Constantinople (KAHN-stant-uhn-oh-puhl), which means "the city of Constantine." Although the empire was still called the Roman Empire, Rome was no longer the real seat of power. Power had moved to the east.

READING CHECK Identifying Cause and Effect
Why did Diocletian divide the Roman Empire?

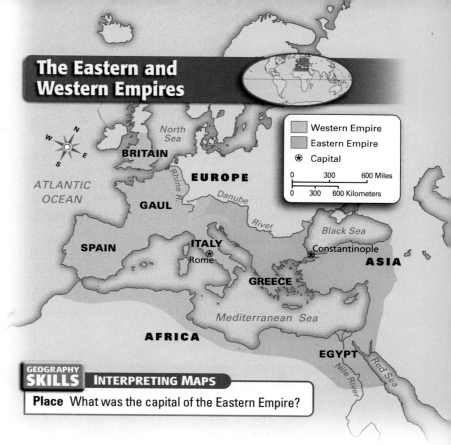

The Eastern and Western Empires

Western Empire
Eastern Empire
⊛ Capital

GEOGRAPHY SKILLS INTERPRETING MAPS

Place What was the capital of the Eastern Empire?

Barbarians Invade Rome

Not long after Constantine moved Rome's capital, German barbarians—people the Romans considered uncivilized—from the north began to raid the Roman Empire. As you have already read, barbarian tribes had settled along the empire's northern border in the 200s. For more than 100 years these tribes mostly stayed out of Roman territory. Late in the 300s, though, the barbarians began raiding deep into the heart of the empire.

Early Invasions

The source of these raids was a new group of people who moved into Europe. Called the Huns, they were fierce warriors from Central Asia.

As you can see on the map on the next page, the Huns invaded southeastern Europe. From there they launched raids on nearby kingdoms. Among the victims of these raids were several groups of people called the Goths.

THE IMPACT TODAY

Constantinople is now called Istanbul. It is Turkey's largest city and a thriving economic center.

The Goths could not defeat the Huns in battle. As the Huns continued to raid their territories, the Goths fled. Trapped between the Huns and Rome, they had nowhere to go but into Roman territory.

ACADEMIC VOCABULARY

strategy a plan for fighting a battle or war

Rome's leaders were afraid that the Goths would destroy Roman land and property. To stop this destruction, the emperors fought to keep the Goths out of Roman lands. In the east the armies were largely successful. They forced the Goths to move farther west. As a result, however, the western armies were defeated by the Goths, who moved into Roman territory.

The Sack of Rome

The Romans fought desperately to keep the Goths away from Rome. They also paid the Goths not to attack them. For many years this **strategy** worked. In 408, however, the Romans stopped making payments. This made the Goths furious. Despite the Romans' best efforts to defend their city, the Goths sacked, or destroyed, Rome in 410.

The destruction of Rome absolutely devastated the Romans. No one had attacked their city in nearly 800 years. For the first time, many Romans began to feel afraid for the safety of their empire.

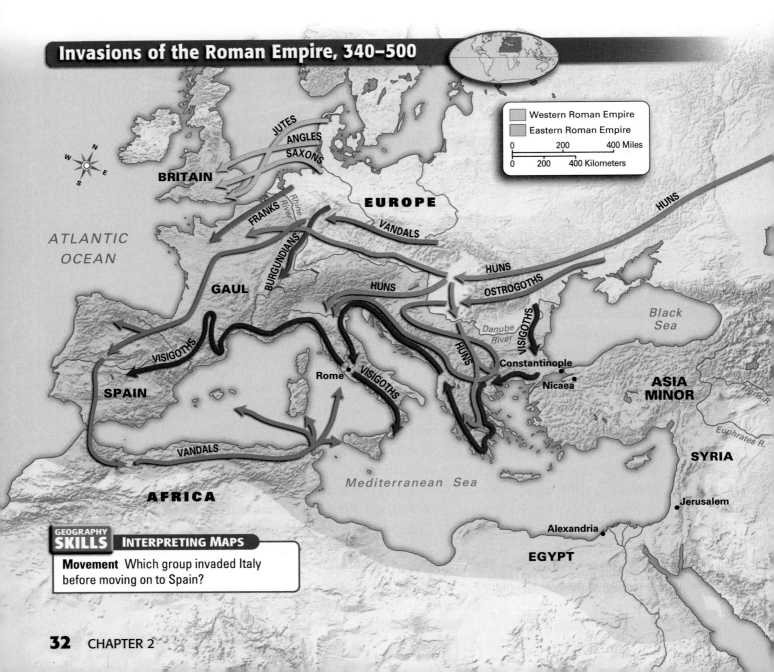

Invasions of the Roman Empire, 340–500

Western Roman Empire
Eastern Roman Empire

0   200   400 Miles
0   200   400 Kilometers

JUTES
ANGLES
SAXONS
BRITAIN
EUROPE
HUNS
FRANKS
Rhine River
VANDALS
ATLANTIC OCEAN
BURGUNDIANS
GAUL
HUNS
HUNS
OSTROGOTHS
Danube River
VISIGOTHS
Black Sea
HUNS
Constantinople
VISIGOTHS
Nicaea
ASIA MINOR
Rome
VISIGOTHS
SPAIN
VISIGOTHS
Tigris R.
Euphrates R.
VANDALS
SYRIA
Mediterranean Sea
AFRICA
Jerusalem
Alexandria
EGYPT

GEOGRAPHY SKILLS **INTERPRETING MAPS**

Movement Which group invaded Italy before moving on to Spain?

The Empire in Chaos

Unfortunately for Rome, the city's fall to the Goths in 410 wasn't the end of the invasions. The Gothic victory served as an example for other barbarian groups to invade the western half of the empire.

In the early 400s the Vandals invaded Spain. Then they crossed into northern Africa and destroyed Roman settlements there. As they passed through Roman areas, the Vandals destroyed nearly everything in their path. At about the same time, the Angles, Saxons, and Jutes invaded Britain, and the Franks invaded Gaul.

By the 480s a Frankish king named **Clovis** had built a huge kingdom in Gaul. Clovis, a Christian, was one of the most powerful of all the German kings.

Meanwhile, the Huns, under a new leader named **Attila** (AT-uhl-uh), raided Roman territory in the east. Attila was a brilliant leader and a very scary enemy. Here is one description that shows why he was so terrifying.

> " He was a man born into the world to shake the nations, the scourge of all lands, who in some way terrified all mankind by the dreadful rumors noised abroad concerning him. "
>
> –Jordanes, from *History of the Goths*

THE IMPACT TODAY

We still use the word *vandal* today to describe someone who destroys property.

The Goths and Huns were just two of the groups that invaded the Roman Empire. In this illustration, a Goth warrior is shown on the right, and a Hun is shown on the left. These invaders also battled each other, as Huns attacked Goths and fought for territory and riches.

Key Events in Roman History

c. 509 BC
Rome sets up a republic.

500 BC

264–146 BC
Rome battles Carthage during the Punic Wars.

27 BC
The Roman Republic becomes the Roman Empire.

BC 1 AD

AD 117
The Roman Empire reaches its height.

Attila led the Huns in raids against Constantinople, Greece, Gaul, and parts of northern Italy. But because he was told that diseases ran wild in southern Italy, he decided not to go south to Rome.

The End of the Western Empire

Rome needed strong leaders to survive these constant attacks, but the emperors of the 400s were weak. As attacks on Rome's borders increased, military leaders took power away from the emperors. By the 450s military leaders ruled Rome.

Unfortunately for Rome, most of these military leaders were too busy fighting among themselves to protect the empire. Barbarian leaders took advantage of this situation and invaded Rome. In 476 a barbarian general overthrew the last emperor in Rome and named himself king of Italy. Many historians consider this event the end of the western Roman Empire.

ACADEMIC VOCABULARY

efficient
(i-FI-shuhnt)
productive and not wasteful

READING CHECK **Analyzing** Why did Rome fall to barbarians in the 400s?

Factors in Rome's Fall

There were many causes for the decline of Rome, including barbarian invasions, corruption of governmental officials, inflation and a weakening economy, and the power of the military to make and remove emperors.

One cause of Rome's decline was the vast size of the empire. In some ways, Rome had simply grown too big to govern. Communication among various parts of the empire was difficult, even in peaceful times. During times of conflict it became even more difficult.

Political crises also contributed to the decline. By the 400s **corruption**, the decay of people's values, had become widespread in Rome's government. Corrupt officials used threats and bribery to achieve their goals, often ignoring the needs of Roman citizens. Because of officials like these, Rome's government was no longer as **efficient** as it had been in the past.

In the face of this corruption, many wealthy citizens fled the city of Rome for their country estates. This action created a series of causes and effects that further weakened the empire.

AD 286
Diocletian divides the Roman Empire in two.

AD 381
All non-Christian religions are banned in Rome.

500

AD 410
The Goths sack Rome.

AD 476 The western Roman Empire falls.

Why Rome Fell

Problems Inside the Empire

- Large size made communication difficult.
- Corruption became common.
- Rich citizens left Rome for country estates.
- Taxes and prices rose.

Problems Outside the Empire

- Barbarians began invading the empire.

ANALYSIS SKILL **READING TIME LINES**

About how long did the Roman Empire last?

Outside Rome, many landowners used slaves or serfs to work on their lands. To protect their estates and their wealth, many landowners created their own armies. Ambitious landowners used these personal armies to overthrow emperors and take power for themselves.

As wealthy citizens abandoned Rome and other cities, city life became more difficult for those who remained. Rome's population decreased, and schools closed. At the same time taxes and prices soared, leaving more and more Romans poor. By the end of the 400s Rome was no longer the city it had once been. As it changed, the empire slowly collapsed around it.

READING CHECK **Finding Main Ideas** How did corruption alter Roman society in the 400s?

SUMMARY AND PREVIEW By the early 500s Rome no longer ruled western Europe. But as you will read in the next section, the empire in the east continued to prosper for several hundred years.

---

go.hrw.com
Online Quiz
KEYWORD: SQ7 CH2

Section 2 Assessment

Reviewing Ideas, Terms, and People **HSS** 7.1.2

1. **a. Recall** Where did **Constantine** move Rome's capital?
   b. Explain Why did **Diocletian** divide the empire in two?
2. **a. Identify** Who was **Attila**?
   b. Summarize Why did the Goths move into the Roman Empire in the 300s?
   c. Elaborate Why do you think the sack of Rome was so devastating?
3. **a. Describe** What kinds of problems did Rome's size cause for its emperors?
   b. Make Generalizations How did **corruption** weaken Rome in the 400s?

Critical Thinking

4. **Drawing Conclusions**
   Draw a word web like the one shown on the right. In each of the outer circles, list a factor that helped lead to the fall of the western Roman Empire. You may add more circles if needed.

   Fall of the Western Roman Empire

FOCUS ON SPEAKING

5. **Adding Details** Make a list of the most important events that led to the fall of the western Roman Empire. Then circle the events you will mention in your poem.

THE FALL OF ROME **35**

The Byzantine Empire

What You Will Learn...

Main Ideas

1. Eastern emperors ruled from Constantinople and tried but failed to reunite the whole Roman Empire.
2. The people of the eastern empire created a new society that was very different from society in the west.
3. Byzantine Christianity was different from religion in the west.

The Big Idea

The Roman Empire split into two parts, and the eastern Roman Empire prospered for hundreds of years after the western empire fell.

Key Terms and People

Justinian, *p. 36*
Theodora, *p. 37*
Byzantine Empire, *p. 38*
mosaics, *p. 39*

HSS 7.1.3 Describe the establishment by Constantine of the new capital in Constantinople and the development of the Byzantine Empire, with an emphasis on the consequences of the development of two distinct European civilizations, Eastern Orthodox and Roman Catholic, and their two distinct views on church-state relations.

If **YOU** were there...

You are a trader visiting Constantinople. You have traveled to many cities but have never seen anything so magnificent. The city has huge palaces and stadiums for horse races. In the city center you enter a church and stop, speechless with amazement. Above you is a vast, gold dome lit by hundreds of candles.

How does the city make you feel about its rulers?

BUILDING BACKGROUND Even before the western empire fell to the Goths, power had begun to shift to the richer, more stable east. The people of the eastern empire considered themselves Romans, but their culture was very different from that of Rome itself.

Emperors Rule from Constantinople

Constantinople was built on the site of an ancient Greek trading city called Byzantium (buh-ZAN-shuhm). It lay near both the Black Sea and the Mediterranean Sea. This location between two seas protected the city from attack and let the city control trade between Europe and Asia. Constantinople was in an ideal place to grow in wealth and power.

Justinian

After Rome fell in 476, the emperors of the eastern Roman Empire dreamed of taking it back and reuniting the old Roman Empire. For **Justinian** (juh-STIN-ee-uhn), an emperor who ruled from 527 to 565, reuniting the empire was a passion. He couldn't live with a Roman Empire that didn't include the city of Rome, so he sent his army to retake Italy. In the end this army conquered not only Italy but also much land around the Mediterranean.

Justinian's other passions were the law and the church. He ordered officials to examine all of Rome's laws and remove any out-of-date or unchristian laws. He then organized all the laws

The Byzantine Empire, 1025

EUROPE

Adriatic Sea

Danube River

Black Sea

Rome
ITALY

Constantinople

ASIA

ASIA MINOR

Ionian Sea

GREECE

Aegean Sea

Athens

Euphrates River

Tigris River

Antioch
SYRIA

Mediterranean Sea

Crete

Cyprus

Byzantine Empire

0   150   300 Miles
0 150   300 Kilometers

GEOGRAPHY SKILLS | **INTERPRETING MAPS**

Location Where was Constantinople?

into a legal system called Justinian's Code. By simplifying Roman law, this code helped guarantee fair treatment for all.

Despite his achievements, Justinian made many enemies. Two groups of these enemies joined together and tried to overthrow him in 532. These groups led riots in the streets and set fire to buildings. Scared for his life, Justinian prepared to leave Constantinople.

Justinian was stopped from leaving by his wife, **Theodora** (thee-uh-DOHR-uh). She convinced Justinian to stay in the city. Smart and powerful, Theodora helped her husband rule effectively. With her advice, he found a way to end the riots. Justinian's soldiers killed all the rioters—some 30,000 people—and saved the emperor's throne.

The Empire after Justinian

After the death of Justinian in 565, the eastern empire began to decline. Faced with invasions by barbarians, Persians, and Muslims, later emperors lost all the land

City walls

Harbor

Forum

Hippodrome

Hagia Sophia

Imperial Palace

Constantinople was strategically located where Europe and Asia meet. As a result, the city was in a perfect location to control trade routes between the two continents.

Justinian had gained. The eastern empire remained a major power for several hundred years, but it never regained its former strength.

The eastern empire's struggles finally ended nearly 700 years after the death of Justinian. In 1453 a group called the Ottoman Turks captured Constantinople. With this defeat the 1,000-year history of the eastern Roman Empire came to an end.

READING CHECK **Drawing Conclusions**
Why did Justinian reorganize Roman law?

A New Society

In many ways Justinian was the last Roman emperor of the eastern empire. After he died, non-Roman influences took hold throughout the empire. People began to speak Greek, the language of the eastern empire, rather than Latin. Scholars studied Greek, not Roman, philosophy. Gradually, the empire lost its ties to the old Roman Empire, and a new society developed.

The people who lived in this society never stopped thinking of themselves as Romans. But modern historians have given their society a new name. They call the society that developed in the eastern Roman Empire after the west fell the **Byzantine** (BI-zuhn-teen) **Empire**, named after the Greek town of Byzantium.

Outside Influence

One reason eastern and western Roman society was different was the Byzantines' interaction with other groups. This interaction was largely a result of trade. Because Constantinople's location was ideal for trading between Europe and Asia, it became the greatest trading city in Europe.

Merchants from all around Europe, Asia, and Africa traveled to Constantinople to trade. Over time Byzantine society began to reflect these outside influences as well as its Roman and Greek roots.

Government

The forms of government that developed in the eastern and western empires also created differences. Byzantine emperors had

History Close-up

The Glory of Constantinople

Constantinople was a crossroads for traders, a center of Christianity, and the capital of an empire. It was a magnificent city filled with great buildings, palaces, and churches. The city's rulers led processions, or ceremonial walks, to show their wealth and power.

This procession went from the church to the royal palace. The procession showed the power and importance of the emperor as head of the church.

more power than western emperors did. They liked to show off their great power. For example, people could not stand while they were in the presence of the eastern emperor. They had to crawl on their hands and knees to talk to him.

The power of an eastern emperor was greater, in part, because the emperor was considered the head of the church as well as the political ruler. The Byzantines thought the emperor had been chosen by God to lead both the empire and the church. In the west the emperor was limited to political power. Popes and bishops were the leaders of the church.

READING CHECK **Contrasting** What were two ways in which eastern and western Roman society were different?

Byzantine Christianity

Just as it was in the west, Christianity was central to the Byzantines' lives. From the beginning, nearly everyone who lived in the Byzantine Empire was Christian.

To show their devotion to God and the Christian Church, Byzantine artists created beautiful works of religious art. Among the grandest works were **mosaics**, pictures made with pieces of colored stone or glass. Some mosaics sparkled with gold, silver, and jewels.

The procession began at Hagia Sophia, the Byzantines' famous church.

Citizens and visitors crowded the square to see the royal rulers pass by.

ANALYSIS SKILL **ANALYZING VISUALS**

Where did the procession begin and end?

QUICK FACTS

The Western Roman and Byzantine Empires

In the Western Roman Empire . . .

- Popes and bishops led the church, and the emperor led the government.
- Latin was the main language.

In the Byzantine Empire . . .

- Emperors led the church and the government.
- Greek was the main language.

THE IMPACT TODAY

The Eastern Orthodox Church is still the main religion in Russia, Greece, and other parts of Eastern Europe.

Even more magnificent than their mosaics were Byzantine churches, especially Hagia Sophia (HAH-juh soh-FEE-uh). Built by Justinian in the 530s, its huge domes rose high above Constantinople. According to legend, when Justinian saw the church he exclaimed in delight

" Glory to God who has judged me worthy of accomplishing such a work as this! O Solomon, I have outdone you! "

–Justinian, quoted in *The Story of the Building of the Church of Santa Sophia*

As time passed, people in the east and west began to interpret and practice Christianity differently. For example, eastern priests could get married, while priests in the west could not. Religious services were performed in Greek in the east. In the west they were held in Latin.

For hundreds of years, church leaders from the east and west worked together peacefully despite their differences. However, the differences between their ideas continued to grow. In time the differences led to a split within the Christian Church. In the 1000s Christians in the east broke away from the rest of the church and formed what became known as the Eastern Orthodox Church. As a result, eastern and western Europe were completely divided.

READING CHECK **Contrasting** What led to a split in the Christian Church?

SUMMARY AND PREVIEW The Roman Empire and the Christian Church both divided into two parts. The Eastern Orthodox Church became a major force in the Byzantine Empire. Before long, though, Orthodox Christians encountered members of a religious group they had never met before, the Muslims.

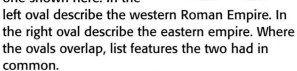

go.hrw.com
Online Quiz
KEYWORD: SQ7 CH2

Section 3 Assessment

Reviewing Ideas, Terms, and People HSS 7.1.3

1. **a. Describe** Where was Constantinople located?
   b. Summarize What were two of **Justinian**'s major accomplishments?
   c. Elaborate What do you think **Theodora**'s role in the government says about women in the eastern empire?
2. **a. Identify** What was one major difference between the powers of emperors in the east and the west?
   b. Explain How did contact with other cultures help change the **Byzantine Empire**?
3. **a. Define** What is a **mosaic**?
   b. Make Generalizations What led to the creation of two different Christian societies in Europe?

Critical Thinking

4. **Comparing and Contrasting** Draw a Venn diagram like the one shown here. In the left oval describe the western Roman Empire. In the right oval describe the eastern empire. Where the ovals overlap, list features the two had in common.

FOCUS ON SPEAKING

5. **Organizing Dates** Add key events from Byzantine history to the list you made in the last section. Once you have your list complete, arrange the events on your list in the order they happened.

Justinian and Theodora

How would you rebuild a fallen empire?

When did they live? Justinian, c. 483–565; Theodora, c. 500–548

Where did they live? Constantinople

What did they do? As Byzantine emperor, Justinian reconquered parts of the fallen western empire and simplified Roman laws. He also ordered the building of many beautiful public buildings and churches, including Hagia Sophia.

KEY EVENTS

- **525** Justinian and Theodora are married.

- **527** Justinian becomes emperor and names Theodora empress.

- **532** Theodora persuades Justinian not to flee Constantinople during riots.

- **534** Justinian's Code is produced.

- **534–565** Justinian's armies reconquer parts of the Roman Empire, from North Africa to Italy to Spain.

Why are they important?

Justinian and Theodora worked together to restore the power, beauty, and strength of the Roman Empire. They made Constantinople into a grand capital city and the center of a strong empire. While Justinian tried to reconquer the west, Theodora helped create laws to aid women and children and to end government corruption.

Evaluating Which of Justinian and Theodora's accomplishments do you find most impressive? Why?

Hagia Sophia rises high above Istanbul, Turkey, the city once called Constantinople.

41

Social Studies Skills

 HSS Analysis HI 4 Students recognize the role of chance, oversight, and error in history.

Analysis | Critical Thinking | Participation | Study

Chance, Error, and Oversight in History

Understand the Skill

History is nothing more than what people thought and did in the past, and the people of the past were just as human as people today. Like us, they occasionally forgot or overlooked things. They made mistakes in their decisions or judgments. Unexpected things happened that they couldn't control. Sometimes, these oversights, errors, and just plain luck shaped history.

Learn the Skill

This chapter notes several examples of the role of error, chance, and oversight in history.

1 **Error:** The Gothic chief Alaric offered peace with Rome in return for land and supplies for his people. Rome's leaders paid for many years, but then they stopped. Stopping the payments was a mistake, because Alaric attacked and looted Rome in 410. For the first time in 800 years, Rome fell to an outside invader.

2 **Chance:** In 452 Attila the Hun attacked northern Italy. After several victories, however, he halted his invasion and turned back. Southern Italy was suffering from a plague, and Attila did not want to risk weakening his army by entering the region. If not for this chance occurrence, Rome might have been conquered again.

3 **Oversight:** Emperor Justinian's subjects failed to appreciate his wife's importance. Theodora was a commoner, so they gave her little respect. When they launched a revolt in 532, Justinian was ready to flee. However, Theodora gave a powerful speech about the rewards of risking one's life for a great cause. Her speech inspired Justinian's supporters to attack and defeat the rebels.

Practice and Apply the Skill

As you read in the chapter, military leaders ruled the western empire by the 450s. Analyze the reasons for this development. Write a paragraph to explain how chance, error, or oversight influenced this shift in power in Rome.

42 CHAPTER 2

Standards Review

Visual Summary

Use the visual summary below to help you review the main ideas of the chapter.

QUICK FACTS

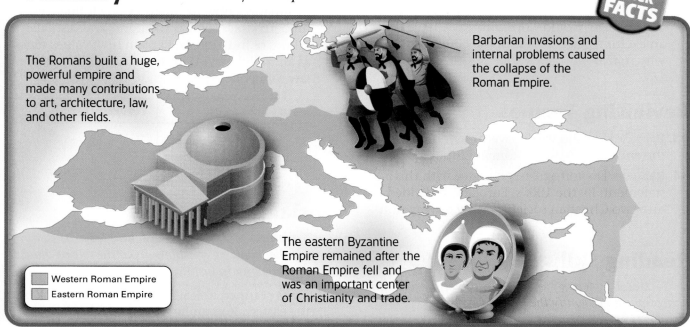

The Romans built a huge, powerful empire and made many contributions to art, architecture, law, and other fields.

Barbarian invasions and internal problems caused the collapse of the Roman Empire.

The eastern Byzantine Empire remained after the Roman Empire fell and was an important center of Christianity and trade.

Western Roman Empire
Eastern Roman Empire

Reviewing Vocabulary, Terms, and People

Unscramble each group of letters below to spell a term that matches the given definition.

1. **anzbtinye**—name given to the eastern half of the Roman Empire
2. **latcodeiin**—emperor who divided the Roman Empire into two parts
3. **zticeins**—people who had the right to participate in Rome's government
4. **ohtradoe**—empress of the Byzantine Empire
5. **rcotponiur**—the decay of people's values
6. **smiacso**—pictures made from pieces of colorful glass or stone
7. **ugsatusu**—the first emperor of Rome
8. **tatali**—leader of the Huns who invaded Rome in the 400s
9. **njiasunti**—Byzantine emperor who tried to reunite the entire Roman Empire

Comprehension and Critical Thinking

SECTION 1 *(Pages 24–29)* **HSS** 7.1.1

10. **a. Recall** What new religion appeared in the Roman Empire in the first century AD?

 b. Analyze What did it mean to be a Roman citizen?

 c. Elaborate Many historians have observed that the Romans were a practical people. How did that quality show in Roman engineering, architecture, and philosophy?

SECTION 2 *(Pages 30–35)* **HSS** 7.1.2

11. **a. Identify** Who were the Huns? Who were the Goths?

 b. Compare and Contrast What did Diocletian and Constantine have in common? How did their actions differ?

 c. Evaluate Of all the causes for the fall of the western Roman Empire, which, if any, could have been prevented? Explain your answer.

SECTION 3 *(Pages 36–40)* **HSS** 7.1.3

12. a. Identify Who were Justinian and Theodora, and what did they accomplish?

b. Contrast In what ways was the Byzantine Empire different from the western Roman Empire?

c. Elaborate Would Constantinople have been an exciting place to visit in the 500s? Why or why not?

Reviewing Themes

13. Politics How did weak government help lead to the end of the western Roman Empire?

14. Religion Do you agree or disagree with this statement: By the 1000s, Europe was divided into two Christian societies. Why or why not?

Reading Skills

Understanding Main Ideas *Read each of the following paragraphs and identify the main idea.*

15. Roads were only one thing the Romans were good at making. The Romans were skilled engineers and builders. They built excellent bridges, aqueducts, and buildings.

16. Many groups invaded the Roman Empire in the 300s and 400s. Among them were the Goths and the Vandals. These groups caused a great deal of damage.

17. Huge churches with large domes were built in Constantinople and other parts of the Byzantine Empire. Byzantine artists also created beautiful works of religious art. Many of their paintings and sparkling mosaics covered the walls of churches. These paintings and mosaics often showed Jesus, angels, and scenes from the Bible.

Using the Internet

18. Activity: Summarizing Most law students are required to learn about Justinian's Code because it had such a strong influence on modern law. Enter the keyword. Then create a chart that summarizes how Justinian's Code influences modern issues such as the rights and responsibilities of individuals. Explain how values such as an individual's right to equality before the law influenced the world.

Justinian's Code	Modern Law

Social Studies Skills

Recognizing Chance, Oversight, and Error in History
Answer the following questions about the role of chance, oversight, or error in history.

19. Attila planned to lead the Huns in an attack on the eastern Roman Empire in 453, but he died of a nosebleed the night of his wedding that year. How might history have been different if Attila had not happened to die?

20. How might the revolt against Justinian in 532 have been caused by an oversight on his part? What might he have done to prevent the revolt?

FOCUS ON SPEAKING

21. Presenting a Narrative Poem Look back over the details and events you listed while reading this chapter. Choose five or six of these events to include in your poem. Write your poem. In the first one or two lines, introduce the poem's subject. Write five or six more lines, each about one event that occurred during Rome's decline. Then present your poem, altering your voice and rhythm as you do so to make your poem more interesting.

Standards Assessment

DIRECTIONS: Read each question, and write the letter of the best response.

1

> - Empire is ruled by all-powerful emperors.
> - Emperors are both religious leaders and political leaders.
> - Women have significant roles in government.
> - Greek, Egyptian, and Muslim cultural influences shape society.
> - People practice the Orthodox Christian religion.
> - People identify themselves as Romans.

The six characteristics listed above describe

A the eastern Roman Empire.

B the western Roman Empire.

C both the eastern and western empires.

D neither the eastern nor the western empire.

2 Byzantine artists were known especially for creating colorful

A statues.

B mosaics.

C frescoes.

D pottery.

3 Which of the following was *not* a reason for the fall of the Roman Empire?

A the empire's vast size

B corruption in Roman government

C pressure on the Goths from the Huns

D the influence of Greek government

4 The eastern Roman Empire is also known as the

A Holy Roman Empire.

B Eastern Orthodox Empire.

C Ottoman Empire.

D Byzantine Empire.

5 In 410 the city of Rome was destroyed for the first time in 800 years by the army of a foreign people called the

A Huns.

B Vandals.

C Goths.

D Franks.

Connecting with Past Learnings

6 Constantine unified the entire Roman Empire and introduced a new religion into the Roman government. Which leader that you learned about in Grade 6 is known for his similar accomplishments?

A Asoka

B Hammurabi

C Alexander

D Piankhi

7 In Grade 6 you learned that the Persians threatened Greek civilization for a time. All of the following peoples played a similar role in Roman history *except* the

A Byzantines.

B Goths.

C Vandals.

D Huns.

Write a description of the Roman Colosseum or the Hagia Sophia in Constantinople.

TIP **Identifying Details** Here are some questions to help you identify details for your description.

- What color or colors best describe it?
- What size is it?
- What shapes can you describe?
- If you touched a wall, how might it feel—gritty, smooth, cold, warm?

ELA **Writing 7.2.0** Students write descriptive texts of at least 500–700 words.

A Description of Ancient Architecture

Have you ever seen something so amazing that you just *had* to describe it to your best friend? A descriptive essay is one way to do that. A good description paints a detailed, vivid picture, one so clear that readers can see it in their minds.

1. Prewrite

Picking a Subject and Choosing Details

Use your textbook, the library, and/or the Internet to find information and illustrations of the Colosseum and the Hagia Sophia. Choose the one that seems most interesting to you and begin to take notes about the building. Look for information about

- the outside of the building,
- the inside of it,
- its size,
- the materials from which it was made,
- any decorations or artwork it contained.

Think about the feeling you want your readers to have about the building. Do you want them to think it was beautiful, cold, huge, or comfortable? Make that feeling part of your big idea and choose details to help create it.

Organizing Your Information

Choose one of two ways to organize your description.

- **Spatial Order:** from front to back, top to bottom, outside to inside
- **Order of Importance:** from least important part to most important part

2. Write

Here is a framework that can help you write a first draft.

A Writer's Framework

Introduction	Body	Conclusion
- Identify your subject and your big idea. - Give your readers any background information they might need.	- Describe your subject, using details to help your readers visualize it. - Organize your details by space or importance.	- Briefly summarize the most important details about the building. - Restate your big idea.

3. Evaluate and Revise

Evaluating

Use the following questions to discover ways to improve your paper.

Evaluation Questions for a Description

- Does your introduction identify your subject and your big idea?
- Does your introduction give readers any needed background information?
- Do the details and information work together to help your readers visualize your subject?

- Are the details and information clearly organized by spatial order or order of importance?
- Does your conclusion summarize the most important details about the building?
- Do you restate your big idea in different words?

Revising

If your description seems a little dull, look for places to replace general words with exact verbs, nouns, and adjectives. They will make your description more interesting and help your reader visualize the building.

General *an interesting roof*

Exact *a huge central dome surrounded by two half-domes and several smaller domes*

Check your description to see whether you could make some details clearer with comparisons. Compare the building, or a part of it, to something your readers can picture in their minds. (See the tip to the right.)

4. Proofread and Publish

Proofreading

Check to be sure you have used a comma after a long group of words at the beginning of a sentence.

Example *To the west of the central dome, you can see a half-dome.*

Publishing

Attach a picture of the building you have described and exchange papers with another student. Discuss which is clearer—the picture or the written description. Make a list of the advantages of the picture and the advantages of the written description.

● Practice and Apply

Use the steps and strategies outlined in this workshop to write your description of the Colosseum or the Hagia Sophia.

TIP **Using Comparisons** To help readers understand a subject, you might compare it to something they know—the dome on the cathedral to the dome on the state capital, for example.

You can also help them understand by comparing two things that are really not alike. These comparisons can help your readers see things in a new way.

Example The center dome rises above the rest of the roof like a mushroom sticking out of the ground.

TIP **Showing Where Things Are** To show where features are located in or on your building, you may use words or groups of words like *below, beside, down, above, over, next to, to the right,* and *to the left.*

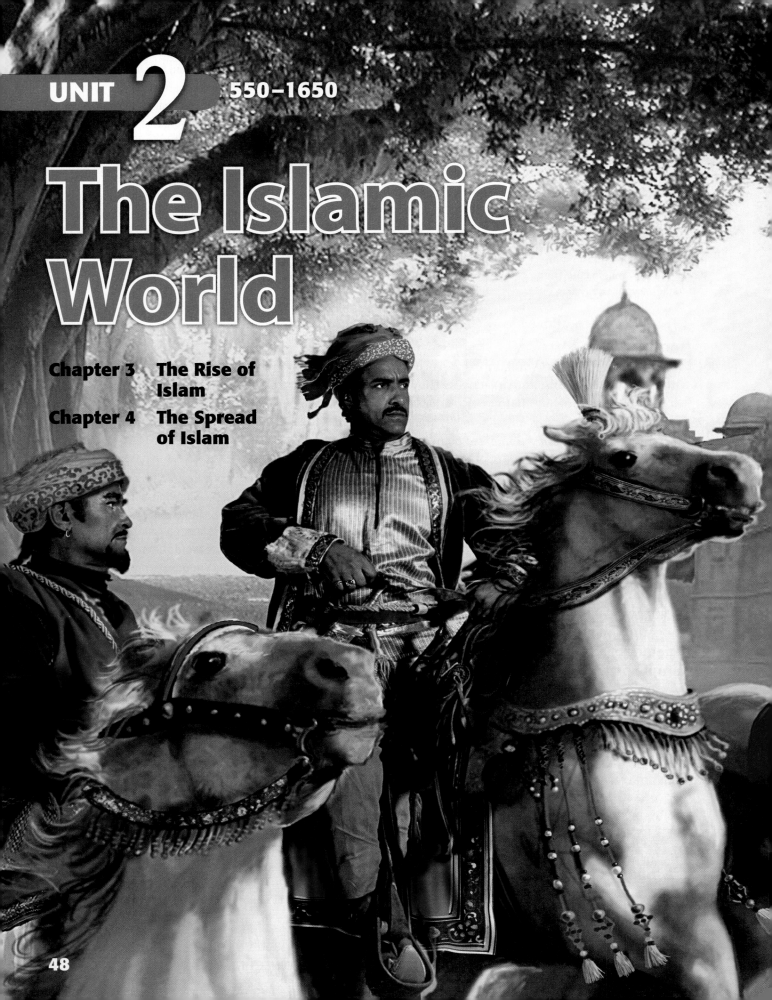

The Islamic World

The rise and spread of Islam was a major development in world history. In a very short time, the religion spread across large parts of Asia and Africa and into Europe. Islam has remained a powerful force in most of these regions to this day.

In the next two chapters, you will learn about the origins of Islam in the life and teachings of Muhammad, a prophet from Mecca. You will also learn about Islamic beliefs and practices, the development of powerful empires, and a rich culture.

Explore the Art
In this scene, the young ruler of the Islamic Mughal Empire, Akbar the Great, leaves his palace on a hunting trip. What does this scene show about Akbar's life?

The Rise of Islam

California Standards

History–Social Science

7.2 Students analyze the geographic, political, economic, religious, and social structures of the civilizations of Islam in the Middle Ages.

Analysis Skills

HI 2 Understand sequence in historical events.

CS 1 Explain how major events are related to one another in time.

CS 2 Construct various time lines of key events, people, and periods of the historical era.

English–Language Arts

Writing 7.1.3 Use strategies of notetaking, outlining, and summarizing to impose structure.

Reading 7.2.0 Students read and understand grade-level-appropriate material.

FOCUS ON WRITING

Designing a Web Site Design a Web site to tell children about the life of the prophet Muhammad and the religion of Islam. You'll design four pages: a home page and three links—Muhammad's Homeland, Who Was Muhammad?, and What Is Islam? As you read, think about what information will be most intriguing to your audience.

CHAPTER EVENTS

c. 550 Trade routes cross Arabia.

550

WORLD EVENTS

562 The Maya city of Calakmul defeats neighboring Tikal.

HOLT

History's Impact

▶ **video series**
Watch the video to understand the impact of Mecca on Islam.

What You Will Learn...

In this chapter you will learn about a religion called Islam. This photo shows thousands of people praying in Mecca, the place where Islam began. Mecca is the most sacred place in the Islamic world.

c. 570
Muhammad is born in Mecca.

613
Muhammad begins teaching people about Islam.

622
Muhammad leaves Mecca.

632
Muhammad dies.

575

600

625

650

593 Prince Shotoku begins to rule Japan.

597 The first Christian missionaries go to England.

618 The Tang dynasty begins in China.

51

Reading Social Studies

Economics | Geography | Politics | Religion | Society and Culture | Science and Technology

Focus on Themes This chapter explains the rise of the Islam **religion**, which began in Arabia in the early 600s. First you'll learn about Arabia, where it is and how the desert climate affected trade in the area. Then, you'll learn about Muhammad, the person who brought the Islam religion to the Arabs. Finally, you will see how Islam guides its followers in their religious practices and their daily lives. Studying the rise of Islam helps you understand the faith of the Muslims.

Chronological Order

Focus on Reading To really understand history and the events that shaped the world, we have to know in what order those events happened. In other words, we need to see how events are related in time.

Understanding Chronological Order The word **chronological** means "related to time." Events discussed in this history book are discussed in **sequence**, in the order in which they happened. To understand history better, you can use a sequence chain to take notes about events in the order they happened.

Additional reading support can be found in the

Inter active

Reader and Study Guide

Sequence Chain

The prophet Muhammad reveals the teachings of Islam.

↓

Islam spreads through Arabia and parts of Southwest Asia.

↓

From Arabia, Islam moves into northern Africa.

↓

From Africa, Islam crosses into Spain.

TIP Writers sometimes signal chronological order, or sequence, by using words or phrases like these:

first, before, then, later, soon, after, before long, next, eventually, finally

You Try It!

The following passage is from the chapter you are about to read. As you read the passage, look for words that show you the order in which events took place.

> Muhammad was born into an important family in Mecca around 570. Muhammad's early life was not easy. His father, a merchant, died before he was born; and his mother died later, when he was six.
>
> With his parents gone, Muhammad was first raised by his grandfather and later by his uncle. When he was a child, he traveled with his uncle's caravans, visiting places such as Syria and Jerusalem. Once he was grown, he managed a caravan business owned by a wealthy woman named Khadijah. Eventually, at age 25, Muhammad married Khadijah.
>
> *From Chapter 3, p. 59*

After you read the passage, answer the following questions.

1. Who raised Muhammad immediately after his mother died? Who raised him after that? Which signal words help you answer those questions?

2. Which signal word begins the phrase that lets you know when Muhammad went to Syria and Jerusalem? What happens if you change that signal word to *after*?

3. Find the sentence that begins with the word *once*. Study the list on the opposite page. What words could you use instead of *once* so that the meaning would stay the same? Which words would change the meaning?

4. Make a sequence chain of events of Muhammad's life. Which signal words help you know where to place events?

Key Terms and People

Chapter 3

Section 1
sand dunes *(p. 56)*
oasis *(p. 56)*
sedentary *(p. 56)*
caravan *(p. 56)*
souk *(p. 56)*

Section 2
Muhammad *(p. 59)*
Islam *(p. 60)*
Muslim *(p. 60)*
Qur'an *(p. 60)*
shrine *(p. 62)*
pilgrimage *(p. 62)*
mosque *(p. 63)*

Section 3
jihad *(p. 67)*
Sunnah *(p. 67)*
Five Pillars of Islam *(p. 68)*

Academic Vocabulary

Success in school is related to knowing academic vocabulary— the words that are frequently used in school assignments and discussions. In this chapter, you will learn the following academic words:

features *(p. 56)*
influence *(p. 63)*

As you read Chapter 3, be on the lookout for words that signal shifts in time. Use those words to help keep events in the right order.

Geography and Life in Arabia

What You Will Learn...

Main Ideas

1. Arabia is mostly a desert land.
2. Two ways of life—nomadic and sedentary—developed in the desert.

The Big Idea

Life in Arabia was influenced by the harsh desert climate of the region.

Key Terms

sand dunes, *p. 56*
oasis, *p. 56*
sedentary, *p. 56*
caravan, *p. 56*
souk, *p. 56*

If **YOU** were there...

Your town is a crossroads for traders and herders. You have always lived in town, but sometimes you envy the freedom of the desert travelers. Your uncle, a trader, says you are old enough to join his caravan. It would mean traveling many days by camel. Your parents don't like the idea but will let you decide.

Will you join the caravan? Why or why not?

BUILDING BACKGROUND For thousands of years, traders have crossed Arabia on routes between Europe, Asia, and Africa. Travel through Arabia was not easy. Travelers had to cross wide deserts with scorching temperatures and little water.

A Desert Land

The Arabian Peninsula, or Arabia, is mostly a hot and dry desert land. Scorching temperatures and a lack of water make life difficult. But in spite of the difficulty, people have lived in Arabia for thousands of years. During this time, Arabia's location, physical features, and climate have shaped life in the region.

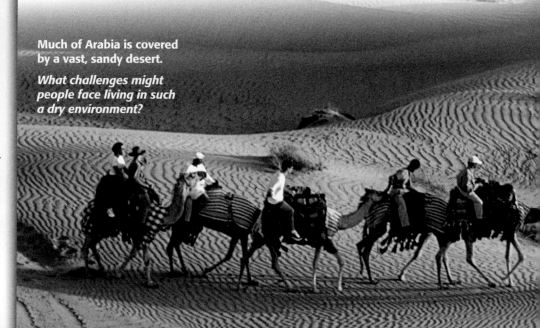

Much of Arabia is covered by a vast, sandy desert.

What challenges might people face living in such a dry environment?

HSS 7.2.1 Identify the physical features and describe the climate of the Arabian peninsula, its relationship to surrounding bodies of land and water, and nomadic and sedentary ways of life.

A Crossroads Location

The Arabian Peninsula is located in the southwest corner of Asia. As you can see on the map, it lies near the intersection of three continents—Africa, Asia, and Europe. Trade routes linking the three continents have passed through the region for thousands of years. Geographers call Arabia a "crossroads" location.

Merchants carried goods such as spices, silk, and gold along the trade routes. Some of these trade routes were on land. Others were water routes along the coast or across the seas. Trade brought many different groups of people through Arabia. These people introduced products and ideas from around the world, influencing Arabian culture and society.

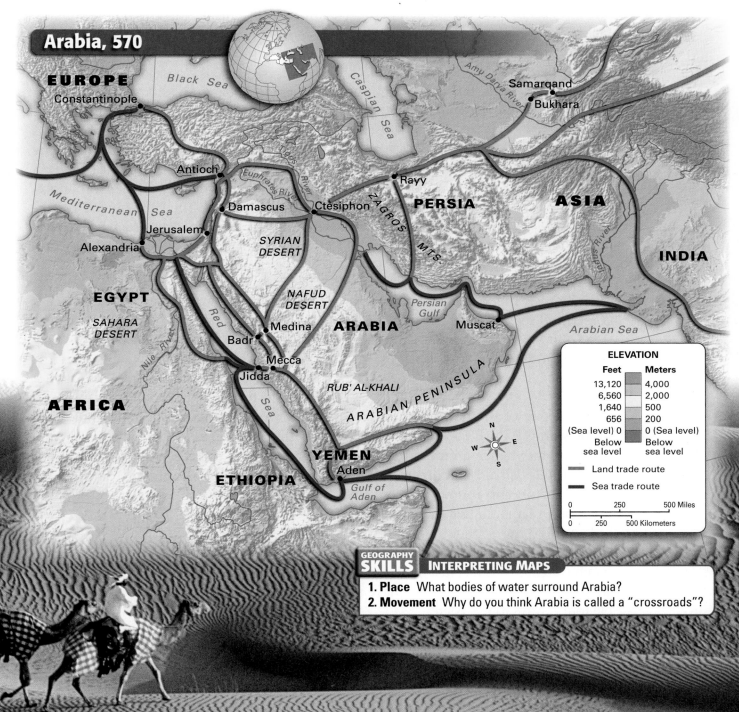

Arabia, 570

EUROPE
Black Sea
Constantinople
Antioch
Mediterranean Sea
Damascus
Jerusalem
Alexandria
SYRIAN DESERT
EGYPT
SAHARA DESERT
Nile River
NAFUD DESERT
Medina
Badr
Mecca
Jidda
Red Sea
AFRICA
RUB' AL-KHALI
ARABIA
ARABIAN PENINSULA
ETHIOPIA
YEMEN
Aden
Gulf of Aden
Caspian Sea
Amu Darya River
Samarqand
Bukhara
Rayy
Ctesiphon
Euphrates River
Tigris River
ZAGROS MTS.
PERSIA
ASIA
Indus River
INDIA
Persian Gulf
Muscat
Arabian Sea

ELEVATION

Feet	Meters
13,120	4,000
6,560	2,000
1,640	500
656	200
(Sea level) 0	0 (Sea level)
Below sea level	Below sea level

—— Land trade route
—— Sea trade route

| 0 | 250 | 500 Miles |
| 0 | 250 | 500 Kilometers |

GEOGRAPHY SKILLS **INTERPRETING MAPS**

1. **Place** What bodies of water surround Arabia?
2. **Movement** Why do you think Arabia is called a "crossroads"?

Physical Features

Arabia's location has also shaped its physical **features**. It lies in a region with hot and dry air. This climate has created a band of deserts across Arabia and northern Africa.

Huge, sandy deserts cover large parts of Arabia. **Sand dunes**, or hills of sand shaped by the wind, can rise to 800 feet high and stretch for hundreds of miles! The world's largest sand desert, the Rub' al-Khali (ROOB ahl-KAH-lee), covers much of southern Arabia. Rub' al-Khali means "Empty Quarter," a name given to the desert because there is so little life there.

Arabia's deserts have a very limited amount of water. There are no permanent lakes or rivers. Water exists mainly in oases scattered across the deserts. An **oasis** is a wet, fertile area in a desert. These wet areas form where underground water bubbles to the surface. Oases have long been key stops along Arabia's overland trade routes.

Although deserts cover much of the interior of Arabia, other landforms appear along the edges of the peninsula. Mountains border the southern and western coasts, and marshy land lies near the Persian Gulf. Most of the settlement in Arabia has been in these milder coastal regions.

Desert Climate

Arabia is one of the hottest, driest places in the world. With a blazing sun and clear skies, summer temperatures in the interior reach 100°F daily. This climate makes it hard for plants and animals to survive.

Desert plants do live in areas that get little rain. Many of them have roots that stretch deep or spread out far to collect as much water as possible. Just as plants have adapted to life in Arabia, so too have people found ways to live there.

READING CHECK **Summarizing** What are the main physical features of Arabia's environment?

Two Ways of Life

To live in Arabia's difficult desert environment, people developed two main ways of life. Some people lived a nomadic life, moving from place to place. Others lived a **sedentary**, or settled, life in towns.

Nomads

Nomads lived in tents and raised herds of sheep, goats, and camels. The animals provided milk, meat, and skins for the nomads' tents. Nomads traveled with their herds across the desert, moving along regular routes as seasons changed, to get food and water for their animals. They depended on camels for transportation and milk.

Among the nomads, camels and tents belonged to individuals. Water and grazing land belonged to tribes. Membership in a tribe, a group of related people, was important to nomads. The tribe offered protection from desert dangers, such as violence that often took place when people competed for water and grazing land.

Townspeople

While nomads moved around the desert, other people settled in oases where they could farm. These settlements, particularly the ones in oases along trade routes, became towns. Most people in Arabia lived in towns. Merchants and craftspeople lived there and worked with people in the caravan trade. A **caravan** is a group of traders that travel together.

Trade Centers

Towns became centers of trade for both nomads and townspeople. Many towns had a **souk** (SOOK)—a market or bazaar. In the market, nomads traded animal products and desert herbs for goods such as cooking supplies and clothing. Merchants sold spices, gold, leather, and other goods brought by the caravans.

Nomads and Townspeople

The city of Mecca is shown here as it might have looked in the late 500s. Nomads from the desert and merchants from distant countries all came to trade at Mecca. Trade made some Meccan merchants wealthy.

Towns developed near oases, where access to water allowed people to grow food.

Towns became centers of trade for both nomads and townspeople. Merchants traded goods like leather, food, spices, and blankets.

Nomads traveled across Arabia, moving their animals as the seasons changed.

ANALYSIS SKILL **ANALYZING VISUALS**

How can you tell which figures are nomads and which figures are townspeople?

Shopping

Did you know that the mall you go to today is similar in some ways to the souks in early Arabia? For example, souks sold clothing, home goods, and food. Often, similar products were grouped in differ-ent areas, sort of like restaurants in a mall are often grouped together in a food court. Souks were open and busy during the day but closed at night. The larger ones were covered with a roof. People went to souks to socialize as well as to shop.

Souks weren't just the same as malls are, however. The shops in souks were smaller than most shops in modern malls, and prices were not fixed. Instead, the buyer and seller bargained to try to agree on a price.

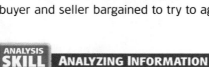
ANALYSIS SKILL **ANALYZING INFORMATION**

Why might people want to shop at a souk or a mall?

Arabian towns were important stations on the trade routes linking India with Northeast Africa and the Mediterranean. Trade brought Arabs into contact with peo-ple and ideas from around the world.

READING CHECK **Categorizing** What two ways of life were common in Arabia?

SUMMARY AND PREVIEW The geogra-phy of Arabia encouraged trade and influenced the development of nomad-ic and sedentary lifestyles. In the next section, you will read about a religion that began to influence many people in Arabia.

go.hrw.com
Online Quiz
KEYWORD: SQ7 HP3

Section 1 Assessment

Reviewing Ideas, Terms, and People HSS 7.2.1

1. **a. Define** What is an **oasis**?
   b. Explain How has Arabia's "crossroads" location affected its culture and society?
   c. Elaborate How might modern developments have changed trade routes through Arabia since the 500s?

2. **a. Identify** Where were nomads and townspeople likely to interact?
   b. Make Generalizations Why did towns often develop near oases?
   c. Elaborate What are some possible reasons nomads chose to live in the desert?

Critical Thinking

3. **Comparing and Contrasting** Draw a graphic organizer like this one. Use it to show some differences and similarities between nomadic and sedentary lifestyles in Arabia.

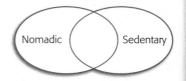
Nomadic   Sedentary

FOCUS ON WRITING

4. **Creating a Word Web** Write *Arabia* in the cen-ter of a word web, and then fill in the web with words and phrases that best describe the geogra-phy and life of Arabia.

Origins of Islam

If **YOU** were there...

You live in a town in Arabia, in a large family of wealthy merchants. Your family's house is larger than most others in the town. You have beautiful clothes and many servants to wait on you. Many townspeople are poor, but you have always taken such differences for granted. Now you hear that some people are saying the rich should give money to the poor.

How might your family react to this idea?

> **BUILDING BACKGROUND** The idea that people should help the poor is one important teaching of a religion called Islam. When Islam was introduced to the people of Arabia, many of its teachings seemed new and different.

Muhammad Becomes a Prophet

A man named **Muhammad** brought a different religion to the people of Arabia. Historians don't know much about Muhammad. What they do know comes from religious writings.

Muhammad's Early Life

Muhammad was born into an important family in Mecca around 570. Muhammad's early life was not easy. His father, a merchant, died before he was born; and his mother died later, when he was six.

With his parents gone, Muhammad was first raised by his grandfather and later by his uncle. When he was a child, he traveled with his uncle's caravans, visiting places such as Syria and Jerusalem. Once he was grown, he managed a caravan business owned by a wealthy woman named Khadijah (ka-DEE-jah). Eventually, at age 25, Muhammad married Khadijah.

The caravan trade made Mecca a rich city. But most of the wealth belonged to just a few people. Poor people had hard lives. Traditionally, wealthy people in Mecca had helped the poor. But as Muhammad was growing up, many rich merchants began to ignore the poor and keep their wealth for themselves.

What You Will Learn...

Main Ideas
1. Muhammad became a prophet and introduced a religion called Islam in Arabia.
2. Muhammad's teachings had similarities to Judaism and Christianity, but they also presented new ideas.
3. Islam spread in Arabia after being rejected at first.

The Big Idea
Muhammad, a merchant from Mecca, introduced a major world religion called Islam.

Key Terms and People
Muhammad, *p. 59*
Islam, *p. 60*
Muslim, *p. 60*
Qur'an, *p. 60*
shrine, *p. 62*
pilgrimage, *p. 62*
mosque, *p. 63*

HSS 7.2.2 Trace the origins of Islam and the life and teachings of Muhammad, including Islamic teachings on the connection with Judaism and Christianity.

2000 BC	1000 BC	BC 1 AD

Beginnings
of Judaism

Beginnings
of Christianity

Three Religions

The three main monotheistic religions in the world are Judaism, Christianity, and Islam. Each religion has its own particular beliefs and practices. Yet they also have important similarities. For example, all three began in the same part of the world—Southwest Asia. Also, all three religions teach similar ideas about kindness to fellow people and belief in one God.

The Torah, part of the
Hebrew Bible, the
holy book of Judaism

The Christian Bible,
the holy book of
Christianity

The Qur'an, the holy
book of Islam

A Message for Muhammad

FOCUS ON READING
What signal words on this page give you clues about chronological order?

Concerned about the changing values in Mecca, Muhammad often went by himself to the hills outside the city to pray and meditate. One day, when he was about 40 years old, Muhammad went to meditate in a cave. Then, according to Islamic teachings, something happened that changed his life forever. An angel appeared and spoke to Muhammad, telling him to "Recite! Recite!" Confused at first, Muhammad asked what he should recite. The angel answered:

❝Recite in the name of your Lord who created,
created man from clots of blood!
Recite! Your Lord is the Most Bountiful One,
Who by the pen taught man what he did
not know.❞

–From *The Koran*, translated by N. J. Dawood

Muslims believe that God had spoken to Muhammad through the angel and had made him a prophet, a person who tells of messages from God. At first Muhammad was afraid and didn't tell anyone except his wife about the voice in the cave. A few years later, in 613, Muhammad began to tell other people about the messages.

The messages Muhammad received form the basis of the religion called **Islam**. The word *Islam* means "to submit to God." A follower of Islam is called a **Muslim**. Muslims believe that Muhammad continued receiving messages from God for the rest of his life. These messages were collected in the **Qur'an** (kuh-RAN), the holy book of Islam.

READING CHECK **Analyzing** How did Muhammad bring Islam to Arabia?

60 CHAPTER 3

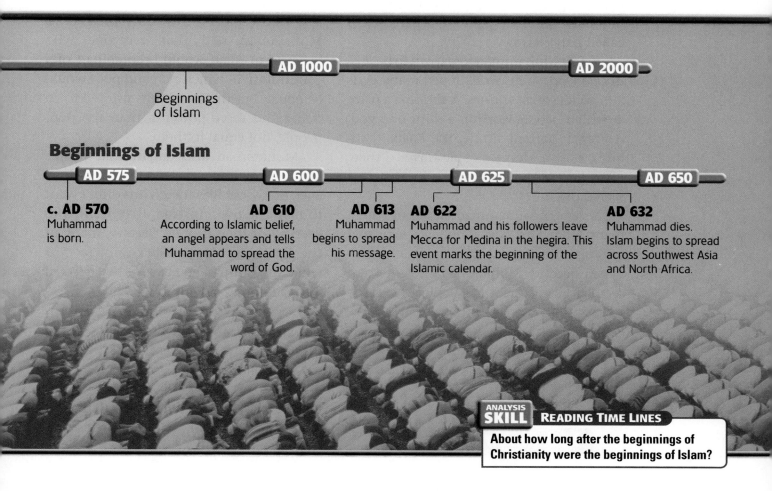

Beginnings
of Islam

Beginnings of Islam

AD 575 **AD 600** **AD 625** **AD 650**

c. AD 570
Muhammad
is born.

AD 610
According to Islamic belief,
an angel appears and tells
Muhammad to spread the
word of God.

AD 613
Muhammad
begins to spread
his message.

AD 622
Muhammad and his followers leave
Mecca for Medina in the hegira. This
event marks the beginning of the
Islamic calendar.

AD 632
Muhammad dies.
Islam begins to spread
across Southwest Asia
and North Africa.

ANALYSIS SKILL **READING TIME LINES**

About how long after the beginnings of
Christianity were the beginnings of Islam?

Muhammad's Teachings

Not all of Muhammad's early teachings
were new. In fact, some were much like the
teachings of Judaism and Christianity. But
Muhammad's teachings challenged and
upset the people of Arabia. These teachings
brought changes to many aspects of life in
Arabia.

A Belief in One God

Muhammad taught that there was only
one God, Allah, which means "the God"
in Arabic. In that way, Islam is like Judaism and Christianity. It is a monotheistic
religion, a religion based on a belief in one
God. Although people of all three religions
believe in one God, their beliefs about God
are not all the same.

Jews, Christians, and Muslims also
recognize many of the same prophets.
Muhammad taught that prophets such as
Abraham, Moses, and Jesus had lived in
earlier times. Unlike Christians, Muslims
do not believe Jesus was the son of God,
but they do believe many stories about his
life. Muhammad told stories about these
prophets similar to the stories in the Torah
and the Christian Bible. Muhammad
respected Jews and Christians as "people of
the Book" because their holy books taught
many of the same ideas that Muhammad
taught.

A Challenge to Old Ideas

Some of Muhammad's teachings would
have seemed familiar to Jews and Christians, but they were new to most Arabs.

For example, most people in Arabia believed in many different gods, a belief system called polytheism.

Before Muhammad told them to believe in one God, Arabs worshipped many gods and goddesses at shrines. A **shrine** is a place at which people worship a saint or a god. A very important shrine, the Kaaba (KAH-buh), was in Mecca. People traveled there every year on a **pilgrimage**, a journey to a sacred place.

Several of Muhammad's teachings upset many Arabs. First, they didn't like being told to stop worshipping their gods and goddesses. Second, Muhammad's new religion seemed like a threat to people who made money from the yearly pilgrimages to the Kaaba. Mecca's powerful merchant leaders thought they would lose business if people didn't worship their gods at the Kaaba.

Another of Muhammad's teachings also worried Mecca's wealthy merchants. Muhammad said that everyone who believed in Allah would become part of a community in which rich and poor would be equal. But the merchants wanted to be richer and more powerful than the poor people, not equal to them.

Muhammad also taught that people should give money to help the poor. However, many wealthy merchants didn't want to help the poor. Instead, they wanted to keep all of their money. Because many of the people in Mecca didn't want to hear what Muhammad had to say, they rejected his teachings.

READING CHECK **Comparing** How were Islamic teachings like the teachings of Judaism and Christianity?

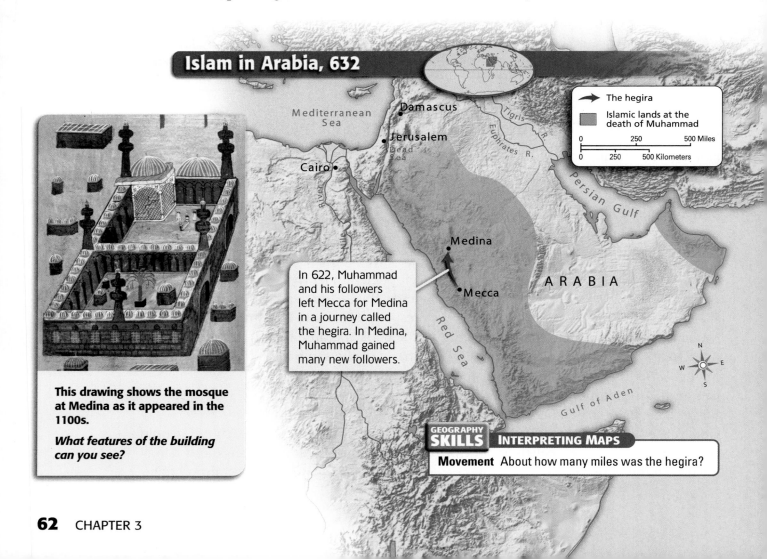

Islam in Arabia, 632

The hegira

Islamic lands at the death of Muhammad

0   250   500 Miles
0   250   500 Kilometers

Mediterranean Sea

Damascus

Jerusalem

Dead Sea

Cairo

Tigris R.

Euphrates R.

Persian Gulf

Medina

In 622, Muhammad and his followers left Mecca for Medina in a journey called the hegira. In Medina, Muhammad gained many new followers.

Mecca

ARABIA

Red Sea

Nile River

Gulf of Aden

N E W S

This drawing shows the mosque at Medina as it appeared in the 1100s.

What features of the building can you see?

GEOGRAPHY SKILLS **INTERPRETING MAPS**

Movement About how many miles was the hegira?

Islam Spreads in Arabia

At first Muhammad did not have many followers. Mecca's merchants refused to believe in a single God and rejected the idea of equality. They even made Muhammad leave Mecca for a while. Eventually, however, Muhammad's teachings began to take root.

From Mecca to Medina

Slowly, more people began to listen to Muhammad's ideas. But as Islam began to **influence** people, the rulers of Mecca became more and more worried. They began to threaten Muhammad and his small group of followers with violence. They even planned to kill Muhammad. As a result, Muhammad had to look for support outside of Mecca.

A group of people from a city north of Mecca invited Muhammad to live in their city. As the threats from Mecca's leaders got worse, Muhammad accepted the invitation. In 622 he and many of his followers, including his daughter Fatimah, left Mecca and went to Medina (muh-DEE-nuh). Named after Muhammad, Medina means "the Prophet's city" in Arabic, the language of the Arabs. Muhammad's departure from Mecca became known in Muslim history as the hegira (hi-JY-ruh), or journey.

From Medina to the Rest of Arabia

Muhammad's arrival in Medina holds an important place in Islamic history. There he became both a spiritual and a political leader. His house became the first **mosque** (MAHSK), or building for Muslim prayer. The year of the hegira, 622, became so important to the development of Islam that Muslims made it the first year in the Islamic calendar.

According to Islamic belief, in Medina Muhammad reported new revelations about rules for Muslim government, society and worship. For example, God told Muhammad that Muslims should face Mecca when they pray. Before, Muslims faced Jerusalem like Christians and Jews did. Muslims recognized the importance of Mecca as the home of the Kaaba. They believe the Kaaba is a house of worship that Abraham built and dedicated to the worship of one God.

As the Muslim community in Medina grew stronger, other Arab tribes in the region began to accept Islam. However, conflict with the Meccans increased. In 630, after several years of fighting, the people of Mecca gave in. They welcomed Muhammad back to the city and accepted Islam as their religion.

In Mecca Muhammad and his followers destroyed the statues of the gods and goddesses in the Kaaba. Soon most of the Arabian tribes accepted Muhammad as their spiritual leader and became Muslims.

ACADEMIC VOCABULARY
influence change, or have an effect on

THE IMPACT TODAY
Muslims all over the world still look toward Mecca when they pray.

Muhammad taught that there was only one God. This Arabic writing says "There is no god but God, and Muhammad is his prophet."

The Prophet's Mosque

This photo shows people praying at the mosque in Medina, where Muhammad died. Muhammad's tomb is located in this mosque, called the Holy Mosque of the Prophet.

What shows that this is a house of worship?

Muhammad died in 632 at his home in Medina. Although he didn't live long after Mecca became Muslim, the religion he taught would soon spread to lands far beyond Arabia.

READING CHECK **Summarizing** How did Islam spread in Arabia?

SUMMARY AND PREVIEW You have just read about some of Muhammad's teachings and how people in Arabia reacted to them. Many people in Arabia accepted Islam and became Muslims. In the next section, you will learn more about the main Islamic teachings and beliefs.

go.hrw.com
Online Quiz
KEYWORD: SQ7 HP3

Section 2 Assessment

Reviewing Ideas, Terms, and People HSS 7.2.2

1. **a. Recall** When did **Muhammad** begin teaching people about **Islam**?
   b. Explain According to Islamic belief, what was the source of Islamic teachings and how did Muhammad receive them?
2. **a. Identify** What is one key Islamic belief about God?
   b. Compare In what ways are Islamic beliefs similar to those of Judaism and Christianity?
3. **a. Recall** Where was the first **mosque**?
   b. Explain Why did Muhammad go to Medina?

Critical Thinking

4. **Sequencing** Draw a time line like the one below. Use it to identify key dates in Muhammad's life.

FOCUS ON WRITING

5. **Taking Notes about Muhammad** Take notes to answer the question, "Who was Muhammad?" You might organize your notes under three headings: "Early Life," "Muhammad the Prophet," and "Muhammad's Teachings."

Fatimah

How did a prophet's daughter become famous herself?

When did she live? Fatimah is believed to have lived from the early 600s to 633.

Where did she live? Fatimah grew up in the city of Mecca, in Arabia. When her father, Muhammad, had to leave Mecca, Fatimah followed him to the city of Medina.

What did she do? Fatimah married Ali, a cousin of her father. Their two sons were Muhammad's only descendants. Fatimah's long family line later became known as the Fatimid dynasty.

Why is she important? Fatimah holds a place of honor in the Islamic religion. Stories describe Fatimah as a loyal daughter who cared for her father. She is said to have suffered hunger and other hardships with him as he preached. Fatimah can also be linked, through her husband, Ali, to the origin of the split between Sunni and Shia Muslims. Members of the Shia branch of Islam believe that Muhammad wanted Ali to be the next leader of Islam. Those who did not believe that Ali was the rightful leader formed the Sunni branch of Islam.

KEY EVENTS

- **c. 595** Muhammad marries Khadijah, who later gives birth to Fatimah.

- **610** Muhammad receives the word of God, according to Islamic belief.

- **619** Muhammad's wife Khadijah dies.

- **622** Muhammad and his followers are forced to leave Mecca for Medina.

- **624** Fatimah marries Ali.

- **633** Fatimah dies in the year following her father's death.

Drawing Inferences From what you read about Fatimah, what qualities do you think made her worthy of being honored?

The Hand of Fatimah can be found on doors in places like Egypt and Morocco. Some Muslims believe this good luck symbol will protect the household.

Islamic Beliefs and Practices

What You Will Learn...

Main Ideas

1. The Qur'an guides Muslims' lives.
2. The Sunnah tells Muslims of important duties expected of them.
3. Islamic law is based on the Qur'an and the Sunnah.

The Big Idea

Sacred texts called the Qur'an and the Sunnah guide Muslims in their religion, daily life, and laws.

Key Terms

jihad, *p. 67*
Sunnah, *p. 67*
Five Pillars of Islam, *p. 68*

HSS 7.2.3 Explain the significance of the Qur'an and the Sunnah as the primary sources of Islamic beliefs, practice, and law, and their influence in Muslims' daily life.

If YOU were there...

Your family owns a hotel in Mecca. Usually business is pretty calm, but this week your hotel is packed. Travelers have come from all over the world to visit your city. One morning you leave the hotel and are swept up in a huge crowd of these visitors. They speak many different languages, but everyone is wearing the same white robes. They are headed to the mosque.

What might draw so many people to your city?

BUILDING BACKGROUND One basic Islamic belief is that everyone who can must make a trip to Mecca sometime during his or her lifetime. More Islamic teachings can be found in Islam's holy books—the Qur'an and the Sunnah.

The Qur'an

During Muhammad's life, his followers memorized his messages from God along with his words and deeds. After Muhammad's death, they collected his teachings and wrote them down to form the book known as the Qur'an. Muslims consider the Qur'an to be the exact word of God as it was told to Muhammad.

Beliefs

The central teaching in the Qur'an is that there is only one God—Allah—and that Muhammad is his prophet. The Qur'an says people must obey Allah's commands. Muslims learned of these commands from Muhammad.

Islam teaches that the world had a definite beginning and will end one day. Muhammad said that on the final day God will judge all people. Those who have obeyed his orders will be granted life in paradise. According to the Qur'an, paradise is a beautiful garden full of fine food and drink. People who have not obeyed God, however, will suffer.

Studying the Qur'an
The Qur'an plays a central role in the lives of many Muslims. Children study and memorize verses from the Qur'an at home, at Islamic schools, and in mosques. Muslims who memorize the entire book are respected as "Keepers" of the Qur'an.

Where do you think these children are studying the Qur'an?

Guidelines for Behavior

Like holy books of other religions, the Qur'an describes acts of worship, guidelines for moral behavior, and rules for social life. Muslims look to the Qur'an for guidance in their daily lives. For example, the Qur'an describes how to prepare for worship. Muslims must wash themselves before praying so they will be pure before Allah. The Qur'an also says what Muslims shouldn't eat or drink. Muslims aren't allowed to eat pork or drink alcohol.

In addition to guidelines for individual behavior, the Qur'an describes relations among people. Many of these ideas changed Arabian society. For example, before Muhammad's time many Arabs owned slaves. Although slavery didn't disappear among Muslims, the Qur'an encourages Muslims to free slaves. Also, women in Arabia had few rights. The Qur'an describes rights of women, including rights to own property, earn money, and get an education. However, most Muslim women still have fewer rights than men.

Another important subject in the Qur'an has to do with **jihad** (ji-HAHD), which means "to make an effort, or to struggle." Jihad refers to the inner struggle people go through in their effort to obey God and behave according to Islamic ways. Jihad can also mean the struggle to defend the Muslim community, or, historically, to convert people to Islam. The word has also been translated as "holy war."

READING CHECK **Analyzing** Why is the Qur'an important to Muslims?

The Sunnah

The Qur'an is not the only source of Islamic teachings. Muslims also study the hadith (huh-DEETH), the written record of Muhammad's words and actions. This record is the basis for the Sunnah. The **Sunnah** (SOOH-nuh) refers to the way Muhammad lived, which provides a model for the duties and the way of life expected of Muslims. The Sunnah guides Muslims' behavior.

Saying "There is no god but God, and Muhammad is his prophet"

Praying five times a day

Giving to the poor and needy

Fasting during the holy month of Ramadan

Traveling to Mecca at least once on a hajj

ANALYSIS SKILL **ANALYZING VISUALS**

Which of the five pillars shows how Muslims are supposed to treat other people?

The Five Pillars of Islam

The first duties of a Muslim are known as the **Five Pillars of Islam**, which are five acts of worship required of all Muslims. The first pillar is a statement of faith. At least once in their lives, Muslims must state their faith by saying, "There is no god but God, and Muhammad is his prophet." Muslims say this when they accept Islam. They also say it in their daily prayers.

The second pillar of Islam is daily prayer. Muslims must pray five times a day: before sunrise, at midday, in late afternoon, right after sunset, and before going to bed. At each of these times, a call goes out from a mosque, inviting Muslims to come pray. Muslims try to pray together at a mosque. They believe prayer is proof that someone has accepted Allah.

The third pillar of Islam is a yearly donation to charity. Muslims must pay part of their wealth to a religious official. This money is used to help the poor, build mosques, or pay debts. Helping and caring for others is important in Islam.

The fourth pillar is fasting—going without food and drink. Muslims fast daily during the holy month of Ramadan (RAH-muh-dahn). The Qur'an says Allah began his revelations to Muhammad in the month of Ramadan. During Ramadan, most Muslims will not eat or drink anything between dawn and sunset. Muslims believe fasting is a way to show that God is more important than one's own body. Fasting also reminds Muslims of people in the world who struggle to get enough food.

The fifth pillar of Islam is the hajj (HAJ), a pilgrimage to Mecca. All Muslims must travel to Mecca at least once in their lives if they can. The Kaaba, in Mecca, is Islam's most sacred place.

The Sunnah and Daily Life

In addition to the five pillars, the Sunnah has other examples of Muhammad's actions and teachings. These form the basis for rules about how to treat others. According to Muhammad's example, people should treat guests with generosity.

In addition to describing personal relations, the Sunnah provides guidelines for relations in business and government. For example, one Sunnah rule says that it is bad to owe someone money. Another rule says that people should obey their leaders.

READING CHECK **Generalizing** What do Muslims learn from the Sunnah?

Islamic Law

The Qur'an and the Sunnah are important guides for how Muslims should live. They also form the basis of Islamic law, or Shariah (shuh-REE-uh). Shariah is a system based on Islamic sources and human reason that judges the rightness of actions an individual or community might take. These actions fall on a scale ranging from required to accepted to disapproved to forbidden. Islamic law makes no distinction between religious beliefs and daily life, so Islam affects all aspects of Muslims' lives.

Shariah sets rewards for good behavior and punishments for crimes. It also describes limits of authority. It was the basis for law in Muslim countries until modern times.

Sources of Islamic Beliefs			QUICK FACTS
Qur'an	**Sunnah**	**Shariah**	
Holy book that includes all the messages Muhammad received from God	Muhammad's example for the duties and way of life expected of Muslims	Islamic law, based on interpretations of the Qur'an and Sunnah	

Most Muslim countries today blend Islamic law with Western legal systems like we have in the United States.

Islamic law is not found in one book. Instead, it is a set of opinions and writings that have changed over the centuries. Different ideas about Islamic law are found in different Muslim regions.

READING CHECK **Finding Main Ideas** What is the purpose of Islamic law?

SUMMARY AND PREVIEW The Qur'an, the Sunnah, and Shariah teach Muslims how to live their lives. In the next chapter you will learn more about Muslim culture and the spread of Islam from Arabia to other lands.

Section 3 Assessment

go.hrw.com
Online Quiz
KEYWORD: SQ7 HP3

Reviewing Ideas, Terms, and People HSS 7.2.3

1. **a. Recall** What is the central teaching of the Qur'an?
   b. Explain How does the Qur'an help Muslims obey God?
2. **a. Recall** What are the **Five Pillars of Islam**?
   b. Make Generalizations Why do Muslims fast during Ramadan?
3. **a. Identify** What is Islamic law called?
   b. Make Inferences How is Islamic law different from law in the United States?
   c. Elaborate What is a possible reason that opinions and writings about Islamic law have changed over the centuries?

Critical Thinking

4. **Categorizing** Draw a chart like the one to the right. Use it to name three teachings from the Qur'an and three teachings from the Sunnah.

Qur'an	Sunnah

FOCUS ON WRITING

5. **Describing Islam** Answer the following questions to help you write a paragraph describing Islam. What is the central teaching of the Qur'an? How do Muslims honor God? What is the function of the Sunnah?

from
The Qur'an

The Merciful   Sura 55:1–55

About the Reading *The Qur'an, the holy book of Islam, is divided into 114 chapters called suras (SUR-uhs). The suras vary widely in length. In general, the longest suras are at the beginning of the Qur'an, and the shortest are at the end. Each sura opens with the same phrase, translated here as "In the Name of Allah, the Compassionate, the Merciful."*

AS YOU READ **Look for words and phrases that are repeated within the text. Think about the reasons for this repetition.**

In the Name of Allah, the Compassionate, the Merciful

It is the Merciful who has taught the Qur'an.

He created man and taught him articulate speech.

The sun and the moon pursue their ordered course. The plants and the trees bow down in adoration.

He raised the heaven on high and set the balance of all things, that you might not transgress it. Give just weight and full measure.

He laid the earth for His creatures, with all its fruits and blossom-bearing palm, chaff-covered grain and scented herbs. ❶ Which of your Lord's blessings would you deny?

He created man from potter's clay and the jinn from smokeless fire. Which of your Lord's blessings would you deny?

The Lord of the two easts is He, and the Lord of the two wests. ❷ Which of your Lord's blessings would you deny?

He has let loose the two oceans: they meet one another. Yet between them stands a barrier which they cannot overrun. Which of your Lord's blessings would you deny?

Pearls and corals come from both. Which of your Lord's blessings would you deny?

His are the ships that sail like banners upon the ocean. Which of your Lord's blessings would you deny?

All who live on earth are doomed to die. But the face of your Lord will abide for ever, in all its majesty and glory. Which of your Lord's blessings would you deny?

All who dwell in heaven and earth beseech Him. Each day some new task employs Him. Which of your Lord's blessings would you deny?

GUIDED READING

WORD HELP

compassionate caring

merciful kind

articulate clear and understandable

adoration praise

transgress violate

jinn (plural) or jinnee (singular) a type of spirit

abide last

beseech beg

❶ Palms, grain, and herbs are among the small number of plants that grow in the Arabian desert.

❷ "The two easts" and "the two wests" refer to the different locations where the sun appears to rise and set in summer and winter. The "two oceans" are fresh water and salt water.

What is the Qur'an saying in this passage?

ELA Reading 7.3.1 Articulate the expressed purposes and characteristics of different forms of prose.

Mankind and jinn, ❸ We shall surely find the time to judge you! Which of your Lord's blessings would you deny?

Mankind and jinn, if you have power to penetrate the confines of heaven and earth, then penetrate them! But this you shall not do except with Our own authority. Which of your Lord's blessings would you deny?

Flames of fire shall be lashed at you, and molten brass. There shall be none to help you. Which of your Lord's blessings would you deny?

When the sky splits asunder and reddens like a rose or stainéd leather (which of your Lord's blessings would you deny?), on that day neither man nor jinnee shall be asked about his sins. Which of your Lord's blessings would you deny?

The wrongdoers shall be known by their looks; ❹ they shall be seized by their forelocks and their feet. Which of your Lord's blessings would you deny?

That is the Hell which the sinners deny. They shall wander between fire and water fiercely seething. Which of your Lord's blessings would you deny?

❺ But for those that fear the majesty of their Lord there are two gardens (which of your Lord's blessings would you deny?) planted with shady trees. Which of your Lord's blessings would you deny?

Each is watered by a flowing spring. Which of your Lord's blessings would you deny?

Each bears every kind of fruit in pairs. Which of your Lord's blessings would you deny?

They shall recline on couches lined with thick brocade, and within their reach will hang the fruits of both gardens. Which of your Lord's blessings would you deny?

Muslims read about Allah in the Qur'an.

GUIDED READING

WORD HELP

asunder into parts
brocade a rich silk fabric with woven patterns

❸ Jinn are spirits that appear in many Arabic tales. In English, the word is also spelled djinn or genies.

❹ *What does the Qur'an say will happen to bad people when they die?*

❺ This section of the Qur'an describes the Muslim idea of paradise.

What is paradise like, according to the Qur'an?

CONNECTING SACRED TEXTS TO HISTORY

1. **Analyzing** Muslims believe that Allah created the world. What words and phrases in this passage illustrate that belief?

2. **Analyzing** The first Muslims lived in an area that was mostly desert. How does this passage reflect the early Muslims' desert location?

Social Studies Skills

HSS **Analysis CS 2** Students explain how major events are related to one another in time.

| Analysis | Critical Thinking | Participation | Study |

Using Time Lines

Understand the Skill

Time lines are visual summaries of what happened when. They show events in chronological order—that is, the sequence in which events occurred. Time lines also illustrate how long after one event another event took place. They help you to see relationships between events and to remember important dates.

Learn the Skill

A time line covers a span of years. Some time lines cover a great number of years or centuries. Other time lines, such as the one below, cover much shorter periods of time. Time lines can be horizontal or vertical. Whichever direction they run, time lines should always be read from the earliest date to the latest date.

Follow these steps to interpret a time line.

1 Determine the time line's framework. Note the range of years covered and the intervals of time into which it is divided.

2 Study the order of events on the time line. Note the length of time between events.

3 Supply missing information. Think about the people, places, and other events associated with each item on the time line.

4 Note relationships. Ask yourself how an event relates to earlier or later events on the time line. Look for cause-and-effect relationships and long-term developments.

Practice and Apply the Skill

Study the time line below about Muhammad and the early spread of Islam. Use it to answer the following questions.

1. What is the framework of this time line?

2. How long was it before Muhammad told many people in Mecca about the messages?

3. For how long did Muhammad spread his teachings in Mecca before going to Medina?

4. What event or events led to warfare between Mecca and Medina?

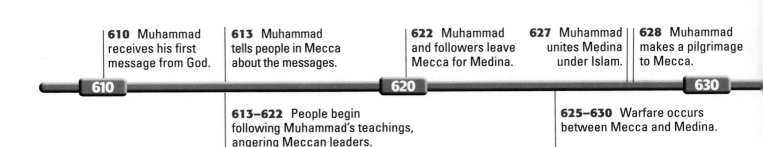

610 Muhammad receives his first message from God.

613 Muhammad tells people in Mecca about the messages.

622 Muhammad and followers leave Mecca for Medina.

627 Muhammad unites Medina under Islam.

628 Muhammad makes a pilgrimage to Mecca.

613–622 People begin following Muhammad's teachings, angering Meccan leaders.

625–630 Warfare occurs between Mecca and Medina.

Standards Review

Visual Summary

Use the visual summary below to help you review the main ideas of the chapter.

QUICK FACTS

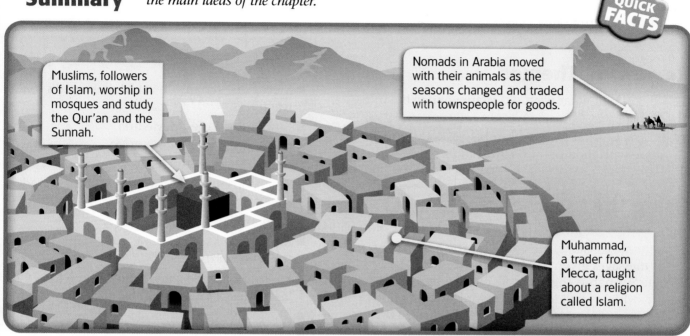

Muslims, followers of Islam, worship in mosques and study the Qur'an and the Sunnah.

Nomads in Arabia moved with their animals as the seasons changed and traded with townspeople for goods.

Muhammad, a trader from Mecca, taught about a religion called Islam.

Reviewing Vocabulary, Terms, and People

*For each statement below, write **T** if it is true and **F** if it is false. If the statement is false, write the correct term that would make the sentence a true statement.*

1. Muslims gather to pray at a souk.

2. Traders often traveled in caravans to take their goods to markets.

3. An Islam is a person who submits to God and follows the teachings of Muhammad.

4. According to Islamic belief, God's messages to Muhammad during his lifetime make up the Sunnah.

5. Some people might worship gods or saints at a shrine.

6. A hill of sand shaped by the wind is called an oasis.

7. Jihad is a journey to a sacred place.

8. Someone who is sedentary does not move around very much.

Comprehension and Critical Thinking

SECTION 1 *(Pages 54–58)* **HSS** 7.2.1

9. **a. Describe** What are some important characteristics of the Arabian Peninsula's physical geography?

   b. Contrast What are the two main ways of life that developed in Arabia? How are they different?

   c. Predict How would Arabia's location affect its trade relationships?

SECTION 2 *(Pages 59–64)* **HSS** 7.2.2

10. **a. Recall** What is the holy book of Islam?

    b. Compare and Contrast How did Muhammad's teachings compare to Judaism and Christianity? How did they contrast with common Arab beliefs of the time?

    c. Elaborate Why is 622 an important year in Islamic history?

11. a. Define What is the hajj?

  b. Analyze How are the Qur'an and the Sunnah connected to Shariah?

  c. Elaborate How do the Five Pillars of Islam affect Muslims' daily lives?

Reviewing Themes

12. Religion In what ways did Islam change life in Arabia?

13. Religion What teachings or beliefs does Islam share with Judaism and Christianity?

Using the Internet

go.hrw.com
KEYWORD: SQ7 WH3

14. Activity: Researching the Qur'an and the Sunnah In Islam, the Qur'an is the collection of messages given to Muhammad from God. The Sunnah is the example of Muhammad's life, which provides a model for the duties and the way of life expected of Muslims. The Sunnah includes the Five Pillars of Islam. Enter the activity keyword and research the significance of the Qur'an and the Sunnah. Pay attention to how they affect Muslims' daily life. Create a three-dimensional object to illustrate what you have learned.

Reading and Analysis Skills

Understanding Chronological Order Answer the following questions about the order of events in the development of Islam.

15. What did Muhammad do after he heard the voice in the cave?

16. Which town—Mecca or Medina—was the first to accept Islam on a large scale?

17. What two monotheistic religions were practiced before Islam?

Social Studies Skills

18. Using Time Lines Copy the time line shown. Use it to show relationships among the following people and events from Section 2. Include dates on your time line when you know them.

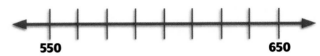

550   650

- Mecca's merchants reject Muhammad's teachings.
- Muhammad dies in Medina.
- Muhammad begins to tell other people about the messages from God.
- The people of Mecca welcome Muhammad back to their city.
- Muhammad is born in Mecca.
- Muhammad tells his wife, Khadijah, about the voice in the cave.
- Muhammad and some followers are forced to leave Mecca for Medina.
- The people of Medina accept Islam.
- Muhammad hears a voice in a cave.

FOCUS ON WRITING

19. Creating Your Web Site Look back over your notes from this chapter. Then, design a home page and the three links named Muhammad's Homeland, Who Was Muhammad?, and What Is Islam? Write four or five sentences for each link on your Web site. You may design the pages either online or on a large sheet of paper.

  Remember that your audience is children, so you should keep your text simple. To keep the children interested in your topic and explain your ideas, use color and pictures or drawings of Arabia and important sites in the history of Islam.

Standards Assessment

DIRECTIONS: Read each question, and write the letter of the best response.

1

> The office of Imam was set up in order to replace the office of Prophet in the defense of the faith and the government of the world. . . . One group says it derives from reason, since it is the nature of reasonable men to submit to a leader who will prevent them from injuring one another and who will settle quarrels and disputes . . . Another group says that the obligation derives from Holy Law and not from reason, since the Imam deals with matters of Holy Law . . .
>
> –Abu al-Hasan al-Mawardi (972–1058)

From the passage, it can be concluded that Imams in early Islam were

A religious leaders.

B government leaders.

C both religious and government leaders.

D neither religious nor government leaders.

2 Which of the following responsibilities of Muslims is *not* one of the Five Pillars of Islam?

A jihad

B frequent prayer

C hajj

D giving to the poor

3 What is the *main* reason some early peoples of Arabia developed the nomadic life that their descendants follow today?

A Trade has long been an important part of life in the region.

B The prophet Muhammad was a nomad.

C No towns developed in Arabia.

D Resources are scarce in the region's desert geography.

4 Medina is probably *best* known as a

A trade city.

B tourist city.

C religious city.

D educational city.

5 The teachings of Muhammad are found *mainly* in the Qur'an and the

A Commentaries.

B Sunnah.

C Jihad.

D Old Testament.

Connecting with Past Learnings

6 Muslims believe that Muhammad revealed Allah's teachings to the world. Which of the following leaders that you learned about in Grade 6 did *not* reveal a religion's teachings to his people?

A Moses

B Hammurabi

C Buddha

D Jesus

7 Islamic society first appeared in Southwest Asia, east of the Mediterranean Sea. Which of the following civilizations also appeared in that area?

A Greek

B Roman

C Egyptian

D Hebrew

The Spread of Islam

California Standards

History–Social Science

7.2 Students analyze the geographic, political, economic, religious, and social structures of the civilizations of Islam in the Middle Ages.

Analysis Skills

HR 1 Frame questions for study and research.

HR 5 Determine the context in which statements were made.

English–Language Arts

Writing 7.2.5a Include the main ideas and most significant details.

Reading 7.2.0 Students read and understand grade-level-appropriate material.

FOCUS ON WRITING

Writing an "I Am" Poem Many intriguing people were involved in the early days of Islam. After reading this section, you will write an "I Am" poem about one person—real or imaginary—from this period.

	634 Muslim forces unite Arabia.	**756** Córdoba becomes the capital of Muslim Spain.
CHAPTER EVENTS		

650

WORLD EVENTS		**700s** Viking raids begin in northern Europe.

HOLT

History's Impact

▶ **video series**
Watch the video to understand the impact of Mecca on Islam.

What You Will Learn...

In the chapter you will learn about the spread of Islam into lands outside of Arabia. This photo shows Muslims in Nigeria, a country in western Africa, celebrating an Islamic holiday.

1325
Ibn Battutah begins his world travels.

1453
The Ottomans capture Constantinople.

1501
The Safavids conquer Persia.

1631
Shah Jahan begins building the Taj Mahal.

900

1150

1650

1215
English nobles force King John to accept Magna Carta.

1521
Cortés conquers the Aztec Empire.

1588
England defeats the Spanish Armada.

Reading Social Studies

by Kylene Beers

| Economics | Geography | **Politics** | Religion | Society and Culture | Science and Technology |

Focus on Themes In this chapter, you will learn about the spread of Islam after Muhammad's death. You will read about great conquests and powerful empires. As you read, you will learn how **political** leaders made laws. You will also see how Muslim scholars increased the world's knowledge of **science**, especially in astronomy, geography, math, and medicine.

Questioning

Focus on Reading Asking yourself questions is a good way to be sure that you understand what you are reading. You should always ask yourself the W questions—**who** the most important people are, **when** and **where** they lived, and **what** they did.

Analytical Questions Questions like **why** and **how** can also help you make sense of what happened in the past. Asking questions about how and why things happened will help you better understand historical events.

Additional reading support can be found in the

Inter active

Reader and Study Guide

Who?
Emperor Akbar

Where?
India

Why?
He didn't think any single religion could provide people with everything they needed.

Growth of Territory

[The Mughal Empire in India] grew in the mid-1500s under an emperor named Akbar. He . . . began a tolerant religious policy. Akbar believed that no single religion, including Islam, had all the answers. He got rid of the tax on non-Muslims and invited Hindus to be part of the Mughal government.

What?
began tolerant religious policies

When?
the mid-1500s

How?
Akbar removed penalties from non-Muslims and granted them new opportunities.

HSS Analysis HR 1 Frame questions that can be answered by historical study and research.
ELA 7.2.0 Read and evaluate grade-level-appropriate material.

You Try It!

Read the following passage and then answer the questions below.

Geography

During the mid-1100s, a Muslim geographer named al-Idrisi collected information from Arab travelers. He was writing a geography book and wanted it to be very accurate. When al-Idrisi had a question about where a mountain, river, or coastline was, he sent trained geographers to figure out its exact location. Using the information the geographers brought back, al-Idrisi made some important discoveries. For example, he proved that land did not go all the way around the Indian Ocean as many people thought.

From Chapter 4, p. 95

Answer these questions based on the passage you just read.

1. Who is this passage about?

2. What is he famous for doing?

3. When did he live?

4. Why did he do what he did?

5. How did he accomplish his task?

6. How can knowing this information help you understand the past?

Academic Vocabulary

Success in school is related to knowing academic vocabulary—the words that are frequently used in school assignments and discussions. In this chapter, you will learn the following academic words:

development *(p. 83)*
establish *(p. 91)*

As you read Chapter 4, ask questions like who, what, when, where, why, and how to help you understand what you are reading.

Early Expansion

What You Will Learn...

Main Ideas

1. Muslim armies conquered many lands into which Islam slowly spread.
2. Trade helped Islam spread into new areas.
3. A mix of cultures was one result of Islam's spread.
4. Islamic influence encouraged the growth of cities.

The Big Idea

Conquest and trade led to the spread of Islam, the blending of cultures, and the growth of cities.

Key Terms and People

Abu Bakr, p. 80
caliph, p. 80
tolerance, p. 83

HSS 7.2.4 Discuss the expansion of Muslim rule through military conquests and treaties, emphasizing the cultural blending within Muslim civilization and the spread and acceptance of Islam and the Arabic language.

7.2.5 Describe the growth of cities and the establishment of trade routes among Asia, Africa, and Europe, the products and inventions that traveled along these routes (e.g., spices, textiles, paper, steel, new crops), and the role of merchants in Arab society.

If YOU were there...

You are a farmer living in a village on the coast of India. For centuries, your people have raised cotton and spun its fibers into a soft fabric. One day, a ship arrives in the harbor, bringing traders from far away. They bring interesting goods you have never seen before. They also bring new ideas.

What ideas might you learn from the traders?

BUILDING BACKGROUND You know that for years traders traveled through Arabia to markets far away. Along the way, they picked up new goods and ideas, and they introduced these to the people they met. Some of the new ideas the traders spread were Islamic ideas.

Muslim Armies Conquer Many Lands

After Muhammad's death, many of the Muslim leaders chose **Abu Bakr** (uh-boo-BAK-uhr), one of Muhammad's first converts, to be the next leader of Islam. He was the first **caliph** (KAY-luhf), a title that Muslims use for the highest leader of Islam. In Arabic, the word *caliph* means "successor." As Muhammad's successors, the caliphs had to follow the prophet's example. This meant ruling according to the Qur'an. Unlike Muhammad, however, early caliphs were not religious leaders.

Though not a religious leader, Abu Bakr was a political and military leader. Under his rule, the Muslims began a series of wars in which they conquered many lands outside of Arabia.

Time Line

The Spread of Islam

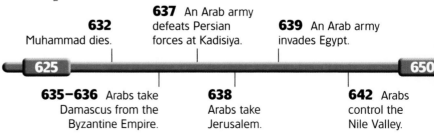

632 Muhammad dies.

637 An Arab army defeats Persian forces at Kadisiya.

639 An Arab army invades Egypt.

625

650

635–636 Arabs take Damascus from the Byzantine Empire.

638 Arabs take Jerusalem.

642 Arabs control the Nile Valley.

Beginnings of an Empire

Abu Bakr directed a series of battles against Arab tribes who did not follow Muhammad's teachings. By his death in 634, he had made Arabia a unified Muslim state.

With Arabia united, Muslim leaders turned their attention elsewhere. Their armies, strong after their battles in Arabia, won many stunning victories. They defeated the Persian and Byzantine empires, which were weak from years of fighting.

When the Muslims conquered lands, they made treaties with any non-Muslims there. These treaties listed rules that conquered people—often Jews and Christians—had to follow. For example, some non-Muslims could not build places of worship in Muslim cities or dress like Muslims. In return, the Muslims would not attack them.

One such treaty was the Pact of Umar, named after the second caliph. It was written about 637 after Muslims conquered Syria.

During this period, differences between groups of Muslims solidified into what became the Shia–Sunni split. One prominent incident was the killing of Hussein, grandson of Muhammad and carrier of the hopes of the Shia Muslim branch.

Growth of the Empire

Many early caliphs came from the Umayyad (oom-EYE-yuhd) family. The Umayyads moved their capital from Medina to Damascus and continued to expand the empire. They took over lands in Central Asia and in northern India. The Umayyads also gained control of trade in the eastern Mediterranean and conquered part of North Africa.

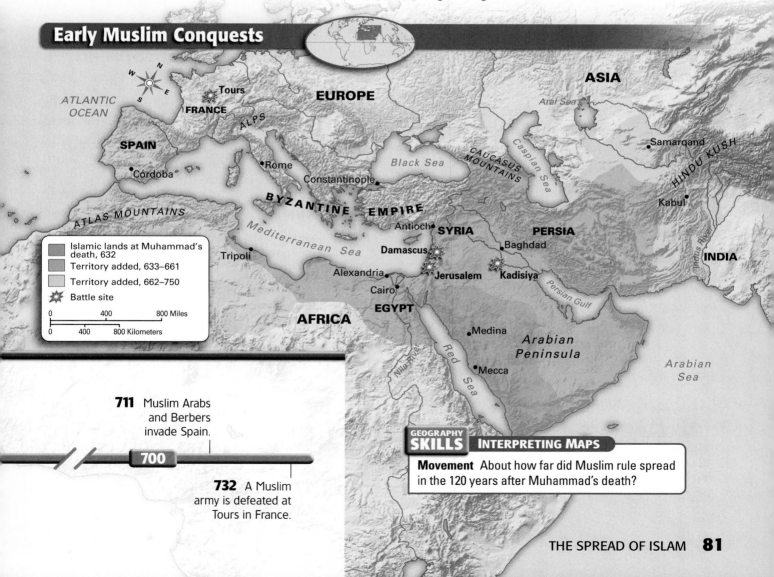

Early Muslim Conquests

Islamic lands at Muhammad's death, 632
Territory added, 633–661
Territory added, 662–750
★ Battle site

0   400   800 Miles
0   400   800 Kilometers

ATLANTIC OCEAN
Tours
FRANCE
EUROPE
ASIA
Aral Sea
SPAIN
ALPS
Rome
Black Sea
CAUCASUS MOUNTAINS
Caspian Sea
Samarqand
HINDU KUSH
Córdoba
Constantinople
BYZANTINE EMPIRE
Kabul
ATLAS MOUNTAINS
Mediterranean Sea
Antioch
SYRIA
PERSIA
Indus River
Tripoli
Damascus
Baghdad
INDIA
Alexandria
Jerusalem
Kadisiya
Cairo
Persian Gulf
EGYPT
Medina
Arabian Peninsula
Nile River
Red Sea
Mecca
Arabian Sea
AFRICA

711 Muslim Arabs and Berbers invade Spain.

700

732 A Muslim army is defeated at Tours in France.

GEOGRAPHY SKILLS | **INTERPRETING MAPS**

Movement About how far did Muslim rule spread in the 120 years after Muhammad's death?

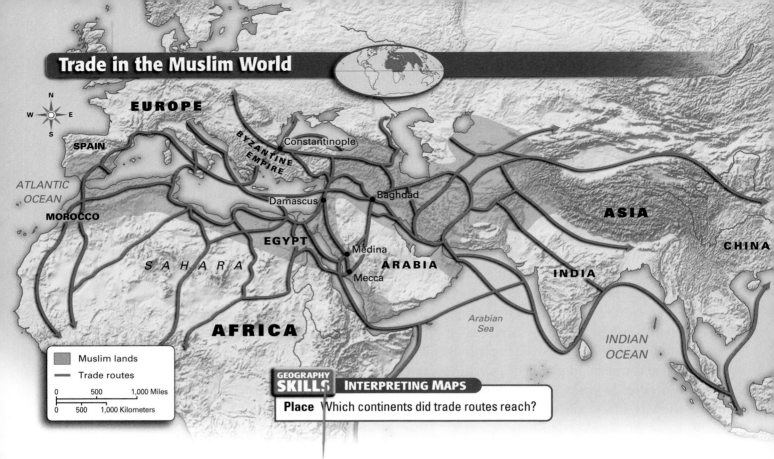

Trade in the Muslim World

EUROPE

SPAIN

ATLANTIC
OCEAN

MOROCCO

BYZANTINE
EMPIRE
Constantinople

Damascus
Baghdad

ASIA

CHINA

EGYPT

SAHARA

Medina
Mecca

ARABIA

INDIA

AFRICA

Arabian
Sea

INDIAN
OCEAN

Muslim lands

Trade routes

0   500   1,000 Miles
0   500   1,000 Kilometers

GEOGRAPHY SKILLS **INTERPRETING MAPS**

Place Which continents did trade routes reach?

In the late 600s, battles with the Berbers slowed the growth of Muslim rule in North Africa. The Berbers are the native people of North Africa. After years of fighting, many Berbers converted to Islam. Following their conversion, they joined the Arabs in their efforts to spread Islam.

Next the Muslims tried to expand their empire into Europe. A combined Arab and Berber army invaded Spain in 711 and quickly conquered it. The army moved on into what is now France, but it was stopped by a Christian army near the city of Tours (TOOR). Despite this defeat, Muslims called Moors continued to rule parts of Spain for the next 700 years.

In continuing the expansion, a new dynasty, the Abbasids (uh-BAS-idz), came to power in 750. The Abbasids reorganized the government to make it easier to rule such a large region.

THE IMPACT TODAY

Indonesia now has the largest Muslim population in the world.

READING CHECK **Analyzing** What role did armies play in spreading Islam?

Trade Helps Islam Spread

Islam gradually spread through areas the Muslims conquered. At the same time trade helped spread Islam into other areas as well. Arabia's crossroads location gave Muslim merchants easy access to South Asia, Europe, and Africa.

Merchants and the Spread of Islam

Along with their trade goods, Arab merchants took Islamic beliefs to new lands. For example, merchants introduced Islam into India. Although many Indian kingdoms remained Hindu, coastal trading cities soon had large Muslim communities. In Africa, societies often had both African and Muslim customs. For example, Arabic influenced local African languages. Also, many African leaders converted to Islam.

Between 1200 and 1600, Muslim traders carried Islam as far east as what are now Malaysia and Indonesia. Even today, Islam is a major influence on life there.

A far-reaching trade network brought wealth and new knowledge to the Muslim world and helped spread Islam. Above, an Arab trader prepares perfume, a valuable trade good.

Products and Inventions

In addition to helping spread Islam, trade brought new products to Muslim lands and made many people rich. First, new products and inventions created by other peoples made their way to the Muslim world. For example, Arabs learned from the Chinese how to make paper and use gunpowder. New crops such as cotton, rice, and oranges arrived from India, China, and Southeast Asia. Second, traders made money on trade between regions.

In addition to trade with Asia, African trade was important to Muslim merchants. Many merchants set up businesses next to African market towns. They wanted African products such as ivory, cloves, and slaves. In return they offered fine white pottery called porcelain from China, cloth goods from India, and iron from Southwest Asia and Europe. Arab traders even traveled south across the Sahara, the world's largest desert, to get gold. In exchange, they brought the Africans salt, which was scarce south of the desert.

READING CHECK **Finding Main Ideas** How did trade affect the spread of Islam?

A Mix of Cultures

As Islam spread through trade, warfare, and treaties, Arabs came in contact with people who had different beliefs and lifestyles than they did. Muslims generally practiced religious **tolerance**, or acceptance, with regard to people they conquered. In other words, the Muslims did not ban all religions other than Islam in their lands. Jews and Christians in particular kept many of their rights, since they shared some beliefs with Muslims.

Although Jews and Christians were allowed to practice their own religions, they had to pay a special tax. They also had to follow the rules of the treaties governing conquered peoples.

Many people conquered by the Arabs converted to Islam. Along with Islamic beliefs, these people often adopted other parts of Arabic culture. For example, many people started speaking Arabic. The Arabs also adopted some of the customs of the people they conquered. For example, they copied a Persian form of bureaucracy in their government.

As Islam spread, language and religion helped unify the many groups that became part of the Islamic world. Cultural blending changed Islam from a mostly Arab religion into a religion of many different cultures.

READING CHECK **Evaluating** Did Muslim tolerance encourage or limit the spread of Islam?

The Growth of Cities

The growing cities of the Muslim world reflected this blending of cultures. Trade had brought people, products, and ideas together. It had also created wealth, which supported great cultural **development** in cities such as Baghdad in what is now Iraq and Córdoba (KAWR-doh-bah) in Spain.

ACADEMIC VOCABULARY

development the process of growing or improving

The City of Córdoba

Córdoba, Spain, was a great center of Islamic learning. In fact, in the early AD 900s, it was one of the richest and most educated cities in Europe.

Córdoba

Baghdad

Baghdad became the capital of the Islamic Empire in 762. Located near both land and water routes, it was a major trading center. In addition to trade, farming contributed to a strong economy. Dates and grains grew well in the fertile soil. Trade and farming made Baghdad one of the world's richest cities in the late 700s and early 800s.

The center of Baghdad was known as the round city, because three round walls surrounded it. Within the walls was the caliph's palace, which took up one-third of the city. Outside the walls were houses and souks for the city's huge population.

Caliphs at Baghdad supported science and the arts. For example, they built a hospital and an observatory. They also built a library that was used as a university and housed Arabic translations of many ancient Greek works. Because Baghdad was a center of culture and learning, many artists and writers went there. Artists decorated the city's public buildings, while writers wrote literature that remains popular today.

Córdoba

Córdoba, too, became a great Muslim city. In 756 Muslims chose it to be the capital of what is now Spain. Like Baghdad, Córdoba had a strong economy based on agriculture and trade. Córdoba exported textiles and jewelry, which were valued throughout Europe.

By the early 900s Córdoba was the largest and most advanced city in Europe. It had mansions and mosques, busy markets and shops, and aqueducts. It also had public water and lighting systems.

Córdoba was a great center of learning. Men and women from across the Muslim world and Europe came to study at the university there. They studied Greek and Roman scientific writings and translated them into Arabic. In addition, they studied writings produced in the Muslim world and translated them from Arabic to Latin. As a result, Arabic writings on such subjects as mathematics, medicine, astronomy, geography, and history could be studied throughout Europe.

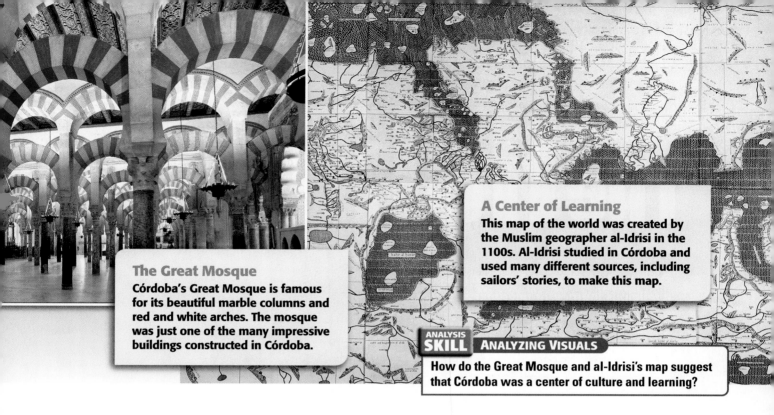

The Great Mosque
Córdoba's Great Mosque is famous for its beautiful marble columns and red and white arches. The mosque was just one of the many impressive buildings constructed in Córdoba.

A Center of Learning
This map of the world was created by the Muslim geographer al-Idrisi in the 1100s. Al-Idrisi studied in Córdoba and used many different sources, including sailors' stories, to make this map.

ANALYSIS SKILL ANALYZING VISUALS

How do the Great Mosque and al-Idrisi's map suggest that Córdoba was a center of culture and learning?

Córdoba was also a center of Jewish culture. Many Jews held key jobs in the government. Jewish poets, philosophers, and scientists made great contributions to Córdoba's cultural growth.

READING CHECK **Comparing** What did Baghdad and Córdoba have in common?

SUMMARY AND PREVIEW Through wars and treaties, Muslim territory grew tremendously and Islam spread gradually through this territory. In the next section you will learn about three empires that grew up and continued to work to spread Islam.

---

go.hrw.com
Online Quiz
KEYWORD: SQ7 HP4

Section 1 Assessment

Reviewing Ideas, Terms, and People **HSS** 7.2.4, 7.2.5

1. **a. Define** What is a **caliph**?
   b. Sequence To what regions, and in what general order, had Islam spread by 750?
2. **a. Recall** What were three places Islam spread to through trade?
   b. Explain How did trade help spread Islam?
3. **Identify** What helped unify the many groups that became part of the Islamic world?
4. **a. Identify** What were two important cities in the Islamic world?
   b. Analyze How did life in Córdoba show a mix of cultures?
   c. Evaluate Do you think tolerance is a good or bad policy for governing people? Why?

Critical Thinking

5. **Identifying Cause and Effect** Draw a graphic organizer like the one below. Use it to identify two ways Arab traders affected the Islamic world.

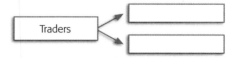

Traders

FOCUS ON WRITING

6. **Taking Notes on Important People** Draw a table with three columns. In the first column, list key people you read about in this section. In the second column, identify who each person was. In the third column, list one contribution of each to Islam.

THE SPREAD OF ISLAM **85**

The Hajj

Every year, as many as 2 million Muslims make a religious journey, or pilgrimage, to Mecca, Saudi Arabia. This journey, called the hajj, is one of the Five Pillars of Islam—all Muslims are expected to make the journey at least once in their lifetime if they can.

Mecca is the place where Muhammad lived and taught more than 1,300 years ago. As a result, it is the holiest city in Islam. The pilgrims who travel to Mecca each year serve as a living reminder of the connection between history and geography.

Europe and the Americas Many countries in Europe and the Americas have a Muslim population. These pilgrims are from Germany.

On the Road to Mecca

- Before entering Mecca, pilgrims undergo a ritual cleansing and put on special white garments.

- At Mecca, guides help pilgrims through religious rituals.

- One important ritual is the "Standing," on Mount Arafat, near Mecca. Pilgrims stand for hours, praying, at a place where Muhammad is said to have held his last sermon.

- Pilgrims then participate in a three-day ritual of "Stoning," in which they throw pebbles at three pillars.

- Finally, pilgrims complete their journey by returning to the Grand Mosque in Mecca, where a great feast is held.

Africa Pilgrims also come from Africa. These pilgrims are from Nigeria, just one of the African countries home to a large Muslim population.

Southeast Asia These pilgrims are from Indonesia, in Southeast Asia. Like all pilgrims, they wear simple white garments that symbolize the equality and unity of all Muslims.

Persian Gulf

MECCA

SAUDI ARABIA

Red Sea

Southwest Asia Pilgrims from Southwest Asia live closest to Mecca. Because of their close relative location, some are able to make the hajj more than once.

Arabian Sea

GEOGRAPHY
SKILLS **INTERPRETING MAPS**

1. **Movement** What are some of the places from which Muslims begin their journey to Mecca?
2. **Place** Why is Mecca the holiest city in Islam?

Muslim Empires

What You Will Learn...

Main Ideas

1. The Ottoman Empire covered a large area in eastern Europe.
2. The Safavid Empire blended Persian cultural traditions with Shia Islam.
3. The Mughal Empire in India left an impressive cultural heritage.

The Big Idea

After the early spread of Islam, three large Islamic empires formed—the Ottoman, Safavid, and Mughal.

Key Terms and People

Janissaries, *p. 88*
Mehmed II, *p. 89*
sultan, *p. 89*
Suleyman I, *p. 90*
harem, *p. 90*
Shia, *p. 90*
Sunni, *p. 90*

HSS 7.2.4 Discuss the expansion of Muslim rule through military conquests and treaties, emphasizing the cultural blending within Muslim civilization and the spread and acceptance of Islam and the Arabic language.

If YOU were there...

You are one of several advisors to the leader of a great empire. His armies have conquered many lands and peoples. But the ruler wants to be known for something other than his military conquests. He wants to be remembered as a wise ruler who united the empire. How can he do this? Some of his advisors tell him to rule strictly. Others urge him to be tolerant of the different peoples in the empire. Now it is your turn.

What advice will you give the ruler?

BUILDING BACKGROUND As Islam spread, leaders struggled to build strong empires. Some were tolerant of those they conquered. Others wanted more control. The policies of leaders affected life in the Ottoman, Safavid, and Mughal empires.

The Ottoman Empire

Centuries after the early Arab Muslim conquests, Muslims ruled several powerful empires containing various peoples. Rulers and military leaders in Persian empires spoke Persian, Turkish leaders spoke Turkish, while Arabic continued as a language of religion and scholarship. One of these empires was the Ottoman Empire, which controlled much of Europe, Asia, and Africa. Built on conquest, the Ottoman Empire was a political and cultural force.

Growth of the Empire

In the mid-1200s Muslim Turkish warriors known as Ottomans began to take land from the Christian Byzantine Empire. As the map shows, they eventually ruled lands from eastern Europe to North Africa and Arabia.

The key to the empire's expansion was the Ottoman army. The Ottomans trained Christian boys from conquered towns to be soldiers. These slave soldiers, called **Janissaries**, converted to Islam and became fierce fighters. Besides these slave troops, the Ottomans were aided by new gunpowder weapons—especially cannons.

In 1453 Ottomans led by **Mehmed II** used huge cannons to conquer Constantinople. With the city's capture, Mehmed defeated the Byzantine Empire. He became known as "the Conqueror." Mehmed made Constantinople, which the Ottomans called Istanbul, his new capital. He also turned the Byzantines' great church, Hagia Sophia, into a mosque.

A later **sultan**, or Ottoman ruler, continued Mehmed's conquests. He expanded the empire to the east through the rest of Anatolia, another name for Asia Minor. His armies also conquered Syria and Egypt. Soon afterward the holy cities of Mecca and Medina accepted Ottoman rule as well. These triumphs made the Ottoman Empire a major world power.

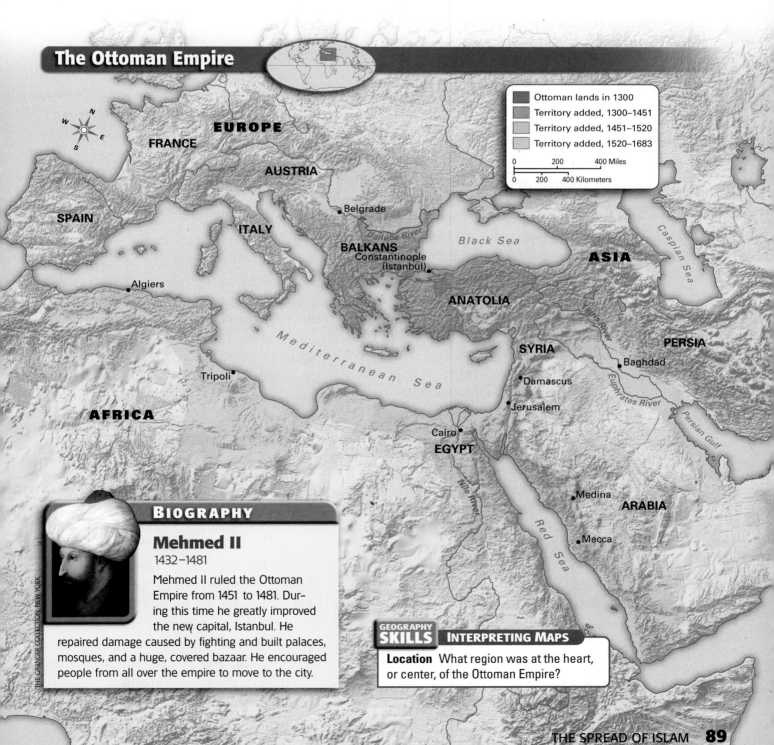

The Ottoman Empire

Legend:
- Ottoman lands in 1300
- Territory added, 1300–1451
- Territory added, 1451–1520
- Territory added, 1520–1683

0 200 400 Miles
0 200 400 Kilometers

EUROPE
FRANCE
AUSTRIA
SPAIN
ITALY
Belgrade
Danube River
Black Sea
BALKANS
Constantinople (Istanbul)
ASIA
Caspian Sea
Algiers
ANATOLIA
Mediterranean Sea
SYRIA
PERSIA
Tigris River
Baghdad
Tripoli
Damascus
Euphrates River
Jerusalem
Persian Gulf
AFRICA
Cairo
EGYPT
Nile River
Medina
ARABIA
Red Sea
Mecca

THE GRANGER COLLECTION, NEW YORK

BIOGRAPHY

Mehmed II
1432–1481

Mehmed II ruled the Ottoman Empire from 1451 to 1481. During this time he greatly improved the new capital, Istanbul. He repaired damage caused by fighting and built palaces, mosques, and a huge, covered bazaar. He encouraged people from all over the empire to move to the city.

GEOGRAPHY SKILLS **INTERPRETING MAPS**

Location What region was at the heart, or center, of the Ottoman Empire?

FOCUS ON
READING
What questions
could you ask to
take notes on this
discussion?

The Ottoman Empire reached its height under **Suleyman I** (soo-lay-MAHN), "the Magnificent." During Suleyman's rule, from 1520 to 1566, the Ottomans took control of the eastern Mediterranean and pushed farther into Europe, areas they would control until the early 1900s.

Also during Suleyman's rule, the Ottoman Empire reached its cultural peak. Muslim poets wrote beautiful works, and architects worked to turn Istanbul from a Byzantine city into a Muslim one.

THE IMPACT TODAY

Most Muslims today belong to the Sunni branch of Islam.

Ottoman Government and Society

The sultan issued laws and made all major decisions in the empire. Most Ottoman law was based on Shariah, or Islamic law, but sultans also made laws of their own.

Ottoman society was divided into two classes. Judges and other people who advised the sultan on legal and military matters were part of the ruling class. Members of the ruling class had to be loyal to the sultan, practice Islam, and understand Ottoman customs.

People who didn't fit these requirements made up the other class. Many of them were Christians or Jews from lands the Ottomans had conquered. Christians and Jews formed religious communities, or millets, within the empire. Each millet had its own leaders and religious laws.

Ottoman society limited the freedom that women enjoyed, especially women in the ruling class. These women usually had to live apart from men in an area of a household called a **harem**. By separating women from men, harems kept women out of public life. However, wealthy women could still own property or businesses. Some women used their money to build schools, mosques, and hospitals.

READING CHECK **Analyzing** How did the Ottomans gain land for their empire?

The Safavid Empire

As the Ottoman Empire reached its height, a group of Persian Muslims known as the Safavids (sah-FAH-vuhds) was gaining power to the east. Before long the Safavids came into conflict with the Ottomans and other Muslims.

The conflict came from an old disagreement among Muslims about who should be caliph. In the mid-600s, Islam split into two groups. The two groups were the Shia (SHEE-ah) and the Sunni (SOO-nee).

The **Shia** were Muslims who thought that only members of Muhammad's family could become caliphs. On the other hand, the **Sunni** didn't think caliphs had to be related to Muhammad as long as they were good Muslims and strong leaders. Over time, religious differences developed between the two groups as well.

Growth of the Empire

The Safavid Empire began in 1501 when the Safavid leader Esma'il (is-mah-EEL) conquered Persia. He took the ancient Persian title of shah, or king.

As shah, Esma'il made Shiism—the beliefs of the Shia—the official religion of the empire. This act worried Esma'il's advisors because most people in the empire were Sunnis. But Esma'il said:

> "I am committed to this action; God and the Immaculate Imams (pure religious leaders) are with me, and I fear no one; by God's help, if the people utter one word of protest, I will draw the sword and leave not one of them alive."
> –Esma'il, quoted in *A Literary History of Persia, Volume 4*, by Edward G. Browne

Esma'il dreamed of conquering other Muslim territories and converting all Muslims to Shiism. He battled the Uzbeks to the north, but he suffered a crushing defeat by the Ottomans, who were Sunni. Esma'il died in 1524, and the next leaders struggled to keep the empire together.

In 1588 the greatest Safavid leader, 'Abbas, became shah. He strengthened the military and gave his soldiers modern gunpowder weapons. Copying the Ottomans, 'Abbas trained foreign slave boys to be soldiers. Under 'Abbas's rule the Safavids defeated the Uzbeks and took back land that had been lost to the Ottomans. 'Abbas also made great contributions to the Safavid culture and economy.

Culture and Economy

The Safavids blended Persian and Muslim traditions. They built beautiful mosques in their capital, Esfahan (es-fah-HAHN). People admired the colorful tiles and large dome of the Shah's mosque, built for 'Abbas. Esfahan was considered one of the world's most magnificent cities in the 1600s.

Safavid culture played a role in the empire's economy because 'Abbas encouraged the manufacturing of traditional products. Handwoven carpets became a major export. Other textiles, such as silk and velvet, were made in large workshops and also sold to other peoples. In addition, the Safavids were admired for their skills in making ceramics and metal goods, especially goods made from steel. Merchants came from as far away as Europe to trade for these goods. Such trade brought wealth to the Safavid Empire and helped **establish** it as a major Islamic civilization. It lasted until the mid-1700s.

ACADEMIC VOCABULARY

establish to set up or create

READING CHECK **Contrasting** What are two ways in which the Safavid and Ottoman empires were different?

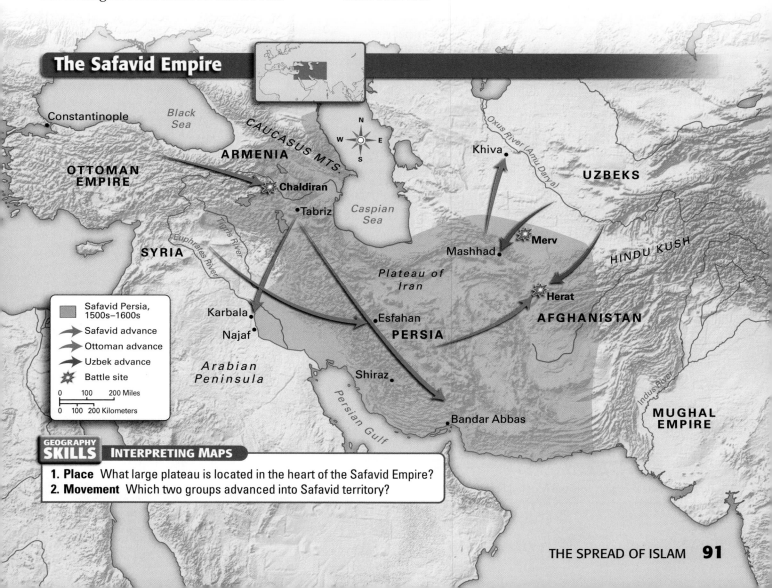

The Safavid Empire

GEOGRAPHY SKILLS **INTERPRETING MAPS**

1. **Place** What large plateau is located in the heart of the Safavid Empire?
2. **Movement** Which two groups advanced into Safavid territory?

THE SPREAD OF ISLAM **91**

The Mughal Empire

East of the Safavid Empire, in India, lay the Mughal (MOO-guhl) Empire. Like the Ottomans, the Mughals united a large and diverse empire. They left a cultural heritage known for poetry and architecture.

Growth of the Empire

The Mughals were Turkish Muslims from Central Asia. The founder of the Mughal Empire was called Babur (BAH-boohr), or "tiger." He tried for years to make an empire in Central Asia. When he didn't succeed there, he decided to build an empire in northern India instead. There Babur established the Mughal Empire in 1526.

The empire grew in the mid-1500s under an emperor named Akbar. He conquered many new lands and worked to make the Mughal government stronger. He also began a tolerant religious policy. Akbar believed that no single religion, including Islam, had all the answers. He got rid of the tax on non-Muslims and invited Hindus to be part of the Mughal government. Akbar's tolerant policies helped unify the empire.

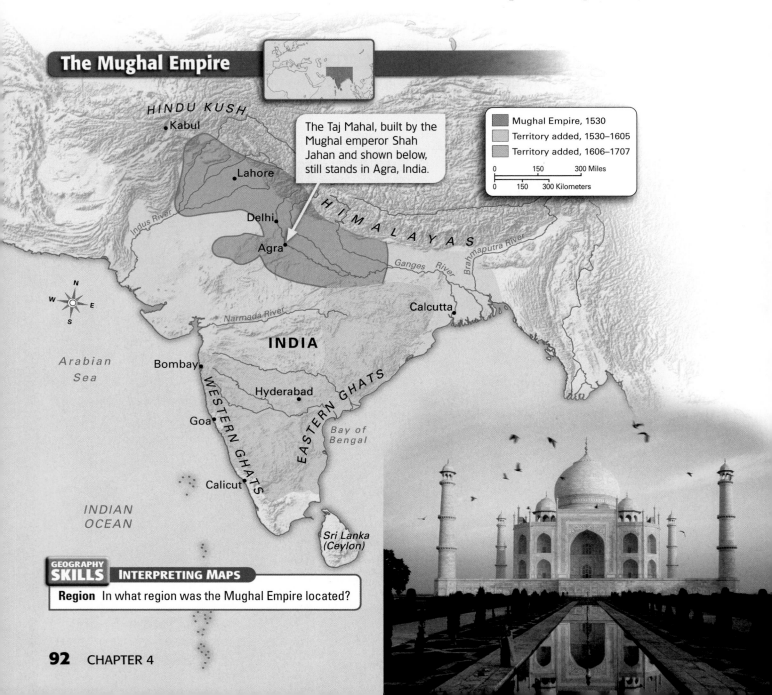

The Mughal Empire

HINDU KUSH
Kabul
Lahore
Delhi
Agra
HIMALAYAS
Indus River
Ganges River
Brahmaputra River
Narmada River
Calcutta
INDIA
Arabian Sea
Bombay
Hyderabad
Goa
WESTERN GHATS
EASTERN GHATS
Bay of Bengal
Calicut
INDIAN OCEAN
Sri Lanka (Ceylon)

The Taj Mahal, built by the Mughal emperor Shah Jahan and shown below, still stands in Agra, India.

- Mughal Empire, 1530
- Territory added, 1530–1605
- Territory added, 1606–1707

0   150   300 Miles
0   150   300 Kilometers

GEOGRAPHY SKILLS | INTERPRETING MAPS

Region In what region was the Mughal Empire located?

In the 1600s Mughal emperors expanded the empire to control almost all of India. Look at the map to see how it grew. This period of expansion was not a peaceful time. In the late 1600s a new emperor changed the tolerant religious policies Akbar had established. The new emperor ordered people to obey strict religious laws and destroyed Hindu temples throughout India. He also persecuted non-Muslims and made them pay a special tax. One persecuted group was the Sikhs, a religious group that had formed from Hinduism after its leaders rejected some Hindu beliefs. When people gathered to protest, he sent war elephants to crush them. As a result of the harsh policies, violent revolts occurred in much of the empire in the late 1600s. The Mughal Empire soon fell apart.

Cultural Achievements

A conflict of cultures led to the end of the Mughal Empire. For much of the empire's history, however, Muslims and Hindus lived together peacefully. Persians and Indians lived and worked in the same communities. As a result, elements of their cultures blended together. The result was a culture unique to the Mughal Empire.

For example, during Akbar's rule, the Persian language and Persian clothing styles were popular. At the same time, however, Akbar encouraged people to write in Indian languages such as Hindi and Urdu. Also, many of the buildings constructed blended Persian, Islamic, and Hindu styles.

The Mughal Empire is known for its monumental architecture—particularly the Taj Mahal. The Taj Mahal is a dazzling tomb built between 1631 and 1647 by Akbar's grandson Shah Jahan for his wife. He brought workers and materials from all over India and Central Asia to build the Taj Mahal. The buildings of the palace include a main gateway and a mosque. Gardens with pathways and fountains add beauty to the palace grounds. Many of the monuments the Mughals built have become symbols of India today.

READING CHECK Summarizing What cultures blended in the Mughal Empire to create a distinct culture?

SUMMARY AND PREVIEW The Ottomans, Safavids, and Mughals built great empires and continued the spread of Islam. In Section 3 you will learn about some other achievements of the Islamic world.

THE IMPACT TODAY
Persecution would later lead many Sikhs to move to California.

go.hrw.com
Online Quiz
KEYWORD: SQ7 HP4

Section 2 Assessment

Reviewing Ideas, Terms, and People **HSS** 7.2.4

1. **a. Define** Who were the **Janissaries**?
   b. Analyze In what ways was the Ottoman society tolerant and in what ways was it not?
2. **a. Recall** When did the Safavid Empire begin?
   b. Explain How was Safavid culture part of the empire's economy?
   c. Elaborate How might people have reacted to Esma'il's decision to make the Safavid Empire **Shia**?
3. **a. Recall** Where was the Mughal Empire located?
   b. Contrast How did Akbar's religious policy in the mid-1500s differ from the religious policy of a different emperor in the late 1600s?

Critical Thinking

4. **Comparing and Contrasting** Draw the graphic organizer below. Use it to compare and contrast different characteristics of the Ottoman, Safavid, and Mughal empires.

	Ottoman	Safavid	Mughal
Leader			
Location			
Religious policy			

FOCUS ON WRITING

5. **Writing about Important People** Add Janissaries, Mehmed II, Suleyman I, Esma'il, 'Abbas, and Akbar to your table. Write a brief description of each. Make a note of who you find most intriguing.

Cultural Achievements

What You Will Learn...

Main Ideas

1. Muslim scholars made advances in various fields of science and philosophy.
2. Islam influenced styles of literature and the arts.

The Big Idea

Muslim scholars and artists made contributions to science, art, and literature.

Key Terms and People

Ibn Battutah, *p. 95*
Sufism, *p. 96*
Omar Khayyám, *p. 97*
patrons, *p. 97*
minaret, *p. 97*
calligraphy, *p. 98*

HSS **7.2.6** Understand the intellectual exchanges among Muslim scholars of Eurasia and Africa and the contributions Muslim scholars made to later civilizations in the areas of science, geography, mathematics, philosophy, medicine, art, and literature.

If YOU were there...

You are a servant in the court of a powerful ruler. Your life at court is comfortable, though not one of luxury. Now the ruler is sending your master to explore unknown lands and distant kingdoms in Africa. The dangerous journey will take him across oceans and deserts. He can take only a few servants with him. He has not ordered you to come but has given you a choice.

Will you join your master's expedition or stay home? Why?

BUILDING BACKGROUND Muslim explorers traveled far and wide to learn about new places. They used what they learned to make maps. Their contributions to geography were just one way Muslim scholars made advancements in science and learning.

Science and Philosophy

The empires of the Islamic world contributed to the achievements of Islamic culture. Muslim scholars made advances in astronomy, geography, math, and science. Scholars at Baghdad and Córdoba translated many ancient writings on these subjects into Arabic.

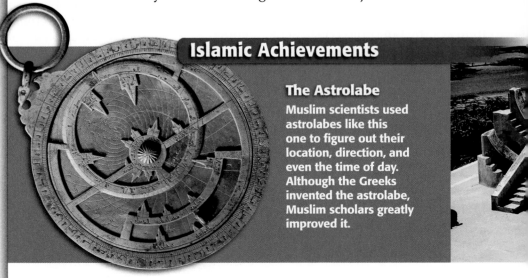

Islamic Achievements

The Astrolabe
Muslim scientists used astrolabes like this one to figure out their location, direction, and even the time of day. Although the Greeks invented the astrolabe, Muslim scholars greatly improved it.

Having a common language helped scholars throughout the Islamic world share what they learned, even though many scholars came from different cultures and spoke other languages.

Astronomy

Many cities in the Muslim world had observatories where people could study astronomy—the sun, moon, and stars. Scientists studied astronomy to better understand time and clockmaking. Muslim scientists also improved the astrolabe, which the Greeks had invented to chart the position of the stars. Arab scholars used the astrolabe to figure out their location on earth. This helped Muslims know what direction to turn so they could face Mecca for their prayers. The astrolabe would later become an important contribution to the exploration of the seas.

Geography

Studying astronomy also helped Muslims explore the world. As people learned to use the stars to calculate time and location, merchants and explorers began to travel widely. For example, **Ibn Battutah** traveled to Africa, India, China, and Spain in the 1320s. To help travelers on their way, Muslim geographers made more accurate maps than were available before. They also developed better ways of calculating distances.

Primary Source

BOOK
Travels in Asia and Africa

Ibn Battutah wrote detailed descriptions of his pilgrimage to Mecca. In the passage below, he talks about crossing the desert from Syria to Medina.

From Tabuk the caravan travels with great speed night and day, for fear of this desert. Halfway through is the valley of al–Ukhaydir. . . . One year the pilgrims suffered terribly here from the samoom–wind; the water–supplies dried up and the price of a single drink rose to a thousand dinars, but both seller and buyer perished. Their story is written on a rock in the valley.

–Ibn Battutah, from *The Travels*

ANALYSIS SKILL **ANALYZING PRIMARY SOURCES**
What parts of Ibn Battutah's description would be useful to a mapmaker?

During the mid-1100s, a Muslim geographer named al-Idrisi (uhl-i-DREE-see) collected information from Arab travelers. He was writing a geography book and wanted it to be very accurate. When al-Idrisi had a question about where a mountain, river, or coastline was, he sent trained geographers to figure out its exact location. Using the information the geographers brought back, al-Idrisi made some important discoveries. For example, he proved that land did not go all the way around the Indian Ocean as many people thought.

Astronomy
Muslim scientists made remarkable advances in astronomy. This observatory was built in the 1700s in Delhi, the capital of Mughal India.

THE GRANGER COLLECTION, NEW YORK

Geography
Muslim travelers collected much information about the world, some of which was used to make this map. New and better maps led to even more travel and a greater understanding of the world's geography.

Math

Muslim scholars also made advances in mathematics. In the 800s they combined the Indian number system, including the use of zero, with the Greek science of mathematics. The Muslim mathematician al-Khwarizmi (al-KWAHR-iz-mee) then used these new ideas to write a math textbook on what he called *al-jabr*, or "algebra." It laid the foundation for the modern algebra that students around the world learn today. When the book was brought to Europe in the 1500s, Europeans called the new numbers "Arabic" numerals.

THE IMPACT TODAY

We still call the numerals 0, 1, 2, 3, 4, 5, 6, 7, 8, and 9 Arabic or Hindu-Arabic numerals.

Medicine

Muslims made many advances in other sciences, but their greatest scientific achievements may have come in medicine. They studied Greek and Indian medicine, adding to this knowledge with discoveries of their own.

As early as the 800s, Muslim doctors in Baghdad began to improve medicine. As they studied, Muslim doctors

- created tests for doctors to pass before they could treat people,
- made encyclopedias of drugs with descriptions of each drug's effects,
- wrote descriptions of diseases,
- started the first pharmacy school to teach people how to make medicines.

The first Muslim public hospital was built in Baghdad. In that hospital, a doctor named Ar-Razi discovered how to diagnose and treat the deadly disease smallpox. Another doctor, Ibn-Sina, who was known in the West as Avicenna (av-uh-SEN-uh), wrote a medical encyclopedia. This encyclopedia, which was translated into Latin and used throughout Europe until the 1600s, is one of the most famous books in the history of medicine.

Philosophy

Many Muslim doctors and scientists also studied the ancient Greek philosophy of reason and rational thought. Other Muslims developed a new philosophy. Worried about the growing interest in worldly things, they focused on spiritual issues. Many of them lived a simple life of devotion to God.

The focus on spiritual issues led to a movement called Sufism (SOO-fi-zuhm). People who practice Sufism are called Sufis (SOO-feez). **Sufism** teaches that people can find God's love by having a personal relationship with God. They focus on loving God and call him their Beloved. Sufism had a strong impact on Islam.

READING CHECK **Evaluating** In your opinion, what was the most important advance in science and learning in the Muslim world?

Islamic Achievements (continued)

Math

Muslim mathematicians combined Indian and Greek ideas with their own to dramatically increase human knowledge of mathematics. The fact that we call our numbers today "Arabic numerals" is a reminder of this contribution.

Medicine

Muslim doctors made medicines from plants like this mandrake plant, which was used to treat pain and illnesses. Muslim doctors developed better ways to prevent, diagnose, and treat many diseases.

Literature and the Arts

The blending of traditional Islam and the cultures of conquered peoples produced fresh approaches to art, architecture, and writing. As a result, literature and the arts flourished in the Islamic world.

Literature

Two forms of literature were popular in the Muslim world—poetry and short stories. Poetry was influenced by Sufism. Some Sufis wrote poems about their loyalty to God. Through their poetry, the mystical ideas of Sufism spread among other Muslims. One of the most famous Sufi poets was **Omar Khayyám** (oh-mahr-ky-AHM). In a book of poems known as *The Rubáiyát*, Khayyám wrote about faith, hope, and other emotions. Some of his poems express deep sadness or despair. Others, like the one below, describe lighter, happier scenes.

> *" A book of verse, underneath the bough, A jug of wine, a loaf of bread—and thou, Beside me singing in the wilderness—Ah, wilderness were paradise enow (enough)! "*
>
> –Omar Khayyám, from *The Rubáiyát*, translated by Edward FitzGerald

Muslims also enjoyed reading short stories. One famous collection of short stories is *The Thousand and One Nights*. It includes stories about legendary heroes and characters. A European compiler later added short stories that were not part of the medieval Arabic collection. Among these were some of the most famous, such as "Sinbad the Sailor," "Aladdin," and "Ali Baba and the 40 Thieves." Many of these tales came from India, Egypt, and other lands that had become part of the Muslim world.

Architecture

Architecture was one of the most important Muslim art forms. Most people would say that the greatest architectural achievements of the Muslim empires were mosques. Like the great medieval cathedrals in Europe, mosques honored God and inspired religious followers.

The first mosques were simple. They were built to look like the courtyard of Muhammad's house in Medina where he had led the community in prayer. As the Muslim world grew richer, rulers became great **patrons**, or sponsors, of architecture. They used their wealth to pay for elaborately decorated mosques.

The main part of a mosque is a huge hall where people gather to pray. Many mosques have a dome and a **minaret**, or narrow tower from which Muslims are called to prayer. Some mosques, such as the Blue Mosque in Istanbul, have many domes and minarets. Great mosques were built in major cities such as Mecca, Cairo, Baghdad, and Córdoba.

Philosophy
Muslim philosophy led to the development of Sufism. Sufis celebrated their love of God through music and dance. These dancers whirl in circles as they dance with joy.

BIOGRAPHY

Omar Khayyám
c. 1048–1131

Omar Khayyám was a Persian mathematician, astronomer, and poet. During his lifetime, he was famous for his achievements in math and science. For example, he developed a calendar that was more accurate than the one we use today. Now, however, he is best known for his poetry. Khayyám's four-line poems have been translated into almost every language.

In addition to the mosques, Muslim architects built palaces, marketplaces, and libraries. These buildings have complicated domes and arches, colored bricks, and decorated tiles. Muslim architecture is known for these features.

Art

Although Muslim buildings are often elaborately decorated with art, most of this art does not show any animals or humans. Muslims think only Allah can create humans and animals or their images. As a result, most Muslim artists didn't include people or animals in their works.

Because they couldn't represent people or animals in paintings, Muslim artists turned **calligraphy**, or decorative writing, into an art form. They used calligraphy to make sayings from the Qur'an into great works of art that they could use to decorate mosques and other buildings. They also painted decorative writing on tiles, wove it into carpets, and hammered it into finely decorated steel sword blades.

Muslim art and literature show the influence of Islamic beliefs and practices. They also reflect the regional traditions of the places Muslims conquered. This mix of Islam with cultures from Asia, Africa, and Europe gave literature and the arts a unique style and character.

READING CHECK **Generalizing** What two architectural elements were usually part of a mosque?

SUMMARY AND PREVIEW As Islam spread through Europe and Asia, powerful new empires developed. These empires blended Islamic traditions with the traditions of conquered peoples. The result was a new kind of Islamic culture, unified by a common language and religion, but not specifically Arab in character. In the next chapter you will learn about another area whose culture was greatly influenced by Muslim ideas and traditions. That area was West Africa.

go.hrw.com
Online Quiz
KEYWORD: SQ7 HP4

Section 3 Assessment

Reviewing Ideas, Terms, and People   HSS 7.2.6

1. **a. Identify** Who traveled to India, Africa, China, and Spain and contributed his knowledge to the study of geography?
   b. Explain How did Muslim scholars help preserve learning from the ancient world?
   c. Rank In your opinion, what was the most important Muslim scientific achievement? Why?
2. **a. Describe** What function do **minarets** play in mosques?
   b. Summarize What did **patrons** do for art and architecture in the Muslim world?
   c. Summarize How did Muslim artists create art without showing humans or animals?

Critical Thinking

3. **Analyzing Information** Draw a graphic organizer like the one shown on the right. In the second column, identify one important achievement or development the Muslims made in each category listed in the first column.

Category	Achievement or development
Astronomy	*Improved astrolabe*
Geography	
Math	
Medicine	
Philosophy	

FOCUS ON WRITING

4. **Noting Muslim Accomplishments** The people you've read about so far have mostly contributed to Islam through military accomplishments. Now take some notes about scholars and artists who contributed to Islamic culture.

The Blue Mosque

The Blue Mosque in Istanbul was built in the early 1600s for an Ottoman sultan. It upset many people at the time it was built because they thought its six minarets—instead of the usual four—were an attempt to make it as great as the mosque in Mecca.

Domes are a common feature of Islamic architecture. Huge columns support the center of this dome, and more than 250 windows let light into the mosque.

The mosque gets its name from its beautiful blue Iznik tiles.

Tall towers called minarets are a common feature of many mosques.

The most sacred part of a mosque is the mihrab, the niche that points the way to Mecca. These men are praying facing the mihrab.

ANALYSIS SKILL **ANALYZING VISUALS**

Why do you think the decoration of the Blue Mosque is so elaborate?

Social Studies Skills

| Analysis | Critical Thinking | Participation | Study |

Determining the Context of Statements

Understand the Skill

A *context* is the circumstances under which something happens. *Historical context* includes values, beliefs, conditions, and practices that were common in the past. At times, some of these were quite different than what they are today. To truly understand a historical statement or event, you have to take its context into account. It is not right to judge what people in history did or said based on present-day values alone. To be fair, you must also consider the historical context of the statement or event.

Learn the Skill

To better understand something a historical figure said or wrote, use the following guidelines to determine the context of the statement.

1 Identify the speaker or writer, the date, and the topic and main idea of the statement.

2 Determine the speaker's or writer's attitude and point of view about the topic.

3 Review what you know about beliefs, conditions, or practices related to the topic that were common at the time. Find out more about those times if you need to.

4 Decide how the statement reflects the values, attitudes, and practices of people living at that time. Then determine how the statement reflects values, attitudes, and practices of today.

Applying these guidelines will give you a better understanding of a clash between Muslim and European armies in 1191. The following account of this clash was written by Baha' ad-Din, an advisor to the Muslim leader Saladin. He witnessed the battle.

> " The [king of the] Franks [the Muslim term for all Europeans] …ordered all the Musulman [Muslim] prisoners …to be brought before him. They numbered more than three thousand and were all bound with ropes. The Franks then flung themselves upon them all at once and massacred them with sword and lance in cold blood. "
>
> –Baha' ad-Din, from *The Crusade of Richard I*, by John Gillingham

By modern standards this event seems barbaric. But such massacres were not uncommon in those times. Plus, the description is from one side's point of view. This context should be considered when making judgments about the event.

Practice and Apply the Skill

Baha' ad-Din also described the battle itself. Read the following passage. Then answer the questions.

> " The center of the Muslim ranks was broken, drums and flags fell to the ground …Although there were almost 7,000 …killed that day God gave the Muslims victory over their enemies. He [Saladin] stood firm until …the Muslims were exhausted, and then he agreed to a truce at the enemy's request. "
>
> –Baha' ad-Din, from *Arab Historians of the Crusades*, translated by E. J. Costello

1. What happened to Saladin's army? Why do you think the writer calls the battle a Muslim victory?

2. History records this battle as a European victory. Plus, this account is part of a larger statement written in praise of Saladin. Does this additional context change your understanding and answer to the first question? Explain how or why not.

Standards Review

Visual Summary

Use the visual summary below to help you review the main ideas of the chapter.

QUICK FACTS

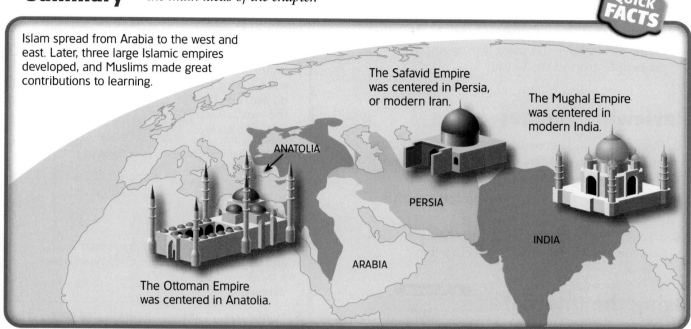

Islam spread from Arabia to the west and east. Later, three large Islamic empires developed, and Muslims made great contributions to learning.

The Safavid Empire was centered in Persia, or modern Iran.

The Mughal Empire was centered in modern India.

ANATOLIA

PERSIA

INDIA

ARABIA

The Ottoman Empire was centered in Anatolia.

Reviewing Vocabulary, Terms, and People

For each group of terms below, write the letter of the term that does not relate to the others. Then write a sentence that explains how the other two terms are related.

1. a. caliph
   b. sultan
   c. harem

2. a. Abu Bakr
   b. Mehmed II
   c. Suleyman I

3. a. tolerance
   b. Janissaries
   c. Akbar

4. a. Shia
   b. Sufism
   c. Sunni

Comprehension and Critical Thinking

SECTION 1 *(Pages 80–85)* **HSS** 7.2.4, 7.2.5

5. a. Identify Who was Abu Bakr, and what did he do?

   b. Draw Conclusions How did trade affect the Arab world?

   c. Elaborate What was Baghdad like in the early 800s? What was Córdoba like in the early 900s?

SECTION 2 *(Pages 88–93)* **HSS** 7.2.4

6. a. Identify Who were Mehmed II, Suleyman I, 'Abbas, and Akbar?

   b. Compare How did the Ottoman, Safavid, and Mughal empires compare in terms of location and size?

   c. Evaluate Which of the three empires seems to have been the most successful? On what do you base your answer?

7. a. Describe What were the major contributions of Ibn Battutah and Omar Khayyám?

b. Make Inferences What is the connection between Islamic belief and calligraphy?

c. Predict Of all the accomplishments of Muslim scholars and artists, which do you think would have the most lasting impact on people around the world?

Reviewing Themes

8. Politics Do you agree or disagree with this statement: "Muslim leaders were tolerant of those they conquered." Defend your answer.

9. Politics How did a religious division affect the Safavid Empire?

10. Science and Technology How did Muslim scholars contribute to science and technology?

Using the Internet

go.hrw.com
KEYWORD: SQ7 WH4

11. Activity: Describing Inventions Muslim advances in science, math, and art were spread around the world by explorers and traders. Enter the activity keyword and learn about these advances. Choose an object created by Muslim scholars in the 600s and 700s and write a paragraph that explains its roots, how it spread to other cultures, and its uses in modern times.

Reading and Analysis Skills

Asking Questions for Understanding Imagine that you are a historian who has just finished reading this chapter and wants to learn more about the spread of Islam. For each of the topics listed below, write one question to which you could attempt to find an answer in your research.

12. Suleyman the Magnificent

13. growth of the Ottoman Empire

14. Muslim achievements in math

15. culture and learning in Baghdad

Social Studies Skills

16. Determining Historical Context Read each of the statements in List A below. Decide which of the people in List B would have been the most likely writer of each statement.

List A	List B
1. "Although I was not allowed to go outside, I hear the weather was beautiful today."	a. a Muslim soldier
2. "Today we fought another Berber army."	b. a Safavid trader
3. "I want to build the finest palace in India."	c. a Sufi poet
4. "In truth everything and everyone is a shadow of the Beloved."	d. a woman in an Ottoman harem
5. "Once again I am heading to Europe. I hope the people there will buy my ceramics."	e. a Mughal emperor

FOCUS ON WRITING

17. Writing Your "I Am" Poem Look back over your chart, and choose one person to write about. You might choose an actual person, such as Omar Khayyám, or an imaginary person, such as a Janissary or a Muslim merchant. Read over the text carefully to find details about the person, and then fill in information with your imagination. Your poem should be six lines long. The lines should begin, "I am," "I believe," "I see," "I feel," "I want," and "I am."

Standards Assessment

DIRECTIONS: Read each question, and write the letter of the best response.

1

> Akbar himself is dressed in . . . a closely-rolled turban hiding his hair . . . . Four times in twenty-four hours Akbar prays to God. . . . He eats but one meal a day . . . . and but little meat, less and less as he grows older. "Why should we make ourselves a sepulchre [burial tomb] for beasts?" is one of his sayings. Rice and sweetmeats [candied items] are the chief of his diet, and fruit, of which he is extremely fond. . . . He will sit far into the night absorbed in discussions on religion: this is one of his clear delights.
>
> —a European's description of Akbar, Mughal emperor of India, 1556-1605

Based on this passage, Akbar

A was not interested in religion.

B loved to eat meat.

C almost never prayed.

D liked to discuss religion.

2 Two of the greatest early centers of Muslim culture and learning were Baghdad and

A Jerusalem.

B Córdoba.

C Tripoli.

D Paris.

3 Most Christians and Jews who were conquered by Arab armies in the AD 600s and 700s were

A allowed to practice their religions.

B sold to North African slave traders.

C moved to northern Europe.

D forced to dress like Muslims.

4 Which area of the world was *least* influenced by Muslim conquest and trade between the AD 600s and 1600s?

A North Africa

B Southwest Asia

C Northern Europe

D Indonesia

5 Which of the following people was not a Muslim scholar?

A Ibn Battutah

B Avicenna

C al-Idrisi

D Hypatia

6 Muslim scholars are credited with developing

A geometry.

B algebra.

C calculus.

D physics.

Connecting with Past Learnings

7 You have learned that Muslim architects were known for their use of the dome. Which culture that you studied in Grade 6 also used many domes?

A Chinese

B Egyptian

C Greek

D Roman

A Summary of a History Lesson

Assignment

Write a summary of one section in a chapter you read in this unit, "The Islamic World."

After you read something, do you have trouble recalling what it was about? Many people do. Writing a summary briefly restating the main ideas and details of something you have read can help you remember it.

1. Prewrite

Reading to Understand

The first thing you need to do is to read the section at least twice.

- **Read** it straight through the first time to see what it is about.
- **Reread** it as many times as necessary to be sure you understand the main topic of the whole section.

Identifying the Main Idea

Next, identify the main idea in each paragraph or for each heading in the chapter. Look back at the facts, examples, quotations, and other information in each of them. Ask yourself, *What is the main idea that they all support, or refer to?* State this idea in your own words.

Noting Details

Note the information that directly and best supports each main idea. Often, several details and examples are given to support a single idea. Choose only those that are most important and provide the strongest support.

2. Write

As you write your summary, refer to the framework below to help you keep on track.

TIP **How Long Is a Summary?**

Here are some guidelines you can use to plan how much to write in a summary. If you are summarizing

- only a few paragraphs, your summary should be about one third as long as the original.
- longer selections such as an article or textbook chapter, write one sentence for each paragraph or heading in the original.

ELA **Writing 7.2.5** Write summaries of reading materials.

A Writer's Framework

Introduction
- Give the section number and title.
- State the main topic of the section.
- Introduce the first main heading in the section and begin your summary by identifying the main idea and supporting information under it.

Body
- Give the main idea, along with its most significant supporting details, for each heading in the section.
- Use words and phrases that show connections between ideas.
- Use your own words as much as you can, and limit quotations in number and length.

Conclusion
- Restate the main idea of the section.
- Comment on maps, charts, other visual content, or other features that were especially important or useful.

3. Evaluate and Revise

Now you need to evaluate your summary to make sure that it is complete and accurate. The following questions can help you decide what to change.

Evaluation Questions for a Summary

- Does your introduction identify the number and title of the section and its main topic?
- Do you identify the main idea of the section?
- Do you include supporting details for each heading or paragraph in the section?
- Do you connect ideas and information by using words that show how they are related?

- Have you written the summary in your own words and limited the number and length of your quotations?
- Does your conclusion state the underlying meaning, or main idea, of the section?

TIP **Finding Main Ideas in a History Chapter** Boldfaced headings in textbooks usually tell what subject is discussed under those headings. The first and last sentences of paragraphs under headings can also be a quick guide to what is said about a subject.

4. Proofread and Publish

Proofreading

Be sure to enclose all quotations in quotation marks and to place other marks of punctuation correctly before or after closing quotation marks.

- **Commas** and **periods** go **inside** closing quotation marks.
- **Semicolons** and **dashes** go **outside** closing quotation marks.
- **Question marks** and **exclamation points** go **inside** closing quotation marks **when they are part of the quotation** and **outside when they are not**.

TIP **Using Special Historical Features** Don't forget to look at maps, charts, timelines, pictures, historical documents, and even study questions and assignments. They often contain important ideas and information.

Publishing

Team up with classmates who have written summaries on different sections of the same chapter you have. Review each other's summaries. Make sure the summaries include all the main ideas and most significant details in each section.

Collect all the summaries to create a chapter study guide for your team. If possible, make copies for everyone on the team. You may also want to make extra copies so that you can trade study guides with teams who worked on other chapters.

● Practice and Apply

Use the steps and strategies outlined in this workshop to write a summary of one section of a chapter in this unit.

West African Civilizations

What You Will Learn...

West Africa is a region rich in natural resources, and its people have long been traders. They traded a wide variety of goods, such as gold, ivory, salt, and food.

Rich resources and extensive trade brought fabulous wealth to West Africa. With this wealth, West African rulers created large trading empires and built magnificent cities.

In the next two chapters, you will learn about the early peoples of West Africa and the vibrant trading empires of Ghana, Mali, and Songhai.

Explore the Art

In this scene, a young traveler named Leo Africanus visits an official of the Songhai Empire in the West African city of Timbuktu. What does this scene show about the city of Timbuktu?

Early West African Societies

California Standards

History–Social Science
7.4 Students analyze the geographic, political, economic, religious, and social structures of the sub-Saharan civilizations of Ghana and Mali in Medieval Africa.

English–Language Arts
Writing 7.2.1b Develop complex major and minor characters and a definite setting.

Reading 7.2.0 Describe and connect essential ideas, arguments, and perspectives of text using knowledge of text structure, organization, and purpose.

FOCUS ON WRITING

Writing a Journal Entry Many people feel that recording their lives in journals helps them to understand their own experiences. Writing a journal entry from someone else's point of view can help you to understand what that person's life is like. In this chapter, you will read about the land and people of early West Africa. Then you will imagine a character and write a journal entry from his or her point of view.

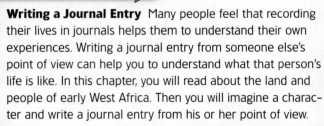

CHAPTER EVENTS

c. 3000 BC
West Africa's climate starts to get drier.

3000 BC

WORLD EVENTS

c. 3000 BC
Egyptians begin to write using hieroglyphics.

HOLT

History's Impact
▶ **video series**
Watch the video to under-
stand the impact of the salt
trade.

What You Will Learn...

In this chapter you will learn about the geography
and early cultures of West Africa. This photo shows
West African villagers performing a traditional dance.

c. 500 BC
The Nok culture
begins using iron and
makes clay sculptures.

c. AD 200
Camels are first
used in North
Africa, making
Saharan
trade easier.

600 BC	300 BC	BC 1 AD	AD 300

c. 480 BC
Greece defeats
Persia in the
Persian Wars.

44 BC
Julius Caesar is
assassinated in Rome.

AD 100s
Trade routes
link the Roman
Empire and
Mediterranean
with East Asia.

EARLY WEST AFRICAN SOCIETIES **109**

Reading Social Studies

by Kylene Beers

Focus on Themes In this chapter, you will read about West Africa—its physical **geography** and early cultures. You will see West Africa is a land of many resources and varied features. One feature, the Niger River, has been particularly important in the region's history, providing water, food, and transportation for people. In addition, salt and iron deposits can be found in the region. Such resources were the basis for a **technology** that allowed people to create strong tools and weapons.

Organization of Facts and Information

Focus on Reading How are books organized in the library? How are the groceries organized in the store? Clear organization helps us find the product we need, and it also helps us find facts and information.

Understanding Structural Patterns Writers use structural patterns to organize information in sentences or paragraphs. What's a structural pattern? It's simply a way of organizing information. Learning to recognize those patterns will make it easier for you to read and understand social studies texts.

Additional reading support can be found in the

Inter active
Reader and Study Guide

Patterns of Organization		
Pattern	**Clue Words**	**Graphic Organizer**
Cause-effect shows how one thing leads to another	as a result, because, therefore, this led to	Cause → Effect, Effect, Effect
Chronological Order shows the sequence of events or actions.	after, before, first, then, not long after, finally	First → Next → Next → Last
Listing presents information in categories such as size, location or importance.	also, most important, for example, in fact	Category • Fact • Fact • Fact

To use text structure to improve your understanding, follow these steps:

1. Look for the main idea of the passage you are reading.

2. Then look for clues that signal a specific pattern.

3. Look for other important ideas and think about how the ideas connect. Is there any obvious pattern?

4. Use a graphic organizer to map the relationships among the facts and details.

You Try It!

The following passages are from the chapter you are about to read. As you read each set of sentences, ask yourself what structural pattern the writer used to organize the information.

Recognizing Structural Patterns

A. "Living in present day Nigeria, the Nok made iron farm tools. One iron tool, the hoe, allowed farmers to clear the land more quickly and easily than they could do with earlier tools. As a result, they could grow more food." (p. 118)

B. "Thousands of years ago, West Africa had a damp climate. About 5,000 years ago the climate changed, though, and the area became drier. As more land became desert, people had to leave areas where they could no longer survive. People who had once lived freely began to live closer together. Over time they settled in villages." (p. 116)

C. "Four different regions make up the area surrounding the Niger River . . . The northern band across West Africa is the southern part of the Sahara . . . The next band is the semiarid Sahel (sah-HEL), a strip of land that divides the desert from wetter areas . . . Farther south is a band of savannah or open grassland . . . The fourth band gets heavy rain." (p. 114)

After you read the passages, answer the questions below:

1. What structural pattern did the writer use to organize the information in passage A? How can you tell?

2. What structural pattern did the writer use to organize the information in passage B? How can you tell?

3. What structural pattern did the writer use to organize the information in passage C? How can you tell?

Key Terms and People

Chapter 5

Section 1
rifts *(p. 112)*
sub-Saharan Africa *(p. 112)*
Sahel *(p. 114)*
savannah *(p. 114)*
rain forests *(p. 114)*

Section 2
extended family *(p. 116)*
animism *(p. 117)*

Academic Vocabulary

Success in school is related to knowing academic vocabulary—the words that are frequently used in school assignments and discussions. In this chapter, you will learn the following academic words:

impact *(p. 114)*
traditional *(p. 117)*

As you read Chapter 5, think about the organization of the ideas. Look for signal words and ask yourself why the author has arranged the text in the way he or she did.

Geography of Africa

What You Will Learn...

Main Ideas

1. The landforms, water, climate, and plant life affected history in West Africa.
2. West Africa's resources included farmland, gold, and salt.

The Big Idea

West Africa has varied environments and valuable resources.

Key Terms

rifts, *p. 112*
sub-Saharan Africa, *p. 112*
Sahel, *p. 114*
savannah, *p. 114*
rain forests, *p. 114*

HSS 7.4.1 Study the Niger River and the relationship of vegetation zones of forest, savannah, and desert to trade in gold, salt, food, and slaves; and the growth of the Ghana and Mali empires.

If YOU were there...

You live in a village near a great bend of the Niger River in Africa in about AD 800. The river is full of life—birds, fish, and crocodiles. You use its water to grow crops and raise cattle. Traders use the river to bring wood, gold, and other products from the forests.

Why is this a good place to live?

> **BUILDING BACKGROUND** The continent of Africa is so large that it includes many varied kinds of terrain, from barren deserts to thick rain forests. Each region has a different climate and provides different resources for the people who live there. In each area different cultures and ways of life developed.

Landforms, Water, Climate, and Plant Life

Africa is a big place. In fact, it is the second-largest continent on earth. Only Asia is bigger. This vast land is shaped roughly like a soup bowl. Forming the bowl's northwestern rim are the Atlas Mountains. The Drakensberg range forms the southeastern edge. In eastern Africa mountains extend alongside great rifts. These **rifts** are long, deep valleys formed by the movement of the earth's crust. From all these mountains the land dips into plateaus and wide, low plains.

The plains of **sub-Saharan Africa**, or Africa south of the Sahara, are crossed by mighty rivers. Among the main rivers are the Congo, the Zambezi, and the Niger. Along the Niger River in West Africa great civilizations arose. The role this river played in the development of civilizations is one example of the way the physical geography of West Africa affected history there.

West Africa's Great River

Look closely at the map on the next page and find the Niger River. As a source of water, food, and transportation, the river allowed many people to live in the area.

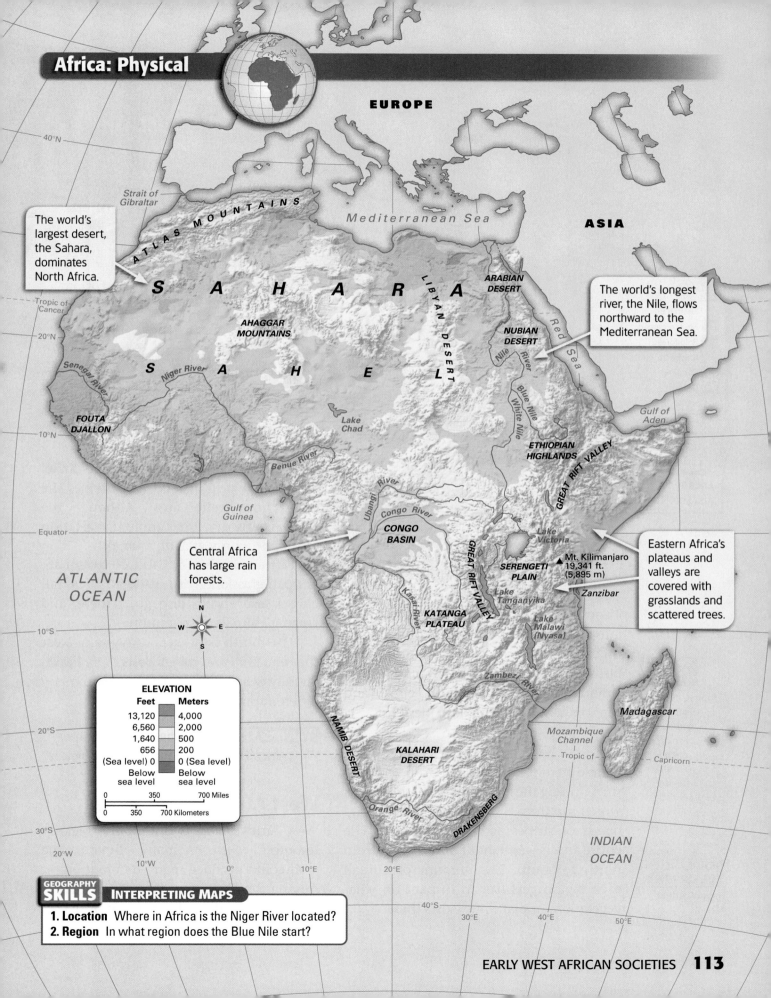

Africa: Physical

EUROPE

ASIA

Strait of Gibraltar

Mediterranean Sea

ATLAS MOUNTAINS

The world's largest desert, the Sahara, dominates North Africa.

S A H A R A

ARABIAN DESERT

LIBYAN DESERT

Red Sea

The world's longest river, the Nile, flows northward to the Mediterranean Sea.

AHAGGAR MOUNTAINS

NUBIAN DESERT

Nile

S A H E L

Senegal River

Niger River

FOUTA DJALLON

Lake Chad

Blue Nile

White Nile

Benue River

ETHIOPIAN HIGHLANDS

Gulf of Aden

Ubangi River

Congo River

Gulf of Guinea

CONGO BASIN

GREAT RIFT VALLEY

Central Africa has large rain forests.

ATLANTIC OCEAN

Lake Victoria

▲ Mt. Kilimanjaro 19,341 ft. (5,895 m)

SERENGETI PLAIN

Zanzibar

Eastern Africa's plateaus and valleys are covered with grasslands and scattered trees.

Kasai River

KATANGA PLATEAU

Lake Tanganyika

GREAT RIFT VALLEY

Lake Malawi (Nyasa)

Zambezi River

Madagascar

Mozambique Channel

NAMIB DESERT

KALAHARI DESERT

Tropic of Capricorn

ELEVATION

Feet		Meters
13,120		4,000
6,560		2,000
1,640		500
656		200
(Sea level) 0		0 (Sea level)
Below sea level		Below sea level

0   350   700 Miles
0   350   700 Kilometers

Orange River

DRAKENSBERG

INDIAN OCEAN

GEOGRAPHY **SKILLS** **INTERPRETING MAPS**

1. **Location** Where in Africa is the Niger River located?
2. **Region** In what region does the Blue Nile start?

EARLY WEST AFRICAN SOCIETIES **113**

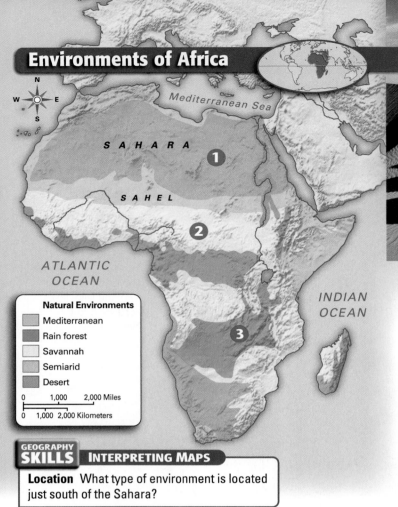

Environments of Africa

SAHARA ①

SAHEL ②

③

ATLANTIC OCEAN

Mediterranean Sea

INDIAN OCEAN

Natural Environments
- Mediterranean
- Rain forest
- Savannah
- Semiarid
- Desert

0   1,000   2,000 Miles

0   1,000 2,000 Kilometers

GEOGRAPHY SKILLS **INTERPRETING MAPS**

Location What type of environment is located just south of the Sahara?

① Desert The huge Sahara covers most of North Africa. Here, a traveler crosses a giant sea of sand.

The northern band across West Africa is the southern part of the Sahara. This huge expanse of sand and gravel is the world's largest desert. Temperatures can climb above 120°F. Rain is very rare.

The next band is the semiarid **Sahel** (sah-HEL), a strip of land that divides the desert from wetter areas. Although the Sahel is fairly dry, it has enough vegetation to support hardy grazing animals.

Farther south is a band of **savannah**, or open grassland with scattered trees. Tall grasses and shrubs also grow there, and grazing animals are common.

The fourth band gets heavy rain. Near the equator are **rain forests**, or moist, densely wooded areas. They contain many different plants and animals.

READING CHECK **Summarizing** What are West Africa's four climate and vegetation regions?

West Africa's Resources

West Africa's land is one of the region's resources. With its many climates, the land could produce many different crops. Among the traditional West African crops are dates raised in desert oases and kola

---

Along the Niger's middle section is a low-lying area of lakes and marshes. This watery region is called the inland delta. Though it looks much like the area where a river flows into the sea, it is hundreds of miles from the coast. Many animals and birds find food and shelter in the area. Among them are crocodiles, geese, and hippopotamus. Fish are also plentiful.

THE IMPACT TODAY

Human activities like logging and farming are rapidly destroying Africa's rain forest.

ACADEMIC VOCABULARY

impact effect, result

West Africa's Climates and Plants

Four different regions make up the area surrounding the Niger River. These regions, which run from east to west, are like broad bands or stripes across West Africa. The entire area is warm, but rainfall varies from north to south. The amount of rainfall each region gets has an **impact** on what vegetation, or plant life, exists there.

2 **Savannah** Much of Africa is covered by grasslands called savannah. Scattered across the savannah are clumps of trees like these acacia trees.

3 **Rain Forest** Thick rain forests like this one are found in central and western Africa. The rain forests' tall trees provide homes for many different animals.

nuts, used for medicines, from the forests' trees. Along the Niger, farmers could use the water to grow many food crops.

Other resources were minerals. People who live mainly on plant foods, like many early Africans, must add salt to their diets. The Sahara was a source of this precious mineral. When ancient lakes there dried up, they left salt behind. Workers mined the salt by digging deep into the earth.

Gold was another mineral resource of West Africa. Although gold is soft and therefore useless for tools or weapons, it makes beautiful jewelry and coins. Gold came from the southern forests. Miners kept the exact locations of the gold mines a secret. To this day, no one knows exactly where the mines were located, but gold became a valuable trade good.

READING CHECK **Finding Main Ideas** What are some of West Africa's major resources?

SUMMARY AND PREVIEW You have read about the physical geography of Africa. Next you will learn how physical features had an impact on culture and trade in early West Africa.

go.hrw.com
Online Quiz
KEYWORD: SQ7 HP5

Section 1 Assessment

Reviewing Ideas, Terms, and People **HSS** 7.4.1

1. **a. Define** What is a **savannah**?
   b. Contrast How might living in the **Sahel** be different from living in a **rain forest**?
   c. Evaluate In which African climate region would you most like to live? Why?
2. **a. Identify** What were two of early West Africa's important mineral resources?
   b. Explain How were these resources related to West Africa's physical geography?
   c. Elaborate Why do you think miners kept the location of the gold mines a secret?

Critical Thinking

3. **Summarizing** Create a chart like the one below. Use it to describe the characteristics of West Africa's four climate regions.

Climate region	Characteristics

FOCUS ON WRITING

4. **Taking Notes on West Africa's Geography** Review this section and take notes on the geography of West Africa. Remember that part of this land is your character's daily environment. What does he or she see every day? What challenges does the environment present?

Early Culture and Trade

What You Will Learn...

Main Ideas

1. Family and religion influenced daily life in early West African society.
2. Iron technology changed life in West Africa.
3. Trade shaped the history of West Africa.

The Big Idea

Family ties, religion, iron technology, and trade all contributed to the growth of West African societies.

Key Terms

extended family, *p. 116*
animism, *p. 117*

HSS 7.4.2 Analyze the importance of family, labor specialization, and regional commerce in the development of states and cities in West Africa.

If YOU were there...

You and your family are farmers in West Africa in about 400 BC. Farming is hard work. You use a sharp, wooden stick to dig the soil and put seeds in the ground. One day a trader brings farm tools made of a dark metal you've never seen before. These fine tools are so strong you can't break them! They have clean, sharp edges.

How will these new tools change your life?

BUILDING BACKGROUND The different climate regions of West Africa provided people with a variety of rich resources. Rivers provided water to grow crops in drier areas. The land was also a rich source of minerals, especially gold and iron. These two resources played a large role in the development of African cultures.

Families, Religion, and Daily Life

Thousands of years ago, West Africa had a damp climate. About 5,000 years ago the climate changed, though, and the area became drier. As more land became desert, people had to leave areas where they could no longer survive. People who had once roamed freely began to live closer together. Over time they settled in villages. At the heart of village life was the family.

Families, Villages, and Loyalties

A typical West African family was an extended family. Usually the **extended family** included the father, mother, children, and close relatives in one household. West African society expected each person to be loyal to his or her extended family.

In some areas people took part in another type of group. In these groups—called age-sets—men who had been born within the same two or three years formed special bonds. Men in the same age-set had a duty to help each other. Women, too, sometimes formed age-sets.

Village Life
Families were an important part of West African village society. Here a family gathers in a Nigerian village.

Village Society

Families
Families were the basic group of village society.

Extended Families
Extended families included grandparents, aunts, uncles, cousins, and their families.

Village Chiefs
Extended families often had a male leader who served as a village chief.

Council of Elders
Sometimes, village chiefs formed a council of elders that led the village.

Loyalty to family and age-sets helped the people of a village work together. Everyone had specific duties. The men hunted and farmed. Among the crops that men tended were millet and sorghum. These hardy grains grew well in the savannah in spite of the poor soil there. After being harvested, the grain could be made into a thick paste or ground into flour to make bread. Cattle could eat the grain. Farmers also raised goats and sheep.

Like the men, West African women worked very hard. They farmed, collected firewood, ground grain, and carried water. Women also cared for children.

Even the very young and the very old had their own tasks. For example, the elders, or old people, taught the family's traditions to younger generations. Through songs, dances, and stories, elders passed on the community's history and values. Among the values that children learned was the need for hard work. Children began working beside older family members as soon as they were able.

Religion and Culture

Another central feature of village life was religion. Some religious practices were similar from village to village. A **traditional** belief showed the importance of families. Many West Africans believed that the unseen spirits of their ancestors stayed nearby. To honor these spirits, families marked places as sacred spaces by putting specially carved statues there. Family members gathered in these places to share news and problems with the ancestors. Families also offered food to the ancestors' spirits. Through these practices they hoped to keep the spirits happy. In return, they believed, these spirits would protect the village from harm.

Another common West African belief had to do with nature. We call it **animism**— the belief that bodies of water, animals, trees, and other natural objects have spirits. Animism reflected West Africans' dependence on the natural world for survival.

ACADEMIC VOCABULARY
traditional customary, time-honored

READING CHECK **Generalizing** What role did families play in traditional West African culture?

Technology and Change

As time passed, the people of West Africa developed advanced and diverse cultures. Changes in technology helped some early communities grow.

Sometime around 500 BC West Africans made a discovery that would change their region forever. They found that they could heat certain kinds of rock to get a hard metal. This metal was iron. By heating the iron again, they could shape it into useful things. Stronger than other metals, iron was good for making tools.

One of the earliest peoples to use this new technology was the Nok. Living in present-day Nigeria, the Nok made iron farm tools. One iron tool, the hoe, allowed farmers to clear the land more quickly and easily than they could with earlier tools.

As a result, they could grow more food. The Nok also used iron tips for arrows and spears. Iron weapons provided a better defense against invaders and helped in hunting. As better-equipped farmers, hunters, and warriors, the Nok gained power. They also became known for fine sculptures of animals and human heads they made from clay.

Iron tools also provided another benefit. They helped West Africans live in places where they couldn't live before. Iron blades allowed people to cut down trees to clear land for farms. Because they had more places to live and more farms for growing food, the population of West Africa grew.

READING CHECK **Finding Main Ideas** How did technology change life in West Africa?

FOCUS ON READING
What structural pattern is used to organize information in the second column on this page?

Trade in West Africa
For centuries, West Africans have traded goods in markets like this one. At these regional markets, people could get local goods like food and clothing, as well as more valuable goods from far away.

What goods can you see in this photo?

Trade and West Africa

As the people of West Africa grew more food, communities had more than they needed to survive. West Africans began to trade the area's resources with buyers who lived thousands of miles away.

Desert Trade

For a long time, West Africans had ventured into the desert for trade. However, those early travelers could only make short trips from oasis to oasis. Their horses couldn't go far without water.

In the AD 200s, the situation changed. At about that time, Romans started to use camels to carry goods throughout northern Africa. These long-legged animals could store water and energy in their bodies for long periods of time. They could also carry heavy loads.

With camels people could cross the Sahara in two months. Traders formed caravans to make the trip. A North African people called the Berbers used their knowledge of the desert to lead the caravans. Even with camels and the Berbers' skills, crossing the Sahara was dangerous. Supplies could run out, thieves could attack, and caravans could lose their way.

Trade in Gold and Salt

Despite these dangers, West Africa's gold and salt mines became a source of great wealth. Camels carried salt from the mines of the Sahara to the south to trade for gold. Traders then took the gold north, to Europe and the Islamic world. Along with gold and salt, traders carried cloth, copper, silver, and other items. They also bought and sold human beings as slaves.

Some of the places where people gathered to trade grew into towns. Timbuktu (tim-buk-TOO), for example, began as a camp for traders in about 1100. Within two centuries, it would become a bustling city and a center of culture and learning. It would lie at the center of great empires that rose to power through the riches of the trans-Sahara trade.

READING CHECK Generalizing What trade goods were a source of West Africa's wealth?

SUMMARY AND PREVIEW Families and religion were central to early West African cultures. When West Africans developed iron technology, communities grew. Trade in gold and salt expanded into a wider area. In the next chapter, you will read about the West African empires based on this trade.

Section 2 Assessment

go.hrw.com
Online Quiz
KEYWORD: SQ7 HP5

Reviewing Ideas, Terms, and People HSS 7.4.2

1. **a. Identify** What are two groups to which a person in early West Africa may have owed loyalty?
   b. Analyze How did **animism** reflect what was important to early West African peoples?
2. **a. Describe** How did the use of iron change farming?
   b. Make Inferences What evidence do you think historians have for how the Nok people lived?
3. **a. Identify** What animal made trade across the Sahara easier?
   b. Summarize In what directions did the main trade items of West Africa move?

Critical Thinking

4. **Identifying Cause and Effect** Draw a diagram like the one below. Use it to identify two reasons towns grew.

```
┌──────────┐
│  Cause   │──────┐
└──────────┘      │   ┌─────────────────────────┐
                  ├──▶│ Effect: growth of towns │
┌──────────┐      │   └─────────────────────────┘
│  Cause   │──────┘
└──────────┘
```

FOCUS ON WRITING

5. **Taking Notes on West Africa's Early Culture** Review this section and take notes on the early West Africans' way of life. This section covers more than one time period and location, so be sure to note when and where particular activities took place.

Crossing the Sahara

Crossing the Sahara has never been easy. Bigger than the entire continent of Australia, the Sahara is one of the hottest, driest, and most barren places on earth. Yet for centuries, people have crossed the Sahara's gravel-covered plains and vast seas of sand. Long ago, West Africans crossed the desert regularly to carry on a rich trade.

Salt, used to preserve and flavor food, was available in the Sahara. Traders from the north took salt south. Camel caravans carried huge slabs of salt weighing hundreds of pounds.

Tindouf

Akjoujt

Taghaza

Walata

Koumbi Saleh

Timbuktu

Es-Souk

Gao

Taked

AFRICA

In exchange for salt, people in West Africa offered other valuable trade goods, especially gold. Gold dust was measured with special spoons and stored in boxes. Ivory, from the tusks of elephants, was carved into jewelry.

Gulf of Guinea

ATLANTIC OCEAN

E U R O P E

Some goods that were traded across the Sahara, like silk and spices, came all the way from Asia along the Silk Road. These luxury items were traded for West African goods like gold and ivory.

MEDITERRANEAN SEA

● Ghadames

Ghat ●

Zawilah ●

S A H A R A

● Bilma

Daima ●

A Difficult Journey

Temperature Temperatures soared to well over 100°F during the day and below freezing at night. Dying of heat or cold was a real danger.

Water Most areas of the Sahara get less than one inch of rain per year. Travelers had to bring lots of water or they could die of thirst.

Distance The Sahara is huge, and the trade routes were not well marked. Travelers could easily get lost.

Bandits Valuable trade goods were a tempting target for bandits. For protection, merchants traveled in caravans.

RED SEA

──── Trade route

● Settlement

Scale varies on this map.

GEOGRAPHY SKILLS **INTERPRETING MAPS**

1. **Movement** What were some goods traded across the Sahara?
2. **Human-Environment Interaction** Why was salt a valued trade good?

Social Studies Skills

Analysis	Critical Thinking	Participation	Study

Making Group Decisions

Understand the Skill

Making decisions as a group is a complicated and difficult skill to learn. However, it is an important skill at all levels of society—from governing a nation to choosing a movie to see with friends. At every level, success is based on the ability of group members to work together in effective and cooperative ways.

Learn the Skill

In Chapter 5 you learned about the cultures of the early peoples of West Africa. In some of these cultures, group decision making was central to the government. For example, the Yoruba of present-day Nigeria, Benin, and Togo lived in independent towns in which all decisions were made by a town council. The council met daily, and each of the town's families had one member on it.

This system of government worked well, largely because it forced council members to overcome their differences, compromise on goals and actions, and accept group decisions they might not have agreed with personally. Like the members of those Yoruba town councils, being part of an effective group requires certain behaviors.

❶ Be an active member. Take part in setting the group's goals and in making its decisions.

❷ Take a position. State your views and work to persuade other members to accept them. However, also be open to negotiating and compromising to settle differences within the group.

❸ Be willing to take charge if leadership is needed. But also be willing to follow the leadership of other members.

Practice and Apply the Skill

Imagine you are a part of a Yoruba town council. An invader is threatening the area. You are representing your town at a meeting of representatives of nearby towns—your classmates. Together, you must decide what to do about the threat. Remember that your town is very independent. If you agree to something that upsets the people, they may not support it. When your group has finished, answer the following questions.

1. Did your group create a plan for completing its task? Did it discuss what to do about the problem? What did you contribute toward the plan?

2. How well did your group work together? What role did you play in that?

3. Was your group able to make a decision? If not, why? If so, was compromise involved? Do you support the decision? Explain why or why not.

Standards Review

Visual Summary

Use the visual summary below to help you review the main ideas of the chapter.

QUICK FACTS

Africa's geography influenced people's way of life.

The family was the basic unit of society in West Africa.

Reviewing Vocabulary, Terms, and People

Choose the letter of the answer that best completes each statement below.

1. An area near the equator that has many trees and heavy rainfall may be called a
- **a.** tropical area.
- **b.** rain forest.
- **c.** savannah.
- **d.** woodland.

2. The belief that natural objects have spirits is called
- **a.** animism.
- **b.** vegetism.
- **c.** animalism.
- **d.** naturalism.

3. The entire region south of a large North African desert is called
- **a.** Drakensberg.
- **b.** extended Africa.
- **c.** sub-Saharan Africa.
- **d.** the sub-savannah.

4. Between the Sahara and the savannah lies the
- **a.** rain forest.
- **b.** inland delta.
- **c.** Zambezi.
- **d.** Sahel.

5. Long, deep valleys formed by the movement of the earth's crust are called
- **a.** chasms.
- **b.** rifts.
- **c.** volcanoes.
- **d.** earthquake zones.

6. A grassland with few trees where grazing animals may live is a
- **a.** savannah.
- **b.** Sahara.
- **c.** desert.
- **d.** meadow.

7. If aunts, uncles, parents, grandparents, children, and cousins live together in the same household, these people are members of
- **a.** a group household.
- **b.** a kinship home.
- **c.** an age-set.
- **d.** an extended family.

8. If a group of people has followed a certain custom for a long time, we may say that the custom is
- **a.** timely.
- **b.** in an age-set.
- **c.** traditional.
- **d.** based on animism.

Comprehension and Critical Thinking

SECTION 1 *(Pages 112–115)* **HSS** 7.4.1

9. a. Identify Along what river did great civilizations develop in early West Africa?

b. Analyze How does Africa's climate affect vegetation?

c. Elaborate Today salt is not nearly as valuable as gold. Why do you think salt was so important in West Africa?

SECTION 2 *(Pages 116–119)* **HSS** 7.4.2

10. a. Describe What effect did the growth of trade have on some West African towns?

b. Analyze What hard metal changed daily life in West Africa? How did this metal change farming? How did it change hunting?

c. Evaluate Which role in the extended family do you think was the most important? Explain your answer.

Reviewing Themes

11. Geography What are the four main geographic regions of West Africa? In which regions were West Africa's two main resources found?

12. Technology How did the development of iron technology affect life in West Africa?

Reading Skills

Understanding Structural Patterns of Text
Read the passage below and use it to answer the questions that follow.

> "Because people who live mainly on plant foods must add salt to their diets, salt was a valuable mineral in West Africa. The Sahara was a source of salt. Therefore, traders crossed the Sahara to get salt. Another mineral resource was gold. Gold is beautiful but soft. As a result, people used it to make jewelry and coins but not tools or weapons."

13. What structural pattern did the writer use to organize the information in the passage?

14. What signal words helped you determine the structural pattern of the information?

go.hrw.com
KEYWORD: SQ7 WH5

Using the Internet

15. Activity: Writing Newspaper Articles Your group of reporters is assigned to write about West Africa. Enter the activity keyword. Then research the land, people, languages, and cultures of West Africa. Write two newspaper articles to present your research.

Social Studies Skills

16. Solving Problems Imagine you are a member of an extended family of West Africa. Consider the tasks and responsibilities of each family member, and then decide what role you will play—mother, father, elder, teenager, or young child. Then imagine a challenge that your family must face, such as a dangerous wild animal, crop failure, or loss of hunting grounds. With a partner, discuss how your family will face the problem by using decision-making and planning skills. Then, on your own, write 4–5 sentences explaining the problem and how you and your partner decided to deal with it. You may want to use a chart like the one below to help you organize your thoughts.

Problem	Possible Action	Result

 FOCUS ON WRITING

17. Writing Your Journal Entry Review your notes and choose an imaginary character. You might choose, for example, a Berber caravan leader, someone who trades goods with a nearby village, or a woman or man of the Nok culture. Then match that person with a place. Finally, write 5–6 sentences as your journal entry. Include details on what the character sees, feels, and does on a typical day.

Standards Assessment

DIRECTIONS: Read each question, and write the letter of the best response.

1 Use the map to answer the following question.

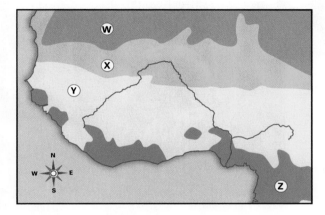

Which letter on the map indicates the Sahara?

A W

B X

C Y

D Z

2 The region of open grasslands where most grazing of cattle and other livestock takes place is the

A rain forest.

B Sahara.

C savannah.

D Sahel.

3 Life in early West Africa was changed by all of the following events *except*

A the use of camels in trade.

B the discovery of how to make iron tools and weapons.

C the development of trade with people to the north.

D the damming of rivers to control flooding and allow farming.

4 How were social groups defined in traditional West African cultures?

A by family and age-set

B by religion and family

C by age-set, family, and religion

D by extended family only

5 West Africans supplied all of the following trade goods to Europe and the Islamic world *except*

A salt.

B gold.

C marble.

D copper.

Connecting with Past Learnings

6 In Grade 6 you learned about early civilizations that developed along the Tigris and Euphrates rivers and along the Huang He in ancient China. Such developments can be compared to changes along which river in West Africa?

A the Congo

B the Niger

C the Nile

D the Sahel

7 Which East African civilization that you learned about in Grade 6 was similar to the Nok in their discovery and use of iron to make tools?

A the Kushite civilization

B the Mesolithic civilization

C the Paleolithic civilization

D the Sumerian civilization

West African Empires

California Standards

History–Social Science

7.4 Students analyze the geographic, political, economic, religious, and social structures of the sub-Saharan civilizations of Ghana and Mali in Medieval Africa.

Analysis Skills

CS 3 Use a variety of maps to explain the expansion and disintegration of empires.

HR 2 Distinguish fact from opinion.

English–Language Arts

Speaking 7.2.1 Deliver narrative presentations.

Reading 7.2.0 Students read and understand grade-level-appropriate material.

FOCUS ON SPEAKING

A Praise Song For centuries, the history of West Africa's peoples and rulers has been kept alive by griots, performers who memorize the histories of their people. At the end of this chapter, you will pretend to be a griot and perform your own song of praise about one of the empires or leaders.

CHAPTER EVENTS

1060s
The Empire of Ghana reaches its height.

1000

WORLD EVENTS

1066
William the Conqueror invades England.

HOLT

History's Impact
▶ video series
Watch the video to understand
the impact of the salt trade.

What You Will Learn...

In this chapter you will learn about the great
empires of West Africa, which grew rich from
trade. This photo shows women in front of a
mosque in the city of Djenné, in the modern
country of Mali.

c. 1235
The empire of
Mali is
established.

1324
Mansa Musa
leaves Mali
on a hajj to
Mecca.

1464
Sunni Ali
conquers
Timbuktu.

1590s
Moroccan
invaders
begin their
conquest of
Songhai.

1200

1400

1600

1281 The
Mongols'
attempt to
conquer
Japan fails.

1337
The Hundred
Years' War
begins in
France.

1521
Spanish
explorers
conquer
the Aztec
Empire.

WEST AFRICAN EMPIRES **127**

Reading Social Studies

by Kylene Beers

Economics	Geography	Politics	Religion	Society and Culture	Science and Technology

Focus on Themes This chapter describes three powerful empires that ruled West Africa between the years 300 and 1600—Ghana, Mali, and Songhai. As you read about each empire, you will learn who its greatest leaders were and how these leaders encouraged the development of their civilizations, civilizations honored for centuries through songs and stories. You will also learn how the **geography** of West Africa affected trade, the basis for the region's **economy**.

Facts and Opinions about the Past

Focus on Reading Every statement you read can be classified as either a fact or an opinion. When you read history, it is important to focus on the facts. Why? By studying facts you can learn what really happened in the past.

Identifying Facts and Opinions A statement is a **fact** if it can be proved or disproved. For example, research can prove the following statement: "Mali was an empire in West Africa." But research can't prove the following statement because it is just an **opinion,** or someone's belief: "Emperor Mansa Musa of Mali was one of the wisest leaders in African history."

Use the process below to decide whether a statement is fact or opinion.

Additional reading support can be found in the

Inter active

Reader and Study Guide

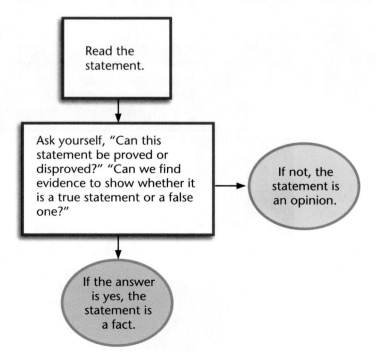

Read the statement.

Ask yourself, "Can this statement be proved or disproved?" "Can we find evidence to show whether it is a true statement or a false one?"

If not, the statement is an opinion.

If the answer is yes, the statement is a fact.

HSS Analysis HR 2 Distinguish fact from opinion.
ELA Reading 7.2.0 Read and understand grade-level-appropriate material.

You Try It!

The following passage tells about how the rulers of Ghana, an empire in West Africa, made money. All the statements in this passage are facts. What makes them facts and not opinions?

Taxes and Gold

With so many traders passing through their lands, Ghana's rulers looked for ways to make money from them. One way they raised money was by forcing traders to pay taxes. Every trader who entered Ghana had to pay a special tax on the goods he carried. Then he had to pay another tax on any goods he took with him when he left.

From Chapter 6, p. 133

Traders were not the only people who had to pay taxes. The people of Ghana also had to pay taxes. In addition, Ghana conquered many small neighboring tribes, then forced them to pay tribute. Rulers used the money from taxes and trade to support Ghana's growing army.

Not all of Ghana's wealth came from taxes and tribute. Ghana's rich mines produced huge amounts of gold. Some of this gold was carried by traders to lands as far away as England, but not all of Ghana's gold was traded. Ghana's kings kept huge stores of gold for themselves.

Identify each of the following as a fact or an opinion and then explain your choice.

1. Ghana's rulers made money by taxing the traders who came to Ghana.

2. This taxation was unfair to traders.

3. The rulers of Ghana were too greedy.

4. None of the people who lived in nearby tribes thought they should have to pay taxes.

5. People shouldn't have to pay taxes to leave a country.

Academic Vocabulary

Success in school is related to knowing academic vocabulary—the words that are frequently used in school assignments and discussions. In this chapter, you will learn the following academic words:

process *(p. 132)*
various *(p. 145)*

As you read Chapter 6, you will learn about several important leaders. As you read facts about these leaders, think of how the facts could be used to support opinions.

Empire of Ghana

If YOU were there...

You are a trader, traveling in a caravan from the north into West Africa in about 1000. The caravan carries many goods, but the most precious is salt. Salt is so valuable that people trade gold for it! You have never met the mysterious men who trade you the gold. You wish you could talk to them to find out where they get it.

Why do you think the traders are so secretive?

BUILDING BACKGROUND The various regions of Africa provide people with different resources. West Africa, for example, was rich in both fertile soils and minerals, especially gold and iron. Other regions had plentiful supplies of other resources, such as salt. Over time, trade developed between regions with different resources. This trade led to the growth of the first great empire in West Africa.

Ghana Controls Trade

For hundreds of years, trade routes crisscrossed West Africa. For most of that time, West Africans did not profit much from the Saharan trade because the routes were run by Berbers from northern Africa. Eventually, that situation changed. Ghana (GAH-nuh), an empire in West Africa, gained control of the valuable routes. As a result, Ghana became a powerful state.

As you can see on the map on the following page, the empire of Ghana lay between the Niger and Senegal rivers. This location was north and west of the location of the modern nation that bears the name Ghana.

Ghana's Beginnings

Archaeology provides some clues to Ghana's early history, but we do not know much about its earliest days. Historians think the first people in Ghana were farmers. Sometime after 300 these farmers, the Soninke (soh-NING-kee), were threatened by nomadic herders. The herders wanted to take the farmers' water and pastures. For protection, groups of Soninke families began to band together. This banding together was the beginning of Ghana.

What You Will Learn...

Main Ideas

1. Ghana controlled trade and became wealthy.
2. Through its control of trade, Ghana built an empire.
3. Ghana's decline was caused by attacking invaders, over-grazing, and the loss of trade.

The Big Idea

The rulers of Ghana built an empire by controlling the salt and gold trade.

Key Terms and People

silent barter, *p. 132*
Tunka Manin, *p. 134*

HSS 7.4.1 Study the Niger River and the relationship of vegetation zones of forest, savannah, and desert to trade in gold, salt, food, and slaves; and the growth of the Ghana and Mali empires.

7.4.2 Analyze the importance of family, labor specialization, and regional commerce in the development of states and cities in West Africa.

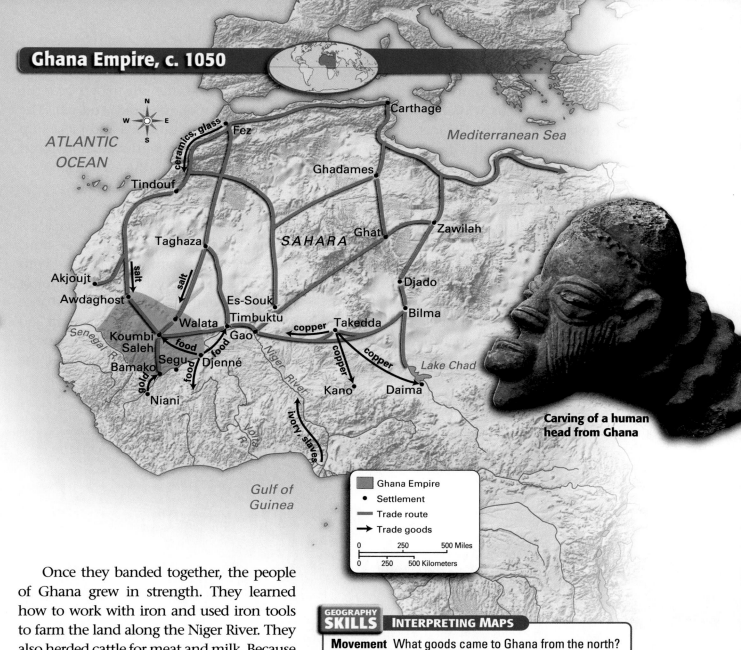

Ghana Empire, c. 1050

ATLANTIC OCEAN

Mediterranean Sea

Carthage

Fez

ceramics, glass

Ghadames

Tindouf

SAHARA

Taghaza

Ghat

Zawilah

salt

salt

Akjoujt

Djado

Awdaghost

Es-Souk

Bilma

Walata

Timbuktu

copper

Takedda

Koumbi Saleh

Gao

copper

Bamako

Segu

food

Djenné

copper

Lake Chad

Senegal R.

food

food

Niger River

gold

Niani

Kano

Daima

Volta R.

ivory, slaves

Gulf of Guinea

Carving of a human head from Ghana

Legend:
- Ghana Empire
- Settlement
- Trade route
- Trade goods

0   250   500 Miles
0   250   500 Kilometers

GEOGRAPHY SKILLS INTERPRETING MAPS

Movement What goods came to Ghana from the north?

Once they banded together, the people of Ghana grew in strength. They learned how to work with iron and used iron tools to farm the land along the Niger River. They also herded cattle for meat and milk. Because these farmers and herders could produce plenty of food, the population of Ghana increased. Towns and villages grew.

Besides farm tools, iron was also useful for making weapons. Other armies in the area had weapons made of bone, wood, and stone. These were no match for the iron spear points and blades used by Ghana's army.

Trade in Valuable Goods

Ghana lay between the vast Sahara Desert and deep forests. In this location, they were in a good position to trade in the region's most valuable resources—gold and salt. Gold came from the south, from mines near the Gulf of Guinea and along the Niger. Salt came from the Sahara in the north.

People wanted gold for its beauty. But they needed salt in their diets to survive. Salt, which could be used to preserve food, also made bland food tasty. These qualities made salt very valuable. In fact, Africans sometimes cut up slabs of salt and used the pieces as money.

The exchange of gold and salt sometimes followed a **process** called silent barter. **Silent barter** is a process in which people exchange goods without ever contacting each other directly. The method made sure that the traders did business peacefully. It also kept the exact location of the gold mines secret from the salt traders.

In the silent barter process, salt traders went to a riverbank near gold fields. There they left slabs of salt in rows and beat a drum to tell the gold miners that trading had begun. Then the salt traders moved back several miles from the riverbank.

Soon afterward, the gold miners arrived by boat. They left what they considered a fair amount of gold in exchange for the salt. Then the gold miners also moved back several miles so the salt traders could return. If they were happy with the amount of gold left there, the salt traders beat the drum again, took the gold, and left. The gold miners then returned and picked up their salt. Trading continued until both sides were happy with the exchange.

Growth of Trade

As the trade in gold and salt increased, Ghana's rulers gained power. Over time, their military strength grew as well. With their armies they began to take control of this trade from the merchants who had once controlled it. Merchants from the north and south met to exchange goods in Ghana. As a result of their control of trade routes, the rulers of Ghana became wealthy.

Salt and Gold

Additional sources of wealth and trade were developed to add to Ghana's wealth. Wheat came from the north. Sheep, cattle, and honey came from the south. Local products, including leather and cloth, were also traded for wealth. Among the prized special local products were tassels made from golden thread.

As trade increased, Ghana's capital grew as well. The largest city in West Africa, Koumbi Saleh (KOOM-bee SAHL-uh) was an oasis for travelers. These travelers could find all the region's goods for sale in its markets. As a result, Koumbi Saleh gained a reputation as a great trading center.

READING CHECK **Generalizing** How did trade help Ghana develop?

Ghana's rulers got rich by controlling the trade in salt and gold. Salt came from the north in large slabs like the ones shown at left. Gold, like the woman above is wearing, came from the south.

Ghana Builds an Empire

By 800 Ghana was firmly in control of West Africa's trade routes. Nearly all trade between northern and southern Africa passed through Ghana. Traders were protected by Ghana's army, which kept trade routes free from bandits. As a result, trade became safer. Knowing they would be protected, traders were not scared to travel to Ghana. Trade increased, and Ghana's influence grew as well.

Taxes and Gold

With so many traders passing through their lands, Ghana's rulers looked for ways to make money from them. One way they raised money was by forcing traders to pay taxes. Every trader who entered Ghana had to pay a special tax on the goods he carried. Then he had to pay another tax on any goods he took with him when he left.

Traders were not the only people who had to pay taxes. The people of Ghana also had to pay taxes. In addition, Ghana conquered many small neighboring tribes, then forced them to pay tribute. Rulers used the money from taxes and tribute to support Ghana's growing army.

Not all of Ghana's wealth came from taxes and tribute. Ghana's rich mines produced huge amounts of gold. Some of this gold was carried by traders to lands as far away as England, but not all of Ghana's gold was traded. Ghana's kings kept huge stores of gold for themselves. In fact, all the gold produced in Ghana was officially the property of the king.

Knowing that rare materials are worth far more than common ones, the rulers banned anyone else in Ghana from owning gold nuggets. Common people could own only gold dust, which they used as money. This ensured that the king was richer than his subjects.

Expansion of the Empire

Ghana's kings used their great wealth to build a powerful army. With this army the kings of Ghana conquered many of their neighbors. Many of these conquered areas were centers of trade. Taking over these areas made Ghana's kings even richer.

Ghana's kings didn't think that they could rule all the territory they conquered by themselves. Their empire was quite large, and travel and communication in West Africa could be difficult. To keep order in their empire, they allowed conquered kings to retain much of their power. These kings acted as governors of their territories, answering only to the king.

The empire of Ghana reached its peak under **Tunka Manin** (TOOHN-kah MAH-nin). This king had a splendid court where he displayed the vast wealth of the empire. A Spanish writer noted the court's splendor.

FOCUS ON READING
Does this quotation express a fact or the writer's opinion? How can you tell?

"The king adorns himself . . . round his neck and his forearms, and he puts on a high cap decorated with gold and wrapped in a turban of fine cotton. Behind the king stand ten pages holding shields and swords decorated with gold."

–al-Bakri, from *The Book of Routes and Kingdoms*

READING CHECK **Summarizing** How did the rulers of Ghana control trade?

BIOGRAPHY

Tunka Manin
Ruled around 1068

All we know about Tunka Manin comes from the writings of a Muslim geographer who wrote about Ghana. From his writings, we know that Tunka Manin was the nephew of the previous king, a man named Basi. Kingship and property in Ghana did not pass from father to son, but from uncle to nephew. Only the king's sister's son could inherit the throne. Once he did become king, Tunka Manin surrounded himself with finery and many luxuries.

Contrasting How was inheritance in Ghana different from inheritance in other societies you have studied?

Ghana's Decline

In the mid-1000s Ghana was rich and powerful, but by the end of the 1200s, the empire had collapsed. Three major factors contributed to its end.

Invasion

The first factor that helped bring about Ghana's end was invasion. A Muslim group called the Almoravids (al-moh-RAH-vidz) attacked Ghana in the 1060s in an effort to force its leaders to convert to Islam.

The people of Ghana fought hard against the Almoravid army. For 14 years they kept the invaders at bay. In the end, however, the Almoravids won. They destroyed the city of Koumbi Saleh.

The Almoravids didn't control Ghana for long, but they certainly weakened the empire. They cut off many trade routes through Ghana and formed new trading partnerships with Muslim leaders instead. Without this trade Ghana could no longer support its empire.

Overgrazing

A second factor in Ghana's decline was a result of the Almoravid conquest. When the Almoravids moved into Ghana, they brought herds of animals with them. These animals ate all the grass in many pastures, leaving the soil exposed to hot desert winds. These winds blew away the soil, leaving the land worthless for farming or herding. Unable to grow crops, many farmers had to leave in search of new homes.

Internal Rebellion

A third factor also helped bring about the decline of Ghana's empire. In about 1200 the people of a country that Ghana had conquered rose up in rebellion. Within a few years the rebels had taken over the entire empire of Ghana.

Overgrazing

Too many animals grazing in one area can lead to problems, such as the loss of farmland that occurred in West Africa.

❶ Animals are allowed to graze in areas with lots of grass.

❷ With too many animals grazing, however, the grass disappears, leaving the soil below exposed to the wind.

❸ The wind blows the soil away, turning what was once grassland into desert.

Once in control, however, the rebels found that they could not keep order in Ghana. Weakened, Ghana was attacked and defeated by one of its neighbors. The empire fell apart.

READING CHECK **Identifying Cause and Effect** Why did Ghana decline in the 1000s?

SUMMARY AND PREVIEW The empire of Ghana in West Africa grew rich and powerful through its control of trade routes. The empire lasted for centuries, but eventually Ghana fell. In the next section you will learn that it was replaced by a new empire, Mali.

Section 1 Assessment

go.hrw.com
Online Quiz
KEYWORD: SQ7 HP6

Reviewing Ideas, Terms, and People **HSS** 7.4.1, 7.4.2

1. a. **Identify** What were the two most valuable resources traded in Ghana?
   b. **Explain** How did the **silent barter** system work?
2. a. **Identify** Who was **Tunka Manin**?
   b. **Generalize** What did Ghana's kings do with the money they raised from taxes?
   c. **Elaborate** Why did the rulers of Ghana not want everyone to have gold?
3. a. **Identify** What group invaded Ghana in the late 1000s?
   b. **Summarize** How did overgrazing help cause the fall of Ghana?

Critical Thinking

4. **Identifying Cause and Effect** Draw a diagram like the one shown here. Use it to identify factors that helped Ghana's trade grow and those that led to its decline.

FOCUS ON SPEAKING

5. **Gathering Information** Look back through this section for information on Ghana and Tunka Manin. Is there anything in this section you might include in your song?

WEST AFRICAN EMPIRES **135**

Empire of Mali

If YOU were there...

You are a servant of the great Mansa Musa, ruler of Mali. You've been chosen as one of the servants who will travel with him on a pilgrimage to Mecca. The king has given you all fine new clothes of silk for the trip. He will carry much gold with him. You've never left your home before. But now you will see the great city of Cairo, Egypt, and many other new places.

How do you feel about going on this journey?

What You Will Learn...

Main Ideas
1. A ruler named Sundiata made Mali into an empire.
2. Mali reached its height under the ruler Mansa Musa.
3. Mali fell to invaders in the late 1400s.

The Big Idea
The wealthy and powerful Mali Empire ruled West Africa after the fall of Ghana.

Key People
Sundiata, *p. 136*
Mansa Musa, *p. 138*

HSS **7.4.3** Describe the role of the trans-Saharan caravan trade in the changing religious and cultural characteristics of West Africa and the influence of Islamic beliefs, ethics, and law.

7.4.4 Trace the growth of the Arabic language in government, trade, and Islamic scholarship in West Africa.

BUILDING BACKGROUND Mansa Musa was one of Africa's greatest rulers, and his empire, Mali, was one of the largest in the continent's history. Rising from the ruins of Ghana, Mali took over the trade routes of West Africa and grew into a powerful state.

Sundiata Makes Mali an Empire

Like Ghana, Mali (MAH-lee) lay along the upper Niger River. This area's fertile soil helped Mali grow. In addition, Mali's location on the Niger allowed its people to control trade on the river. Through this control of trade, the empire became rich and powerful. According to legend, Mali's rise to power began under a ruler named **Sundiata** (soohn-JAHT-ah).

Beginnings of the Empire

Since written records about Mali are scarce, the details of its rise to power are unclear. Many legends about this period exist, though. According to these legends, Sundiata, Mali's first strong leader, was both a mighty warrior and a magician. According to the legends, he had to overcome great hardships before he could build his empire.

Sundiata was the son of a previous king of Mali. When he was a boy, however, Mali was conquered by a powerful king who treated the people of Mali badly. Sundiata grew up hating him. When he reached adulthood, Sundiata built up a huge army and won his country's independence. Then he set about conquering many nearby kingdoms, including Ghana.

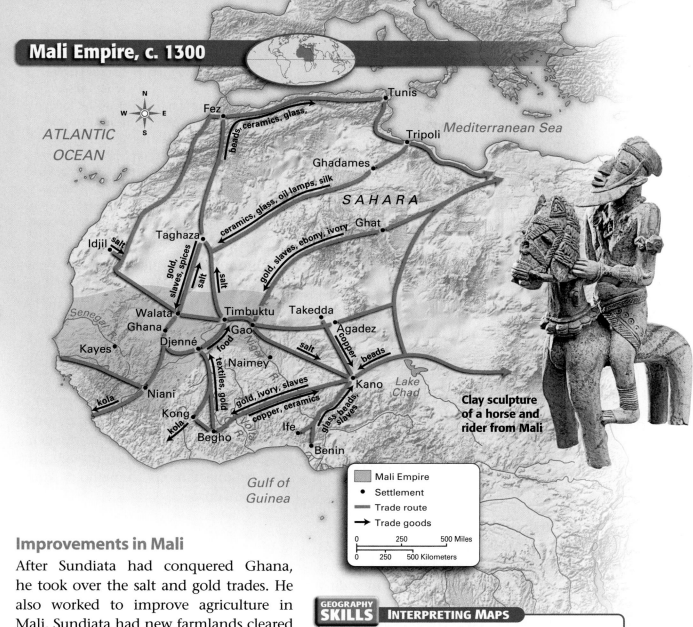

Mali Empire, c. 1300

ATLANTIC OCEAN

Mediterranean Sea

Tunis

Fez

beads, ceramics, glass,

Tripoli

Ghadames

SAHARA

ceramics, glass, oil lamps, silk

Ghat

Idjil — salt

Taghaza

gold, slaves, spices

salt

salt

gold, slaves, ebony, ivory

Senegal R.

Walata

Ghana

Timbuktu

Takedda

Gao

Agadez

copper

Djenné

food

Kayes

Naimey

salt

beads

textiles, gold

Kano

Lake Chad

Niani

gold, ivory, slaves

copper, ceramics

Volta R.

kola

Kong

kola

Begho

Ife

glass beads, slaves

Benin

Gulf of Guinea

Clay sculpture of a horse and rider from Mali

Legend
- Mali Empire
- • Settlement
- — Trade route
- → Trade goods

0   250   500 Miles
0   250   500 Kilometers

Improvements in Mali

After Sundiata had conquered Ghana, he took over the salt and gold trades. He also worked to improve agriculture in Mali. Sundiata had new farmlands cleared for beans, onions, rice, and other crops. He even introduced a new crop to Mali—cotton. People used cotton to make clothing that was comfortable in the warm climate. Realizing its value, they also sold cotton to other people.

To help feed the people of his new empire, legend says that Sundiata put some soldiers to work in the fields. Once Mali's enemies had been defeated, the soldiers didn't need to fight, so they worked alongside slaves on large farms. Using conquered people as slaves was a common practice in the kingdoms of West Africa.

GEOGRAPHY SKILLS **INTERPRETING MAPS**

Location On what river are Timbuktu and Gao located?

Consolidation of Power

Under Sundiata's guidance, Mali grew into a prosperous kingdom. To keep order and protect his authority, Sundiata took power away from local leaders. These local leaders had borne the title *mansa* (MAHN-sah), a title Sundiata now took for himself.

Mansas had both political and religious roles in society. By taking on the religious authority of the *mansas*, Sundiata gained even more power in Mali.

The religious role of the *mansa* grew out of traditional Malian beliefs. According to these beliefs, the people's ancestors had made an agreement with the spirits of the land. The spirits would make sure that the land provided plenty of food. By keeping in touch with their ancestors, the people could contact these spirits.

Sundiata died in 1255. His son, who was the next ruler of Mali, also took the title of *mansa*, as did the empire's later rulers. Unlike Sundiata, though, most of these later rulers were Muslims.

READING CHECK **Sequencing** What steps did Sundiata take to turn Mali into an empire?

Mansa Musa

Mali's most famous ruler was a Muslim king named **Mansa Musa** (MAHN-sah moo-SAH). Under his skillful leadership, Mali reached the height of its wealth, power, and fame in the 1300s. Because of Mansa Musa's influence, Islam spread through a large part of West Africa.

Mansa Musa ruled Mali for about 25 years. During that time, his army captured many important trade cities, including Timbuktu (tim-buhk-TOO), Gao (GOW), and Djenné (je-NAY). These cities became part of Mali's empire.

The World Learns about Mali

Religion was very important to Mansa Musa. In 1324, he left Mali on a pilgrimage to Mecca. Making such a journey, or hajj, is a spiritual duty of all Muslims.

Mansa Musa's first stop on his hajj was Cairo, Egypt. According to one account, he arrived in the city with nearly 100 camels, each loaded with 300 pounds of gold. Some 60,000 men traveled with him. About 10 years later, a historian spoke to an official who had met him:

THE IMPACT TODAY

Some of the mosques built by Mansa Musa can still be seen in West Africa today.

" He did me extreme honor and treated me with the greatest courtesy. He addressed me, however, only through an interpreter despite his perfect ability to speak in the Arabic tongue. Then he forwarded [sent] to the royal treasury many loads of unworked native gold and other valuables . . . He left no court emir nor holder of a royal office without the gift of a load of gold. The Cairenes [people of Cairo] made incalculable [uncountable] profits out of him. "
–Shihad ad-Din Ahmad Ibn Fadl Allah al-Umari, from *Sight-Seeing Journeys*

This historian says that Mansa Musa gave away so much gold in Egypt that gold was no longer rare there, even 10 years later! As a result, its value dropped steeply.

Through his journey, Mansa Musa introduced the empire of Mali to the world. Before he came to power, only a few people outside of West Africa had ever heard of Mali, even though it was one of the world's largest empires. Mansa Musa made such a great impression on people, though, that Mali became famous throughout Africa, Asia, and Europe.

Learning and Religion in Mali

Just as he supported his faith, Mansa Musa supported education. In his first years as ruler, he sent scholars to study in Morocco. These scholars later set up schools in Mali for studying the Qur'an. Timbuktu became famous for its schools.

Mansa Musa wanted Muslims to be able to read the Qur'an. Therefore, he stressed the importance of learning to read and write the Arabic language. Arabic became the main language not only for religious study but also for government and trade.

Mansa Musa wanted to spread Islam in West Africa. To encourage this spread, he hired architects from other Muslim countries to build mosques throughout his empire. Elaborate mosques were built in Timbuktu, Djenné, and other cities.

Timbuktu

Timbuktu became a major trading city at the height of Mali's power under Mansa Musa. Traders came to Timbuktu from the north and south to trade for salt, gold, metals, shells, and many other goods.

Mansa Musa and later rulers built several large mosques in the city, which became a center of Islamic learning.

Winter floods allowed boats to reach Timbuktu from the Niger River.

Timbuktu's walls and build-ings were mostly built with bricks made of dried mud. Heavy rains could soften the bricks and destroy buildings.

At crowded market stalls, people traded for goods like sugar, kola nuts, and glass beads.

Camel caravans from the north brought goods like salt, cloth, books, and slaves to trade at Timbuktu.

ANALYSIS SKILL **ANALYZING VISUALS**

How did traders from the north bring their goods to Timbuktu?

Mansa Musa hoped that people would accept Islam as he had, but he did not want to force people to convert. Still, during his reign Islam became very popular in Mali. Following their king's example, many people from Mali went to Mecca. In turn, many Muslims from Asia, Egypt, and other parts of Africa visited Mali. These journeys between regions helped create more trade and made Mali even richer.

READING CHECK Identifying Cause and Effect How did Mansa Musa spread Islam?

The Fall of Mali

Mali's success depended on strong leaders. Unfortunately, some of Mali's leaders were not strong. Their poor leadership weakened the empire.

When Mansa Musa died, his son Maghan (MAH-gan) took the throne. Unlike his father, however, Maghan was a weak ruler. When raiders poured into Mali, he couldn't stop them. The raiders set fire to Timbuktu's great schools and mosques. Mali never fully recovered from this terrible blow. Weakened, the empire gradually declined.

One reason the empire declined was its size. The empire had become so large that the government could no longer control it. Parts of the empire began to break away. For example, the city of Gao declared its independence in the 1400s.

Invaders also helped weaken the empire. In 1431 the Tuareg (TWAH-reg), nomads from the Sahara, attacked and seized Timbuktu. Soon afterward, the kingdom of Takrur (TAHK-roohr) in northern Mali declared its independence. Gradually, the people living at the edges of Mali's empire broke away. By 1500, nearly all of the lands the empire had once ruled were lost. Only a small area of Mali remained.

READING CHECK Evaluating How did Mali's growth eventually weaken the empire?

SUMMARY AND PREVIEW Through the leadership of people like Sundiata and Mansa Musa, Mali became a large empire. In time, it became famous for its wealth and its centers of learning. In the next section you will learn about the empire that took over much of Mali's wealth and its great cities. That empire was called Songhai.

Section 2 Assessment

go.hrw.com
Online Quiz
KEYWORD: SQ7 HP6

Reviewing Ideas, Terms, and People HSS 7.4.3, 7.4.4

1. a. **Identify** Who was **Sundiata**?
   b. **Sequence** How did Sundiata turn Mali into an empire?
2. a. **Identify** What became the main language of government, trade, and Islamic scholarship in West Africa?
   b. **Summarize** How did **Mansa Musa**'s journey change people's perceptions of Mali?
   c. **Elaborate** How did Islam help turn Mali into a center of learning?
3. a. **Identify** What group invaded Mali in 1431?
   b. **Explain** How did Mali's size lead to its fall?

Critical Thinking

4. **Finding Main Ideas** Draw two boxes. In them, list three major accomplishments of Sundiata and Mansa Musa.

Sundiata	Mansa Musa

FOCUS ON SPEAKING

5. **Taking Notes on Mali** Add to the notes you took earlier your thoughts on Sundiata and Mansa Musa. Compare the leaders of Mali with those of Ghana. Start thinking about which you will choose for your poem.

Mansa Musa

How could one man's travels become a major historic event?

When did he live? the late 1200s and early 1300s

Where did he live? Mali

What did he do? Mansa Musa, the ruler of Mali, was one of the Muslim kings of West Africa. He became a major figure in African and world history largely because of a pilgrimage he made to the city of Mecca.

Why is he important? Mansa Musa's spectacular journey attracted the attention of the Muslim world and of Europe. For the first time, other people's eyes turned to West Africa. During his travels, Mansa Musa gave out huge amounts of gold. His spending made people eager to find the source of such wealth. Within 200 years, European explorers would arrive on the shores of western Africa.

Identifying Points of View How do you think Mansa Musa changed people's views of West Africa?

THE GRANGER COLLECTION, NEW YORK

KEY FACTS

According to chroniclers of the time, Mansa Musa was accompanied on his journey to Mecca by some 60,000 people. Of those people,

- **12,000** were servants to attend to the king.
- **500** were servants to attend to his wife.
- **14,000** more were slaves wearing rich fabrics such as silk.
- **500** carried staffs heavily decorated with gold. Historians have estimated that the gold Mansa Musa gave away on his trip would be worth more than $100 million today.

This Spanish map from the 1300s shows Mansa Musa sitting on his throne.

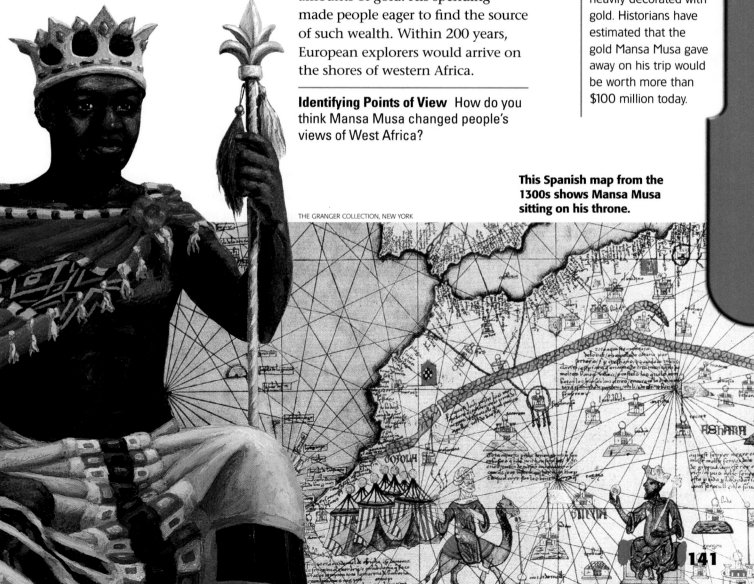

Empire of Songhai

What You Will Learn...

Main Ideas

1. The Songhai built a new empire in West Africa.
2. Askia the Great ruled Songhai as an Islamic empire.
3. Songhai fell to Moroccan invaders, ending the great era of West African empires.

The Big Idea

The Songhai Empire strengthened Islam in West Africa.

Key People

Sunni Ali, *p. 143*
Askia the Great, *p. 144*

HSS 7.4.3 Describe the role of the trans-Saharan caravan trade in the changing religious and cultural characteristics of West Africa and the influence of Islamic beliefs, ethics, and law.

If YOU were there...

You are a farmer in the Niger River Valley in about 1500. You're making your first visit to the great city of Timbuktu. You stare around you at the buildings with their tall towers. In the streets you hear people talking in many different languages. They must be students from other countries, come to study in the universities here. From the tower of a mosque, you hear the call to prayer.

How does the great city make you feel?

BUILDING BACKGROUND Timbuktu was the greatest city in Mali. But as the empire of Mali grew weaker and fell, the city did not. As a new empire arose in West Africa, its rulers recognized the greatness of Timbuktu. Just as it had been the major city of Mali's empire, so it was the greatest city in Mali's replacement—Songhai.

The Songhai Build an Empire

Even as the empire of Mali was reaching its height, a rival power was growing in the area. That rival was the Songhai (SAHNG-hy) kingdom. From their capital at Gao, the Songhai participated in the same trade that had made Ghana and Mali so rich.

By the 1300s the Songhai had become rich and powerful enough to draw the attention of Mali's rulers. Mansa Musa sent his army to conquer the Songhai and make their lands part of his empire. As you have already seen, Gao became one of the most important cities in all of Mali.

The Birth of the Empire

Songhai did not remain part of Mali's empire for long. As Mali's government grew weaker, the people of Songhai rose up against it and regained their freedom.

Even before they were conquered by Mali, the leaders of the Songhai had become Muslims. As such, they shared a common religion with many of the Berbers who crossed the Sahara to trade in West Africa. Because of this shared religion, the Berbers were willing to trade with the Songhai, who began to grow richer.

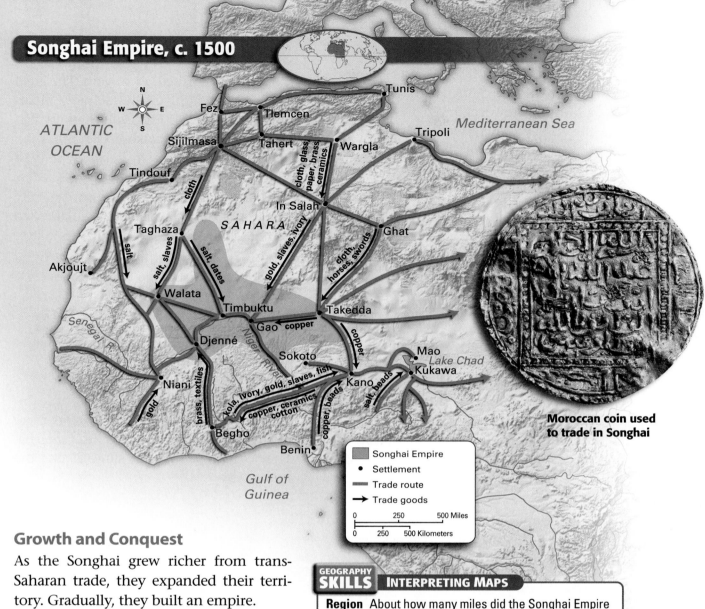

Songhai Empire, c. 1500

ATLANTIC OCEAN

Mediterranean Sea

Tunis
Fez
Tlemcen
Tripoli
Sijilmasa
Tahert
Wargla
Tindouf
cloth
In Salah
cloth, glass, paper, brass, ceramics
SAHARA
Ghat
Taghaza
salt
salt, slaves
gold, slaves, ivory
cloth, horses, swords
Akjoujt
salt, dates
Walata
Senegal R.
Timbuktu
Takedda
copper
Gao
copper
Djenné
Niger River
Sokoto
copper
Mao
Lake Chad
Kukawa
Niani
brass, textiles
gold
kola, ivory, gold, slaves, fish
copper, ceramics, cotton
Kano
copper, beads
salt, beads
Begho
Benin

Gulf of Guinea

Moroccan coin used to trade in Songhai

	Songhai Empire
•	Settlement
—	Trade route
→	Trade goods

0   250   500 Miles
0   250   500 Kilometers

GEOGRAPHY SKILLS INTERPRETING MAPS

Region About how many miles did the Songhai Empire stretch from west to east?

Growth and Conquest

As the Songhai grew richer from trans-Saharan trade, they expanded their territory. Gradually, they built an empire.

Songhai's growth was largely the work of one man, **Sunni Ali** (SOOH-nee ah-LEE), who became the ruler of Songhai in 1464. Before Ali took over, the Songhai state had been disorganized and poorly run. As ruler, he worked constantly to unify, strengthen, and enlarge it.

Much of the land that Sunni Ali added to his empire had been part of Mali. For example, he conquered the wealthy trade cities of Timbuktu and Djenné. In 1468 the rulers of Mali asked Sunni Ali to help fight off Tuareg invaders who were about to capture Timbuktu. Ali agreed, but once he had driven off the invaders he decided to keep the city for himself. From there he launched attacks against Djenné, which he finally captured five years later.

As king, Sunni Ali encouraged all people in his empire to work together. To build peace between religions, he participated in both Muslim and local religions. As a result, he brought peace and stability to Songhai.

READING CHECK **Finding Main Ideas** What did Sunni Ali achieve as ruler of the Songhai?

Askia the Great

Sunni Ali died in 1492. He was followed as king by his son, Sunni Baru, who was not a Muslim. However, most of the people of the empire's towns were. They were afraid that if Sunni Baru didn't support Islam they would lose power in the empire, and trade with other Muslim lands would suffer. As a result, they rebelled against Sunni Baru.

The leader of the people's rebellion was a general named Muhammad Ture (moo-HAH-muhd too-RAY). After overthrowing Sunni Baru, he took the title *askia*, a title of high military rank. Eventually, he became known as **Askia the Great**.

Religion and Education

Like Mansa Musa, the famous ruler of Mali, Askia the Great took his Muslim faith very seriously. After he defeated Sunni Baru, Askia made a pilgrimage to Mecca, just as Mansa Musa had 200 years earlier.

Also like Mansa Musa, Askia worked to support education. Under his rule the city of Timbuktu flourished once again. The great city contained universities, schools, libraries, and mosques. Especially famous was the University of Sankore (san-KOH-rah). People arrived there from all over West Africa to study mathematics, science, medicine, grammar, and law. In the early 1500s, a Muslim traveler and scholar called Leo Africanus wrote this about Timbuktu:

> "There are in Timbuktu numerous judges, teachers and priests, all properly appointed by the king. He greatly honors learning. Many hand-written books imported from Barbary [North Africa] are also sold. There is more profit made from this commerce [trade] than from all other merchandise."
>
> –Leo Africanus, from *History and Description of Africa*

Djenné also became a center of learning, especially for medicine. Doctors there discovered that mosquitoes spread malaria. They even performed surgery on the human eye.

The people of Songhai depended on the Niger River for many things. It was an important transportation route and provided fertile lands and a source of water for farming.

Trade and Government

Timbuktu and Djenné were centers of learning, but they were also trading centers. Merchants from distant lands came to these cities and to Gao.

Most of Songhai's traders were Muslim, and as they gained influence in the empire so did Islam. Askia the Great, himself a devout Muslim, encouraged the growth in Islamic influence. Many of the laws he made were similar to those of Muslim nations across the Sahara.

To help maintain order, Askia set up five provinces within Songhai. He removed local leaders and appointed new governors who were loyal to him. One such governor ran the empire for Askia when he was away on pilgrimage to Mecca. When he returned, Askia brought even more Muslim influence into his government.

Askia also created special departments to oversee certain tasks. These departments worked much like government offices do today. He created a standing professional army, the first in West Africa.

READING CHECK **Evaluating** What do you think was Askia's greatest accomplishment?

Songhai Falls to Morocco

After Askia the Great lost power to his son in 1528, other *askias* ruled Songhai. The empire did not survive for long, though. Areas along the empire's borders started to nibble away at Songhai's power.

The Moroccan Invasion

One of Songhai's northern neighbors, Morocco, wanted to control the Saharan salt mines. To get those mines, Moroccan troops invaded Songhai. With them they brought a terrible new weapon—the arquebus (AHR-kwih-buhs). The arquebus was an early form of a gun.

BIOGRAPHY

Askia the Great
c. 1443–1538

Askia the Great became the ruler of Songhai when he was nearly 50 years old. He ruled Songhai for about 35 years. During his reign the cities of Songhai gained power over the countryside.

When he was in his 80s, Askia went blind. His son Musa forced him to leave the throne. Askia was sent to live on an island. He lived there for nine years until another of his sons brought him back to the capital, where he died. His tomb is still one of the most honored places in all of West Africa.

Drawing Inferences Why do you think Askia the Great's tomb is still considered an honored place?

The Moroccans wanted control of the salt mines because they needed money. Not long before the fight over the mines, Morocco had defended itself against huge invading armies from Portugal and Spain. The Moroccans had eventually defeated the Europeans, but the defense had nearly ruined Morocco financially. Knowing of Songhai's wealth, the Moroccan ruler decided to attack Songhai for its rich deposits of salt and gold.

The Moroccan army set out for the heart of Songhai in 1591. Not all of the troops were Moroccan, though. About half were actually Spanish and Portuguese war prisoners. These prisoners had agreed to fight against Songhai rather than face more time in prison. Well trained and disciplined, these soldiers carried **various** weapons, including the deadly new guns. The Moroccans even dragged a few small cannons across the desert with them.

ACADEMIC VOCABULARY
various of many types

West African Empires

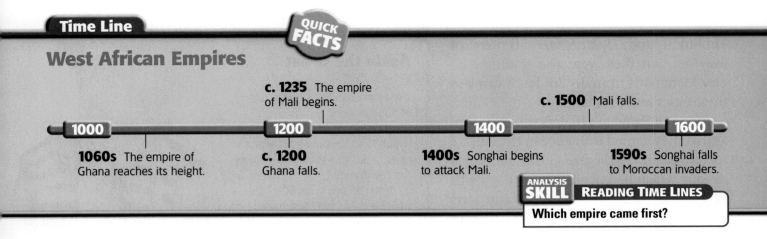

c. 1235 The empire of Mali begins.

c. 1500 Mali falls.

1000

1200

1400

1600

1060s The empire of Ghana reaches its height.

c. 1200 Ghana falls.

1400s Songhai begins to attack Mali.

1590s Songhai falls to Moroccan invaders.

ANALYSIS SKILL **READING TIME LINES**

Which empire came first?

The Destruction of Songhai

The Moroccans' guns and cannons brought disaster to Songhai. The swords, spears, and bows carried by Songhai's warriors were no match for firearms.

The Moroccans attacked Timbuktu and Gao, looting and taking over both cities. The Moroccans didn't push farther into Songhai, but the damage was done. Songhai never recovered from the loss of these cities and the income they produced.

Changes in trade patterns completed Songhai's fall. Overland trade declined as port cities north and south of the old empire became more important. For example, people who lived south of Songhai began to trade along the Atlantic coast. European traders preferred to sail to Atlantic ports than to deal with Muslim traders. Slowly, the period of great West African empires came to an end.

READING CHECK **Predicting** What do you think happened to the people of West Africa after the empire of Songhai was defeated?

SUMMARY AND PREVIEW The empire of Songhai was known for its wealth, culture, and learning. In the next section you will read more about the major West African cultures and how we know about them.

Section 3 Assessment

go.hrw.com
Online Quiz
KEYWORD: SQ7 HP6

Reviewing Ideas, Terms, and People **HSS** 7.4.3

1. **a. Identify** In what part of West Africa did Songhai begin?
   b. Summarize What did **Sunni Ali** accomplish?
2. **a. Identify** What religion gained influence in Songhai under **Askia the Great**?
   b. Analyze How did contact with other cultures change Songhai's government?
3. **a. Identify** Which group of people invaded the Songhai Empire in the 1590s?
   b. Predict How might West Africa's history have been different if the invaders who conquered Songhai had not had firearms?

Critical Thinking

4. **Analyzing**
   Copy the graphic organizer on the right. In each oval, describe an important development in Songhai during the rule of Askia the Great.

   Askia the Great

FOCUS ON SPEAKING

5. **Evaluating** Add information to your notes for Songhai's leaders. What were their achievements? Compare the Songhai achievements with those of Ghana and Mali.

Historical and Artistic Traditions

If YOU were there...

You are the youngest and smallest in your family. People often tease you about not being very strong. In the evenings, when work is done, the people of your village gather to listen to storytellers. One of your favorites is about the hero Sundiata. As a boy he was small and weak, but he grew to be a great warrior and hero.

How does the story of Sundiata make you feel?

BUILDING BACKGROUND Although trading empires rose and fell in West Africa, many traditions continued through the centuries. In every town and village, storytellers passed on the people's histories, legends, and wise sayings. These were at the heart of West Africa's arts and cultural traditions.

Storytellers Maintain Oral History

Although cities like Timbuktu and Djenné were known for their universities and libraries, writing was never very common in West Africa. In fact, none of the major early civilizations of West Africa developed a written language. Arabic was the only written language they used. Many Muslim traders, government officials, and religious leaders could read and write Arabic.

The lack of a written language does not mean that the people of West Africa didn't know their history, though. They passed along information through oral histories. An **oral history** is a spoken record of past events. The task of remembering West Africa's history was entrusted to storytellers.

The Griots

West African storytellers were called **griots** (GREE-ohz). They were highly respected in their communities because the people of West Africa were very interested in the deeds of their ancestors. Griots helped keep this history alive for each new generation.

What You Will Learn...

Main Ideas

1. Storytellers helped maintain the oral history of the cultures of West Africa.
2. Visitors to West Africa from other lands wrote histories and descriptions of what they saw there.
3. Traditionally, West Africans have valued the arts.

The Big Idea

Because the people of West Africa did not have a written language, their culture has been passed down through oral history, writings by other people, and the arts.

Key Terms

oral history, *p. 147*
griots, *p. 147*
proverbs, *p. 148*
kente, *p. 151*

HSS **7.4.4** Trace the growth of the Arabic language in government, trade, and Islamic scholarship in West Africa.

7.4.5 Describe the importance of written and oral traditions in the transmission of African history and culture.

Oral Traditions
West African storytellers called griots had the job of remembering and passing on their people's history. In this photo, everyone wears their best clothes and gathers around a griot to listen.

The griots' stories were entertaining as well as informative. They told of past events and of the deeds of people's ancestors. For example, some stories explained the rise and fall of the West African empires. Other stories described in detail the actions of powerful kings and warriors. Some griots made their stories more lively by acting out events from the past like scenes in a play.

In addition to stories, the griots recited **proverbs**, or short sayings of wisdom or truth. They used proverbs to teach lessons to the people. For example, one West African proverb warns, "Talking doesn't fill the basket in the farm." This proverb reminds people that they must work to accomplish things. They can't just talk about what they want to do. Another proverb advises, "A hippopotamus can be made invisible in dark water." It warns people to remain alert. Just as it can be hard to see animals in a deep pool, people don't always see the problems they will face.

In order to recite their stories and proverbs, the griots memorized hundreds of names and events. Through this memorization process the griots passed on West African history from generation to generation. However, some griots confused names and events in their heads. When this happened, specific facts about some historical events became distorted. Still, the griots' stories tell us a great deal about life in the West African empires.

West African Epics

Some of the griot poems are epics—long poems about kingdoms and heroes. Many of these epic poems are collected in the *Dausi* (DAW-zee) and the *Sundiata*.

The *Dausi* tells the history of Ghana. Intertwined with historical events, though, are myths and legends. For example, one story is about a terrifying seven-headed snake god named Bida. This god promised that Ghana would prosper if the people sacrificed a young woman to him every year. One year a mighty warrior killed Bida. But as the god died, he cursed Ghana. The griots say that it was this curse that caused the empire of Ghana to fall.

Like the *Dausi*, the *Sundiata* is about the history of an empire, Mali. It is the story of Sundiata, Mali's legendary first ruler. According to the epic, when Sundiata was still a boy, a conqueror captured Mali and killed Sundiata's father and 11 brothers. He didn't kill Sundiata because the boy was sick and didn't seem like a threat. However, Sundiata grew up to be an expert hunter and warrior. Eventually he overthrew the conqueror and became king.

READING CHECK **Drawing Conclusions** Why were oral traditions important in West Africa?

Visitors Write Histories

The people of West Africa left no written histories of their own. Visitors to West Africa from other parts of the world, however, did write about the region. Much of what we know about early West Africa comes from the writings of travelers and scholars from Muslim lands such as Spain and Arabia.

One of the first people to write about West Africa was an Arab scholar named al-Masudi (ahl-mah-SOO-dee). He visited the region in the 900s. In his writings, al-Masudi described the geography, customs, history, and scientific achievements of West Africa.

About 100 years later, another writer, Abu Ubayd al-Bakri, wrote about West Africa. He lived in Córdoba, Spain, where he met many people who had been to West Africa. Based on the stories these people told him, al-Bakri wrote about life in West African kingdoms.

More famous than either of these two writers was Ibn Battutah, a tireless traveler who described most of the Muslim world.

From 1353 to 1354 Ibn Battutah traveled through West Africa. His account of this journey describes the political and cultural lives of West Africans in great detail.

The last of the major Muslim visitors to West Africa was a young man called Leo Africanus (LEE-oh af-ri-KAY-nuhs), or Leo the African. Born in what is now Spain, Leo traveled through northern and western Africa on missions for the government. On his way home, however, pirates captured Leo and brought him to Rome as a prisoner. Although he was freed, he stayed in Rome for many years. There he wrote a description of what he had seen in Africa. Because Leo lived and wrote in Europe, for a long time his work was the only source about life in Africa available to Europeans.

READING CHECK **Generalizing** Why were the written histories of West Africa written by people from other lands?

Primary Source

BOOK
A Description of Mali

In the 1300s, Ibn Battutah traveled through much of Asia and Africa. This passage describes the people of Mali, one of the places he visited in Africa.

❝[They] possess some admirable qualities. They are seldom unjust, and have a greater abhorrence [hatred] of injustice than any other people. Their sultan [ruler] shows no mercy to anyone who is guilty of the least act of it. There is complete security in their country. Neither traveler nor inhabitant in it has anything to fear from robbers or men of violence . . . They are careful to observe the hours of prayer, and assiduous [careful] in attending them in congregations [gatherings], and in bringing up their children to them.❞

–Ibn Battutah, from *Travels in Asia and Africa 1325–1354*

ANALYSIS SKILL **ANALYZING PRIMARY SOURCES**

Why may Ibn Battutah have been particularly interested in security within Mali?

West Africans Value Arts

Like most peoples, West Africans valued the arts. The art they produced took many forms. Common West African art forms included sculpture, mask- and cloth-making, music, and dance.

Sculpture

Of all the visual art forms, the sculpture of West Africa is probably the best known. West Africans made ornate statues and carvings out of wood, brass, clay, ivory, stone, and other materials.

Most statues from West Africa are of people—often the sculptor's ancestors. In most cases, these statues were made for religious rituals, to ask for the ancestors' blessings. Sculptors made other statues as gifts for the gods. These sculptures were kept in holy places. They were never meant to be seen by people.

Because their statues were often used in religious rituals, many African artists were deeply respected. People thought artists had been blessed by the gods.

Long after the decline of Ghana, Mali, and Songhai, West African art is still admired. Museums around the world today display African art. In addition, African sculpture helped inspire some European artists of the 1900s, including Henri Matisse and Pablo Picasso.

Masks and Clothing

In addition to statues, the artists of West Africa carved elaborate masks. Made of wood, these masks bore the faces of animals such as hyenas, lions, monkeys, and antelopes. Artists often painted the masks after carving them. People wore these masks during rituals as they danced around fires. The way firelight reflected off the masks made them look fierce and lifelike.

LINKING TO TODAY

Music From Mali to Memphis

Did you know that the music you listen to today may have begun with the griots? From the 1600s to the 1800s, many people from West Africa were brought to America as slaves. In America, these slaves continued to sing the way they had in Africa. They also continued to play traditional instruments such as the *kora* played by Senegalese musician Soriba Kouyaté, the son of a griot (right). Over time, this music developed into a style called the blues, made popular by such artists as B. B. King (left). In turn, the blues shaped other styles of music, including jazz and rock. So, the next time you hear a Memphis blues track or a cool jazz tune, listen for its ancient African roots!

ANALYSIS SKILL **ANALYZING INFORMATION**

How did West African music affect modern American music?

Many African societies were also famous for the cloth they wove. The most famous of these cloths is called kente (ken-TAY). **Kente** is a hand-woven, brightly colored fabric. The cloth was woven in narrow strips that were then sewn together. Kings and queens in West Africa wore garments made of kente for special occasions.

Music and Dance

In many West African societies, music and dance were as important as the visual arts. Singing and dancing were great forms of entertainment, but they also helped people honor their history and were central to many celebrations. For example, music was played when a ruler entered a room.

Dance has long been a central part of African society. Many West African cultures used dance to celebrate specific events or ceremonies. For example, they may have performed one dance for weddings and another for funerals. In some parts of West Africa, people still perform dances similar to those performed hundreds of years ago.

READING CHECK **Summarizing** Summarize how traditions were preserved in West Africa.

Like their music and dance, many West African crafts have been handed down for generations. This woman in the modern nation of Ghana is weaving traditional baskets.

SUMMARY AND PREVIEW The societies of West Africa never developed written languages, but their histories and cultures have been passed on through traditions and customs. You will next read about another culture in which traditions are important—China.

go.hrw.com
Online Quiz
KEYWORD: SQ7 HP6

Section 4 Assessment

Reviewing Ideas, Terms, and People HSS 7.4.4, 7.4.5

1. **a. Define** What is **oral history**?
   b. Generalize Why were **griots** and their stories important in West African society?
   c. Evaluate Why may an oral history provide different information than a written account?
2. **a. Identify** Name one writer who wrote about West Africa.
   b. Infer How do you think these writers' views of West Africa may have differed from the views of West Africans?
3. **Identify** What were two forms of visual art popular in West Africa?

Critical Thinking

4. **Categorizing** Create a chart like the one here. Use it to describe the *Dausi* and the *Sundiata*.

Great Epics of West Africa	
Dausi	*Sundiata*

FOCUS ON SPEAKING

5. **Writing about Oral and Written Traditions** Take notes on how griots and musicians wrote and played to get ideas for your own performance. Consider these questions: How dramatic should my praise song be? How can I make the performance of my praise song more interesting?

from
Sundiata

by D. T. Niane, as told by Djeli Mamoudou Kouyaté
Translated by G. D. Pickett

About the Reading *For almost 900 years, West African griots have been telling the story of Sundiata, king and founder of the Mali Empire. Like other ancient epics, this one is a blend of history and legend. Some parts of the story are based on fact—such as Sundiata's defeat of the tyrant-king Sumanguru, which took place in about 1235. Other elements, though, were added over time for dramatic effect. In the following episode, for example, an almost superhuman Sundiata swoops down upon Sumanguru's capital city, Sosso, vowing to destroy it in a single morning.*

AS YOU READ Imagine the sequence of events.

Sosso was a magnificent city. In the open plain her triple rampart with awe-inspiring towers reached into the sky. The city comprised a hundred and eighty-eight fortresses and the palace of Soumaoro loomed above the whole city like a gigantic tower. ❶ Sosso had but one gate; colossal and made of iron, the work of the sons of fire. Noumounkeba hoped to tie Sundiata down outside of Sosso, for he had enough provisions to hold out for a year.

The sun was beginning to set when Sogolon Djata appeared before Sosso the Magnificent. ❷ From the top of a hill, Djata and his general staff gazed upon the fearsome city of the sorcerer-king. The army encamped in the plain opposite the great gate of the city and fires were lit in the camp. Djata resolved to take Sosso in the course of a morning . . .

At daybreak the towers of the ramparts were black with sofas. ❸ Others were positioned on the ramparts themselves. They were the archers. The Mandingoes were masters in the art of storming a town. ❹ In the front line Sundiata placed the sofas of Mali, while those who held the ladders were in the second line protected by the shields of the spearmen. The main body of the army was to attack the city gate. When all was ready, Djata gave the order to attack. The drums resounded, the horns blared and like a tide the Mandingo front line

GUIDED READING

WORD HELP

rampart a protective bank or wall
colossal gigantic
provisions supplies

❶ *Soumaoro* is another name for Sumanguru. Noumounkeba is one of his assistants.

❷ *Sogolon Djata* is another name for Sundiata.

Imagine that you are one of Sundiata's warriors. How do you feel as you look down on the city of Sosso?

❸ A *sofa* is a warrior.

❹ The Mandingoes were the people of Mali.

ELA Reading 7.3.2 Identify events that advance the plot and determine how each event explains past or present action(s) or foreshadows future action(s).

moved off, giving mighty shouts. With their shields raised above their heads the Mandingoes advanced up to the foot of the wall, then the Sossos began to rain large stones down on the assailants. From the rear, the bowmen of Wagadou shot arrows at the ramparts. The attack spread and the town was assaulted at all points . . . On one knee the archers fired flaming arrows over the ramparts. Within the walls the thatched huts took fire and the smoke swirled up. The ladders stood against the curtain wall and the first Mandingo sofas were already at the top. Seized by panic through seeing the town on fire, the Sossos hesitated a moment. The huge tower surmounting the gate surrendered, for Fakoli's smiths had made themselves the masters of it. ❺ They got into the city where the screams of women and children brought the Sossos' panic to a head. They opened the gates to the main body of the enemy.

Then began the massacre. Women and children in the midst of fleeing Sossos implored mercy of the victors. Djata and his cavalry were now in front of the awesome tower palace of Soumaoro. Noumounkeba, conscious that he was lost, came out to fight. With his sword held aloft he bore down on Djata, but the latter dodged him and, catching hold of the Sosso's braced arm, forced him to his knees whilst the sword dropped to the ground. He did not kill him but delivered him into the hands of Manding Bory . . . ❻

Just as he had wished, Sundiata had taken Sosso in the course of a morning. When everything was outside of the town and all that there was to take had been taken out, Sundiata gave the order to complete its destruction. The last houses were set fire to and prisoners were employed in the razing of the walls. Thus, as Djata intended, Sosso was destroyed to its very foundations.

GUIDED READING

WORD HELP

assailants attackers
surmounting rising above
razing tearing down

❺ Fakoli, Soumaoro's nephew, had rebelled against his uncle.

❻ Manding Bory is Sundiata's half-brother and best friend.

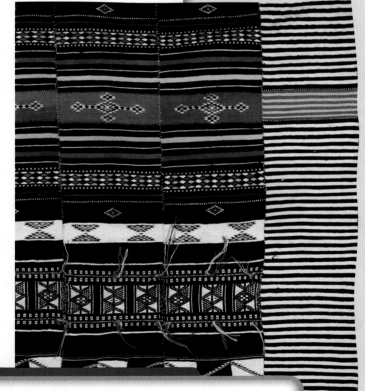

This blanket was woven by the Fulani people of modern Mali, the descendants of Sumanguru and his subjects.

CONNECTING LITERATURE TO HISTORY

1. **Analyzing** West African epics sometimes included both elements of truth and fictional embellishments. Which details in this excerpt sound like they could be true? Which were probably invented later? What makes you think that?

2. **Making Decisions** Griots had to commit to memory hundreds of events in order to tell their stories. They would sometimes act stories out like plays. If you were a griot, how might you bring the action in this excerpt to life?

HSS Analysis CS 3 Use maps to explain the expansion and disintegration of empires.

Analysis	Critical Thinking	Participation	Study

Interpreting Maps: Expansion of Empires

Understand the Skill

Many types of maps are useful in the study of history. *Physical maps* show natural features on the earth's surface. *Political maps* show human cultural features such as cities, states, and countries. Modern political maps show the present-day borders of states and countries. Historical political maps show what cultural features were in the past.

Some historical political maps show how boundaries and features changed over time. Being able to interpret such maps makes the growth and disintegration of countries and empires easier to visualize and understand.

Learn the Skill

Use these guidelines to interpret maps that show political change.

❶ Read the title to find out what the map is about.

❷ Read the legend. The map's title may state the time period covered by the map. However, in this type of map, information about dates is often found in the legend.

❸ Study the legend carefully to be sure you understand what each color or symbol means. Pay special attention to colors or symbols that might indicate changes in borders, signs of the growth or loss of a country's territory.

❹ Study the map itself. Compare the colors and symbols in the legend to those on the map. Note any labels, especially those that may show political change. Look for other indications of political changes on the map.

Practice and Apply the Skill

Interpret the map below to answer the following questions about the Mali and Songhai empires.

1. Which empire was older? Which empire expanded the most?

2. Was Songhai ever part of the Mali Empire? Explain how the map provides this information.

3. Who controlled the city of Gao in the year 1100? in 1325? in 1515?

4. By what date do you know for sure that the Mali Empire had disintegrated? How do you know?

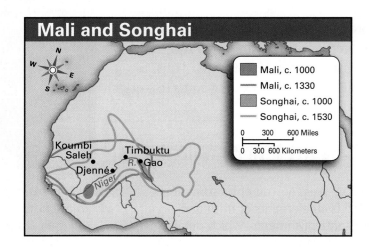

Mali and Songhai

Koumbi Saleh
Timbuktu
Djenné
Niger R. • Gao

Mali, c. 1000
Mali, c. 1330
Songhai, c. 1000
Songhai, c. 1530

0   300   600 Miles
0   300 600 Kilometers

Visual Summary

Use the visual summary below to help you review the main ideas of the chapter.

QUICK FACTS

The Ghana Empire developed in West Africa and controlled the trade in salt and gold.

Mali's kings built an empire and spread Islam in West Africa.

The Songhai Empire continued to spread Islam.

The history of West Africa has been preserved through storytelling, writing, music, and art.

Reviewing Vocabulary, Terms, and People

Imagine that these terms and people from the chapter are correct answers to items in a crossword puzzle. Write the clues for the answers. Then make the puzzle with some answers written down and some across.

1. silent barter
2. Tunka Manin
3. Sundiata
4. Mansa Musa
5. various
6. Askia the Great
7. oral history
8. griots
9. proverbs
10. kente
11. Sunni Ali
12. process

Comprehension and Critical Thinking

SECTION 1 *(Pages 130–135)* **HSS** 7.4.1, 7.4.2

13. **a. Identify** What were the two major trade goods that made Ghana rich? Where did each come from?

b. Draw Conclusions Why did merchants in Ghana not want other traders to know where their gold came from?

c. Evaluate Who do you think was more responsible for the collapse of Ghana, the people of Ghana or outsiders? Why?

SECTION 2 *(Pages 136–140)* **HSS** 7.4.3, 7.4.4

14. **a. Describe** How did Islam influence society in Mali?

b. Compare and Contrast How were Sundiata and Mansa Musa similar? How were they different?

c. Elaborate How did Mali's growth and power help lead to its downfall?

SECTION 3 *(Pages 142–146)* **HSS** **7.4.3**

15. a. Identify What ruler led Songhai in its conquest of Mali?

b. Make Inferences Why did Muhammad Ture become known as Askia the Great?

c. Evaluate Which do you think played more of a role in Songhai's society, warriors or traders? Why?

SECTION 4 *(Pages 147–151)* **HSS** **7.4.4, 7.4.5**

16. a. Describe Who were the griots? What role did they play in West African society?

b. Make Inferences Why do you think music and dance were so important in West African society?

c. Evaluate Which do you think is a more reliable source about life in the Mali Empire—a story told by a modern griot or an account written by a Muslim scholar who had spoken to travelers from Mali? Defend your answer.

Reviewing Themes

17. Geography How did the location of the West African empires affect their success at trade?

18. Economics How did economics shape the governments and societies of West African empires?

Using the Internet

go.hrw.com
KEYWORD: SQ7 WH6

19. Activity: Writing Proverbs Does the early bird get the worm? If you go outside at sunrise to check, you missed the fact that it's a proverb that means "The one that gets there first can earn something good." Griots created many proverbs that expressed wisdom or truth. Enter the activity keyword. Then use the Internet resources to write three proverbs that might have been said by griots during the time of the great West African empires. Make sure your proverbs are written from the point of view of a West African person living during those centuries.

Reading and Analysis Skills

Distinguishing Fact and Opinion *Read the primary source and answer the questions that follow.*

> "The interpreter Dugha ...plays on an instrument made of reeds, with some small calabashes at its lower end, and chants a poem in praise of the sultan, recalling his battles and deeds of valor ...after Dugha has finished his display, the poets come in. Each of them is inside a figure resembling a thrush, made of feathers, and provided with a wooden head with a red beak, to look like a thrush's head. They stand in front of the sultan in this ridiculous make-up and recite their poems."

20. Is the first sentence of this passage a fact or an opinion? How do you know?

21. What words or phrases display Ibn Battutah's opinions about the poets of Mali?

Social Studies Skills

Understanding Political Change *Study the maps of Ghana, Mali, and Songhai on pages 137 and 143 and answer the following questions.*

22. Which empire appears to have included the largest area?

23. Which empire seems to have contained the most trading cities?

24. How did the government of Timbuktu change over time?

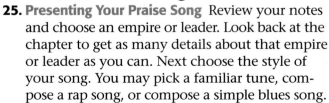
FOCUS ON SPEAKING

25. Presenting Your Praise Song Review your notes and choose an empire or leader. Look back at the chapter to get as many details about that empire or leader as you can. Next choose the style of your song. You may pick a familiar tune, compose a rap song, or compose a simple blues song.

Now write words to go with your song's music. Be sure that your song identifies the empire or leader and tells about important accomplishments. Practice your song until you can sing it without looking at the words. Once you have prepared your song, perform it. You don't have to sing. You can chant or speak if you prefer.

Standards Assessment

DIRECTIONS: Read each question, and write the letter of the best response.

1

> Well placed for the caravan trade, it was badly situated to defend itself from the Tuareg raiders of the Sahara. These restless nomads were repeatedly hammering at the gates of Timbuktu, and often enough they burst them open with disastrous results for the inhabitants. Life here was never quite safe enough to recommend it as the centre [center] of a big state.
>
> –Basil Davidson, from *A History of West Africa*

In this quote, the author is discussing why Timbuktu was

A a good place for universities.

B not a good place for a capital city.

C a good location for trade.

D not a good location for the center of the Tuareg state.

2 In the second sentence of the passage above, what does the phrase *hammering at the gates of Timbuktu* mean?

A driving nails into Timbuktu's gates

B knocking on the door to get in the city

C trying to get into and conquer the city

D making noise to anger the inhabitants

3 Which of the following rivers helped the development of the West African empires?

A Niger

B Congo

C Nile

D Zambezi

4 The wealth of Ghana, Mali, and Songhai was based on

A raiding other tribes.

B the gold and salt trade.

C trade in ostriches and elephant tusks.

D making iron tools and weapons.

5 The two rulers who were most responsible for spreading Islam were

A Sunni Ali and Mansa Musa.

B Sundiata and Sunni Ali.

C Ibn Battutah and Leo Africanus.

D Mansa Musa and Askia the Great.

6 Griots contributed to West African societies by

A fighting battles.

B collecting taxes.

C preserving oral history.

D trading with the Berbers.

Connecting with Past Learnings

7 You learned earlier about the fall of the Roman Empire. Mali fell for some of the same reasons that the Roman Empire ended. Of the following, which is *not* one of those reasons?

A invasions by other peoples

B large size of the empire

C lack of strong leadership

D lack of products for trade

Assignment

Write a paper explaining one of these topics:

- how the introduction of iron changed life in early West African civilizations
- why the empire of Mali declined and fell

TIP **Using a Clear Order** Essays explaining how or why should be written in a clear and consistent order. Consider using one of these:

- **chronological order,** or the order that events occurred
- **order of importance,** going from the most important information or point to the least important, or from the least important to the most important

ELA **Writing 7.2.0** Students write expository texts.

How and Why in History

Why were the pyramids built? How did early West Africans get water for their crops? Often the first question we ask about something begins with *why* or *how*. One way we can answer *how* or *why* questions is by writing an explanation.

1. Prewrite

Considering Topic and Audience

As soon as you choose one of the two topics to write about, you need to convert it to a big idea. For example, your big idea might be "The introduction of iron changed life in early West African civilizations in three important ways."

You also need to think about the people who will read your essay. In this case, your audience will be middle school students. What background information will they need to understand your explanation? What details or information might cause confusion?

Collecting and Organizing Information

Scan the material in your textbook, looking for information about your topic. Use that information to start a plan for your paper and to organize the support for your big idea. For example, look for two or three ways in which iron changed life in early West Africa or two or three factors that caused Mali to fall. If you need more information, check your library or the Internet for sources on early West Africa.

2. Write

Here is a framework that can help you write a first draft.

A Writer's Framework

Introduction	Body	Conclusion
■ Start with an interesting fact or question.	■ Create at least one paragraph for each point supporting your big idea.	■ Summarize your main points.
■ Identify your big idea.	■ Include facts and details to explain and illustrate each point.	■ Restate your big idea in different words.
■ Include important background information.	■ Use chronological order or order of importance to present your support.	

3. Evaluate and Revise

Evaluating

Clear, straightforward language is the key to writing effective explanations. Use the following questions to discover ways to improve your paper.

Evaluation Questions for an Explanation of How or Why

- Do you begin with an interesting fact or question?
- Does your introduction identify your big idea and provide any background information your readers might need?
- Do you have at least one paragraph for each point you are using to support the big idea?

- Do you include facts and details to explain and illustrate each point?
- Do you use chronological order or order of importance to organize your main points?
- Does your conclusion summarize the main points and restate the big idea of your paper?

TIP **Using Bulleted Lists** The items in a bulleted list should always be in the same word forms or structures.

Not the same:

Askia the Great was important because he

- supported education,
- reorganization of government,
- standardized weights.

The same:

Askia the Great was important because he

- supported education,
- reorganized government,
- standardized weights.

Revising

Look back through your paper to see whether you have any paragraphs that are confusing or packed too full with information. To make explanations clearer, you may want to

- take the facts or details from three or more sentences,
- introduce them in one sentence, and
- break them out into a bulleted or numbered list.

4. Proofread and Publish

Proofreading

Special formatting—such as *italics*, **boldface**, underlining, numbering, or bullets—can help make your ideas clear. Using special formatting inconsistently, however, will only confuse your reader. As you proofread your paper, ask yourself these questions to look for formatting errors.

- Have you used boldface or italic type for headings, important information, or key terms in a consistent (unchanging) way?
- In a list of items, have you consistently used numbers or bullets?
- In a list of numbered steps, have you missed any numbers?

Publishing

Share your explanation with students from another class. Ask them if your explanation makes sense to them.

● Practice and Apply

Use the steps and strategies outlined in this workshop to write your explanation.

Asian
Civilizations

Chapter 7   China
Chapter 8   Japan

The Asian civilizations of China and Japan were great centers of learning and culture. In China, a series of dynasties ruled a large and unified empire. China made many advances during this time. For example, the Chinese invented paper money, porcelain, and gunpowder, and made many improvements in transportation and agriculture.

To the east, Japan reached a golden age of art and literature during the Heian Period. During this period, the Japanese produced beautiful art, poetry, and the world's first known novel. Later, the country developed a military government run by generals called shogun and warriors known as samurai.

In the next two chapters, you will learn about the history and culture of the Chinese and Japanese people.

Explore the Art

In this scene, a young Japanese girl is shown writing in her journal. What does the scene suggest about Japanese society?

China

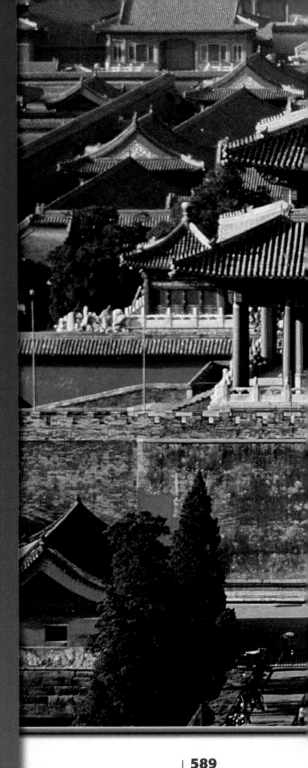

California Standards

History–Social Science

7.3 Students analyze the geographic, political, economic, religious, and social structures of the civilizations of China in the Middle Ages.

Analysis Skills

HI 6 Students conduct cost-benefit analyses of economic and political issues.

English–Language Arts

Writing 7.2.0 Write expository texts.

Reading 7.2.0 Students read and understand grade-level-appropriate material.

FOCUS ON WRITING

A Magazine Article In this chapter you will read about a great period in the history of China. You will learn about many important accomplishments made during this period, and then you will write a magazine article about them. The purpose of the article will be to explain Chinese contributions to world society.

CHAPTER EVENTS

589 China is reunified under the Sui dynasty.

600

WORLD EVENTS

613 Muhammad begins teaching the basic beliefs of Islam.

故宫博物院

What You Will Learn...

In this chapter you will learn about Chinese history from the 500s to the 1600s. The magnificent Forbidden City, shown in this photo, was built during this time as a royal palace. Today it is a museum.

730s–760s
Li Bo and Du Fu write some of the greatest poems in Chinese history.

1279
Mongols found the Yuan dynasty in China.

1644
The Ming dynasty ends.

800 **1000** **1200** **1400** **1600**

794 The Japanese court is established at Heian.

1060s
The empire of Ghana reaches its height.

1347
The Black Death strikes Europe.

CHINA **163**

Reading Social Studies

by Kylene Beers

Focus on Themes This chapter will explore the history of China from the late 500s until the 1400s. As you read, you will discover that many different dynasties ruled the country during that period, leading to great political changes. Some of those dynasties supported trade, leading to great **economic** growth and stability. Others favored isolation, limiting Chinese contact with the rest of the world. You will also learn that this period saw huge leaps forward in **science and technology**.

Drawing Conclusions about the Past

Focus on Reading You have no doubt heard the phrase, "Put two and two together." When people say that, they don't mean "two + two = four." They mean, "Put the information together."

Using Background Knowledge to Draw Conclusions A **conclusion** is a judgment you make by combining information. You put information from what you are reading together with what you already know, your background knowledge.

Additional reading support can be found in the

Inter active

Reader and Study Guide

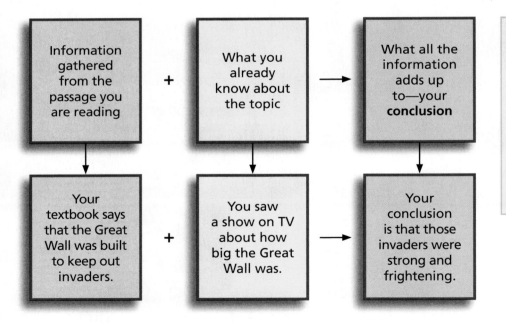

| Information gathered from the passage you are reading | + | What you already know about the topic | → | What all the information adds up to—your **conclusion** |

| Your textbook says that the Great Wall was built to keep out invaders. | + | You saw a show on TV about how big the Great Wall was. | → | Your conclusion is that those invaders were strong and frightening. |

Steps for Drawing Conclusions

1. Read the passage, looking for information the author gives you about the topic.

2. Think about what you already know about the topic. Consider things you've studied, books you've read, or movies you've seen.

3. Put your background knowledge together with what the passage says.

You Try It!

The following passage is from the chapter you are getting ready to read. As you read the passage, look for facts about China.

Advances in Agriculture

Chinese civilization had always been based on agriculture. Over thousands of years, the Chinese had become expert farmers. In the north farmers grew wheat, barley, and other grains. In the warmer and wetter south they grew rice.

From Chapter 7, p. 170

During the Song dynasty, though, Chinese farming reached new heights. The improvement was largely due to new irrigation techniques. For example, some farmers dug underground wells. A new irrigation device, the dragon backbone pump, allowed one person to do the work of several. With this light and portable pump, a farmer could scoop up water and pour it into an irrigation canal. Using these new techniques, farmers created elaborate irrigation systems.

After you have finished the passage, answer the questions below, drawing conclusions about what you have read.

1. Think back on what you've learned about irrigation systems in other societies. What do you think irrigation was like in China before the Song dynasty?

2. What effect do you think this improved irrigation had on Chinese society? Why do you think this?

3. Based on this passage, what kinds of conditions do you think rice needs to grow? How does this compare to the conditions wheat needs?

4. Which crop was most likely grown near the Great Wall—wheat or rice? Why do you think so?

Key Terms and People

Academic Vocabulary

Success in school is related to knowing academic vocabulary—the words that are frequently used in school assignments and discussions. In this chapter, you will learn the following academic words:

function (p. 177)
incentive (p. 178)
consequences (p. 186)

As you read Chapter 7, think about what you already know about China and draw conclusions to fill gaps in what you are reading.

CHINA **165**

China Reunifies

What You Will Learn...

Main Ideas

1. The Period of Disunion was a time of war and disorder that followed the end of the Han dynasty.
2. China was reunified under the Sui, Tang, and Song dynasties.
3. The Age of Buddhism saw major religious changes in China.

The Big Idea

The Period of Disunion was followed by reunification by rulers of the Sui, Tang, and Song dynasties.

Key Terms and People

Period of Disunion, *p. 166*
Grand Canal, *p. 167*
Empress Wu, *p. 168*

HSS 7.3.1 Describe the reunification of China under the Tang Dynasty and reasons for the spread of Buddhism in Tang China, Korea, and Japan.

If YOU were there...

You are a peasant in China in the year 264. Your grandfather often speaks of a time when all of China was united, but all you have known is warfare among rulers. A man passing through your village speaks of even more conflict in other areas.

Why might you want China to have just one ruler?

BUILDING BACKGROUND Most of China's history is divided into dynasties. The first dynasties ruled China for centuries. But when the Han dynasty collapsed in 220, China plunged into disorder.

The Period of Disunion

When the Han dynasty collapsed, China split into several rival kingdoms, each ruled by military leaders. Historians sometimes call the time of disorder that followed the collapse of the Han the **Period of Disunion**. It lasted from 220 to 589.

Although war was common during the Period of Disunion, peaceful developments also took place at the same time. During this period, nomadic peoples settled in northern China. Some Chinese people adopted the nomads' culture, while the invaders adopted some Chinese practices. For example, one former nomadic ruler ordered his people to adopt Chinese names, speak Chinese, and dress like the Chinese. Thus, the culture of the invaders and traditional Chinese mixed.

A similar cultural blending took place in southern China. Many northern Chinese, unwilling to live under the rule of the nomadic invaders, fled to southern China. There, northern Chinese culture mixed with the more southern cultures.

As a result of this mixing, Chinese culture changed. New types of art and music developed. New foods and clothing styles became popular. The new culture spread over a wider geographic area than ever before, and more people became Chinese.

READING CHECK **Finding Main Ideas** How did Chinese culture change during the Period of Disunion?

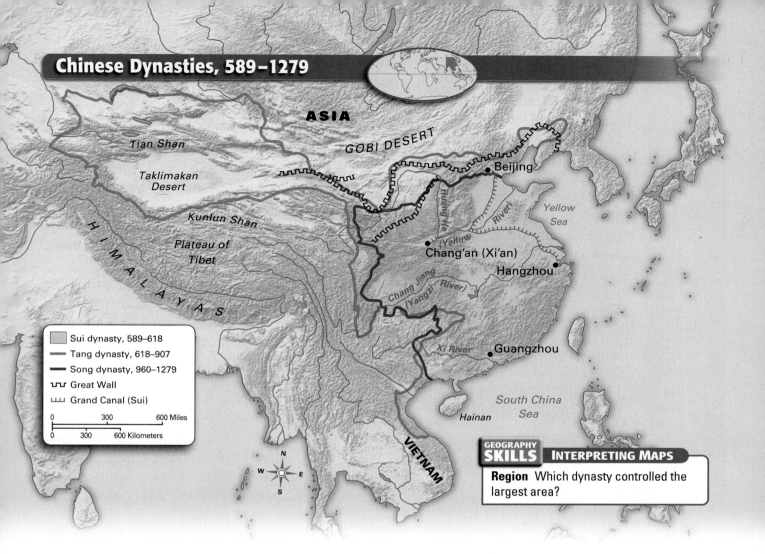

Chinese Dynasties, 589–1279

ASIA

GOBI DESERT

Tian Shan

Taklimakan Desert

Kunlun Shan

Plateau of Tibet

HIMALAYAS

Beijing

Huang He (Yellow River)

Yellow Sea

Chang'an (Xi'an)

Hangzhou

Chang Jiang (Yangzi River)

Xi River

Guangzhou

South China Sea

Hainan

VIETNAM

Sui dynasty, 589–618
Tang dynasty, 618–907
Song dynasty, 960–1279
Great Wall
Grand Canal (Sui)

0   300   600 Miles
0   300   600 Kilometers

N W E S

GEOGRAPHY SKILLS | **INTERPRETING MAPS**

Region Which dynasty controlled the largest area?

The Sui, Tang, and Song

Finally, after centuries of political confusion and cultural change, China was reunified. For about 700 years, it remained unified under a series of powerful dynasties.

The Sui Dynasty

The man who finally ended the Period of Disunion was a northern ruler named Yang Jian (YANG jee-EN). In 589, he conquered the south, unified China, and created the Sui (SWAY) dynasty.

The Sui dynasty didn't last long, only from 589 to 618. During that time, though, its leaders restored order to China and began the **Grand Canal**, a canal linking northern and southern China.

The Tang Dynasty

A new dynasty arose in China in 618 when a former Sui official overthrew the old government. This dynasty, the Tang, would rule for nearly 300 years. As you can see on the map, China grew under the Tang dynasty to include much of eastern Asia, as well as large parts of Central Asia.

Historians view the Tang dynasty as a golden age of Chinese civilization. One of its greatest rulers was Taizong (TY-tzoong). He helped unify China through his programs, including reform of the military, creation of law codes, and a land reform policy known as the equal field system. Another brilliant Tang ruler was Xuanzong (SHOO-AN-tzoong). During his reign, culture flourished. Many of China's finest poets wrote while Xuanzong ruled.

The Tang dynasty also included the only woman to rule China—**Empress Wu**. Her methods were sometimes vicious, but she was intelligent and talented.

After the Tang dynasty fell, China entered another brief period of chaos and disorder, with separate kingdoms competing for power. In fact, China was so divided during this period that it is known as Five Dynasties and Ten Kingdoms. The disorder only lasted 53 years, though, from 907 to 960.

The Song Dynasty

In 960, China was again reunified, this time by the Song dynasty. Like the Tang, the Song ruled for about 300 years, until 1279. Also like the Tang, the Song dynasty was a time of great accomplishments.

READING CHECK **Sequencing** When was China reunified? When was China not unified?

BIOGRAPHY

Empress Wu
625–705

Married to a sickly emperor, Empress Wu became the virtual ruler of China in 655. After her husband died, Wu decided her sons were not worthy of ruling. She kept power for herself, and ruled with an iron fist. Those who threatened her power risked death. Unlike many earlier rulers, she chose advisors based on their abilities rather than their ranks. Although she was not well liked, Wu was respected for bringing stability and prosperity to China.

Drawing Conclusions Why do you think Empress Wu was never very popular?

The Age of Buddhism

While China was experiencing changes in its government, another major change was taking place in Chinese culture. A new religion was spreading quickly throughout the vast land.

Buddhism is one of the world's major religions, originating in India around 500 BC. Buddhism first came to China during the Han dynasty. But for some time, there were few Buddhists in China.

Buddhism's status changed during the Period of Disunion. During this troubled time, many people turned to Buddhism. They took comfort in the Buddhist teaching that people can escape suffering and achieve a state of peace.

By the end of the Period of Disunion, Buddhism was well established in China. As a result, wealthy people donated land and money to Buddhist temples, which arose across the land. Some temples were architectural wonders and housed huge statues of the Buddha.

Buddhism continued to influence life in China after the country was reunified. In fact, during the Sui and Tang dynasties, Buddhism continued to grow and spread. Chinese missionaries, people who travel to spread their religion, introduced Buddhism to Japan, Korea, and other Asian lands.

Buddhism influenced many aspects of Chinese culture, including art, literature, and architecture. In fact, so important was Buddhism in China that the period from about 400 to about 845 can be called the Age of Buddhism.

This golden age of Buddhism came to an end when a Tang emperor launched a campaign against the religion. He burned many Buddhist texts, took lands from Buddhist temples, destroyed many temples, and turned others into schools.

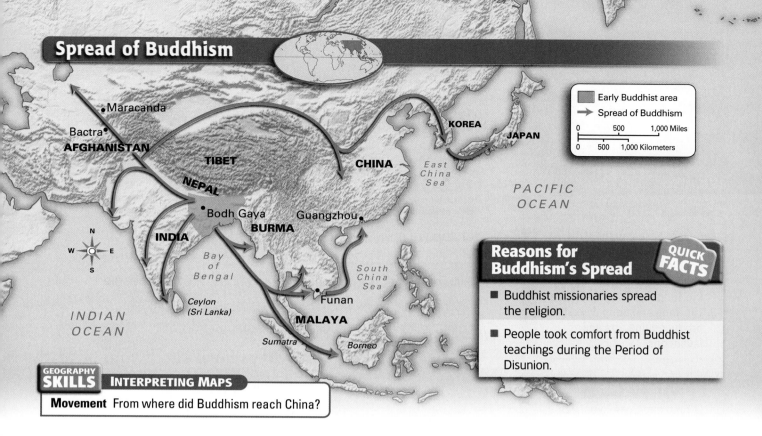

Spread of Buddhism

Early Buddhist area
→ Spread of Buddhism

0   500   1,000 Miles
0   500   1,000 Kilometers

Maracanda
Bactra
AFGHANISTAN
TIBET
NEPAL
Bodh Gaya
INDIA
CHINA
KOREA
JAPAN
East China Sea
PACIFIC OCEAN
Guangzhou
BURMA
Bay of Bengal
Ceylon (Sri Lanka)
INDIAN OCEAN
Funan
South China Sea
MALAYA
Sumatra
Borneo

Reasons for Buddhism's Spread QUICK FACTS

■ Buddhist missionaries spread the religion.

■ People took comfort from Buddhist teachings during the Period of Disunion.

GEOGRAPHY SKILLS **INTERPRETING MAPS**

Movement From where did Buddhism reach China?

The emperor's actions weakened the influence of Buddhism in China, but they did not destroy it completely. Buddhism continued to play a key role in Chinese society for centuries. As it had during the early Tang period, it continued to shape Chinese art and literature. But even as it influenced life in China, Buddhism changed. People began to blend elements of Buddhism with elements of other philosophies, especially Confucianism and Daoism, to create a new way of thinking.

READING CHECK **Identifying Cause and Effect** Why did Buddhism spread more easily during the Period of Disunion?

SUMMARY AND PREVIEW From the disorder that followed the fall of the Han dynasty, new dynasties arose to restore order in China. You will read about their many advances in the next section.

Section 1 Assessment

go.hrw.com
Online Quiz
KEYWORD: SQ7 HP7

Reviewing Ideas, Terms, and People HSS 7.3.1

1. **a. Define** What was the **Period of Disunion**?
   b. Explain How did Chinese culture change during the Period of Disunion?
2. **a. Identify** Who was **Empress Wu**? What did she do?
   b. Evaluate How do you think the reunification of China affected the common people?
3. **a. Identify** When was the Age of Buddhism in China?
   b. Explain Why did people turn to Buddhism during the Period of Disunion?
   c. Elaborate How did Buddhism influence Chinese culture?

Critical Thinking

4. **Sequencing** Draw a time line like this one. Use it to place the main events described in this section in order.

200   1300

FOCUS ON WRITING

5. **Getting an Overview** In this section you read an overview of three major dynasties and the contributions of Buddhism. Make a note of any ideas or contributions that you might want to include in your article.

Tang and Song Achievements

What You Will Learn...

Main Ideas

1. Advances in agriculture led to increased trade and population growth.
2. Cities and trade grew during the Tang and Song dynasties.
3. The Tang and Song dynasties produced fine arts and inventions.

The Big Idea

The Tang and Song dynasties were periods of economic, cultural, and technological accomplishments.

Key Terms

porcelain, *p. 173*
woodblock printing, *p. 174*
gunpowder, *p. 174*
compass, *p. 174*

HSS 7.3.2 Describe agricultural, technological, and commercial developments during the Tang and Song periods.

7.3.5 Trace the historic influence of such discoveries as tea, the manufacture of paper, wood-block printing, the compass, and gunpowder.

If YOU were there...

It is the year 1270. You are a rich merchant in a Chinese city of about a million people. The city around you fills your senses. You see people in colorful clothes among beautiful buildings. Glittering objects lure you into busy shops. You hear people talking—discussing business, gossiping, laughing at jokes. You smell delicious food cooking at a restaurant down the street.

How do you feel about your city?

BUILDING BACKGROUND The Tang and Song dynasties were periods of great wealth and progress. Changes in farming formed the basis for other advances in Chinese civilization.

Advances in Agriculture

Chinese civilization had always been based on agriculture. Over thousands of years, the Chinese had become expert farmers. In the north farmers grew wheat, barley, and other grains. In the warmer and wetter south they grew rice.

During the Song dynasty, though, Chinese farming reached new heights. The improvement was largely due to new irrigation techniques. For example, some farmers dug underground wells. A new irrigation device, the dragon backbone pump, allowed one person to do the work of several. With this light and portable pump, a farmer could scoop up water and pour it into an irrigation canal. Using these new techniques, farmers created elaborate irrigation systems.

Under the Song, the amount of land under cultivation increased. Lands along the Chang Jiang that had been wild now became farmland. Farms also became more productive, thanks to the discovery of a new type of fast-ripening rice. Because it grew and ripened quickly, this rice enabled farmers to grow two or even three crops in the time it used to take to grow just one.

Chinese farmers also learned to grow new crops, such as cotton, efficiently. Workers processed cotton fiber to make clothes and other goods. The production of tea, which had been grown in China for centuries, also increased.

Agricultural surpluses helped pay taxes to the government. Merchants also traded food crops. As a result, food was abundant not just in the countryside but also in the cities. Because food was plentiful, China's population grew. During the Tang dynasty, the population had been about 60 million. During the Song dynasty, the farmers of China fed a country of nearly 100 million people. At the time, China was the largest country in the world.

READING CHECK **Identifying Cause and Effect** How did agricultural advances affect population growth?

THE IMPACT TODAY

China is still the world's most populous country. More than 1.3 billion people live there today.

Growing Rice

Rice has long been a vital crop in southern China, where the warm, wet climate is perfect for rice growing.

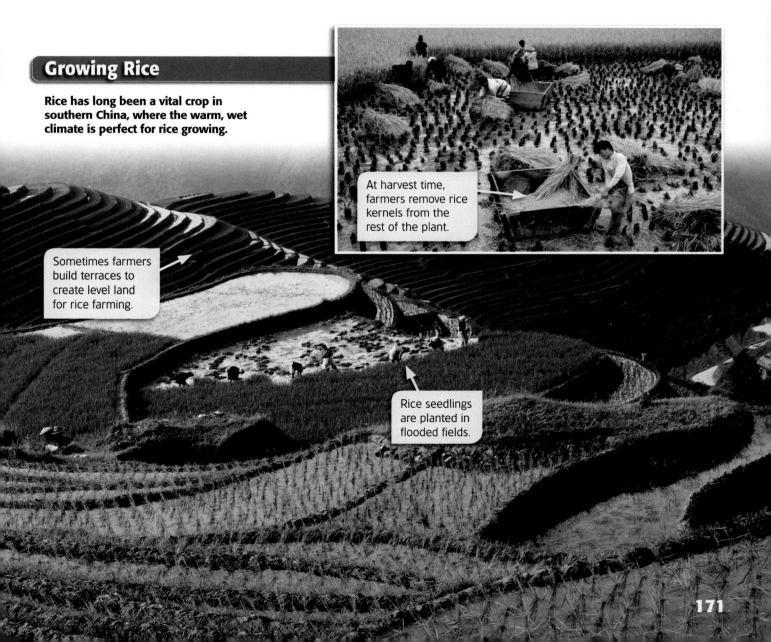

At harvest time, farmers remove rice kernels from the rest of the plant.

Sometimes farmers build terraces to create level land for rice farming.

Rice seedlings are planted in flooded fields.

Cities and Trade

Throughout the Tang and Song dynasties, much of the food grown on China's farms flowed into the growing cities and towns. China's cities were crowded, busy places. Shopkeepers, government officials, doctors, artisans, entertainers, religious leaders, and artists made them lively places as well.

City Life

FOCUS ON READING
What can you conclude about the link between Grand Canal and the growth of cities?

China's capital and largest city during the Tang dynasty was Chang'an (chahng-AHN), a huge, bustling trade center. With a population of more than a million, it was by far the largest city in the world at the time.

Chang'an, like other trading cities, had a mix of people from many cultures—China, Korea, Persia, Arabia, and Europe. It was also known as a religious and philosophical center, not just for Buddhists and Daoists but for Asian Christians as well.

Cities continued to grow under the Song. Several cities, including the northern Song capital, Kaifeng (KY-fuhng), had about a million people. A dozen more had populations of close to half a million.

Trade in China and Beyond

Trade grew along with Chinese cities. This trade, combined with China's agricultural base, made China richer than ever before.

Much trade took place within China itself. Traders used the country's rivers to ship goods on barges and ships.

The Grand Canal, a series of waterways that linked major cities, carried a huge amount of trade goods, especially farm products. Construction on the canal had begun during the Sui dynasty. During the Tang dynasty, it was improved and expanded. The Grand Canal allowed the Chinese to move goods and crops from distant agricultural areas into cities.

The Grand Canal

The Chinese also carried on trade with other lands and peoples. During the Tang dynasty, most foreign trade was over land routes leading west to India and Southwest Asia, though Chinese traders also went to Korea and Japan in the east. The Chinese exported many goods, including tea, rice, spices, and jade. However, one export was especially important—silk. So valuable was silk that the Chinese tried to keep the method of making it secret. In exchange for their exports, the Chinese imported different foods and plants, wool, glass, gold, and silver.

During the Song dynasty, maritime trade, or sea trade, became more important. China opened its Pacific ports to foreign traders. The sea-trade routes connected China to many other countries. During this time, the Chinese also developed another valuable product—a thin, beautiful type of pottery called **porcelain**.

China's Grand Canal (left) is the world's longest human-made waterway. It was built largely to transport rice and other foods from the south to feed China's cities and armies in the north. Barges like the one above crowd the Grand Canal, which is still an important transportation link in China.

All of this trade helped create a strong economy. As a result, merchants became important members of Chinese society during the Song dynasty. Also as a result of the growth of trade and wealth, the Song invented the world's first system of paper money in the 900s.

READING CHECK Summarizing How far did China's trade routes extend?

Arts and Inventions

While China grew rich economically, its cultural riches also increased. In literature, art, and science, China made huge advances.

Artists and Poets

The artists and writers of the Tang dynasty were some of China's greatest. Wu Daozi (DOW-tzee) painted murals that celebrated Buddhism and nature. Li Bo and Du Fu wrote poems that readers still enjoy for their beauty. This poem by Li Bo expresses the homesickness that one feels late at night:

" Before my bed
there is bright moonlight
So that it seems
like frost on the ground:
Lifting my head
I watch the bright moon,
Lowering my head
I dream that I'm home "
–Li Bo, "Quiet Night Thoughts"

Also noted for its literature, the Song period produced Li Qingzhao (ching-ZHOW), perhaps China's greatest female poet. She once said that the purpose of her poetry was to capture a single moment in time.

Artists of both the Tang and Song dynasties made exquisite objects in clay. Tang figurines of horses clearly show the animals' strength. Song artists made porcelain items covered in a pale green glaze called celadon (SEL-uh-duhn).

THE IMPACT TODAY
Porcelain became so popular in the West that it became known as chinaware, or just china.

Paper

Invented during the Han dynasty around 105, paper was one of the greatest of all Chinese inventions. It gave the Chinese a cheap and easy way of keeping records and made printing possible.

Porcelain

Porcelain was first made during the Tang dynasty, but it wasn't perfected for many centuries. Chinese artists were famous for their work with this fragile material.

Woodblock printing

The Chinese invented printing during the Tang dynasty, centuries before it was known in Europe. Printers could copy drawings or texts quickly, much faster than they could be copied by hand.

Gunpowder

Invented during the late Tang or early Song dynasty, gunpowder was used to make fireworks and signals. The Chinese did not generally use it as a weapon.

Movable type

Inventors of the Song dynasty created movable type, which made printing much faster. Carved letters could be rearranged and reused to print many different messages.

Magnetic compass

Invented no later than the Han period, the compass was greatly improved by the Tang. The new compass allowed sailors and merchants to travel vast distances.

Paper money

The world's first paper money was invented by the Song. Lighter and easier to handle than coins, paper money helped the Chinese manage their growing wealth.

Important Inventions

The Tang and Song dynasties produced some of the most remarkable—and most important—inventions in human history. Some of these inventions influenced events around the world.

According to legend, a man named Cai Lun invented paper in the year 105 during the Han dynasty. A later Tang invention built on Cai Lun's achievement—**woodblock printing**, a form of printing in which an entire page is carved into a block of wood. The printer applies ink to the block and presses paper against the block to create a printed page. The world's first known printed book was printed in this way in China in 868.

Another invention of the Tang dynasty was gunpowder. **Gunpowder** is a mixture of powders used in guns and explosives. It was originally used only in fireworks, but it was later used to make small bombs and rockets. Eventually, gunpowder was used to make explosives, firearms, and cannons. Gunpowder dramatically altered how wars were fought and, in doing so, changed the course of human history.

One of the most useful achievements of Tang China was the perfection of the magnetic **compass**. This instrument, which uses the earth's magnetic field to show direction, revolutionized travel. A compass made it possible to find direction more accurately than ever before. The perfection of the compass had far-reaching effects. Explorers the world over used the compass to travel vast distances. The navigators of trading ships and warships also came to rely on the compass. Thus, the compass has been a key factor in some of the most important sailing voyages in history.

The Song dynasty also produced many important inventions. Under the Song, the Chinese invented movable type. Movable type is a set of letters or characters that are

The Paper Trail

The dollar bill in your pocket may be crisp and new, but paper money has been around a long time. Paper money was printed for the first time in China in the AD 900s and was in use for about 700 years, through the Ming dynasty, when the bill shown here was printed. However, so much money was printed that it lost value. The Chinese stopped using paper money for centuries. Its use caught on in Europe, though, and eventually became common. Most countries now issue paper money.

ANALYSIS SKILL **ANALYZING INFORMATION**

What are some advantages of paper money?

used to print books. Unlike the blocks used in block printing, movable type can be rearranged and reused to create new lines of text and different pages.

The Song dynasty also introduced the concept of paper money. People were used to buying goods and services with bulky coins made of metals such as bronze, gold, and silver. Paper money was far lighter and easier to use. As trade increased and many people in China grew rich, paper money became more popular.

READING CHECK **Finding Main Ideas** What were some important inventions of the Tang and Song dynasties?

SUMMARY AND PREVIEW The Tang and Song dynasties were periods of great advancement. Many great artists and writers lived during these periods. Tang and Song inventions also had dramatic effects on world history. In the next section you will learn about the government of the Song dynasty.

---

go.hrw.com
Online Quiz
KEYWORD: SQ7 HP7

Section 2 Assessment

Reviewing Ideas, Terms, and People **HSS** 7.3.2, 7.3.5

1. **a. Recall** What advances in farming occurred during the Song dynasty?
   b. Explain How did agricultural advancements affect China's population?
2. **a. Describe** What were the capital cities of Tang and Song China like?
   b. Draw Conclusions How did geography affect trade in China?
3. **a. Identify** Who was Li Bo?
   b. Draw Conclusions How may the inventions of paper money and **woodblock printing** have been linked?
   c. Rank Which Tang or Song invention do you think was most important? Defend your answer.

Critical Thinking

4. **Categorizing** Copy the chart at right. Use it to identify facts about the Tang and Song dynasties.

	Tang Dynasty	Song Dynasty
Agriculture		
Cities		
Trade		
Art		
Inventions		

FOCUS ON WRITING

5. **Identifying Achievements** You have just read about the achievements of the Tang and Song dynasties. Make a list of those you might include in your article.

Confucianism and Government

What You Will Learn...

Main Ideas

1. Confucianism underwent changes and influenced Chinese government.
2. Scholar-officials ran China's government during the Song dynasty.

The Big Idea

Confucian thought influenced the Song government.

Key Terms

bureaucracy, *p. 178*
civil service, *p. 178*
scholar-official, *p. 178*

HSS **7.3.3** Analyze the influences of Confucianism and changes in Confucian thought during the Song and Mongol periods.

7.3.6 Describe the development of the imperial state and the scholar-official class.

If **YOU** were there...

You are a student in China in 1184. Night has fallen, but you cannot sleep. Tomorrow you have a test. It will be, you know, the most important test of your entire life. You have studied for it, not for days or weeks or even months—but for *years.* As you toss and turn, you think about how your entire life will be determined by how well you do on this one test.

How could a single test be so important?

BUILDING BACKGROUND The Song dynasty ruled China from 960 to 1279. This was a time of improvements in agriculture, growing cities, extensive trade, and the development of art and inventions. It was also a time of major changes in Chinese government.

Confucianism

The dominant philosophy in China, Confucianism is based on the teachings of Confucius. He lived more than 1,500 years before the Song dynasty. His ideas, though, had a dramatic effect on the Song system of government.

Confucian Ideas

Confucius's teachings focused on ethics, or proper behavior, for individuals and governments. He said that people should conduct their lives according to two basic principles. These principles were *ren*, or concern for others, and *li*, or appropriate behavior. Confucius argued that society would **function** best if everyone followed *ren* and *li*.

Confucius thought that everyone had a proper role to play in society. Order was maintained when people knew their place and behaved appropriately. For example, Confucius said that young people should obey their elders and that subjects should obey their rulers.

The Influence of Confucianism

After his death, Confucius's ideas were spread by his followers, but they were not widely accepted. In fact, the Qin dynasty officially suppressed Confucian ideas and teachings. By the time of the Han dynasty, Confucianism had again come into favor, and Confucianism became the official state philosophy.

During the Period of Disunion, which followed the Han dynasty, Confucianism was overshadowed by Buddhism as the major tradition in China. As you recall, many Chinese people turned to Buddhism for comfort during these troubled times. In doing so, they largely turned away from Confucian ideas and outlooks.

Later, during the Sui and early Tang dynasties, Buddhism was very influential. Unlike Confucianism, which stressed ethical behavior, Buddhism stressed a more spiritual outlook that promised escape from suffering. As Buddhism became more popular in China, Confucianism lost some of its influence.

ACADEMIC VOCABULARY
function work or perform

PHOTOGRAPH © 2004 MUSEUM OF FINE ARTS, BOSTON

In addition to ethics, Confucianism stressed the importance of education. This painting, created during the Song period, shows earlier Confucian scholars during the Period of Disunion sorting scrolls containing classic Confucian texts.

Civil Service Exams

This painting from the 1600s shows civil servants writing essays for China's emperor. Difficult exams were designed to make sure that government officials were chosen by ability—not by wealth or family connections.

Difficult Exams

- Students had to memorize entire Confucian texts.

- To pass the most difficult tests, students might study for more than 20 years!

- Some exams lasted up to 72 hours, and students were locked in private rooms while taking them.

- Some dishonest students cheated by copying Confucius's works on the inside of their clothes, paying bribes to the test graders, or paying someone else to take the test for them.

- To prevent cheating, exam halls were often locked and guarded.

Neo-Confucianism

Late in the Tang dynasty, many Chinese historians and scholars again became interested in the teachings of Confucius. Their interest was sparked by their desire to improve Chinese government and society.

During and after the Song dynasty, a new philosophy called Neo-Confucianism developed. Based on Confucianism, Neo-Confucianism was similar to the older philosophy in that it taught proper behavior. For example, Neo-Confucian scholars discussed such issues as what made human beings do bad things even if their basic nature was good. In addition, it also emphasized spiritual matters that incorporated Buddhist and Daoist concepts about the meaning of life.

Neo-Confucianism became much more appealing and influential under the Song. Later its influence grew even more. In fact, the ideas of Neo-Confucianism became official government teachings after the Song dynasty.

ACADEMIC VOCABULARY

incentive something that leads people to follow a certain course of action

READING CHECK Contrasting How did Neo-Confucianism differ from Confucianism?

Scholar-Officials

The Song dynasty took another major step that affected China for centuries. They improved the system by which people went to work for the government. These workers formed a large **bureaucracy**, or a body of unelected government officials. They joined the bureaucracy by passing civil service examinations. **Civil service** means service as a government official.

To become a civil servant, a person had to pass a series of written examinations. The examinations tested students' grasp of Confucianism and related ideas.

Because the tests were so difficult, students spent years preparing for them. Only a very small fraction of the people who took the tests would reach the top level and be appointed to a position in the government. However, candidates for the civil service examinations had a strong **incentive** for studying hard. Passing the tests meant life as a **scholar-official**—an educated member of the government.

Scholar-Officials

First rising to prominence under the Song, scholar-officials remained important in China for centuries. These scholar-officials, for example, lived during the Qing dynasty, which ruled from the mid-1600s to the early 1900s. Their typical responsibilities might include running government offices; maintaining roads, irrigation systems, and other public works; updating and maintaining official records; or collecting taxes.

Scholar-officials were elite members of society. They performed many important jobs in the government and were widely admired for their knowledge and ethics. Their benefits included considerable respect and reduced penalties for breaking the law. Many also became wealthy from gifts given by people seeking their aid.

The civil service examination system helped ensure that talented, intelligent people, including commoners, could hope to become scholar-officials. The civil service system was a major factor in the stability of the Song government.

READING CHECK **Analyzing** How did the Song dynasty change China's government?

SUMMARY AND PREVIEW During the Song period, Confucian ideas helped shape China's government. In the next section, you will read about the two dynasties that followed the Song—the Yuan and the Ming.

go.hrw.com
Online Quiz
KEYWORD: SQ7 HP7

Section 3 Assessment

Reviewing Ideas, Terms, and People **HSS** 7.3.3, 7.3.6

1. **a. Identify** What two principles did Confucius believe people should follow?
   b. Explain What was Neo-Confucianism?
   c. Elaborate Why do you think Neo-Confucianism appealed to many people?
2. **a. Define** What was a **scholar-official**?
   b. Explain Why would people want to become scholar-officials?
   c. Evaluate Do you think **civil service** examinations were a good way to choose government officials? Why or why not?

Critical Thinking

3. **Sequencing** Draw a graphic organizer like the one shown. Use it to describe the effects of Confucianism on government and the changes it went through.

Confucianism → Neo-Confucianism → Government bureaucracy

FOCUS ON WRITING

4. **Gathering Ideas about Confucianism and Government** In this section you read about Confucianism and new ideas about government. What did you learn that you could add to your list of achievements?

The Yuan and Ming Dynasties

What You Will Learn...

Main Ideas

1. The Mongol Empire included China, and the Mongols ruled China as the Yuan dynasty.
2. The Ming dynasty was a time of stability and prosperity.
3. China under the Ming saw great changes in its government and relations with other countries.

The Big Idea

The Chinese were ruled by foreigners during the Yuan dynasty, but they threw off Mongol rule and prospered during the Ming dynasty.

Key Terms and People

Genghis Khan, *p. 180*
Kublai Khan, *p. 181*
Zheng He, *p. 183*
isolationism, *p. 186*

HSS **7.3.4** Understand the importance of both overland trade and maritime expeditions between China and other civilizations in the Mongol Ascendancy and Ming Dynasty.

If **YOU** were there...

You are a farmer in northern China in 1212. As you pull weeds from a wheat field, you hear a sound like thunder. Looking toward the sound, you see hundreds—no, *thousands*—of armed horsemen on the horizon, riding straight toward you. You are frozen with fear. Only one thought fills your mind—the dreaded Mongols are coming.

What can you do to save yourself?

BUILDING BACKGROUND Throughout its history, northern China had been attacked over and over by nomadic peoples. During the Song dynasty these attacks became more frequent and threatening.

The Mongol Empire

Among the nomadic peoples who attacked the Chinese were the Mongols. For centuries, the Mongols had lived as separate tribes in the vast plains north of China. Then in 1206, a powerful leader, or khan, united them. His name was Temüjin. When he became leader, though, he was given a new title: "Universal Ruler," or **Genghis Khan** (JENG-guhs KAHN).

The Mongol Conquest

Genghis Khan organized the Mongols into a powerful army and led them on bloody expeditions of conquest. The brutality of the Mongol attacks terrorized people throughout much of Asia and Eastern Europe. Genghis Khan and his army killed all of the men, women, and children in countless cities and villages. Within 20 years, he ruled a large part of Asia.

Genghis Khan then turned his attention to China. He first led his armies into northern China in 1211. They fought their way south, wrecking whole towns and ruining farmland. By the time of Genghis Khan's death in 1227, all of northern China was under Mongol control.

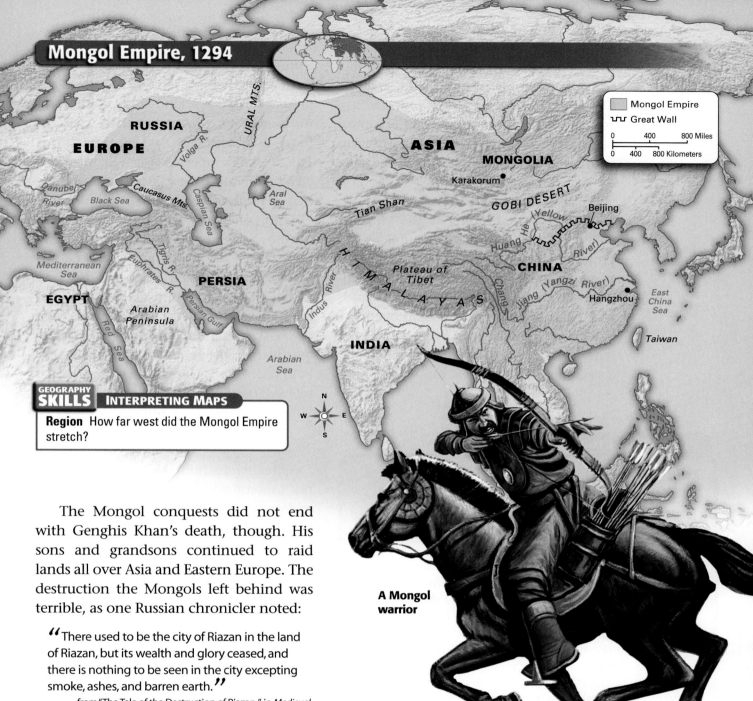

Mongol Empire, 1294

Legend:
- Mongol Empire
- Great Wall

0   400   800 Miles
0   400   800 Kilometers

Labels on map: RUSSIA, EUROPE, ASIA, MONGOLIA, Karakorum, GOBI DESERT, Beijing, URAL MTS., Volga R., Danube River, Black Sea, Caucasus Mts., Caspian Sea, Aral Sea, Tian Shan, Yellow (River), Huang He, CHINA, Mediterranean Sea, Tigris R., Euphrates R., Persian Gulf, PERSIA, Plateau of Tibet, HIMALAYAS, Chang Jiang (Yangzi River), Hangzhou, East China Sea, EGYPT, Arabian Peninsula, Red Sea, Indus River, INDIA, Arabian Sea, Taiwan

GEOGRAPHY SKILLS **INTERPRETING MAPS**

Region How far west did the Mongol Empire stretch?

A Mongol warrior

The Mongol conquests did not end with Genghis Khan's death, though. His sons and grandsons continued to raid lands all over Asia and Eastern Europe. The destruction the Mongols left behind was terrible, as one Russian chronicler noted:

"There used to be the city of Riazan in the land of Riazan, but its wealth and glory ceased, and there is nothing to be seen in the city excepting smoke, ashes, and barren earth."
–from "The Tale of the Destruction of Riazan," in *Medieval Russia's Epics, Chronicles, and Tales*, edited by Serge Zenkovsky

In 1260 Genghis Khan's grandson **Kublai Khan** (KOO-bluh KAHN) became ruler of the Mongol Empire. He completed the conquest of China and in 1279 declared himself emperor of China. This began the Yuan dynasty, a period that some people also call the Mongol Ascendancy. For the first time in its long history, foreigners ruled all of China.

Life in Yuan China

Kublai Khan and the Mongol rulers he led belonged to a different ethnic group than the Chinese did. They spoke a different language, worshipped different gods, wore different clothing, and had different customs. The Chinese resented being ruled by these foreigners, whom they saw as rude and uncivilized.

However, Kublai Khan did not force the Chinese to accept Mongol ways of life. Some Mongols even adopted aspects of the Chinese culture, such as Confucianism. Still, the Mongols made sure to keep control of the Chinese. They prohibited Confucian scholars from gaining too much power in the government, for example. The Mongols also placed heavy taxes on the Chinese.

Much of the tax money the Mongols collected went to pay for vast public-works projects. These projects required the labor of many Chinese people. The Yuan extended the Grand Canal and built new roads and palaces. Workers also improved the roads that were part of China's postal system. In addition, the Yuan emperors built a new capital, Dadu, near modern Beijing.

Mongol soldiers were sent throughout China to keep the peace as well as to keep a close watch on the Chinese. The soldiers' presence kept overland trade routes safe for merchants. Sea trade between China, India, and Southeast Asia continued, too. The Mongol emperors also welcomed foreign traders at Chinese ports. Some of these traders received special privileges.

Part of what we know about life in the Yuan dynasty comes from one such trader, an Italian merchant named Marco Polo. Between 1271 and 1295 he traveled in and around China. Polo was highly respected by the Mongols and even served in Kublai Khan's court. When Polo returned to Europe, he wrote of his travels. Polo's descriptions of China fascinated many Europeans. His book sparked much European interest in China.

The End of the Yuan Dynasty

Despite their vast empire, the Mongols were not content with their lands. They decided to invade Japan. A Mongol army sailed to Japan in 1274 and 1281. The campaigns, however, were disastrous. Violent storms and fierce defenders destroyed most of the Mongol force.

The failed campaigns against Japan weakened the Mongol military. The huge, expensive public-works projects had already weakened the economy. These weaknesses, combined with Chinese resentment, made China ripe for rebellion.

In the 1300s many Chinese groups rebelled against the Yuan dynasty. In 1368 a former monk named Zhu Yuanzhang (JOO yoo-ahn-JAHNG) took charge of a rebel army. He led this army in a final victory over the Mongols. China was once again ruled by the Chinese.

READING CHECK Finding Main Ideas How did the Mongols come to rule China?

Primary Source

BOOK
A Chinese City

In this passage Marco Polo describes his visit to Hangzhou (HAHNG-JOH), a city in southeastern China.

❝Inside the city there is a Lake . . . and all round it are erected [built] beautiful palaces and mansions, of the richest and most exquisite [finest] structure that you can imagine . . . In the middle of the Lake are two Islands, on each of which stands a rich, beautiful and spacious edifice [building], furnished in such style as to seem fit for the palace of an Emperor. And when any one of the citizens desired to hold a marriage feast, or to give any other entertainment, it used to be done at one of these palaces. And everything would be found there ready to order, such as silver plate, trenchers [platters], and dishes, napkins and table-cloths, and whatever else was needful. The King made this provision for the gratification [enjoyment] of his people, and the place was open to every one who desired to give an entertainment.❞

–Marco Polo, from *Description of the World*

ANALYSIS SKILL **ANALYZING PRIMARY SOURCES**

From this description, what impression might Europeans have of Hangzhou?

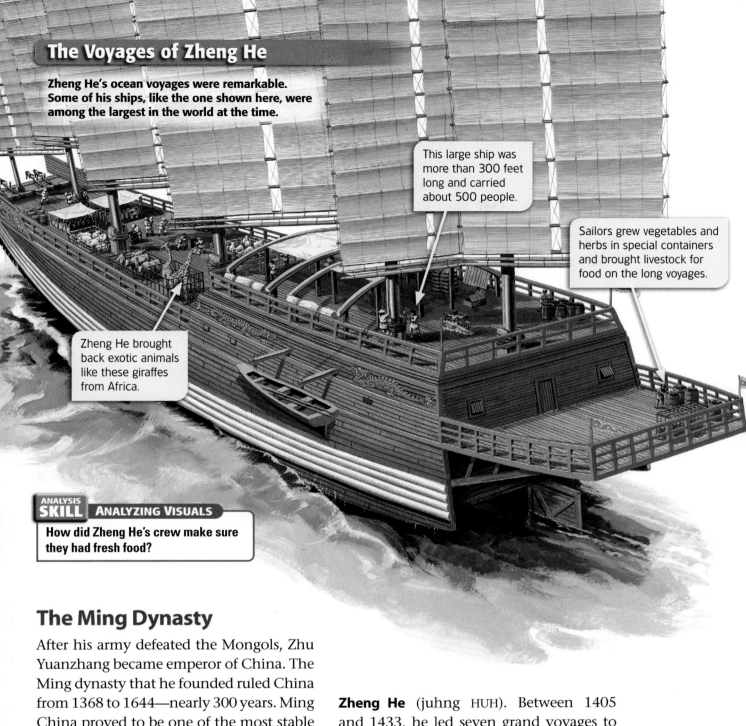

The Voyages of Zheng He

Zheng He's ocean voyages were remarkable. Some of his ships, like the one shown here, were among the largest in the world at the time.

This large ship was more than 300 feet long and carried about 500 people.

Sailors grew vegetables and herbs in special containers and brought livestock for food on the long voyages.

Zheng He brought back exotic animals like these giraffes from Africa.

ANALYSIS SKILL **ANALYZING VISUALS**

How did Zheng He's crew make sure they had fresh food?

The Ming Dynasty

After his army defeated the Mongols, Zhu Yuanzhang became emperor of China. The Ming dynasty that he founded ruled China from 1368 to 1644—nearly 300 years. Ming China proved to be one of the most stable and prosperous times in Chinese history. The Ming expanded China's fame overseas and sponsored incredible building projects across China.

Great Sea Voyages

During the Ming dynasty, the Chinese improved their ships and their sailing skills. The greatest sailor of the period was

Zheng He (juhng HUH). Between 1405 and 1433, he led seven grand voyages to places around Asia. Zheng He's fleets were huge. One included more than 60 ships and 25,000 sailors. Some of the ships were gigantic too, perhaps more than 300 feet long. That is longer than a football field!

In the course of his voyages Zheng He sailed his fleet throughout the Indian Ocean. He sailed as far west as the Persian Gulf and the easternmost coast of Africa.

Everywhere his ships landed, Zheng He presented leaders with beautiful gifts from China. He boasted about his country and encouraged foreign leaders to send gifts to China's emperor. From one voyage, Zheng He returned to China with representatives of some 30 nations, sent by their leaders to honor the emperor. He also brought goods and stories back to China.

Zheng He's voyages rank among the most impressive in the history of seafaring. Although they did not lead to the creation of new trade routes or the exploration of new lands, they served as a clear sign of China's power.

Great Building Projects

The Ming were also known for their grand building projects. Many of these projects were designed to impress both the Chinese people and their enemies to the north.

In Beijing, for example, Ming emperors built the Forbidden City. This amazing palace complex included hundreds of imperial residences, temples, and other government buildings. Within the buildings were some 9,000 rooms. The name "Forbidden City" came from the fact that the common people were not even allowed to enter the complex. For centuries, this city within a city was a symbol of China's glory.

The Forbidden City

The Forbidden City is not actually a city. It's a huge complex of almost 1,000 buildings in the heart of China's capital. The Forbidden City was built for the emperor, his family, his court, and his servants, and ordinary people were forbidden from entering.

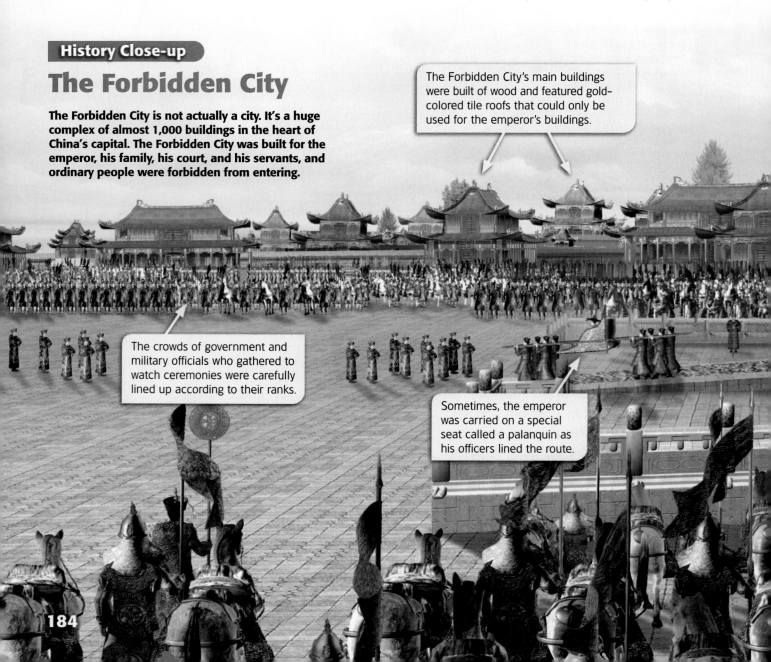

The Forbidden City's main buildings were built of wood and featured gold-colored tile roofs that could only be used for the emperor's buildings.

The crowds of government and military officials who gathered to watch ceremonies were carefully lined up according to their ranks.

Sometimes, the emperor was carried on a special seat called a palanquin as his officers lined the route.

Ming rulers also directed the restoration of the famous Great Wall of China. Large numbers of soldiers and peasants worked to rebuild collapsed portions of walls, connect existing walls, and build new ones. The result was a construction feat unmatched in history. The wall was more than 2,000 miles long. It would reach from San Diego to New York! The wall was about 25 feet high and, at the top, 12 feet wide. Protected by the wall—and the soldiers who stood guard along it—the Chinese people felt safe from invasions by the northern tribes.

READING CHECK **Generalizing** In what ways did the Ming dynasty strengthen China?

China Under the Ming

During the Ming dynasty, Chinese society began to change. This change was largely due to the efforts of the Ming emperors. Having expelled the Mongols, the Ming emperors worked to eliminate all foreign influences from Chinese society. As a result, China's government and relations with other countries changed dramatically.

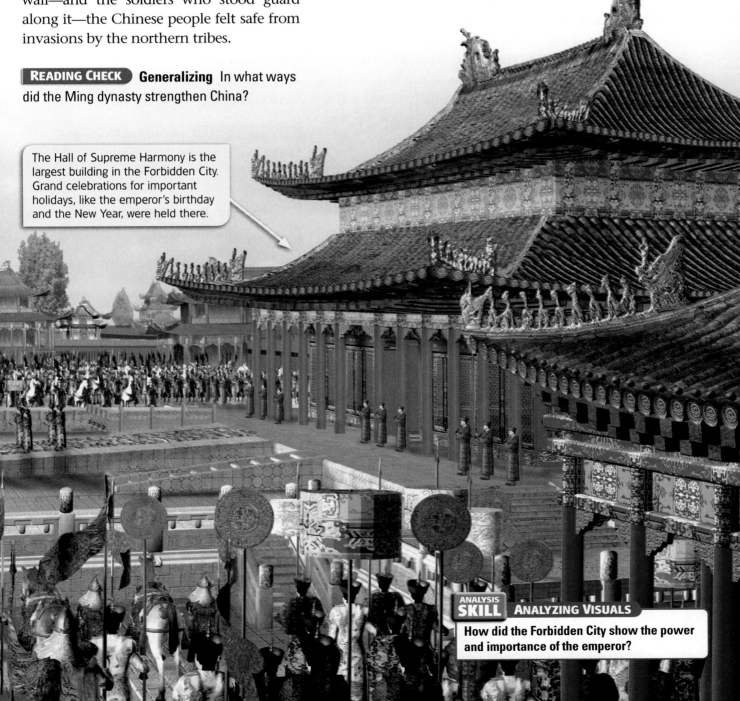

The Hall of Supreme Harmony is the largest building in the Forbidden City. Grand celebrations for important holidays, like the emperor's birthday and the New Year, were held there.

ANALYSIS SKILL **ANALYZING VISUALS**
How did the Forbidden City show the power and importance of the emperor?

185

Government

When the Ming took over China, they adopted many government programs that had been created by the Tang and the Song. However, the Ming emperors were much more powerful than the Tang and Song emperors had been. They abolished the offices of some powerful officials and took a larger role in running the government themselves. These emperors fiercely protected their power, and they punished anyone whom they saw as challenging their authority.

Despite their personal power, though, the Ming did not disband the civil service system. Because he personally oversaw the entire government, the emperor needed officials to keep his affairs organized.

The Ming also used examinations to appoint censors. These officials were sent throughout China to investigate the behavior of local leaders and to judge the quality of schools and other institutions. Censors had existed for many years in China, but under the Ming their power and influence grew.

ACADEMIC VOCABULARY
consequences effects of a particular event or events

Relations with Other Countries

In the 1430s a new Ming emperor made Zheng He return to China and dismantle his fleet. At the same time, he banned foreign trade. China entered a period of isolationism. **Isolationism** is a policy of avoiding contact with other countries.

In the end, this isolationism had great **consequences** for China. In 1644 the Ming dynasty was overthrown. By the late 1800s the Western world had made huge leaps in technological progress. Westerners were then able to gain influence in Chinese affairs. Partly due to its isolation and lack of progress, China was too weak to stop them.

READING CHECK **Identifying Cause and Effect** How did isolationism affect China?

SUMMARY AND PREVIEW Under the Yuan and Ming dynasties, Chinese society changed. Eventually, the Ming began a policy of isolationism. In the next chapter you will read about Japan, another country that was isolated at times.

go.hrw.com
Online Quiz
KEYWORD: SQ7 HP7

Section 4 Assessment

Reviewing Ideas, Terms, and People HSS 7.3.4

1. **a. Identify** Who was **Genghis Khan**?
   b. Explain How did the Mongols gain control of China?
   c. Evaluate Judge this statement: "The Mongols should never have tried to invade Japan."
2. **a. Identify** Who was **Zheng He**, and what did he do?
   b. Analyze What impression do you think the Forbidden City had on the residents of Beijing?
   c. Draw Conclusions How may the Great Wall have both helped and hurt China?
3. **a. Define** What is **isolationism**?
   b. Explain How did the Ming change China?
   c. Develop How might a policy of isolationism have both advantages and disadvantages?

Critical Thinking

4. **Categorizing** Draw a graphic organizer like the one below. Use it to identify key facts about China under the Yuan and Ming dynasties.

Yuan Dynasty	Ming Dynasty

FOCUS ON WRITING

5. **Identifying Achievements of the Later Dynasties** Make a list of the achievements of the Yuan and Ming dynasties. Then look back over all your notes and rate the achievements or inventions. Which three do you think are the most important?

Kublai Khan

How did a Mongol nomad settle down to rule a vast empire?

When did he live? 1215–1294

Where did he live? Kublai came from Mongolia but spent much of his life in China. His capital, Dadu, was near the modern city of Beijing.

What did he do? Kublai Khan completed the conquest of China that Genghis Khan had begun. He ruled China as the emperor of the Yuan dynasty.

Why is he important? The lands Kublai Khan ruled made up one of the largest empires in world history. It stretched from the Pacific Ocean to Eastern Europe. As China's ruler Kublai Khan welcomed foreign visitors, including the Italian merchant Marco Polo and the Arab historian Ibn Battutah. The stories these two men told helped create interest in China and its products among Westerners.

Generalizing How did Kublai Khan's actions help change people's views of China?

KEY FACTS

- Unified all of China under his rule
- Established peace, during which China's population grew
- Extended the Grand Canal so that food could be shipped from the Huang He (Yellow River) to his capital near modern Beijing
- Linked China to India and Persia with better roads
- Increased contact with the West

This painting from the 1200s shows Kublai Khan hunting on horseback.

187

The Great Wall

The Great Wall of China is one of the longest structures ever built. It stretches for many miles across China's northern lands. Along the way, the Great Wall crosses mountains, deserts, plains, and valleys.

Why did the Chinese build such a gigantic wall? The answer is for defense. For centuries, the people of China had been attacked by nomadic horsemen from Mongolia and other lands to the north. The Great Wall was built to keep these invaders—and their horses—out.

Great Facts about The Great Wall

- Parts of the Great Wall have been built and rebuilt for more than 2,000 years. Most of the wall that stands today was built during the Ming dynasty (1368–1644).

- The Great Wall was also used for communication. Soldiers marched along the wall, and guards used smoke signals and torches to send messages along it.

- Many people died building the Great Wall. Some historians estimate that as many as 8 million people died working on the wall over the years.

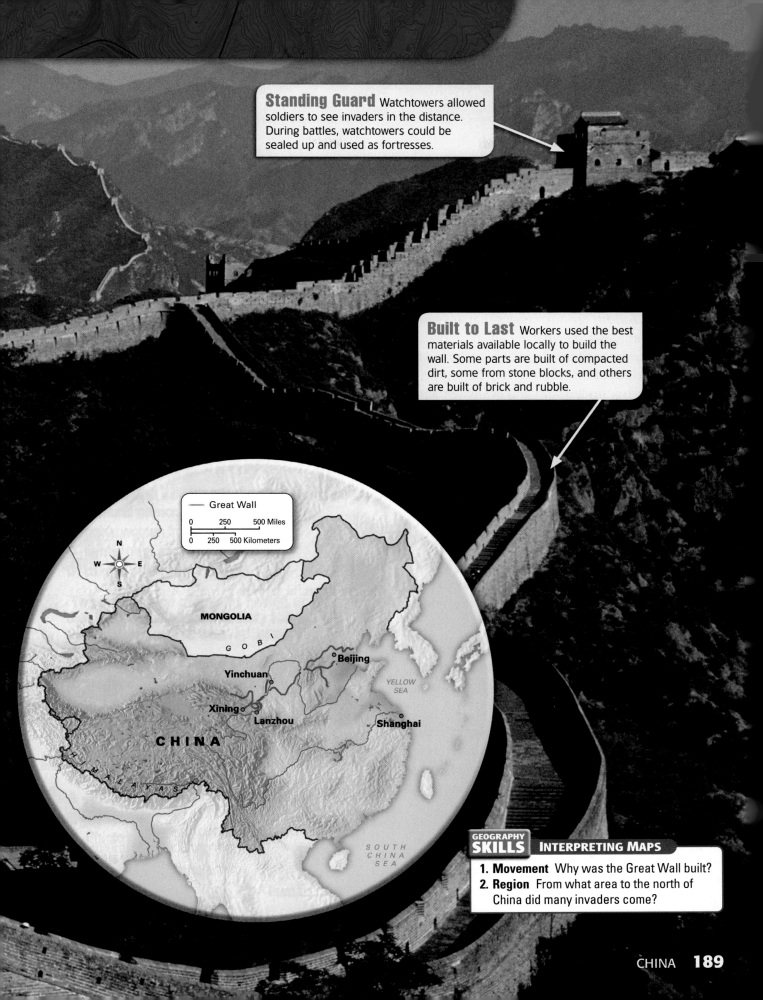

Standing Guard Watchtowers allowed soldiers to see invaders in the distance. During battles, watchtowers could be sealed up and used as fortresses.

Built to Last Workers used the best materials available locally to build the wall. Some parts are built of compacted dirt, some from stone blocks, and others are built of brick and rubble.

Great Wall

0   250   500 Miles
0 250 500 Kilometers

MONGOLIA

G O B I

Beijing

Yinchuan

YELLOW SEA

Xining

Lanzhou

Shanghai

C H I N A

HIMALAYAS

SOUTH CHINA SEA

GEOGRAPHY SKILLS | **INTERPRETING MAPS**

1. **Movement** Why was the Great Wall built?
2. **Region** From what area to the north of China did many invaders come?

Social Studies Skills

Analysis | **Critical Thinking** | **Participation** | **Study**

Analyzing Benefits and Costs

Understand the Skill

Every action we take has both benefits and costs attached to it. This was as true of people in the past as it is today. *Benefits* are advantages that are gained from an action. *Costs* are what are given up or sacrificed in order to obtain benefits. Analyzing the benefits and costs of developments in history will help you to better understand and evaluate them.

Cost-benefit analysis is also a valuable life skill. Weighing an action's benefits against its costs can help you decide whether to take the action.

Learn the Skill

Follow these steps to conduct a simple cost-benefit analysis of a historical development or event.

1 Determine what the people who took the action hoped to accomplish. This will help you decide which effects of the action were benefits and which were costs.

2 Look for positive or successful results of the action. These are its benefits. Remember that benefits can be more than just the goals of an action. Unexpected gains are benefits too.

3 Consider the negative or unsuccessful effects of the action or development. In addition, think about what positive things would have happened if the development had *not* taken place. These things are also part of its costs.

4 Make a chart of the costs and benefits. By comparing the list of benefits to the list of costs, you can better understand the development or action and evaluate its overall merits.

For example, an analysis of a public works program under the Sui dynasty might produce a chart like this one.

Benefits	Costs
System of canals	Drain on China's human resources
Roadways linking communities	Drain on China's financial resources
Reinforcing of the Great Wall	Fall of the Sui dynasty
Jobs for peasants	
Unification of China	

This chart shows more benefits than costs. However, in evaluating the program, you must also consider what the Sui hoped to accomplish. If they wanted to make the dynasty popular, they failed. If it was to improve transportation in China, this cost-benefit analysis shows that they were successful.

Practice and Apply the Skill

Apply the guidelines above and information from the chapter to conduct a cost-benefit analysis of the Song or Tang dynasty. Compile a chart similar to the one above. Then use your chart to write an evaluation of the dynasty you analyzed.

Visual Summary

Use the visual summary below to help you review the main ideas of the chapter.

QUICK FACTS

China was reunified, and Buddhism spread during the Sui and Tang dynasties.

Farming and trade grew under the Tang and Song dynasties.

Confucian thought influenced Chinese government and education.

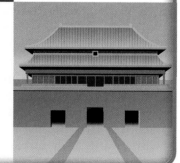

The powerful Yuan and Ming dynasties strengthened China and expanded trade, but then China became isolated.

Reviewing Vocabulary, Terms, and People

Match the words or names with their definitions or descriptions.

a. Kublai Khan   **g.** compass

b. movable type   **h.** porcelain

c. scholar-official   **i.** Genghis Khan

d. Empress Wu   **j.** isolationism

e. bureaucracy   **k.** incentive

f. Zheng He   **l.** gunpowder

1. ruthless but effective Tang dynasty ruler
2. a set of letters or characters that can be moved to create different lines of text
3. leader who united the Mongols and began invasion of China
4. body of unelected government officials
5. thin, beautiful pottery
6. a device that indicates direction
7. policy of avoiding contact with other countries
8. founder of the Yuan dynasty
9. a mixture of powders used in explosives
10. commanded huge fleets of ships
11. educated government worker
12. something that leads people to follow a certain course of action

Comprehension and Critical Thinking

SECTION 1 *(Pages 166–169)* **HSS** 7.3.1

13. **a.** **Identify** What period did China enter after the Han dynasty collapsed? What dynasty brought an end to this period?

    b. **Analyze** Why is the Tang dynasty considered a golden age of Chinese civilization?

    c. **Predict** How might Chinese culture have been different in the Tang and Song dynasties if Buddhism had not been introduced to China?

SECTION 2 (Pages 170–175) [HSS] 7.3.2, 7.3.5

14. a. Describe What did Wu Daozi, Li Bo, Du Fu, and Li Qingzhao contribute to Chinese culture?

b. Analyze What led to the growth of cities in China? What were China's cities like during the Tang and Song dynasties?

c. Evaluate Which Chinese invention has had a greater effect on world history—the magnetic compass or gunpowder? Why do you think so?

SECTION 3 (Pages 176–179) [HSS] 7.3.3, 7.3.6

15. a. Define What is Confucianism? How did it change during and after the Song dynasty?

b. Make Inferences Why do you think the civil service examination system was created?

c. Elaborate Why were China's civil service examinations so difficult?

SECTION 4 (Pages 180–186) [HSS] 7.3.4

16. a. Describe How did the Mongols create their huge empire? What areas were included in it?

b. Draw Conclusions How did Marco Polo and Zheng He help shape ideas about China?

c. Elaborate Why do you think the Ming emperors spent so much time and money rebuilding and enlarging the Great Wall?

Using the Internet

go.hrw.com
KEYWORD: SQ7 WH7

17. Activity: Creating a Mural The Tang and Song periods saw many agricultural, technological, and commercial developments. New irrigation techniques, movable type, and gunpowder were a few of them. Enter the activity keyword and learn more about such developments. Imagine that a city official has hired you to create a mural showing all of the great things the Chinese developed during the Tang and Song dynasties. Create a large mural that depicts as many advances as possible.

Reviewing Themes

18. Science and Technology How did Chinese inventions alter the course of world history?

19. Economics How did the strong agricultural and trading economy of Tang and Song China affect the country?

Reading Skills

20. Drawing Conclusions Read the statements about the Ming below. For each conclusion that follows, decide whether the statements provide sufficent evidence to justify the conclusion.

> The Ming ruled China from 1368 to 1644.
>
> Zhu Yuanzhang was a Ming emperor.
>
> The Great Wall was rebuilt by the Ming.

a. The Great Wall is located in China.

b. Zhu Yuanzhang was a good emperor.

c. Zhu Yuanzhang ruled sometime between 1368 and 1644.

d. Zhu Yuanzhang rebuilt the Great Wall.

Social Studies Skills

21. Analyzing Costs and Benefits Analyze the costs and benefits of the Chinese emperor's decision to isolate his country. To help with your analysis, create a chart like the one below. In the left column, list the plan's costs—factors that will hurt China's economy. In the right column, list its benefits—factors that will help the economy. Once you have completed your chart, decide whether the emperor's decision was a good idea or a bad idea. Support your answer.

Costs	Benefits

FOCUS ON WRITING

22. Writing a Magazine Article Now that you have identified three achievements or inventions you want to write about, begin your article. Open with a sentence that states your main idea. Include two or three sentences about each achievement or invention you have chosen. These sentences should describe the achievement or invention and explain why it was so important. End your article with a sentence or two summarizing China's importance to the world.

Standards Assessment

DIRECTIONS: Read each question, and write the letter of the best response.

1

This object displays Chinese expertise at working with

A woodblocks.

B gunpowder.

C cotton fibers.

D porcelain.

2 Trade and other contact with peoples far from China stopped under which dynasty?

A Ming

B Yuan

C Song

D Sui

3 Which of the following was *not* a way that Confucianism influenced China?

A emphasis on family and family values

B expansion of manufacturing and trade

C emphasis on service to society

D well-educated government officials

4 What was a major cause for the spread of Buddhism to China and other parts of Asia?

A the teachings of Kublai Khan

B the writings of Confucius

C the travels of Buddhist missionaries

D the support of Empress Wu

5 All of the following flourished during *both* the Tang and the Song dynasties, *except*

A art and culture.

B sea voyages of exploration.

C science and technology.

D trade.

Connecting with Past Learnings

6 In Grade 6, you learned about the deeds of emperor Shi Huangdi. He had laborers work on a structure that Ming rulers improved. What was that structure?

A the Great Wall

B the Great Tomb

C the Forbidden City

D the Temple of Buddha

7 In Grade 6, you learned that the ancient Egyptians increased food production by digging irrigation canals to water their fields. Under which dynasty did the Chinese develop new irrigation techniques to increase their production of food?

A Han

B Ming

C Song

D Sui

Japan

California Standards

History–Social Science

7.5 Students analyze the geographic, political, economic, religious, and social structures of the civilizations of Medieval Japan.

English–Language Arts

Writing 7.1.2 Support all statements and claims with anecdotes, descriptions, facts and statistics, and specific examples.

Reading 7.2.6 Assess the adequacy, accuracy, and appropriateness of the author's evidence to support claims and assertions, noting instances of bias and stereotyping.

FOCUS ON WRITING

Writing a Travel Brochure You've been hired to create a travel brochure called "Japan's Rich History." Your brochure will describe tourist attractions in Japan that show the country's fascinating past. As you read this chapter, think about how you might encourage people to visit Japan.

CHAPTER EVENTS

c. 550 Buddhism is introduced into Japan.

550

WORLD EVENTS

632–661 Arab armies conquer Southwest Asia.

HOLT

History's Impact

▶ **video series**
Watch the video to understand the impact of the samurai tradition on Japan today.

What You Will Learn...

In this chapter, you will learn about the geography and history of early Japan. This photo shows Mount Fuji, a snow-covered **volcano** that has long been a symbol of Japan.

c. 1000
Lady Murasaki Shikibu writes *The Tale of Genji*.

1192
The first shogun rules Japan.

1603–1868
The Tokugawa shoguns rule Japan.

825

1100

1375

1650

768–814
Charlemagne rules much of western Europe.

1279
The Mongols take over China.

1588
England defeats the Spanish Armada.

195

Reading Social Studies

by Kylene Beers

Economics	Geography	Politics	Religion	Society and Culture	Science and Technology

Focus on Themes As you read this chapter, you will step into the world of early Japan. You will learn about the first Japanese people and their religion, Shinto, and about how the people of Korea and China began to influence the growth of Japanese culture. As you read about the history of Japan, you will learn how the development of their **politics** not only affected the laws of the land but also shaped the **society and culture** of the people.

Stereotypes and Bias in History

Focus on Reading Historians today try to be impartial in their writing. They don't let their personal feelings affect what they write.

Writers in the past, however, didn't always feel the need to be impartial. Their writings were sometimes colored by their attitudes about other people, places, and ideas.

Identifying Stereotypes and Bias Two ways in which writing can be colored by the author's ideas are stereotypes and bias. A **stereotype** is a generalization about whole groups of people. **Bias** is an attitude that one group is superior to another. The examples below can help you identify stereotypes and bias in the things you read.

Stereotypes suggest that all members of a group act, think, or feel the same.

Stereotypes can often hurt or offend members of a group.

Some stereotypes encourage the reader to think about a group in a certain way.

Examples of Stereotypes

- Japanese people are hardworking, dedicated, and proud of their history.
- Japanese daimyo were selfish, greedy rulers who didn't care about anyone but themselves.
- Japan's early emperors were wise men who deserved to rule the country.

Examples of Bias

- The Japanese culture is far superior to other cultures that developed in Asia.
- Personally, I think that the Japanese created the best form of government in all of history.
- Compared to the Japanese, the Koreans were weak and culturally backward.

A biased statement obviously favors one person or group over another.

Bias is based on the author's opinions, not facts.

Bias is often the result of an author's dislike of a particular group.

Additional reading support can be found in the

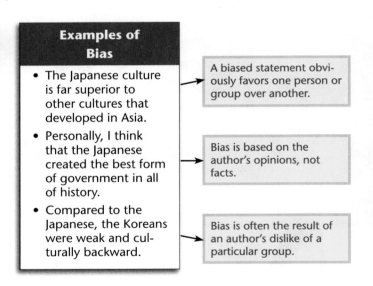

Inter~active Reader and Study Guide

ELA **Reading 7.2.6** Assess the adequacy, accuracy, and appropriateness of the author's evidence to support claims and assertions, noting instances of bias and stereotyping.

You Try It!

The following passage is taken from the journal of a noble woman who lived in Japan in the 1000s. As you read the passage, look for signs of stereotypes and bias in her writing.

The Pillow Book

Often the common people who come to Hasadera show a gross lack of respect for the better sort of visitors, lining up in front of one's pew so close that they brush one with the tails of their coats . . . impatient to gaze at last upon the glorious countenance [face] of Buddha, it is exasperating to find my view barred by a parcel of common white-robed priests and country-people, swarming like caterpillars, who plant themselves there without the slightest regard for those behind them. Often, while they were performing their prostrations [bows], I have come near to rolling them over sideways!

–Sei Shonagon, *The Pillow Book,*
translated by Arthur Waley

Review the graphic organizer on the previous page. Then answer the following questions about the passage you just read.

1. Does the author show a bias in favor of one group within Japanese society?

2. What opinion of Japan's common people does the first sentence of the passage suggest the author holds?

3. What stereotypes about non-nobles did the author include in her writing?

4. How do you think a Japanese priest or country person would feel about this passage? Why?

Key Terms and People

Chapter 8

Academic Vocabulary

Success in school is related to knowing academic vocabulary—the words that are frequently used in school assignments and discussions. In this chapter, you will learn the following academic words:

As you read Chapter 8, notice how the authors of this book have avoided making stereotypes about the Japanese people.

Geography and Early Japan

What You Will Learn...

Main Ideas

1. Geography shaped life in Japan.
2. Early Japanese society was organized in clans, which came to be ruled by an emperor.
3. Japan learned about language, society, and government from China and Korea.

The Big Idea

Japan's early societies were both isolated from and influenced by China and Korea.

Key Terms and People

clans, *p. 200*
Shinto, *p. 200*
Prince Shotoku, *p. 202*
regent, *p. 202*

HSS 7.5.1 Describe the significance of Japan's proximity to China and Korea and the intellectual, linguistic, religious, and philosophical influence of those countries on Japan.

7.5.2 Discuss the reign of Prince Shotoku of Japan and the characteristics of Japanese society and family life during his reign.

If YOU were there...

You live in a small farming village on one of the islands of Japan. You're very happy with your life. The sea is nearby and food is plentiful. You have a large, extended family to protect and take care of you. Your grandmother says that life in your village has not changed for hundreds of years, and that is good. But now you have heard that some people from across the sea are coming to your village. They are bringing new ideas and new ways of doing things.

How do you feel about these changes?

BUILDING BACKGROUND Japan is a large group of islands located east of the Asian mainland. Life in Japan has always been influenced by many factors. The islands' geography and location shaped how people lived there, and as you read above, visitors from other lands also affected Japanese society.

Geography Shapes Life in Japan

The islands of Japan are really just the tops of undersea mountains and volcanoes, sticking up out of the ocean. Those mountains, as you can see on the map, cover nearly all of Japan. Only about 20 percent of the land is flat. Because it is difficult to live and farm on mountain slopes, most Japanese people have always lived in those flat areas, the coastal plains.

In addition to the mountains and the lack of flat land, the nearness of the sea shaped the lives of Japanese people. Their homes were never far from the sea. Naturally, they turned to the sea for food. They learned to prepare all kinds of seafood, from eel to shark to octopus to seaweed. As a result, seafood has been a key part of the Japanese diet for thousands of years.

The islands' location affected the Japanese people in another way as well. Because they lived on islands, the Japanese were separated from the other people of Asia. This separation allowed

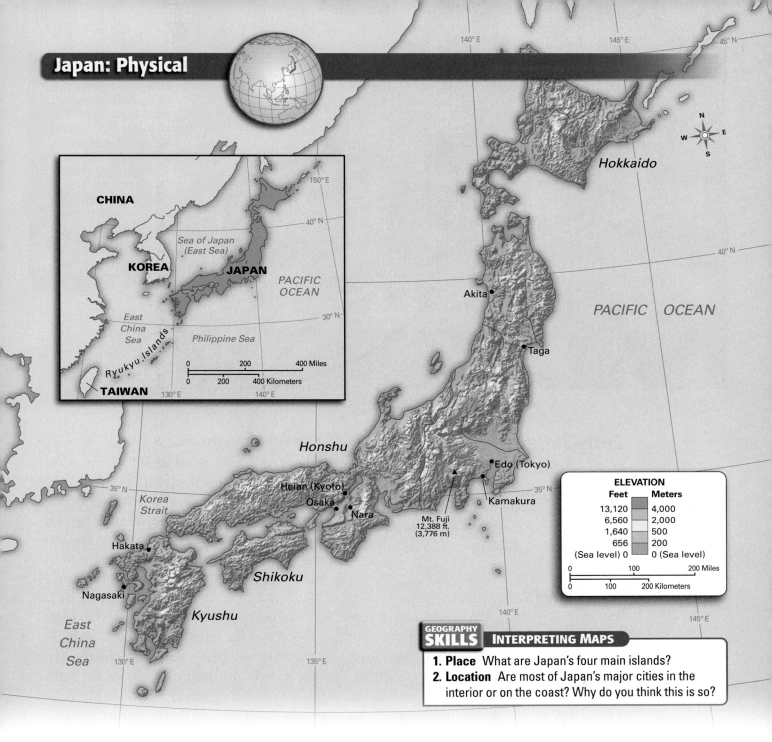

CHINA

Sea of Japan
(East Sea)

KOREA   JAPAN

PACIFIC
OCEAN

East
China
Sea

Philippine Sea

Ryukyu Islands

TAIWAN

Hokkaido

Akita

PACIFIC   OCEAN

Taga

Honshu

Edo (Tokyo)

Heian (Kyoto)

Osaka

Nara

Kamakura

Mt. Fuji
12,388 ft.
(3,776 m)

ELEVATION

Feet		Meters
13,120		4,000
6,560		2,000
1,640		500
656		200
(Sea level) 0		0 (Sea level)

0   100   200 Miles

0   100   200 Kilometers

Korea
Strait

Hakata

Shikoku

Nagasaki

East
China
Sea

Kyushu

0   200   400 Miles

0   200   400 Kilometers

GEOGRAPHY SKILLS | **INTERPRETING MAPS**

1. **Place** What are Japan's four main islands?
2. **Location** Are most of Japan's major cities in the interior or on the coast? Why do you think this is so?

the Japanese to develop their own culture. For example, they created a religion and a social **structure** very different from those in other parts of Asia. This separation has always been an important part of Japanese society.

Japan isn't totally isolated, however. Look at the inset map above to find Korea and China. As you can see, neither country is very far from the Japanese islands. Korea is only about 100 miles away from Japan. China is about 400 miles away. Those short distances allowed the older Korean and Chinese cultures to influence the new culture of Japan.

READING CHECK **Summarizing** What is Japan's geography like?

ACADEMIC VOCABULARY

structure the way something is set up or organized

A Shinto Shrine
Entering a Shinto shrine, these people walk through a gate called a torii (TOR-ee). The torii marks the boundary of a shrine or other sacred Shinto site. Over time, the torii has become a symbol of Shinto, Japan's ancient religion.

What elements of nature can you see in this painting?

Early Japanese Society

Korea and China did play a major part in shaping Japanese society, but not at first. Early Japan was home to two different cultures, neither of which had any contact with the rest of Asia.

The Ainu

One culture that developed in Japan was the Ainu (EYE-noo). Historians aren't sure exactly when or how the Ainu moved to Japan. Some people think they came from what is now Siberia in eastern Russia. Wherever they came from, the Ainu spoke a language unlike any other language in eastern Asia. They also looked different from the other people of Japan.

Over time, the Ainu began to fight with other people for land. They lost most of these fights, and so they lost their land as well. Eventually the Ainu were driven back onto a single island, Hokkaido. Over time the Ainu culture almost disappeared. Many people gave up the Ainu language and adopted new customs.

THE IMPACT TODAY
Few Ainu remain in Japan today, and most of them live on Hokkaido.

The First Japanese

The people who lived south of the Ainu eventually became the Japanese. They lived mostly in small farming villages. These villages were ruled by powerful **clans**, or extended families. Other people in the village, including farmers and workers, had to obey and respect members of these clans.

At the head of each clan was a chief. In addition to his political power, each chief also had religious duties. The Japanese believed that their clan chiefs were descended from nature spirits called *kami* (KAH-mee). Clan chiefs led their clans in rituals that honored their *kami* ancestors.

Over time, these rituals became a central part of the traditional religion of Japan, **Shinto**. According to Shinto teachings, everything in nature—the sun, the moon, trees, waterfalls, and animals—has *kami*. Shintoists believe that some *kami* help people live and keep them from harm. They build shrines to *kami* and perform ceremonies in which they ask the *kami* to bless them.

The First Emperors

The clans of early Japan weren't all equal. Some clans were larger and more powerful than others. In time a few of these powerful clans built up armies and set out to conquer their neighbors.

One clan that gained power in this way lived in the Yamato region, the western part of Japan's largest island, Honshu. In addition to military might, the Yamato rulers claimed to have a glorious family history. They believed they were descended from the most powerful of all *kami*, the goddess of the sun.

By the 500s the Yamato rulers had extended their control over much of Honshu. Although they didn't control the whole country, the leaders of the Yamato clan began to call themselves the emperors of all Japan.

READING CHECK Sequencing How did emperors take power in Japan?

Japan Learns from China and Korea

Early Japanese society received very little influence from cultures on the Asian mainland. Occasionally, officials from China, Korea, or other parts of Asia visited Japan. For the most part, however, these visits didn't have a great impact on the Japanese way of life.

By the mid-500s, though, some Japanese leaders thought that Japan could learn a great deal from other cultures. In particular, they wanted to learn more about the cultures of China and Korea.

To learn what they wanted to know, the rulers of Japan decided to send representatives to China and Korea to gather information about their cultures. They also invited people from China and Korea to move to Japan. The emperors hoped that these people could teach the Japanese new ways of working and thinking.

Influences from China and Korea

QUICK FACTS

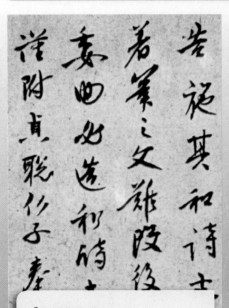

Language
The earliest Japanese writing used Chinese characters.

Philosophy
The ideas of the Chinese philosopher Confucius helped shape Japanese culture and family life.

THE GRANGER COLLECTION, NEW YORK

Religion
Buddhism came to Japan from Korea.

Changes in Language

One of the first things the Japanese learned from China and Korea was language. The early Japanese didn't have a written language. Therefore, many learned to write in Chinese. They continued to speak in Japanese, however, which is very different from Chinese. It wasn't until about 200 years later that people devised a way of writing in Japanese. They used Chinese characters to represent the sounds used in Japanese.

As Japan's contact with China increased, some Japanese people—especially rich and well-educated people—began to write in the Chinese language. Japanese writers used Chinese for their poems and stories. One of the first histories of Japan, written in the 700s, is in Chinese. For many years Chinese was even the official language of Japan's government.

Changes in Religion and Philosophy

One of the people most influential in bringing Chinese ideas to Japan was **Prince Shotoku** (shoh-toh-koo). He served from 593 to 621 as regent (REE-juhnt) for his aunt, the empress. A **regent** is a person who rules a country for someone who is unable to rule alone.

All his life, Prince Shotoku admired Chinese culture. As regent, Shotoku saw a chance for Japan to adopt more Chinese ideas. He sent scholars to China to learn all they could about Chinese society.

The ideas these scholars brought back changed Japanese society. For example, they taught the Japanese about Confucianism.

BIOGRAPHY

Prince Shotoku
573–621

Prince Shotoku was one of Japan's greatest leaders. He helped rule Japan when he was only 20 years old. For many centuries, people have admired him. Legends have developed about his wisdom. According to one early biography, Shotoku was able to talk as soon as he was born and never made a wrong decision.

Prince Shotoku's Japan

Under Prince Shotoku, Buddhism spread across Japan. Shotoku ordered beautiful Buddhist temples to be built, such as the one below in Nara, Japan. The spread of Buddhism changed many areas of Japanese culture during Prince Shotoku's time.

Horyuji Temple in Nara, Japan

Among other things, Confucianism outlined how families should behave. Confucius taught that fathers should rule their families. He believed that wives should obey their husbands, children should obey their parents, and younger brothers should obey older brothers. Families in China lived according to these rules. As Confucian ideas spread through Japan, the Japanese began to live by them as well.

More important than these social changes, though, were the vast religious changes Shotoku made in Japan. He was a Buddhist, and he wanted to spread Buddhism throughout his country. Buddhism wasn't new to Japan. Korean visitors had introduced the religion to Japan about 50 years earlier. But it was not very popular. Most people preferred to keep their traditional religion, Shinto.

Shotoku worked to change people's minds about Buddhism. He built a grand Buddhist temple that still stands today. He also wrote commentaries on Buddhist teachings. Largely because of his efforts, Buddhism became very popular, especially among Japanese nobles.

Statue of the Buddha in Horyuji

Changes in Government

Shotoku also wanted to change Japan's government to be more like China's. He especially wanted Japan's emperors to have more power, like China's emperors did.

Afraid that they would lose power to the emperor, many clan leaders opposed Shotoku's government plans. As a result, Japan's emperors gained little power.

READING CHECK **Categorizing** What aspects of Chinese society did Shotoku bring to Japan?

> **SUMMARY AND PREVIEW** In this section, you learned how early Japan grew and developed. Next you'll see how Japan's emperors encouraged nobles to create great works of art and literature.

go.hrw.com
Online Quiz
KEYWORD: SQ7 HP8

Section 1 Assessment

Reviewing Ideas, Terms, and People HSS 7.5.1, 7.5.2

1. **a. Recall** What types of landforms cover most of Japan?
   b. Explain How did Japan's location both separate it from and tie it to China and Korea?
2. **a. Define** What is **Shinto**?
   b. Sequence How did the Yamato rulers gain power?
3. **a. Explain** How did **Prince Shotoku** help spread Buddhism in Japan?
   b. Rate What do you think was the most important idea the Japanese borrowed from China or Korea? Why?

Critical Thinking

4. **Categorizing** Draw a graphic organizer like this one. In the circle, list ideas that developed in Japan with no outside influence. In the arrow, list ideas that the Japanese borrowed from other people.

FOCUS ON WRITING

5. **Taking Notes on Early Japan** Think about the section you have just read. Which details from this section might be appealing to tourists? Write down some thoughts in your notebook. Plan to include them in a section of your travel brochure called "Fun Facts."

Art and Culture in Heian

What You Will Learn...

Main Ideas

1. Japanese nobles created great art in their court at Heian.
2. Buddhism changed in Japan during the Heian period.

The Big Idea

Japanese culture experienced a golden age during the Heian period of the 800s to the 1100s.

Key Terms and People

court, p. 204
Lady Murasaki Shikibu, p. 205
Zen, p. 208

HSS **7.5.4** Trace the development of distinctive forms of Japanese Buddhism.

7.5.5 Study the ninth and tenth centuries' golden age of literature, art, and drama and its lasting effects on culture today, including Murasaki Shikibu's *Tale of Genji*.

If YOU were there...

You are a noble, serving the empress of Japan and living in the capital city. While walking in the garden one day, she gives you a small book with blank pages. When you ask her why, she says the book is a diary for you to write in. She tells you that nobles, both men and women, keep diaries to record their lives.

What will you write in your new diary?

BUILDING BACKGROUND In 794 the emperor and empress of Japan moved to Heian (HAY-ahn), a city now called Kyoto. Many nobles, like the one you just read about, followed their rulers to the new city. These nobles loved art and beauty, and they tried to make their new home a beautiful place.

Japanese Nobles Create Great Art

The nobles who followed Japan's emperor to Heian wanted to win his favor by living close to him. In Heian, these nobles created an imperial **court**, a group of nobles who live near and serve or advise a ruler.

Members of the noble court had little to do with the common people of Heian. They lived apart from poorer citizens and seldom left the city. These nobles enjoyed their lives of ease and privilege. In fact, their lives were so easy and so removed from the rest of Japan that many nobles called themselves "dwellers among the clouds."

The nobles of this court loved beauty and elegance. Because of this love, many nobles were great supporters of the arts. As a result, the court at Heian became a great center of culture and learning. In fact, the period between 794 and 1185 was a golden age of the arts in Japan.

Heian (Kyoto)

JOURNAL ENTRY
The Pillow Book

Sei Shonagon (SAY shoh-nah-gohn), author of The Pillow Book, *served Japan's empress from 991 to 1000. The Pillow Book was her journal. In it she wrote poems and thoughts about nature as well as descriptions of daily events. Here she describes the first time she met the empress.*

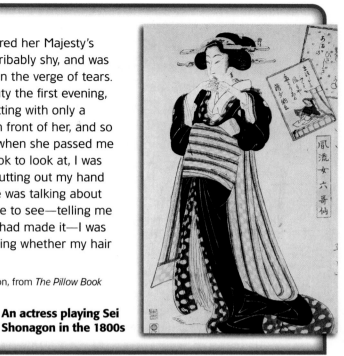

An actress playing Sei Shonagon in the 1800s

"When I first entered her Majesty's service I felt indescribably shy, and was indeed constantly on the verge of tears. When I came on duty the first evening, the Empress was sitting with only a three-foot screen in front of her, and so nervous was I that when she passed me some picture or book to look at, I was hardly capable of putting out my hand to take it. While she was talking about what she wanted me to see—telling me what it was or who had made it—I was all the time wondering whether my hair was in order."

−Sei Shonagon, from *The Pillow Book*

ANALYSIS SKILL **ANALYZING PRIMARY SOURCES**

How did Sei Shonagon feel when she met the empress?

Fashion

The nobles' love of beauty began with their own appearances. They had magnificent wardrobes full of silk robes and gold jewelry. Nobles loved elaborate outfits. For example, women wore long gowns made of 12 layers of colored silk cleverly cut and folded to show off many layers at once.

To complete their outfits, nobles often carried delicate decorative fans. These fans were painted with flowers, trees, and birds. Many nobles also attached flowers and long silk cords to their fans.

Literature

In addition to how they looked, Japanese nobles took great care with how they spoke and wrote. Writing was very popular among the nobles, especially among the women. Many women wrote diaries and journals about their lives at court. In their diaries, these women carefully chose their words to make their writing beautiful.

Unlike men, who usually wrote in Chinese, noble women wrote in the Japanese language. As a result, many of the greatest works of early Japanese literature were written by women.

One of the greatest writers in early Japanese history was **Lady Murasaki Shikibu** (moohr-ah-sahk-ee shee-kee-boo). Around 1000, she wrote *The Tale of Genji*. Many historians consider this book to be the world's first full-length novel. Many readers also consider it one of the best.

The Tale of Genji is the story of a prince named Genji and his long quest for love. During his search he meets women from many different social classes.

Many people consider *The Tale of Genji* one of Japan's greatest novels. The characters it describes are very colorful and seem real. In addition, Lady Murasaki's writing is clear and simple but graceful at the same time. She describes court life in Japan with great detail.

Most early Japanese prose was written by women, but both men and women wrote poetry. Nobles loved to read and write poems. Some nobles held parties at which they took turns writing poetry and reading their poems aloud to each other.

Poems from this time usually had only five lines. They followed a specific structure that outlined how many syllables each line could include. Most were about love or nature, but some described everyday events. Here is an example of a nature poem about the end of winter:

> " The breezes of spring
> Are blowing the ripples astray
> Along the water—
> Today they will surely melt
> The sheet of ice on the pond. "
>
> –Kino Tomonori, from the *Gosenshu*

Visual Art

Besides literature, Japan's nobles also loved the visual arts. The most popular art forms of the period were painting, calligraphy, and architecture.

In their paintings, the nobles of Heian liked bright, bold colors. They also liked paintings that illustrated stories. In fact, many of the greatest paintings from this period illustrate scenes from literature, such as *The Tale of Genji*. Other paintings show scenes from nature or from court life. Many artists painted on doors and furniture rather than on paper.

Another popular form of art in Heian was calligraphy, or decorative writing. Calligraphers spent hours carefully copying poems. They wanted the poems to look as beautiful as they sounded.

The Arts in Heian

Heian was Japan's capital for many centuries. The wealthy nobles who lived there were great supporters of the arts. With their support, literature, painting, calligraphy, and other arts flourished in Heian.

A favorite theme in Japanese painting was *The Tale of Genji*. In this illustration of a scene from the novel, Genji's son is reading a letter as his wife approaches.

Architecture

The nobles of Heian worked to make their city beautiful. They greatly admired Chinese architecture and modeled Heian after the Chinese capital, Chang'an. They copied Chinese building styles, especially in the many temples they built. These styles featured buildings with wooden frames that curved slightly upward at the ends. The wooden frames were often left unpainted to look more natural. Thatched roofs also added to the natural feel.

For other buildings, the nobles liked simple, airy designs. Most buildings were made of wood with tiled roofs and large, open spaces inside. To add to the beauty of these buildings, the nobles surrounded them with elegant gardens and ponds. Similar gardens are still popular in Japan.

Performing Arts

The performing arts were also popular in Japan during the Heian period. The roots of later Japanese drama can be traced back to this time. People often gathered to watch performances by musicians, jugglers, and acrobats. These performances were wild and fun. Especially popular were the plays in which actors skillfully mimicked other people.

In later centuries, these types of performances developed into a more serious form of drama called Noh. Created in the 1300s, Noh plays combine music, speaking, and dance. These plays often tell about great heroes or figures from Japan's past.

THE IMPACT TODAY

Noh plays are still popular in Japan today.

READING CHECK **Categorizing** What forms of art were popular in the Heian period?

Japanese writing could be an art form in itself. This album made in the shape of a fan is covered in text and pictures.

The Buddha was a popular subject for statues in the Heian period.

ANALYSIS SKILL **ANALYZING VISUALS**

How does art from this period reflect the culture of Heian?

Many Zen gardens like this one include raked gravel shaped to look like water and small boulders arranged like mountains.

One new form of Buddhism was very popular with Japan's common people. It was called Pure Land Buddhism and didn't require any special rituals. Instead, Pure Land Buddhists chanted the Buddha's name over and over to achieve an enlightened state.

In the 1100s another popular new form of Buddhism called **Zen** arrived from China. Zen Buddhists believed that neither faith nor good behavior led to wisdom. Instead, people seeking wisdom should practice self-discipline and meditation, or quiet thinking. These ideas appealed to many Japanese, especially warriors. As these warriors gained more influence in Japan, so did Zen Buddhism.

Buddhism Changes

Religion became something of an art form in Heian. The nobles' religion reflected their love of elaborate rituals. Most of the common people in Japan, though equally religious, didn't have the time or money for elaborate rituals. As a result, different forms of Buddhism developed in Japan.

READING CHECK **Finding Main Ideas** How did Buddhism change in Japan?

SUMMARY AND PREVIEW At Heian, Japan's emperors presided over an elegant court. In the next section, you'll learn what happened when emperors and the court lost power and prestige.

Section 2 Assessment

go.hrw.com
Online Quiz
KEYWORD: SQ7 HP8

Reviewing Ideas, Terms, and People HSS 7.5.4, 7.5.5

1. **a. Recall** Where did Japan's **court** move in the late 700s?
   b. Make Generalizations Why are the 800s to the 1100s considered a golden age for Japanese literature and art?
   c. Evaluate Do you think women in Heian had more rights and freedoms than women in other societies? Why or why not?
2. **a. Identify** What were two forms of Buddhism that developed in Japan?
   b. Compare and Contrast How was religion among Japan's nobles different from religion among the common people?
   c. Elaborate Why do you think Pure Land Buddhism was popular with common people?

Critical Thinking

3. **Summarizing** Draw a Japanese fan like the one shown here. In each section of the fan, list two contributions that the Japanese made in one of the arts.

Fashion
Visual Art
Literature
Architecture
Performing Arts

FOCUS ON WRITING

4. **Writing about Japanese Art** Japan's nobles left a legacy of beautiful art that today's visitors can still enjoy. Choose two art forms described in this section and take notes for your brochure. What kinds of pictures could you use to illustrate your text?

Lady Murasaki Shikibu

How would you describe the people you observe in life every day?

When did she live? around 1000

Where did she live? Heian

What did she do? Lady Murasaki was a noble and a servant to the Empress Akiko. While in the empress's service, she wrote lively observations of court life in her diaries. She also wrote the novel *The Tale of Genji*.

Why is she important? *The Tale of Genji* is one of the world's oldest novels, and—some would argue—one of the best. Besides entertaining readers for hundreds of years, *The Tale of Genji* describes the daily lives, customs, and attitudes of Japanese nobles of the time.

Drawing Conclusions What qualified Lady Murasaki to comment on upper-class life in Japan?

KEY IDEAS

Observations of Lady Murasaki Shikibu

- " Lady Dainagon is very small and refined . . . Her hair is three inches longer than her height. "

- " Lady Senji is also a little person, and haughty . . . She puts us to shame, her carriage is so noble. "

- " Lady Koshosho, all noble and charming. She is like a weeping-willow tree at budding time. Her style is very elegant and we all envy her her manners. "

–from The Diary of Lady Murasaki Shikibu, in *Anthology of Japanese Literature*, edited by Donald Keene

This painting from the 1600s is an illustration of court life from *The Tale of Genji*.

from The Tale of Genji

by Lady Murasaki Shikibu
translated by Edward G. Seidensticker

About the Reading *The Tale of Genji was written by Lady Murasaki Shikibu at the height of Japan's golden age. This thousand-page novel traces the life and adventures—especially in love—of a noble known as "the shining Genji." Although Genji is the favorite son of the emperor, his mother is only a commoner, so Genji cannot inherit the throne. Instead, it passes first to his half-brother Suzaku (soo-zah-koo) and then to Genji's own son. Here, Genji's son and his half-brother Suzaku visit Genji's mansion in Rokujo (roh-koo-joh), a district of Heian.*

> **AS YOU READ** Look for details that describe the lives of Japanese nobles.

The emperor paid a state visit to Rokujo late in the Tenth Month. ❶ Since the colors were at their best and it promised to be a grand occasion, the Suzaku emperor accepted the invitation of his brother, the present emperor, to join him. It was a most extraordinary event, the talk of the whole court. The preparations, which occupied the full attention of everyone at Rokujo, were unprecedented in their complexity and in the attention to brilliant detail.

Arriving late in the morning, the royal party went first to the equestrian grounds, where the inner guards were mustered for mounted review in the finery usually reserved for the iris festival. There were brocades spread along the galleries and arched bridges and awnings over the open places when, in early afternoon, the party moved to the southeast quarter. The royal cormorants had been turned out with the Rokujo cormorants on the east lake, where there was a handsome take of small fish. Genji hoped that he was not being a fussy and overzealous host, but he did not want a single moment of the royal progress to be dull. ❷ The autumn leaves were splendid, especially in Akikonomu's southwest garden. Walls had been taken down and gates opened, and not so much as an autumn mist was permitted to obstruct the royal view. Genji showed his guests to seats on a higher level than his own. The emperor ordered this mark of inferiority dispensed with, and thought again what a satisfaction it would be to honor Genji as his father.

GUIDED READING

WORD HELP

unprecedented having no equal

equestrian related to horses

mustered gathered together

brocades rich cloths with designs woven into them

cormorants large diving birds

inferiority lower rank

❶ *What kind of modern-day American event might be compared to the emperor's visit?*

❷ *What do Genji's thoughts and actions tell you about his attitude toward his guests?*

HSS **7.5.5** Study the ninth and tenth centuries' golden age of literature, art, and drama and its lasting effects on culture today, including Murasaki Shikibu's *The Tale of Genji*.

ELA Reading **7.3.3** Analyze characterization as delineated through a character's thoughts, words, speech patterns, and actions; the narrator's description; and the thoughts, words, and actions of other characters.

The lieutenants of the inner guards advanced from the east and knelt to the left and right of the stairs before the royal seats, one presenting the take from the pond and the other a brace of fowl taken by the royal falcons in the northern hills. To no Chujo received the royal command to prepare and serve these delicacies. ❸ An equally interesting repast had been laid out for the princes and high courtiers. The court musicians took their places in late afternoon . . . The concert was quiet and unpretentious and there were court pages to dance for the royal guests. It was as always the excursion to the Suzaku Palace so many years before that people remembered. One of To no Chujo's sons, a boy of ten or so, danced "Our Gracious Monarch" most elegantly. The emperor took off a robe and laid it over his shoulders, and To no Chujo himself descended into the garden for ritual thanks . . .

A painting of Lady Murasaki Shikibu from around 1700

The evening breeze had scattered leaves of various tints to make the ground a brocade as rich and delicate as the brocades along the galleries. The dancers were young boys from the best families, prettily dressed in coronets and the usual grayblues and roses, with crimsons and lavenders showing at their sleeves. They danced very briefly and withdrew under the autumn trees, and the guests regretted the approach of sunset. The formal concert, brief and unassuming, was followed by impromptu music in the halls above, instruments having been brought from the palace collection. As it grew livelier a koto was brought for each of the emperors and a third for Genji. ❹ . . . It was cause for general rejoicing that the two houses should be so close.

GUIDED READING

WORD HELP

brace pair
repast meal
unpretentious simple; modest
coronets small crowns

❸ To no Chujo is Genji's best friend. During the Heian period, food preparation was considered an art, and chefs were highly honored for their skill.

❹ A koto is a stringed instrument sometimes called a Japanese harp.

CONNECTING LITERATURE TO HISTORY

1. **Summarizing** The nobles of the court at Heian loved beauty and elegance. Because of this love, many nobles were great supporters of the arts. Based on this passage, what specific arts did Japanese nobles enjoy?

2. **Generalizing** The nobles enjoyed their lives of ease and privilege. What details suggest that Japanese nobles lived lives of luxury?

3. **Evaluating** After reading this passage, what is your overall impression of Japanese court life?

Growth of a Military Society

What You Will Learn...

Main Ideas

1. Samurai and shoguns took over Japan as emperors lost influence.
2. Samurai warriors lived honorably.
3. Order broke down when the power of the shoguns was challenged by invaders and rebellions.
4. Strong leaders took over and reunified Japan.

The Big Idea

Japan developed a military society led by generals called shoguns.

Key Terms and People

daimyo, *p. 212*
samurai, *p. 212*
figurehead, *p. 213*
shogun, *p. 213*
Bushido, *p. 214*

HSS 7.5.3 Describe the values, social customs, and traditions prescribed by the lord-vassal system consisting of *shogun, daimyo,* and *samurai* and the lasting influence of the warrior code throughout the twentieth century.

7.5.6 Analyze the rise of a military society in the late twelfth century and the role of the samurai in that society.

If YOU were there...

You are a Japanese warrior, proud of your fighting skills. For many years you've been honored by most of society, but you face an awful dilemma. When you became a warrior, you swore to protect and fight for both your lord and your emperor. Now your lord has gone to war against the emperor, and both sides have called for you to join them.

How will you decide whom to fight for?

BUILDING BACKGROUND Wars between lords and emperors were not uncommon in Japan after 1100. Closed off from society at Heian, emperors had lost touch with the rest of Japan. As a result, order broke down throughout the islands.

Samurai and Shoguns Take Over Japan

By the late 1100s, Heian was the great center of Japanese art and literature. But in the rest of Japan, life was very different. Powerful nobles fought each other over land. Rebels fought against imperial officials. This fighting destroyed land, which made it difficult for peasants to grow food. Some poor people became bandits or thieves. Meanwhile, Japan's rulers were so focused on courtly life, they didn't notice the many problems growing in their country.

The Rise of the Samurai

With the emperor distracted by life in his court, Japan's large landowners, or **daimyo** (DY-mee-oh), decided that they needed to protect their own lands. They hired **samurai** (SA-muh-ry), or trained professional warriors, to defend them and their property. The samurai wore light armor and fought with swords and bows. Most samurai came from noble families and inherited their positions from their fathers.

The word *samurai* comes from the Japanese word for "to serve." Every samurai, from the weakest soldier to the most powerful warrior, was supposed to serve his lord. Because all lords in Japan were supposed to serve the emperor, all samurai were required to be loyal to him.

An army of samurai was expensive to support. Few lords could afford to buy armor and weapons for their warriors. As a result, lords paid their samurai with land or food.

Only the most powerful samurai got land for their service. Most of these powerful samurai didn't live on the land they received, but they did profit from it. Every year, the peasant farmers who worked on the land gave the samurai money or food. Samurai who received no land were given food—usually rice—as payment.

Shoguns Rule Japan

Many of the nobles outside Heian were unhappy with the way Japan's government was being run. Frustrated, these nobles wanted a change of leadership. Eventually a few very strong noble clans decided to try to take power for themselves.

Two of these powerful clans went to war with each other in the 1150s. For almost 30 years, the two clans fought. Their fighting was terrible, destroying land and property and tearing families apart.

In the end, the Minamoto clan won. Because he had a very powerful army, and because the emperor was still busy in Heian, the leader of the Minamoto clan was the most powerful man in Japan. He decided to take over ruling the country.

He didn't, however, want to get rid of the emperor. He kept the emperor as a **figurehead**, a person who appears to rule even though real power rests with someone else. As a samurai, the Minamoto leader was supposed to be loyal to the emperor, but he decided to rule in the emperor's place. In 1192 he took the title **shogun**, a general who ruled Japan in the emperor's name. When he died, he passed his title and power on to one of his children. For about the next 700 years, one shogun would rule in Japan.

READING CHECK **Sequencing** How did the shogun rise to power in Japan?

Samurai Society

QUICK FACTS

Emperor
The emperor was a figurehead for the powerful shogun.

Shogun
A powerful military leader, the shogun ruled in the emperor's name.

Daimyo and Samurai
Daimyo were powerful lords who often led armies of samurai. Samurai warriors served the shogun and daimyo.

Peasants
Most Japanese were poor peasants who had no power.

ANALYSIS SKILL **ANALYZING VISUALS**
Who was the most powerful person in Japan's samurai society?

Samurai Live Honorably

FOCUS ON READING
As you read this section, notice how the author avoids using bias or stereotypes.

Under the shogun, who were military rulers, samurai warriors became more central to Japanese society. As a result, samurai enjoyed many social privileges. Common people had to treat the samurai with respect. Anyone who disrespected a samurai could be killed.

At the same time, tradition placed restrictions on samurai. For example, they couldn't attend certain types of entertainment, such as theater, which were considered beneath them. They also couldn't take part in trade or commerce.

Bushido

More importantly, all samurai had to follow a strict code of rules that taught them how to behave. The samurai code of rules was known as **Bushido** (BOOH-shi-doh). This name means "the way of the warrior." Both men and women from samurai families had to follow Bushido rules.

Bushido required samurai to be brave and honorable fighters. Both men and women of samurai families learned how to fight, though only men went to war. Women learned to fight so they could protect their homes from robbers.

Japan's Samurai

The samurai were bold, highly trained warriors. They followed a strict code of behavior called Bushido, or "the way of the warrior."

What equipment did samurai have to protect themselves?

Samurai wore armor and special helmets. Many carried two swords.

Samurai were often called on to fight, like in the scene above. They were expected to serve with honor and loyalty in battle. The samurai in the scene to the right is writing a poem on a cherry tree. Writing poetry helped train the samurai to concentrate.

Samurai were expected to live simple, disciplined lives. They believed that self-discipline made them better warriors. To improve their discipline, many samurai participated in peaceful rituals that required great concentration. Some created intricate flower arrangements or grew miniature bonsai trees. Others held elaborate tea ceremonies. Many samurai also adopted Zen Buddhism, which stressed self-discipline and meditation.

More than anything else, Bushido required a samurai to be loyal to his lord. Each samurai had to obey his master's orders without hesitation, even if it caused the samurai or his family to suffer. One samurai expressed his duties in this way:

❝If one were to say in a word what the condition of being a samurai is, its basis lies first in seriously devoting one's body and soul to his master.❞

–Yamamoto Tsunetomo, from *Hagakure*

Obeying his lord was important to the samurai's sense of honor. Honor was the most important thing in a samurai's life. If he did anything to lose honor, a samurai was expected to commit suicide rather than living with his shame. Such shame might be caused by disobeying an order, losing a fight, or failing to protect his lord.

Bushido and Modern Japan

Although it was created as a code for warriors, Bushido influenced much of Japanese society. Even today, many Japanese feel a connection to the samurai. For example, the samurai's dedication and discipline are still greatly admired in Japan. <u>Values</u> such as loyalty and honor, the central ideas of the samurai code, remain very important in modern Japan.

ACADEMIC VOCABULARY

values ideas that people hold dear and try to live by

READING CHECK **Finding Main Ideas** What customs did samurai follow?

LINKING TO TODAY

Modern Samurai

Although the samurai class disappeared from Japan at the end of the 1800s, samurai images and values live on. Fierce samurai appear on posters, in advertisements and movies, and in video games, challenging foes with their sharp swords and deadly skills. Many people study the same martial arts, such as sword fighting, that the samurai practiced. In addition, the loyalty that samurai felt toward their lords is still a key part of Japanese society. Many Japanese feel that same loyalty toward other groups—their families, companies, or favorite sports teams. Samurai values such as hard work, honor, and sacrifice have also become deeply rooted in Japanese society.

ANALYSIS SKILL **ANALYZING INFORMATION**

How are Japan's samurai values still alive today?

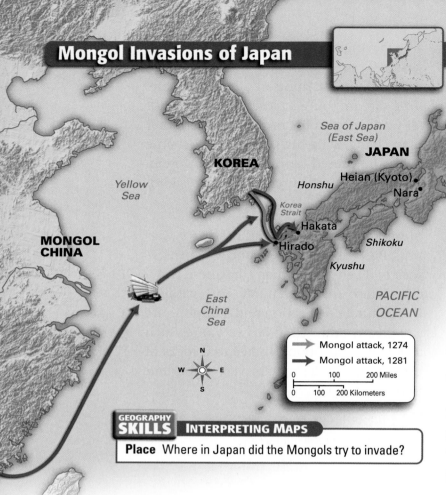

Mongol Invasions of Japan

Sea of Japan (East Sea)

JAPAN

KOREA

Yellow Sea

Honshu

Heian (Kyoto)

Nara

Korea Strait

Hakata

Hirado

Shikoku

Kyushu

MONGOL CHINA

East China Sea

PACIFIC OCEAN

Mongol attack, 1274
Mongol attack, 1281

0   100   200 Miles
0   100   200 Kilometers

N S E W

GEOGRAPHY SKILLS   INTERPRETING MAPS

Place Where in Japan did the Mongols try to invade?

In 1281 the Mongols invaded again. This time they sent two huge armies and threatened to overwhelm the Japanese warriors. For weeks, the two armies were locked in deadly combat.

Once again, though, the weather helped the Japanese. A huge storm swept over Japan, sinking most of the Mongol fleet. Many Mongol soldiers drowned, and many more returned to China. The grateful Japanese called the storm that had saved them the kamikaze (kah-mi-kah-zee), or "divine wind." They believed the gods had sent the storm to save Japan.

But many nobles were left unhappy by the war. They didn't think the shogun gave them enough credit for their part in the fighting. Many came to resent the shogun's power over them.

Internal Rebellion

After the Mongol invasion, new problems arose for the shogun. The emperor, tired of having no say in the government, began to fight the shogun for control of the country. At the same time daimyo, the nobles who owned much of Japan's land, fought to break free of the shogun's control. During these struggles for power, small wars broke out all over Japan.

By the 1400s the shoguns had lost most of their authority. The emperor was still largely powerless, and daimyo ruled much of Japan. Each daimyo controlled his own territory. Within that territory, he made laws and collected taxes. There was no powerful central authority of any sort to impose order in Japan.

READING CHECK   **Summarizing** What challenges appeared to the shogun's authority?

Order Breaks Down

For about a century, the shoguns kept order in Japan. Supported by the samurai, the shoguns were able to put down challenges to their authority. Eventually, however, more serious challenges arose that brought this order to an end.

Foreign Invasion

One of the greatest challenges to the shoguns was an invasion by the Mongols from China. China's emperor, Kublai Khan, sent an army to conquer the islands in 1274. Faced with invasion, the shogun sent troops to fight the Mongols. In addition, Japan's warring nobles put aside their differences to fight the enemy. The Japanese warriors were aided by a great storm. The storm sank many Mongol ships and forced the Mongols to flee.

Strong Leaders Take Over

Soon new leaders rose to power. They began as local rulers, but these men wanted more power. In the 1500s, each fought to unify all of Japan under his control.

Unification

The first such leader was Oda Nobunaga (ohd-ah noh-booh-nah-gah). Oda gave his soldiers guns that had been brought to Japan by Portuguese traders. This was the first time guns had been used in Japan. With these new weapons, Oda easily defeated his opponents.

After Oda died, other leaders continued his efforts to unify Japan. By 1600, one of them, Tokugawa Ieyasu (toh-koohg-ah-wuh ee-e-yahs-ooh), had conquered his enemies. In 1603 Japan's emperor made Tokugawa shogun. From his capital at Edo (AY-doh)—now Tokyo—Tokugawa ruled all of Japan.

Tokugawa's rise to power began the Tokugawa shogunate (SHOH-guhn-uht), or rule by shoguns of the Tokugawa family. Early in this period, which lasted until 1868, Japan traded with other countries and let Christian missionaries live in Japan.

Isolation

Not all of the shoguns who followed Tokugawa liked this contact with the world, though. Some feared that Japan would become too much like Europe, and the shoguns would lose their power. To prevent such a thing from happening, in the 1630s the ruling shogun closed Japan off from the rest of the world.

Japan's rulers also banned guns. They feared that peasants with guns could defeat their samurai armies. The combination of isolation from the world and limited technology helped extend the samurai period in Japan until the 1800s, far longer than it might have otherwise lasted.

READING CHECK **Drawing Conclusions** How did Japan change in the Tokugawa shogunate?

SUMMARY AND PREVIEW By the 1100s, the growing power of shoguns, daimyo, and samurai had turned Japan into a military society. In the next chapter you will read about a similar military society that developed in Europe.

Section 3 Assessment

go.hrw.com
Online Quiz
KEYWORD: SQ7 HP8

Reviewing Ideas, Terms, and People **HSS** 7.5.3, 7.5.6

1. **a. Recall** What was the relationship between **samurai** and **daimyo**?
   b. Elaborate Why do you think the first **shogun** wanted to keep the emperor as a **figurehead**?
2. **a. Define** What was **Bushido**?
   b. Explain Why did samurai take up pursuits like flower arranging?
3. **a. Identify** Who invaded Japan in the 1270s and 1280s?
   b. Summarize How did the daimyo help weaken the shoguns?
4. **Identify** What strong leaders worked to unify Japan in the late 1500s?

Critical Thinking

5. **Analyzing Information** Draw a word web like the one here. In the center, write a sentence that describes the samurai. In each outer circle, write one of the samurai's jobs, duties, or privileges.

FOCUS ON WRITING

6. **Describing the Samurai** A Japanese history museum will offer a special exhibit on the samurai warrior. Add notes about the samurai to encourage tourists to visit the exhibit. Tell who they were, what they did, and how they lived.

Social Studies Skills

Solving Problems

Understand the Skill

Problem solving is a process for finding good solutions to difficult situations. It involves asking questions, identifying and evaluating information, comparing and contrasting, and making judgments. It is useful in studying history because it helps you better understand problems a person or group faced in the past and how they dealt with those issues.

The ability to understand and evaluate how people solved problems in the past also can help in solving similar problems today. The skill can be applied to many other kinds of difficulties besides historical ones. It is a method for thinking through almost any situation.

Learn the Skill

Using the following steps will help you to better understand and solve problems.

1 **Identify the problem.** Ask questions of yourself and others. This first step helps you to be sure you know exactly what the situation is. It also helps you understand why it is a problem.

2 **Gather information.** Ask other questions and do research to learn more about the problem. For example, what is its history? What caused the problem? What contributes to it?

3 **List options.** Based on the information you have gathered, identify possible options for solving the problem. It will be easier to find a good solution if you have several options.

4 **Evaluate the options.** Weigh each option you are considering. Think of the advantages it has as a solution. Then think of its potential disadvantages. It may help you to compare your options if you make a list of advantages and disadvantages for each possible solution.

5 **Choose and apply a solution.** After comparing the advantages and disadvantages of each possible solution, choose the one that seems best and apply it.

6 **Evaluate the solution.** Once the solution has been tried, evaluate how effective it is in solving the problem. This step will tell you if the solution was a good one, or if you should try another of the options instead. It will also help you know what to do in the future if you happen to face the same problem again.

Practice and Apply the Skill

Read again the "If you were there" in Section 3. Imagine that you are the samurai warrior with this problem. You can apply the steps for solving problems to help you decide what to do. Review the information in the section about the samurai and this time period in Japan's history. Then, in the role of the samurai warrior, answer the questions below.

1. What is the specific problem that you face? Why is it a problem?

2. What events led to your problem? What circumstances and conditions have contributed to it?

3. What options can you think of to solve your problem? List the advantages and disadvantages of each.

4. Which of your options seems to be the best solution for your problem? Explain why. How will you know if it is a good solution?

Visual Summary

Use the visual summary below to help you review the main ideas of the chapter.

QUICK FACTS

Japan's early culture was influenced by China and Korea.

A golden age of Japanese art and culture occurred during Japan's Heian Period.

After the Heian Period, the Japanese created a military society.

Reviewing Vocabulary, Terms, and People

Unscramble each group of letters below to spell a term that matches the given definition.

1. **etrgne**—a person who rules in someone else's name

2. **misaaru**—a Japanese warrior

3. **aclsn**—large, extended families

4. **elauvs**—ideas that people hold dear

5. **uctro**—a group of nobles who surround a ruler

6. **nguosh**—a great Japanese general who ruled instead of the emperor

7. **enz**—a form of Japanese Buddhism

8. **osnith**—a nature religion that began in Japan

9. **odmiya**—Japanese lords who gave land to samurai

10. **kosouth**—prince who introduced many Chinese ideas to Japan

11. **rctusrteu**—the way something is set up

Comprehension and Critical Thinking

SECTION 1 *(Pages 198–203)* **HSS** 7.5.1, 7.5.2

12. **a. Identify** Who was Prince Shotoku, and what did he do?

   b. Compare and Contrast Why was Japan isolated from China and Korea? How did China and Korea still affect Japan?

   c. Predict How would Japan's physical geography affect the development of Japanese government and society?

SECTION 2 *(Pages 204–208)* **HSS** 7.5.4, 7.5.5

13. **a. Recall** Why is Murasaki Shikibu a major figure in the history of Japanese culture?

   b. Analyze What made the period between the 800s and the 1100s a golden age of the arts in Japan?

   c. Evaluate Would you like to have been a member of the imperial court at Heian? Why or why not?

SECTION 3 *(Pages 212–217)* **HSS** 7.5.3, 7.5.6

14. a. Define What was the Tokugawa shogunate?

b. Analyze How did Japan develop into a military society? What groups made up that society?

c. Elaborate What was daily life like for the samurai?

Reviewing Themes

15. Politics What role did warriors play in Japan's government after the 1100s?

16. Society and Culture How was society under the shoguns different from society during the Heian period?

17. Society and Culture How did Bushido affect modern Japanese culture?

Reading Skills

Identifying Bias and Stereotypes *The passage below is from a Chinese history written in the 500s. It describes Japan, which the Chinese called Wa. Read the passage and then answer the questions that follow.*

> " During the reigns of Huan-di (147–168) and Ling-di (168–189), the country of Wa was in a state of great confusion, war and conflict raging on all sides. For a number of years, there was no ruler. Then a woman named Pimiko appeared. Remaining unmarried, she occupied herself with magic and sorcery and bewitched the populace. Thereupon they placed her on the throne. She kept one thousand female attendants, but few people saw her. "

18. Do you think the writer of this passage shows bias against Pimiko as a ruler?

19. What words or phrases from the passage support your opinion?

20. What does this passage suggest about ancient Chinese stereotypes of unmarried women?

Using the Internet

go.hrw.com KEYWORD: SQ7 WH8

21. Activity: Drawing a Comic Strip A strong military influence affected the governing structure of Japan. Eventually, warriors and generals gained power in Japan as emperors lost some of it. Enter the activity keyword and create a comic strip, similar in style to Japanese anime, about the people who held power. Your characters should include a shogun, a daimyo, a samurai, and an emperor.

Social Studies Skills

22. Solving Problems Imagine that you are a samurai warrior who has been called upon to help fight the Mongol invasion. You are stationed in a small village that is directly in the path of the Mongol army. Some people in the village want to stay and fight the Mongols, but you know they will be killed if they try to fight. The town's leaders want your opinion about what they should do. Write down one or two ideas you might suggest for how to save the people of the village. For each idea, make notes about what consequences your proposed action may have.

FOCUS ON WRITING

23. Creating Your Travel Brochure Look back over your notes from this chapter, and then create a travel brochure that describes Japan's historic attractions. Keep your writing brief—remember that you have to get your audience's attention with just a few words. To help get their attention, draw or find pictures to illustrate your travel brochure.

Standards Assessment

DIRECTIONS: *Read each question, and write the letter of the best response.*

1

> I was brought up in a distant province which lies farther than the farthest end of the Eastern Road. I am ashamed to think that inhabitants of the Royal City will think me an uncultured girl.
>
> Somehow I came to know that there are such things as romances in the world and wished to read them. When there was nothing to do by day or at night, one tale or another was told me by my elder sister or stepmother, and I heard several chapters about the shining Prince Genji.

From the content of this passage, it can be concluded that its author was a

A samurai warrior.

B noble woman from Heian.

C farmer from northern Japan.

D daimyo.

2 The importance of loyalty, honor, and discipline in Japanese society today are *mainly* the result of what influence in Japan's history?

A the code of the samurai

B the teachings of Shinto

C the reforms of Prince Shotoku

D the spread of Chinese Buddhism

3 Most great works of early Japanese literature were written by

A Buddhist scholars.

B samurai warriors.

C Shinto priests.

D noble women.

4 The influence of China and Korea on Japan's history, culture, and development is found in all of the following *except*

A Japan's first writing system.

B the traditional Japanese diet.

C early rules for family behavior.

D the practice of Buddhism.

5 The main function of samurai in Japanese society was to

A write poetry.

B manage farmland.

C defend lords.

D conquer China.

Connecting with Past Learnings

6 Early Japanese society under the clans was not a single unified country but many small states. This type of government *most* resembled that of

A the early city-states of ancient Greece.

B the Roman Empire during the Pax Romana.

C the Old Kingdom of ancient Egypt.

D the New Kingdom of ancient Egypt.

7 The nobles of Heian placed great emphasis on art and learning, just like the people of which ancient Greek city-state that you learned about in Grade 6?

A Sparta

B Athens

C Macedonia

D Troy

Comparing Cultures and People

Assignment

Write a paper comparing and contrasting one of the following: (1) the achievements of the Tang and Song dynasties in China, (2) the life of nobles in the Heian court and the life of samurai warriors.

TIP **Looking for Points of Comparison** As you collect information, look for two or three characteristics you can compare. For example, you might compare Tang and Song art, inventions, and government. You might compare the pastimes, privileges, and contributions to society of the Heian nobles and the samurai.

ELA **Writing 7.2.0** Students write expository text of at least 500–700 words.

To understand people and events of the past, we often compare and contrast them. When we study how two things or people are alike and different, we learn more about each of them. We begin to see them both more clearly.

1. Prewrite

Getting Started

Begin by choosing one of the topics in the assignment. Then collect some information on the topic you have chosen. Use that information to decide on your big idea. Here are two examples of big ideas on these topics:

- Both the Tang and the Song dynasties brought technical and cultural advancements to China.
- Both the nobles of Heian and the samurai had many social privileges, but they lived very different lives.

Organizing Your Information

Essays that compare and contrast usually are organized one of two ways.

- **Block Style** For example, write everything you have to say about the Tang dynasty. Then write everything you have to say about the Song dynasty. Discuss the points of comparison in the same order for each dynasty.
- **Point-by-Point Style** Discuss the points of comparison one at a time. Explain how the dynasties are alike and different on one point of comparison, then another, then another. Discuss the two dynasties in the same order for each point of comparison.

2. Writing

Here is a framework you can use to write your first draft.

A Writer's Framework

Introduction	Body	Conclusion
■ Begin with a question or interesting fact related to the two subjects you are comparing and contrasting. ■ State your big idea, or thesis, about the two subjects.	■ Use block or point-by-point organization. ■ Use three points of comparison. ■ Support your points with specific historical facts, details, and examples.	■ Summarize the points you made. ■ Restate your big idea in different words.

3. Evaluate and Revise

Evaluating

Use these questions to discover ways to improve your draft.

Evaluation Questions for a Comparison/Contrast Paper

- Do you begin with a question or interesting fact related to the two subjects?
- Do you state your big idea, or thesis, in the introduction?
- Do you use at least three points of comparison/contrast?
- Do you organize your points of comparison with either the block style or point-by-point style?

- Do you support your points of comparison with appropriate historical facts, details, and examples?
- Do you summarize your points of comparison in the conclusion?
- Do you restate your big idea in different words?

TIP **Using Relevant Facts**

When you read your draft, look for and remove irrelevant facts. These are facts that are not directly related to the topic.

One culture that developed in Japan was the Ainu. Historians aren't sure exactly when or how the Ainu moved to Japan. [*relevant*] The people who lived south of the Ainu were farmers. [*irrelevant*] Wherever the Ainu came from, they spoke a language unlike any other in eastern Asia. [*relevant*]

Revising

Read your essay out loud. If you run out of breath before you get to the end of a sentence, you may have some "stringy" sentences. Stringy sentences have many ideas connected with *and*, *but*, *or* or *so*. You can fix a stringy sentence by breaking it up into separate sentences.

Stringy The Ainu began to fight with other people for land but they lost most of these fights and so they lost their land and were driven back to an island.

Not Stringy The Ainu began to fight with others for land. Because they lost most of these fights, they lost their land as well. They were driven back to an island.

4. Proofread and Publish

Proofread

If you break a stringy sentence up into separate sentences, be sure to use correct end punctuation and capitalization. Check to be sure you have capitalized the first word in each new sentence and ended with a period, question mark, or exclamation point.

Publish

Compare your paper with another student's paper on the same topic. How are your papers similar? How are they different?

● Practice and Apply

Use the steps and strategies outlined in this workshop to write your comparison/contrast paper.

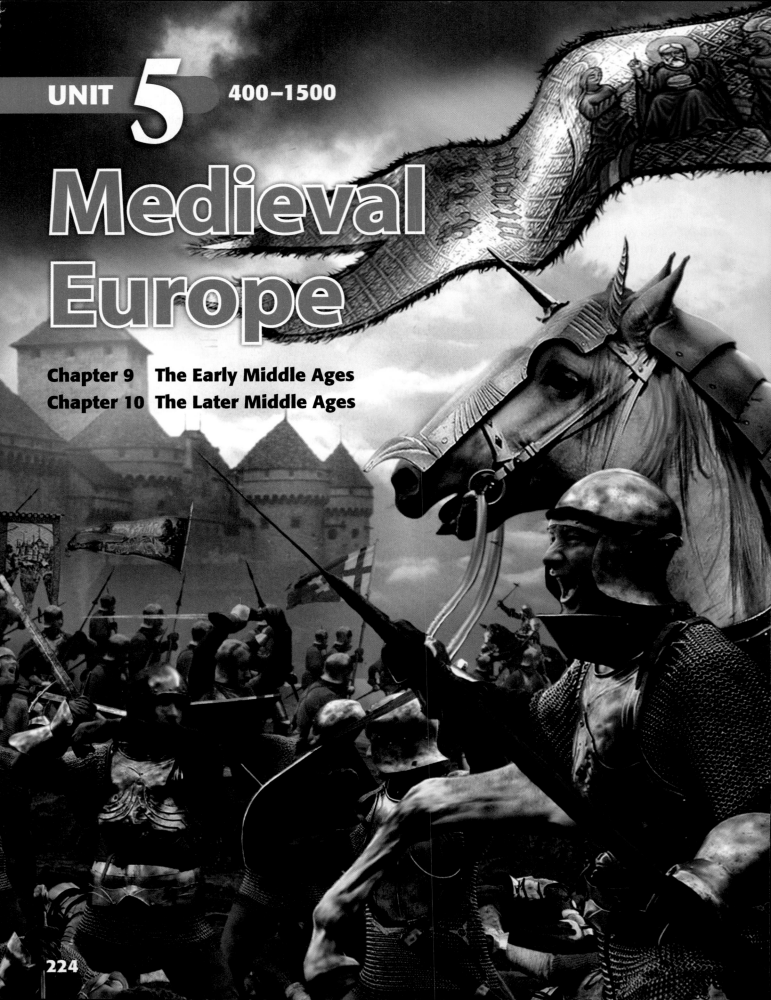

Medieval Europe

When the Roman Empire collapsed, Europe lost its center of power and a new period of history began. That period, called the Middle Ages or medieval times, is the period between ancient and modern times.

During the Middle Ages, Europe saw the growth of empires and the development of new ways of governing. It saw a new economic system and the spread of Christianity. It also saw long, difficult religious wars and early stirrings of democratic thought.

In the next two chapters, you will learn about this period of dramatic struggle and great change.

Explore the Art

In this scene, French teenager Joan of Arc carries a religious flag as she leads an army into battle. What does the scene suggest about the struggles of the Middle Ages?

The Early Middle Ages

California Standards

History–Social Science

7.6 Students analyze the geographic, political, economic, religious, and social structures of the civilizations of Medieval Europe.

Analysis Skills

HR 4 Analyze primary and secondary sources.

English–Language Arts

Writing 7.2.4c Anticipate and address reader concerns and counter-arguments.

Reading 7.2.0 Students read and understand grade-level-appropriate material.

FOCUS ON WRITING

A Job Advertisement In the 900s nobles needed knights, or warriors, to help protect their property. As you read this chapter, imagine what it would be like to be one of those nobles. Then you will write a job ad seeking knights to help you defend your land.

CHAPTER EVENTS

c. 430 Saint Patrick brings Christianity to Ireland.

400

WORLD EVENTS

476 Rome falls.

What You Will Learn...

In this chapter you will learn about the social and economic systems in Europe during a time called the Middle Ages. This photo shows Caernarfon Castle in Wales. Built in the late 1200s, the castle showed the king's power and provided defense from invasions.

700s–800s
The Vikings raid Europe.

800
Charlemagne is crowned emperor of much of Europe.

1066
Feudalism is introduced into Britain.

600

800

1000

1200

613
Muhammad begins teaching people about Islam.

794
Heian becomes the capital of Japan.

1000s
The Chinese invent gunpowder.

1076
Ghana falls to Muslim invaders.

THE EARLY MIDDLE AGES   **227**

Reading Social Studies

by Kylene Beers

Focus on Themes In this chapter you will read about Europe during the early Middle Ages. You will learn how the geography of the land affected growth and trade and see how the Christian **religion** spread throughout northern Europe during this time. You will learn about the invaders who tried to conquer the land and see how the feudal system developed. As you read, you will understand how this feudal system shaped the entire **society and culture** of the people.

Evaluating Sources

Focus on Reading As you have already learned, historians study both primary and secondary sources to learn about the past. By studying both types, they can get a better picture of what life was like.

Assessing Primary and Secondary Sources However, not all sources are accurate or reliable. You need to be careful when you read historical sources. Checklists like the ones below can help you judge which sources are reliable and worth using in your research.

Additional reading support can be found in the

Inter active

Reader and Study Guide

Checklist for Primary Sources

✔ Who is the author? Does he or she seem trustworthy?

✔ Was the author actually present for the event described in the source?

✔ How soon after the event occurred was the source written?

✔ Can the information in the source be verified in other primary or secondary sources?

Historians in the past were not always careful about what they put in their books. Some included rumors, gossip, or hearsay.

The more time that passed between the event and the writing, the greater the chance of errors or distortion in the description.

Not everyone who writes about history is a good historian. Try to use sources by qualified writers.

Good historians will always tell you where they got their information. If information isn't documented, you can't always trust that it is true or accurate.

Checklist for Secondary Sources

✔ Who is the author? What are his or her credentials, or qualifications for writing?

✔ Where did the author get his or her information?

✔ Is the information in the source properly documented?

✔ Has the author drawn valid conclusions from his or her sources?

HSS **Analysis HR 4** Assess primary and secondary sources.
ELA **Reading 7.2.0** Read and understand grade-level-appropriate material.

You Try It!

The following passage of a primary source can be found in the chapter you are about to read. As you read this passage, ask yourself if what you could learn from this source.

> ## The Benedictine Rule
>
> For bedding, a mattress, a blanket, a coverlet and a pillow are enough. The beds should be frequently inspected by the Abbot as a precaution against private possessions. If anyone is found to have anything which was not given him by the Abbot, he is to undergo the severest punishment; and that this vice of personal ownership may be totally eliminated, everything necessary should be given by the Abbot; namely a cowl, a tunic, stockings, shoes, a belt, a knife, a pen, a needle, a handkerchief and writing tablets, so that all excuses about necessity are removed.
>
> *From Chapter 9, page 236*

After you read the passage, answer the following questions.

1. The passage you have just read is from a code of rules that monks lived by in the early 500s. If a historian wanted to study how monks lived at that time, would this be a good source to use? Why or why not?

2. Where else might a historian look to verify the information found in this source?

3. Would this be a good source to study to learn how monks live today? Why or why not?

Key Terms and People

Chapter 9

Section 1
Eurasia *(p. 230)*
topography *(p. 230)*

Section 2
Middle Ages *(p. 234)*
medieval *(p. 234)*
Patrick *(p. 235)*
monks *(p. 236)*
monasteries *(p. 236)*
Benedict *(p. 236)*
Charlemagne *(p. 237)*

Section 3
knights *(p. 242)*
vassal *(p. 243)*
feudalism *(p. 243)*
William the Conqueror *(p. 244)*
manor *(p. 245)*
serfs *(p. 245)*
Eleanor of Aquitaine *(p. 246)*

Section 4
chivalry *(p. 249)*
haiku *(p. 250)*

Academic Vocabulary

Success in school is related to knowing academic vocabulary— the words that are frequently used in school assignments and discussions. In this chapter, you will learn the following academic words:

role *(p. 246)*
elements *(p. 250)*

As you read Chapter 9, look at the primary sources included in the chapter. Why do you think these sources were chosen to be included?

Geography of Europe

What You Will Learn...

Main Ideas

1. The physical features of Europe vary widely from region to region.
2. Geography has shaped life in Europe, including where and how people live.

The Big Idea

Because Europe has many types of landforms and climates, different ways of life have developed there.

Key Terms

Eurasia, *p. 230*
topography, *p. 230*

HSS **7.6.1** Study the geography of Europe and the Eurasian land mass, including their location, topography, waterways, vegetation, and climate and their relationship to ways of life in Medieval Europe.

If YOU were there...

Your village is on the banks of a river. The river has created a flat plain where you can grow crops. The river also gives you a way to get to the sea and to trade with villages farther inland. You love your village and think it's the perfect place to live. But your favorite uncle, the one everyone looks up to, says he is very worried. Your village is in a very dangerous place.

Why do you think your uncle is worried?

BUILDING BACKGROUND Many villages in Europe were built on rivers. But rivers were only one of the physical features that affected where and how people lived in Europe. All of Europe's features—its landforms, its waterways, and its climates—played roles in shaping people's lives.

The Physical Features of Europe

Europe is a small continent, but it is very diverse. Many different landforms, water features, and climates can be found there.

Although we call Europe a continent, it is actually part of **Eurasia**, the large landmass that includes both Europe and Asia. Geographers consider the Ural Mountains to be the boundary between the two continents.

Landforms and Waterways

Look at the map of Europe. You can see that different parts of Europe have very different features. In other words, Europe's topography (tuh-PAH-gruh-fee) varies widely from place to place. **Topography** refers to the shape and elevation of land in a region.

Mountain ranges cover much of southern Europe. Some peaks in the Alps reach higher than 15,000 feet. The highest mountains have large snowfields and glaciers.

Europe: Physical

ARCTIC OCEAN

Iceland

ASIA

Norwegian Sea

SCANDINAVIAN PENINSULA

URAL MOUNTAINS

20°W

20°E

30°E

40°E

70°N

60°N

50°N

40°N

British Isles

PENNINES

North Sea

Gulf of Bothnia

Baltic Sea

N. Dvina River

Kama River

Ural River

NORTHERN EUROPEAN PLAIN

Vistula River

Don River

Volga River

ATLANTIC OCEAN

English Channel

Paris

Rhine River

Elbe River

Oder River

Danube River

Dnieper River

Dnestr River

CARPATHIAN MTS.

Bay of Biscay

Mont Blanc 15,781 ft. (4,810 m)

ALPS

Mt. Elbrus 18,510 ft. (5,642 m)

Caspian Sea

PYRENEES

Rhône River

Po River

ITALIAN PENINSULA

Adriatic Sea

CAUCASUS MTS.

Black Sea

IBERIAN PENINSULA

Corsica

Sardinia

Balearic Islands

Tyrrhenian Sea

BALKAN PENINSULA

ASIA

Strait of Gibraltar

Sicily

Aegean Sea

Crete

Mediterranean Sea

ELEVATION

Feet		Meters
13,120		4,000
6,560		2,000
1,640		500
656		200
(Sea level) 0		0 (Sea level)
Below sea level		Below sea level

Ice cap

0   250   500 Miles

0   250   500 Kilometers

GEOGRAPHY SKILLS INTERPRETING MAPS

1. **Region** What four peninsulas do you see labeled?
2. **Movement** How might the Alps have affected the movement of peoples?

North of the Alps, the land is much flatter than in southern Europe. In fact, most of northern Europe is part of the vast Northern European Plain. As you can see on the map, this plain stretches all the way from the Atlantic Ocean in the west to the Ural Mountains in the east. In the past, this huge expanse of land was covered with thick forests. Many types of trees grew well in the plain's rich, fertile soils.

The Northern European Plain is also the location of most of Europe's major rivers. Many of these rivers begin with melting snow in the southern mountains and flow out across the plain on their way northward to the sea.

If you travel even farther north from the Northern European Plain, the land starts to rise again. Far northern Europe has many rugged hills and low mountains.

Geography and Living

Europe's geography has influenced the development of different ways of life. It has influenced, for example, what crops people have grown and where cities have developed.

3 Norway

2 Germany

1 Italy

1 Farmers have long grown olives and other hardy crops in the drier, warmer areas along the Mediterranean in southern Europe.

You can see these hills and mountains in the northern part of the British Isles and in Scandinavia, Europe's largest peninsula. Scandinavia is only one of Europe's many peninsulas. Smaller peninsulas extend into the sea from many parts of Europe. These peninsulas give Europe a very long, jagged coastline.

Climate and Vegetation

Like its landforms, Europe's climates and vegetation vary widely from region to region. For example, southern Europe is largely warm and sunny. As a result, shrubs and trees that don't need a lot of water are common there.

Most of northwestern Europe, in contrast, has a mild and cooler, wetter climate. Cold winds from the north and northeast can bring freezing weather in winter.

Freezing weather is much more common in Scandinavia, though. That region is very cold throughout the year. Snow falls for much of the year, and few plants can survive the region's cold climates.

READING CHECK **Summarizing** How do Europe's landforms and climates vary by region?

Geography Shapes Life

As in other parts of the world, geography has affected history in Europe. It influenced where and how people lived.

Southern Europe

In southern Europe, most people lived on coastal plains or in river valleys where the land was flat enough to farm. People grew crops like grapes and olives that could survive the region's dry summers. In the mountains where the land was steep or rocky, people raised sheep and goats.

Because southern Europe has many peninsulas, people there don't live far from the sea. As a result, many became traders and seafarers.

Northern Europe

Most people in northern Europe lived farther from the sea. They still had access to the sea, however, through northern Europe's rivers. Because rivers were an easy method of transportation, towns grew up along them. Rivers also provided protection. The city of Paris, France, for example, was built on an island in a river to make the city hard for raiders to reach.

2 Cities have grown along rivers such as the Rhine in Germany. Rivers have been routes for moving people and goods.

3 Many people in cold, snowy Scandinavia have settled on the coasts, looking to the sea and lands beyond for the resources they need.

In the fields around cities, farmers grew all sorts of crops. These fields were excellent farmlands, but the flat land also made an easy route for invaders to follow. No mountains blocked people's access to northern Europe, and as a result, the region was frequently invaded.

READING CHECK **Contrasting** How did geography influence where people lived in Europe?

SUMMARY AND PREVIEW You have just read about the role Europe's geography played in its history. Because Europe has so many types of landforms and climates, many different ways of life developed there. Also, northern Europe had few natural barriers to prevent invasions. In the next section, you will learn how Europe changed when invasions did occur.

Section 1 Assessment

go.hrw.com
Online Quiz
KEYWORD: SQ7 HP9

Reviewing Ideas, Terms, and People **HSS** 7.6.1

1. **a. Define** What is **topography**?
   b. Compare and Contrast How is southern Europe's climate like or unlike your climate?
2. **a. Describe** Where do most people in southern Europe live?
   b. Draw Conclusions Do you think Europe's major farming regions are in the north or the south? Why?
   c. Elaborate How might the region's climate affect how people live in Scandinavia?

Critical Thinking

3. **Categorizing** Draw a chart like the one to the right. Use it to list the landforms, climates, and vegetation of northern Europe, southern Europe, and Scandinavia.

	Landforms	Climates	Vegetation
Northern Europe			
Southern Europe			
Scandinavia			

FOCUS ON WRITING

4. **Thinking about Geography** If you were a noble living in northern Europe, what might your life be like? How would the landforms and climate affect people in your area? Why might you need the protection of knights? Write some ideas down in your notebook.

Europe after the Fall of Rome

What You Will Learn...

Main Ideas

1. Christianity spread to northern Europe through the work of missionaries and monks.
2. The Franks, led by Charlemagne, created a huge Christian empire and brought together scholars from around Europe.
3. Invaders threatened much of Europe in the 700s and 800s.

The Big Idea

Despite the efforts of Christians to maintain order, Europe was a dangerous place after the fall of Rome.

Key Terms and People

Middle Ages, *p. 234*
medieval, *p. 234*
Patrick, *p. 235*
monks, *p. 236*
monasteries, *p. 236*
Benedict, *p. 236*
Charlemagne, *p. 237*

HSS **7.6.2** Describe the spread of Christianity north of the Alps and the roles played by the early church and by monasteries in its diffusion after the fall of the western half of the Roman Empire.

If YOU were there...

You're returning to your village in northern Europe after a hard day working in the fields. But as you reach the top of a hill, you smell smoke. Alarmed, you break into a run. Finally, your village comes into sight, and your fears are realized. Your village is on fire! In the distance, you can see sails moving away on the river.

What do you think has happened to your village?

BUILDING BACKGROUND Europe was a dangerous place after Rome fell. Without the Roman government, Europe had no central authority to keep order. As a result, outlaws and bandits became common. At the same time, new groups of people were moving into Europe. Violence was common. Distressed, people looked for ways to bring order and comfort into their lives.

Christianity Spreads to Northern Europe

As the Roman Empire fell, various groups from the north and east moved into former Roman lands. As they moved in, these groups created their own states. The rulers of these states, usually powerful warlords, began to call themselves kings. These kings often fought among themselves. As a result, by the early 500s Europe was divided into many small kingdoms.

The creation of these kingdoms marked the beginning of the **Middle Ages**, a period that lasted from about 500 to about 1500. We call this time the "middle" ages because it falls between ancient times and modern times. Another name for the Middle Ages is the **medieval** (mee-DEE-vuhl) period, from the Latin words for "middle age."

At the beginning of the Middle Ages, many of the kingdoms of northern Europe were not Christian. Christianity was only common in places that had been part of the Roman Empire, such as Italy and Spain. As time passed, however, Christianity

The Spread of Christianity

ATLANTIC
OCEAN

North
Sea

IRELAND
BRITAIN
Whitby
Canterbury
Aachen
Cologne
Paris
GERMANY
Tours
GAUL
(FRANCE)
Lyon
Milan
Marseille
SPAIN
Toledo
ITALY
Rome
Naples
Caesarea
Carthage
Syracuse
Corinth
Athens
Constantinople
Nicaea
Ephesus
ASIA
MINOR
Antioch
Black Sea
Caspian Sea
Danube River
Tigris River
Euphrates River
Damascus
Mediterranean Sea
Cyrene
Jerusalem
Alexandria
Memphis
EGYPT
Nile River
Red Sea

BIOGRAPHY

Saint Patrick
AD 400s

Saint Patrick was a monk who helped convert the Irish to Christianity. As a teenager, Patrick was kidnapped in Britain and taken to Ireland, where he was forced to work as a shepherd. After six years, he escaped. But later he returned to Ireland to spread Christianity. According to legend, he won favor with the Irish by driving all of the snakes in Ireland into the sea.

Mainly Christian by AD 325
Mainly Christian by AD 600
■ Centers of Christian spread

0   250   500 Miles
0   250   500 Kilometers

GEOGRAPHY SKILLS | INTERPRETING MAPS

Place How far north had Christianity spread by AD 600?

slowly spread farther north. This spread was largely through the efforts of two groups of Christians—missionaries and monks.

Missionaries

Perhaps the most powerful force that helped spread Christianity into northern Europe was the pope. Over the years, many popes sent missionaries to teach people in northern kingdoms about Christianity. Missionaries are people who try to convert others to a particular religion. Some missionaries traveled great distances to spread Christianity to new lands. For their devotion to Christianity, many missionaries were named saints.

Saint is a religious title given to people famous for their holiness.

One of the first places to which popes sent missionaries was Britain. These missionaries traveled all over the island, and eventually most people in Britain became Christian. From Britain, other missionaries carried Christianity into what are now France and Germany.

Not all missionaries, though, were sent by the pope. In fact, one of the first missionaries to travel to northern Europe was **Patrick**, who took it upon himself to teach people about Christianity. In the mid-400s Patrick traveled from Britain to Ireland to convert the people there.

Unlike most missionaries, Patrick traveled alone. Although he faced resistance to his teachings, he eventually converted the Irish people to Christianity.

Monks

While missionaries traveled to spread Christian teachings, men called monks were equally dedicated to their faith. **Monks were religious men who lived apart from society in isolated communities.** In these communities, monks spent their time in prayer, work, and meditation.

Communities of monks, or **monasteries**, were built all over Europe in the Middle Ages. Life in a monastery was strictly organized. The monks had to follow rules that were intended to help them live as good Christians. These rules outlined the day-to-day affairs of the monastery, including how monks should dress and what they should eat.

Most European monasteries followed a set of rules created in the early 500s by an Italian monk named **Benedict**. His code was called the Benedictine Rule, and those who followed it were called Benedictine monks. But not all monks in Europe were Benedictines. Different groups of monks created their own rules. For example, monks in Ireland were very different from monks in France or Germany.

Even though they lived apart from society, monks had a big influence on Europe. Monks performed many services, both inside and outside of monasteries. Monasteries sometimes provided basic services, such as health care, that were unavailable to many members of their communities. The poor and needy would arrive at a monastery and the monks would give them aid.

In addition to giving aid to people in their communities, monks

- ran schools and copied books for those who couldn't read or write,
- collected and saved ancient writings from Greece and Rome,
- served as scribes and advisors to local rulers.

Monks also helped spread Christian teachings into new areas. Many monasteries were built in remote locations where Christians had never traveled before. People living near the monasteries learned about Christianity from the monks.

READING CHECK **Summarizing** How did missionaries and monks help spread Christianity into new areas?

Primary Source

HISTORIC DOCUMENT
The Benedictine Rule

The Benedictine Order was the largest group of monks in Europe in the early Middle Ages. In his rule, Saint Benedict listed the guidelines monks had to follow. Here he describes what each monk was allowed to own.

> Monks were not allowed to own any property.

> An abbot is the head of a monastery.

"For bedding, a mattress, a blanket, a coverlet and a pillow are enough. The beds should be frequently inspected by the Abbot as a precaution against private possessions. If anyone is found to have anything which was not given him by the Abbot, he is to undergo the severest punishment; and that this vice [wickedness] of personal ownership may be totally eliminated, everything necessary should be given by the Abbot; namely, a cowl [hood], a tunic [long shirt], stockings, shoes, a belt, a knife, a pen, a needle, a handkerchief and writing tablets, so that all excuses about necessity are removed.**"**

–from *The Rule of Saint Benedict,* translated by Abbot Parry

ANALYSIS SKILL **ANALYZING PRIMARY SOURCES**

Why do you think Benedictine monks were only allowed a few simple possessions?

The Franks Build an Empire

As Christianity was spreading into northern Europe, political changes were also taking place. In the 480s a powerful group called the Franks conquered Gaul, the region we now call France. Under a ruler named Clovis, the Franks became Christian and created one of the strongest kingdoms in Europe.

As strong as the Franks were under Clovis, though, they had yet to reach their greatest power. That power would not come until the late 700s, when a leader named **Charlemagne** (SHAHR-luh-mayn) appeared. Charlemagne was a brilliant warrior and a strong king, and he led the Franks in building a huge empire.

To build this empire, Charlemagne spent much of his time at war. He led his armies into battle against many neighboring kingdoms and conquered them. By the time he was finished, Charlemagne's empire included all of what is now France. It also stretched into modern Germany, Austria, Italy, and northern Spain.

Charlemagne, a Christian king, had conquered parts of the former Roman Empire. For that reason, on Christmas Day in 800, Pope Leo III crowned Charlemagne Emperor of the Romans. This title symbolized a return to the greatness of the Roman Empire.

Charlemagne didn't spend all of his energy on warfare, however. A great admirer of education, he built schools across Europe. He also brought scholars to teach in his capital at Aachen (AH-kuhn), now in western Germany. Among these scholars were some of the greatest religious scholars and teachers of the Middle Ages. Their teachings helped shape religious and social life in Europe for centuries.

READING CHECK Finding Main Ideas What were Charlemagne's major accomplishments?

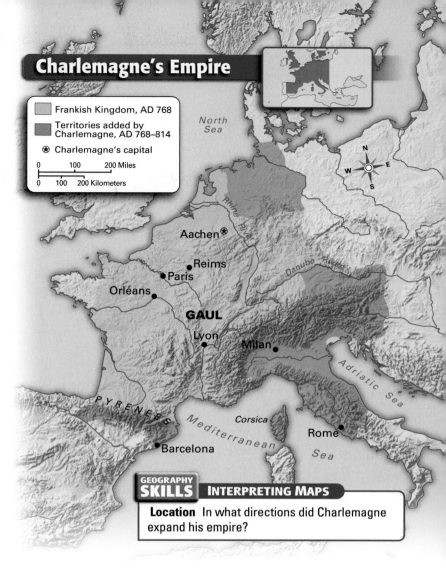

Charlemagne's Empire

Frankish Kingdom, AD 768

Territories added by Charlemagne, AD 768–814

⊛ Charlemagne's capital

0   100   200 Miles

0   100   200 Kilometers

North Sea

Aachen ⊛

Reims

Paris

Orléans

GAUL

Lyon

Milan

PYRENEES

Mediterranean Sea

Corsica

Rome

Barcelona

Adriatic Sea

Rhine River

Danube River

GEOGRAPHY SKILLS INTERPRETING MAPS

Location In what directions did Charlemagne expand his empire?

Invaders Threaten Europe

Even while Charlemagne was building his empire, though, new threats appeared in Europe. Invaders began to attack settlements all over the continent. Muslim armies poured into southern France and northern Italy. Fierce warriors called the Magyars swept into Europe from the east, attacking towns and destroying fields. From Scandinavia came perhaps the most frightening invaders of all, the Vikings.

The Vikings raided Britain, Ireland, and other parts of western Europe. They looted towns and monasteries and took prisoners to sell into slavery. The attacks were swift and savage, and Europeans lived in terror of Viking raids.

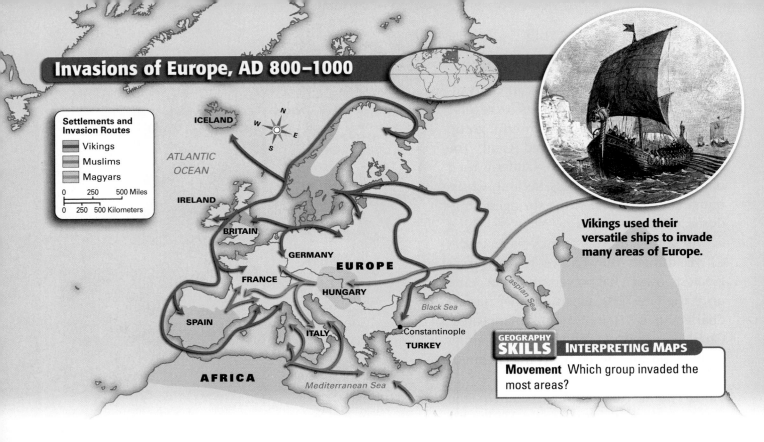

Invasions of Europe, AD 800–1000

Settlements and Invasion Routes
- Vikings
- Muslims
- Magyars

0   250   500 Miles
0 250 500 Kilometers

ICELAND

ATLANTIC OCEAN

IRELAND

BRITAIN

GERMANY

EUROPE

FRANCE

HUNGARY

SPAIN

ITALY

AFRICA

Mediterranean Sea

Black Sea

Caspian Sea

Constantinople

TURKEY

Vikings used their versatile ships to invade many areas of Europe.

GEOGRAPHY SKILLS   INTERPRETING MAPS

Movement Which group invaded the most areas?

Because Vikings could sail their ships up rivers, their raids weren't limited to coastal areas. The Vikings also reached inland cities and attacked cities in the Iberian and Italian peninsulas.

READING CHECK Finding the Main Idea
What groups invaded Europe in the 700s and 800s?

SUMMARY AND PREVIEW After the fall of Rome, northern Europe gradually became Christian. But Europe could still be a dangerous place. Invaders threatened Europeans constantly. In the next section, you will learn about ways people tried to protect themselves from invaders.

Section 2 Assessment

go.hrw.com
Online Quiz
KEYWORD: SQ7 HP9

Reviewing Ideas, Terms, and People   **HSS** 7.6.2

1. **a. Describe** How are **monks** and **monasteries** related?
   b. Explain Why did missionaries travel to northern Europe?
   c. Elaborate Why do you think monks followed such strict rules?
2. **a. Recall** What is **Charlemagne** famous for?
   b. Evaluate What do you think Charlemagne's greatest accomplishment was? Why?
3. **a. Identify** What areas of Europe did the Vikings raid?
   b. Make Generalizations Why were people in Europe so frightened of Viking raids?

Critical Thinking

4. **Summarizing** Copy this outline of a monastery. Inside, list two rules that monks had to follow. Outside, list three contributions that monks made to society.

1. _____   1. _____
2. _____   2. _____
           3. _____

FOCUS ON WRITING

5. **Considering Life Then** Now you see why you might need the protection of knights. Look back at your list and add to it. What services might you hire knights to perform?

Charlemagne

What would you do if you ruled much of Europe?

When did he live? 742–814

Where did he live? Charlemagne, or Charles the Great, ruled most of what are now France and Germany. He lived mainly in his capital, Aachen, near the modern city of Cologne, Germany.

What did he do? Through his wars of conquest, Charlemagne united many of the tribes of central and western Europe into a single empire.

Why is he important? While Europe was still reeling from the collapse of Rome, Charlemagne brought people together. He helped Europeans realize that they shared common bonds, such as Christianity, that linked them. In other words, he helped people see themselves as Europeans, not members of tribes.

Drawing Conclusions How did this change in view affect later European society?

KEY EVENTS

771 Charlemagne becomes king of the Franks.

773 Charlemagne becomes an ally of the pope after rescuing him from invaders.

794 Charlemagne makes Aachen his capital.

800 Pope Leo III names Charlemagne emperor.

This painting shows Charlemagne being crowned by the pope in AD 800.

from

Beowulf

translated by Burton Raffel

About the Reading *The story of a mighty hero, Beowulf was composed in the 700s but probably not written down until much later. The hero of the story, Beowulf, is a Geat, a member of a group that lived in what is now Sweden. One day he hears of a terrible monster, Grendel, who has killed and eaten many Danish warriors in Britain. To help the Danish king—and to prove his own valor—Beowulf sails across the sea and promises to rid the Danes of their enemy. One night, he lies in wait for Grendel inside Herot, the hall of the Danish king, ready to kill the monster.*

AS YOU READ Look for details that reflect Beowulf's heroism.

GUIDED READING

WORD HELP

bogs wet, spongy lands
bolted swallowed whole

❶ Grendel creeps out of his den in the swamp and makes his way to Herot, where Beowulf is waiting.

What do you think was going through Beowulf's mind while he waited for Grendel?

❷ Beowulf is only pretending to sleep, hoping to catch Grendel by surprise.

ELA Reading 7.3.0 Students read and respond to historically and culturally significant works of literature that reflect and enhance their studies of history and social science.

Out from the marsh, from the foot of misty
Hills and bogs, bearing God's hatred,
Grendel came, hoping to kill
Anyone he could trap on this trip to high Herot . . . ❶
Eyes were watching his evil steps,
Waiting to see his swift hard claws.
Grendel snatched at the first Geat
He came to, ripped him apart, cut
His body to bits with powerful jaws,
Drank the blood from his veins, and bolted
Him down, hands and feet; death
And Grendel's great teeth came together,
Snapping life shut. Then he stepped to another
Still body, clutched at Beowulf with his claws,
Grasped at a strong-hearted wakeful sleeper ❷
—And was instantly seized himself . . .
   That shepherd of evil, guardian of crime,
Knew at once that nowhere on earth
Had he met a man whose hands were harder. . . .
  All of Beowulf's
Band had jumped from their beds, ancestral
Swords raised and ready, determined

Danish swords

To protect their prince if they could. ❸ Their courage
Was great but wasted: They could hack at Grendel
From every side, trying to open
A path for his evil soul, but their points
Could not hurt him, the sharpest and hardest iron
Could not scratch at his skin. . . .
Now he discovered—once the afflictor
Of men, tormentor of their days—what it meant
To feud with Almighty God: Grendel
Saw that his strength was deserting him, his claws
Bound fast, Higlac's brave follower ❹ tearing at
His hands. The monster's hatred rose higher,
But his power had gone. He twisted in pain,
And the bleeding sinews deep in his shoulder
Snapped, muscle and bone split
And broke. The battle was over, Beowulf
Had been granted new glory: Grendel escaped,
But wounded as he was could flee to his den,
His miserable hole at the bottom of the marsh,
Only to die, to wait for the end
Of all his days. And after that bloody
Combat the Danes laughed with delight.
He who had come to them from across the sea,
Bold and strong-minded, had driven affliction
Off, purged Herot clean. He was happy,
Now, with that night's fierce work; the Danes
Had been served as he'd boasted he'd serve them; Beowulf,
A prince of the Geats, had killed Grendel,
Ended the grief, the sorrow, the suffering
Forced on Hrothgar's helpless people
By a bloodthirsty fiend. No Dane doubted
The victory, for the proof, hanging high
From the rafters where Beowulf had hung it, was the monster's
Arm, claw and shoulder and all. ❺

GUIDED READING

WORD HELP

afflictor one who causes suffering

tormentor one who causes pain

sinews tendons or connective tissues

purged rid

❸ The author of *Beowulf*—and his Germanic ancestors—belonged to a warrior society. This society was based on the loyalty of warriors to their leader.

What was a warrior's main responsibility?

❹ "Higlac's brave follower" is Beowulf. Higlac was the name of Beowulf's lord.

❺ Hrothgar is the king of the Danes. To show his people that they no longer have to fear—and as a trophy of his victory—Beowulf hangs Grendel's arm from the ceiling.

How do you think the Danes feel toward Beowulf after the battle?

CONNECTING LITERATURE TO HISTORY

1. **Analyzing** In 597 the pope sent a group of missionaries to Britain. They traveled throughout the island, spreading Christianity. What words or phrases in this passage tell you that its author was Christian?

2. **Generalizing** By the early 500s western Europe was divided into small kingdoms that were often at war. Based on the passage, what qualities do you think were most valued in warriors of the early Middle Ages?

Feudalism and Manor Life

What You Will Learn...

Main Ideas

1. Feudalism governed how knights and nobles dealt with each other.
2. Feudalism spread through much of Europe.
3. The manor system dominated Europe's economy.
4. Towns and trade grew and helped end the feudal system.

The Big Idea

A complex web of duties and obligations governed relationships between people in the Middle Ages.

Key Terms and People

knights, *p. 242*
vassal, *p. 243*
feudalism, *p. 243*
William the Conqueror, *p. 244*
manor, *p. 245*
serfs, *p. 245*
Eleanor of Aquitaine, *p. 246*

HSS 7.6.3 Understand the development of feudalism, its role in the medieval European economy, the way in which it was influenced by physical geography (the role of the manor and the growth of towns), and how feudal relationships provided the foundation of political order.

If YOU were there...

You are a peasant in the Middle Ages, living on the land of a noble. Although you and your family work very hard for many hours of the day, much of the food you grow goes to the noble and his family. Your house is very small, and it has a dirt floor. Your parents are tired and weak, and you wish you could do something to improve their lives.

Is there any way you could change your life?

BUILDING BACKGROUND Hard work was a constant theme in the lives of peasants in the Middle Ages. They worked long hours and had to obey the wishes of nobles. But most nobles weren't free to live as they chose either. They were sworn to obey more powerful nobles, who had to obey the wishes of the king. Life in the Middle Ages was one big web of duties and obligations.

Feudalism Governs Knights and Nobles

When the Vikings, Magyars, and Muslims began their raids in the 800s, the Frankish kings were unable to defend their empire. Their army was too slow to defend against the lightning-fast attacks of their enemies. Because they couldn't depend on protection from their kings, nobles had to defend their own lands. As a result, the power of nobles grew, and kings became less powerful. In fact, some nobles became as powerful as the kings themselves. Although these nobles remained loyal to the king, they ruled their lands as independent territories.

Knights and Land

To defend their lands, nobles needed soldiers. The best soldiers were **knights**, warriors who fought on horseback. However, knights needed weapons, armor, and horses. This equipment was expensive, and few people had money in the early Middle Ages.

As a result, nobles gave knights fiefs (FEEFS), or pieces of land, instead of money for their military service. A noble who gave land to a knight in this way was called a lord.

In return for the land, a knight promised to support the noble in battle or in other matters. A knight who promised to support a lord in exchange for land was called a **vassal**. The vassal swore that he would always remain loyal to his lord. Historians call this system of promises that governed the relationships between lords and vassals **feudalism** (FYOO-duh-lih-zuhm).

A Lord's Duties

The ties between lords and vassals were the heart of feudalism. Each group had certain responsibilities toward the other. A lord had to send help to his vassals if an enemy attacked. In addition, he had to be fair toward his vassals. He couldn't cheat them or punish them for no reason. If a lord failed to do what he was supposed to, his vassals could break all ties with him.

To defend their lands, many lords built castles. A castle is a large building with strong walls that can easily be defended against attacks. Early castles didn't look like the towering structures we see in movies and storybooks. Those great castles were built much later in the Middle Ages. Most early castles were made of wood, not stone. Nevertheless, these castles provided security in times of war.

A Vassal's Duties

When a lord went to war, he called on his vassals to fight with him. But fighting wasn't a vassal's only duty. For example, vassals had to give their lords money on special occasions, such as when a lord's son became a knight or when his daughter got married. A vassal also had to give his lord food and shelter if he came to visit. If a vassal gained enough land, he could become a lord. In this way a person might be both a lord and a vassal. A knight could also accept fiefs from two different lords and become a vassal to both. Feudal obligations could become confusing.

READING CHECK **Sequencing** What led to the creation of feudalism?

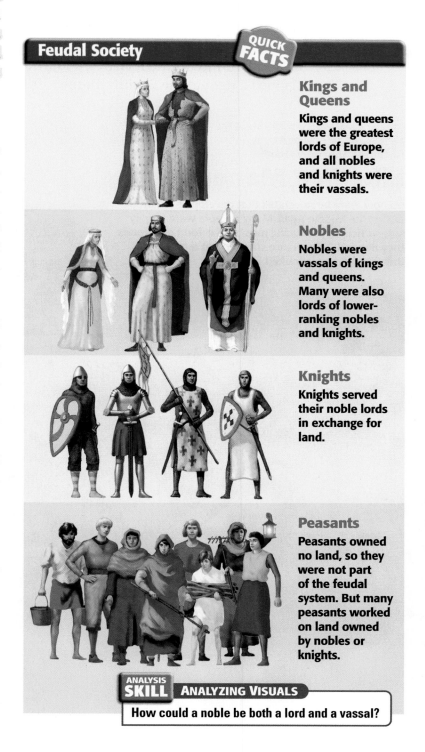

Feudal Society QUICK FACTS

Kings and Queens

Kings and queens were the greatest lords of Europe, and all nobles and knights were their vassals.

Nobles

Nobles were vassals of kings and queens. Many were also lords of lower-ranking nobles and knights.

Knights

Knights served their noble lords in exchange for land.

Peasants

Peasants owned no land, so they were not part of the feudal system. But many peasants worked on land owned by nobles or knights.

ANALYSIS SKILL **ANALYZING VISUALS**

How could a noble be both a lord and a vassal?

Feudalism Spreads

Feudalism was first created by the Franks. Before long the system began to spread into other kingdoms. In the 1000s, Frankish knights introduced feudalism into northern Italy, Spain, and Germany. Feudalism then spread into eastern Europe.

Feudalism also reached Britain in the 1000s. It was brought there by a French noble named William, who was the duke of Normandy in northern France, and who claimed a right to the English throne.

In 1066, William and his knights sailed into England and defeated the English king at the Battle of Hastings. After winning the battle, William declared himself the new king of England. He became known as **William the Conqueror**. To reward his knights for their part in the victory, William gave them large estates of land in his new country. This was the beginning of feudalism in England.

READING CHECK Sequencing How did feudalism spread to England?

History Close-up

Life on a Manor

Manors were large estates that developed in Europe during the Middle Ages. Many manors were largely self-sufficient, producing most of the food and goods they needed. This picture shows what a manor in Britain might have looked like.

The lord of the manor lived in a large stone house called the manor house.

Peasants grew vegetables in small gardens near their houses.

In the fall, peasants worked to harvest crops like wheat.

The Manor System

When a knight received a fief from his lord, he needed a way to farm it. Knights were fighters who didn't have time to work in the fields. At the same time, peasants, or small farmers, needed to grow food to live. Very few peasants, however, owned any land.

As a result, a new economic system developed. Under this system, knights allowed peasants to farm land on their large estates. In return, the peasants had to give the knights food or other payment.

The large estate owned by a knight or lord was called a **manor**. In general, each manor included a large house or castle, pastures, fields, and forests. It also had a village where the peasants who worked on the manor lived.

Peasants, Serfs, and Other Workers

Most medieval lords kept about one-fourth to one-third of their land for their own use. The rest of the land was divided among peasants and **serfs**—workers who were tied to the land on which they lived.

The village church was built on a small piece of land that belonged to the lord.

Sheep grazed on grassy fields, and villagers used sheep's wool to make clothes.

The village black-smith made iron tools for farming.

Harvested wheat was taken to the mill and ground into flour, which was used to make bread.

ANALYSIS SKILL **ANALYZING VISUALS**

What goods can you see being produced on this manor?

Although they weren't slaves, serfs weren't allowed to leave their land without the lord's permission. Serfs spent much of their time working in their lords' fields. In return for this work, they got a small piece of land to farm for themselves. They also received their lords' protection against outlaws and raiders.

The lives of serfs and peasants weren't easy. Farm labor was hard, and they often worked in the fields late into the night. Men did most of the farming. Women made clothing, cooked, grew vegetables, and gathered firewood. Even children worked, tending sheep and chickens.

In addition to peasants and serfs, most manors had several skilled workers. These workers traded their goods and services to the peasants in exchange for food. Lords wanted the people who lived on the manor to produce everything they needed, including food and clothing.

ACADEMIC VOCABULARY
role assigned behavior

Manor Lords

The lord of a manor controlled everything that happened on his lands. His word was law. The lord resolved any disputes that arose on the manor and punished people who misbehaved. He also collected taxes from the people who lived on his manor.

As you would expect, manor lords and ladies lived more comfortably than other people on the manor. They had servants and large houses. Still, their lives weren't easy. Lords who survived diseases faced the possibility of being killed in war.

Women in the Middle Ages

Regardless of their social class, women in the Middle Ages had fewer rights than men. Women generally had to obey the wishes of their fathers or husbands. But women still had important **roles** in society. As you have read, peasant women worked to support their families. Noblewomen also had duties. They ran manor households and supervised servants. Women governed manors when their husbands went to war. Some noblewomen, like the French woman **Eleanor of Aquitaine**, had great political power. Other women who wanted power and influence joined the most powerful of institutions, the Christian Church.

READING CHECK **Contrasting** How were the lives of nobles and peasants different?

Towns and Trade Grow

In the Middle Ages, most people lived on manors or on small farms, not in towns. As a result, most towns were small. After about 1000, however, this situation began to change. Some towns became big cities. At the same time, new towns appeared.

What led to the growth of medieval towns? For one thing, Europe's population increased, partly because more food was

BIOGRAPHY

Eleanor of Aquitaine
1122?–1204

Eleanor of Aquitaine was one of the most powerful people of the Middle Ages. She ruled Aquitaine, a region in southwestern France, as the king's vassal. In 1137 Eleanor became queen of France when she married King Louis VII. Later, she divorced Louis and became queen of England by marrying King Henry II of England. Even while she was queen of England, she spent much of her time ruling her own territory. Eleanor had many children, and two of her sons later became kings of England.

Drawing Conclusions
Why do you think Eleanor had more power than other women in the Middle Ages?

available. New technology helped farmers produce larger harvests than ever before. Among these improvements was a heavier plow. With this plow farmers could dig deeper into the soil, helping their plants grow better. Another new device, the horse collar, allowed farmers to plow fields using horses. In times past, farmers had used oxen, which were strong but slow. With horses, farmers could tend larger fields, grow more food, and feed more people.

Towns also grew because trade increased. As Europe's population grew, so did trade. Trade routes spread all across Europe. Merchants also brought goods from Asia and Africa to sell in markets in Europe. The chance to make money in trade led many people to leave their farms and move to cities, causing cities to grow even larger.

In time, the growth of trade led to the decline of feudalism. Knights began to demand money for their services instead of land. At the same time, serfs and peasants left their manors for towns, slowly weakening the manor system.

READING CHECK **Identifying Cause and Effect** Why did towns and trade grow in the Middle Ages?

Medieval Market

In the Middle Ages, some towns held large trade fairs each year. This illustration shows a bishop blessing a trade fair in France.

SUMMARY AND PREVIEW In this section, you learned about European feudalism and the social and economic relationships it created among people. In the next section, you'll read about how this system compares to one that developed halfway around the world in Japan.

Section 3 Assessment

go.hrw.com
Online Quiz
KEYWORD: SQ7 HP9

Reviewing Ideas, Terms, and People   HSS 7.6.3

1. **a. Define** What was a **knight**?
   b. Explain Why did **vassals** have to serve lords?
   c. Elaborate Do you think knights or lords benefited more from **feudalism**? Why?
2. **Explain** How did **William the Conqueror** help spread feudalism?
3. **a. Describe** What was a typical **manor** like?
   b. Elaborate How do you think most **serfs** felt about the manor system?
4. **a. Recall** What led to the growth of Europe's population in the Middle Ages?
   b. Draw Conclusions Why do you think many peasants left their farms for cities?

Critical Thinking

5. **Analyzing** Draw a flow chart like the one below. In each box, list the responsibilities that each group had toward the other.

Lords	Knights	Serfs

FOCUS ON WRITING

6. **Writing about Knights** Take notes on the knights described in this section and how what you've learned will affect your search for knights. What kinds of people will you hire? How will you pay them? Write your answers in your notebook.

Feudal Societies

If YOU were there...

You want to be a squire, a young person who trains to be a knight. Your best friend thinks you are foolish. He says that you'll have to swear a vow of loyalty to your lord, and you'll have to fight in battles for him. Your sister tells you that you will have to follow a strict code of honor. But you still want to be a knight.

Why do you want to be a knight?

BUILDING BACKGROUND Knights were an important part of feudal society. People who wanted to be knights did have to swear vows of loyalty, fight in battles, and follow a code of honor. But European knights were not the only people who had to live by these rules. Half a world away, Japanese samurai lived under similar obligations. In fact, if you look at these two societies, you will see that many striking similarities existed between them.

What You Will Learn...

Main Ideas

1. Feudal societies shared common elements in Europe and Japan.
2. Europe and Japan differed in their cultural elements such as religion and art.

The Big Idea

Although the feudal systems of Europe and Japan were similar, their cultures were very different.

Key Terms

chivalry, *p. 249*
haiku, *p. 250*

Feudal Societies Share Common Elements

Feudalism was not unique to Europe. As you have already read, the Japanese developed a very similar system halfway around the world from Europe at about the same time. But how similar were the two societies?

Lords and Vassals

In Europe, the basis for the feudal system was land. Kings and lords gave land to knights. In return, the knights promised to serve their lords and fight for them when necessary. Many knights owned large manors. Peasants and serfs worked on the manors and paid the lords in food.

A very similar system existed in Japan. There, the emperor gave land to great lords who were later called daimyo. In turn, these lords employed warriors called samurai. Like European knights, the samurai promised to serve and fight for their lords. In exchange, the samurai received rice and grain. Lords got the grain from peasants who farmed their land. Peasants had to pay their lords in grain.

Samurai and Knights

Although Japanese samurai and European knights never actually met, they had much in common. Both were the elite warriors of their time and place.

ANALYSIS SKILL   ANALYZING VISUALS

How are the samurai and knight similar? How are they different?

Knights and Samurai

The lives of knights and samurai were, in many ways, very similar. Both had to swear vows of loyalty to their lords. These lords expected them to fight well and to be fearless in battle. The lords also expected their knights or samurai to live disciplined and honorable lives.

Both European knights and Japanese samurai had to follow strict codes of honor that governed how they behaved. You have already learned about Bushido, the Japanese code of the samurai. Europeans called their code of honorable behavior for knights **chivalry** (SHIV-uhl-ree). Like Bushido, chivalry required knights to be brave and loyal but humble and modest at the same time. It also required them to be kind and generous when dealing with people, especially women.

Because of their loyalty and dedication, both knights and samurai were greatly admired by other members of their societies. This admiration can often be seen in literary descriptions of the men, such as this description of the French knight Roland and his comrades who are greatly outnumbered by their enemies:

> "The battle is fearful and full of grief.
> Oliver and Roland strike like good men,
> the Archbishop, more than a thousand blows,
> and the Twelve Peers do not hang back, they strike!
> the French fight side by side, all as one man.
> The pagans die by hundreds, by thousands:
> whoever does not flee finds no refuge from death,
> like it or not, there he ends his days."
> –from *The Song of Roland,* translated by Frederick Goldin

FOCUS ON READING

Why is a primary source included here?

Even though Roland and the others were almost certain that they would die, they continued to fight. They became heroes, admired for their courage and bravery.

ACADEMIC
VOCABULARY
elements parts

The Japanese also admired their warriors for their courage. A passage from a Japanese text shows a similar admiration for warriors fighting impossible odds:

"Where Naozane galloped, Sueshige followed; where Sueshige galloped, Naozane followed. Neither willing to be outdone, they dashed in by turns, whipping their horses and attacking until the sparks flew… Naozane pulled out the arrows that were lodged in his own armor, tossed them aside, faced the stronghold with a scowl, and shouted in a mighty voice, 'I am Naozane, the man who left Kamakura last winter determined to give his life for Lord Yoritomo… Confront me! Confront me!'"

–from *The Tale of the Heike*, translated by Helen Craig McCullough

READING CHECK **Comparing** How were European knights and Japanese samurai similar?

Europe and Japan Differ

Although European and Japanese societies were the same in some ways, in most ways they were not. Their two cultures were also very different.

Perhaps the main difference between medieval Europeans and Japanese was religion. Nearly all Europeans were Christian, while the Japanese blended **elements** of Buddhism, Shinto, and Confucianism. European and Japanese religions taught very different ways of looking at the world. People in those places, therefore, did not act the same way.

The differences between Europe and Japan can also be seen in the artistic forms popular in each place. European art in the Middle Ages dealt mostly with religious themes. Paintings showed scenes from the Bible, and writers tried to inspire people with stories about great Christians.

In Japan, on the other hand, most art dealt with natural themes. Paintings of nature were common, and people built many gardens. Buildings blended with nature, rather than standing out. Japanese literature also celebrated nature. For example, Japanese poets in the 1600s created **haiku** (HY-koo), short, three-line poems of 17 syllables that describe nature scenes.

Art in Europe and Japan

The medieval arts of Europe and Japan were very different. European art often emphasized religion, while Japanese art often emphasized nature.

In what ways are these two paintings different?

Feudal Europe

- Christianity
- Religious themes in art and literature

- Feudal government
- Royalty (kings and queens, emperor)
- Nobles (lords, daimyo)
- Warriors (knights, samurai)
- Warrior codes of honor (chivalry, Bushido)
- Peasants worked land

Feudal Japan

- Buddhism, Shinto, Confucianism
- Nature themes in art and literature

Here is one example of haiku:

> Very soon they die—
> but of that there is no sign
> in the locust-cry.
>
> –Matsuo Basho, from *Anthology of Japanese Literature*, edited by Donald Keene

Although European and Japanese feudal systems seemed similar, the cultures that lay behind them were different. Still, it is remarkable to think that feudal systems so similar could exist so far apart.

READING CHECK **Contrasting** How were feudal European and Japanese cultures different?

SUMMARY AND PREVIEW In this section you learned how to compare feudalism in Europe and Japan. Although both Europe and Japan had feudal societies, there were many differences in the two societies. Feudalism lasted much longer in Japan than it did in Europe, not disappearing until the 1800s. In the next chapter you will learn about how European society changed after feudalism disappeared in the later Middle Ages. One major change was the growing importance of religion.

Section 4 Assessment

go.hrw.com
Online Quiz
KEYWORD: SQ7 HP9

Reviewing Ideas, Terms, and People

1. **a. Define** What was **chivalry**?
   b. Compare What were three characteristics knights and samurai shared?
   c. Develop Why do you think feudal systems developed in both Europe and Japan?
2. **a. Identify** What religion were most people in medieval Europe? What religions influenced most people in Japan?
   b. Contrast How were the subjects of **haiku** different from medieval European poems?
   c. Evaluate In your opinion, were European and Japanese societies more similar to or different from each other? Explain your answer.

Critical Thinking

3. **Comparing and Contrasting** Draw a chart like the one below. List two similarities and one key difference between knights and samurai.

Similarities	Difference
1.	1.
2.	

FOCUS ON WRITING

4. **Describing Chivalry** Think about what you've just learned about chivalry. What kinds of rules will you expect your knights to follow? How will you explain these rules to them?

Social Studies Skills

Interpreting Diagrams

Understand the Skill

Diagrams are drawings that use lines and labels to explain or illustrate something. Different types of diagrams have different purposes. *Pictorial diagrams* show an object in simple form, much like it would look if you were viewing it. *Cutaway diagrams* show the "insides" of an object. *Component diagrams* show how an object is organized by separating it into parts. Such diagrams are sometimes also called *schematic drawings*. The ability to interpret diagrams will help you to better understand a historical object, its function, and how it worked.

Learn the Skill

Use these basic steps to interpret a diagram:

❶ Determine what type of diagram it is.

❷ Read the diagram's title or caption to find out what it represents.

❸ Look for any labels and read them carefully. Most diagrams include text that identifies the object's parts or explains relationships between the parts.

❹ If a legend is present, study it to identify and understand any symbols and colors that are used in the diagram.

❺ Look for numbers or letters that might indicate a sequence of steps. Also look for any arrows that might show direction or movement.

An Early Castle

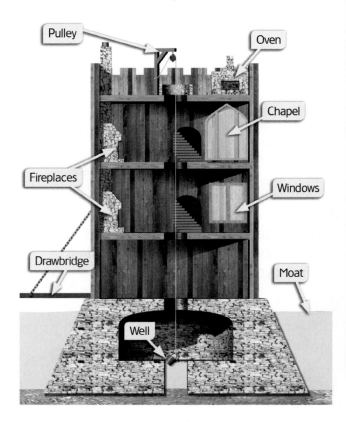

Pulley · Oven · Chapel · Fireplaces · Windows · Drawbridge · Moat · Well

Practice and Apply the Skill

Interpret the diagram of an early castle, and answer the following questions.

1. What type of diagram is this?
2. What labels in the diagram suggest how the castle was heated?
3. What was the purpose of the pulley?
4. Of what materials was the castle made?
5. What features of the castle helped make it secure against attack?

Visual Summary

Use the visual summary below to help you review the main ideas of the chapter.

QUICK FACTS

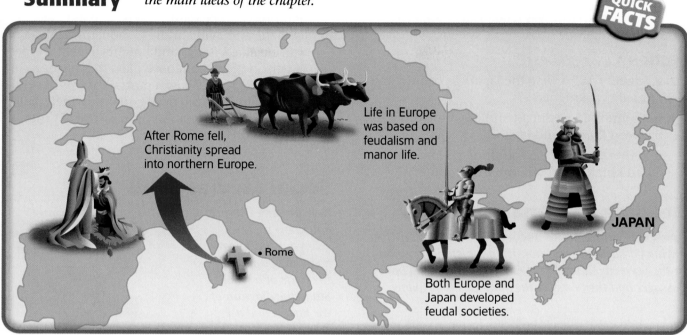

After Rome fell, Christianity spread into northern Europe.

Life in Europe was based on feudalism and manor life.

• Rome

JAPAN

Both Europe and Japan developed feudal societies.

Reviewing Vocabulary, Terms, and People

Write each word defined below, circling each letter that is marked by a star. Then write the word these letters spell.

1. ***** _ _ _ _—religious men who lived in isolated communities

2. ***** _ _ _ _ _ _ _ of Aquitaine—one of the most powerful women of the Middle Ages

3. _ _ _ ***** _ _ _ _ _ _—a political system in which land is given for military service

4. _ _ ***** _ _ _ _ _ _—a code of behavior that knights had to follow

5. _ ***** _ _ _—farm workers who were tied to the land they worked

6. ***** _ _ _ _ _—someone who received land in exchange for military service

7. _ ***** _ _ _—a large estate

8. _ _ _ _ _ ***** _ _ _ _ _ _ _—Frankish king who created a huge empire

Comprehension and Critical Thinking

SECTION 1 *(Pages 230–233)* **HSS** 7.6.1

9. **a. Identify** What region of Europe has the best land for farming?

b. Analyze How have rivers and seas influenced life in Europe?

c. Evaluate Based on its geography, in which part of Europe would you want to live? Why would you want to live there?

SECTION 2 *(Pages 234–238)* **HSS** 7.6.2

10. **a. Identify** What two groups of people were largely responsible for the northern spread of Christianity?

b. Compare In what way was the empire of the Franks under Charlemagne like the Roman Empire?

c. Elaborate How do you think the building of new monasteries helped spread Christianity?

SECTION 3 *(Pages 242–247)* **HSS** 7.6.3

11. a. Describe What were women's lives like during the Middle Ages?

b. Analyze How did knights and lords try to make their manors self-sufficient?

c. Elaborate How was feudalism related to medieval Europe's economic system?

SECTION 4 *(Pages 248–251)*

12. a. Identify Who were the Japanese counterparts of medieval knights?

b. Contrast How did art and literature differ between Europe and Japan?

c. Elaborate Why do you think people wrote about knights and samurai in literature?

Reading and Analysis Skills

Analyzing Primary and Secondary Sources *The following passages are both taken from historians writing in the 800s about the life of Charlemagne. Read both passages and then answer the questions that follow.*

> "I consider that it would be foolish for me to write about Charlemagne's birth and childhood …for nothing is set down in writing about this and nobody can be found still alive who claims to have any personal knowledge of these matters. I have therefore decided to leave out what is not really known …"
>
> –Einhard, from *Two Lives of Charlemagne*, translated by Lewis Thorpe

> "When I was a child, he was already a very old man. He brought me up and used to tell me about these events. I was a poor pupil, and I often ran away, but in the end he forced me to listen."
>
> –Notker, from *Two Lives of Charlemagne*, translated by Lewis Thorpe

13. Are these passages primary or secondary sources?

14. Which historian do you think would be the most credible, or believable?

Reviewing Themes

15. Religion Do you think religion helped to unify or divide Europeans in the Middle Ages? Why?

16. Society and Culture Do you think religion or government had more influence on medieval societies? Why?

Using the Internet

17. Activity: Researching Daily Life Feudalism created a web of relationships and duties between different people in medieval Europe. Enter the activity keyword and research the lives of monks and peasants, rulers such as Charlemagne and William the Conqueror, and warriors like Vikings and knights. Pick the type of person you would have liked to have been in the Middle Ages. Draw a portrait of this person. Then write 5–6 sentences explaining their daily life. Include information on how they fit into the political order of society.

Social Studies Skills

Interpreting Diagrams *You know there are many types of diagrams. Some diagrams show the parts of a whole. Study the diagram of the knight and use it to answer the questions that follow.*

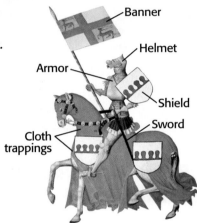

18. Which parts of a knight's outfit were used for protection? Which might help him be recognized in battle?

19. What did a knight use as a weapon?

20. Why might a knight carry a banner?

FOCUS ON WRITING

21. Writing a Job Ad "Wanted: Brave and Loyal Knights." Use your notes from this chapter to write a job ad. Start your ad by explaining why you need knights to help you. Then write a description of the type of people who will be suitable for the job and how they will be expected to behave. Be sure to mention in your ad what knights will receive in exchange for their service.

Standards Assessment

DIRECTIONS: Read each question, and write the letter of the best response.

1

PERSON A

Obligations to Person B
- Provide Protection
- Provide Land

PERSON B

Obligations to Person A
- Provide Loyalty
- Provide Military Service

In this diagram, Person B is probably a
A lord.
B vassal.
C serf.
D peasant.

2 One thing that continued to grow and spread across Europe after the fall of the Roman Empire was
A Christianity.
B Roman culture.
C Bushido.
D republican government.

3 Why would feudalism have taken hold more strongly in northern Europe than in southern Europe?
A Fewer geographic barriers protected northern Europeans from invasion by enemies.
B Southern Europeans were more interested in fishing than in farming.

C A larger number of towns grew up along the rivers of northern Europe.
D Most people in southern Europe lived along the region's long coastlines.

4 Which of these descriptions does *not* apply to feudalism as it developed in Europe?
A growing power of kings
B powerful nobles
C clearly defined roles in society
D duties and obligations

5 One way in which society developed *differently* in Europe and Japan was in
A the relationship between lords and vassals.
B the duties and obligations in each system.
C the themes of their art and literature.
D the behavior of knights and samurai.

Connecting with Past Learnings

6 Charlemagne was a brilliant warrior and a strong king. The achievements of which ancient figure have the *least* in common with those of Charlemagne?
A Julius Caesar
B Alexander the Great
C Aristotle
D Shi Huangdi

7 Serfs were tied to the land on which they worked. A serf in medieval Europe held a place in society that was *most* like
A a Brahman in ancient India.
B a peasant in ancient China.
C a Christian in ancient Rome.
D a trader in ancient Egypt.

The Later Middle Ages

California Standards

History–Social Science

7.6 Students analyze the geographic, political, economic, religious, and social structures of the civilizations of Medieval Europe.

Analysis Skills

CS 3 Identify physical and cultural features.

HI 2 Understand and distinguish cause and effect.

English–Language Arts

Writing 7.1 Students write clear, coherent, and focused essays.

Reading 7.2.3 Analyze text that uses the cause-and-effect organizational pattern.

FOCUS ON WRITING

A Historical Article Your friend is the editor of a magazine for young children. He wants you to write an article on the most important people in Europe in the Middle Ages. As you read, collect information to help you write this article.

CHAPTER EVENTS

1066 The Battle of Hastings is fought.

1000

WORLD EVENTS

1055 The Seljuk Turks take control of Baghdad.

What You Will Learn...

In this chapter, you will learn about life in Europe during the later Middle Ages. Christianity was a major influence on people's lives during these years. This photo shows the monastery at Mont St. Michel in France.

1096–1291
Crusaders battle for control of the Holy Land.

1347–1351
The Black Death kills about 25 million people in Europe.

1492
The Spanish drive the Jews out of Spain.

1100

1200

1300

1400

1500

1192 The first shogun takes power in Japan.

1405–1433
Admiral Zheng He leads Chinese sea expeditions of Asia and Africa.

1492
Christopher Columbus lands in the Americas.

THE LATER MIDDLE AGES **257**

Reading Social Studies

by Kylene Beers

Economics | Geography | Politics | Religion | Society and Culture | Science and Technology

Focus on Themes The later Middle Ages in Europe were a time of change. As the Christian church grew stronger, popes challenged kings for power, and people who disagreed with Christian teachings were punished. Beautiful churches and religious art were created, while soldiers set out to fight wars over religious issues. As you can see, **religion** was a major force in people's lives. It was one of the most important factors that shaped Europe's **society and culture** during this period.

Causes and Effects in History

Focus on Reading No event happens for no reason. To really understand past events, you should try to figure out what made them occur.

Identifying Causes and Effects A **cause** is something that makes another thing happen. An **effect** is the result of something else that happened. Most historical events have a number of causes as well as a number of effects.

1. *Many people in Italy looked to the pope as their leader. As a result, some popes began to live like royalty. They became rich and built huge palaces. At the same time, they came into conflict with Europe's other political leaders, kings.* (p. 261)

TIP Sometimes writers use words that signal a cause or an effect:

Cause—*reason, basis, because, motivated, as*

Effect—*therefore, as a result, for that reason, so*

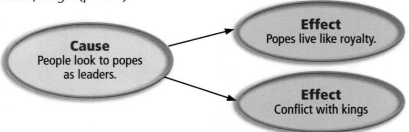

Cause
People look to popes as leaders.

Effect
Popes live like royalty.

Effect
Conflict with kings

2. *As popes worked to increase their power, they often came into conflict with kings. For example, kings thought they should be able to select bishops in their countries. Popes, on the other hand, argued that only they could choose religious officials.* (p. 263)

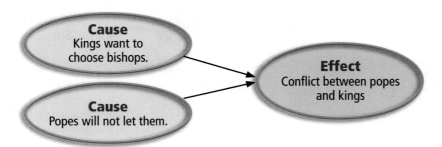

Cause
Kings want to choose bishops.

Cause
Popes will not let them.

Effect
Conflict between popes and kings

Additional reading support can be found in the

Inter active

Reader and Study Guide

ELA Reading 7.2.3 Analyze text that uses the cause-and-effect organizational pattern.

HSS Analysis HI 2 Understand and distinguish cause and effect.

You Try It!

The following passage from this chapter describes a series of actions taken by Pope Gregory VII and Holy Roman Emperor Henry IV. Read closely to see the causes and results of these actions.

Kings and Popes Clash

In 1073 a new pope came to power in Rome. His name was Pope Gregory VII. Trouble arose when Gregory disapproved of a bishop chosen by the Holy Roman Emperor Henry IV. Angry because the pope questioned his authority, Henry convinced Germany's bishops that they should remove Gregory as pope. In response, the pope excommunicated Henry. He called on the empire's nobles to overthrow Henry.

Desperate to stay in power, Henry went to Italy to ask the pope for forgiveness. Gregory refused to see him. For three days Henry stood barefoot in the snow outside the castle where Pope Gregory was staying. Eventually, Gregory accepted Henry's apology.

From Chapter 10, p. 263

After you read the passage, draw a chart like the one below in your notebook, filling in the missing causes and effects.

Causes	Effects
Gregory disapproved of bishop.	1. _____
	2. _____
3. _____	Gregory excommunicates Henry.
Henry wants to stay in power.	4. _____
5. _____	Henry stands barefoot in snow.

As you read **Chapter 10,** look for words that signal causes or effects. Make a chart like the one above to keep track of how causes and effects are related.

Academic Vocabulary

Success in school is related to knowing academic vocabulary— the words that are frequently used in school assignments and discussions. In this chapter, you will learn the following academic words:

authority (p. 262)
policy (p. 284)

Popes and Kings

What You Will Learn...

Main Ideas

1. Popes and kings ruled Europe as spiritual and political leaders.
2. Popes fought for power, leading to a permanent split within the church.
3. Kings and popes clashed over some issues.

The Big Idea

Popes and kings dominated European society in the Middle Ages.

Key Terms and People

excommunicate, *p. 261*
Pope Gregory VII, *p. 263*
Emperor Henry IV, *p. 263*

HSS 7.6.4 Demonstrate an understanding of the conflict and cooperation between the Papacy and European monarchs (e.g., Charlemagne, Gregory VII, Emperor Henry IV).

If **YOU** were there...

You are 13 years old, the youngest child of the king of France. One day your father announces that he wants to make an alliance with a powerful noble family. To seal the alliance, he has arranged for you to marry one of his new ally's children. Your father wants you to be happy and asks what you think of the idea. You know the alliance will make your father's rule more secure, but it means leaving home to marry a stranger.

What will you say to your father?

BUILDING BACKGROUND In the Middle Ages, kings were some of the most powerful men in Europe. Many kings, like the one described above, looked for ways to increase their power. But in their search for power, these kings had to deal with other powerful leaders, including popes. These other leaders had their own plans and goals.

Popes and Kings Rule Europe

In the early Middle Ages, great nobles and their knights held a great deal of power. As time passed, though, this power began to shift. More and more, power came into the hands of two types of leaders, popes and kings. Popes had great spiritual power, and kings had political power. Together, popes and kings controlled most of European society.

The Power of the Popes

In the Middle Ages, the pope was the head of the Christian Church in Western Europe. Since nearly everyone in the Middle Ages belonged to this church, the pope had great power. People saw the pope as God's representative on Earth. They looked to him for guidance about how to live and pray.

Because the pope was seen as God's representative, it was his duty to decide what the church would teach. From time to time, a pope would write a letter called a bull to explain a religious teaching or outline a church policy. In addition, the pope decided when someone was acting against the church.

If the pope felt someone was working against the church, he could punish the person in many ways. For serious offenses, the pope or other bishops could choose to **excommunicate**, or cast out from the church, the offender. This punishment was deeply feared because Christians believed that a person who died while excommunicated would not get into heaven.

In addition to spiritual power, many popes had great political power. After the Roman Empire collapsed, many people in Italy looked to the pope as their leader. As a result, some popes began to live like royalty. They became rich and built huge palaces. At the same time, they came into conflict with Europe's other political leaders, kings.

The Power of Kings

As you can see on the map below, Europe in 1000 was divided into many small states. Most of these states were ruled by kings, some of whom had little real power. In a few places, though, kings had begun to take firm control of their countries. Look at the map to find England, France, and the Holy Roman Empire. At this time, Europe's most powerful kings ruled those three countries.

In England and France, kings inherited their thrones from their fathers. At times, nobles rebelled against the kings, but the kings usually reestablished order fairly quickly. They maintained this order through alliances as well as warfare.

THE IMPACT TODAY

Hundreds of millions of people around the world consider the pope their spiritual leader.

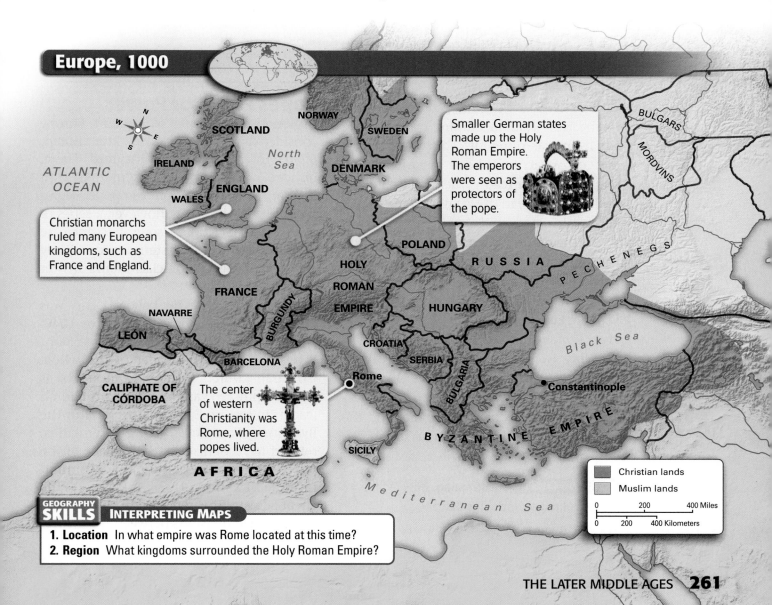

Europe, 1000

Smaller German states made up the Holy Roman Empire. The emperors were seen as protectors of the pope.

Christian monarchs ruled many European kingdoms, such as France and England.

The center of western Christianity was Rome, where popes lived.

NORWAY
SCOTLAND
SWEDEN
North Sea
IRELAND
DENMARK
ATLANTIC OCEAN
ENGLAND
WALES
POLAND
HOLY
ROMAN
EMPIRE
RUSSIA
BULGARS
MORDVINS
PECHENEGS
FRANCE
BURGUNDY
HUNGARY
NAVARRE
LEÓN
CROATIA
SERBIA
BULGARIA
Black Sea
BARCELONA
Rome
Constantinople
CALIPHATE OF CÓRDOBA
BYZANTINE EMPIRE
SICILY
AFRICA
Mediterranean Sea

Christian lands
Muslim lands

0   200   400 Miles
0   200   400 Kilometers

GEOGRAPHY SKILLS | **INTERPRETING MAPS**

1. **Location** In what empire was Rome located at this time?
2. **Region** What kingdoms surrounded the Holy Roman Empire?

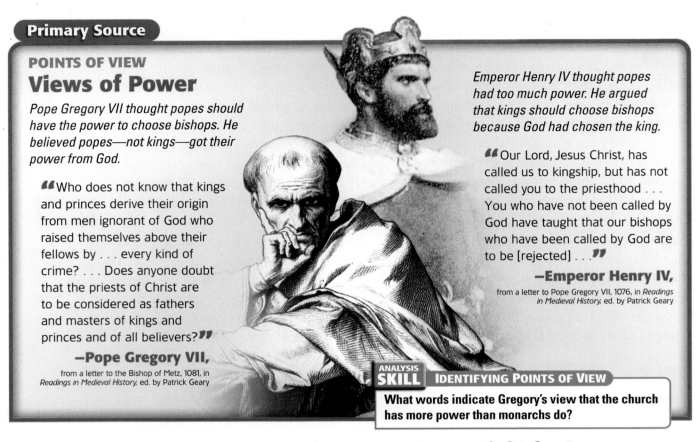

Primary Source

POINTS OF VIEW
Views of Power

Pope Gregory VII thought popes should have the power to choose bishops. He believed popes—not kings—got their power from God.

❝Who does not know that kings and princes derive their origin from men ignorant of God who raised themselves above their fellows by . . . every kind of crime? . . . Does anyone doubt that the priests of Christ are to be considered as fathers and masters of kings and princes and of all believers?❞

—Pope Gregory VII,
from a letter to the Bishop of Metz, 1081, in *Readings in Medieval History,* ed. by Patrick Geary

Emperor Henry IV thought popes had too much power. He argued that kings should choose bishops because God had chosen the king.

❝Our Lord, Jesus Christ, has called us to kingship, but has not called you to the priesthood . . . You who have not been called by God have taught that our bishops who have been called by God are to be [rejected] . . .❞

—Emperor Henry IV,
from a letter to Pope Gregory VII, 1076, in *Readings in Medieval History,* ed. by Patrick Geary

ANALYSIS SKILL **IDENTIFYING POINTS OF VIEW**

What words indicate Gregory's view that the church has more power than monarchs do?

The Holy Roman Empire

In the Holy Roman Empire, however, the situation was different. This empire grew out of what had been Charlemagne's empire. As you read earlier, Charlemagne built his empire in the 700s with the pope's approval.

In the mid-900s, another emperor took the throne with the approval of the pope. Because the empire was approved by the pope and people saw it as a rebirth of the Roman Empire, it became known as the Holy Roman Empire.

Holy Roman emperors didn't inherit their crowns. Instead, they were elected by the empire's nobles. Sometimes, these elections led to fights between nobles and the emperor. In the worst of these squabbles, emperors had to call on the pope for help.

READING CHECK **Contrasting** How did the powers of popes and kings differ?

ACADEMIC VOCABULARY

authority power, right to rule

Popes Fight for Power

Although the people of western Europe considered the pope the head of the church, people in eastern Europe disagreed. There, bishops controlled religious matters with little or no guidance from the pope. Beginning in the mid-1000s, however, a series of clever and able popes sought to increase their **authority** over eastern bishops. They believed all religious officials should answer to the pope.

Among those who believed this was Pope Leo IX, who became pope in 1049. He argued that because the first pope, Saint Peter, had been the leader of the whole Christian Church, later popes should be as well. Despite Leo's arguments, many church leaders in eastern Europe, most notably the Byzantine Patriarch Michael Cerularius, refused to recognize the supremacy of the pope. The pope responded by excommunicating him in 1054. This is known as the Great Schism. It is reflected in the cultural and political divisions between the Orthodox and Catholic parts of Europe today.

Leo's decision created a permanent split within the church. Christians who agreed with the bishop of Constantinople formed the Orthodox Church. Those who supported Leo's authority became known as Roman Catholics. With their support, the pope became head of the Roman Catholic Church and one of the most powerful figures in western Europe.

READING CHECK Generalizing How did Leo IX try to increase popes' authority?

Kings and Popes Clash

As popes worked to increase their power, they often came into conflict with kings. For example, kings thought they should be able to select bishops in their countries. Popes, on the other hand, argued that only they could choose religious officials.

In 1073 a new pope came to power in Rome. His name was **Pope Gregory VII**. Trouble arose when Gregory disapproved of a bishop chosen by the Holy Roman **Emperor Henry IV**. Angry because the pope questioned his authority, Henry convinced Germany's bishops that they should remove Gregory as pope. In response, the pope excommunicated Henry. He called on the empire's nobles to overthrow Henry.

Desperate to stay in power, Henry went to Italy to ask the pope for forgiveness. Gregory refused to see him. For three days Henry stood barefoot in the snow outside the castle where Pope Gregory was staying. Eventually, Gregory accepted Henry's apology and allowed the emperor back into the church. Gregory had proven himself more powerful than the emperor, at least for that moment.

The fight over the right to choose bishops continued even after Henry and Gregory died. In 1122 a new pope and emperor reached a compromise. They decided that church officials would choose all bishops and abbots. The bishops and abbots, however, would still have to obey the emperor.

This compromise did not end all conflict. Kings and popes continued to fight for power throughout the Middle Ages, changing lives all over Europe.

READING CHECK Identifying Causes and Effects What caused Gregory and Henry's power struggle?

SUMMARY AND PREVIEW In this section you read about the powers of popes and kings. In many cases, these powers led to conflict between the two. In the next section, though, you will read about popes and kings working together against a common enemy.

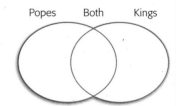

Section 1 Assessment

go.hrw.com
Online Quiz
KEYWORD: SQ7 HP10

Reviewing Ideas, Terms, and People HSS 7.6.4

1. **a. Describe** What was the pope's role in the Roman Catholic Church?
   b. Draw Conclusions How did cooperation with the pope help kings like Charlemagne and the early Holy Roman Emperors?
2. **Explain** Why did Pope Leo IX **excommunicate** the bishop of Constantinople?
3. **a. Identify** With whom did **Pope Gregory VII** clash?
   b. Elaborate Why do you think the pope made **Emperor Henry IV** wait for three days before forgiving him?

Critical Thinking

4. **Comparing** Draw a Venn diagram like the one shown here. Use it to compare the power of the popes to the power of the kings.

Popes   Both   Kings

FOCUS ON WRITING

5. **Taking Notes on the Popes and Kings** Who were the popes and kings you read about in this section? Why were they important? Start a list of important people.

The Crusades

If YOU were there...

You belong to a noble family that has produced many great knights. One day your uncle, the head of the family, tells you that the pope has called on warriors to defend holy places in a faraway land. Your uncle is too old to fight, so it falls on you to answer the pope's call to war. The journey will be long and dangerous. Still, you will see new places and possibly win glory for your family.

How do you feel about joining this war?

What You Will Learn...

Main Ideas

1. The pope called on Crusaders to invade the Holy Land.
2. Despite some initial success, the later Crusades failed.
3. The Crusades changed Europe forever.

The Big Idea

The Christian and Muslim cultures fought over holy sites during a series of medieval wars.

Key Terms and People

Crusades, *p. 264*
Holy Land, *p. 264*
Pope Urban II, *p. 264*
King Richard I, *p. 266*
Saladin, *p. 266*

HSS **7.6.6** Discuss the causes and course of the religious Crusades and their effects on the Christian, Muslim, and Jewish populations in Europe, with emphasis on the increasing contact by Europeans with cultures of the Eastern Mediterranean world.

> **BUILDING BACKGROUND** In the early Middle Ages few people traveled far from home. They spent most of their lives in a single village or farm. As time passed, however, Europeans learned of other people and places. Their contacts with some of these people were peaceful. With others, though, the contact was not peaceful. Wars broke out. The most famous of these wars were the Crusades.

Crusaders Invade the Holy Land

The **Crusades** were a long series of wars between Christians and Muslims in Southwest Asia. They were fought over control of Palestine, a region of Southwest Asia. Europeans called Palestine the **Holy Land** because it was the region where Jesus had lived, preached, and died.

Causes of the Crusades

For many years, Palestine had been in the hands of Muslims. In general, the Muslims did not bother Christians who visited the region. In the late 1000s, though, a group of Turkish Muslims entered the area and captured the city of Jerusalem. Pilgrims returning to Europe said that these Turks had attacked them in the Holy Land, which was no longer safe for Christians.

Before long, the Turks began to raid the Byzantine Empire. The Byzantine emperor, fearing an attack on Constantinople, asked **Pope Urban II** of the Roman Catholic Church for help. Although the Byzantines were Orthodox Christians and not Catholic, the pope agreed to the request.

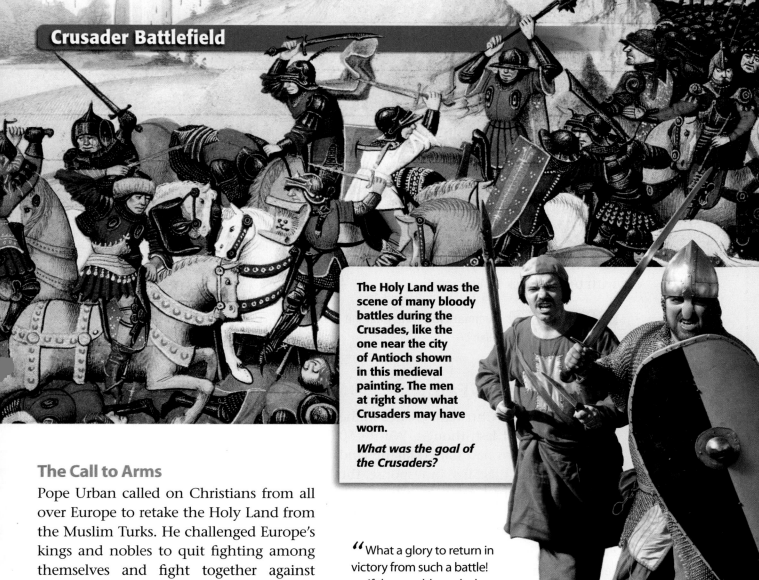

Crusader Battlefield

The Holy Land was the scene of many bloody battles during the Crusades, like the one near the city of Antioch shown in this medieval painting. The men at right show what Crusaders may have worn.

What was the goal of the Crusaders?

The Call to Arms

Pope Urban called on Christians from all over Europe to retake the Holy Land from the Muslim Turks. He challenged Europe's kings and nobles to quit fighting among themselves and fight together against the Turks. In response, people joined the pope's army by the thousands.

Crusaders from all over Europe flocked to France to prepare for their long journey. They sewed crosses onto their clothing to show that they were fighting for God. In fact, the word *crusade* comes from the Latin for "marked with a cross." As they marched off to war, the Crusaders yelled their rallying cry, "God wills it!"

Why would people leave home to fight in a distant land? Some just hoped to save their souls or to do what they thought God wanted. They thought that God would look favorably on them for fighting his enemies, as one French abbot noted:

"What a glory to return in victory from such a battle! . . . if they are blessed who die in the Lord, how much more are they who die for the Lord!"
—Saint Bernard of Clairvaux, from *In Praise of the New Knighthood*

Other Crusaders wanted land and treasure. Still others were looking for something to do. Adventure called to them.

The First Crusade

About 5,000 Crusaders left Europe for the Holy Land in 1096. Some of the first ones to set out were peasants, not soldiers. On their way to the Holy Land, these peasant Crusaders attacked Jews in Germany. They blamed the Jews for Jesus's death.

Before they even reached the Holy Land, Turkish troops killed most of these untrained, poorly equipped peasants.

The nobles and knights fared better. When they reached Jerusalem in 1099, they found the Muslim army disorganized and unready to fight. After about a month of fighting, the Crusaders took Jerusalem.

After the Europeans took Jerusalem, they set up four small kingdoms in the Holy Land. The rulers of these kingdoms created lord and vassal systems like they had known at home. They also began to trade with people back in Europe.

READING CHECK Summarizing What did the First Crusade accomplish?

Later Crusades Fail

The kingdoms the Christians created in the Holy Land didn't last, though. Within 50 years the Muslims had started taking land back from the Christians. In response, the Europeans launched more Crusades.

The Second and Third Crusades

French and German kings set off in 1147 to retake land from the Muslims. This Second Crusade was a terrible failure. Poor planning and heavy losses on the journey to the Holy Land led to the Christians' total defeat. Ashamed, the Crusaders returned to Europe in less than a year.

The Third Crusade began after the Muslims retook Jerusalem in 1189. The rulers of England, France, and the Holy Roman Empire led their armies to the Holy Land to fight for Jerusalem, but problems soon arose. The German king died, and the French king left. Only **King Richard I** of England stayed in the Holy Land.

King Richard's main opponent in the Third Crusade was **Saladin**, the leader of the Muslim forces. Saladin was a brilliant

BIOGRAPHY

Richard I
1157–1199

Called "Lion Heart" for his courage, Richard I was a skilled soldier and a great general. He did not succeed in taking Jerusalem during the Third Crusade, but he earned the respect of Muslims and Christians alike. Since his death, he has become the hero of countless stories and legends.

ATLANTIC OCEAN

leader. Even Crusaders respected his kindness toward fallen enemies. In turn, the Muslims admired Richard's bravery.

For months, Richard and Saladin fought and negotiated. Richard captured a few towns and won protection for Christian pilgrims. In the end, however, he returned home with Jerusalem still in Muslim hands.

The Fourth Crusade

In 1201 French knights arrived in Venice ready to sail to the Holy Land to begin a Fourth Crusade. However, the knights didn't have money to pay for the voyage. For payment the Venetians asked the knights to conquer Zara, a rival trade city. The knights agreed. Later they also attacked Constantinople and carried off many treasures. The city that had been threatened by Muslims before the Crusades had been sacked by Christians!

The End of the Crusades

Other Crusades followed, but none were successful. By 1291 the Muslim armies had taken back all of the Holy Land, and the

The Major Crusades, 1096–1204

ENGLAND
Dover
Paris
Vézelay
Lyon
Clermont
Marseille
Corsica
Sardinia
Mediterranean Sea
HOLY ROMAN EMPIRE
Regensburg
Vienna
Trieste
Venice
Genoa
Zadar
Rome
Sicily
Crete
BYZANTINE EMPIRE
Black Sea
Constantinople
SELJUK TURKS
Edessa
Antioch
Tripoli
Acre
Jerusalem
HOLY LAND
North Sea

Legend:
- Western Christian lands, 1095
- Eastern Christian lands, 1095
- Islamic lands, 1095
- First Crusade, 1096–1099
- Second Crusade, 1147–1149
- Third Crusade, 1189–1192
- Fourth Crusade, 1201–1204

0   100   200 Miles
0   100   200 Kilometers

BIOGRAPHY

Saladin
1137–1193

Saladin is often called one of the greatest generals of the Middle Ages. The Muslim leader successfully held Jerusalem against Richard I in the Third Crusade. Saladin's people considered their leader a wise ruler. Crusaders respected his sometimes kind treatment of fallen enemies. Many Christians saw him as a model of knightly chivalry.

GEOGRAPHY SKILLS INTERPRETING MAPS

1. **Place** From which countries did the first three Crusades start out?
2. **Movement** About how far was the journey from Paris to Jerusalem?

Crusades had ended. Why did the Crusades fail? There were many reasons.

- The Crusaders had to travel huge distances just to reach the war. Many died along the way.
- Crusaders weren't prepared to fight in Palestine's desert climate.
- The Christians were outnumbered by their well-led and organized Muslim foes.

- Christian leaders fought among themselves and planned poorly.

Whatever the reasons for their failure, the Crusades ended just as they had begun so many years before, with the Holy Land under Muslim control.

READING CHECK Analyzing How did geography limit the success of the Crusades?

Crusades Change Europe

Although the Crusades failed, they changed Europe forever. Trade between Europe and Asia grew. Europeans who went to the Holy Land learned about products such as apricots, rice, and cotton cloth. Crusaders also brought ideas of Muslim thinkers to Europe.

Politics in Europe also changed. Some kings increased their power because many nobles and knights had died in the Holy Land. These kings seized lands that were left without clear owners. During the later Crusades, kings also gained influence at the popes' expense. The popes had wanted the church to be in charge of all the Crusades. Instead, rulers and nobles took control.

The Crusades had lasting effects on relations among peoples as well. Because some Crusaders had attacked Jews, many Jews distrusted Christians. In addition, tension between the Byzantines and western Christians increased, especially after Crusaders attacked Constantinople.

The greatest changes occurred with Christian and Muslim relationships. Each group learned about the other's religion and culture. Sometimes this led to mutual respect. In general, though, the Crusaders saw Muslims as unbelievers who threatened innocent Christians. Most Muslims viewed the Crusaders as vicious invaders. Some historians think that the distrust that began during the Crusades still affects Christian and Muslim relationships today.

READING CHECK Finding Main Ideas What were some results of the Crusades?

SUMMARY AND PREVIEW In this section you learned how religious beliefs led to a series of wars. In the next section you will learn about the role of religion in most people's daily lives in the Middle Ages.

QUICK FACTS

The Crusades	
Causes	**Effects**
■ Turks take control of the Holy Land in 1071.	■ Trade between Europe and Asia increases.
■ Turks threaten Constantinople in the 1090s.	■ Kings become more powerful.
■ Byzantine emperor asks pope for help.	■ Tension between Christians, Jews, and Muslims grows.

Section 2 Assessment

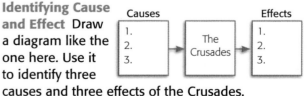

go.hrw.com
Online Quiz
KEYWORD: SQ7 HP10

Reviewing Ideas, Terms, and People HSS 7.6.6

1. **a. Recall** What did **Pope Urban II** ask Christians to do?
   b. Elaborate Why do you think so many people were willing to go on a Crusade?
2. **a. Identify** In which Crusade did **Saladin** and **King Richard I** fight?
   b. Rank Which Crusade do you think was the least successful? Why?
3. **a. Identify** What new products were introduced to Europe after the Crusades?
   b. Draw Conclusions Why did the Crusades change relationships between Christians and other groups?

Critical Thinking

4. **Identifying Cause and Effect** Draw a diagram like the one here. Use it to identify three causes and three effects of the Crusades.

Causes		Effects
1. 2. 3.	The Crusades	1. 2. 3.

FOCUS ON WRITING

5. **Thinking about the Crusades** Look back through what you've just read and make a list of people who were important in the Crusades. What made them important?

Christianity and Medieval Society

SECTION 3

If YOU were there...

You are a stone carver, apprenticed to a master builder. The bishop has hired your master to design a huge new church. He wants the church to inspire and impress worshippers with the glory of God. Your master has entrusted you with the decoration of the outside of the church. You are excited by the challenge.

What kind of art will you create for the church?

BUILDING BACKGROUND Thousands of churches were built across Europe in the Middle Ages. People took great pride in their churches because religion was very important to them. In fact, Christianity was a key factor in shaping medieval society.

The Church Shapes Society and Politics

Nearly everyone who lived in Europe during the Middle Ages was Christian. In fact, Christianity was central to every part of life. Church officials, called **clergy**, and their teachings were very influential in European culture and politics.

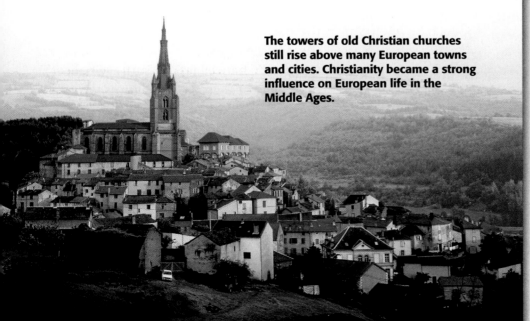

The towers of old Christian churches still rise above many European towns and cities. Christianity became a strong influence on European life in the Middle Ages.

What You Will Learn...

Main Ideas

1. The Christian Church shaped society and politics in medieval Europe.
2. Orders of monks and friars did not like the church's political nature.
3. Church leaders helped build the first universities in Europe.
4. The church influenced the arts in medieval Europe.

The Big Idea

The Christian Church was central to life in the Middle Ages.

Key Terms and People

clergy, *p. 269*
religious order, *p. 272*
Francis of Assisi, *p. 272*
friars, *p. 272*
Thomas Aquinas, *p. 273*
natural law, *p. 274*

HSS 7.6.8 Understand the importance of the Catholic church as a political, intellectual, and aesthetic institution (e.g., founding of universities, political and spiritual roles of the clergy, creation of monastic and mendicant religious orders, preservation of the Latin language and religious texts, St. Thomas Aquinas's synthesis of classical philosophy with Christian theology, and the concept of "natural law").

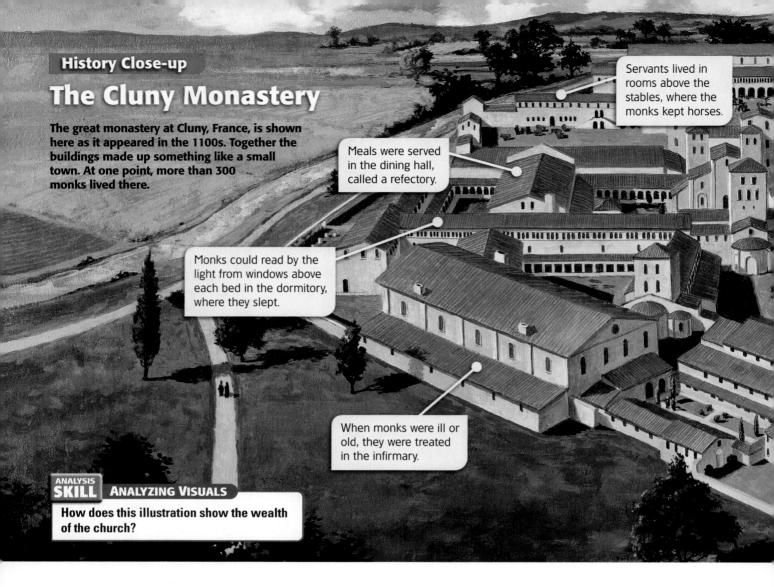

History Close-up
The Cluny Monastery

The great monastery at Cluny, France, is shown here as it appeared in the 1100s. Together the buildings made up something like a small town. At one point, more than 300 monks lived there.

Servants lived in rooms above the stables, where the monks kept horses.

Meals were served in the dining hall, called a refectory.

Monks could read by the light from windows above each bed in the dormitory, where they slept.

When monks were ill or old, they were treated in the infirmary.

ANALYSIS SKILL **ANALYZING VISUALS**

How does this illustration show the wealth of the church?

The Church and Society

In the Middle Ages, life revolved around the local church. Markets, festivals, and religious ceremonies all took place there.

For some people, however, the local church was not enough. They wanted to see important religious sites—the places where Jesus lived, where holy men and women died, and where miracles happened. The church encouraged these people to go on pilgrimages, journeys to religious locations. Among the most popular destinations were Jerusalem, Rome, and Compostela, in northwestern Spain. Each of these cities had churches that Christians wanted to visit.

Another popular pilgrimage destination was Canterbury, near London in England. Hundreds of visitors went to the cathedral in Canterbury each year. One such visit is the basis for one of the greatest books of the Middle Ages, *The Canterbury Tales* by Geoffrey Chaucer (CHAW-suhr). Chaucer's book tells of a group of pilgrims who feel drawn, like many people, to Canterbury:

"When in April the sweet showers fall
And pierce the drought of March to the root . . .
Then people long to go on pilgrimages
And palmers long to seek the stranger strands
Of far-off saints, hallowed in sundry lands
And specially, from every shire's end
Of England, down to Canterbury they wend."
—Geoffrey Chaucer, from *The Canterbury Tales*

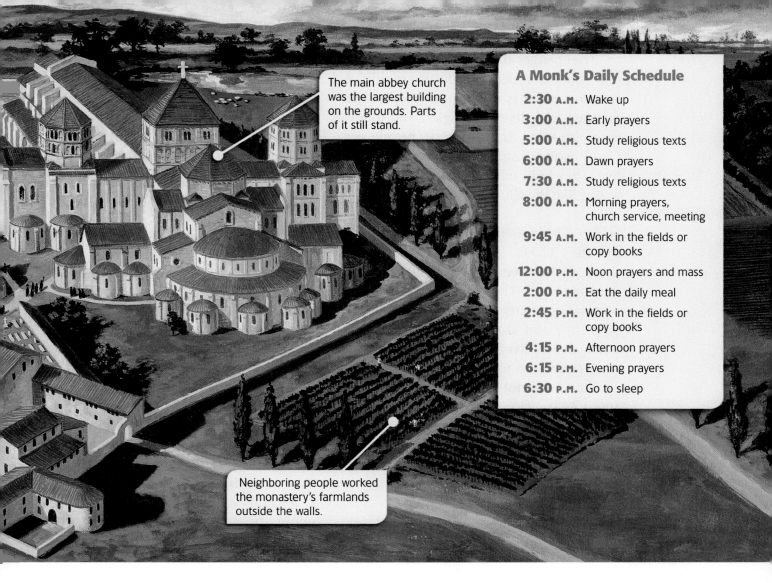

The main abbey church was the largest building on the grounds. Parts of it still stand.

Neighboring people worked the monastery's farmlands outside the walls.

A Monk's Daily Schedule

2:30 A.M.	Wake up
3:00 A.M.	Early prayers
5:00 A.M.	Study religious texts
6:00 A.M.	Dawn prayers
7:30 A.M.	Study religious texts
8:00 A.M.	Morning prayers, church service, meeting
9:45 A.M.	Work in the fields or copy books
12:00 P.M.	Noon prayers and mass
2:00 P.M.	Eat the daily meal
2:45 P.M.	Work in the fields or copy books
4:15 P.M.	Afternoon prayers
6:15 P.M.	Evening prayers
6:30 P.M.	Go to sleep

The Church and Politics

The church also gained political power during the Middle Ages. Many people left land to the church when they died. In fact, the church was one of the largest landholders in Europe. Eventually, the church divided this land into fiefs. In this way, it became a feudal lord.

Of all the clergy, bishops and abbots were most involved in political matters. They often advised local rulers. Some clergy got so involved with politics that they spent little time dealing with religious affairs.

READING CHECK **Analyzing** In what ways were clergy members important political figures?

Monks and Friars

Some people were unhappy with the political nature of the church. They thought the clergy should focus only on spiritual matters. These people feared that the church had become obsessed with wealth and power.

The Monks of Cluny

Among those unhappy with the church were a group of French monks. In the early 900s they started a monastery in the town of Cluny (KLOO-nee). The monks of Cluny followed a strict schedule of prayers and religious services. They paid little attention to the world, concerning themselves only with religious matters.

The changes at Cluny led to the creation of a religious order, the Cluniac monks. A **religious order** is a group of people who dedicate their lives to religion and follow common rules. Across Europe, people saw Cluny as an example of how monks should live. They built new monasteries and tried to live like the Cluniacs.

Other New Orders

By the 1100s, though, some monks thought that even Cluny's rules weren't strict enough. They created new orders with even stricter rules. Some took vows of silence and stopped speaking to each other. Others lived in tiny rooms and left them only to go to church services.

Men were not the only ones to create and join religious orders. Women were allowed to join these kinds of orders as well. Communities of nuns called convents appeared across Europe. Like monks, these nuns lived according to a strict set of rules. The nuns of each convent prayed and worked together under the watchful eyes of an abbess, the convent's leader.

Although monks and nuns lived apart from other people, they did a great deal for society. For example, they collected and stored texts that explained Christian teachings. Monks spent hours copying these documents, and they sent copies to monasteries across Europe.

The Friars

Not everyone who joined a religious order wanted to live apart from society. Some wanted to live in cities and spread Christian teachings. As a result, two new religious orders were begun in the early 1200s.

These orders were the Dominicans and the Franciscans, named for their founders, Dominic de Guzmán and **Francis of Assisi**. Because they didn't live in monasteries, members of these orders were not monks. They were **friars**, people who belonged to religious orders but lived and worked among the general public.

Friars lived simply, wearing plain robes and no shoes. Like monks, they owned no property. They roamed about, preaching and begging for food. For that reason, friars were also called mendicants, from a Latin word for beggars.

The main goal of the friars was to teach people how to live good Christian lives. They taught people about generosity and kindness. A prayer credited to Francis illustrates what the friars hoped to do:

> *"*Lord, make me an instrument of your peace. Where there is hatred, let me sow love; where there is injury, pardon; where there is doubt, faith; where there is despair, hope; where there is darkness, light; and where there is sadness, joy.*"*
> –Francis of Assisi, from *The Prayer of Saint Francis*

READING CHECK **Summarizing** Why did people create new religious orders?

BIOGRAPHY

Saint Francis of Assisi
1182?–1226

Born in Assisi, Italy, Francis was the son of a wealthy merchant. As a young man, however, Francis gave all his money and possessions away and left his father's house. He lived a simple life, preaching and tending to people who were poor or ill. Francis considered everyone his brother or sister, including animals. He encouraged people to take care of animals just as they would take care of other people. Within a few years other people had begun to copy his lifestyle. In 1210 they became the first members of the Franciscan Order.

Making Generalizations How do you think Francis's generosity and compassion might inspire Christians to follow the church's teachings?

School Days

Did you know that many customs that schools and universities follow today began in the Middle Ages? For example, medieval teachers taught groups of students instead of individuals. Classes ran according to a fixed schedule, and students had to take tests. At night, students went to their rooms to study and complete assignments. Many students participated in sports such as races and ball games after classes. At graduation, students dressed up in caps and gowns. All of these customs are still common today.

Medieval universities were not exactly the same as universities are now, however. Medieval students entered the university at age 14, and only boys could attend.

ANALYSIS SKILL | **ANALYZING INFORMATION**

Why do you think some customs followed by universities in the Middle Ages have lasted until today?

Universities Are Built

While some people were drawing away from the world in monasteries and convents, others were looking for ways to learn more about it. In time, their search for knowledge led to the creation of Europe's first universities.

Some of the earliest universities were created by the church. The church's goal was to teach people about religion. Other universities were created by groups of students who went searching for teachers who could tell them about the world.

Most teachers in these universities were members of the clergy. Besides religion, schools taught law, medicine, astronomy, and other courses. All classes were taught in Latin. Although relatively few people in Europe spoke Latin, it was the language of scholars and the church.

As people began to study new subjects, some of them developed new ideas about the world. In particular, they wondered how human reason and Christian faith were related. In the past, people had believed that some things could be proven with reason, but other things had to be taken on faith. Some people in universities, though, began to wonder if the two ideas could work together.

One such person was the Dominican philosopher **Thomas Aquinas** (uh-KWY-nuhs). Thomas was a teacher at the University of Paris. He argued that rational thought could be used to support Christian beliefs. For example, he wrote an argument to prove the existence of God.

Thomas also believed that God had created a law that governed how the world operated. He called it **natural law**. If people could study and learn more about this law, he argued, they could learn to live the way God wanted.

READING CHECK Generalizing How did universities help create new ideas?

The Church and the Arts

In addition to politics and education, the church was also a strong influence on art and architecture. Throughout the Middle Ages, religious feeling inspired artists and architects to create beautiful works of art.

Religious Architecture

Many of Europe's churches were incredible works of art. The grandest of these churches were cathedrals, large churches in which bishops led religious services. Beginning in the 1100s Europeans built their cathedrals using a dramatic new style called Gothic architecture.

Gothic cathedrals were not only places to pray, but also symbols of people's faith.

Gothic Architecture

One of the most beautiful of all Gothic cathedrals is in Chartres (SHAHRT), near Paris, France. At 112 feet high it is about as tall as a 10-story building.

As a result, they were towering works of great majesty and glory.

What made these Gothic churches so unusual? For one thing, they were much taller than older churches. The walls often rose up hundreds of feet, and the ceilings seemed to reach to heaven. Huge windows of stained glass let sunlight pour in, filling the churches with dazzling colors. Many of these amazing churches still exist. People continue to worship in them and admire their beauty.

Religious Art

Medieval churches were also filled with beautiful objects created to show respect for God. Ornate paintings and tapestries covered the walls and ceilings. Even the clothing priests wore during religious services was marvelous. Their robes were often highly decorated, sometimes with threads made out of gold.

Many of the books used during religious ceremonies were beautiful objects. Monks had copied these books carefully.

BIOGRAPHY

Saint Thomas Aquinas
1225–1274

Though he was born in Italy, Thomas Aquinas lived most of his life in France. As a student and then a teacher at the University of Paris, Thomas spent most of his time in study.

He wrote a book called the *Summa Theologica,* in which he argued that science and religion were related.

Although some people did not like Thomas's ideas, most considered him the greatest thinker of the Middle Ages. Later teachers modeled their lessons after his ideas.

Making Generalizations Why might people believe someone is a great thinker even if they disagree with his or her ideas?

Flying buttresses support heavy walls.

Pointed arches support the high ceilings.

Huge stained glass windows called rose windows are found in many Gothic cathedrals.

ANALYSIS SKILL **ANALYZING VISUALS**

What would it have been like to travel from a small farm and see this cathedral for the first time?

They also decorated them using bright colors to adorn the first letters and the borders of each page. Some monks added thin sheets of silver and gold to the pages. Because the pages seem to glow, we use the word *illuminated* to describe them.

READING CHECK **Generalizing** How were medieval art and religion related?

SUMMARY AND PREVIEW Besides its religious role, the church played important roles in politics, education, and the arts. The church changed as time passed. In the next section, you will learn about other changes that took place in Europe at the same time. These changes created new political systems around the continent.

Section 3 Assessment

go.hrw.com
Online Quiz
KEYWORD: SQ7 HP10

Reviewing Ideas, Terms, and People **HSS** 7.6.8

1. a. **Recall** What are church officials called?
   b. **Explain** Why did people go on pilgrimages?
2. a. **Identify** What new monastery founded in France in the 900s served as an example to people around Europe?
   b. **Contrast** How were **friars** different from monks?
3. **Analyze** How did **Thomas Aquinas** think reason and faith could work together?
4. a. **Identify** What new style of religious architecture developed in Europe in the 1100s?
   b. **Elaborate** Why do you think so much of the art created in the Middle Ages was religious?

Critical Thinking

5. **Categorizing** Draw a chart like the one below. Use it to list the roles the church played in politics, education, and the arts in the Middle Ages.

Politics	Education	The Arts

FOCUS ON WRITING

6. **Taking Notes on Church Leaders** In this section, you've read about at least two people who became saints. Add them to your list and note why they're important.

Political and Social Change

What You Will Learn...

Main Ideas

1. Magna Carta caused changes in England's government and legal system.
2. The Hundred Years' War led to political changes in England and France.
3. The Black Death, which swept through Europe in the Middle Ages, led to social changes.

The Big Idea

Europe's political and social systems underwent great changes in the late Middle Ages.

Key Terms and People

Magna Carta, *p. 276*
Parliament, *p. 277*
Hundred Years' War, *p. 278*
Joan of Arc, *p. 278*
Black Death, *p. 279*

HSS 7.6.5 Know the significance of developments in medieval English legal and constitutional practices and their importance in the rise of modern democratic thought and representative institutions (e.g., Magna Carta, parliament, development of habeas corpus, an independent judiciary in England).

7.6.7 Map the spread of the bubonic plague from Central Asia to China, the Middle East, and Europe and describe its impact on global population.

If **YOU** were there...

You are a baron, one of England's great nobles, living in northern Britain. Winter is approaching, and it looks like it will be very cold soon. To prepare for the winter, you send some of your servants to a forest on your land to gather firewood. When they return, though, they don't have much wood. The king has chopped down many of the trees in your forest to build a new castle. Dismayed, you send a messenger to ask the king to pay a fair price for the wood, but he refuses.

How can you get the king to respect your rights?

BUILDING BACKGROUND Beginning with William the Conqueror, the kings of England fought to increase their power. By the 1200s, the kings felt that they could do as they pleased, whether their nobles agreed with them or not. The kings' attitudes upset many nobles, especially when kings began to create new taxes or take the nobles' property. Some nobles began to look for ways to limit kings' powers and protect their own rights.

Magna Carta Causes Change in England

In 1215 a group of nobles decided to force the king to respect their rights. In the middle of a field called Runnymede near London, they made King John approve a document they had written. This document listing rights that the king could not ignore was called **Magna Carta**. Its name is a Latin phrase meaning "Great Charter."

William the Conqueror

HISTORIC DOCUMENT
Magna Carta

Magna Carta was one of the first documents to protect the rights of the people. Magna Carta was so influential that the British still consider it part of their constitution. Some of its ideas are also in the U.S. Constitution. Included in Magna Carta were 63 demands that English nobles made King John agree to follow. A few of these demands are listed here.

Demand 31 defended people's right to own any property, not just wood.

Magna Carta guaranteed that everyone had the right to a fair trial.

To all free men of our kingdom we have also granted, for us and our heirs for ever, all the liberties written out below, to have and to keep for them and their heirs, of us and our heirs.

(16) No man shall be forced to perform more service for a knight's 'fee,' or other free holding of land, than is due from it.

(31) Neither we nor any royal official will take wood for our castle, or for any other purpose, without the consent [permission] of the owner.

(38) In future no official shall place a man on trial upon his own unsupported statement, without producing credible [believable] witnesses to the truth of it.

—Magna Carta, from a translation by the British Library

ANALYSIS SKILL   ANALYZING PRIMARY SOURCES

In what ways do you think the ideas listed above influenced modern democracy?

The Effects of Magna Carta

Magna Carta required the king to honor certain rights. Among these rights was habeas corpus (HAY-bee-uhs KOHR-puhs), a Latin phrase meaning "you have the body." The right of habeas corpus meant that people could not be kept in jail without a reason. They had to be charged with a crime and convicted at a jury trial before they could be sent to prison. Before, kings could arrest people for no reason at all.

More importantly, Magna Carta required that everyone—even the king—had to obey the law. The idea that everyone must follow the law became one of the basic principles of English government.

Changes after Magna Carta

Magna Carta inspired the English to find more ways to limit the king's power. A council of nobles was created to advise the king. In time, the council developed into **Parliament** (PAHR-luh-muhnt), the lawmaking body that governs England today. Over the years, membership in Parliament was opened to knights and town leaders. By the late Middle Ages, kings could do little without Parliament's support.

The English continued to work to secure and protect their rights. To ensure that everyone was treated fairly, people demanded that judges be free of royal control. Many people believed judges chosen by the king would always side with him. Eventually, in the late 1600s, the king agreed to free the courts of his control. This creation of an independent judicial system was a key step in bringing democracy to England.

READING CHECK **Summarizing** How did Magna Carta and Parliament limit the king's power?

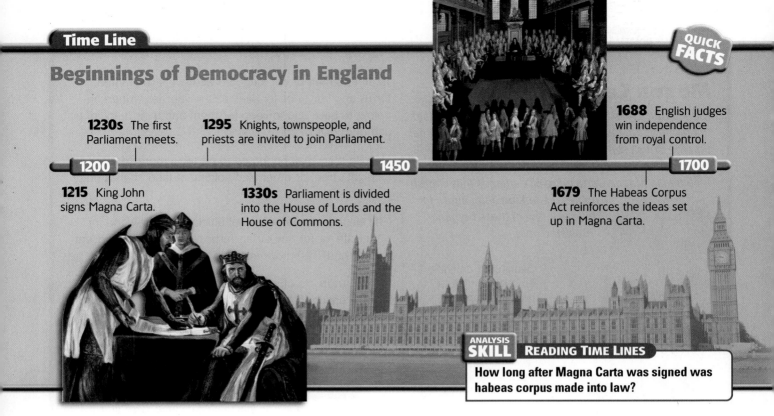

Beginnings of Democracy in England

QUICK FACTS

1230s The first Parliament meets.

1295 Knights, townspeople, and priests are invited to join Parliament.

1688 English judges win independence from royal control.

1200 — 1450 — 1700

1215 King John signs Magna Carta.

1330s Parliament is divided into the House of Lords and the House of Commons.

1679 The Habeas Corpus Act reinforces the ideas set up in Magna Carta.

ANALYSIS SKILL **READING TIME LINES**

How long after Magna Carta was signed was habeas corpus made into law?

THE IMPACT TODAY

Joan of Arc is still a national hero in France.

The Hundred Years' War

Although Magna Carta changed England's government, it had no effect outside of that country. Kings in other parts of Europe continued to rule as they always had. Eventually, however, these kings also had to face great political changes.

The Course of the War

One of the countries in which political change occurred was France. In 1328 the king of France died with no sons, and two men claimed his throne. One was French. The other was the king of England. In the end, the French man became king.

This did not sit well with the English king, and a few years later he invaded France. This invasion began a long conflict between England and France that came to be called the **Hundred Years' War**.

At first the English armies did well, winning most of the battles. After nearly 100 years of fighting, however, a teenage peasant girl, **Joan of Arc**, rallied the French troops. Although the English eventually captured and killed Joan, it was too late. The French drove the English from their country in 1453.

Results of the War

The Hundred Years' War changed the governments of both England and France. In England, Parliament's power grew because the king needed Parliament's approval to raise money to pay for the costly war. As Parliament gained more influence, the king lost power.

In France, on the other hand, the king's power grew. During the war, the king had become popular with his nobles. Fighting the English had created a bond between them. As a result, the nobles supported the king after the war as well.

READING CHECK **Contrasting** How did the governments of England and France change after the war?

The Black Death

While the English and French fought the Hundred Years' War, an even greater crisis arose. This crisis was the **Black Death**, a deadly plague that swept through Europe between 1347 and 1351.

The plague originally came from central and eastern Asia. Unknowingly, traders brought rats carrying the disease to Mediterranean ports in 1347. From there it quickly swept throughout much of Europe. Fleas that feasted on the blood of infected rats passed on the plague to people.

The Black Death was not caused by one disease but by several different forms of plague. One form called bubonic plague (byoo-BAH-nik PLAYG) could be identified by swellings called buboes that appeared on victims' bodies. Another even deadlier form could spread through the air and kill people in less than a day.

The Black Death killed so many people that many were buried quickly without priests or ceremonies. In some villages nearly everyone died or fled as neighbors fell ill. In England alone, about 1,000 villages were abandoned.

The plague killed millions of people in Europe and millions more around the world. Some historians think Europe lost about a third of its population—perhaps 25 million people. This huge drop in population caused sweeping changes in Europe.

In most places, the manor system fell apart completely. There weren't enough people left to work in the fields. Those peasants and serfs who had survived the plague found their skills in high demand. Suddenly, they could demand wages for their labor. Once they had money, many fled their manors completely, moving instead to Europe's growing cities.

READING CHECK **Identifying Cause and Effect** What effects did bubonic plague have in Europe?

SUMMARY AND PREVIEW Magna Carta, the Hundred Years' War, and the Black Death changed European society. In the next section, you will learn about other changes in society, changes brought about by religious differences.

Section 4 Assessment

Reviewing Ideas, Terms, and People **HSS** 7.6.5, 7.6.7

1. **a. Identify** What document did English nobles hope would limit the king's power?
   b. Explain How was the creation of **Parliament** a step toward the creation of democracy in England?
2. **a. Identify** Who rallied the French troops during the **Hundred Years' War**?
   b. Elaborate The Hundred Years' War caused much more damage in France than in England. Why do you think this was the case?
3. **a. Describe** What was the **Black Death**?
   b. Explain How did the Black Death contribute to the decline of the manor system?
   c. Elaborate Why do you think the Black Death was able to spread so quickly through Europe?

Critical Thinking

go.hrw.com
Online Quiz
KEYWORD: SQ7 HP10

4. **Identifying Cause and Effect** Draw a scroll like the one shown here. Inside the scroll, list two ideas contained in Magna Carta. Next to the scroll, write two sentences about Magna Carta's effects on England's government.

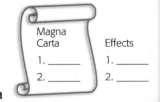

Magna Carta
1. _____
2. _____

Effects
1. _____
2. _____

FOCUS ON WRITING

5. **Rating Importance** After reading this section, you'll probably want to add King John to your list. You should also start to think about which people were the most important. Rank the people on your list from most to least important.

The Black Death

"And they died by the hundreds," wrote one man who saw the horror, "both day and night." The Black Death had arrived. The Black Death was a series of deadly plagues that hit Europe between 1347 and 1351, killing millions. People didn't know what caused the plague. They also didn't know that geography played a key role in its spread—as people traveled to trade, they unwittingly carried the disease with them to new places.

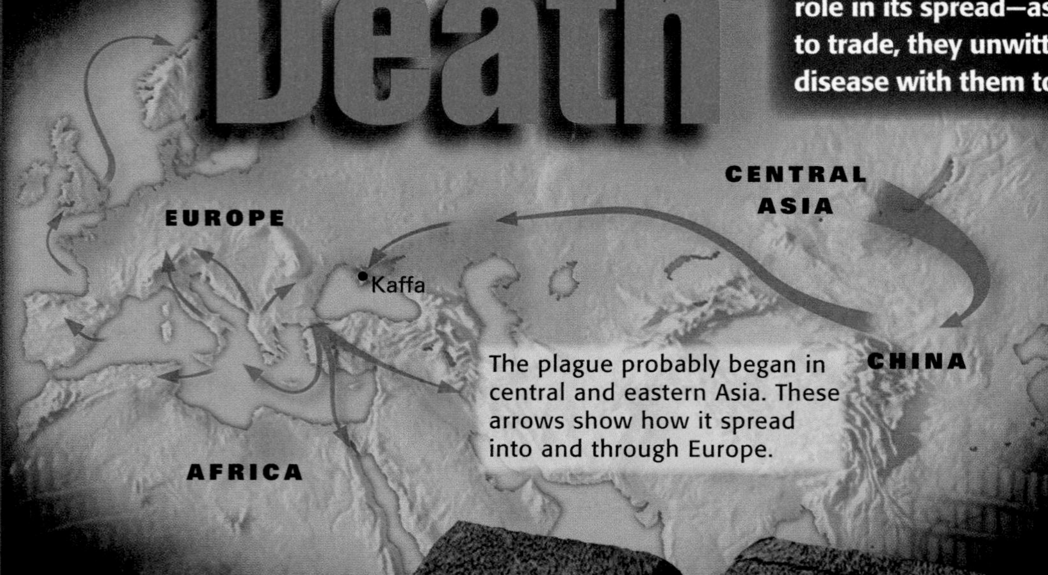

CENTRAL ASIA

EUROPE

Kaffa

CHINA

AFRICA

The plague probably began in central and eastern Asia. These arrows show how it spread into and through Europe.

This ship has just arrived in Europe from the east with trade goods—and rats with fleas.

The fleas carry the plague and jump onto a man unloading the ship. Soon, he will get sick and die.

The plague is so terrifying that many people think it's the end of the world. They leave town for the country, spreading the Black Death even farther.

People dig mass graves to bury the dead. But often, so many victims are infected that there is no one left to bury them.

The garbage and dirty conditions in the town provide food and a home for the rats, allowing the disease to spread even more.

So many people die so quickly that special carts are sent through the streets to gather the bodies.

GEOGRAPHY
SKILLS   INTERPRETING MAPS

1. How did the Black Death reach Europe from Asia?
2. What helped spread the plague within Europe?

Challenges to Church Authority

What You Will Learn...

Main Ideas

1. The church reacted to challengers by punishing people who opposed its teachings.
2. Christians fought Moors in Spain and Portugal in an effort to drive all Muslims out of Europe.
3. Jews faced discrimination across Europe in the Middle Ages.

The Big Idea

In the Middle Ages, the Christian Church dealt harshly with people who did not respect its authority.

Key Terms and People

heresy, *p. 282*
Reconquista, *p. 283*
King Ferdinand, *p. 284*
Queen Isabella, *p. 284*
Spanish Inquisition, *p. 284*

HSS 7.6.9 Know the history of the decline of Muslim rule in the Iberian Peninsula that culminated in the Reconquista and the rise of Spanish and Portuguese kingdoms.

If YOU were there...

You are a student at a university in Córdoba, Spain. Your fellow students include Christians, Muslims, and Jews. But a new king and queen want all Muslims and Jews to leave Spain.

How will the rulers' decision affect your friends?

BUILDING BACKGROUND As you have read, most Europeans in the Middle Ages belonged to the Catholic Church. As Christianity spread in Europe, many Jews and Muslims were pressured to become Christian or leave their homes. At the same time, others openly challenged the church's authority.

The Church Reacts to Challengers

By around 1100, some Christians had begun to question church teachings. They felt that the clergy focused more on money and land than on God. Others didn't agree with the church's ideas. They began to preach their own ideas about religion.

Religious ideas that oppose accepted church teachings are called **heresy** (HER-uh-see). People who hold such ideas are called heretics. Church officials sent priests and friars throughout Europe to find possible heretics. Most of these priests and friars tried to be fair. A few tortured people until they confessed to heresy, even if they were innocent. Most people found guilty in these trials were fined or put in prison. Others were killed.

In the early 1200s, Pope Innocent III decided that heresy was too great a threat to ignore. He called a crusade against heretics in southern France. With this call, the pope encouraged the king of France and his knights to rid their country of heretics. The result was a bloody war that lasted about 20 years. The war destroyed towns and cost thousands of people their lives.

READING CHECK **Finding Main Ideas** How did church leaders try to fight heresy?

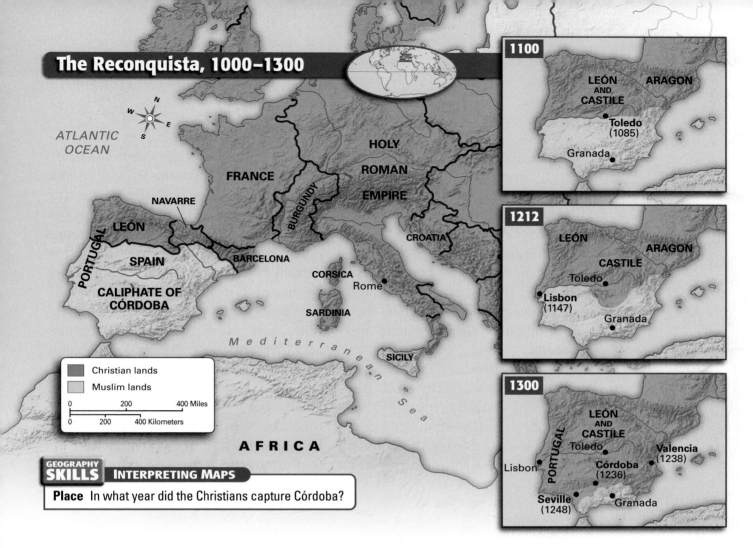

The Reconquista, 1000–1300

ATLANTIC OCEAN

FRANCE

NAVARRE

LEÓN

PORTUGAL

SPAIN

BARCELONA

CALIPHATE OF CÓRDOBA

HOLY ROMAN EMPIRE

BURGUNDY

CROATIA

CORSICA

Rome

SARDINIA

Mediterranean Sea

SICILY

AFRICA

Christian lands
Muslim lands

0   200   400 Miles
0   200   400 Kilometers

1100

LEÓN AND CASTILE

ARAGON

Toledo (1085)

Granada

1212

LEÓN

CASTILE

ARAGON

Toledo

Lisbon (1147)

Granada

1300

LEÓN AND CASTILE

PORTUGAL

Toledo

Valencia (1238)

Lisbon

Córdoba (1236)

Seville (1248)

Granada

GEOGRAPHY **SKILLS** | **INTERPRETING MAPS**

Place In what year did the Christians capture Córdoba?

Christians Fight the Moors

France was not the only place where Christians fought people they saw as the church's enemies. In Spain and Portugal, armed Christian warriors fought to drive the Muslim Moors out of their lands.

The Weakening of Muslim Control

By the late 900s the once powerful Muslim government of Spain had begun to weaken. Political and religious leaders fought each other for power. Various ethnic groups also fought each other.

In 1002 the Muslim government fell apart completely. Caught up in fighting among themselves, Muslim leaders were too busy to guard against the Christian kingdoms of northern Spain.

The Fight against the Moors

For centuries, the kingdoms of northern Spain had been small and weak. But as the Moors' power declined, these little Christian kingdoms seized the opportunity to attack. Slowly, they took land away from the Moors. They called their efforts to retake Spain from the Moors the **Reconquista** (reh-kahn-KEES-tuh), or reconquest.

In 1085 Castile (ka-STEEL), the largest of the Spanish kingdoms, won a great victory against the Moors. The Castilian victory inspired other Christian kingdoms to fight the Moors. The kingdoms of Aragon and Portugal soon joined the fight.

The Christian armies won victory after victory. By the 1250s, the victorious Christian armies had nearly pushed the Moors completely out of Europe.

THE IMPACT TODAY

Although the Moors were driven out, many places in Spain and Portugal still bear names that came from Arabic, the language the Moors spoke.

The only territory still under Muslim control was a small kingdom called Granada (grah-NAH-dah).

The Rise of Portugal and Spain

As a result of their victories, both Portugal and Spain grew more powerful than before. Portugal, once a part of Castile, broke free and declared its independence. Meanwhile, Castile and Aragon decided to unite.

In 1469 Ferdinand, the prince of Aragon, married Isabella, a Castilian princess. Ten years later, they became king and queen of their countries. Together, they ruled all of Spain as **King Ferdinand** and **Queen Isabella**.

Ferdinand and Isabella finally brought an end to the Reconquista. In 1492 their army conquered Granada, the last Muslim stronghold in Spain. That same year, they required all Spanish Jews to convert to Christianity or leave the country. A few years later, they banned the practice of Islam as well. Through this **policy**, all of Spain became Christian.

The Spanish Inquisition

Ferdinand and Isabella wanted only Christians in their kingdom. To ensure that Christianity alone was practiced, they created the **Spanish Inquisition**, an organization of priests that looked for and punished anyone in Spain suspected of secretly practicing their old religion. Later, the Inquisition spread to Portugal as well.

The Spanish and Portuguese Inquisitions were ruthless in seeking heretics, Muslims, and Jews. People found guilty of heresy were sentenced in public ceremonies. Many of those found guilty were killed. They were often burned to death. In total, the Spanish sentenced about 2,000 people to die. Almost 1,400 more were put to death by the Portuguese Inquisition.

READING CHECK **Summarizing** What was the purpose of the Spanish Inquisition?

BIOGRAPHY

Queen Isabella
1451–1504

Although she is considered one of the greatest monarchs in Spanish history, Isabella was never actually the queen of Spain. She was the queen of Castile, but she had no official power in her husband's kingdom, Aragon. In practice, however, the two ruled both kingdoms together.

In addition to her role in the Reconquista, Isabella made great contributions to Spanish society. She encouraged religion and education and supported many artists. She also helped pay for the transatlantic voyages of Christopher Columbus, during which he landed in America.

Analyzing How did Isabella help promote Spanish culture?

Jews Face Discrimination

Heretics and Muslims were not the only groups punished for their beliefs in the Middle Ages. European Jews also suffered. This suffering was caused by Christians who believed that the Jews had been responsible for the death of Jesus. These Christians thought Jews should be punished.

You have already read about how Jews were killed during the Crusades. You have also read that Jews were forced to leave their homes in Spain. Similar things happened all over Europe. Rulers, supported by the church, forced Jews to leave their countries. For example, in 1290, the king of England arrested all English Jews and forced them to leave the country. The same thing happened in France in 1306 and again in 1394.

The Spanish Inquisition

The painting shows accused heretics, in the pointed hats, before the Spanish Inquisition. The Spanish artist Francisco Goya painted it in the early 1800s.

How did the artist show what the accused heretics are feeling?

In the Holy Roman Empire, frightened people blamed Jews for the arrival of the Black Death. Many Jews had to flee their homes to escape angry mobs. Because the Jews were not Christian, many Europeans didn't want them in their towns.

READING CHECK **Summarizing** How were Jews discriminated against in the Middle Ages?

SUMMARY AND PREVIEW During the Middle Ages, religion shaped how people thought, what they did, and where they lived. In some places religion led to wars and punishment for those who didn't agree with the Catholic Church. In the next chapter, you will learn about the era that followed the Middle Ages.

Section 5 Assessment

go.hrw.com
Online Quiz
KEYWORD: SQ7 HP10

Reviewing Ideas, Terms, and People **HSS** 7.6.9

1. **a. Define** What is **heresy**?
   b. Explain Why did the church send priests and friars to find heretics?
2. **a. Identify** Who did Spanish Christians try to drive out of their lands?
   b. Explain What was the purpose of the **Spanish Inquisition**?
   c. Predict How might Spanish history have been different if the Spanish had not defeated the Moors?
3. **Summarize** How did kings and other rulers punish Jews in the Middle Ages?

Critical Thinking

4. **Categorizing** Draw a chart like the one shown here. Use it to describe Christians' reactions to different groups in the Middle Ages.

Heretics	Moors	Jews

FOCUS ON WRITING

5. **Choosing Important People** There are two more people in this section whose names you can add to your list. Where do they go on the list of most-to-least important? Who is most important?

Social Studies Skills

HSS Analysis CS 3 Use maps to identify physical and cultural features of neighborhoods and cities.

Analysis	Critical Thinking	Participation	Study

Interpreting Maps: Cultural Features

Understand the Skill

Maps show features on the earth's surface. *Physical maps* show natural features, such as mountains and rivers. *Political maps* show human features. They may contain such things as boundaries, roads, and settlements. *Historical maps* are political maps that show their subject as it was in the past.

Maps can be of large regions, such as countries or continents. They can also be of smaller places, such as battlefields or towns. Being able to interpret maps can help you understand more about history and geography.

Learn the Skill

Follow these steps to gain information from a map.

1 Read the title to determine what the map is about and the time period it covers.

2 Study the map's legend or key to understand what the colors or symbols on the map mean. Note its scale, which measures distances.

3 Pay attention to the map's other features. Maps may contain labels or information in addition to what is explained in the legend or key.

You can apply these guidelines to interpret the map of the Old City of Jerusalem that appears here. Modern Jerusalem covers many square miles. Near its center lies the Old City, the ancient part of Jerusalem. The Old City contains places sacred to Jews, Christians, and Muslims. These places made it an important battleground during the Crusades.

One sacred place in the Old City of Jerusalem is Temple Mount—a temple built by ancient Israel's King Solomon. Its Western Wall is the holiest place in Judaism. Also located on Temple Mount is the rock from which Muslims believe Muhammad ascended into heaven. Nearby is the Church of the Holy Sepulchre. This 1,700-year-old church was built on the site where Christians believe Jesus was crucified, buried, and arose. See if you can find these places on the map below.

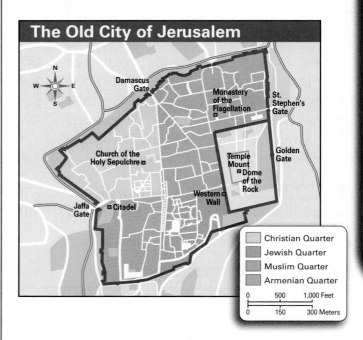

Practice and Apply the Skill

Interpret the map above to answer the following questions.

1. Into what different neighborhoods was the city divided?

2. How far is the Western Wall from the Jaffa Gate?

3. What is the dark line that surrounds the city? How do you know? What are the white lines on the map?

Visual Summary

Use the visual summary below to help you review the main ideas of the chapter.

QUICK FACTS

Government
The church and monarchy often worked together but sometimes were rivals.

Crusades
The pope called for Christians to retake the Holy Land.

The Church
The church was a powerful influence in the later Middle Ages.

Education and Society
The church helped guide learning and reacted to challenges to its authority.

Art and Architecture
Christianity inspired great forms of art and architecture.

Reviewing Vocabulary, Terms, and People

Match the words with their definitions.

1. excommunicate
2. religious order
3. Crusades
4. clergy
5. heresy
6. Thomas Aquinas
7. Magna Carta
8. Spanish Inquisition

a. church officials
b. punished non-Christians in Spain
c. religious ideas that oppose church teachings
d. an English document limiting the king's powers
e. cast out from the church
f. thought faith and reason could be used together
g. a group of people who dedicate their lives to religion, live together, and follow the same rules
h. wars fought to regain the Holy Land

Comprehension and Critical Thinking

SECTION 1 *(Pages 260–263)* **HSS** 7.6.4

9. **a. Describe** What was the relationship between Charlemagne and the pope like?

b. Contrast How did the opinions of popes like Gregory VII about power differ from those of kings like Henry IV?

c. Evaluate Do you think conflict with kings strengthened or weakened medieval popes? Why?

SECTION 2 *(Pages 264–268)* **HSS** 7.6.6

10. **a. Identify** What was the main goal of the Crusades?

b. Draw Conclusions Why do you think the Crusades changed the relationships between Christians and other groups?

c. Evaluate Which Crusade do you think was most successful? Which was least successful? Why?

SECTION 3 *(Pages 269–275)* **HSS** **7.6.8**

11. a. Describe How did Christianity shape art and education in the Middle Ages?

b. Analyze Why was Christianity so influential in so many areas of medieval life?

c. Elaborate How were the changes that took place in the medieval church related to its growing power and wealth?

SECTION 4 *(Pages 276–279)* **HSS** **7.6.5, 7.6.7**

12. a. Describe What was the Black Death, and how did it affect Europe?

b. Make Inferences Why do some people consider Magna Carta to represent the beginning of democracy in England?

c. Predict How might Europe's history have been different if England had won the Hundred Years' War?

SECTION 5 *(Pages 282–285)* **HSS** **7.6.9**

13. a. Identify What were the results of the Reconquista?

b. Draw Conclusions Why were the Spanish and Portuguese Inquisitions so feared?

c. Elaborate Why do you think some Christians considered heresy such a threat?

Reviewing Themes

14. Religion In what ways did the Crusades demonstrate the power of the church in Europe?

15. Society and Culture How did the church affect the lives of ordinary people?

Using the Internet

16. Activity: Evaluating Sources A challenge for anyone trying to understand the Middle Ages is evaluating the primary and secondary sources. Enter the activity keyword, and then rate the listed sources. Explain whether the source is a primary or secondary source, whether you think it is believable, and your reasoning.

Reading and Analysis Skills

17. Understanding Cause and Effect Match a cause in list A with an effect in list B. One effect will not be used.

> **List A**
>
> 1. Some people opposed church teachings.
> 2. The pope excommunicated a bishop who didn't agree that the pope was the head of the Catholic Church.
> 3. The Turks took control of the Holy Land and seemed ready to attack Constantinople.
> 4. Some people gave land to the church when they died.

> **List B**
>
> a. The clergy became active outside the church in political affairs.
> b. The church created the Inquisition.
> c. Pope Urban II called on Christians to join a Crusade.
> d. Kings gained more power.
> e. The Eastern Orthodox Church was formed.

Social Studies Skills

18. Using City Maps Locate a map of your town either in print or on the Internet. Look at the map to find places that serve the same functions as the following locations in medieval towns: a cathedral, a market, the local lord's house, and the mill. What other places can you find in your town that are similar to medieval places? Make a list and compare it with your classmates' lists.

FOCUS ON WRITING

19. Writing Your Article Review your notes. Be sure you've identified the three people you think are the most important and why they're important. Now write an article explaining why these people were so important to Europe in the Middle Ages. Keep your article short: one or two sentences to introduce your topic, a sentence or two about each important person, and a one- or two-sentence conclusion.

Standards Assessment

DIRECTIONS: Read each question, and write the letter of the best response.

1

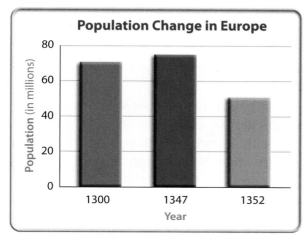

Population Change in Europe

What historical event was responsible for the population trend shown in the graph?

A the Crusades

B the Black Death

C the Hundred Years' War

D the Spanish Inquisition

2 Which of the following had the *greatest* influence on the lives of most Europeans during the Middle Ages?

A towns and trade

B the king

C religion and the church

D universities

3 One reason the Crusades failed to conquer the Holy Land permanently was because

A the fighting was a long distance from Europe.

B Crusader armies had better weapons than the Muslims did.

C religion was not important to most Europeans.

D the power of the popes declined.

4 Which statement *best* describes the relationship between popes and kings during Europe's Middle Ages?

A Popes became more powerful than kings.

B Many popes became kings, and many kings became popes.

C Popes and kings often disagreed with each other.

D Kings had more power than popes did.

5 Before the Reconquista, most of the Iberian Peninsula was controlled by

A Spaniards.

B Portuguese.

C Crusaders.

D Muslims.

Connecting with Past Learnings

6 Muslim culture spread all the way to Spain through conquest and trade. Which culture spread across much of the ancient world in the same way?

A Japanese

B Harappan

C Roman

D Sumerian

7 Magna Carta helped introduce democratic ideas to England. The first democracy in the ancient world arose in

A Greece.

B China.

C India.

D Rome.

A Historical Narrative

Assignment
A narrative is a story that may be true or fictional. Write a fictional historical narrative set in Europe during the Middle Ages.

What was life like in Europe in the Middle Ages? Where did people live? How did they spend their days? You can learn more about history by researching and writing a narrative that is set in a different time and place.

1. Prewrite

Planning Character and Setting
You should write your narrative from the point of view of someone who lived during that time.

- **The Narrator** Is the person telling your story a knight, a peasant, or a priest? A lady or a lady's maid?
- **The Event** What event or incident will your narrator experience? A jousting tournament? A Viking invasion? A religious pilgrimage? A famine or fire in the village?
- **The Setting** How will the time, between 800 and 1200 AD, and place, somewhere in Europe, affect this person? What will he or she want out of life or would fear or admire?

Developing a Plot
Select an event or incident, and then ask yourself these questions.

- How would the event have unfolded? In other words, what would have happened first, second, third, and so on?
- What problem might face your narrator during this event? How could your narrator solve this problem?

2. Write

Have your narrator tell what happened in the first person, using *I, me, we, us,* etc. For example, *I woke up early. We stopped by a stream.* Then use the framework below to help you write your first draft.

TIP **Adding Details** Help your audience get a feel for the setting by using sensory details. As you think about everyday life in the Middle Ages, make note of details that describe how things might have looked, felt, sounded, smelled, or tasted.

ELA Writing 7.2.1 Write fictional or autobiographical texts.

A Writer's Framework

Introduction	Body	Conclusion
■ Grab the reader's attention. ■ Offer needed background information about the place and the people involved in the event.	■ Start with the beginning of the incident or event, and present the actions in the order they happen. ■ Build to a suspenseful moment when the outcome is uncertain.	■ Show how the narrator solves his or her problem. ■ Explain how the narrator changes or how his or her life changes.

3. Evaluate and Revise

Evaluating

Read through the first draft of your narrative. Then use the guidelines below to consider its content and organization.

Evaluation Questions for a Fictional Historical Narrative

- Do you grab the reader's attention at the very beginning?
- Do you include background information to explain the time, place, and people involved in the event?
- Do you use first-person pronouns to show that your narrator is the central person in the event?

- Do you tell the actions in the order they happen or happened?
- Do you show how the narrator solves the problem or how it is solved for him or her?
- Do you explain how the narrator changes as a result of the event?

Revising

Before you share your narrative with others, have a classmate read it and retell the narrative to you. Add details at any point where his or her retelling seems uncertain or dull. Add transitions to show how events are connected in time.

4. Proofread and Publish

Proofreading

Weak word choice can drain the life from your narrative. Vague nouns and adjectives do little to spark the interest and imagination of readers. In contrast, precise words make your story come alive. They tell readers exactly what the characters and setting are like.

- **Vague Nouns or Pronouns** Words like *man* and *it* tell your readers little. Replace them with precise words, like *peasant* or *cottage*.
- **Vague adjectives** Would you prefer an experience that is *nice* or *fun*, or one that is *thrilling, exhilarating, or stirring*?

Publishing

You can publish your historical narrative by reading it aloud in class or by posting it on a class authors' wall. You may also publish all the narratives in your class as an Internet page or in a photocopied literary magazine.

Practice and Apply

Use the steps and strategies outlined in this workshop to write your historical narrative.

TIP **Describing Actions** We communicate not only with our words but also with our actions. By describing specific actions—movements, gestures, and facial expressions—you can make people in your narrative live and breathe.

TIP **Connecting Events** To improve your narrative, use transitions such as *next, later,* and *finally* to show the order in which the events and actions happen or happened.

Renewal in Europe

As the Middle Ages drew to a close, Europe entered a new period of creativity and learning called the Renaissance. During the Renaissance, artists and scholars rediscovered the ideas of ancient Greece and Rome. They hoped to build on the achievements of these classical civilizations.

Some Renaissance scholars and thinkers clashed with church officials. These clashes led to a struggle in Christianity called the Reformation. Other thinkers, searching for the truth about nature and humanity, invented modern science.

In the next three chapters, you will read about how these developments dramatically reshaped Europe and the world.

Explore the Art

In this scene, the young singer Francesca Caccini performs at a private gathering in Italy. What features of daily life can you see in this illustration?

The Renaissance

California Standards

History–Social Science

7.8 Students analyze the origins, accomplishments, and geographic diffusion of the Renaissance.

Analysis Skills

CS 3 Use maps to identify the migration of people and the growth of economic systems.

English–Language Arts

Writing 7.2.4b Describe the points in support of the proposition, employing well-articulated evidence.

Reading 7.1.2 Use knowledge of Greek, Latin, and Anglo-Saxon roots and affixes to understand content-area vocabulary.

FOCUS ON WRITING

A Movie Proposal You have a great idea for a movie set during the Renaissance. To get your film made, you need to convince a studio that the period is interesting and exciting. As you read this chapter, look for people and ideas that you could include in your movie.

CHAPTER EVENTS

WORLD EVENTS

1200

1271 Marco Polo travels to China.

1281 The *kamikaze* saves Japan from a Mongol invasion.

What You Will Learn...

In this chapter you will learn how the Renaissance changed life in Europe. The Renaissance began in Italy's great trading cities like Venice, shown here. Venice is an island city crisscrossed with canals, so its "streets" are actually waterways.

1321
Dante completes *The Divine Comedy.*

1368
The Ming dynasty begins in China.

c. 1455
Gutenberg develops his printing press.

1453
The Ottomans conquer Constantinople.

1508–1512
Michelangelo paints the ceiling of the Sistine Chapel.

1464
Sunni Ali founds the Songhai Empire in West Africa.

1594–1595
Shakespeare writes *Romeo and Juliet.*

1300   1400   1500   1600

Reading Social Studies

by Kylene Beers

| Economics | Geography | Politics | Religion | Society and Culture | Science and Technology |

Focus on Themes This chapter takes you into Italy in the 1300s and 1400s. At that time scholars, artists, and scientists built on classical Greek and Roman roots to make new advances in **science and technology** and the arts. You will read how Italy's **geographical** location, along with the invention of the printing press and the reopening of routes between China and Europe made the Renaissance a worldwide event with effects far beyond Italy.

Greek and Latin Word Roots

Focus on Reading During the Renaissance, scientists and scholars became interested in the history and languages of ancient Greece and Rome. Many of the words we use every day are based on words spoken by people in these ancient civilizations.

Common roots The charts below list some Greek and Latin roots found in many English words. As you read the charts, try to think of words that include each root. Then think about how the words' meanings are related to their roots.

Common Latin Roots		
Root	**Meaning**	**Sample words**
-aud-	hear	audience, audible
liter-	writing	literature, literary
re-	again	repeat, redo
-script-	write	script, manuscript
sub-	below	submarine, substandard
trans-	across	transport, translate

Common Greek Roots		
Root	**Meaning**	**Sample words**
anti-	against	antifreeze, antiwar
astr-	star	asteroid, astronaut
-chron-	time	chronicle, chronology
dia-	across, between	diagonal, diameter
micr-	small	microfilm, microscope
-phono-	sound	telephone, symphony

Additional reading support can be found in the

Inter*active Reader and Study Guide

ELA Reading 7.1.2 Use knowledge of Greek, Latin, and Anglo-Saxon roots and affixes to understand content-area vocabulary.

You Try It!

Each of the following sentences is taken from the chapter you are about to read. After you've read the sentences, answer the questions at the bottom of the page.

Using Word Origins

1. In their luggage these scholars carried rare, precious works of <u>literature</u>. *(p. 305)*
2. Among the ideas that Italian scholars wanted to <u>revive</u> were subjects that the Greeks and Romans had studied. *(p. 306)*
3. Later <u>astronomers</u> built on this discovery to lay the foundation for modern astronomy. *(p. 310)*
4. Although church leaders fought strenuously against it, the Bible was eventually <u>translated</u> and printed. *(p. 313)*
5. Also, straight lines, such as on floor tiles, appear <u>diagonal</u>. *(p. 307)*

Answer the following questions about the underlined words. Use the Common Roots charts on the opposite page for help.

1. Which of the underlined words has a root word that means "writing?" How does knowing the root word help you figure out what the word means?

2. What does the root word *astr-* mean? How does that help you figure out the meaning of *astronomy?*

3. In the second sentence, what do you think *revive* means? How could this be related to the root *re-?*

4. What's the root word in *translation?* What does *translation* mean? How is that definition related to the meaning of the root word?

5. What does the word *diagonal* mean? How is that meaning related to the meaning of *dia-?*

6. How many more words can you think of that use the roots in the charts on the previous page? Make a list and share it with your classmates.

Academic Vocabulary

Success in school is related to knowing academic vocabulary—the words that are frequently used in school assignments and discussions. In this chapter, you will learn the following academic words:

classical *(p. 305)*
affect *(p. 310)*

As you read Chapter 11, be on the lookout for words with Greek and Latin root words like those listed in the chart on the opposite page. Use the chart to help you figure out what words mean.

Origins of the Renaissance

What You Will Learn...

Main Ideas

1. European trade with Asia increased in the 1300s.
2. Trade cities in Italy grew wealthy and competed against each other.
3. As Florence became a center for arts and learning, the Renaissance began.

The Big Idea

The growth of wealthy trading cities in Italy led to a new era called the Renaissance.

Key Terms and People

Marco Polo, *p. 299*
interest, *p. 302*
Cosimo de' Medici, *p. 302*
Renaissance, *p. 303*

HSS **7.8.2** Explain the importance of Florence in the early stages of the Renaissance and the growth of independent trading cities (e.g., Venice), with emphasis on the cities' importance in the spread of Renaissance ideas.

7.8.3 Understand the effects of the reopening of the ancient "Silk Road" between Europe and China, including Marco Polo's travels and the location of his routes.

If YOU were there...

You are a historian living in Florence, Italy, in the late 1300s. In your writing you describe the wonders of your city. But the place was very different only about 50 years before. At that time, the Black Death was sweeping through the city. In fact, your own grandfather was killed by the terrible disease. Some 50,000 of the city's other citizens also died from plague. Now, though, Florence is known for its beauty, art, and learning.

How did your city change so quickly?

BUILDING BACKGROUND By the late 1300s the Black Death's horrors had passed. In Europe the stage was set for great changes. Europeans could worry less about dying and concentrate more on living. They wanted to enjoy life's pleasures—art, literature, and learning. Increased trade with faraway lands would help spark new interest in these activities.

Trade with Asia

It seems strange that the Black Death could have had any positive results, but that is what happened. You may remember that workers who survived could charge more money for their labor. In addition, the disease didn't damage farmland, buildings, ships, machines, or gold. People who survived could use these things to raise more food or make new products. They did just that. Europe's economy began to grow again.

As more goods became available, prices went down. People could buy more of the things they wanted. Trade increased, and new products appeared in the markets. Some of these goods came from India, China, and other lands to the east. How did these items move thousands of miles over high mountains and wide deserts? To learn more, we need to go back in time.

The Silk Road Reopens

The Chinese and Romans did business together from about AD 1 to 200. Products moved east and west along the Silk Road. This caravan route started in China and ended at the Mediterranean Sea.

When the Roman Empire and the Han dynasty fell, soldiers no longer protected travelers between Europe and Asia. As a result, use of the Silk Road declined. Then in the 1200s the Mongols took over China.

They once again made the roads safer for travelers and traders. Among these traders were a remarkable man from Venice named **Marco Polo** and his family.

Look at the map to follow the route of the Polo family's trip. Part of the journey was along the old Silk Road. When the Polos arrived in China, they met with the Mongol emperor Kublai Khan. He invited them to stay in his court and even made Marco Polo a government official.

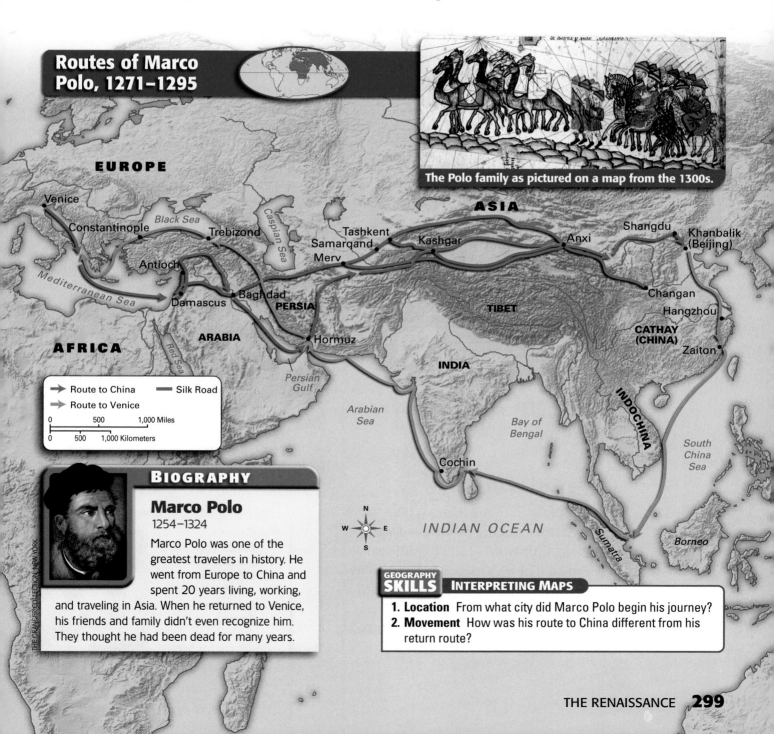

Routes of Marco Polo, 1271–1295

The Polo family as pictured on a map from the 1300s.

Route to China → **Silk Road** ━━ **Route to Venice** →

0 500 1,000 Miles
0 500 1,000 Kilometers

BIOGRAPHY

Marco Polo
1254–1324

Marco Polo was one of the greatest travelers in history. He went from Europe to China and spent 20 years living, working, and traveling in Asia. When he returned to Venice, his friends and family didn't even recognize him. They thought he had been dead for many years.

THE GRANGER COLLECTION, NEW YORK

GEOGRAPHY SKILLS | INTERPRETING MAPS

1. **Location** From what city did Marco Polo begin his journey?
2. **Movement** How was his route to China different from his return route?

The Polos saw many amazing things in China. For example, the Chinese used paper money in addition to the coins that Europeans used. The Polos were also fascinated by an unusual fuel source, which Marco later described:

> "It is a fact that throughout the province of Cathay [China] there is a sort of black stone, which is dug out of veins in the hillsides and burns like logs. These stones keep a fire going better than wood."
>
> –Marco Polo, from *A Description of the World*

This is the first known description of coal by a European.

While his father and uncle stayed in China, Marco Polo visited India and Southeast Asia. He traveled as a messenger for the emperor. Marco Polo spent 20 years living and traveling in Asia.

Eventually, the Polos returned to Venice. There a writer helped Marco Polo record his journey. At the time, many people didn't believe Polo's stories. Some people thought he had never set foot in China! Over the years his reputation grew, however. Polo's description made many Europeans curious about Asia. As their curiosity grew, people began to demand goods from Asia. Trade between Asia and Europe increased. Italian merchants organized much of this trade.

READING CHECK Finding Main Ideas What ancient trade route did the Polos travel?

Trade Cities in Italy

By the 1300s four northern Italian cities had become trading centers—Florence, Genoa (JEN-uh-wuh), Milan (muh-LAHN), and Venice. These cities bustled with activity. Shoppers there could buy beautiful things from Asia. Residents could meet strangers from faraway places and hear many languages on the streets.

Ports and Craft Centers

Italian cities played two very important roles in trade. One role was as ports on the Mediterranean Sea. Venice and Genoa were Italy's main port cities. Merchant ships brought spices and other luxuries from Asia into the cities' harbors. From there, merchants shipped the goods across Europe.

The other role was as manufacturing centers. Cities specialized in certain crafts. Venice produced glass. Workers in Milan made weapons and silk. Florence was a center for weaving wool into cloth. All of this economic activity put more money in merchants' pockets. Some Italian merchant families became incredibly wealthy. Eventually, this wealth would help make Italy the focus of European culture. How did this happen?

1 Milan
This castle in Milan was built in the mid-1400s. It shows the wealth and power of Italy's trading cities.

2 Genoa
Genoa is on the Mediterranean. This location enabled Genoa to become rich through overseas trade.

Separate States and Rival Rulers

Look at the map below. Notice that in the 1300s Italy was not a single country. Instead, it was made up of independent states. These states had different forms of government. For example, Venice was a republic, while the pope ruled the Papal States as a monarchy.

In most big Italian cities, a single rich merchant family controlled the government. This type of government was called a *signoria* (seen-yohr-EE-uh). The head of the family, the *signore* (seen-YOHR-ay), ruled the city. Under the *signori*, trade grew in Italy. In fact, the *signori* competed against each other to see whose city could grow richest from trade. They also competed for fame. Each one wanted to be known as powerful, wise, and devoted to his city.

READING CHECK **Summarizing** What were the four great trade cities of Italy in the 1300s?

Major Trading Cities in Renaissance Italy

Milan
Po River
Genoa
Venice
Adriatic Sea
Pisa
Florence
Tiber River
Corsica
Rome
Sardinia
Tyrrhenian Sea
Naples
Mediterranean Sea
Ionian Sea
Sicily

3 Venice
Venice is an island city. Like Genoa, Venice grew rich from its sea trade.

4 Florence
Florence was a banking and trade center. The city's wealthy leaders used their money to beautify the city with impressive buildings and art.

Florence
Genoa
Milan
Naples
Papal States
Venice

0   50   100 Miles
0   50   100 Kilometers

GEOGRAPHY SKILLS **INTERPRETING MAPS**

Location In what part of Italy are all four major trading cities located?

Florence

A market buzzes with activity in this scene showing what Florence may have looked like in the late 1300s.

Merchants traded goods from Europe and Asia in the city's markets.

Cloth was a major trade good in Florence.

Bankers kept detailed records of their investments.

Florence

In the 1300s, trade goods from Asia poured into Europe. Many of those items came through Italian ports. As a result, the merchant families in these cities made money. As the families grew rich and powerful, they wanted everyone to see what their money could buy. Although these factors affected most big Italian cities, one city—Florence—stands out as an example of trade and wealth at this time.

The Medici Family

THE IMPACT TODAY

Renaissance bankers in Florence developed a bookkeeping system that bankers still use today.

Although Florence's wealth began with the wool trade, banking increased that wealth. Bankers in Florence kept money for merchants from all over Europe. The bankers made money by charging interest. **Interest** is a fee that borrowers pay for the use of someone else's money. This fee is usually a certain percentage of the loan.

The greatest bankers in Florence were the Medici (MED-i-chee) family. In the early 1400s they were Florence's richest family, and by 1434 **Cosimo de' Medici** (KOH-zee-moh day MED-i-chee) ruled the city.

As ruler, Cosimo de' Medici wanted Florence to be the most beautiful city in the world. He hired artists to decorate his palace. He also paid architects to redesign many of Florence's buildings.

Cosimo de' Medici also valued education. After all, his banks needed workers who could read, write, and understand math. To improve education, he also built libraries and collected books.

During the time that the Medici family held power, Florence became the center of Italian art, literature, and culture. In other Italian cities, rich families tried to outdo the Medicis—and each other—in their support of the arts and learning.

City leaders hired architects and artists to create beautiful buildings like this famous church called the Duomo.

Visitors to Florence helped spread Renaissance ideas throughout Europe.

ANALYSIS SKILL **ANALYZING VISUALS**

What can you see in this illustration that shows the wealth of Florence?

Beginning of the Renaissance

This love of art and education was a key feature of a time we call the Renaissance (REN-uh-sahns). The word **Renaissance** means "rebirth" and refers to the period that followed Europe's Middle Ages.

What was being "reborn"? Interest in Greek and Roman writings was revived. Also new was an emphasis on people as individuals. These ideas were very different from the ideas of the Middle Ages.

READING CHECK Finding Main Ideas How did Florence help begin the Renaissance?

SUMMARY AND PREVIEW Changes in Italy led to the beginning of an era called the Renaissance. In the next section you'll learn about the Italian Renaissance—its ideas, people, and arts.

go.hrw.com
Online Quiz
KEYWORD: SQ7 HP11

Section 1 Assessment

Reviewing Ideas, Terms, and People **HSS** 7.8.2, 7.8.3

1. **a. Recall** What road did **Marco Polo** travel to Asia?
   b. Summarize How did the Polos affect trade with Asia?
2. **a. Identify** What were the four major trade cities of Italy?
   b. Analyze How were these cities important economically?
3. **a. Identify** What is one reason why education was important to **Cosimo de' Medici**?
   b. Analyze How did Florence rise to fame?

Critical Thinking

4. **Sequencing** Draw a graphic organizer like the one below. Use it to describe the results of increased trade with Asia.

$$\bigcirc \rightarrow \bigcirc \rightarrow \bigcirc \rightarrow \text{Beginnings of the Renaissance}$$

FOCUS ON WRITING

5. **Choosing a Setting** In this section, you read about the setting in which the Renaissance developed: Italy in the 1200s and 1300s. How could you use this setting to make your movie interesting?

The Italian Renaissance

What You Will Learn...

Main Ideas

1. During the Italian Renaissance, people found new ways to see the world.
2. Italian writers contributed great works of literature.
3. Italian art and artists were among the finest in the world.
4. Science and education made advances during this time.

The Big Idea

New ways of thinking created a rebirth of the arts and learning in Italy.

Key Terms and People

humanism, *p. 304*
Dante Alighieri, *p. 306*
Niccolo Machiavelli, *p. 306*
perspective, *p. 307*
Michelangelo, *p. 308*
Leonardo da Vinci, *p. 308*
Petrarch, *p. 310*

HSS **7.8.1** Describe the way in which the revival of classical learning and the arts fostered a new interest in humanism (i.e., a balance between intellect and religious faith).

7.8.5 Detail advances made in literature, the arts, science, mathematics, cartography, engineering, and the understanding of human anatomy and astronomy (e.g., by Dante Alighieri, Leonardo da Vinci, Michelangelo di Buonarroti Simoni, Johann Gutenberg, William Shakespeare).

If YOU were there...

You are an apprentice working in the studio of a famous painter. You admire him but think some of his ideas are old-fashioned. Most of the time, your job is to paint the background of the master's pictures. Now, though, you have finished a painting of your own. You are proud of it and want the world to know who made it. But the master says an artist should never put his name on a painting.

Will you sign your painting?

BUILDING BACKGROUND The Renaissance period brought new ways of thinking. Like this young painter, people began to value individuals and their personal achievements. This was a big change from the way people thought during the Middle Ages.

New Ways to See the World

During the Middle Ages, most people in Europe had devoted themselves entirely to Christianity. People looked to the church for answers to problems in their lives, and most of Europe's brilliant and influential thinkers were church figures.

By the late 1300s, however, scholars had begun to study subjects besides religion. They studied history, literature, public speaking, and art, subjects that emphasized the actions and abilities of humans. Together, these subjects are called the humanities. The study of the humanities led to a new way of thinking and learning known as **humanism**.

Humanism and Religion

The humanists of the Renaissance were no less religious than people had been before. Like the people of the Middle Ages, they were devout Christians. At the same time, however, people in the Renaissance were interested in ideas besides religion.

People's newfound interest in the humanities led them to respect those who could write, create, or speak well. As a result, talented writers and artists won great fame and honor. This too was a great change from the Middle Ages, when most people had worked only to glorify God.

Rediscovering the Past

The popularity of the humanities was due in large part to a new interest in ancient history. This interest had been caused by the rediscovery of many ancient writings that Europeans had thought to be lost.

During the 1300s, Turks had conquered much of the Byzantine Empire. Scholars seeking to escape the Turks fled to Italy. In their luggage these scholars carried rare, precious works of literature.

Many of the works they brought to Italy were ancient **classical** writings, such as works by Greek thinkers. You may remember some of their names—Plato and Thucydides, for example. Europeans had thought that these ancient writings were lost forever. Excited by their return, scholars then went looking for ancient texts in Latin. They discovered many Latin texts in monasteries, where the monks had preserved works by Roman writers. As Italian scholars read the ancient texts, they rediscovered the glories of Greece and Rome. As a result, they longed for a renewal of classical culture.

ACADEMIC VOCABULARY

classical referring to the cultures of ancient Greece or Rome

Rebirth of Classical Ideas

These two statues were carved about 1,500 years apart, yet they share many features. To the left is an ancient Roman statue of the emperor Augustus. To the right is a statue of Moses by the Renaissance artist Michelangelo.

Features of Classical and Renaissance Statues

- Both figures are shown in realistic, lifelike poses.

- Both statues look as though the subject could start moving at any moment.

- Both statues show the human body in great detail.

- Both figures wear clothing that appears to drape and fold like real cloth.

BOOK
The Prince

In The Prince, *Machiavelli offers advice for rulers on how to stay in power. In this famous passage, he explains why in his view it is better for rulers to be feared than to be loved.*

❝A controversy has arisen about this: whether it is better to be loved than feared, or vice versa. My view is that it is desirable to be both loved and feared; but it is difficult to achieve both and, if one of them has to be lacking, it is much safer to be feared than loved . . . For love is sustained by a bond of gratitude which, because men are excessively self-interested, is broken whenever they see a chance to benefit themselves. But fear is sustained by a dread of punishment that is always effective.❞

ANALYSIS SKILL **ANALYZING PRIMARY SOURCES**

Do you think that Machiavelli gave good advice in this passage? Why or why not?

FOCUS ON READING

What does the root **re-** in **revive** mean? What other word on this page has the same root?

Among the ideas that Italian scholars wanted to <u>revive</u> were subjects that the Greeks and Romans had studied. These subjects included grammar, speaking, poetry, history, and the Greek and Latin languages—the humanities.

Other ancient sources of inspiration for Renaissance artists and architects were all around. Roman ruins still stood in Italy. Fine classical statues were on display, and more were being found every day. Throughout the Renaissance, Italian artists studied these ancient statues. They tried to make their own works look like the works of the Romans and Greeks. In fact, some artists wanted their works to look ancient so badly that they buried their statues in the ground to make them look older!

READING CHECK **Summarizing** What sources inspired Renaissance artists and scholars?

Italian Writers

Many Italian writers contributed great works of literature to the Renaissance. The earliest was the politician and poet named **Dante Alighieri** (DAHN-tay ahl-eeg-YEH-ree), or simply Dante. Before Dante, most medieval authors had written in Latin, the language of the church. But Dante wrote in Italian, which was the common language of the people. By using Italian, Dante showed that he considered the people's language to be as good as Latin. Later writers continued to use common languages in their works of literature.

Dante's major work was *The Divine Comedy*. It describes an imaginary journey he took through the afterlife. On this journey, Dante meets people from his past as well as great figures from history. In fact, the Roman poet Virgil is one of the guides on the journey. In the course of his writing, Dante described many of the problems he saw in Italian society.

A later Italian writer was also a politician. His name was **Niccolo Machiavelli** (neek-koh-LOH mahk-yah-VEL-lee). In 1513 Machiavelli wrote a short book called *The Prince*. It gave leaders advice on how they should rule.

Machiavelli didn't care about theories or what *should* work. In his writings, he argued that rulers had to focus on the "here and now," not theories, to be successful. He was only interested in what really happened in both war and peace. For example, Machiavelli thought that sometimes rulers had to be ruthless to keep order. In this way, Machiavelli serves as a good example of Renaissance interest in human behavior and society.

READING CHECK **Drawing Conclusions** How did Dante and Machiavelli reflect the ideas of the Renaissance?

Italian Art and Artists

During the Renaissance Italian artists created some of the most beautiful paintings and sculptures in the world. Rich families and church leaders hired the artists to create these works. New techniques made their work come alive.

New Methods for a New Era

Renaissance ideas about the value of human life are reflected in the art of the time. Artists showed people more realistically than medieval artists had done. Renaissance artists studied the human body and drew what they saw. However, because artists often used classical statues as their guides, many of the human beings they drew were as perfect as Greek gods.

Artists also used a new discovery—**perspective**, a method of showing a three-dimensional scene on a flat surface so that it looks real. Perspective uses various techniques. For example, people in the background are smaller than those in front. Also, straight lines, such as on floor tiles, appear diagonal. Colors could also show distance. So mountains in the background of a picture are a hazy blue.

Great Artists

In the work of the greatest Italian artists the people shown are clearly individuals. In this way, the art reflects the Renaissance idea of the value of human beings. For example, the figures in the painting below by the artist Raphael have clear personalities.

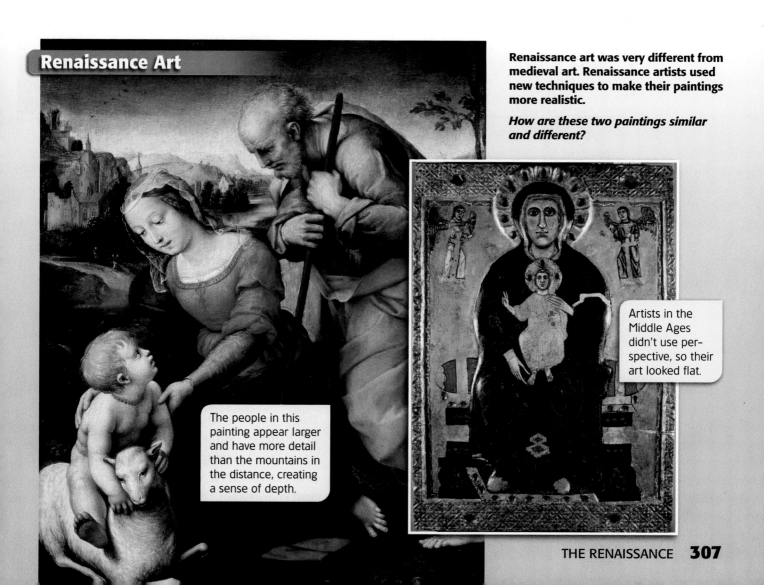

Renaissance Art

Renaissance art was very different from medieval art. Renaissance artists used new techniques to make their paintings more realistic.

How are these two paintings similar and different?

The people in this painting appear larger and have more detail than the mountains in the distance, creating a sense of depth.

Artists in the Middle Ages didn't use perspective, so their art looked flat.

The Genius of Leonardo da Vinci

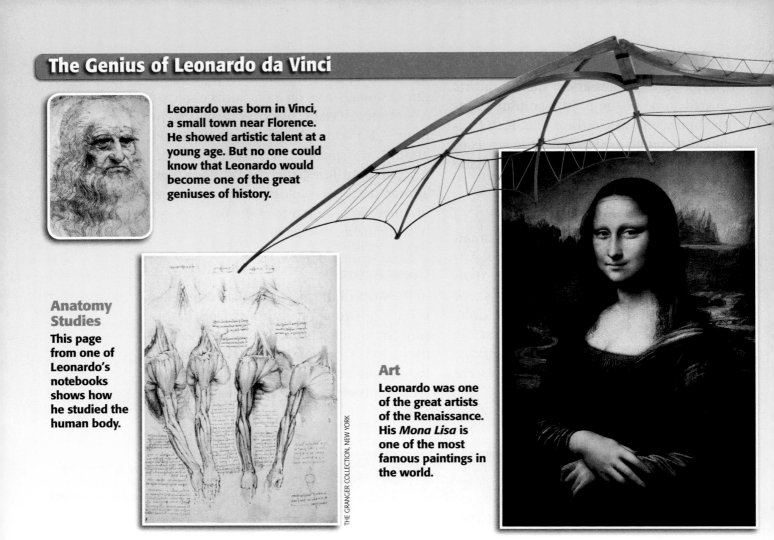

Leonardo was born in Vinci, a small town near Florence. He showed artistic talent at a young age. But no one could know that Leonardo would become one of the great geniuses of history.

Anatomy Studies

This page from one of Leonardo's notebooks shows how he studied the human body.

THE GRANGER COLLECTION, NEW YORK

Art

Leonardo was one of the great artists of the Renaissance. His *Mona Lisa* is one of the most famous paintings in the world.

Sandro Botticelli (bot-ti-CHEL-lee), a painter from Florence, also showed respect for people. Many of his paintings show scenes from Roman myths. But he painted everyone—whether ancient gods, saints, angels, or farmers—in fine detail.

The work of Titian (TISH-uhn), the finest artist of Venice, reflects interest in the past. Like Botticelli, he often painted scenes from classical myths. For Venice's churches, though, Titian painted colorful scenes from Christian teachings.

Two Masters

Of all the Italian Renaissance artists, two stand above the rest. Each is what we call a Renaissance person—someone who can do practically anything well.

One of the greatest Italian artists was **Michelangelo** (mee-kay-LAHN-jay-loh). He had many talents. Michelangelo designed buildings, wrote poetry, carved sculptures, and painted magnificent pictures. Perhaps his most famous work is a painting that covers the ceiling of the Sistine Chapel in the Vatican. The muscular human figures in this immense painting remind the viewer of Greek or Roman statues.

The true genius of the Renaissance was **Leonardo da Vinci**. In fact, some call him the greatest genius that has ever lived. In addition to being an expert painter, Leonardo was a sculptor, architect, inventor, and engineer. He was even a town planner and mapmaker.

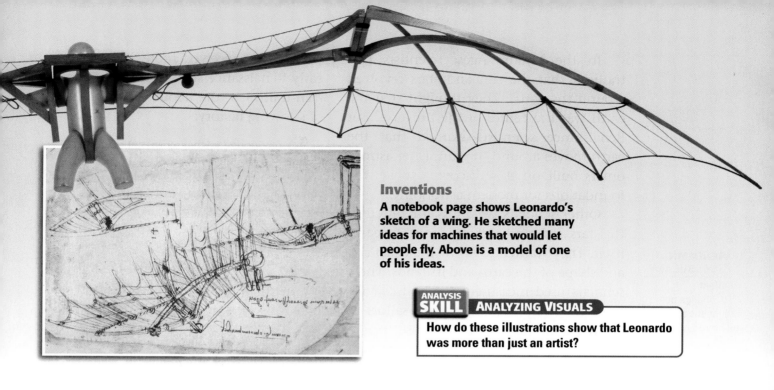

Inventions

A notebook page shows Leonardo's sketch of a wing. He sketched many ideas for machines that would let people fly. Above is a model of one of his ideas.

ANALYSIS SKILL **ANALYZING VISUALS**

How do these illustrations show that Leonardo was more than just an artist?

Both nature and technology fascinated Leonardo. Detailed drawings of plants, animals, and machines fill his sketchbooks. To make his art more real, Leonardo studied anatomy, or the structure of human bodies. He dissected corpses to see how bones and muscles worked. Yet Leonardo's paintings also show human emotions. For example, people who see his *Mona Lisa* can't help wondering what made the lady smile.

READING CHECK **Categorizing** Who were some of the great artists of the Italian Renaissance?

Science and Education

Many of the texts rediscovered in the 1300s dealt with science. For the first time in centuries, Europeans could read works by ancient scientists. After reading these works, Renaissance scholars went on to make their own scientific advances.

Mathematics

Some scholars thought mathematics could help them understand the universe. They studied ancient math texts and built upon the ideas in them. In the process, they created symbols we still use in math today. For example, they created symbols for the square root ($\sqrt{}$) and for positive ($+$) and negative ($-$) numbers.

Engineering and Architecture

Advances in math led to advances in other fields of science. For example, engineers and architects used new mathematical formulas to strengthen buildings.

One Renaissance architect who used these new ideas was Filippo Brunelleschi (broo-nayl-LAYS-kee). He designed a huge dome for a cathedral in Florence. But Brunelleschi ran into a problem. The dome that he wanted to build was so big that it would be too heavy for the cathedral's walls to support. To solve the problem, he built the dome out of two thin, light layers instead of one thick, heavy one.

Astronomy and Cartography

Other Renaissance scientists wanted to know more about the sky and what was in it. They studied astronomy to learn about the sun, stars, and planets.

In the Middle Ages, scientists had thought that the sun and stars revolved around the earth. They thought that the earth was the center of the universe. But Renaissance scientists learned that the earth moves around the sun. Later astronomers built on this discovery to lay the foundations for modern astronomy.

Other scholars were less interested in the stars and more curious about the earth itself. They wanted to know the exact size and shape of the earth and its lands. These scholars used measurements and calculations made by merchants and sailors to create better, more accurate maps.

Changes in Education

In time, these changes in literature, art, science, and technology would spread beyond Italy. For these changes to spread, however, required changes in education.

During the Middle Ages, students had concentrated on religious subjects. During the Renaissance, students learned about the humanities as well. History was one subject that received more attention. An early Renaissance scholar named **Petrarch** (PEH-trahrk), wrote about the importance of knowing history:

> " O inglorious age! that scorns antiquity, its mother, to whom it owes every noble art . . . What can be said in defense of men of education who ought not to be ignorant of antiquity [ancient times] and yet are plunged in . . . darkness and delusion? "
>
> –Francesco Petrarch, from a 1366 letter to Boccaccio

Petrarch's ideas would **affect** education for many years to come. Education and new ways of spreading information would take the Renaissance far beyond Italy.

READING CHECK **Predicting** How do you think Renaissance ideas would change as they spread to other countries?

SUMMARY AND PREVIEW A great rebirth of art, literature, and learning began in Italy in the late 1300s. Renaissance ideas changed as they spread across Europe.

ACADEMIC VOCABULARY

affect
to change or influence

THE IMPACT TODAY

Many American universities grant degrees in the humanities.

Section 2 Assessment

go.hrw.com
Online Quiz
KEYWORD: SQ7 HP11

Reviewing Ideas, Terms, and People **HSS** 7.8.1, 7.8.5

1. **a. Identify** What are some basic ideas of **humanism**?
   b. Summarize How did ancient texts and statues affect Renaissance scholars?
2. **a. Recall** What set **Dante** apart from earlier Italian writers?
   b. Draw Conclusions Why may a historian call **Niccolo Machiavelli** "the first modern Italian"?
3. **a. Identify** What are three techniques for showing **perspective**?
   b. Summarize What are some characteristics of art by Raphael, Botticelli, and Titian?
   c. Evaluate Which artist would you rather have met in real life—**Michelangelo** or **Leonardo da Vinci**? What is the reason for your choice?

4. **a. Identify** Name one Renaissance achievement in each category of mathematics, architecture, astronomy, and cartography.
   b. Summarize How did the choice of school subjects change during the Renaissance?

Critical Thinking

5. **Identifying Cause and Effect** Draw a graphic organizer like the one shown here. Use it to show how Turkish conquests east of Europe contributed to the growth of the Renaissance.

FOCUS ON WRITING

6. **Thinking about Characters** The Renaissance was full of great writers, artists, and scholars. How could you use the people you read about in this section to make your movie interesting?

Michelangelo

Why is an Italian artist from the 1500s still popular today?

When did he live? 1475–1564

Where did he live? Michelangelo di Buonarroti Simoni was born in Florence, but he also lived and worked in Rome and Bologna.

What did he do? Michelangelo created some of the most famous works of art in world history. Many of these works he created for the Roman Catholic Church. Popes, bishops, and other church officials hired Michelangelo to decorate their churches with his brilliant statues and paintings.

Why is he important? Michelangelo represents the ideas of the Renaissance in many ways. He strove for perfection in his works and considered them ruined if he found even the tiniest flaw. In the end his perfectionism paid off, for his art leaves people in awe today just as it did in the artist's own time.

Make Generalizations How was Michelangelo an example of the ideal Renaissance person?

KEY EVENTS

1498 Michelangelo is hired to carve a statue of Jesus and Mary for the Vatican.

1501 He is asked to carve a statue of the Hebrew king David for Florence's cathedral.

1508 Pope Julius II hires Michelangelo to paint the ceiling of the Sistine Chapel.

1527 Michelangelo helps plan the defense of Florence, which is under attack.

1534 Michelangelo returns to Rome, where he redesigns St. Peter's Cathedral.

This painting by Michelangelo decorates part of the ceiling of the Sistine Chapel in Rome.

The Renaissance beyond Italy

What You Will Learn...

Main Ideas

1. Paper, printing, and new universities led to the spread of new ideas.
2. The ideas of the Northern Renaissance differed from those of the Italian Renaissance.
3. Literature beyond Italy also thrived in the Renaissance.

The Big Idea

The Renaissance spread far beyond Italy and changed in the process.

Key Terms and People

Johann Gutenberg, *p. 313*
Christian humanism, *p. 314*
Desiderius Erasmus, *p. 314*
Albrecht Dürer, *p. 315*
Miguel de Cervantes, *p. 316*
William Shakespeare, *p. 316*

HSS 7.8.4 Describe the growth and effects of new ways of disseminating information (e.g., the ability to manufacture paper, translation of the Bible into the vernacular, printing).

7.8.5 Detail advances made in literature, the arts, science, mathematics, cartography, engineering, and the understanding of human anatomy and astronomy (e.g., by Dante Alighieri, Leonardo da Vinci, Michelangelo di Buonarroti Simoni, Johann Gutenberg, William Shakespeare).

If YOU were there...

You are a student from Holland, studying law at the university in Bologna, Italy. Life in Renaissance Italy is so exciting! You've met artists and writers and learned so much about art and literature. You can hardly wait to tell people at home about everything you've learned. But now a lawyer in Bologna has offered you a chance to stay and work in Italy.

Will you stay in Italy or return to Holland?

BUILDING BACKGROUND By the late 1400s the Renaissance spirit was spreading from Italy to other parts of Europe. Artists, writers, and scholars came to Italy to study. Then they taught others what they had learned and brought paintings and sculptures from Italy back home. Along with works of art, they picked up new ideas. Soon, printing and books made these new ideas available to even more people.

Time Line

Printing in Europe

1000 Printing has not developed in Europe yet. Books are copied by hand, usually by monks.

1000 **1300**

1300s Factories in Europe begin making paper using techniques introduced from Asia.

Spread of New Ideas

Travelers and artists helped spread the Renaissance throughout Europe. But the development of printing was a giant step in spreading ideas. For the first time ever, thousands of people could read books and share ideas about them.

Paper and Printing

By the late 700s papermaking had spread from China to the Middle East. From there it came to Europe. European factories were making paper by the 1300s. Because it was cheaper and easier to prepare, paper soon replaced the animal skins on which people had written before.

Then in the mid-1400s a German man, **Johann Gutenberg** (GOOT-uhn-berk), developed a printing press that used movable type. That is, each letter was a separate piece. A worker could fit letters into a frame, spread ink on the letters, and press a sheet of paper against the letters. In this way, an entire page was printed at once. Then the worker could rearrange letters in the frame to create a new page. How much faster printing was than writing!

The first printed book was a Bible printed in the Latin language in about 1455. Soon, some thinkers began to call for the Bible to be translated into common languages. Although church leaders fought strenuously against it, the Bible was eventually translated and printed. Bibles were suddenly available to more people. Because the Bible was available to read, more people learned to read. Then, they wanted more education.

New Universities

Students from around Europe traveled to Italy to study at Italian universities. By the early 1500s most of the teachers in these universities were humanists. Students from northern Europe who studied with these teachers took Renaissance ideas back with them to their home countries.

Over time, many of the new scholars became teachers in Europe's universities. In addition, new universities opened in France, Germany, and the Netherlands. Because these schools were set up by humanists, Renaissance ideas about the value of people spread throughout Europe.

THE IMPACT TODAY

The demand for more books led to improvements in printing and binding that have made modern books cheap and easily available.

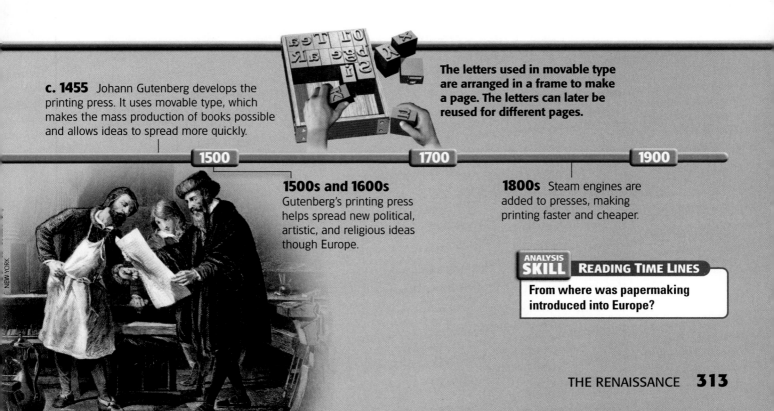

c. 1455 Johann Gutenberg develops the printing press. It uses movable type, which makes the mass production of books possible and allows ideas to spread more quickly.

The letters used in movable type are arranged in a frame to make a page. The letters can later be reused for different pages.

1500 **1700** **1900**

1500s and 1600s
Gutenberg's printing press helps spread new political, artistic, and religious ideas though Europe.

1800s Steam engines are added to presses, making printing faster and cheaper.

ANALYSIS SKILL READING TIME LINES

From where was papermaking introduced into Europe?

NEW YORK

Although only men could attend universities, women also helped spread these ideas. Many noble families educated their daughters at home. They encouraged young women to study classical literature, philosophy, and the arts. Some educated women became powerful political figures. They married nobles from around Europe and encouraged the spread of Renaissance ideas in their husbands' lands.

READING CHECK **Analyzing** How did travel and marriage spread Renaissance ideas?

The Northern Renaissance

As humanism spread, scholars in northern Europe became more interested in history. Northern scholars, however, focused not on Greece and Rome but on the history of Christianity. The resulting combination of humanist and religious ideas is called **Christian humanism**.

Many northern scholars felt that the church was corrupt and no longer true to the spirit of Jesus's teachings anymore. They began to call for church reform.

A Northern Scholar

A Dutch priest named **Desiderius Erasmus** (des-i-DEER-ee-uhs i-RAZ-mus) was the most important of these scholars. In 1509 he published a book, *The Praise of Folly,* in which he criticized corrupt clergy. Erasmus also wanted to get rid of some church rituals that he considered meaningless. Instead of rituals, he emphasized devotion to God and the teachings of Jesus.

Northern Renaissance Art

Northern Europeans also changed some Renaissance ideas about art. For one thing, the humans in northern paintings don't look like Greek gods. Instead, they are realistic, with physical flaws.

Northern artists embraced realism in another way, too. They painted objects, from rocks to flowers, so clearly that the objects don't look like they were painted at all. They almost appear to be the real thing, glued to the painting.

Biblical scenes and classical myths were the traditional subjects of Italian Renaissance art. In contrast, northern artists painted scenes of daily life. For example, look at the painting below of hunters returning home. It was painted by Pieter Brueghel (BROY-guhl) the Elder, an artist from what is now Belgium. Some of Brueghel's other paintings show people working in fields, dancing, or eating. His son, called Brueghel the Younger, later used his father's ideas in his own works.

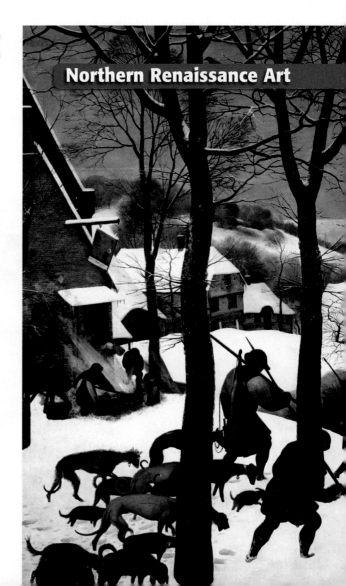

Northern Renaissance Art

Albrecht Dürer (AWL-brekt DYUR-uhr) was a famous northern artist from Germany. Like Italian artists, Dürer studied anatomy so he could paint people more realistically. Like his fellow northerners, Dürer showed objects in great detail. A lover of nature, Dürer drew even a patch of weeds so clearly that today scientists can identify the plant species.

Dürer created religious paintings for churches. But he is most famous for his prints. A print is a work of art reproduced from an original. First, Dürer carved the image into either a metal sheet or a wooden block. Then he covered the image with ink and pressed a sheet of paper down onto it. The image transferred to the paper. Dürer sold his prints at fairs and markets.

Among other great artists of the Northern Renaissance were two portrait painters—Hans Holbein (HAWL-byn) and Jan van Eyck (yahn van YK). Holbein grew up in Switzerland but moved to England. There he painted a portrait of King Henry VIII. Among van Eyck's works are many religious scenes. Van Eyck worked in oil paints, a new invention. The colors in his paintings seem to glow from within.

READING CHECK **Categorizing** Who were some major artists of the Northern Renaissance?

Northern Renaissance artists often painted realistic scenes from daily life, like *Return of the Hunters*, painted by Pieter Brueghel in 1565. Albrecht Dürer created *The Four Horsemen of the Apocalypse* shown above in 1597 and 1598. It is a woodcut—a print made from a detailed carving in a block of wood.

What scenes of daily life can you see in Brueghel's painting?

Literature beyond Italy

Writers in other countries besides Italy also included Renaissance ideas in their works. Like Dante, they wrote in the languages of their home countries. In Spain **Miguel de Cervantes** (mee-GEL day ser-VAHN-tays) wrote *Don Quixote* (kee-HOH-tay). In this book Cervantes poked fun at romantic tales of the Middle Ages. His main character is an old man who decides to become a knight, a decision that Cervantes mocks.

> "At last, when his wits were gone beyond repair, he came to conceive the strangest idea that ever occurred to any madman in this world. It now appeared to him fitting and necessary, in order to win a greater amount of honor for himself and serve his country at the same time, to become a knight-errant and roam the world on horseback, in a suit of armor."
>
> –Miguel de Cervantes, from *Don Quixote*, translated by Samuel Putnam

Like many writers of his day, Cervantes thought his own time was much better than the Middle Ages.

In France, too, writers poked fun at the ideas of the Middle Ages. The greatest of these French Renaissance writers was François Rabelais (fran-swah RAB-uh-lay). Like many Renaissance figures, Rabelais was a person of many trades. In addition to being a writer, he was a doctor and a priest. But it is for his writing that he is best known. Rabelais wrote a series of novels about characters named Gargantua and Pantagruel. Through his characters' actions, Rabelais mocks the values of the Middle Ages as well as events that had happened to him in his own life.

Readers around the world consider **William Shakespeare** the greatest writer in the English language. Although he also wrote poems, Shakespeare is most famous

Don Quixote

In one of the most famous scenes from *Don Quixote*, the confused knight tilts, or charges at, a windmill that he believes to be a fierce giant. Because of this scene, we still use the phrase "tilting at windmills" to describe someone attempting an impossible task.

How does this scene mock medieval ideas of bravery and knighthood?

for his plays. Shakespeare wrote more than 30 comedies, tragedies, and histories. London audiences of the late 1500s and early 1600s packed the theatre to see them. Ever since, people have enjoyed the beauty of Shakespeare's language and his understanding of humanity. The following passage reflects the Renaissance idea that each human being is important. Shakespeare compares people to the actors in a play who should be watched with great interest:

" All the world's a stage,
And all the men and women merely players.
They have their exits and their entrances;
And one man in his time plays many parts,
His acts being seven ages. "
–William Shakespeare, from *As You Like It*, Act 2, Scene 7

The works of Cervantes, Rabelais, and Shakespeare have been translated into dozens of languages. Through these translations, their Renaissance spirit lives on.

READING CHECK **Comparing** How does the choice of language used by Cervantes and Shakespeare compare to that of Italian writers?

BIOGRAPHY

William Shakespeare
1564–1616

Many people consider William Shakespeare the greatest playwright of all time. His plays are still hugely popular around the world. Shakespeare was such an important writer that he even influenced the English language. He invented common phrases such as *fair play* and common words such as *lonely.* In fact, Shakespeare is probably responsible for more than 2,000 English words.

Drawing Inferences How do you think Shakespeare invented new words and phrases?

SUMMARY AND PREVIEW The making of paper, the printing press, and new universities helped spread the Renaissance beyond Italy into lands where its ideas changed. In the next chapter, you will read about religious ideas that swept through Europe at about the same time.

Section 3 Assessment

Reviewing Ideas, Terms, and People   HSS 7.8.4, 7.8.5

1. **a. Identify** What two inventions helped spread the Renaissance beyond Italy?
   b. Explain How did **Johann Gutenberg**'s machine work?
2. **a. Describe** What was **Desiderius Erasmus**'s position on church rituals?
   b. Contrast How did **Christian humanism** differ from the earlier form of humanism that developed in Italy?
   c. Elaborate What is the connection between humanism and painting people working in the fields?
3. **a. Compare** What is one thing that **Miguel de Cervantes** and **William Shakespeare** had in common with Dante?
   b. Elaborate Why have Shakespeare's works remained popular around the world for centuries?

Critical Thinking

4. **Summarizing** Copy the chart below to describe the works of Northern Renaissance artists. Add rows as needed.

Artist	Artist's Work

FOCUS ON WRITING

5. **Outlining a Plot** This section introduced you to a whole new set of places and people you could use for your movie. Will you use any of these places or people? Think back to the ideas you had after reading the last two sections, and start to plan the story for your movie. Where will it be set? Who will be in it? Draw up a short, rough outline that explains the movie's plot.

from Romeo and Juliet

by William Shakespeare

About the Reading *Shakespeare's plays spotlight an enormous range of human experiences—including love, loss, and everything in between. Even though* Romeo and Juliet *ends in disaster, its message is a hopeful one. Its main characters, two teenaged members of warring families, meet at a party and fall instantly in love. In this scene, which takes place later that evening, a troubled Romeo spies Juliet on her balcony.*

AS YOU READ Notice the words Romeo uses to describe Juliet's beauty.

Rom. But soft, what light through yonder window breaks?
It is the east, and Juliet is the sun. ❶
Arise, fair sun, and kill the envious moon,
Who is already sick and pale with grief
That thou, her maid, art far more fair than she . . .
Two of the fairest stars in all the heaven,
Having some business, do entreat her eyes
To twinkle in their spheres till they return.
What if her eyes were there, they in her head?
The brightness of her cheek would shame those stars,
As daylight doth a lamp; her eyes in heaven
Would through the airy region stream so bright
That birds would sing and think it were not night.
See how she leans her cheek upon her hand!
O that I were a glove upon that hand,
That I might touch that cheek!
Jul. Ay me!
Rom. She speaks!
O, speak again, bright angel, for thou art
As glorious to this night, being o'er my head,
As is a winged messenger of heaven
Unto the white-upturned wond'ring eyes
Of mortals that fall back to gaze on him,

GUIDED READING

WORD HELP

envious jealous
entreat beg

❶ Romeo compares Juliet to the sun and claims that even the moon will be jealous of her beauty.

To what else does he compare her in this speech?

ELA Reading 7.3.3 Analyze characterization as delineated through a character's thoughts, words, speech patterns, and actions; the narrator's description; and the thoughts, words, and actions of other characters.

When he bestrides the lazy puffing clouds,
And sails upon the bosom of the air.
Jul. O Romeo, Romeo, wherefore art thou Romeo? ❷
Deny thy father and refuse thy name;
Or, if thou wilt not, be but sworn my love,
And I'll no longer be a Capulet.
Rom. [Aside.] Shall I hear more, or shall I speak at this?
Jul. 'Tis but thy name that is my enemy;
Thou art thyself, though not a Montague.
What's Montague? It is nor hand nor foot,
Nor arm nor face, nor any other part
Belonging to a man. O, be some other name!
What's in a name? That which we call a rose
By any other word would smell as sweet;
So Romeo would, were he not Romeo call'd,
Retain that dear perfection which he owes
Without that title. Romeo, doff thy name,
And for thy name, which is no part of thee,
Take all myself. ❸
Rom. I take thee at thy word.
Call me but love, and I'll be new baptized;
Henceforth I never will be Romeo.
Jul. What man art thou that thus bescreen'd in night
So stumblest on my counsel?
Rom. By a name
I know not how to tell thee who I am.
My name, dear saint, is hateful to myself,
Because it is an enemy to thee;
Had I it written, I would tear the word.
Jul. My ears have not yet drunk a hundred words
Of thy tongue's uttering, yet I know the sound.
Art thou not Romeo, and a Montague?
Rom. Neither, fair maid, if either thee dislike.

GUIDED READING

WORD HELP

bestrides mounts
wherefore why
doff remove
counsel secret thoughts

❷ Juliet is not asking where Romeo is. She is asking why he is Romeo, her family's enemy.

❸ Juliet says that she could be with Romeo if he were from a different family.

What does she ask him to do?

A painting of Romeo and Juliet from the 1800s

CONNECTING LITERATURE TO HISTORY

1. **Evaluating** Renaissance humanists believed that people can achieve great goals if they are willing to work hard. How do the characters of Romeo and Juliet reflect this humanist idea?

2. **Analyzing** Medieval writings often focused on religious topics. But the Renaissance humanists believed that people could write about many different subjects without discussing religion. Based on this passage, what new topic did some humanist writers explore?

Social Studies Skills

Analysis | **Critical Thinking** | **Participation** | **Study**

Understanding Transportation Maps

Understand the Skill

Many of the maps used in the study of history are special-purpose maps. These maps are intended to illustrate specific relationships, developments, or events in history. Transportation maps are one type of special-purpose map. They show routes of travel and trade. These maps help you understand about the movement of people, products, and ideas between places in the world.

Learn the Skill

Follow these steps to interpret a transportation map.

❶ Read the map's title. This will tell you what general information is shown on the map. Study the legend. Look for any symbols that relate to routes or methods of transportation.

❷ Note any lines or arrows on the map. These lines and arrows often indicate routes of movement. Study these carefully. Note their starting and ending points and where they pass in between.

❸ Study the map as a whole. Read all the labels. Transportation maps can tell you a lot about the history of an area. For example, they can show how geography influenced the area's development.

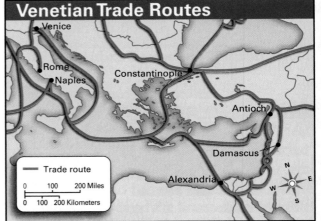

Practice and Apply the Skill

Interpret the map on this page and answer the following questions.

1. How did Constantinople's location make it a trade center?

2. With what cities did Constantinople trade? What means of transportation did these cities' traders use?

3. How would products coming across the Silk Road from Asia reach Venice? What means of transportation would be used?

4. How does this map suggest the cultural influences, exchanges, and connections that existed between Europe and Asia?

Visual Summary

Use the visual summary below to help you review the main ideas in this chapter.

QUICK FACTS

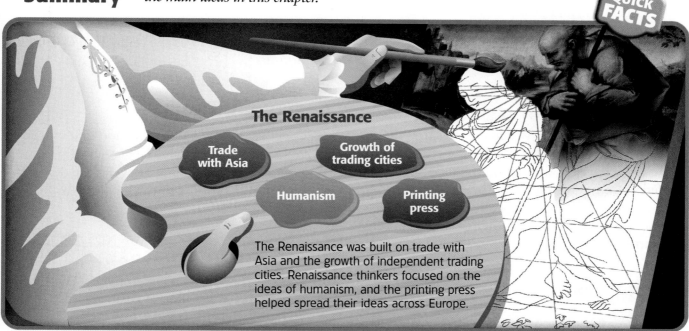

The Renaissance

Trade with Asia

Growth of trading cities

Humanism

Printing press

The Renaissance was built on trade with Asia and the growth of independent trading cities. Renaissance thinkers focused on the ideas of humanism, and the printing press helped spread their ideas across Europe.

Reviewing Key Terms and People

Match the "I" statement with the person or thing that might have made the statement.

a. Cosimo de' Medici
b. Leonardo da Vinci
c. Desiderius Erasmus
d. Miguel de Cervantes
e. humanism
f. Albrecht Dürer
g. Marco Polo
h. Niccolo Machiavelli
i. William Shakespeare
j. Michelangelo

1. "I wrote many comedies, tragedies, and histories in which I examined human emotions."
2. "I am a group of ideas about the value of people and their achievements."
3. "I traveled the Silk Road to China."
4. "I was a rich banker in Florence who paid for great works of art."
5. "I wrote a political book called *The Prince*."
6. "I became famous for printed pictures that I sold at markets and fairs."
7. "I painted the ceiling of the Sistine Chapel."
8. "I thought that the church should give up practices that don't help people."
9. "I wrote *Don Quixote*."
10. "I filled my notebooks with drawings of plants, animals, and machines."

Comprehension and Critical Thinking

SECTION 1 *(Pages 298–303)* **HSS** 7.8.2, 7.8.3

11. **a.** **Identify** Who was Marco Polo, and how did he affect trade?

b. **Compare** How were the four great trading cities of northern Italy similar?

c. **Evaluate** Did the Black Death help bring about the Renaissance? Why or why not?

SECTION 2 *(Pages 304–310)* **HSS** 7.8.1, 7.8.5

12. a. Describe What contributions did Dante Alighieri and Niccolo Machiavelli make to the Renaissance?

b. Compare What are some characteristics that Michelangelo and Leonardo da Vinci shared?

c. Elaborate A historian has said that the Renaissance "created something new from something old." What does this statement mean?

SECTION 3 *(Pages 312–317)* **HSS** 7.8.4, 7.8.5

13. a. Recall What were two main ways that the Renaissance spread beyond Italy?

b. Contrast How was Northern European art different from Italian art?

c. Evaluate William Shakespeare is often called the greatest writer in the English language. Why is this so?

Reading Skills

Using Greek and Latin Roots *Answer the following questions about the Greek and Latin roots of words from this chapter.*

14. Based on the definition of *perspective*, what do you think the Latin root *spec-* means? Hint: Think about other words that use this root, such as *spectator* and *spectacles*.

a. to feel	**c.** to hear
b. to see	**d.** to understand

15. The prefix *per-* in perspective means "through." Based on this meaning, what do you think the word *permeate* means?

a. to spread through	**c.** to disappear from
b. to dissolve in	**d.** to climb over

Social Studies Skills

Understanding Transportation Maps *Use the map in Section 1 of the Routes of Marco Polo to answer the following questions.*

16. What means of transportation would a trader use to get from Venice to Damascus?

17. How many miles was the route from Cochin to Hormuz?

Reviewing Themes

18. Geography How did the location of Italy's port cities help them develop trade networks?

19. Science and Technology How did the development of the printing press change daily life for many Europeans?

Using the Internet

go.hrw.com
KEYWORD: SQ7 WH11

20. Activity: Supporting a Point of View The Renaissance was a time of great advances in literature, the arts, science, and math. Enter the activity keyword and learn about the important people and events of the Renaissance. Then create a political cartoon about an event or person in the chapter. Pick the point of view of a supporter or critic and use your cartoon to explain how they would have viewed your topic.

FOCUS ON WRITING

21. Writing Your Letter to a Movie Studio Now that you have outlined the plot for your movie, write a letter to the head of a studio to convince him or her to film your movie. In two paragraphs, briefly describe the plot of your movie and include details about the characters and setting. In your last paragraph, explain why you think people will be interested in a movie about the Renaissance. Remember that your audience is a busy executive. You'll need to use descriptive language to keep the studio head interested.

Standards Assessment

DIRECTIONS: Read each question, and write the letter of the best response.

1

> I realize that women have accomplished many good things and that even if evil women have done evil, . . . the benefits accrued [gained] . . . because of good women—particularly the wise and literary ones. . . outweigh the evil. Therefore, I am amazed by the opinion of some men who claim they do not want their daughters, wives, or kinswomen [female relatives] to be educated because their mores [morals] will be ruined as a result.
>
> —Christine de Pizan, from *The Book of the City of Ladies,* 1405

The content of this passage suggests that the person who wrote it was

A a rich Italian merchant.

B Niccolo Machiavelli.

C a supporter of humanism.

D Marco Polo.

2 **Which person's contribution was *most* important in spreading the ideas of the Renaissance beyond Italy?**

A Cosimo de' Medici

B Johann Gutenberg

C Leonardo da Vinci

D Dante Alighieri

3 **In general, the artists and architects of the Renaissance were financially supported by**

A rich families and church leaders.

B large European universities.

C the most powerful nations in Europe.

D the printing industry.

4 **All of the following helped lead to the Italian Renaissance directly or indirectly *except***

A the Black Death.

B the renewal of trade along the Silk Road.

C the Medici family of Florence.

D the unification of Italy.

5 **Which influence was *most* important in inspiring the Renaissance?**

A ancient Greek and Roman culture

B early Christianity

C ancient Judaism

D early Chinese civilization

Connecting with Past Learnings

6 **Italy in the Renaissance was not a unified country but several small independent states. Which culture that you studied in Grade 6 had a similar structure?**

A ancient Greece during the Golden Age

B the Fertile Crescent during the Stone Age

C the New Kingdom of ancient Egypt

D Rome during the Pax Romana

7 **William Shakespeare was a great writer of plays. His contributions to world history and culture are similar to those of which person?**

A Asoka in India

B Confucius in China

C Sophocles in Greece

D Cicero in Rome

The Reformation of Christianity

California Standards

History–Social Science

7.9 Students analyze the historical developments of the Reformation.

English–Language Arts

Writing 7.1.2b Develop the topic with supporting details and precise verbs, nouns, and adjectives to paint a visual image in the mind of the reader.

Reading 7.2.6 Assess the adequacy, accuracy, and appropriateness of the author's evidence to support claims and assertions.

FOCUS ON WRITING

A Book Jacket You work at a publishing company, and you've been asked to design a book jacket for a book about the Reformation. As you read this chapter, consider which main ideas and important details you should include in the description on the back page, which image you might pick for the front, and what you should call the book.

CHAPTER EVENTS

1492 The Spanish Inquisition begins.

1500

WORLD EVENTS

1501 The Safavid Empire begins in Persia.

HOLT
History's Impact
▶ video series
Watch the video to understand the impact of the Renaissance and Reformation.

What You Will Learn...

In this chapter you will learn about the Reformation of Christianity in Europe. The Reformation began in the town of Wittenberg, Germany. In this photo, churchgoers there celebrate Reformation Day services.

1517
Martin Luther criticizes the Catholic Church in his Ninety-Five Theses.

1572
Thousands of French Protestants die in the Saint Bartholomew's Day massacre.

1648
The Thirty Years' War ends the Holy Roman Empire.

1550   1600   1650

1537
Spanish conquistadors conquer the Inca Empire.

1579
Francis Drake stops in California on his way around the world.

1603
The Tokugawa shoguns begin ruling Japan.

1609
Galileo uses a telescope to study planets.

Reading Social Studies

by Kylene Beers

Focus on Themes Look at the title of this chapter. Do you see the word *reformation*? That word comes the word *reform*, which means to reshape or to put into a new form. That is what you will read about in this chapter: how and why the Christian **religion** was reshaped and put into new forms. As you read, you will meet the leaders of that reformation and will see how the reformation affected different **societies and cultures** throughout the world.

Online Research

Focus on Reading Researching history topics on the World Wide Web can lead to valuable information. However, just because information is on the Web doesn't mean it is valuable!

Evaluating Web Sites As you conduct research on the Web, remember to evaluate the Web sites you use. The checklist below can help you determine if the site is worth your time.

Additional reading support can be found in the

Inter**active**

Reader and Study Guide

Evaluating Web-Based Resources

Name of site: _____ URL: _____ Date of access: _____

Rate each item below on a scale of 1 to 3	1 = No	2 = Some	3 = Yes
I. Authority			
a. Authors are clearly identified by name.	1	2	3
b. Contact information is provided for authors.	1	2	3
c. Authors' qualifications are clearly stated.	1	2	3
d. Information on when site was last updated is easy to find.	1	2	3
e. Copyrighted material is clearly labeled as such.			
II. Content			
a. Title on home page explains what site is about.	1	2	3
b. Information is useful to your project.	1	2	3
c. Information at site could be verified through additional research.	1	2	3
d. Graphics are helpful, not just decorative.	1	2	3
III. Design and Technical Elements			
a. Pages are readable and are easy to navigate.	1	2	3
b. Links work and lead to more useful information.	1	2	3
IV. Overall, this site will be useful in my research.	**1**	**2**	**3**

ELA Reading 7.2.6 Assess the adequacy, accuracy, and appropriateness of the author's evidence to support claims and assertions, noting instances of bias and steretyping.

You Try It!

Imagine that the text below is the home page for a Web site about Martin Luther, one of the figures you will learn about in this chapter. Examine the text and then answer the questions below.

Dr. Smith's Martin Luther Page
by Professor John Smith, Ph. D.

"Here I stand; I can do no other. God help me!"
–Martin Luther

Welcome to my web site about Martin Luther, one of the most important individuals in the entire history of Christianity. I've been teaching about Luther for nearly 30 years, and in that time I've learned a great deal about the man that I wanted to share with people.

For a biography of Martin Luther, click here.

For information about his teachings, click here.

To read Luther's writings in Latin, German, **or** English, **click the appropriate link.**

For photos of important sites in his life, click here.

For links to other professors' sites and to the American Lutheran church, click here.

Page last updated: October 31, 2004

After you read the passage, answer the following questions.

1. Who is the author of the site? Does the author seem qualified to write a Web page about Martin Luther?

2. What information about Luther is contained on the site? Do you think that information could be useful? Why or why not?

3. To what other sites does this page link? What might this tell you about the site?

4. What other information is included on the page?

5. Overall, do you think this site could be useful for history students?

Key Terms and People

Chapter 12

Section 1
Reformation (p. 328)
indulgence (p. 329)
purgatory (p. 329)
Martin Luther (p. 330)
Protestants (p. 331)
John Calvin (p. 332)
King Henry VIII (p. 333)

Section 2
Catholic Reformation (p. 334)
Ignatius of Loyola (p. 336)
Jesuits (p. 336)
Francis Xavier (p. 338)

Section 3
Huguenots (p. 342)
Edict of Nantes (p. 343)
Thirty Years' War (p. 344)
congregation (p. 345)
federalism (p. 345)

Academic Vocabulary

Success in school is related to knowing academic vocabulary—the words that are frequently used in school assignments and discussions. In this chapter, you will learn the following academic words:

method (p. 329)
agreement (p. 344)

As you read Chapter 12, think about topics that might be interesting to research further online. How could you judge the quality of the sites you found if you did more research?

The Protestant Reformation

What You Will Learn...

Main Ideas

1. The Catholic Church faced challengers who were upset with the behavior of Catholic clergy and with church practices.
2. Martin Luther urged reform in the Catholic Church, but he eventually broke away from the church.
3. Other reformers built on the ideas of early reformers to create their own churches.

The Big Idea

Unsatisfied with the Roman Catholic Church, religious reformers broke away to form their own churches.

Key Terms and People

Reformation, *p. 328*
indulgence, *p. 329*
purgatory, *p. 329*
Martin Luther, *p. 330*
Protestants, *p. 331*
John Calvin, *p. 332*
King Henry VIII, *p. 333*

HSS **7.9.1** List the causes for the internal turmoil in and weakening of the Catholic church (e.g., tax policies, selling of indulgences).

7.9.2 Describe the theological, political, and economic ideas of the major figures during the Reformation (e.g., Desiderius Erasmus, Martin Luther, John Calvin, William Tyndale).

If YOU were there...

You live in a town in Germany in the 1500s. The Catholic Church has a lot of influence there. Often, church officials clash with local nobles over political issues. The church also makes the nobles pay taxes. Lately, a local priest has been criticizing the way many church leaders act. He wants to make changes.

How do you think the nobles will respond to him?

BUILDING BACKGROUND By the early 1500s Renaissance ideas had caused many Europeans to view their lives with a more critical eye. They thought their lives could be changed for the better. One area that some people thought needed improvement was religion.

The Catholic Church Faces Challengers

By the late Renaissance some people had begun to complain about problems in the Catholic Church. They called on church leaders to erase corruption and to focus on religion. Eventually, their calls led to a reform movement of Western Christianity called the **Reformation** (re-fuhr-MAY-shuhn).

Unpopular Church Practices

The reformers who wanted to change and improve the church had many complaints. Their complaints criticized the behavior of priests, bishops, and popes, as well as church practices.

Some reformers thought priests and bishops weren't very religious anymore. They claimed that many priests didn't even know basic church teachings. Others felt that the pope was too involved in politics, neglecting his religious duties. These people found it difficult to see the pope as their spiritual leader.

Other reformers had no problems with the clergy, but they thought the church had grown too rich. During the Middle Ages the Roman Catholic Church had become one of the richest

ART
German Woodcuts

Many German reformers used woodcut illustrations to spread their ideas among people who couldn't read. Woodcuts were cheap and easy to print, which made them an easy way to spread ideas visually. The two woodcuts on this page attacked the pope by comparing him unfavorably to Jesus.

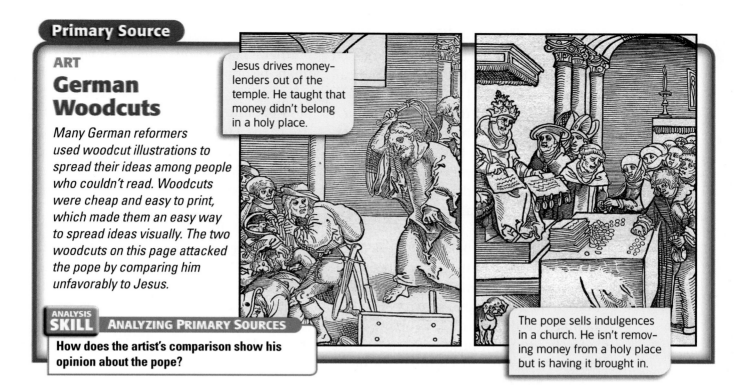

Jesus drives money-lenders out of the temple. He taught that money didn't belong in a holy place.

The pope sells indulgences in a church. He isn't removing money from a holy place but is having it brought in.

ANALYSIS SKILL **ANALYZING PRIMARY SOURCES**

How does the artist's comparison show his opinion about the pope?

---

institutions in Europe. The church used a number of **methods** to raise money, and it had been able to stay rich because it didn't have to pay any taxes.

For many people the worst problems were the methods the church used to raise money. One common method the church used to raise money was the sale of **indulgences**, a relaxation of penalties for sins people had committed.

According to the church some indulgences reduced the punishment that a person would receive for sins in purgatory. In Catholic teachings, **purgatory** was a place where souls went before they went to heaven. In purgatory the souls were punished for the sins that they had committed in life. Once they had paid for these sins, the souls went to heaven. The idea that people could reduce the time that their souls would spend in purgatory by paying for indulgences enraged many Christians. They thought the church was letting people buy their way into heaven.

The Call for Reform

The unpopular practices of the church weakened its influence in many people's lives. By the early 1500s scholars in northern Europe were calling for reforms.

One of the first people to seek reforms in the church was the Dutch priest and writer Desiderius Erasmus. Erasmus thought that the church's problems were caused by lazy clergy. He complained that church officials ignored their duties to lead easy lives:

" Whatever work may be called for . . . is passed along . . . [but] if there's any splendor or pleasure being given out, that our church leaders are willing to take on. And . . . no class of men live more comfortably or with less trouble. "
–Desiderius Erasmus, from *The Praise of Folly*

Erasmus wanted to reform the church from within. His ideas, though, inspired later reformers who chose to break from the church completely.

READING CHECK **Analyzing** What were some complaints that people had with the church?

ACADEMIC VOCABULARY
method a way of doing something

Martin Luther Urges Reform

On October 31, 1517, a priest named **Martin Luther** added his voice to the call for reform. He nailed a list of complaints about the church to the door of a church in Wittenberg (VIT-uhn-berk) in the German state of Saxony. Luther's list is called the Ninety-Five Theses (THEE-seez). Thanks to the newly invented printing press, copies of Luther's complaints spread to neighboring German states.

The Ninety-Five Theses criticized the church and many of its practices, especially the sale of indulgences. The Theses also outlined many of Luther's own beliefs. For example, he didn't think people needed to do charity work or give money to the church. According to Luther, as long as people believed in God and lived by the Bible, their souls would be saved.

A Break from the Church

Luther's complaints angered many German bishops. They sent a copy of the Ninety-Five Theses to Pope Leo X, who also became outraged by Luther's actions. He called Luther a heretic and excommunicated him. In addition, Germany's ruler, the Holy Roman Emperor, ordered Luther to appear before a diet, or council of nobles and church officials, in the German city of Worms (VOHRMS).

Although many of the nobles who attended the council supported Luther, the emperor did not. He declared Luther an outlaw and ordered him to leave the empire. But one noble secretly supported Luther. He got Luther out of Worms and to a castle where he helped Luther hide from the emperor. Luther remained in hiding for more than a year.

Martin Luther's Message

When Martin Luther nailed his Ninety-Five Theses to a church door in Wittenberg, Germany, the Reformation began. Soon, others unhappy with church practices also began to criticize the church.

BIOGRAPHY

Martin Luther
1483–1546

Martin Luther is credited with starting the Reformation, but he never wanted to leave the Catholic Church. He just wanted to correct what he saw as the church's mistakes. After he was excommunicated, Luther began to depart more and more from church teachings. For example, although the Roman Catholic Church didn't let priests get married, Luther married a former nun in 1525. Still, as an old man Luther regretted that his actions had caused a split in the church.

Luther's ideas eventually led to a split in the Roman Catholic Church. Those who sided with Luther and protested against the church became known as **Protestants** (PRAH-tuhs-tuhnts). Those Protestants who also followed Luther's teachings were known as Lutherans.

Luther's Teachings

Luther thought anyone could have a direct relationship with God. They didn't need priests to talk to God for them. This idea is called the priesthood of all believers.

The priesthood of all believers challenged the traditional structure of the church. To Luther, this was a benefit. People's beliefs shouldn't be based on traditions, he argued, but on the Bible. He thought that people should live as the Bible, not priests or the pope, said.

To help people understand how God wanted them to live, Luther translated the Bible's New Testament into German, his native language. For the first time many Europeans who didn't know Greek or Latin could read the Bible for themselves. In addition to translating the Bible, Luther wrote pamphlets, essays, and songs about his ideas, many of them in German.

Many German nobles liked Luther's ideas. They particularly supported Luther's position that the clergy should not interfere with politics. Because these nobles allowed the people who lived on their lands to become Lutheran, the Lutheran Church soon became the dominant church in most of northern Germany.

THE IMPACT TODAY

Many of the songs Luther wrote are still sung in Protestant churches around the world.

READING CHECK **Summarizing** What were Martin Luther's main religious teachings?

Primary Source

HISTORIC DOCUMENT
Luther's Ninety-Five Theses

In Wittenberg, nailing documents to the church door was a common way of sharing ideas with the community. The Ninety-Five Theses Martin Luther posted, however, created far more debate than other such documents. The items listed here, selected from Luther's list, argued against the sale of indulgences.

Luther thought that only God—not the Pope—could grant forgiveness.

Luther thought buying indulgences was useless.

(5) The pope will not, and cannot, remit [forgive] other punishments than those which he has imposed by his own decree [ruling] or according to the canons [laws].

(21) Therefore, those preachers of indulgences err [make a mistake] who say that, by the Pope's indulgence, a man may be exempt from all punishments, and be saved.

(30) Nobody is sure of having repented [been sorry] sincerely enough; much less can he be sure of having received perfect remission of sins.

(43) Christians should be taught that he who gives to the poor, or lends to a needy man, does better than buying indulgences.

(52) It is a vain and false thing to hope to be saved through indulgences, though the commissary [seller]—nay, the pope himself—was to pledge his own soul therefore.

—Martin Luther, from the *Ninety-Five Theses*

ANALYSIS SKILL **ANALYZING PRIMARY SOURCES**

Why did Martin Luther argue against the sale of indulgences?

Modern Reformers

During the Reformation the ideas and actions of single individuals had sweeping effects on European society. Since that time many other individuals have risen up and called for social changes.

In the 1960s a man named Cesar Chavez organized a strike of farm workers in California, refusing to return to work until the workers received fair treatment. At about the same time, Dr. Martin Luther King Jr. worked to gain equal rights for African Americans. Even today individuals are working to fight injustice and corruption around the world. For example, a woman named Aung San Suu Kyi is fighting to bring democracy to her country, Burma.

ANALYSIS SKILL **ANALYZING INFORMATION**

How have people like Cesar Chavez, Martin Luther King Jr., and Aung San Suu Kyi continued the traditions of protest and reform?

Other Reformers

FOCUS ON READING

What kind of a Web site would you go to if you wanted to learn more about reformers?

Even before Luther died in 1546, other reformers across Europe had begun to follow his example. Some of them also broke away from the Catholic Church to form churches of their own.

William Tyndale

Another important reformer was William Tyndale (TIN-duhl), an English professor. Like Luther he thought that everyone should be able to read and interpret the Bible. This belief went against the teachings of the Catholic Church, in which only clergy could interpret the Bible.

Tyndale decided to translate the Bible into English. This upset the English clergy, who tried to arrest him. Tyndale fled the country and continued his translation. He sent copies of his Bible back to England. Tyndale's work angered Catholic authorities, who had him executed.

John Calvin

A more influential reformer than Tyndale was **John Calvin**. One of Calvin's main teachings was predestination, the idea that God knew who would be saved even before they were born. Nothing people did during their lives would change God's plan. However, Calvin also taught that it was important to live a good life and obey God's laws.

In 1541 the people of Geneva, Switzerland, made Calvin their religious and political leader. He and his followers, called Calvinists, passed laws to make people live according to Calvin's teachings. Since Calvin's followers believed that people were generally sinful, they banned many forms of entertainment, such as playing cards and dancing. They thought these activities distracted people from religion. Calvin hoped to make Geneva an example of a good Christian city for the rest of the world.

Henry VIII

In England the major figure of the Reformation was **King Henry VIII.** Because he had no sons and his wife couldn't have any more children, Henry asked the pope to officially end his marriage. Henry wanted to get married again so that he could have a son to whom he could leave his throne.

The pope refused Henry's request. Furious and hurt, Henry decided that he didn't want to obey the pope anymore. In 1534 he declared himself the head of a new church, called the Church of England, or Anglican Church.

Unlike Luther and Calvin, Henry made his break from the Catholic Church for personal reasons rather than religious ones. As a result, he didn't change many church practices. Many rituals and beliefs of the Church of England stayed very much like those of the Catholic Church. Henry's break from the church, however, opened the door for other Protestant beliefs to take hold in England.

READING CHECK **Comparing** How were Tyndale's and Calvin's ideas similar to Luther's?

BIOGRAPHY

John Calvin
1509–1564

Calvin was probably the most influential figure of the Reformation after Luther. Through his writings and preaching, Calvin spread basic Reformation ideas such as the right of the common people to make church policy. Unlike many other religious leaders, Calvin didn't think that the pursuit of profits would keep businesspeople from being saved. This idea would eventually help lead to the growth of capitalism.

Making Inferences Why might Calvin's ideas have been popular with businesspeople?

SUMMARY AND PREVIEW The religious landscape of Europe changed dramatically in the 1500s. The Catholic Church now had many rivals. In Section 2 you will learn how Catholic leaders made some changes in their religion to keep their influence in Europe.

Section 1 Assessment

go.hrw.com
Online Quiz
KEYWORD: SQ7 HP12

Reviewing Ideas, Terms, and People **HSS** 7.9.1, 7.9.2

1. **Recall** What were three complaints people had about the Roman Catholic Church in the early 1500s?

2. **a. Identify** What was **Martin Luther**'s list of complaints about the Roman Catholic Church called?
   b. Contrast How did Luther's ideas about interpreting the Bible differ from Catholics' ideas?

3. **a. Describe** What did **King Henry VIII** do that makes him a Reformation figure?
   b. Summarize How did **John Calvin**'s ideas affect life in Geneva?
   c. Predict How might William Tyndale's life have been different if he had lived after Henry VIII broke away from the Catholic Church?

Critical Thinking

4. **Comparing and Contrasting** Draw a Venn diagram like the one here. Use it to compare and contrast Luther's and Calvin's ideas about reforming the church.

   Luther   Both   Calvin

FOCUS ON WRITING

5. **Finding Key Details** The main idea of this section might be stated, "Unpopular Catholic Church practices led some reformers to start their own churches." Write this main idea in your notebook. What key details in this section support this idea? Write them in your notebook as well.

The Catholic Reformation

Main Ideas

1. The influence of the church created a Catholic culture in Spain.
2. Catholic reforms emerged in response to the Reformation.
3. Missionaries worked to spread Catholic teachings.

The Big Idea

Catholic leaders worked to reform the Catholic Church and spread Catholic teachings.

Key Terms and People

Catholic Reformation, *p. 334*
Ignatius of Loyola, *p. 336*
Jesuits, *p. 336*
Francis Xavier, *p. 338*

HSS **7.9.5** Analyze how the Counter-Reformation revitalized the Catholic church and the forces that fostered the movement (e.g., St. Ignatius of Loyola and the Jesuits, the Council of Trent).

7.9.6 Understand the institution and impact of missionaries on Christianity and the diffusion of Christianity from Europe to other parts of the world in the medieval and early modern periods; locate missions on a world map.

7.9.7 Describe the Golden Age of cooperation between Jews and Muslims in medieval Spain that promoted creativity in art, literature, and science, including how that cooperation was terminated by the religious persecution of individuals and groups (e.g., the Spanish Inquisition and the expulsion of Jews and Muslims from Spain in 1492).

If YOU were there...

You live in a small port city in Portugal in the 1500s. Your parents are fishers, but you have always dreamed of seeing more of the world. One day you learn that several missionaries are planning to set sail for India and Japan. Every sailor knows that the voyage will be long and dangerous. The people in those countries may welcome the missionaries—or attack them. As a result, the ship's captain is paying well for new crew members.

Will you join the crew of the missionaries' ship?

BUILDING BACKGROUND As Protestant ideas swept through northern Europe, Catholic leaders realized that people were unhappy with the clergy and with church policies. They looked for ways to restore people's faith in the church.

Catholic Culture in Spain

The effort to reform the Catholic Church from within is called the **Catholic Reformation,** or the Counter-Reformation. Through the late 1500s and 1600s Catholic Reformation leaders worked to strengthen the Catholic Church and to stop the spread of Protestantism in Europe.

Many of the leaders of the Catholic Reformation came from southern Europe, especially from Spain. Spain's rulers, nobles, and clergy were used to defending the Catholic Church. They had been fighting to make Catholicism the only religion in their kingdoms for hundreds of years.

The Growth of Roman Catholic Spain

For centuries the region we now call Spain had been home to three religions. In many areas Christians, Muslims, and Jews all lived and worked together. Because they cooperated and didn't fight against each other, people of all three religions prospered.

They made some important advancements in art, literature, philosophy, mathematics, and science; this was referred to as the Golden Age.

Eventually, the Roman Catholic rulers decided to force the Muslims and Jews out of Spain. For hundreds of years religious wars tore up the Spanish countryside. Finally, in 1492 the king and queen of Spain defeated the last of the Spanish Muslims. They ordered all Muslims and Jews to convert to Catholicism or leave their kingdom.

The Spanish Inquisition

To enforce their decision, the Spanish monarchs ordered the Spanish Inquisition to find and punish any Muslims or Jews left in Spain. The Inquisition was ruthless in carrying out this duty. Its members hunted down and punished converted Muslims and Jews who were suspected of keeping their old beliefs.

After a time the Inquisition began to turn its attention to Christians as well as to Muslims and Jews. Catholic officials wanted to be sure that everyone in Spain belonged to the Catholic Church. They ordered the Inquisition to seek out Christians, such as Protestants, whose ideas differed from the church's.

Once the Inquisition had punished all Muslims, Jews, and Protestants, the Catholic Church in Spain had no opposition. By the late 1400s and 1500s the Spanish church was very strong. As a result, the ideas of the Reformation did not become as popular in Spain as they did elsewhere. In fact, the Spanish clergy were among the first to fight back against the Protestant Reformation.

READING CHECK **Summarizing** How did the Roman Catholic Church in Spain gain power?

The Surrender of Granada
In 1492 the last Muslim stronghold in Spain, Granada, fell. This painting from the 1800s shows Granada's Muslim ruler surrendering to Spain's Catholic leaders.

Many Catholic leaders responded to Protestant criticisms by working to reform the Catholic Church. Church leaders founded new religious orders and tried to clarify official church teachings.

1534
Ignatius founded the Society of Jesus, or the Jesuits. His goal was to teach young men about Catholic ideas in the hope that they would reject Protestant ones.

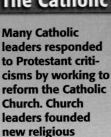

BIOGRAPHY

Saint Ignatius of Loyola
1491–1556

Ignatius of Loyola came from a noble Spanish family. As a young man he became a knight. In 1521 he was wounded in battle and spent several months in bed. During that time he became very religious. When he founded the Jesuits, Ignatius used his military experience. He took the title of general and insisted that his followers were well trained, like soldiers. He thought this would make them better able to fight against the spread of Protestantism.

Catholic Reforms

By the mid-1500s Catholic leaders in Europe were responding to the criticisms of Protestants. They responded in many ways. Some reformers created new religious orders. Others tried to change church policy. Still others tried to stop the spread of Protestant teachings in Catholic areas.

THE IMPACT TODAY

The Jesuit Order runs Catholic schools and universities all around the world.

New Religious Orders

Catholic reformers created many new religious orders in southern Europe in the 1500s. These orders had different rules and customs. But they all shared one important goal—they wanted to win back support for the Catholic Church from people who had turned away.

The first new order was founded in 1534 by a Spanish noble, **Ignatius** (ig-NAY-shuhs) **of Loyola**. This new order was the Society of Jesus, or the Jesuits. The **Jesuits** were a religious order created to serve the pope and the church. Ignatius had been a soldier, and the organization of the Jesuits reflects this background. Jesuits tried to be as disciplined as soldiers in their religious duties. As the Jesuits' leader, Ignatius took the title of general, and he referred to the Jesuits as soldiers.

One of the Jesuits' goals was to teach people about Catholic ideas. They hoped that a strong Catholic education would turn people against Protestant ideas.

Another order was created in 1535 in Italy by Angela Merici (may-REE-chee). Called the Ursuline Order, it was created to teach girls rather than boys. Like the Jesuits, the Ursulines thought Catholic education was the key to strengthening the Catholic Church and limiting the impact of Protestant teachings.

1535
Angela Merici founded the Ursuline Order. Her goal was to teach young women about official Catholic teachings and to give aid and help to people in need.

1545
The Council of Trent met between 1545 and 1563 to clarify church teachings that had been criticized by Protestants. The council played a key role in revitalizing the Catholic Church in Europe.

Results of the Council of Trent QUICK FACTS

- The selling of indulgences is banned.

- Bishops must live in the areas they oversee.

- The ideas of Luther, Calvin, and other Reformation leaders are rejected.

The Council of Trent

The new religious orders were one response to reform, but many Catholic leaders felt that more change was needed. They decided to call together a council of church leaders. Held in Trent, Italy, this council was called the Council of Trent. At this meeting, clergy from across Europe came together to discuss, debate, and eventually reform Catholic teachings.

The Council of Trent actually met three times between 1545 and 1563. The decisions made in these meetings led to major reforms in the Roman Catholic Church. The council restated the importance of the clergy in interpreting the Bible, but it created new rules that clergy had to follow. For example, the council ordered bishops to actually live in the areas they oversaw. Before this decision some bishops had lived far from the churches they ran.

The Council of Trent endorsed Catholic teaching and instituted reform of Catholic practice. From this point on, there was a clear distinction between Catholic and Protestant beliefs and practices.

The Fight against Protestants

Some Catholic Reformation leaders wanted to be more direct in their fight against Protestants. They thought Protestants were heretics who should be punished.

To lead the fight against Protestants, the pope created religious courts to punish any Protestants found in Italy. He also issued a list of books considered dangerous for people to read, including many by Protestant leaders. People reading books on this list could be excommunicated.

READING CHECK **Finding Main Ideas** What were the goals of Catholic Reformation leaders?

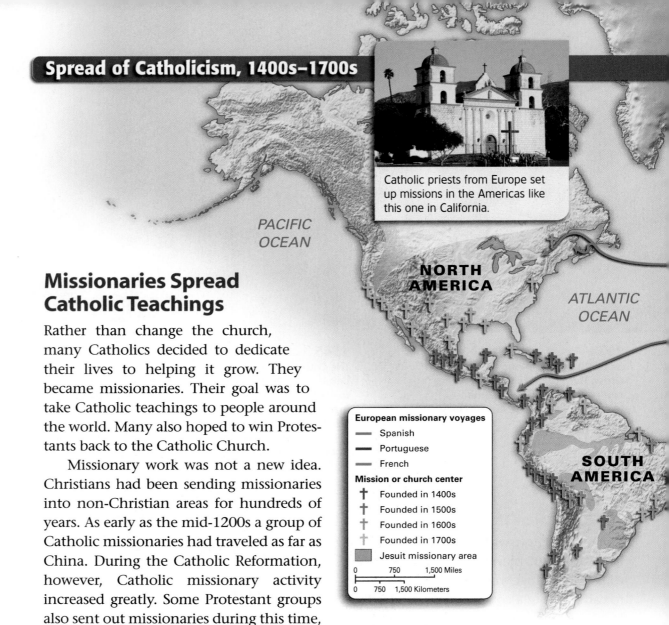

Spread of Catholicism, 1400s–1700s

Catholic priests from Europe set up missions in the Americas like this one in California.

PACIFIC OCEAN

NORTH AMERICA

ATLANTIC OCEAN

SOUTH AMERICA

European missionary voyages
— Spanish
— Portuguese
— French

Mission or church center
† Founded in 1400s
† Founded in 1500s
† Founded in 1600s
† Founded in 1700s
▨ Jesuit missionary area

0   750   1,500 Miles
0   750   1,500 Kilometers

Missionaries Spread Catholic Teachings

Rather than change the church, many Catholics decided to dedicate their lives to helping it grow. They became missionaries. Their goal was to take Catholic teachings to people around the world. Many also hoped to win Protestants back to the Catholic Church.

Missionary work was not a new idea. Christians had been sending missionaries into non-Christian areas for hundreds of years. As early as the mid-1200s a group of Catholic missionaries had traveled as far as China. During the Catholic Reformation, however, Catholic missionary activity increased greatly. Some Protestant groups also sent out missionaries during this time, but they were generally outnumbered by Catholic missionaries.

Many of the new Catholic missionaries were Jesuits. Jesuit priests went to Africa and Asia to teach people about the Catholic Church. In addition, some Jesuits traveled with explorers to America to convert the native peoples there.

Probably the most important missionary of the period was the Jesuit priest **Francis Xavier** (ZAYV-yuhr). He traveled throughout Asia in the mid-1500s, bringing Catholicism to parts of India and Japan. As a result of his efforts, some people in those regions became Catholics.

Around the world Catholic missionaries baptized millions of people. Through their efforts the effects of the Catholic Reformation reached far beyond Europe.

READING CHECK **Finding Main Ideas** What were the goals of Catholic missionaries?

SUMMARY AND PREVIEW Catholic leaders responded to the Reformation in Europe. In the next section you will see what happened when Catholics and Protestants began to interact.

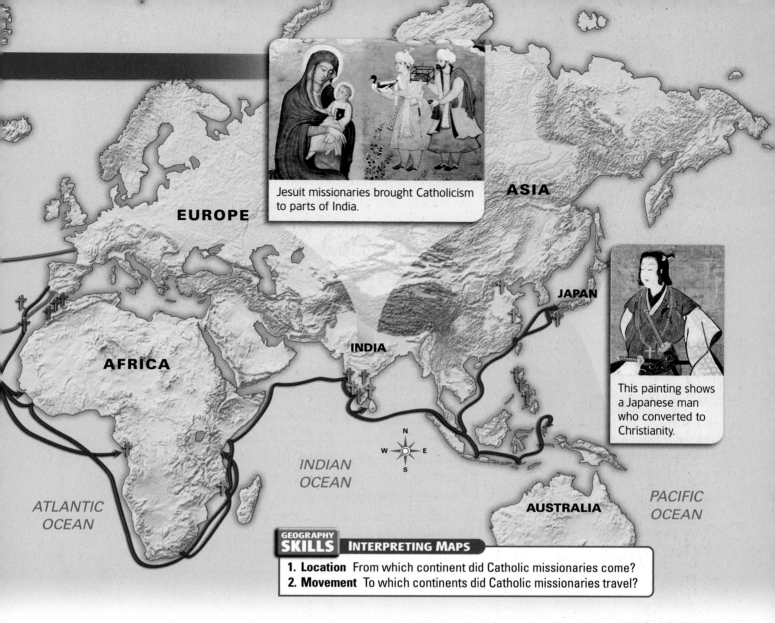

Jesuit missionaries brought Catholicism to parts of India.

EUROPE

ASIA

JAPAN

This painting shows a Japanese man who converted to Christianity.

INDIA

AFRICA

INDIAN OCEAN

ATLANTIC OCEAN

AUSTRALIA

PACIFIC OCEAN

GEOGRAPHY SKILLS **INTERPRETING MAPS**

1. **Location** From which continent did Catholic missionaries come?
2. **Movement** To which continents did Catholic missionaries travel?

Section 2 Assessment

go.hrw.com
Online Quiz
KEYWORD: SQ7 HP12

Reviewing Ideas, Terms, and People HSS 7.9.5, 7.9.6, 7.9.7

1. **a. Define** What was the **Catholic Reformation**?
   b. Explain Why was the Catholic Church stronger in Spain than in many other parts of Europe?

2. **a. Identify** What religious order did **Ignatius of Loyola** create?
   b. Summarize How did the Catholic Church try to fight the spread of Protestant ideas?
   c. Evaluate Which do you think was a better way to reform the Catholic Church, new religious orders or the Council of Trent? Why?

3. **Recall** Where did Catholic missionaries travel?

Critical Thinking

4. **Identifying Cause and Effect** Draw a graphic organizer like the one below. In the first box, write the main cause of the Catholic Reformation. In the third box, list three effects of church reform.

| Cause | | Catholic Reformation | | Effects |

FOCUS ON WRITING

5. **Finding the Main Idea** You already wrote a list of important details to support a main idea. Now find the main idea of this section. Write a sentence that states the main idea. Then write the details that support it.

THE REFORMATION OF CHRISTIANITY **339**

Effects of the Reformation

What You Will Learn...

Main Ideas

1. Religious division occurred within Europe and the Americas.
2. Religious wars broke out between Protestants and Catholics.
3. Social changes were a result of the Reformation.

The Big Idea

The Reformation changed religion in Europe and led to political and cultural conflicts.

Key Terms

Huguenots, *p. 342*
Edict of Nantes, *p. 343*
Thirty Years' War, *p. 344*
congregation, *p. 345*
federalism, *p. 345*

HSS 7.9.3 Explain Protestants' new practices of church self-government and the influence of those practices on the development of democratic practices and ideas of federalism.

7.9.4 Identify and locate the European regions that remained Catholic and those that became Protestant and explain how the division affected the distribution of religions in the New World.

If YOU were there...

You live in central Europe in the 1600s. As far back as you can remember, the countryside has been at war over religion. There have been riots and bloodshed. People have even been killed in the streets of your town. Now your parents have had enough of fighting. They have decided to move the whole family to one of the American colonies, far across the ocean.

How do you feel about moving to America?

BUILDING BACKGROUND The Protestant and Catholic reformations led to religious changes in Europe. These religious changes had other consequences as well. In some places violence broke out. In other places people shifted their attitudes about life and the world. Such changes drove some people to leave their homes for new lands, like those in America.

Religious Division

At the beginning of the 1500s nearly all of Europe was Catholic. As you can see on the map, however, that situation had changed dramatically 100 years later. By 1600, nearly all of southern Europe was still Catholic. But the majority of people in northern Europe had become Protestant.

Division within Europe

In many European countries, like Spain, nearly everyone shared the same religion. In Spain most people were Catholic. In northern countries such as England, Scotland, Norway, and Sweden, most people were Protestant. In the Holy Roman Empire each prince chose the religion for his territory. As a result, the empire became a patchwork of small kingdoms, some Catholic and some Protestant. Keeping peace between kingdoms with different religions was often a difficult task.

Division in the Americas

When explorers and missionaries set out from Europe for other parts of the world, they took their religions with them. In this way, the distribution of religions in Europe shaped religious patterns around the world. For example, some parts of the Americas were settled by people from Catholic countries such as Spain, France, and Portugal. These areas, including parts of Canada and most of Mexico, Central America, and South America, became Catholic. In contrast, places settled by Protestants from England and other countries—including the 13 colonies that became the United States—became mostly Protestant.

READING CHECK **Finding Main Ideas**
Which areas of Europe stayed Catholic after the Reformation?

Religions in Europe, 1600

ICELAND

SWEDEN

NORWAY

SCOTLAND

IRELAND

North Sea

DENMARK

Baltic Sea

RUSSIA

ENGLAND

London

ATLANTIC OCEAN

Wittenberg

POLAND

FRANCE

Paris

Geneva

HUNGARY

PORTUGAL

Madrid

SPAIN

PAPAL STATES

Rome

OTTOMAN

Black Sea

EMPIRE

Mediterranean Sea

OTTOMAN EMPIRE

Protestant	Eastern Orthodox
Roman Catholic	Muslim
Roman Catholic with Protestant minorities	Boundary of the Holy Roman Empire

0   250   500 Miles
0   250   500 Kilometers

GEOGRAPHY SKILLS **INTERPRETING MAPS**

1. **Region** In which part of Europe were most people Protestant?
2. **Place** How were Catholic and Protestant areas arranged in the Holy Roman Empire?

Religious Wars

Disagreements about religion and violence often went hand in hand. During the Reformation, this violence was sometimes tied to political concerns. For example, German peasants rebelled against their rulers in 1534 after reading Luther's Bible. It says that all people are equal, and the peasants wanted equal rights. They began a revolt that was soon defeated.

In most places, though, religious concerns between Catholics and Protestants, not politics, led to conflicts and violence.

France

Although most people in France remained Catholic, some became Protestants. French Protestants were called **Huguenots** (HYOO-guh-nahts). A series of conflicts between Catholics and Huguenots led to years of bloody war. The conflicts began when the French king, who was Catholic, decided to get rid of all the Protestants in France. To accomplish this he banned all Protestant religions in France and punished or exiled any Protestants he found.

The king's efforts to eliminate Protestants increased tensions, but violence didn't break out until 1562. In that year a Catholic noble attacked and killed a group of Protestants in northwestern France. The attack infuriated Protestants throughout France. Angry Protestants rose up in arms against both the noble and France's Catholic monarchy. After about a year of fighting, both sides agreed to stop fighting. As a gesture of peace the king allowed Protestants to remain in France, but only in certain towns.

Time Line

Religious Wars in Europe

1517 Martin Luther posts his Ninety-Five Theses. The Reformation begins.

1500

1550

1534 King Henry VIII of England breaks away from the Catholic Church and founds the Anglican Church.

THE GRANGER COLLECTION, NEW YORK

The peace didn't last for long, though. Fighting soon resumed, and the war continued on and off for almost 20 years.

The worst incident of the war was the St. Bartholomew's Day Massacre. It took place on August 24, 1572, which Catholics called St. Bartholomew's Day. In one night Catholic rioters killed about 3,000 Protestants in Paris. In the days that followed, riots broke out all over France.

The war between French Catholics and Protestants finally ended in 1598. In that year King Henry IV—who was raised a Protestant—issued the **Edict of Nantes** (NAHNT), granting religious freedom in most of France. It allowed Protestants to live and worship anywhere except in Paris and a few other cities. Henry's law stopped the war, but resentment between Catholics and Protestants continued.

The Holy Roman Empire

Religious wars caused even more destruction in the Holy Roman Empire than in France. Major violence there broke out in 1618 when unhappy Protestants threw two Catholic officials out of a window in the city of Prague (PRAHG). Their action was a response to a new policy issued by the king of Bohemia—a part of the empire. The king had decided to make everyone in his kingdom become Catholic. To enforce his decision, he closed all Protestant churches in Bohemia.

The king's decision upset many Protestants. In Prague, unhappy Protestants overthrew their Catholic ruler and replaced him with a Protestant one. Their action did not resolve anything, however. Instead, it added to the religious conflict in the Holy Roman Empire.

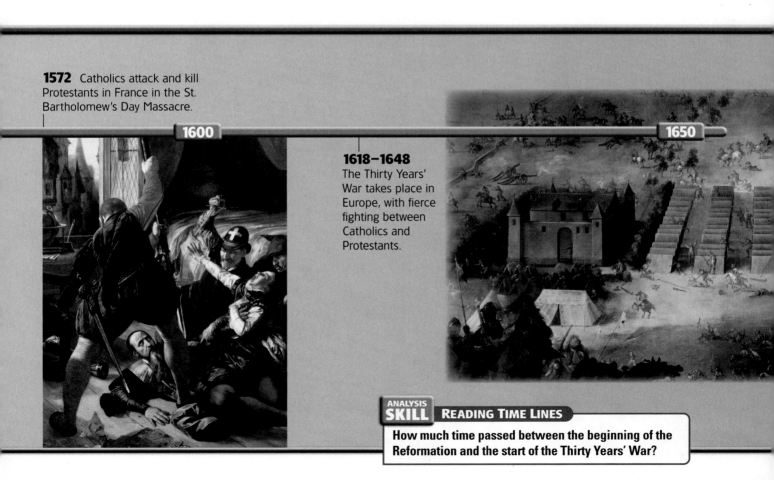

1572 Catholics attack and kill Protestants in France in the St. Bartholomew's Day Massacre.

1600

1618–1648 The Thirty Years' War takes place in Europe, with fierce fighting between Catholics and Protestants.

1650

ANALYSIS SKILL **READING TIME LINES**

How much time passed between the beginning of the Reformation and the start of the Thirty Years' War?

Their revolt quickly spread into other parts of the empire. This rebellion began what is known as the **Thirty Years' War**, a long series of wars that involved many of the countries of Europe.

The war quickly became too much for the Holy Roman Emperor to handle. He sought help from other Catholic countries, including Spain. As the fighting grew worse, the Protestants also looked for help. Some of their allies weren't even Protestant. For example, the Catholic king of France agreed to help them because he didn't like the Holy Roman Emperor.

Although it began as a religious conflict, the Thirty Years' War grew beyond religious issues. Countries fought each other over political rivalries, for control of territory, and about trade rights.

ACADEMIC VOCABULARY

agreement a decision reached by two or more people or groups

After 30 years of fighting, Europe's rulers were ready for the war to end. This was especially true in the German states of the Holy Roman Empire, where most of the fighting had taken place. In 1648 Europe's leaders worked out a peace agreement.

The **agreement** they created, the Treaty of Westphalia, allowed rulers to determine whether their countries would be Catholic or Protestant. The treaty also introduced political changes in Europe. One important change affected the Holy Roman Empire. The states of Germany became independent, with no single ruler over them, and the Holy Roman Empire no longer existed.

READING CHECK **Identifying Cause and Effect** How did Europe change after the Thirty Years' War?

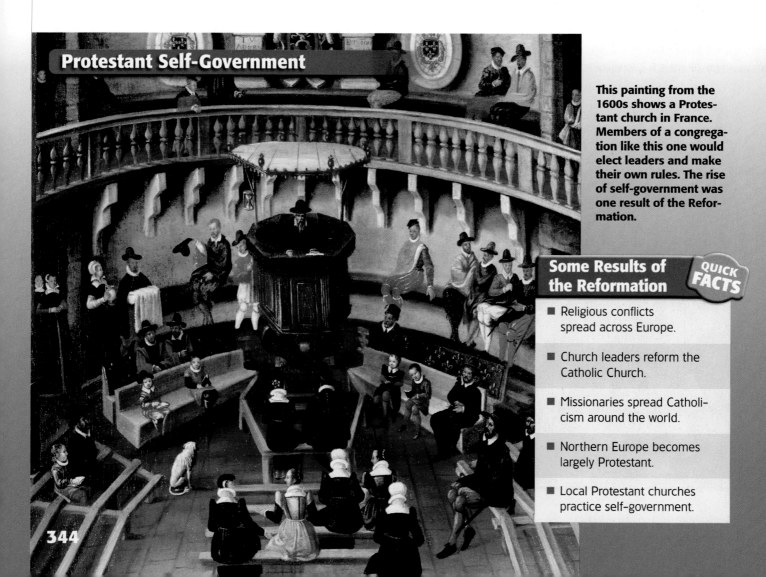

Protestant Self-Government

This painting from the 1600s shows a Protestant church in France. Members of a congregation like this one would elect leaders and make their own rules. The rise of self-government was one result of the Reformation.

Some Results of the Reformation QUICK FACTS

- Religious conflicts spread across Europe.

- Church leaders reform the Catholic Church.

- Missionaries spread Catholicism around the world.

- Northern Europe becomes largely Protestant.

- Local Protestant churches practice self-government.

Social Changes

The religious changes of the Reformation and the political turmoil that followed set other changes in motion. People began to question the role of government and the role of science in their lives.

Self-Government

Before the Reformation most Europeans had no voice in governing the Catholic Church. They simply followed the teachings of their priests and bishops.

Many Protestant churches didn't have priests, bishops, or other clergy. Instead, each **congregation**, or church assembly, made its own rules and elected leaders to make decisions for them. People began to think that their own ideas, not just the ideas of the clergy, were important.

Once people began to govern their churches they also began to want political power. In some places congregations began to rule their towns, not just their churches. In Scotland, England, and some English colonies in America, congregations met to decide how their towns would be run. These town meetings were an early form of self-goverment, in which people rule themselves.

As time passed, some congregations gained more power. Their decisions came to affect more aspects of people's lives or to control events in larger areas. The power of these congregations didn't replace national governments, but national rulers began to share some power with local governments. The sharing of power between local governments and a strong central government is called **federalism**.

New Views of the World

Once people began to think that their own ideas were important, they began to raise questions. They wanted to know more about the natural physical world around them. In addition, more and more people refused to accept information about the world based on someone else's authority. They didn't care if the person was a writer from ancient Greece or a religious leader. The desire to investigate, to figure things out on their own, led people to turn increasingly to science.

READING CHECK **Summarizing** How did the Reformation change European society?

SUMMARY AND PREVIEW The Reformation caused great changes in Europe, and not just in religion. In the next chapter you will learn how the ideas of the Reformation paved the way for the growth of science and the Scientific Revolution.

Section 3 Assessment

go.hrw.com
Online Quiz
KEYWORD: SQ7 HP12

Reviewing Ideas, Terms, and People **HSS** 7.9.3, 7.9.4

1. **a. Recall** Where did more Protestants live, in northern or southern Europe?
   b. Evaluate Why do you think the Catholic Church had more influence in southern Europe?
2. **a. Identify** Where did the **Thirty Years' War** begin?
   b. Explain What started the wars of religion in France?
3. **a. Identify** What were two areas of society that changed as a result of the Reformation?
   b. Sequence How did the Reformation lead to the growth of **federalism**?

Critical Thinking

4. **Identifying Cause and Effect** Draw a series of boxes like the ones shown here. In the first box, identify the cause of religious conflict in Europe. In the last box, list two effects of that conflict.

   Cause → Religious Conflict → Effects

FOCUS ON WRITING

5. **Choosing Important Details** Once again, write the main idea and supporting details of the section in your notebook. Then look over your notes to choose the most important and intriguing details for the book jacket. Put a check mark next to the details you think you'll include.

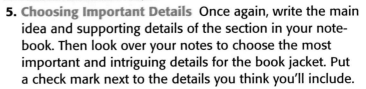

Social Studies Skills

Understanding Graphs

Understand the Skill

Graphs are drawings that display data in a clear, visual form. There are three main types of graphs. *Line graphs* show changes in something over time. *Bar graphs* compare quantities within a category. Some bar graphs may illustrate changes over time as well. *Circle graphs*, also called *pie graphs*, represent the parts that make up a whole of something. Each piece of the circle, or "pie," shows what proportion that part is of the whole.

Graphs let you see relationships more quickly and easily than tables or written explanations do. The ability to read and interpret graphs will help you to better understand and use statistical information in history.

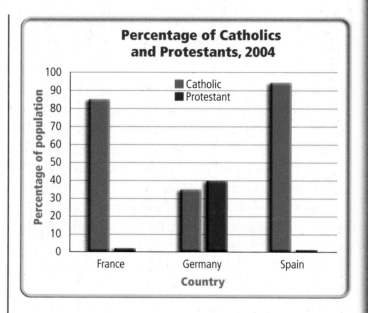

Percentage of Catholics and Protestants, 2004

Learn the Skill

Use the following guidelines to understand and interpret data presented in a graph.

❶ Read the graph's title to identify the subject. Note the kind of graph. This will give you clues about its purpose.

❷ Study the graph's parts and read its labels. Note the subjects or categories that are graphed. Also note the units of measure. If the graph uses different colors, determine what each means.

❸ Analyze the data. Note any increases or decreases in quantities. Look for trends or changes over time. Determine any other relationships in the data that is graphed.

Practice and Apply the Skill

The Reformation brought changes to Christianity in Europe. The effects of these changes can still be seen there today. Interpret the graph to answer the following questions.

1. What kind of graph is this?

2. What is the purpose of the graph?

3. What percentage of the population in France is Catholic?

4. In what country are there more Protestants than Catholics?

Visual Summary

Use the visual summary below to help you review the main ideas of the chapter.

QUICK FACTS

Protestant
Catholic

Unhappy with the Catholic Church, reformers in Europe began to break away and form Protestant churches.

The Protestant Reformation led to efforts to reform the Catholic Church.

The split in the church changed the religious map of Europe.

Reviewing Vocabulary, Terms, and People

Choose the letter of the answer that best completes each statement below.

1. The movement to reform the Roman Catholic Church that created many new religions was the
  a. Council of Trent. **c.** Catholic Reformation.
  b. Thirty Years' War. **d.** Protestant Reformation.

2. The man who began the Reformation by nailing complaints about the church to a church door was
  a. Martin Luther. **c.** Francis Xavier.
  b. John Calvin. **d.** King Henry VIII.

3. People who disagreed with and broke away from the Catholic Church during the Reformation were called
  a. indulgences. **c.** Jesuits.
  b. congregations. **d.** Protestants.

4. Documents that were believed to reduce the time a person's soul would spend in purgatory were called
  a. Huguenots. **c.** indulgences.
  b. missionaries. **d.** Protestants.

5. The founder of the Jesuit Order was
  a. Martin Luther. **c.** Francis Xavier.
  b. John Calvin. **d.** Ignatius of Loyola.

Comprehension and Critical Thinking

SECTION 1 *(Pages 328–333)* **HSS** 7.9.1, 7.9.2

6. a. Describe What were some of the complaints that people had about the Catholic Church in the 1500s?

  b. Analyze How did Martin Luther's teachings affect the beliefs of many people in northern Europe?

SECTION 1 (continued)

c. **Predict** How did William Tyndale and King Henry VIII affect people's lives for hundreds of years to come?

SECTION 2 (Pages 334–339) **HSS** 7.9.5, 7.9.6, 7.9.7

7. a. Identify Who were Ignatius of Loyola, Angela Merici, and Francis Xavier?

b. **Analyze** Why was Spain a leader in the Catholic Reformation?

c. **Evaluate** Why might a historian say that the Protestant Reformation actually helped spread Catholicism around the world?

SECTION 3 (Pages 340–345) **HSS** 7.9.3, 7.9.4

8. a. Recall By the 1600s, which parts of Europe were mostly Catholic? Which parts were mostly Protestant?

b. **Compare and Contrast** How were the wars in France and the Holy Roman Empire similar? How were they different?

c. **Elaborate** How did the Reformation affect other aspects of daily life in Europe and the English colonies in America?

Reviewing Themes

9. Society and Culture What were two non-religious effects of the Reformation?

10. Religion Do you think the Reformation increased or decreased most people's interest in religion? Why?

Using the Internet

go.hrw.com
KEYWORD: SQ7 WH12

11. Activity: Researching Reformers If you walked down the narrow streets in Wittenberg before Luther nailed up his list of complaints, you might have heard an indulgence salesman say "When a coin into the coin box rings, a soul from Purgatory soon will spring." Luther and other Reformation leaders put indulgence sellers on the unemployment line. Enter the keyword above. Then write a profile of a Reformation leader that outlines his life and his impact on the Reformation.

Reading Skills

Online Research *Each question below lists two types of Web sites you could use to answer the question. Decide which Web site is likely to be a more valuable and reliable source of information.*

12. What happened to Martin Luther after he nailed his Ninety-Five Theses to the church door?

a. a movie studio Web site for a movie about Martin Luther's life

b. an online encyclopedia

13. What happened during the Thirty Years' War?

a. a Web site with an excerpt from a book by a university professor about the war

b. a museum Web site for an exhibit about the Holy Roman Empire

Social Studies Skills

14. Understanding Graphs What kind of graph (line, bar, or circle) would you create to show how the number of Protestants in the Netherlands rose and fell during the 1600s? Explain your answer.

FOCUS ON WRITING

15. Designing Your Book Jacket By now you've chosen details about events and people you want to include on your book jacket. Write 7–8 sentences about the Reformation. Include enough detail to hook your readers and make them want to read the book. Once you've completed the summary, think of a catchy title for the book and an image for the front cover.

Standards Assessment

DIRECTIONS: Read each question, and write the letter of the best response.

1 Use the map to answer the following question.

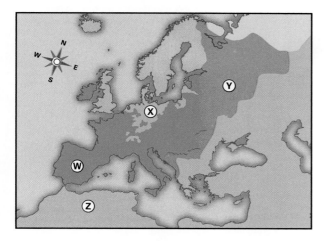

Which letter on the map shows the area of Europe where most people remained Catholic after the Reformation?

A W

B X

C Y

D Z

2 The Reformation had all of the following effects in Europe *except*

A an increased interest in science.

B wars between Catholics and Protestants.

C the growth of federalism.

D the creation of a Holy Roman Empire.

3 Reformers found fault with all of the following practices of the Catholic Church *except*

A the selling of indulgences.

B the Bible appearing only in Latin.

C lazy or corrupt clergy.

D the building of monasteries.

4 One result of the Catholic Reformation in Europe was

A missionary activity that spread the Catholic faith around the world.

B the founding of the Anglican Church and other Protestant faiths.

C the cooperation of European Muslims and Jews to advance the arts and sciences.

D the elimination of the papacy.

5 Which person is generally credited with starting the Reformation?

A Desiderius Erasmus

B Martin Luther

C John Calvin

D King Henry VIII

Connecting with Past Learnings

6 Earlier, you learned that a missionary named Patrick introduced Christianity to Ireland. Which of the following figures played a similar role in other parts of the world?

A Francis Xavier

B King Henry VIII

C Ignatius of Loyola

D King Charles IV

7 In many places in Europe in the 1500s, Protestants were persecuted for their beliefs. Another group that you have studied that were persecuted for what they believed were

A Egyptians under Alexander the Great.

B Hindus in India.

C Christians in the Roman Empire.

D Buddhists in China.

The Scientific Revolution

California Standards

History–Social Science

7.10 Students analyze the historical developments of the Scientific Revolution and its lasting effect on religious, political, and cultural institutions.

English–Language Arts

Speaking 7.2.4b Describe the points in support of the argument and employ well-articulated evidence.

Reading 7.2.0 Students read and understand grade-level-appropriate material.

FOCUS ON SPEAKING

A Defense One of Europe's greatest scientists, Galileo Galilei, has been arrested and is being put on trial for contradicting Church teachings. You think he's innocent, and you've been hired to defend Galileo to the court. As you read this chapter, you will gather information that you can use to give a short speech in the scientist's defense.

CHAPTER EVENTS

1525

1543 Copernicus publishes his theory of the sun-centered solar system.

WORLD EVENTS

1537 Francisco Pizarro conquers the Incas.

HOLT

History's Impact

▶ **video series**
Watch the video to understand the impact of the Renaissance and Reformation.

What You Will Learn...

In this chapter you will learn about the discoveries and inventions of the Scientific Revolution. The Scientific Revolution laid the foundations for modern science. This photo shows a powerful telescope that astronomers use to study the skies.

c.1590
Zacharias Janssen invents the microscope.

1609
Galileo uses his telescope to study planets.

1687
Sir Isaac Newton publishes *Principia Mathematica*.

1575

1625

1675

1725

1620
The *Mayflower* sets sail for North America.

c.1631
Construction begins on the Taj Mahal in India.

1690
John Locke argues that people have certain natural rights.

351

Reading Social Studies

by Kylene Beers

Focus on Themes This chapter will discuss the advances in **science and technology** made during the Scientific Revolution. As you read this chapter you will learn about such great scientists as Nicolaus Copernicus, Galileo, and Isaac Newton—scientists whose ideas are respected and admired even today. They and other scientists like them have greatly influenced **society and culture**, not just in Europe but around the world. Think how much different our lives would be without science!

Comparing and Contrasting Historical Facts

Focus on Reading Comparing and contrasting facts, ideas, or concepts is a good way to learn more about them. That's one reason historians use comparison and contrast to explain people and events in history.

Understanding Comparison and Contrast To **compare** is to look for likenesses, or similarities. To **contrast** is to look for differences. Sometimes writers point out similarities and differences. Other times you have to look for them yourself. You can use a diagram like this one to keep track of similarities and differences as you read.

Additional reading support can be found in the

Inter active

Reader and Study Guide

Science

Before the Scientific Revolution

Differences
- Based on Biblical and church teachings
- No organized method for research
- Not very widespread or popular

Similarities
- Attempt to learn more about the world
- People tried to learn more about the sun and planets

After the Scientific Revolution

Differences
- Based on careful observation and use of reason
- Scientific method for research
- Very widespread and popular

Clues for Comparison-Contrast

Writers sometimes signal comparisons or contrasts with words like these:

Comparison—*similarly, like, in the same way, too*

Contrast—*however, unlike, but, while, although, in contrast*

You Try It!

The following passage is from the chapter you are about to read. Read this passage looking for what two things are being compared and contrasted.

Nicolaus Copernicus

Copernicus was familiar with Ptolemy's theories and writings. Ptolemy had written that the earth was the center of the universe and that the sun and other planets orbited, or circled around, the earth. For 1,400 years, people accepted this belief as fact.

From Chapter 13, pages 359–360

As Copernicus studied the movements of the planets, however, what Ptolemy stated made less and less sense to him. If the planets were indeed orbiting the earth, they would have to be moving in very complex patterns.

So Copernicus tried a different explanation for what he observed in the sky. Copernicus asked, What if the planets actually orbited the sun? Suddenly, complex patterns weren't necessary to make sense of what Copernicus observed. Instead, simple circular orbits would account for the planets' movements.

After you read the passage, answer the following questions.

1. What two figures does this passage compare?

2. What is one way in which Ptolemy and Copernicus were similar? What is one way in which they were different?

3. Draw a diagram like the one on the previous page comparing Ptolemy and Copernicus. How will your information be arranged?

4. Why do you think the author organized this passage as a comparison and contrast?

Key Terms and People

Chapter 13

Section 1
Scientific Revolution *(p. 354)*
science *(p. 355)*
theories *(p. 355)*
Ptolemy *(p. 356)*
rationalists *(p. 356)*
alchemy *(p. 357)*

Section 2
Nicolaus Copernicus *(p. 359)*
Tycho Brahe *(p. 360)*
Johannes Kepler *(p. 360)*
Galileo Galilei *(p. 361)*
Sir Isaac Newton *(p. 362)*
barometer *(p. 363)*

Section 3
Francis Bacon *(p. 364)*
René Descartes *(p. 365)*
scientific method *(p. 365)*
hypothesis *(p. 366)*

Academic Vocabulary

Success in school is related to knowing academic vocabulary— the words that are frequently used in school assignments and discussions. In this chapter, you will learn the following academic words:

logical *(p. 355)*
procedure *(p. 365)*
principles *(p. 366)*

As you read **Chapter 13,** look for examples of text arranged as comparisons and contrasts.

A New View of the World

What You Will Learn...

Main Ideas

1. The Scientific Revolution marked the birth of modern science.
2. The roots of the Scientific Revolution can be traced to ancient Greece, the Muslim world, and Europe.

The Big Idea

Europeans drew on earlier ideas to develop a new way of gaining knowledge about the natural world.

Key Terms and People

Scientific Revolution, *p. 354*
science, *p. 355*
theories, *p. 355*
Ptolemy, *p. 356*
rationalists, *p. 356*
alchemy, *p. 357*

HSS 7.10.1 Discuss the roots of the Scientific Revolution (e.g., Greek rationalism; Jewish, Christian, and Muslim science; Renaissance humanism; new knowledge from global exploration).

If YOU were there...

You are a student in Germany in the early 1500s. You love to watch the changing phases of the moon and draw the star patterns at different times of year. You've asked your teachers many questions: Why does the moon hang in the sky? Why do the stars move? But their answers don't seem convincing to you.

How can you find the answers to your questions?

BUILDING BACKGROUND In the 1500s, Europe was undergoing dramatic changes. The Renaissance was well under way. During the Renaissance, great advances were made in art, writing, and education. The stage was set for another revolution in thinking.

The Birth of Modern Science

During the 1500s and 1600s, a handful of brilliant individuals laid the foundations for science as we know it today. Some historians consider the development of modern science the most important event in the intellectual history of humankind.

A Revolution in Thinking

The series of events that led to the birth of modern science is called the **Scientific Revolution**. It occurred between about 1540 and 1700. Why would the birth of science be called a "revolution"? The answer is that science was a radical new idea. It was a completely different way of looking at the world.

Before the Scientific Revolution, most educated people who studied the world took guidance from the explanations given by authorities like ancient Greek writers and Catholic Church officials. After the Scientific Revolution, educated people placed more importance on what they observed and less on what they were told. They gained knowledge by observing the world around them and coming up with logical explanations for what they saw.

Understanding Science

Science is a particular way of gaining knowledge about the world. In fact, the word *science* comes from a Latin word meaning "knowledge" or "understanding."

Science starts with observation. Scientists observe, or look at, the world. By observing the world they can identify facts about it. A famous scientist once said, "Science is built up with facts, as a house is with stones. But a collection of facts is no more a science than a pile of stones is a house."

So scientists do more than identify facts. They use logic to explain the facts they have observed. The explanations scientists develop based on these facts are called **theories**.

Theories are not accepted on faith. They must be tested to see if they are true. Scientists design experiments to test their theories. If the experiments keep showing that the theory makes sense, the theory is kept. If the experiments do not support the theory, scientists try a new theory. In this way, scientists learn more about the world.

As you can see, scientific knowledge is based on observations, facts, and logical ideas, or theories, about them. Before the Scientific Revolution, this method of gaining knowledge was uncommon.

READING CHECK **Finding Main Ideas** What was the Scientific Revolution?

Roots of the Revolution

Some of the main ideas of science had been expressed long before the Scientific Revolution. In fact, some of the basic ideas of science are ancient.

Greek Thinkers

Many Greek thinkers expressed ideas that, today, we would call scientific. The great philosopher Aristotle, for example, wrote about astronomy, geography, and many other fields. But his greatest contribution to science was the idea that people should observe the world carefully and draw logical conclusions about what they see.

ACADEMIC VOCABULARY
logical
reasoned, well thought out

Philosophers like Plato and Aristotle used reason and logic to understand the world.

Greek Thinkers
The ancient Greeks developed theories about how the world worked that influenced later scientific thinkers. This famous painting from the early 1500s by the Italian artist Raphael shows some influential Greek thinkers.

Pythagoras studied numbers and believed that things could be predicted and measured.

Euclid discovered basic mathematical laws that helped explain the natural world.

Roots of the Scientific Revolution

Greek Ideas
- Importance of observation, logic, and rational thought
- Basic theories about astronomy, geography, and mathematics

Scholars of Three Faiths
- Muslim preservation and study of ancient texts
- Jewish study of Greek ideas and religion
- Christian study of Greek ideas and religion

THE GRANGER COLLECTION, NEW YORK

The use of observation and logic, as you have just read, is important in gaining scientific knowledge.

Another Greek thinker was **Ptolemy** (TAHL-uh-mee), an ancient astronomer. He studied the skies, recorded his observations, and offered theories to explain what he saw. Ptolemy was also a geographer who made the best maps of his time. His maps were based on observations of the real world.

Aristotle, Ptolemy, and other Greek thinkers were **rationalists**, people who looked at the world in a rational, or reasonable and logical, way. During the Renaissance, Europeans studied the works of Greek rationalists. As a result, they began to view the world in a rational way. They began to think like scientists.

Preserving Ancient Knowledge

European scholars could study ancient Greek writings because of the work of others. Muslim scholars translated Greek writings into Arabic. They studied them for centuries and added their own new ideas. Later, the Arabic versions were translated into Latin, which was read in Europe. This work preserved ancient knowledge and spread interest in science to Europe.

Other religious scholars also played a role in preserving Greek ideas. The Jewish scholar Maimonides (my-MAHN-uh-deez) studied and wrote about Aristotle, trying to unite his work with Jewish ideas. The Christian scholar Thomas Aquinas tried to unite the work of Aristotle with Christian ideas. Other Christian scholars studied Greek ideas in Europe's universities.

Developments in Europe

The Scientific Revolution was not just the result of European scholars studying ancient Greek writings. Developments in Europe also helped bring about the Scientific Revolution.

One development that helped lead to the Scientific Revolution was the growth of humanism during the Renaissance. Humanist artists and writers spent much of their time studying the natural world. This interest in the natural world carried forward into the Scientific Revolution.

Renaissance Humanism
- Emphasis on Greek and Roman ideas
- Focus on the importance of education and learning

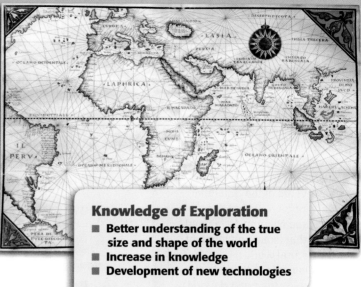

Knowledge of Exploration
- Better understanding of the true size and shape of the world
- Increase in knowledge
- Development of new technologies

Another development was a growing interest in alchemy (AL-kuh-mee). **Alchemy was a forerunner of chemistry.** Alchemists experimented with various natural substances. They were best known for trying to change other metals into gold. Although they failed at that, alchemists succeeded in using experiments to learn more about how nature worked.

All of these developments—the interest in ancient Greek writings, the growth of humanism, the experiments of alchemists—came together in the early 1500s to bring about the Scientific Revolution.

READING CHECK Understanding Cause and Effect How did Greek rationalism help lead to the Scientific Revolution?

SUMMARY AND PREVIEW The Scientific Revolution was the birth of modern science. Greek, Muslim, and European thought all contributed to its beginning. Next you will read about specific events of the Scientific Revolution.

go.hrw.com
Online Quiz
KEYWORD: SQ7 HP13

Section 1 Assessment

Reviewing Ideas, Terms, and People **HSS** 7.10.1

1. **a. Define** What is **science**?
   b. Explain Why was the **Scientific Revolution** important in world history?
   c. Elaborate What might cause scientists to reject a theory?
2. **a. Identify** Who was **Ptolemy**?
   b. Analyze What qualities did Greek **rationalists** have?
   c. Elaborate Why might alchemists have thought they could turn other metals into gold?

Critical Thinking

3. **Identifying Cause and Effect**
   Draw a graphic organizer like the one here. In the boxes to the left, identify four causes of the Scientific Revolution.

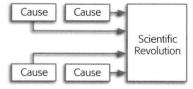

FOCUS ON SPEAKING

4. **Explaining Science** As part of your defense of Galileo, you'll probably need to explain what science is. Look back through this section and take some notes that you might use to explain the basic principles of science.

Discoveries and Inventions

What You Will Learn...

Main Ideas

1. The discovery of the Americas led scholars to doubt ancient Greek ideas.
2. Advances in astronomy were key events of the Scientific Revolution.
3. Sir Isaac Newton developed laws that explained much of the natural world.
4. New inventions helped scientists study the natural world.

The Big Idea

During the Scientific Revolution, new ideas and inventions changed the nature of knowledge.

Key Terms and People

Nicolaus Copernicus, *p. 359*
Tycho Brahe, *p. 360*
Johannes Kepler, *p. 360*
Galileo Galilei, *p. 361*
Sir Isaac Newton, *p. 362*
barometer, *p. 363*

HSS **7.10.2** Understand the significance of the new scientific theories (e.g., those of Copernicus, Galileo, Kepler, Newton) and the significance of new inventions (e.g., the telescope, microscope, thermometer, barometer).

If YOU were there...

You are an innkeeper in Spain in 1498. Many of the guests who stay at your inn are sailors. Today they are telling stories about a vast new land filled with strange peoples, plants, and animals. No one had ever thought such a land really existed before.

How does this news change your view of the world?

BUILDING BACKGROUND During the Scientific Revolution advances in science allowed people to discover new lands and to build new machines. Some of these new machines allowed people to study the world in ways they had never been able to before.

Discovery Leads to Doubt

During the Renaissance, European scholars eagerly read and studied the works of Greek rationalists. Aristotle, Ptolemy, and others were viewed as authorities.

This drawing shows the earth at the center of the universe. Before Copernicus, most people believed that the sun revolved around the earth.

Jupiter

Saturn

Then an event took place that caused Europeans to doubt some of what the Greeks had said. In 1492, Christopher Columbus sailed west across the Atlantic Ocean in hopes of reaching Asia. As a guide, he took the map of the world that Ptolemy had created. Columbus never reached Asia because he ran into North America instead. Within a few years voyages of exploration made it clear that there was an entire continent that Europeans hadn't even known existed.

This discovery stunned Europeans. This continent was not on Ptolemy's map. Ptolemy was wrong. Observation of the real world had disproved the teachings of an ancient authority. Soon, European scholars began to question the accuracy of other Greek authorities. More and more, observations the Europeans made did not fit with what the authorities had described. Such observations helped lead to the Scientific Revolution.

READING CHECK **Identifying Cause and Effect** How did the European discovery of America affect the Scientific Revolution?

Advances in Astronomy

In 1543 an astronomer published a book that contradicted what a Greek authority had written. Many historians think the publication of this book marks the beginning of the Scientific Revolution.

Nicolaus Copernicus

The book thought to have marked the beginning of the Scientific Revolution was written by a Polish astronomer, **Nicolaus Copernicus** (kuh-PUHR-ni-kuhs). His 1543 book was called *On the Revolution of the Celestial Spheres.*

Copernicus was familiar with Ptolemy's theories and writings. Ptolemy had written that the earth was the center of the universe and that the sun and other planets orbited, or circled around, the earth. For 1,400 years, people accepted this belief as fact.

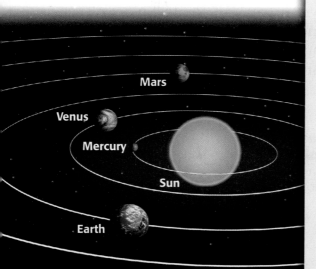

BIOGRAPHY

Nicolaus Copernicus
1473–1543

Nicolaus Copernicus realized that sharing his revolutionary ideas about the universe could be dangerous. He feared persecution or even death at the hands of Church leaders. He was also worried that the scientific community would reject his theories. Eventually, he was persuaded to publish his theories, and the "Copernican system" became a landmark discovery of the Scientific Revolution.

Making Decisions If you were Nicolaus Copernicus would you have published your theories? Why or why not?

As Copernicus studied the movements of the planets, however, what Ptolemy stated made less and less sense to him. If the planets were indeed orbiting the earth, they would have to be moving in very complex patterns.

So Copernicus tried a different explanation for what he observed in the sky. Copernicus asked, What if the planets actually orbited the sun? Suddenly, complex patterns weren't necessary to make sense of what Copernicus observed. Instead, simple circular orbits would account for the planets' movements.

What Copernicus had done was practice science. Instead of trying to make his observations fit an old idea, he came up with a different idea—a different theory—to explain what he observed. Copernicus never proved his theory, but the Scientific Revolution had begun.

Brahe and Kepler

Another important astronomer of the Scientific Revolution was **Tycho Brahe** (TYOO-koh BRAH-huh). Brahe, who was Danish, spent most of his life observing the stars. In the late 1500s, he charted the positions of more than 750 of them.

What Brahe did, however, was less important than *how* he did it. Brahe emphasized the importance of careful observation and detailed, accurate records. Careful recording of information is necessary so that other scientists can use what has previously been learned. In this way, Brahe made an important contribution to modern science.

Brahe was assisted by the German astronomer **Johannes Kepler**. Later, Kepler tried to map the orbits of the planets. But Kepler ran into a problem. According to his observations, the planet Mars did not move in a circle as he expected it to.

Kepler knew that Copernicus had stated that the orbits of the planets were circular. But Kepler's observations showed that Copernicus was mistaken. In 1609 Kepler wrote that Mars—and all other planets—moved in elliptical, or oval, orbits instead of circular ones. Here was a new theory that fit the observed facts. Kepler's work helped

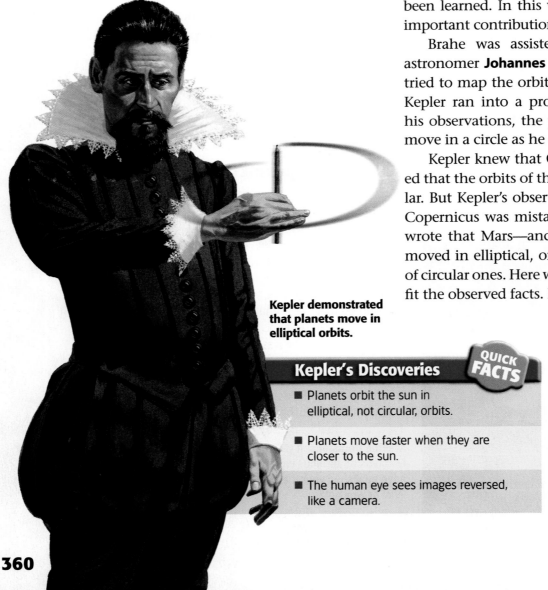

Kepler demonstrated that planets move in elliptical orbits.

Kepler's Discoveries

QUICK FACTS

- Planets orbit the sun in elliptical, not circular, orbits.

- Planets move faster when they are closer to the sun.

- The human eye sees images reversed, like a camera.

prove Copernicus's theory that the planets orbit the sun. In fact, Kepler became one of the first scientists to speak out in support of Copernicus.

Kepler continued to study the planets for the rest of his life. His basic ideas about the planets' movements are still accepted by scientists today.

Galileo Galilei

Galileo Galilei (gal-uh-LEE-oh gal-uh-LAY) was one of the most important scientists of the Scientific Revolution. He was the first person to study the sky with a telescope. With his telescope, Galileo discovered craters and mountains on the moon. He also discovered that moons orbit Jupiter.

Galileo was interested in more than astronomy, however. He also was interested in such things as how falling objects behave. Today, we use the term *mechanics* for the study of objects and motion.

Galileo's biggest contribution to the development of science was the way he learned about mechanics. Instead of just observing things in nature, he set up experiments to test what he observed. Galileo was the first scientist to routinely use experiments to test his theories. For this, he is remembered as the father of experimental science.

READING CHECK **Summarizing** What were two major achievements in astronomy?

THE IMPACT TODAY

Astronomers still study Kepler's ideas, which they call his laws of planetary motion.

Galileo studied the sky and performed experiments to learn about motion mechanics.

Primary Source

LETTER
Galileo Defends His Work

In 1613, Galileo (1564–1642) wrote a letter to the Grand Duchess Christina of Tuscany, the mother of the great banker Cosimo de' Medici. In this letter, he defended himself against attackers who claimed that his ideas went against church teachings. Galileo opened his letter with an explanation of his discoveries.

Galileo points out that many people are unhappy with his discoveries simply because they are new.

Galileo defends his discoveries by pointing out that God created the heavens. Humans can only study what God put there.

❝Some years ago, as Your Serene Highness well knows, I discovered in the heavens many things that had not been seen before our own age. The novelty [newness] of these things, as well as some consequences which followed from them in contradiction [contrast] to the physical notions [ideas] commonly held among academic philosophers, stirred up against me no small number of professors—as if I had placed these things in the sky with my own hands in order to upset nature and overturn the sciences. They seemed to forget that the increase of known truths stimulates [encourages] the investigation, establishment, and growth of the arts; not their diminution [decrease] or destruction.❞

–from *A Letter to the Grand Duchess Christina of Tuscany* from Galileo Galilei, 1615

ANALYSIS SKILL **ANALYZING PRIMARY SOURCES**

How does Galileo justify his search for knowledge?

Sir Isaac Newton

The high point of the Scientific Revolution was marked by the publication of a remarkable book. This book, published in 1687, was *Principia Mathematica*. Its author was the English scientist **Sir Isaac Newton**. Newton was one of the greatest and most influential scientists who ever lived.

Newton studied and simplified the work of earlier scientists. In doing so, he:

- reviewed everything scientists had been learning,
- coupled it with his own observations and ideas, and
- identified four theories that described how the physical world worked.

Some of his theories have been proven so many times that they are no longer called theories, but laws.

One of Newton's laws is called the law of gravity. You may know that gravity is the force that attracts objects to each other. It's the force that makes a dropped apple fall to the ground and that keeps the planets in orbit around the sun.

Newton's other three laws are called the laws of motion. They describe how objects move in space. You may have heard of one of them: "For every action there is an equal and opposite reaction."

Newton proposed that the universe was like a huge machine. Within this machine, all objects follow the laws he identified. In short, Newton explained how the physical world worked—and he was correct. Newton's laws became the foundation of nearly all scientific study until the 1900s.

Newton also invented calculus, an advanced form of mathematics that scientists use to solve complex problems. For this, and for his laws of motion, Newton is remembered as a great scientist.

READING CHECK **Summarizing** Why are Newton's theories called laws?

BIOGRAPHY

Sir Isaac Newton
1642–1727

Sir Isaac Newton was interested in learning about the nature of light, so he conducted a series of experiments. In Newton's time, most people assumed that light was white. Newton proved, however, that light is actually made up of all of the colors of the rainbow. His research on light became the basis for his invention of the reflecting telescope—the type of telescope found in most large observatories today.

Summarizing What did Newton prove about the nature of light?

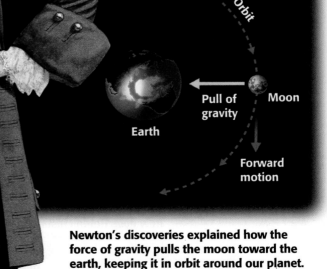

Newton's discoveries explained how the force of gravity pulls the moon toward the earth, keeping it in orbit around our planet.

New Inventions

During the Scientific Revolution, scientists invented new and better instruments. These helped them study the natural world.

Around 1590, a Dutch lens maker named Zacharias Janssen invented a simple microscope. The first person to use a microscope as a scientific instrument, though, was the Dutch scientist Antoni van Leeuwenhoek (LAY-ven-hook) in the mid-1600s. Examining a drop of pond water with his microscope, he saw tiny plants and animals not visible to the naked eye.

In 1593, Galileo invented the thermometer. Thermometers are used to measure temperature. About 50 years later an Italian doctor developed a more accurate model than Galileo's.

The telescope was probably invented by a Dutch lens maker in 1608. The next year, Galileo built a much-improved telescope that he used to make his important astronomical discoveries.

In 1643, the Italian scientist Evangelista Torricelli invented the barometer. A **barometer** is a scientific instrument that measures air pressure. Barometers are used to help forecast the weather.

These instruments—the microscope, the thermometer, the telescope, and the barometer—are very common today. In fact, you have probably used at least one of them yourself. But when they were invented, they were dramatic advances in technology. They gave scientists the tools they needed to make more accurate observations of the world and to conduct experiments. They were the tools of the Scientific Revolution.

READING CHECK Comparing
How are the microscope and the telescope similar?

This early microscope was made around 1675. The lens is protected by cardboard and leather and slides up and down.

SUMMARY AND PREVIEW The work of Copernicus, Brahe, Kepler, Galileo, and Newton was central to the Scientific Revolution. In the next section, you will learn more about the effects of these scientists' accomplishments on society then and now.

Section 2 Assessment

go.hrw.com
Online Quiz
KEYWORD: SQ7 HP13

Reviewing Ideas, Terms, and People HSS 7.10.2

1. **a. Recall** What event caused Europeans to doubt the ideas of ancient Greek authorities?
   b. Explain How did the doubting of Greek authorities help usher in the Scientific Revolution?
2. **a. Identify** Who was **Galileo**?
   b. Summarize How did **Copernicus** and **Kepler** change people's view of the universe?
3. **a. Identify** For what laws is **Isaac Newton** most famous?
   b. Evaluate Why do you think Newton is considered the greatest figure of the Scientific Revolution?
4. **Define** What is a **barometer**?

Critical Thinking

5. **Comparing and Contrasting** Draw a diagram like the one below. Describe each individual's view of how the universe is organized.

Scientist	Ptolemy	Copernicus	Kepler
View			

FOCUS ON SPEAKING

6. **Noting Galileo's Achievements** Now that you've read about Galileo, make a list of some of his major achievements. Then look back at your definiton of science from Section 1. How do Galileo's achievements match the basic goals of science?

Science and Society

What You Will Learn...

Main Ideas

1. The ideas of Francis Bacon and René Descartes helped to clarify the scientific method.
2. Science influenced new ideas about government.
3. Science and religion developed a sometimes uneasy relationship.

The Big Idea

The Scientific Revolution led to the establishment of science as a method of learning, new ideas about government, and conflict with religious authorities.

Key Terms and People

Francis Bacon, *p. 364*
René Descartes, *p. 365*
scientific method, *p. 365*
hypothesis, *p. 366*

HSS **7.10.3** Understand the scientific method advanced by Bacon and Descartes, the influence of new scientific rationalism on the growth of democratic ideas, and the coexistence of science with traditional religious beliefs.

If YOU were there...

You are a scientist conducting an experiment about falling objects. You stand at the base of a tall tower, watching as two of your assistants drop balls from the top. The balls are the same size, but one is made of iron and one of wood. The iron ball is much heavier, so you think that it will hit the ground first. But to your surprise, the two balls appear to hit the ground at the same time! You begin to think that all items will fall at the same speed.

How could you test your new theory?

BUILDING BACKGROUND The great scientists of the Scientific Revolution were pioneers. Even as they made great discoveries, scientists like the one described here had to find ways to explain what they had learned and how it could affect society.

Bacon, Descartes, and the Scientific Method

The Scientific Revolution led to a dramatic change in the way people learned about the world. The new, scientific way of gaining knowledge had far-reaching effects. In fact, the Scientific Revolution still affects us today.

The first effect of the Scientific Revolution was the establishment of science as the most effective way for learning about the natural world. Two individuals played a leading role in gaining this acceptance of science.

Francis Bacon

Francis Bacon was an English philosopher who had read the works of the great scientists of the Scientific Revolution. He was extremely impressed with what he read. He noted how these scientists, using observations, facts, experiments, and theories, were revealing the truth about how nature worked.

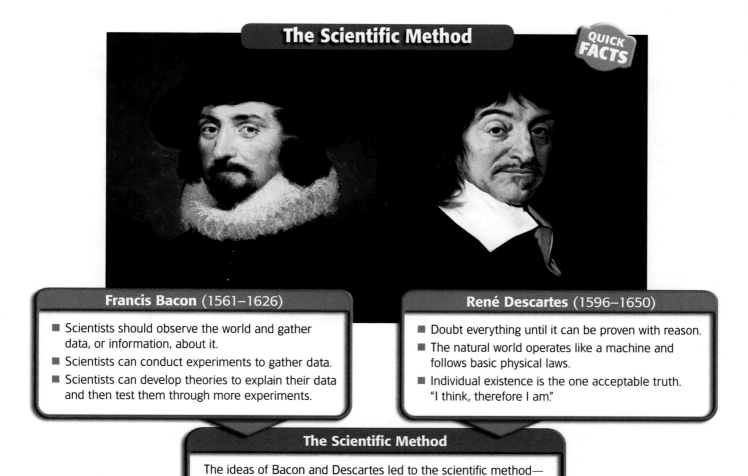

The Scientific Method

QUICK FACTS

Francis Bacon (1561–1626)

- Scientists should observe the world and gather data, or information, about it.
- Scientists can conduct experiments to gather data.
- Scientists can develop theories to explain their data and then test them through more experiments.

René Descartes (1596–1650)

- Doubt everything until it can be proven with reason.
- The natural world operates like a machine and follows basic physical laws.
- Individual existence is the one acceptable truth. "I think, therefore I am."

The Scientific Method

The ideas of Bacon and Descartes led to the scientific method—a method for gathering and testing ideas about the world.

Bacon argued that science should be pursued in a systematic fashion. He even tried to get the king of England to provide money for scientific research. If science were pursued consistently and logically, Bacon wrote, then human knowledge would continually advance over the years. In 1605, Bacon published his ideas in a book titled *The Advancement of Learning*.

René Descartes

Another thinker who made great contributions to the establishment of science was the French philosopher **René Descartes** (ruh-NAY day-CART).

Descartes believed that nothing should be accepted as true if it wasn't proven to be true. This differed from the belief that most European scholars had been supporting for generations. They believed knowledge begins with faith; Descartes said it begins with doubt.

Descartes didn't just mean that observations and experiments were needed for this proof. These things, he said, took place in the material world, and people might be tricked by their senses. Instead, Descartes emphasized that people must use clear thinking and reason to establish proof.

The Scientific Method

Today scientists use a **procedure** called the scientific method when doing their research. The **scientific method** is a step-by-step method for performing experiments and other scientific research.

ACADEMIC VOCABULARY

procedure
a series of steps taken to accomplish a task

Science in School

If you have performed an experiment in science class, then you've seen the scientific method at work. Here, students are performing an experiment to learn about falling objects.

Students and scientists still use the scientific method because it helps them rationally solve problems. They conduct experiments to test their hypotheses. If their experiments don't produce the results they expect, they change their hypotheses and start over. Only after getting the same results time after time do scientists consider their findings conclusive.

 ANALYSIS SKILL **ANALYZING INFORMATION**

How does the scientific method help scientists solve problems?

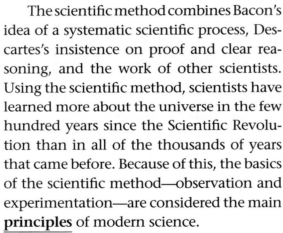

The scientific method combines Bacon's idea of a systematic scientific process, Descartes's insistence on proof and clear reasoning, and the work of other scientists. Using the scientific method, scientists have learned more about the universe in the few hundred years since the Scientific Revolution than in all of the thousands of years that came before. Because of this, the basics of the scientific method—observation and experimentation—are considered the main **principles** of modern science.

There are six basic steps in the scientific method:

1. Stating the problem. The problem is often a question that begins with *why*. For example, Copernicus's problem today would be stated, "Why do the planets move as they do?"

2. Gathering information. This can involve reading what other scientists have written and making observations.

3. Forming a hypothesis. A **hypothesis** is a solution that the scientist proposes to solve the problem. A hypothesis differs from a theory in that a hypothesis has not yet been tested.

4. Testing the hypothesis by performing experiments.

5. Recording and analyzing data gathered from the experiments.

6. Drawing conclusions from the data collected.

After scientists have concluded their experiments, they typically publish their results. This sharing of ideas is very important for two reasons.

First, publishing results lets other scientists try to reproduce the experiments. By reproducing experiments, scientists can determine whether the results are the same. If they are, they can be reasonably sure that the results are accurate.

Second, publishing results spreads scientific knowledge. New scientific knowledge builds on previous knowledge. Sir Isaac Newton once wrote, "If I have seen further it is by standing on the shoulders of Giants."

READING CHECK **Sequencing** What are the steps in the scientific method?

ACADEMIC VOCABULARY

principles basic beliefs, rules, or laws

Science and Government

Some of the most important effects of the Scientific Revolution had nothing to do with science at all. When philosophers began applying scientific thought to other areas of human life, they came up with some startling new ideas.

The Power of Reason

By the end of the Scientific Revolution, one thing had become clear to many European thinkers: human reason, or logical thought, was a powerful tool. After all, scientists using reason had made many discoveries about the universe in a relatively short time.

Since reason had proven itself as a way to learn some of nature's great secrets, might reason also be used to solve the problems facing people? Philosophers decided to use reason when they considered society's problems like poverty and war, or what type of government is best.

This use of reason to consider the problems of society led philosophers to look at the world in a new way. They thought they could use reason to determine how to improve society.

Democratic Ideas

One way in which scientists thought they could improve society was by changing its government. Scientists' use of reason and logic during the Scientific Revolution helped pave the way for the beginnings of democratic thought in Europe.

As scientists like Sir Isaac Newton studied the world, they discovered laws that governed nature. In time, some scientists began to think that there must be laws that governed human behavior as well. Once people learned what these laws were, the scientists argued, they could improve their lives and their societies.

But the idea that people's lives were governed by laws had a deeper meaning as well. If all people were governed by the same laws, then it stood to reason that all people must be equal. This idea of the equality of all people was a fundamental step in the development of democratic ideas in Europe.

READING CHECK **Identifying Cause and Effect** How did the growth of science help lead to the growth of democratic ideas?

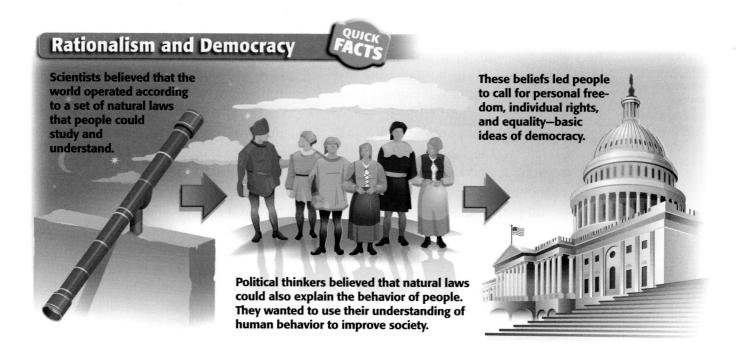

Rationalism and Democracy QUICK FACTS

Scientists believed that the world operated according to a set of natural laws that people could study and understand.

Political thinkers believed that natural laws could also explain the behavior of people. They wanted to use their understanding of human behavior to improve society.

These beliefs led people to call for personal freedom, individual rights, and equality—basic ideas of democracy.

Science and Religion

The Roman Catholic Church was a powerful force in Europe during the time of the Scientific Revolution. The birth and growth of science led to conflicts between scientists and the Church.

Reason for Conflict

FOCUS ON READING

What sentences point to a contrast between scientific and religious ideas?

There were two related parts to the conflict between science and the Church. The first was that the new science was putting forth ideas that contradicted Church teachings. For example, Copernicus's idea that the earth orbited the sun contradicted the Church teaching that the earth was at the center of the universe.

A second part of the conflict was related to the first. When people contradicted the Church's teachings, they weakened the Church. Church officials were afraid that questioning even one Church teaching might lead to more and more questions about the Church. People might even start to doubt key elements of the faith. Church officials feared this would undermine the Church's influence.

The Trial of Galileo

The conflict between science and the Church was illustrated by a trial. Galileo published a book that supported the view that the planets orbit the sun. For this, he was put on trial by the Inquisition, a Church court that investigated people who questioned Church authority.

Catholic officials insisted that Galileo publicly reject his findings and accept Catholic teachings that the earth was the center of the universe and did not move. Under threat of torture, Galileo agreed. Still, legend has it that as Galileo left his trial, he muttered, "And yet it does move."

Although he is remembered for opposing this Church teaching, Galileo was a devout Catholic. He believed that experimentation was a search for an understanding of God's creation.

The painting at left shows Galileo defending himself before Church officials. Still, Galileo and other scientists were deeply religious, like the Italian monk and mathematician above.

touches your life every day. Therefore, the Scientific Revolution ranks as one of the most influential events in history.

READING CHECK Analyzing Why were science and the Catholic Church at odds during the Scientific Revolution?

SUMMARY AND PREVIEW The scientific method became the standard method for all scientific study. New philosophies based on scientific thinking would later influence government. However, scientific teachings would sometimes conflict with religious teachings. In the next unit, you will turn your attention away from Europe and learn about the early civilizations of the Americas.

Knowledge and Belief

Many of the scientists you have been reading about held views similar to Galileo's. For the scientists of the Scientific Revolution, science and traditional religious beliefs could exist at the same time.

Nicolaus Copernicus served as a Church official. Sir Isaac Newton saw a close connection between science and religion. For example, Newton believed that all forces in nature were actions directed by God.

Bacon, too, was a religious man. He wrote that knowledge "is a rich storehouse for the glory of the Creator." Unlike Newton, Bacon stressed the separation of reason and faith. He argued that religious leaders shouldn't try to explain scientific matters. In turn, he said that scientific thinkers shouldn't try to interpret religious matters.

Despite the conflicts, science developed rapidly after the Scientific Revolution. Scientists made—and continue to make—countless discoveries. Scientific knowledge has changed human life dramatically and

go.hrw.com
Online Quiz
KEYWORD: SQ7 HP13

Section 3 Assessment

Reviewing Ideas, Terms, and People **HSS** 7.10.3

1. **a.** Define What is the **scientific method**?
   b. Explain Why did **Francis Bacon** want the king to fund scientific research?
2. **a.** Identify What type of government began to develop using ideas from the Scientific Revolution?
   b. Draw Conclusions Why did political philosophers begin to make greater use of reason in their work?
3. **a.** Recall Why did the Inquisition put Galileo on trial?
   b. Summarize What caused conflict between science and the Roman Catholic Church?

Critical Thinking

4. **Understanding Cause and Effect** Copy the diagram. Identify effects of the Scientific Revolution. Add as many arrows and circles as you need.

Scientific Revolution

FOCUS ON SPEAKING

5. **Planning Your Defense** In this section, you read about the Church's objections to Galileo's ideas. How might you argue against those objections? Look back over your notes from the previous two sections to get some ideas.

Social Studies Skills

Analyzing Tables

Understand the Skill

Like graphs, tables present numerical data. The data are usually listed side by side for easy reference and comparison. A table is especially useful for organizing several different categories of data. Since the data in each row or column are related, you can easily compare numbers and see relationships.

Learn the Skill

Follow these guidelines to read and analyze a table.

1 Read the table's title to determine its subject. All the data presented in the table will be related in some way to this subject.

2 Identify the data. Note the headings and labels of the table's columns and rows. This will tell you how the data are organized. A table may also contain notes in parentheses. These explain the units in which the data should be read.

3 Study the information. Note the numbers in each row and column. Read across rows and down columns.

4 Use critical thinking skills to compare and contrast numbers, identify cause-and-effect relationships, and note statistical trends. Form hypotheses and draw conclusions.

Practice and Apply the Skill

The table below provides information on planets in the solar system. Interpret the table to answer the following questions.

1. Which planets were unknown to Kepler, Galileo, and other scientists of the 1500s and 1600s?

2. What relationship does the table show between the length of a planet's year and its distance from the sun?

3. Why did Pluto remain undiscovered for so long?

Planets of the Solar System					
Planet	When discovered	Diameter (in miles)	Minimum distance from Earth (in millions of miles)	Distance from Sun (in millions of miles)	Length of year (in Earth years)
Mercury	ancient times	3,024	57	36	0.24
Venus	ancient times	7,504	26	67	0.62
Earth	————	7,909	————	93	1.00
Mars	ancient times	4,212	49	141	1.88
Jupiter	ancient times	88,534	390	482	11.86
Saturn	prehistoric times	74,400	792	885	29.46
Uranus	1781	32,488	1,687	1,780	84.01
Neptune	1846	31,279	2,695	2,788	164.80
Pluto	1930	1,364	3,573	3,666	247.70

Visual Summary

Use the visual summary below to help you review the main ideas of the chapter.

The roots of the Scientific Revolution included Greek and Muslim science, Renaissance humanism, and world exploration.

Scientists like Copernicus and Newton made important discoveries about the universe.

The ideas of Bacon and Descartes helped create the scientific method.

Reviewing Vocabulary, Terms, and People

Complete each sentence by filling in the blank with the correct term from the chapter.

1. In science, a logical explanation for observed facts is called a(n) _____.

2. Greek _____ used logic and reason to explain what they observed in nature.

3. The first scientist to argue that the planets orbited the sun was _____.

4. _____ put forth important theories in his book, *Principia Mathematica*.

5. The _____ is a set of steps that scientists follow.

6. One important invention of the Scientific Revolution was the _____, an instrument that measures air pressure.

7. _____ believed that nothing should be accepted as true if it wasn't proven to be true.

Comprehension and Critical Thinking

SECTION 1 *(Pages 354–357)* **HSS** 7.10.1

8. **a. Recall** When did the Scientific Revolution occur?

b. Analyze How did Muslim scholars contribute to the Scientific Revolution?

c. Evaluate Do you agree or disagree with the statement that the Scientific Revolution was the single most important event in the intellectual history of humankind? Why?

SECTION 2 *(Pages 358–363)* **HSS** 7.10.2

9. **a. Describe** What was Nicolaus Copernicus's theory about the planets and the sun?

b. Compare and Contrast How were Copernicus's and Kepler's theories about the movement of the planets similar? How were they different?

c. Elaborate Choose one invention from the Scientific Revolution and explain how it affects your life.

10. a. Describe How did the Scientific Revolution help inspire democratic ideas?

b. Analyze Why did many scientists believe science and religion could exist at the same time?

c. Elaborate What did Sir Isaac Newton mean when he wrote, "If I have seen further it is by standing on the shoulders of Giants"?

Social Studies Skills

Understanding Tables *An invention from the Scientific Revolution—the barometer—is used to record air pressure during a hurricane. Scientists measure the strength of a hurricane on a scale from 1–5, with 5 being the strongest. Study the data in the table below about Hurricane Frances in 2004. Use the table to answer the questions that follow.*

Date and Time	Wind speed (mph)	Air pressure (mb)	Category
9/1 12:00 noon	120	937	4
9/2 12:00 noon	125	939	4
9/3 12:00 noon	110	957	3
9/4 12:00 noon	90	960	2
9/5 11:00 am	80	963	1

11. What happened to the air pressure as the hurricane got weaker?

12. On what days did the air pressure of the hurricane measure 950 mb or greater?

Using the Internet

go.hrw.com
KEYWORD: SQ7 WH13

13. Activity: Researching Scientists and Their Discoveries Imagine a time when the basic understanding of the universe was yet to be revealed and statements like "The sun revolves around the earth" were considered true. Amazing discoveries were made during the Scientific Revolution. Enter the activity keyword. Then create a chart of important scientists of that time, their key discoveries or inventions, the way in which each discovery influenced society, and how information about the discoveries has evolved over the years.

Reviewing Themes

14. Science and Technology How do *you* know the earth orbits the sun? Did you gain that knowledge using methods similar to those used before or during the Scientific Revolution? Explain your answer.

15. Society and Culture How did the birth of science lead to the growth of democratic ideas?

Reading Skills

Understanding Comparison and Contrast *Read the paragraph below and answer the questions that follow.*

Two scientists who played a vital role in the Scientific Revolution were Nicolaus Copernicus and Johannes Kepler. Copernicus, who was Polish, lived from 1473 to 1543. Kepler, who was German, lived from 1571 to 1630. Both men were astronomers. Copernicus's great contribution was his theory that the planets all orbit the sun. Kepler's great contribution was his theory that the orbits of the planets are elliptical, rather than circular. Both of these theories overturned ideas that people had believed for more than 1,400 years.

16. Compare the lives of Copernicus and Kepler by identifying three similarities they had.

17. Contrast the lives of Copernicus and Kepler by identifying three differences between them.

FOCUS ON SPEAKING

18. Giving Your Speech Prepare your speech for defending your client. Begin with an introduction. Then present your main points in support of your claim, supporting your points with reasons or evidence. Try to anticipate the other side's points and address them in your speech. End your speech with a conclusion.

Write sentences describing each of your points. These notes will help you remember what you want to say in your speech. When you give your speech, be sure to make eye contact with your audience, use a pleasant tone of voice, and speak with confidence.

Standards Assessment

DIRECTIONS: Read each question, and write the letter of the best response.

1

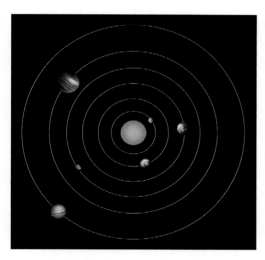

The pioneering work of which early scientist produced this understanding of the solar system?

A Francis Bacon

B Nicolaus Copernicus

C Antoni van Leeuwenhoek

D Isaac Newton

2 The fundamental principles of the modern scientific method are

A logic and mathematical theories.

B common beliefs of science and religion.

C very detailed record keeping.

D observation and experimentation.

3 The basis of the Scientific Revolution of the 1500s and 1600s is found *mainly* in the

A writings of early Catholic popes and monks.

B inventions of the ancient Chinese.

C sponsorship of scientists by powerful European kings.

D work of ancient Greeks and Muslim scholars.

4 Sir Isaac Newton is one of the most important participants in the Scientific Revolution because of his

A observation that objects in the universe follow orderly laws.

B first use of the telescope to study the solar system and the universe.

C application of the scientific method to learn about the organs of the human body.

D invention of the microscope and use of it to discover the existence of bacteria.

5 The two Europeans generally credited with developing the modern scientific method are

A Galileo Galilei and Sir Isaac Newton.

B Sir Isaac Newton and Francis Bacon.

C Francis Bacon and René Descartes.

D René Descartes and Sir Isaac Newton.

Connecting with Past Learnings

6 In Grade 6 you learned about the interest that many ancient civilizations had in astronomy. Which European scientist would have been *least* interested in the ancients' work?

A Tycho Brahe

B Galileo Galilei

C Antoni van Leeuwenhoek

D Johannes Kepler

7 The event you learned about earlier in this course that was *most* responsible for the Scientific Revolution was

A the Renaissance.

B the fall of Rome.

C the development of feudalism.

D the Crusades.

Assignment

Collect information and write an informative report on a topic related to the Renaissance or to the Reformation. Use one of these topics, or choose your own topic:

- The importance of Florence to the Renaissance
- Martin Luther's contributions to the Reformation

TIP **Choosing a Point of View** Your audience should find your report informative and believable. One part of being believable is writing your report from the third-person point of view. That means you never bring yourself or your own opinions into the report. Watch for the pronouns *I*, *me*, and *we*. If you are using those words, you are bringing your own opinion into the report.

ELA **Writing 7.2.3** Write research reports.

A Social Studies Report

You play many roles when you write a research report. As a detective, you track down information about a subject. As a judge, you determine what information is credible. As a reporter, you write clearly about what you have learned. In the process, you can reach a deeper understanding of history.

1. Prewrite

Choosing a Topic

Here are two keys to choosing a good topic for research:

- You find the topic interesting.
- You can find several sources of information on it.

A good topic is broad enough that you can find information, but narrow enough to cover in detail. You can narrow a topic by looking at a small part of it and breaking that part into even smaller parts.

Renaissance → Renaissance Artists → Leonardo's Achievements

Developing a Research Question

Starting with a question helps focus your research. For example, here is a question on the topic "The Achievements of Leonardo da Vinci": *How did Leonardo's achievements reflect the ideas of the Renaissance?* The answer to your question becomes your thesis, or big idea.

Finding Historical Information

Look for answers to your research question in at least three sources of historical information besides your textbook. For each source, write down the kinds of information shown below. To help with taking notes, put a circled number next to each source.

① **Encyclopedia article:** "Article Title." <u>Name of Encyclopedia</u>. Edition or year published.

③ **Magazine or newspaper article:** "Title of Article." <u>Publication name</u>. Date: page number(s).

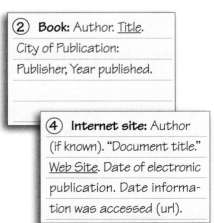

② **Book:** Author. <u>Title</u>. City of Publication: Publisher, Year published.

④ **Internet site:** Author (if known). "Document title." <u>Web Site</u>. Date of electronic publication. Date information was accessed (url).

Taking Notes

As you read your sources, carefully write down facts, details, and quotations related to your research question. Take these types of notes:

Paraphrases The source's ideas in your own words
Summaries The source's main points in your own words
Direct quotations The source's exact words inside quotation marks

Next to each note, write the number of the source and the number of the page that contains the information.

Organizing Your Ideas and Information

How can you organize your research information? Here are two good ways:

- Chronological order (the order that events occurred)
- Order of importance (usually least to most important)

Use one of these orders to organize your notes in an outline. Here is a partial outline of the main body of a paper about Leonardo da Vinci.

> Big Idea: Because of his many talents and interests, Leonardo da Vinci embodied the sprit of the Renaissance.
>
>   I. Leonardo's artistic talents
>   A. Painting
>   B. Sculpture
>   C. Architecture
>   II. Leonardo's other talents
>   A. Inventor
>   B. Engineer
>   C. Town planner
>   III. Leonardo's interest in learning
>   A. Nature
>   B. Technology

TIP **Checking Other Sources** Get a more complete picture of your subject by consulting sources with different opinions. For example, reading both praise and criticism of the Medicis will give you a more balanced view of the family.

2. Write

Here is a framework that can help you as you write a first draft.

A Writer's Framework

Introduction
- Start with a quote or an interesting historical fact.
- State your report's big idea.
- Provide historical background readers need to understand your big idea.

Body
- Present information about at least three sub-points of your big idea.
- Write at least one paragraph for each of these main (or sub-) points.
- Include supporting details, facts, or examples in each paragraph.

Conclusion
- Summarize your main points.
- Restate your big idea in slightly different words.
- You might comment on how the information in your report relates to other historical events.

Studying a Model

Here is a model of a research report. Study it to see how one student developed a paper. The first and last paragraphs are shown in full. The paragraphs in the body of the paper are summarized.

INTRODUCTORY PARAGRAPH

Attention grabber

Statement of Thesis or Big Idea

He may have been the greatest painter of the Renaissance. He was also its greatest sculptor and its greatest architect. In addition, he was a notable inventor, engineer, town planner, and mapmaker. In his spare time, he filled his sketchbook with detailed drawings of plants, animals, and machines. His name was Leonardo da Vinci. Many experts consider him to be the greatest genius in history. With his extraordinary talent and wide-ranging interests, Leonardo da Vinci embodied the spirit of the Renaissance.

Body Paragraphs

In the first paragraph of the body of the research report, the student briefly describes a painting, a sculpture, and a building designed by Leonardo. For each example, the student cites expert opinions about the work's merit.

In the next paragraph, the student discusses Leonardo's non-artistic talents—his inventions and his work as an engineer and town planner. As in the previous paragraph, the student cites expert opinions.

In the last paragraph of the body, the student gives examples of Leonardo's interest in nature and technology. The student also discusses Leonardo's notebooks and quotes expert opinions about the work.

CONCLUDING PARAGRAPH

Summary of Main Points

Statement of Big Idea

General Comment about the Topic

Artist, sculptor, architect, engineer, and observer of nature— Leonardo displayed his genius in a wide variety of fields. A Renaissance person is someone who can do almost anything well. Since Leonardo da Vinci was a genius at almost everything, he embodied the spirit of the Renaissance. He was the ultimate Renaissance person.

Notice that each paragraph uses the same organizational pattern as the entire paper. Each paragraph expresses a main idea, then provides information to support that idea. One difference is that only the last paragraph ends with a concluding statement.

3. Evaluate and Revise

Evaluating and Revising Your Draft

Carefully read your first draft. Ask the questions below to decide which parts of your first draft should be revised.

Evaluating and Revising an Informative Report

- Does the introduction begin with an interesting quotation or fact?
- Does your introduction include a clear statement of your big idea?
- Does your introduction give any needed background information?
- Is the report clearly organized in either chronological order or order of importance?
- Does the body of your report have at least three paragraphs, each developing one point under your big idea?

- Are all facts, details, and examples accurate? Are they clearly related to the ideas they support?
- Does the conclusion summarize the main points?
- Does the conclusion restate the big idea in different words?
- Have you included a list of at least three sources you used?

TIP **Evaluating Sources** Not all sources of information are equal. Some are not reliable or trustworthy.

You have to be especially careful about Internet sources since anyone can create an Internet site. For example, do not use a Web page created by a 10-year-old to find information about Leonardo's art. Look for a reliable source—an art historian or an art museum.

4. Proofread and Publish

Proofreading

After revising your report, read it carefully before sharing it. Look especially for these things.

- Proper spelling and capitalization of names for people, places, things, and events.
- Correct punctuation marks around direct quotations.

Publishing

Choose one or more of these ideas to publish your report.

- Turn your report into an informative speech and share it with classmates.
- Make a display that includes your report and helpful illustrations. Place it in a hallway display case or the library.
- Submit your report to an online discussion group that focuses on the Renaissance or the Reformation. Ask for feedback.

TIP **Identifying Sources**
If your teacher asks you to show your sources in the body of your paper, you can use **parenthetical citations**. Enclose the author's last name (or if no author is given, the first major word of the source title) followed by the page number.

Example
Between 1485 and 1490, Leonardo da Vinci created plans for advanced weapons and submarines (Renaissance 1).

Practice and Apply

Use the steps and strategies outlined in this workshop to research and write a research report on the Renaissance or the Reformation.

Civilization in the Americas

In the Americas, civilizations developed after people learned to grow crops like maize, or corn, and potatoes. Having a steady food supply allowed Native Americans to build large, complex societies.

Three major civilizations developed in the Americas. They were the Maya, Aztec, and Inca civilizations. Each civilization developed farming and trade networks and built large cities and temples.

In the next two chapters, you will learn where the civilizations of the Americas developed and what they were like.

Explore the Art

In this scene, Aztec teenagers attend a special school to learn about the Aztec way of life. What does this scene indicate about education in the Aztec Empire?

The Early Americas

 California Standards

History–Social Science

7.7 Students compare and contrast the geographic, political, economic, religious, and social structures of the Meso-American and Andean civilizations.

Analysis Skill

HR 3 Distinguish relevant from irrelevant, essential from incidental, and verifiable from unverifiable information.

English–Language Arts

Writing 7.1.2 Support all statements and claims with anecdotes, descriptions, facts and statistics, and specific examples.

Reading 7.2.6 Assess the adequacy, accuracy, and appropriateness of the author's evidence.

 FOCUS ON WRITING

A Travel Brochure Each year, millions of people visit the places you'll read about in this chapter. Try your hand at writing part of a brochure for a historical tour of the early Americas. As you read, you'll discover spots you won't want to miss.

CHAPTER EVENTS

c. 12,000–10,000 BC The first people arrive in the Americas.

12,000 BC

WORLD EVENTS

c. 5000 BC Irrigation is used in Mesopotamia and Egypt.

HOLT
History's Impact
▶ **video series**
Watch the video to understand the impact of Mayan achievements on math and astronomy.

What You Will Learn...

In this chapter you will learn about the development of civilization in the Americas. This photo shows the ruins of a great Maya temple in Tikal, Guatemala. More than 1,500 years ago the Maya built large cities in their American homeland.

c. 3500 BC
Maize is domesticated in Mesoamerica.

c. 1200 BC
The Olmec civilization begins in Mesoamerica.

c. AD 200
The Maya begin building large cities in the Americas.

c. AD 900
The Maya Classic Age ends.

| 3000 BC | 2000 BC | 1000 BC | BC 1 AD | AD 1000 |

c. 3000 BC
Egyptians begin to write using hieroglyphics.

c. 500 BC
Athens develops the world's first democracy.

AD 476
The Roman Empire falls.

Reading Social Studies

by Kylene Beers

Economics	Geography	Politics	Religion	Society and Culture	Science and Technology

Focus on Themes In this chapter, you will read about the development of civilizations in Mesoamerica, which is in the southern part of North America, and in the Andes, which is in South America. As you read about the Olmec and Maya in Mesoamerica and Chavín in South America, you will see how the **geography** of the areas affected their way of life. You will learn that these ancient civilizations made interesting advancements in **science and technology**.

Analyzing Historical Information

Focus on Reading History books are full of information. As you read, you are confronted with names, dates, places, terms, and descriptions on every page. Because you're faced with so much information, you don't want to have to deal with unimportant or untrue material in a history book.

Identifying Relevant and Essential Information Information in a history book should be relevant, or related to the topic you're studying. It should also be essential, or necessary, to understanding that topic. Anything that is not relevant or essential distracts from the important material you are studying.

The passage below comes from an encyclopedia, but some irrelevant and nonessential information has been added so that you can learn to identify it.

The Maya

The first sentence of the paragraph expresses the main idea. Anything that doesn't support this idea is nonessential.

This paragraph discusses Maya communication. Any other topics are irrelevant.

Who They Were Maya were an American Indian people who developed a magnificent civilization in Mesoamerica, which is the southern part of North America. They built their largest cities between AD 250 and 900. Today, many people travel to Central America to see Maya ruins.

Communication The Maya developed an advanced form of writing that used many symbols. Our writing system uses 26 letters. They recorded information on large stone monuments. Some early civilizations drew pictures on cave walls. The Maya also made books of paper made from the fig tree bark. Fig trees need a lot of light.

The last sentence does not support the main idea and is nonessential.

The needs of fig trees have nothing to do with Maya communication. This sentence is irrelevant.

Portions of this text and the one on the next page were taken from the 2004 World Book Online Reference Center.

Additional reading support can be found in the

Inter active

Reader and Study Guide

HSS Analysis **HR 3** Distinguish relevant from irrelevant information.
ELA **7.2.6** Assess the adequacy, accuracy, and appropriateness of the author's evidence.

You Try It!

The following passage has some sentences that aren't important, necessary, or relevant. Read the passage and identify those sentences.

The Maya Way of Life

Religion The Maya believed in many gods and goddesses. More than 160 gods and goddesses are named in a single Maya manuscript. Among the gods they worshipped were a corn god, a rain god, a sun god, and a moon goddess. The early Greeks also worshipped many gods and goddesses.

Family and Social Structure Whole families of Maya—including parents, children, and grandparents—lived together. Not many houses today could hold all those people. Each family member had tasks to do. Men and boys, for example, worked in the fields. Very few people are farmers today. Women and older girls made clothes and meals for the rest of the family. Now most people buy their clothes.

After you read the passage, answer the following questions.

1. Which sentence in the first paragraph is irrelevant to the topic? How can you tell?

2. Which three sentences in the second paragraph are not essential to learning about the Maya? Do those sentences belong in this passage?

Key Terms and People

Chapter 14

Section 1
Mesoamerica *(p. 384)*
maize *(p. 387)*

Section 2
obsidian *(p. 390)*
Pacal *(p. 392)*

Section 3
observatories *(p. 398)*
Popol Vuh *(p. 399)*

Academic Vocabulary
Success in school is related to knowing academic vocabulary—the words that are frequently used in school assignments and discussions. In this chapter, you will learn the following academic words:

rebel *(p. 394)*
aspects *(p. 397)*

As you read **Chapter 14**, notice how the writers have left out information that is not essential or relevant to what you are reading.

Geography and Early Cultures

What You Will Learn...

Main Ideas

1. The geography of the Americas is varied with a wide range of landforms.
2. The first people to arrive in the Americas were hunter-gatherers.
3. The development of farming led to early settlements in the Americas.

The Big Idea

The landforms and climate of the Americas affected farming and the development of early cultures.

Key Terms

Mesoamerica, *p. 384*
maize, *p. 387*

HSS 7.7.1 Study the locations, landforms, and climates of Mexico, Central America, and South America and their effects on Mayan, Aztec, and Incan economies, trade, and development of urban societies.

If **YOU** were there...

You are a hunter-gatherer in North America. All of your life you have been moving south, following herds of animals. This year you have found a place where the climate is warmer and there are more kinds of plants to eat. Some people say this would be a good place to stay and make a permanent home. But others think you need to keep moving.

Do you think your people should keep going or settle down in this new place? Why?

BUILDING BACKGROUND The first people to arrive in the Americas were hunter-gatherers. Their ability to find food greatly depended on the geography of this new land.

Geography of the Americas

Two continents—North America and South America—make up the region we call the Americas. These two continents have a wide range of landforms and climates.

The northern continent, North America, has high mountains, desert plateaus, grassy plains, and forests. Look at the map to find the location of some of these physical features. In the northern part of the continent, the climate is cold and icy. Temperatures get warmer toward the south.

In the southern part of North America lies Mesoamerica. **Mesoamerica** is a region that includes the southern part of what is now Mexico and parts of the northern countries of Central America. Steamy rain forests cover some of this region. In some places, volcanoes rise above the forest. Their activity over the years has made the surrounding soil very fertile. Fertile mountain valleys, rivers, and a warm climate make Mesoamerica good for farming. In fact, the first farmers in the Americas domesticated plants in Mesoamerica.

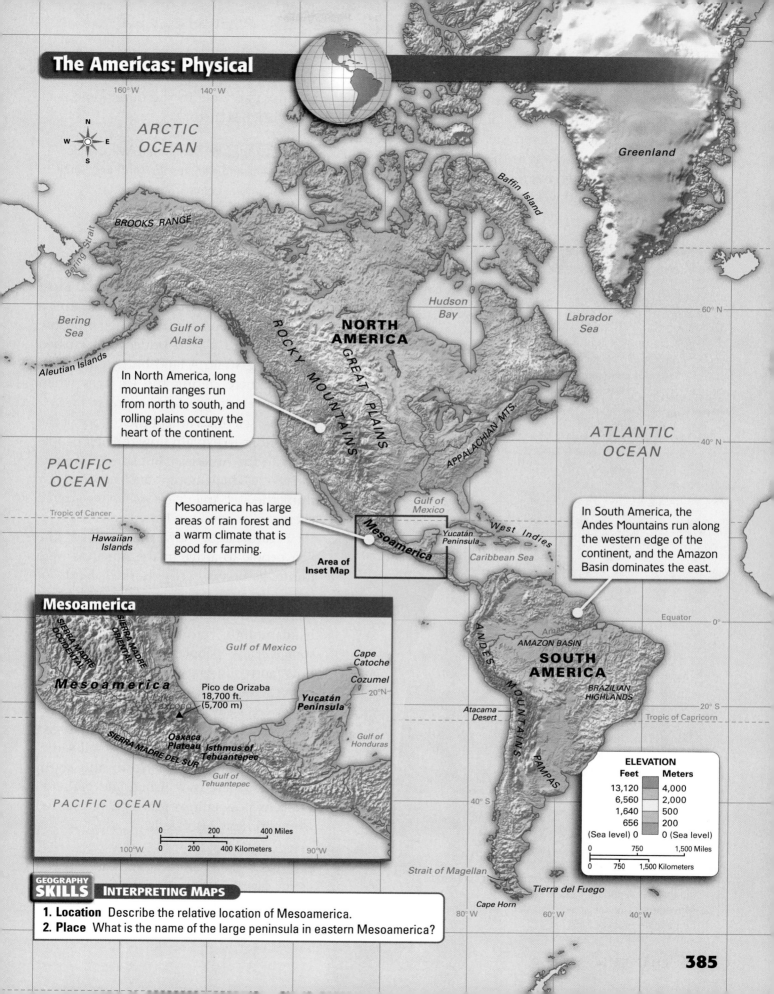

The Americas: Physical

ARCTIC OCEAN

160° W
140° W

Greenland

Baffin Island

BROOKS RANGE

Bering Strait

Bering Sea

Gulf of Alaska

Aleutian Islands

PACIFIC OCEAN

Tropic of Cancer

Hawaiian Islands

ROCKY MOUNTAINS

NORTH AMERICA

GREAT PLAINS

Hudson Bay

Labrador Sea

60° N

APPALACHIAN MTS.

Mississippi

40° N

ATLANTIC OCEAN

In North America, long mountain ranges run from north to south, and rolling plains occupy the heart of the continent.

Mesoamerica has large areas of rain forest and a warm climate that is good for farming.

Gulf of Mexico

Mesoamerica

Yucatán Peninsula

West Indies

Caribbean Sea

Area of Inset Map

In South America, the Andes Mountains run along the western edge of the continent, and the Amazon Basin dominates the east.

Equator 0°

Amazon

AMAZON BASIN

SOUTH AMERICA

BRAZILIAN HIGHLANDS

20° S

Tropic of Capricorn

Atacama Desert

ANDES MOUNTAINS

PAMPAS

40° S

Mesoamerica

SIERRA MADRE OCCIDENTAL

SIERRA MADRE ORIENTAL

Gulf of Mexico

Cape Catoche

Cozumel

Mesoamerica

Pico de Orizaba 18,700 ft. (5,700 m)

Lake Texcoco

Yucatán Peninsula

20°N

SIERRA MADRE DEL SUR

Oaxaca Plateau

Isthmus of Tehuantepec

Gulf of Honduras

Gulf of Tehuantepec

PACIFIC OCEAN

0   200   400 Miles
0   200   400 Kilometers

100°W

90°W

ELEVATION

Feet	Meters
13,120	4,000
6,560	2,000
1,640	500
656	200
(Sea level) 0	0 (Sea level)

0   750   1,500 Miles
0   750   1,500 Kilometers

40° S

Strait of Magellan

Tierra del Fuego

Cape Horn

80° W
60° W
40° W

GEOGRAPHY SKILLS INTERPRETING MAPS

1. **Location** Describe the relative location of Mesoamerica.
2. **Place** What is the name of the large peninsula in eastern Mesoamerica?

Like North America, South America has many different kinds of landforms. The towering Andes Mountains run along the western shore of the continent. There, a narrow desert sits on the edge of rich fishing waters in the Pacific Ocean. East of the Andes lies the Amazon region—a huge, hot, and wet rain forest. The mighty Amazon River drains this region. As you will see, the geography of the Americas played an important role in the development of early societies there.

READING CHECK **Comparing** What kinds of landforms and climates do North and South America have in common?

The First People Arrive

No one is sure how the first people got to the Americas or when they arrived. Most historians think they came to North America from Asia by 12,000 BC. They probably walked across a land bridge that crossed the Bering Strait. A land bridge may have formed there during the ice ages when ocean levels dropped and exposed land.

Most scientists accept the theory of the land bridge to explain how the first people came to the Americas. But some scientists today are challenging that theory. They think the first Americans may have arrived even earlier—perhaps by sea.

Regardless of how they arrived, the first people to arrive in the Americas were hunter-gatherers. They hunted herds of large animals that wandered the land. These animals, including bison and huge woolly mammoths, provided their main food source. Early people also gathered fruits, nuts, and wild grains to eat. Early people didn't settle in one place very long, because they were always looking for food.

Eventually, some early people began to settle down. They formed small settlements on the coasts of North and South America, where they fished and gathered food. As populations grew, people started to experiment with seeds.

READING CHECK **Drawing Inferences** How do you think the geography of the Americas affected early peoples' search for food?

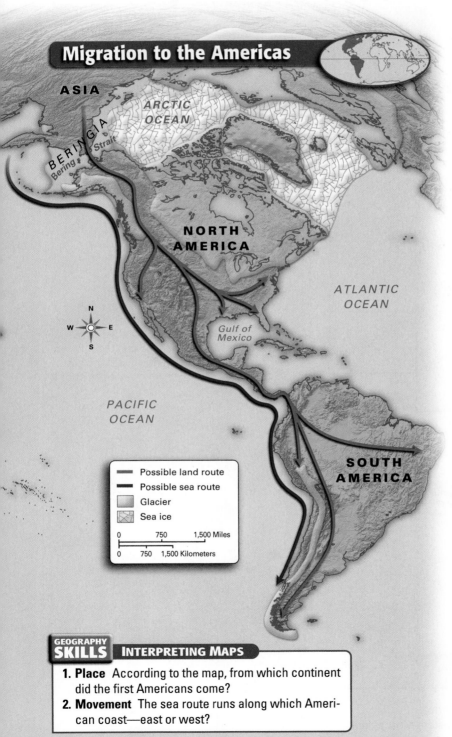

Migration to the Americas

ASIA

ARCTIC OCEAN

BERINGIA
Bering Strait

NORTH AMERICA

ATLANTIC OCEAN

Gulf of Mexico

PACIFIC OCEAN

SOUTH AMERICA

N
W E
S

— Possible land route
— Possible sea route
☐ Glacier
▨ Sea ice

0   750   1,500 Miles
0   750   1,500 Kilometers

GEOGRAPHY SKILLS **INTERPRETING MAPS**

1. **Place** According to the map, from which continent did the first Americans come?
2. **Movement** The sea route runs along which American coast—east or west?

Farming and Settlement

From their experiments with seeds, people eventually learned to farm. Farming allowed people to stop following animal herds and settle permanently in one place.

First Farming Settlements

The first permanent farming settlements in the Americas appeared in Mesoamerica. This region had rich soils, warm temperatures, and plenty of rain. By 3500 BC people in Mesoamerica were growing **maize** (MAYZ), or corn. Later they learned to grow beans and squash. By growing these foods, settlements could support larger populations. More advanced societies grew, and people began to focus on activities such as building, trade, art, and organized religion. Eventually, settlements developed into towns and cities.

The Olmec

The Olmec (OHL-mek) formed the first urban civilization in Mesoamerica around 1200 BC. Most Olmec lived in small villages, but some lived in larger towns. These towns were religious and government centers with temples and plazas. Impressive sculptures and buildings mark the Olmec as the first complex civilization in the Americas. They built the first pyramids in the Americas. They also made sculptures of huge stone heads. Each head probably represented a different Olmec ruler. Other sculptures, such as jaguars, probably represented Olmec gods.

Other factors that may mark the Olmec as a complex civilization are writing and scientific study. Some researchers think the Olmec may have developed the first writing system in the Americas. Scientists recently found an Olmec artifact with symbols that might be an early form of writing. The Olmec may have also had a calendar.

Maize

A man sits on a stack of maize, or corn, in Mexico City. In the early Americas, maize was widely grown and supported large urban populations.

Why was the growing of maize important to urban growth?

The Olmec civilization also had a large trading network. Villages traded with each other and with other peoples farther away. The Olmec may have even established a string of trading colonies along the Pacific coast. Through trade the Olmec got valuable goods such as the stones they used for building and sculpture.

Olmec civilization ended around 400 BC. By then trade had spread Olmec influence around Mesoamerica. Later peoples were able to build on their achievements. Some later peoples in Mesoamerica also followed some Olmec traditions.

Primary Source

POINTS OF VIEW
Views of Writing

Scientists have discovered an Olmec roller used for printing symbols. It may be evidence of the earliest writing system in the Americas. Some people don't believe the Olmec had a written language. Scientists disagree on what defines a written language. Some scientists think written language must include symbols that stand for sounds—not just for images.

❝Even if you have symbols—like a light bulb in a cartoon—that's not writing.❞

—David Grove,
Professor Emeritus of Anthropology,
University of Illinois Urbana–Champaign

Other scientists think a system of symbols is a form of written communication. The symbols do not have to represent sound or spoken language. These scientists think written communication is the same thing as written language.

❝We're not arguing that we have phonetics (sounds). But we say we do have logographs (symbols representing words), and we're arguing the Maya copied this. We have a system here that goes back to the Olmec.❞

—Mary E. D. Pohl,
Professor of Anthropology, Florida State University

ANALYSIS SKILL | **ANALYZING POINTS OF VIEW**
Why might it be hard to define written language?

Farming and the Growth of Other Civilizations

Early civilizations also developed in other parts of the Americas. As in Mesoamerica, people in North and South America formed civilizations after they domesticated plants and learned how to farm.

About the time Mesoamericans started growing maize, South Americans in the Andes started growing potatoes. Later, maize farming spread south into the Andes from Mesoamerica. By about 2000 BC, South Americans were growing maize and beans as well as potatoes.

A number of small civilizations developed in South America, but the first major civilization began in the Andes. It is known as the Chavín (chah-VEEN) culture, and it lasted from about 900 to 200 BC. Its city was a major religious and trading center. The Chavín culture is known for its woven textiles, carved stone monuments, and pottery shaped like animals and humans.

Several hundred years after farming began in South America, maize farming also spread north from Mesoamerica. People began growing maize in what is now the southwestern United States. The dry climate made farming difficult there, so people learned to choose fertile soils and use river water to irrigate their crops. Eventually maize became an important crop to people in the region. It was the main food of people in hundreds of small villages.

FOCUS ON READING
What is the purpose of this paragraph? Are any sentences irrelevant?

This Native American legend reveals the importance of maize, or corn:

"The breaths of the corn maidens blew rain-clouds from their homes in the Summer-land, and when the rains had passed away green corn plants grew everywhere the grains had been planted."

—Zuni legend, quoted in *Kingdoms of Gold, Kingdoms of Jade* by Brian Fagan

The development of farming was important in the growth of civilizations all over the Americas. As with other peoples you have studied, a steady food supply led to population growth. Farming also encouraged people to establish permanent villages and cities.

READING CHECK Finding Main Ideas How did farming influence settlement patterns in the Americas?

SUMMARY AND PREVIEW You have learned that geography affected settlement and farming in the Americas. Early civilizations, such as the Olmec and Chavín, developed there. In Section 2 you will learn about a later civilization influenced by the Olmec—the Maya.

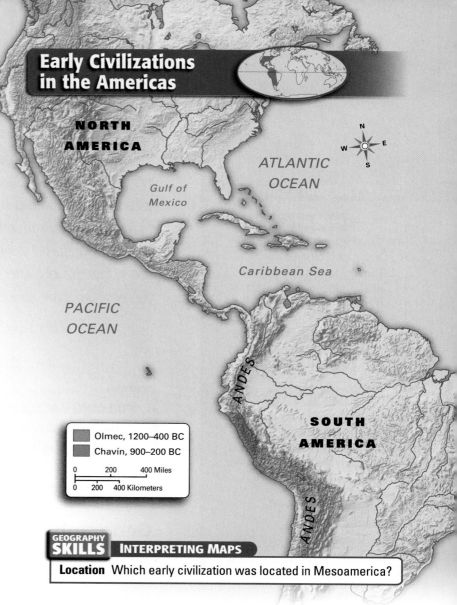

Early Civilizations in the Americas

NORTH AMERICA
ATLANTIC OCEAN
Gulf of Mexico
Caribbean Sea
PACIFIC OCEAN
ANDES
SOUTH AMERICA
ANDES

Olmec, 1200–400 BC
Chavín, 900–200 BC

0   200   400 Miles
0   200   400 Kilometers

GEOGRAPHY SKILLS INTERPRETING MAPS

Location Which early civilization was located in Mesoamerica?

Section 1 Assessment

go.hrw.com
Online Quiz
KEYWORD: SQ7 HP14

Reviewing Ideas, Terms, and People HSS 7.7.1

1. **a. Recall** Where is **Mesoamerica**?
   b. Explain In what ways is the geography of Mesoamerica good for agriculture?
2. **a. Identify** What landform do most scientists think the first people crossed to reach America?
   b. Make Inferences Why do you think scientists aren't sure how the first people came to the Americas?
3. **a. Identify** What was the first crop domesticated in Mesoamerica?
   b. Predict How might the Olmec civilization have influenced later civilizations in Mesoamerica?

Critical Thinking

4. **Sequencing** Draw the graphic organizer below. Use it to show how the development of maize farming laid the foundation for cultural advances.

   Maize Farming → ☐ → ☐ → ☐

FOCUS ON WRITING

5. **Taking Notes about Early Settlements in the Americas** Note where people first settled in the Americas. What sites would show how early hunter-gatherers and farmers lived? What geographical features are important to mention?

The Maya

What You Will Learn...

Main Ideas

1. Geography affected early Maya civilization.
2. The Maya Classic Age was characterized by great cities, trade, and warfare.
3. Maya civilization declined, and historians have several theories as to why.

The Big Idea

Maya civilization was characterized by great cities, trade, and warfare, but it disappeared for reasons that are still unclear.

Key Terms and People

obsidian, *p. 390*
Pacal, *p. 392*

HSS 7.7.1 Study the locations, landforms, and climates of Mexico, Central America, and South America and their effects on Mayan, Aztec, and Incan economies, trade, and development of urban societies.

7.7.3 Explain how and where each empire arose and how the Aztec and Incan empires were defeated by the Spanish.

If **YOU** were there...

You live in a village in the lowlands of Mesoamerica. Your family members have always been weavers, and now your aunts are teaching you to weave cloth from the cotton grown by nearby farmers. Traders from other areas often pass through your village. They tell wonderful stories about strange animals and sights they see in their travels. After talking to the traders who buy your cloth, you begin to think about becoming a trader, too.

Why might you want to become a trader?

BUILDING BACKGROUND Through trade, people get resources unavailable in their own natural environment. The natural environment, or geography, of Mesoamerica affected how a people called the Maya lived.

Geography Affects Early Maya

The Maya (MY-uh) civilization developed in Mesoamerica. Early Maya lived in the lowlands of this region beginning around 1000 BC. Thick forests covered most of the land, so the Maya had to clear wooded areas for farmland. Like earlier Mesoamericans, the Maya grew maize and other crops.

Although the thick forests made farming hard, they provided valuable resources. Forest animals such as deer and monkeys were a source of food. In addition, trees and other plants made good building materials. For example, the Maya used wood poles and vines, along with mud, to build their houses.

The early Maya lived in small villages. Eventually these villages started trading with one another. They traded goods such as cloth and **obsidian**, a sharp, glasslike volcanic rock, that came from different parts of Mesoamerica. As trade helped support larger populations, villages grew. By about AD 200 the Maya were building large cities in the Americas.

READING CHECK Finding Main Ideas What were two ways in which the early Maya relied on their physical environment?

Maya Classic Age

The Maya civilization reached its height between about AD 250 and 900. Historians call this period of Maya history the Classic Age. During the Classic Age, Maya civilization spread to the Yucatán Peninsula and grew to include more than 40 cities of 5,000 to 50,000 people each.

Trade

Maya cities in the highlands traded with those in the lowlands. In this way people all over Maya territory got things that they didn't have nearby.

Look at the trade routes on the map to see the goods that were available in different areas of Mesoamerica. For example, the warm lowlands were good for growing cotton, rubber trees, and cacao (kuh-KOW) beans, the source of chocolate. Cacao beans had great value. Chocolate was known as the food of rulers and of the gods. The Maya even used cacao beans as money.

Lowland crops didn't grow well in the cool highlands. Instead, the highlands had valuable stones such as jade and obsidian. People carried these and other products along Maya trade routes.

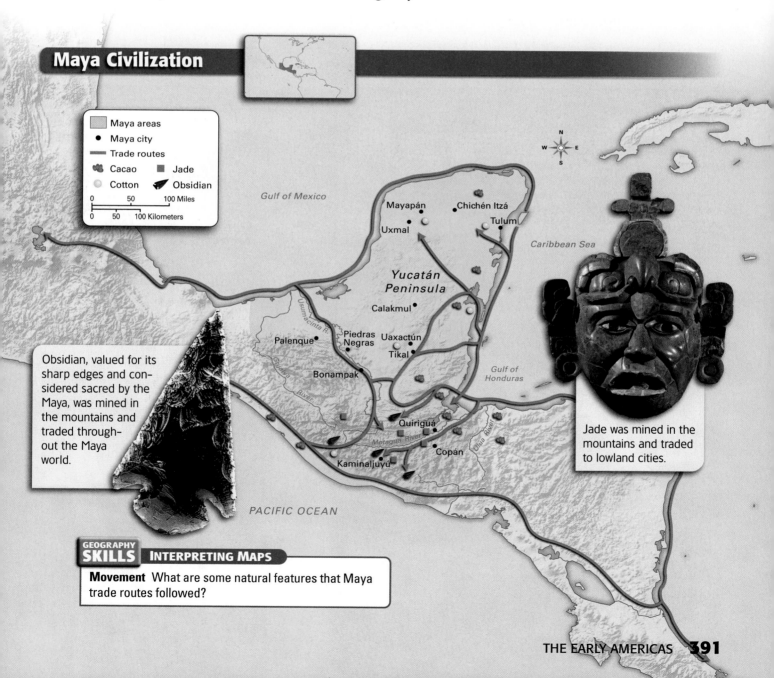

Maya Civilization

Legend:
- Maya areas
- ● Maya city
- ▬ Trade routes
- Cacao
- ■ Jade
- Cotton
- Obsidian

0   50   100 Miles
0   50   100 Kilometers

Gulf of Mexico

Mayapán · Chichén Itzá
Uxmal · Tulum

Caribbean Sea

Yucatán Peninsula

Calakmul

Usumacinta R.

Palenque · Piedras Negras · Uaxactún
Tikal

Gulf of Honduras

Bonampak

Quiriguá
Metagua River · Copán
Ulúa River

Kaminaljuyú

PACIFIC OCEAN

Obsidian, valued for its sharp edges and considered sacred by the Maya, was mined in the mountains and traded throughout the Maya world.

Jade was mined in the mountains and traded to lowland cities.

GEOGRAPHY SKILLS | **INTERPRETING MAPS**

Movement What are some natural features that Maya trade routes followed?

Cities

Maya cities had many grand buildings, including large stone pyramids, temples, and palaces. Some of these buildings honored local Maya kings. For example, in the city of Palenque (pah-LENG-kay), a temple honored the king **Pacal** (puh-KAHL). Pacal had the temple built to record his achievements as a ruler. Maya artists decorated temples and palaces with carvings and colorful paintings.

In addition to temples and palaces, the Maya also built structures to improve life in their cities. For example, builders paved large plazas for public gatherings, and they built canals to control the flow of water through their cities. Farmers shaped nearby hillsides into flat terraces so they could grow crops on them.

Most Maya cities also had a special ball court. People played or watched a type of ball game in these large stone arenas. Using only their heads, shoulders, or hips, players tried to bounce a heavy, hard rubber ball through a stone ring above their heads. Players weren't allowed to use their hands or feet. The winners were awarded jewels and clothing. The losers were sometimes killed. This ball game was one that the Maya had picked up from Olmec traditions.

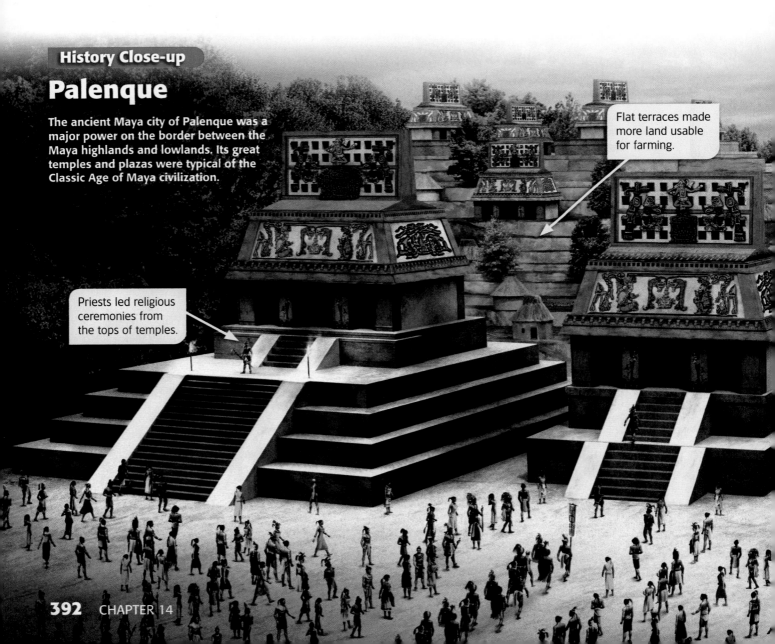

History Close-up

Palenque

The ancient Maya city of Palenque was a major power on the border between the Maya highlands and lowlands. Its great temples and plazas were typical of the Classic Age of Maya civilization.

Flat terraces made more land usable for farming.

Priests led religious ceremonies from the tops of temples.

The Maya cities were really city-states. Each had its own government and its own king. No single ruler united the many cities into one empire.

Warfare

Conflicts between cities often led to fighting. Maya cities usually battled each other to gain power and land. For example, the city of Tikal (tee-KAHL) fought many battles with its rival Calakmul (kah-lahk-MOOL). Both cities wanted to control a smaller city that lay between them. Power shifted back and forth between the two larger cities for years.

Maya warfare was bloody. Warriors fought hand-to-hand using spears, flint knives, and wooden clubs. The Maya often captured enemy prisoners and killed them in religious ceremonies as a sacrifice to their gods. They burned enemy towns and villages. Warfare probably tore up the land and destroyed crops. Maya warfare was so destructive that some scholars think it may have contributed to the end of the Maya civilization.

READING CHECK **Summarizing** What were two ways Maya cities interacted with each other?

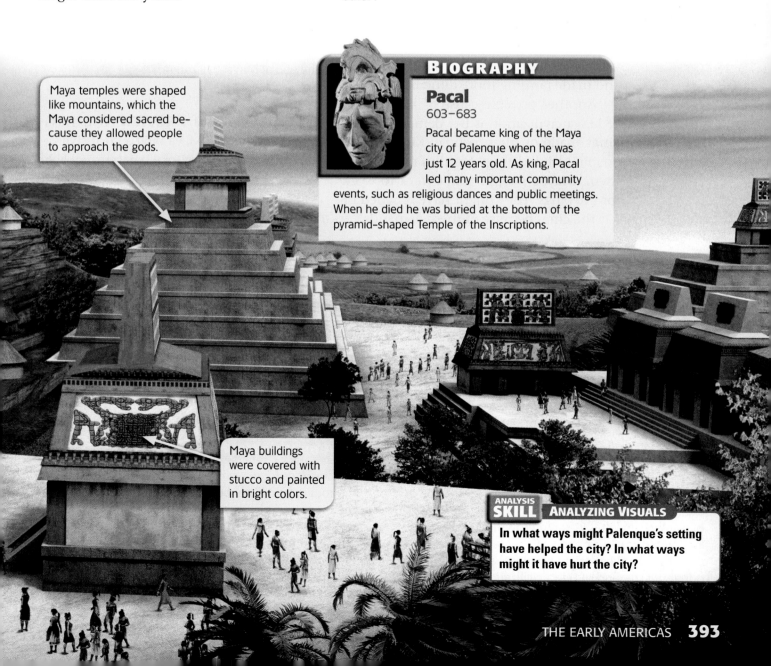

Maya temples were shaped like mountains, which the Maya considered sacred because they allowed people to approach the gods.

BIOGRAPHY

Pacal
603–683

Pacal became king of the Maya city of Palenque when he was just 12 years old. As king, Pacal led many important community events, such as religious dances and public meetings. When he died he was buried at the bottom of the pyramid-shaped Temple of the Inscriptions.

Maya buildings were covered with stucco and painted in bright colors.

ANALYSIS SKILL **ANALYZING VISUALS**

In what ways might Palenque's setting have helped the city? In what ways might it have hurt the city?

Maya Civilization Declines

THE IMPACT TODAY

Many Maya still live in villages throughout Meso-america. Others have moved to big cities.

Maya civilization began to collapse in the 900s. People stopped building temples and other structures. They left the cities and moved back to the countryside. What caused this collapse? Historians aren't sure, but they do have some theories.

One theory says that increased warfare brought about the end of the Maya Classic Age. A related theory is that, as cities grew, perhaps the Maya could not grow enough food to feed everyone. Growing the same crops year after year might have left the soil too weak for farming. As a result, competition between cities for land may have increased. This competition could have led to even more warfare than before. Increased warfare would have destroyed more crops and made farming more difficult.

Another possible cause of the decline of Maya civilization is the demands Maya kings made on their people. Kings forced people to build huge temples or farm for them. Maybe people didn't want to work for the kings. They might have **rebelled** or left the cities because of these demands.

ACADEMIC VOCABULARY

rebel to fight against authority

Some historians also think climate might have played a role in the collapse of Maya civilization. Scientists have learned that the region suffered from a long dry period and droughts for about 150 years. This dry period took place about the time the Maya moved away from their cities. A drier climate and droughts would have made it hard to grow enough food to feed everyone in the cities.

Most researchers agree that there was probably no single event that caused the end of the Classic Age. More likely, a mix of several factors led to the decline of the Maya civilization.

READING CHECK **Drawing Inferences** Why do you think scientists aren't sure what caused the end of Maya civilization?

SUMMARY AND PREVIEW You have learned that the Maya built a great civilization, but it collapsed for what were probably several reasons. In Section 3 you will learn more about what Maya life and society was like at its height.

Section 2 Assessment

go.hrw.com
Online Quiz
KEYWORD: SQ7 HP14

Reviewing Ideas, Terms, and People HSS 7.7.1, 7.7.3

1. **a. Recall** What resources did the Maya get from the forest?
   b. Make Inferences How might the Maya have used **obsidian**?
2. **a. Identify** Who was an important king of Palenque?
   b. Make Generalizations Why did Maya cities fight each other?
3. **a. Describe** What happened to Maya civilization in the 900s?
   b. Analyze In what way did growth of cities, warfare, and drought possibly affect Maya civilization?
   c. Elaborate What might scientists study to find out about the end of Maya civilization?

Critical Thinking

4. **Identifying Cause and Effect** Draw a diagram like the one to the right. Use it to show four possible causes for the decline of the Classic Age in Maya civilization.

[Diagram: four boxes pointing to a box labeled "Decline of Maya Civilization"]

FOCUS ON WRITING

5. **Gathering Information about the Maya** Much of the tour would likely be devoted to the Maya. Use the maps and pictures in this chapter to help you choose which places to write about. What areas and features of each site would you point out? What would you say about the history of these different places?

Maya Life and Society

If YOU were there...

You are a Maya farmer, growing corn on a farm near the city. Often you enter the city to join the crowd at a religious ceremony. You watch the king and his priests, standing at the top of a tall pyramid. They wear capes of brightly colored feathers and many heavy gold ornaments that glitter like the sun. As the king offers a sacrifice to the gods, a ray of sun strikes the pyramid.

How do these ceremonies make you feel about your king?

> **BUILDING BACKGROUND** Fancy clothes and important responsibilities showed the role kings and priests played in Maya society. The roles people played determined what their daily life was like.

Roles in Maya Society

Maya society had a complex class structure. As you might expect, life for the upper social classes differed greatly from life for the lower classes.

Upper Class

The upper class of Maya society included different groups of people. The king held the highest position in society. Priests, warriors, and merchants were also part of the upper class.

Maya society had a rigid class structure.

An attendant brings gifts to two Maya rulers.

What You Will Learn...

Main Ideas

1. Roles in Maya society were based on a complex class structure.
2. Religion in Maya society was often bloody.
3. The Maya made achievements in art, science, math, and writing.

The Big Idea

People played different roles in Maya society, but together they made great achievements in art, science, math, and writing.

Key Terms

observatories, *p. 398*
Popol Vuh, *p. 399*

HSS 7.7.2 Study the roles of people in each society, including class structures, family life, warfare, religious beliefs and practices, and slavery.

7.7.4 Describe the artistic and oral traditions and architecture in the three civilizations.

7.7.5 Describe the Meso-American achievements in astronomy and mathematics, including the development of the calendar and the Meso-American knowledge of seasonal changes to the civilizations' agricultural systems.

The Maya believed their rulers were related to the gods. For this reason, rulers were often involved in religious ceremonies. They also led battles. As the richest people in Maya society, rulers had beautiful clothing and jewelry. Kings wore huge feather headdresses and capes of cotton, jaguar skins, and feathers.

Priests were usually born into their role in Maya society. They led religious ceremonies. They were also the most educated people. Priests used their knowledge of astronomy and math to plan the best times for religious ceremonies.

Professional warriors fought battles against other Maya cities. In battle, these warriors wore animal headdresses, jade jewelry, and jaguar-skin capes. They painted their bodies red and black.

Merchants directed trade among the cities. They organized the transportation and distribution of goods. They also supervised the people who carried goods between cities. Together, the members of the upper class controlled the politics, religion, and economy in Maya society.

Lower Classes

Although the upper classes had the most power, most Maya belonged to the lower classes as farming families. These Maya lived in small houses outside the cities. Girls learned from their mothers how to cook, make yarn, and weave. Women cared for children. Men crafted household tools such as knives. They had to provide food for their family, so they also spent a lot of time hunting and farming. They kept small gardens next to their houses and worked together to farm larger fields.

Farmers had to give some of their crops to their rulers. Lower-class Maya also had to "pay" their rulers with goods such as cloth and salt. They had to work on building temples, palaces, and other buildings.

They also had to serve in the army during times of war. If captured in battle, a lower-class man usually became a slave.

Slaves held the lowest position in society. Orphans, slaves' children, and people who owed money also became slaves. Slaves had to carry trade goods between cities. They also served upper-class Maya by working as farmers or household servants.

The lower class supported the upper class with food and labor, but the upper class also helped the lower class. For example, upper-class Maya led the religious ceremonies that were vital to daily life for all classes of society.

READING CHECK **Identifying Cause and Effect**
How might one become a slave in Maya society?

A Maya King and His Court
The king and his court were the center of Maya government and religious life. This vase painting shows a Maya king relaxing with some of his servants. Kings enjoyed all the luxuries of Maya life, such as music, fine clothing and food, and even chocolate.

Religion

The Maya worshipped many gods related to different **aspects** of their daily life. The most important god was the creator. This god would take many different forms. Others included a sun god, moon goddess, and maize god. The Maya believed their kings communicated with the gods.

According to Maya beliefs, the gods could be helpful or harmful, so people tried to please the gods to get their help. The Maya believed their gods needed blood to prevent disasters or the end of the world. Every person offered blood to the gods by piercing their tongue or skin. The Maya sometimes held special ceremonies to give blood at events such as births, weddings, and funerals.

On special occasions the Maya believed they needed extra amounts of blood. On these occasions they made human sacrifices to their gods. They usually used prisoners captured in battle for this ritual. A priest would offer human hearts to stone carvings of gods. These sacrifices usually took place at a temple.

READING CHECK Generalizing Why did the Maya want to please their gods?

Achievements

The Maya's many artistic and architectural skills are reflected in their sculpture and in their temples. Maya achievements also included discoveries in science and math, as well as developments in writing.

ACADEMIC VOCABULARY

aspects parts

The king is gazing at this mirror, which the Maya believed held magical powers.

A bodyguard stands behind the king.

These vases held a chocolate drink, a favorite of Maya nobles.

The fly whisk in the king's hand is a symbol of authority.

ANALYSIS SKILL ANALYZING VISUALS

What about the king indicates he is an important person?

397

Art and Architecture

Some of the best-known Maya art is their sculpture and their jade and gold jewelry. They carved stone sculptures of kings or gods for their cities.

Maya cities showed the talent of their architects and builders. The Maya built cities without using metal tools. They didn't even have wheeled vehicles to carry supplies. Instead, workers used obsidian tools to cut limestone into blocks. Then, to move the giant blocks, workers rolled them over logs and lifted them with ropes. It took many workers to build Maya cities, perhaps the most recognizable Maya achievement.

Science and Math

Maya achievements in science and math were just as important as their achievements in art and architecture. The Maya built **observatories**, or buildings to study astronomy, so their priests could study the stars. Maya astronomers figured out that a year is about 365 days long. They also learned about the cycles of the moon and how to predict eclipses.

Partly based on their discoveries in astronomy, the Maya developed calendars. They had a religious calendar to plan religious events. The Maya used a different calendar for agriculture. It had symbols for different months tied to farming activities such as planting or harvesting. These activities matched changes in the seasons. The Maya calendar was more accurate than the calendar used in Europe at that time.

To go along with their calendars, the Maya created a number system that included some new concepts in math. For example, the Maya were among the first people with a symbol for zero. The Maya used their number system to record important dates in their history.

Writing and Oral Traditions

The Maya also developed a writing system. It was similar to Egyptian hieroglyphics. Symbols represented both objects and sounds. The Maya created records, especially about achievements of their kings, by carving symbols into large stone tablets. They also wrote in bark-paper books.

Maya Astronomy and Calendars

This photo shows the observatory at the Maya city of Chichén Itzá. The diagram shows the Maya religious and farming calendars. The Maya used these two calendars together to coordinate planting, harvesting, and important religious events.

365-day farming calendar

260-day religious calendar

Primary Source

ART
A Maya Carving

This carving comes from the palace at Yaxchilán (yahsh-chee-LAHN). The Maya recorded historical events on carvings like this one. Historians can now translate most Maya writing. They study the pictures and writings to learn about events in Maya history.

October 28, AD 709

She is letting blood.

Lady Xoc

Lord of Yaxchilán

ANALYSIS SKILL **ANALYZING PRIMARY SOURCES**

Who are the people in this carving?

Stories and poetry got passed down orally from one generation to the next. After the Spanish arrived, Maya legends and history were written in a book called the **Popol Vuh** (poh-pohl VOO). This book provides valuable information about the Maya.

READING CHECK **Analyzing** What activities did the Maya calendar regulate?

SUMMARY AND PREVIEW The Maya had a complex social structure. They also made achievements in art and learning. They left behind many records of their society and history. In the next chapter you will learn about two great empires that developed later in the Americas—the Aztecs and Incas.

Section 3 Assessment

go.hrw.com
Online Quiz
KEYWORD: SQ7 HP14

Reviewing Ideas and Terms **HSS** 7.7.2, 7.7.4, 7.7.5

1. **a. Identify** Who were members of the upper class in Maya society?
   b. Explain In what ways did lower-class Maya support upper-class Maya?
2. **a. Describe** What did the Maya do to try to please their gods?
   b. Explain Why did the Maya practice human sacrifice?
3. **a. Recall** What did the Maya study from **observatories**?
   b. Rank What do you think was the most impressive Maya achievement?

Critical Thinking

4. **Analyzing Information** Draw a diagram like the one to the right. Use it to identify some major achievements of the Maya.

   | Writing system |
   | Achievements |

5. **FOCUS ON WRITING**

5. **Identifying Key Details about Maya Culture** Some sites might have displays of Maya art and tools. There could even be scenes and live performances of how the Maya lived. Make a list of what the people on the tour might see of Maya culture.

THE EARLY AMERICAS   **399**

from the
Popol Vuh

translated by Dennis Tedlock

About the Reading *In the language of the Maya,* Popol Vuh *means "Council Book." This work contains both the myths and the history of a group of Maya. It was first used by Maya kings and lords to help them govern their people. Today, the* Popol Vuh *helps modern readers understand how the Maya lived and what they believed. The following myth, for example, tells us how the gods tried to create people several times before they eventually succeeded.*

AS YOU READ Pay close attention to the behavior of the creator-gods.

Again there comes an experiment with the human work, the human design, by the Maker, Modeler, Bearer, Begetter:

"It must simply be tried again. The time for the planting and dawning is nearing. For this we must make a provider and nurturer. ❶ How else can we be invoked and remembered on the face of the earth? We have already made our first try at our work and design, but it turned out that they didn't keep our days, nor did they glorify us."

"So now let's try to make a giver of praise, giver of respect, provider, nurturer," they said.

So then comes the building and working with earth and mud. They made a body, but it didn't look good to them. It was just separating, just crumbling, just loosening, just softening, just disintegrating, and just dissolving. ❷ Its head wouldn't turn, either. Its face was just lopsided, its face was just twisted. It couldn't look around. It talked at first, but senselessly. It was quickly dissolving in the water.

"It won't last," the mason and sculptor said then. "It seems to be dwindling away, so let it just dwindle. It can't walk and it can't multiply, so let it be merely a thought," they said.

So then they dismantled, again they brought down their work and design. Again they talked:

"What is there for us to make that would turn out well, that would succeed in keeping our days and praying to us?" they said. Then they planned again . . .

GUIDED READING

WORD HELP

disintegrating breaking apart

mason one who works with stone or brick

dismantled took apart

❶ *Why do the gods wish to make human beings?*

❷ *What do the gods use to make the body? What happens to it?*

ELA **Reading 7.3.2** Identify events that advance the plot and determine how each event explains past or present action(s) or foreshadows future action(s).

The creator-gods try again. This time, they produce a group of wooden creatures called "manikins."
They came into being, they multiplied, they had daughters, they had sons, these manikins, woodcarvings. But there was nothing in their hearts and nothing in their minds, no memory of their mason and builder. They just went and walked wherever they wanted. They did not remember the Heart of Sky. ❸

Monkeys were common subjects in Maya carvings.

And so they fell, just an experiment and just a cutout for humankind.

They were not competent, nor did they speak before the builder and sculptor who made them and brought them forth, and so they were killed, done in by a flood:

There came a rain of resin from the sky.

There came the one named Gouger of Faces: he gouged out their eyeballs.

There came Sudden Bloodletter: he snapped off their heads.

There came Crunching Jaguar: he ate their flesh.

There came Tearing Jaguar: he tore them open.

They were pounded down to the bones and tendons, smashed and pulverized even to the bones . . . ❹

Such was the scattering of the human work, the human design. The people were ground down, overthrown. The mouths and faces of all of them were destroyed and crushed. And it used to be said that the monkeys in the forests today are a sign of this. They were left as a sign because wood alone was used for their flesh by the builder and sculptor.

❺ And so this is why monkeys look like people: they are a sign of a previous human work, human design—mere manikins, mere woodcarvings.

GUIDED READING

WORD HELP

competent capable; fit
resin a gooey substance that comes from trees
pulverized crushed

❸ The Heart of Sky is the father-god of the Maya.

❹ *In your own words, explain what happened to the creatures.*

❺ *This myth explains the origin, or beginning, of what animal?*

CONNECTING LITERATURE TO HISTORY

1. **Evaluating** According to Maya beliefs, the gods could be helpful or harmful, so people tried to please the gods to get their help. Are the gods in this myth helpful or harmful? Explain your answer.

2. **Analyzing** By studying Maya records, archaeologists are learning about the achievements of the Maya. What have you learned about the Maya by reading this "record" of their life and society?

Social Studies Skills

Analysis | Critical Thinking | **Participation** | Study

Accepting Social Responsibility

Understand the Skill

"No man is an island entire of itself; every man is a piece of the continent, a part of the main." The great English poet John Donne made this observation almost 400 years ago. It is a famous quotation that remains as true today as when Donne wrote it. It means that no one exists alone. We are all members of society—"a part of the main."

Donne's poem continues, "If a clod be washed away by the sea, Europe is the less." This was Donne's way of saying that a society's strength depends on the contributions of its members. They must be willing to fulfill their roles in that society and to do what is best for it.

Learn the Skill

As a member of society, you have obligations to the people around you. The most obvious obligation is to do nothing that might harm society. This duty can range from small things, such as not littering, to large things, such as not committing a crime.

In addition, you have a duty to participate in society. At the very least, this means using the rights and responsibilities of citizenship. These responsibilities include being informed about important issues in your school, community, and country. Later, when you are older, they will also include serving on juries and voting in elections.

Another level of social responsibility and participation is becoming involved in change to benefit society. It goes beyond just being informed about issues to trying to do something about them. Before you take this important step, however, here are some points to consider.

1 Few changes that benefit society will have everyone's support. Some people always want things to stay the same. They may get upset or treat you badly if you work for change. You must be prepared for this possibility if you decide to take action.

2 Sometimes efforts to improve things involve opposing laws or rules that you believe need to be changed. No matter how just your cause is, if you break laws or rules, you must be willing to accept the consequences of your behavior.

3 Remember that violence is *never* an acceptable method for change. People who use force in seeking change are not behaving in a socially responsible manner, even if their cause is good.

Practice and Apply the Skill

Review the "If You Were There" scene in Section 3. Imagine yourself as that Maya farmer. You respect your king as the leader of your city and its army. War is very important in your culture. Your city is at war nearly all the time, and you feel this fighting is hurting your society. Farming is difficult because farmers must spend so much time in the army. In addition, enemy attacks destroy the crops farmers are able to grow. Food shortages are common.

1. If you did something to try to end the warfare, in what ways might that benefit your society?

2. Why might some people oppose your efforts?

3. What might the consequences be for you if you refuse to fight?

4. If you were this Maya farmer, what would you do? Explain your answer.

Visual Summary

Use the visual summary below to help you review the main ideas of the chapter.

QUICK FACTS

People arrived in the Americas sometime before 10,000 BC.

By 2500 BC people in Mesoamerica had domesticated maize.

The Maya built cities in the Americas during their Classic Age.

The Maya civilization eventually collapsed, but no one knows why.

Reviewing Vocabulary, Terms, and People

Imagine that these terms from the chapter are correct answers to six items in a crossword puzzle. Write the six clues for the answers. Then make the puzzle with some answers written down and some across.

1. Mesoamerica

2. Pacal

3. obsidian

4. observatories

5. maize

6. Popol Vuh

Comprehension and Critical Thinking

SECTION 1 *(Pages 384–389)* **HSS** 7.7.1

7. a. Identify What plants did early farmers in Mesoamerica grow for food? What plants did farmers grow in South America?

b. Make Inferences What do Olmec towns, sculptures, and other items tell us about Olmec society?

c. Evaluate Evaluate this statement: "Global temperature change had a big impact on the history of the Americas."

SECTION 2 *(Pages 390–394)* **HSS** 7.7.1, 7.7.3

8. a. Recall What were two important trade goods for the early Maya?

b. Analyze Why did the Maya civilization decline?

c. Elaborate For which people in Maya society was life probably pleasant and secure? For which people was life less pleasant or secure?

SECTION 3 *(Pages 395–399)* **HSS** 7.7.2, 7.7.4, 7.7.5

9. a. Describe What are some things that happened during Maya religious ceremonies?

b. Contrast How did daily life for the upper and lower classes of Maya society differ?

c. Evaluate Of the Maya's many achievements, which do you think is the most important? Why?

THE EARLY AMERICAS **403**

Reviewing Themes

10. Science and Technology Do you agree or disagree with this statement: "The Maya were clever and talented because they built their cities without the help of metal tools or wheeled vehicles." Why?

11. Geography How did geography play a role in the Maya economy?

Using the Internet

12. Activity: Understanding Maya Math The ancient Maya invented a number system that helped them construct buildings and keep track of their agriculture and commerce. Number glyphs are mostly simple dots and lines. The Maya also used head glyphs, which are more intricate drawings for numbers. Enter the activity keyword. Then visit the Web sites and complete some math problems using Maya numbers.

Reading and Analysis Skills

Analyzing Information In each of the following passages, one underlined selection is irrelevant or nonessential to the meaning of the sentence, or it cannot be verified as true. Identify the irrelevant, nonessential, or unverifiable selection in each sentence.

13. Pacal was greatly honored by the Maya. He was very tall. The Maya built a great temple to record his achievements.

14. Ball games were popular in Maya cities. Players could not use their hands or feet to touch the ball. The Maya would not enjoy modern basketball very much.

15. Chocolate was valuable in Maya society. Only rulers and gods could have chocolate. Today, many people enjoy chocolate every day.

16. The Maya developed an accurate calendar system. They knew that a year had 365 days. The ancient Romans also had a calendar. The Maya calendar used symbols to represent months.

17. Mesoamerica is largely covered by rain forests. Many kinds of plants and animals live in rain forests. The people of Mesoamerica probably liked to watch monkeys playing in the trees.

Social Studies Skills

18. Accepting Responsibility and Consequences Organize your class into groups. Choose one member of your group to represent the ruler of a Maya city. The rest of the group will be his or her advisers. As a group, decide how you will behave toward other cities. Will you go to war, or will you trade? Once you have made your decisions, declare your intentions to other cities. Ask the representatives of those cities how they will respond to your action. As a class, discuss the consequences of the actions you have chosen to take.

FOCUS ON WRITING

19. Writing Your Brochure Travel brochures often feature exciting descriptions of tours. Use your notes to help you write such a description for a historical tour of the ancient Americas.

Choose sites from the most ancient ones to the Maya cities. For each site, write several sentences about the people who lived there. You might tell how they came to live there or how an object there played a part in their lives.

Most travel brochures show lots of pictures. What pictures would you choose to go with what you've written?

Standards Assessment

DIRECTIONS: *Read each question, and write the letter of the best response.*

1 Use the map to answer the following question.

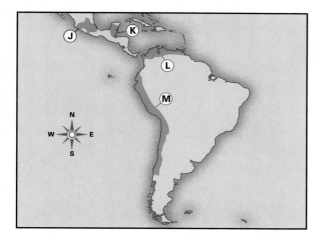

Which of the areas on the map shows the location of the Maya civilization?

A J

B K

C L

D M

2 Mesoamerica contains all of the following geographic features *except*

A mountains.

B rain forests.

C deserts.

D rivers.

3 Which word *best* describes the Maya civilization during its Classic Age?

A peaceful

B religious

C united

D democratic

4 Despite their accomplishments, the Maya did *not* have

A a reliable calendar.

B wheeled vehicles.

C a writing system.

D knowledge of mathematics.

5 Which class of people held the lowest position in Maya society?

A priests

B farmers

C slaves

D merchants

Connecting with Past Learnings

6 In this chapter you read that Maya civilization during the Classic Age included independent city-states. What other civilization that you have studied was organized into city-states?

A ancient Greece

B ancient Persia

C Han China

D the Roman Empire

7 The Maya believed their rulers were related to the gods. What other ancient civilization believed the same thing?

A Jews

B Indians

C Phoenicians

D Egyptians

The Aztec and Inca Empires

California Standards

History–Social Science

7.7 Students compare and contrast the geographic, political, economic, religious, and social structures of the Meso-American and Andean civilizations.

Analysis Skills

CS 3 Students use maps to identify cultural features of neighborhoods, cities, states, and countries.

English–Language Arts

Writing 7.2.1c Use a range of appropriate strategies (e.g., dialogue; suspense; naming of specific narrative action, including movement, gestures, and expressions).

Reading 7.2.0 Students describe and connect the essential ideas, arguments, and perspectives of the text by using their knowledge of text structure, organization, and purpose.

FOCUS ON WRITING

A Lively Dialogue Imagine that a child your age from Tenochtitlán, the capital of the Aztec Empire, met a child from Cuzco, the capital of the Inca Empire, and became friends. What might the children say to each other? As you read this chapter, you'll gather material to write a dialogue between the two children in which they talk about their lives.

CHAPTER EVENTS

c. 1325 The Aztecs set up their capital at Tenochtitlán.

1300

WORLD EVENTS

1337 The Hundred Years' War between France and England begins.

What You Will Learn...

In this chapter you will learn about the accomplishments of the Aztec and Inca empires. The ruins of the Inca city Machu Picchu, shown here, lie high in the Andes Mountains.

c. 1440
Pachacuti begins to expand the Inca Empire.

1502
Moctezuma II becomes emperor of the Aztecs.

1519
Cortés arrives in Mexico.

1537
Pizarro conquers the Inca Empire.

1375   1450   1525   1600

1433
China's emperor ends ocean exploration of Asia and Africa.

1453
The Ottomans conquer Constantinople.

1517
Martin Luther announces his Ninety-Five Theses.

THE AZTEC AND INCA EMPIRES   **407**

Economics	Geography	Politics	Religion	Society and Culture	Science and Technology

Focus on Themes This chapter describes two of the greatest empires in the Americas, the Aztec and Inca empires. You will read about the development of these civilizations, including people's daily lives there. You will also learn about the **political** systems they used to govern their nations and the **scientific and technological** advancements they made. Finally, you will see how both empires were defeated and conquered by invaders from across the sea.

Main Ideas and Their Support

Focus on Reading You know that if you take the legs out from under a table it will fall flat to the floor. In just the same way, a main idea will fall flat without details to support it.

Understanding a Writer's Support for Ideas A writer can support main ideas with several kinds of details. These details might be facts, brief stories, examples, definitions, or comments from experts on the subject.

Additional reading support can be found in the

Inter active

Reader and Study Guide

Notice the types of details the writer uses to support the main idea in the passage below.

The Incas are known for their massive buildings and forts made of huge, stone blocks. Workers cut the blocks so precisely that they didn't have to use cement to hold them together. Inca masonry, or stonework, was of such high quality that even today it is nearly impossible to fit a knife blade between the stones. In fact, many Inca buildings in Cuzco are still being used.

From Chapter 15, p. 430

The **main idea** is stated first.

This is an **example** of the way the Incas cut the stone for their buildings and forts.

The **definition** of masonry helps tie this example to the main idea.

This **fact** about the building helps explain why the Incas would be known for them—they lasted a long time.

ELA **Reading 7.2.0** Students describe and connect the essential ideas, arguments, and perspectives of the text by using their knowledge of text structure, organization, and purpose.

You Try It!

The following passage is from the chapter you are about to read. As you read it, try to identify the writer's proposition and the details that support it.

Tenochtitlán

Through the Aztecs' efforts, Tenochtitlán became the greatest city in the Americas. It had huge temples, a busy market, clean streets, and a magnificent palace. The first Europeans in the city were stunned by what they saw.

From Chapter 15, p. 413

> "These great towns and pyramids and buildings rising from the water, all made of stone, seemed like an enchanted vision . . . It was all so wonderful that I do not know how to describe the first glimpse of things never heard of, seen, or dreamed of before."
>
> —Bernal Diaz del Castillo, from *The Conquest of New Spain*

At its height, Tenochtitlán was one of the world's largest cities, with some 200,000 people.

After you read the passage, answer the following questions.

1. Which sentence best states the main idea of the passage?
   a. The first Europeans were stunned by what they saw.
   b. It had huge temples, a busy market, and a great palace.
   c. Through the Aztecs' efforts, Tenochtitlán became the greatest city in the Americas.

2. Which of the following is a fact used to support the main idea?
   a. At its height, Tenochtitlán was one of the world's largest cities.
   b. "These great towns . . . seemed like an enchanted vision."

3. The quotation in the passage by Bernal Díaz del Castillo is an example of a(n)
   a. fact.
   b. comment from an expert.
   c. definition.
   d. example.

Key Terms and People

Chapter 15

Section 1
causeways *(p. 411)*
conquistadors *(p. 413)*
Hernán Cortés *(p. 413)*
Moctezuma II *(p. 413)*

Section 2
codex *(p. 420)*

Section 3
Pachacuti *(p. 423)*
Quechua *(p. 424)*
llamas *(p. 425)*
Atahualpa *(p. 425)*
Francisco Pizarro *(p. 425)*

Section 4
masonry *(p. 430)*

Academic Vocabulary

Success in school is related to knowing academic vocabulary—the words that are frequently used in school assignments and discussions. In this chapter, you will learn the following academic words:

motive *(p. 413)*
distribute *(p. 425)*

As you read Chapter 15, look for the details that the writer used to support main ideas. What types of details do you see?

The Aztec Empire

What You Will Learn...

Main Ideas

1. The Aztecs built an empire through warfare and trade and created an impressive capital city in Mesoamerica.
2. Hernán Cortés conquered the Aztec Empire.

The Big Idea

The Aztecs built a great empire in central Mexico but were conquered by the Spanish in 1521.

Key Terms and People

causeways, *p. 411*
conquistadors, *p. 413*
Hernán Cortés, *p. 413*
Moctezuma II, *p. 413*

HSS **7.7.1** Study the locations, landforms, and climates of Mexico, Central America, and South America and their effects on Mayan, Aztec, and Incan economies, trade, and development of urban societies.

7.7.3 Explain how and where each empire arose and how the Aztec and Incan empires were defeated by the Spanish.

If YOU were there...

You live in a village in southeast Mexico that is ruled by the powerful Aztec Empire. Each year your village must send many baskets of corn to the emperor. You have to dig gold for him, too. One day some strangers arrive by sea. They tell you they want to overthrow the emperor. They ask for your help.

Should you help the strangers? Why or why not?

BUILDING BACKGROUND The Aztecs ruled a large empire in Mesoamerica. Each village they conquered had to contribute to the Aztec economy. This system helped create a very powerful empire, but one that lasted only about a century.

The Aztecs Build an Empire

The first Aztecs were farmers from northern Mexico. Around the 1100s they migrated south. When they arrived in central Mexico, they found that other tribes had taken all the good farmland. All that was left for the Aztecs was a swampy island in the middle of Lake Texcoco (tays-KOH-koh). To survive, the Aztecs hired themselves out as skilled fighters.

War, Tribute, and Trade

War was a key factor in the Aztecs' rise to power. The fierce Aztec warriors conquered many towns. In addition, the Aztecs sometimes made alliances, or partnerships, to build their empire. For example, in the late 1420s the Aztecs formed a secret alliance with two other cities on Lake Texcoco. With their allies' help, they defeated the other towns around the lake.

The Aztecs made people they conquered pay tribute. Tribute is a payment to a more powerful ruler or country. Conquered tribes had to pay the Aztecs with goods such as cotton, gold, or food. This system was the basis of the Aztec economy.

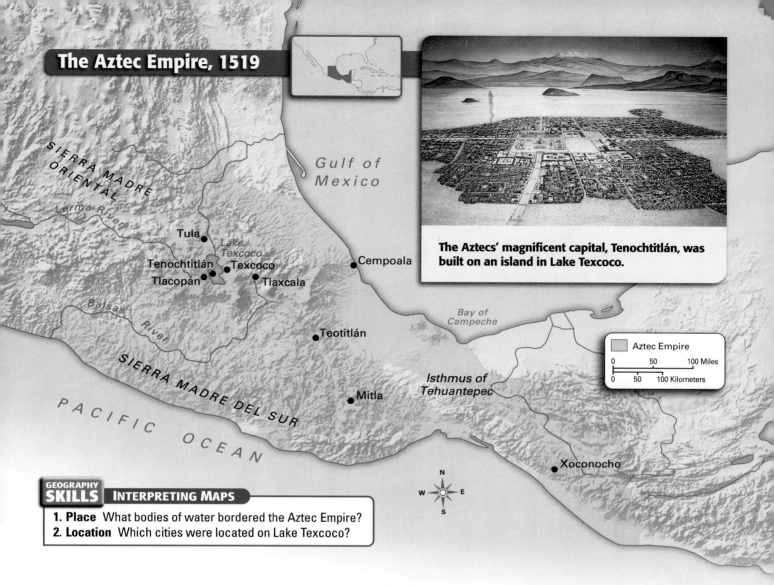

The Aztec Empire, 1519

SIERRA MADRE ORIENTAL

Lerma River

Gulf of Mexico

Tula

Lake Texcoco

Tenochtitlán • Texcoco

Tlacopán • • Tlaxcala

Cempoala

Balsas River

SIERRA MADRE DEL SUR

Teotitlán

Bay of Campeche

PACIFIC OCEAN

Mitla

Isthmus of Tehuantepec

Xoconocho

The Aztecs' magnificent capital, Tenochtitlán, was built on an island in Lake Texcoco.

| | Aztec Empire |
| 0   50   100 Miles |
| 0   50   100 Kilometers |

GEOGRAPHY SKILLS | **INTERPRETING MAPS**

1. **Place** What bodies of water bordered the Aztec Empire?
2. **Location** Which cities were located on Lake Texcoco?

The Aztecs also controlled a huge trade network. Most towns in the empire had a market where local farmers and artisans brought their goods to trade. One enormous market near the capital drew buyers and sellers from all over the Aztec Empire. Merchants carried luxury goods such as gems and rare foods to sell there. Because these merchants dealt with people in many parts of the empire, the emperors used them as spies. These spy merchants reported trouble building in the empire.

War, tribute, and trade made the Aztecs rich. As they grew rich, they grew even stronger and conquered more people. By the early 1500s they ruled the most powerful state in Mesoamerica.

Tenochtitlán

Nowhere was the Aztec Empire's power and wealth more visible than in its capital, Tenochtitlán (tay-NAWCH-teet-LAHN). To build this amazing city, the Aztecs had to overcome many geographical challenges.

The city's island location made travel and trade difficult. To make it easier to get to and from their city, the Aztecs built three wide **causeways**—raised roads across water or wet ground—to connect the island to the shore. The causeways were made of rocks covered with dirt.

Tenochtitlán was surrounded by water, but the water was undrinkable. As a result, the Aztecs built a stone aqueduct, or channel, to bring fresh water to the city.

THE IMPACT TODAY

On the site of Tenochtitlán workers filled the lake to build Mexico City, the modern capital of Mexico.

Tenochtitlán

The Aztecs turned a swampy, uninhabited island into one of the largest and grandest cities in the world. The first Europeans to visit Tenochtitlán were stunned. At the time, the Aztec capital was about five times bigger than London.

The Great Temple stood at the heart of the city. On top of the temple were two shrines—a blue shrine for the rain god and a red shrine for the sun god.

Gold, silver, cloaks, and precious stones were among the many items sold at the market.

A network of canals linked different parts of the city.

Aztec farmers grew crops on "floating gardens" called *chinampas*.

ANALYSIS SKILL **ANALYZING VISUALS**

What is the most important building in this picture?

The city's island location also limited land available for farming. To create more land for farming, they built "floating gardens" called *chinampas* (chee-NAHM-pahs). They made the gardens by putting soil on rafts anchored to trees in the water. The *chinampas* surrounded a central island that was the heart of the city.

Through the Aztecs' efforts, Tenochtitlán became the greatest city in the Americas. It had huge temples, a busy market, clean streets, and a magnificent palace. The first Europeans in the city were stunned by what they saw.

>" These great towns and pyramids and buildings rising from the water, all made of stone, seemed like an enchanted vision . . . It was all so wonderful that I do not know how to describe this first glimpse of things never heard of, seen, or dreamed of before."
> –Bernal Díaz del Castillo, from *The Conquest of New Spain*

At its height, Tenochtitlán was one of the world's largest cities, with some 200,000 people. But the arrival of Europeans soon destroyed both the city and the rest of the Aztec Empire.

READING CHECK **Finding Main Ideas** What was one key factor in the Aztecs' rise to power?

Cortés Conquers the Aztecs

In the late 1400s Spanish explorers and soldiers arrived in the Americas. The soldiers, or **conquistadors** (kahn-kees-tuh-DOHRZ), came to explore new lands, search for gold, and spread their Catholic religion.

Cortés and Moctezuma

A small group of conquistadors led by **Hernán Cortés** (er-NAHN kawr-TAYS) reached Mexico in 1519. They were looking for gold. Hearing of this arrival, the Aztec emperor, **Moctezuma II** (MAWK-tay-SOO-mah), believed Cortés to be a god. According to an Aztec legend, the god Quetzalcoatl (ket-suhl-kuh-WAH-tuhl) was to return to Mexico in 1519. Cortés resembled the god's description from the legend.

Thinking that the god had returned, Moctezuma sent Cortés gifts, including gold. With getting more gold his **motive**, Cortés marched to the Aztec capital. When he got there Moctezuma welcomed him, but Cortés took the emperor prisoner.

Enraged, the Aztecs attacked and drove the Spanish out. In the confusion Moctezuma was killed. Cortés and his men came back, though, with many Indian allies. In 1521 they conquered Tenochtitlán.

ACADEMIC VOCABULARY

motive reason for doing something

BIOGRAPHIES

Hernán Cortés
1485–1547

After arriving on the coast of Mexico, Hernán Cortés burned his ships so his men couldn't return home. They had no choice but to stay and fight with Cortés. In the end they conquered the Aztecs, partly due to Cortés's leadership and determination to find gold.

Drawing Inferences What choices do you think Cortés' men had after he burned the ships?

Moctezuma II
1466–1520

Moctezuma II ruled the Aztec Empire at its height, but he also contributed to its downfall. The tribute he demanded from neighboring tribes made the Aztecs unpopular. In addition, his belief that Cortés was Quetzalcoatl allowed Cortés to capture him and eventually conquer the empire.

Summarizing How did Moctezuma II contribute to the downfall of the Aztec Empire?

Causes of the Defeat of the Aztecs

How did a few conquistadors defeat a powerful empire? Four factors were vital in the Spanish victory: alliances, weapons and horses, geography, and disease.

First, alliances in the region helped the Spanish forces. One important ally was an American Indian woman named Malintzin (mah-LINT-suhn), also known as Malinche. She was a guide and interpreter for Cortés. With her help, he made alliances with tribes who did not like losing battles and paying tribute to the Aztecs. The allies gave the Spaniards supplies, information, and warriors to help defeat the Aztecs.

The Spaniards also had better weapons. The Aztecs couldn't match their armor, cannons, and swords. In addition to these weapons, the Spaniards brought horses to Mexico. The Aztecs had never seen horses and at first were terrified of them.

The third factor, geography, gave the Spanish another advantage. They blocked Tenochtitlán's causeways, bridges, and waterways. This cut off drinking water and other supplies. Thousands of Aztecs died from starvation.

The final factor in the Spanish success was disease. Unknowingly, the Spanish had brought deadly diseases such as smallpox to the Americas. These new diseases swept through Aztec communities. Many Aztecs became very weak or died from the diseases because they didn't have strength to defend themselves.

Together, these four factors gave the Spanish forces a tremendous advantage and weakened the Aztecs. When the Spanish conquered Tenochtitlán, the Aztec Empire came to an end.

READING CHECK **Summarizing** What four factors helped the Spanish defeat the Aztecs?

SUMMARY AND PREVIEW The Aztecs built a powerful empire and established a great capital city on a swampy island in central Mexico. A few hundred years later their empire ended in defeat by Spanish conquistadors. In the next section you will learn about life and society in the Aztec Empire before it was defeated by the Spanish.

Section 1 Assessment

go.hrw.com
Online Quiz
KEYWORD: SQ7 HP15

Reviewing Ideas, Terms, and People **HSS** 7.7.1, 7.7.3

1. **a. Define** What is a **causeway**? Where did the Aztecs build causeways?
   b. Explain How did the Aztecs adapt to their island location?
   c. Elaborate How might Tenochtitlán's location have been both a benefit and a hindrance to the Aztecs?

2. **a. Identify** Who was the ruler of the Aztecs when Cortés and the conquistadors arrived in Mexico?
   b. Make Generalizations How and why did allies help **Cortés** conquer the Aztec Empire?
   c. Evaluate Judge **Moctezuma**'s decisions as the Aztec leader.

Critical Thinking

3. **Evaluating** Draw a diagram like the one shown. On each level of the pyramid, list a factor that led to the growth of a strong Aztec Empire. List the factor you think was most important on the top level and the least important on the bottom. Explain your choices.

Aztec Empire

FOCUS ON WRITING

4. **Thinking about the Aztec Empire** Think about things in this section that you could include in your dialogue. For example, how might an Aztec describe Tenochtitlán to a new friend? What do *chinampas* and other features of the city look like?

Malintzin

Would you have helped a conqueror take control of your people?

When did she live? c. 1501–1550

Where did she live? the Aztec Empire

What did she do? Malintzin became Cortés's companion and interpreter. She played a major role in the Spanish conquest of the Aztec Empire.

Why is she important? Malintzin was from a noble Aztec family but was sold into slavery as a child. While enslaved, Malintzin learned the Mayan language. After she was given to Cortés, Malintzin's knowledge of languages helped him make deals with the Aztecs' enemies.

However, because Malintzin helped the Spanish defeat the native Aztecs, today many Mexicans consider her a traitor. Some Mexicans use the word *malinchista* to describe someone who betrays his or her own people.

Drawing Inferences Why do you think Malintzin helped the Spanish rather than the Aztecs?

KEY FACTS

Communication between Cortés and the Aztecs involved four steps:

1. Cortés spoke in Spanish to his original interpreter, who also spoke Mayan.

2. The original interpreter translated the message from Spanish into Mayan for Malintzin.

3. Malintzin translated the message from Mayan into Nahuatl, the Aztec language.

4. Malintzin spoke Nahuatl to the Aztecs and the Aztecs' enemies.

In this drawing, Cortés makes a treaty with the Aztecs. Malintzin is standing by his side interpreting.

483

Aztec Life and Society

What You Will Learn...

Main Ideas

1. Aztec society was divided by social roles and by class.
2. Aztec religion required human sacrifice for keeping the gods happy.
3. The Aztecs had many achievements in science, art, and language.

The Big Idea

The Aztecs developed complex social, religious, artistic, and scientific systems in their empire.

Key Term

codex, *p. 420*

HSS **7.7.2** Study the roles of people in each society, including class structures, family life, warfare, religious beliefs and practices, and slavery.

7.7.4 Describe the artistic and oral traditions and architecture in the three civilizations.

7.7.5 Describe the Meso-American achievements in astronomy and mathematics, including the development of the calendar and the Meso-American knowledge of seasonal changes to the civilizations' agricultural systems.

If YOU were there...

You belong to an important family of Aztec artisans. You make fine gold jewelry and ornaments for the emperor and his nobles. Your brother wants to break this family tradition and become a warrior. Your family is upset by this news. Your brother asks what you think of his plans.

What will you tell your brother?

BUILDING BACKGROUND Most Aztec children grew up to be what their parents were. The artisan family described above would enjoy many privileges of the upper class. Warriors played an important role in Aztec society, so many young men wanted to be warriors.

Aztec Society

People in Aztec society had clearly defined roles. These roles, along with social class, determined how Aztec men and women lived. Aztec society was organized into groups called *calpullis* (kahl-POOH-yees). A *calpulli* was a community of families that

People in Aztec Society QUICK FACTS

Kings
Aztec kings ruled the empire and lived in luxury.

Nobles
Nobles served as important officials, such as tax collectors and judges.

THE GRANGER COLLECTION, NEW YORK

shared land, schools, and a temple. Each *calpulli* elected a leader who took orders from the king.

Kings and Nobles

The king was the most important person in Aztec society. He lived in a great palace that had gardens, a zoo, and an aviary full of beautiful birds. Some 3,000 servants attended to his every need. Of these servants, 300 did nothing but tend to the animals in the zoo, and 300 more tended to the birds in the aviary! Other servants fed and entertained the emperor.

The king was in charge of law, trade and tribute, and warfare. These were huge responsibilities, and the king couldn't have managed them without people to help. These people, including tax collectors and judges, were Aztec nobles. Noble positions were passed down from fathers to their sons. As a result, young nobles went to special schools to learn the responsibilities they would face as government officials, military leaders, or priests.

Priests and Warriors

Just below the king and his nobles were priests and warriors. Priests in particular had a great influence over Aztecs' lives. They had many duties in society, including:

Primary Source

BOOK
An Aztec Festival

The Aztecs often used the occasion of the crowning of a new king to remind the leaders of their conquered territories just who the true masters were. An observer in Tenochtitlán recalled one such event:

❝The intentions of the Mexicans [Aztecs], in preparing a festival . . . was to make known their king, and to ensure that their enemies . . . should be terrorized and filled with fear; and that they should know, by the . . . wealth of jewels and other presents, given away at the ceremonies, how great was the abundance of Mexico, its valor and its excellence. Finally, all was based on ostentation [extravagance] and vain glory, with the object of being feared, as the owners of all the riches of the earth and of its finest provinces. To this end they ordered these feasts and ceremonies so splendidly.❞

–Fray Diego Durán, from *Historia de Las Indias de Nueva España e Islas de la Tierra Firme*

ANALYSIS SKILL **ANALYZING PRIMARY SOURCES**

Do you think Fray Diego Durán admired the Aztecs? Why or why not?

- keeping calendars and deciding when to plant crops or perform ceremonies,
- passing down Aztec history and stories to keep their tradition alive,
- performing various religious ceremonies, including human sacrifice.

Priests
Priests performed many important duties, such as keeping calendars.

Warriors
Warriors fought to conquer other peoples and capture victims for sacrifice.

Merchants
Aztec merchants traded goods like food, clothing, and tools.

THE GRANGER COLLECTION, NEW YORK

THE GRANGER COLLECTION, NEW YORK

Aztec warriors also had many duties. They fought fiercely to capture victims for religious sacrifices. Partly because they played this role in religious life, warriors had many privileges and were highly respected. Warriors were also respected for the wealth they brought to the empire. They fought to conquer new lands and people, bringing more tribute and trade goods to enrich the Aztec civilization.

Merchants and Artisans

Not really members of the upper class, merchants and artisans fell just below priests and warriors in Aztec society. Merchants gathered goods from all over Mesoamerica and sold them in the main market. By controlling trade in the empire, they became very rich. Many used their wealth to build large, impressive houses and to send their sons to special schools.

Like merchants, most artisans were also rich and important. They made goods like beautiful feather headdresses and gold jewelry that they could sell at high prices. Many of the richest artisans lived in Tenochtitlán. Other artisans, who lived outside the capital and made items for everyday use, lived more like the lower class. Artisans from other tribes often sent crafts to the Aztecs as tribute.

Farmers and Slaves

Farmers and slaves were in the lower class of Aztec society. However, some people could improve their lives and positions by becoming warriors in the army or studying at special schools.

Most of the empire's people were farmers who grew maize, beans, and a few other crops. Farmers did not own their land, and they were very poor. They had to pay so much in tribute that they often found it tough to survive. Farmers lived outside Tenochtitlán in huts made of sticks and mud and wore rough capes.

No one in the Aztec Empire suffered as much as slaves did. Most of the slaves had been captured in battle or couldn't pay their debts. Slaves had little to look forward to. Most were sold as laborers to nobles or merchants. Slaves who disobeyed orders were sacrificed to the gods.

READING CHECK **Summarizing** What groups of people were in the upper class in Aztec society?

Aztec Religion

The Aztecs believed gods ruled all parts of life. Their gods' powers could be seen in nature, such as in trees or storms, and in great people, such as kings or ancestors.

People in Aztec Society (continued)

Artisans
Skilled artisans made a wide variety of goods that people needed.

Farmers
Most Aztecs were farmers who lived in simple huts.

Slaves
Prisoners of war became slaves. They were forced to work or were sacrificed.

Like other Mesoamericans, the Aztecs always tried to please their gods. They believed sacrifice was necessary to keep the gods strong and the world safe.

Aztecs made their greatest number of sacrifices to the war god Huitzilopochtli (wee-tsee-loh-POHCHT-lee) and the rain god Tlaloc (TLAH-lohk). The Aztecs believed the former made the sun rise every day, and the latter made the rain fall. Without them, their crops would die, and they would have no food.

To prevent this, Aztec priests led bloody ceremonies on the top of the Great Temple in Tenochtitlán. These priests cut themselves to give their blood to the gods.

Priests also sacrificed human victims to their gods. Many of the victims for these sacrifices were warriors from other tribes who had been captured in battle. Priests would sacrifice these victims to "feed" their gods human hearts and blood, which they thought would make the gods strong. Aztec priests sacrificed as many as 10,000 victims a year in religious ceremonies.

READING CHECK **Finding Main Ideas** Why was human sacrifice part of Aztec religion?

Science, Art, and Language

The Aztecs valued learning and art. Aztec scientific achievements, artistic traditions, and language contributed to their culture.

Scientific Achievements

The Aztecs made several advances in science. Many of these they accomplished by building on the achievements of the peoples they conquered. The Aztec system of tribute and their large trading network allowed them to learn skills from people all over the empire. For example, they learned how to build their floating gardens called *chinampas* from neighboring tribes.

Aztec Gods

The Aztecs worshipped hundreds of gods. Two of the most important were Tlaloc and Huitzilopochtli, who are shown below.

Tlaloc was the Aztec god of rain. The Aztecs believed he made the rain fall. A mask of Tlaloc decorates this vessel.

Huitzilopochtli was the Aztec god of war. The Aztecs believed he made the sun rise. The eyes of this statue of Huitzilopochtli are made of shell and obsidian.

419

Aztec Arts

Aztec artists were very skilled. They created detailed and brightly colored items like the ones you see here. Many were used in religious ceremonies.

What are some features of Aztec art that you can see in these pictures?

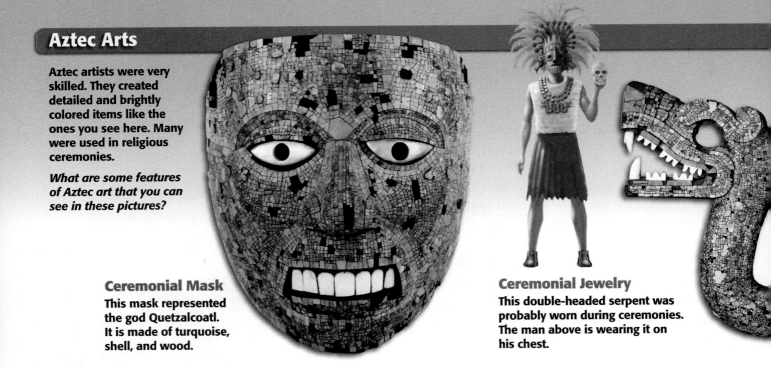

Ceremonial Mask
This mask represented the god Quetzalcoatl. It is made of turquoise, shell, and wood.

Ceremonial Jewelry
This double-headed serpent was probably worn during ceremonies. The man above is wearing it on his chest.

The Aztecs also studied astronomy and created a calendar much like the Maya one. The calendar helped the Aztecs choose the best days for ceremonies, for battles, or for planting and harvesting crops. The Aztecs also knew many different uses for plants. For example, they knew of more than 100 plants that could be used as medicines.

Artistic Traditions

FOCUS ON READING
What information supports the main idea of this section?

In addition to their achievements in science, the Aztecs had a rich artistic tradition that included architecture, sculpture, and jewelry. Both the architecture and the sculpture made use of stone. Workers built bridges and lined canals with stone. Carpenters and stonecutters built huge pyramid-shaped stone temples. Hundreds of such temples stood in Tenochtitlán.

Talented Aztec artisans used turquoise mosaics to decorate knife handles and masks. Artisans also used gold and colorful feathers to make jewelry. Aztec women wove cloth from cotton and other fibers and embroidered it with colorful designs.

Writing and Literature

The Aztecs had a complex writing system. They kept written historical records in books made of separate pages. Another name for this type of ancient book is a **codex** (KOH-deks). Many pages of Aztec books were made of bark or animal skins.

In addition to their written records, the Aztecs had a strong oral tradition. They considered fine speeches very important, and they also enjoyed riddles. These were some popular Aztec riddles at the time when the Spaniards arrived:

"What is a little blue-green jar filled with popcorn? Someone is sure to guess our riddle: it is the sky.

What is a mountainside that has a spring of water in it? Our nose."
–Bernardino de Sahagún, from *Florentine Codex*

Knowing the answers to riddles showed that one had paid attention in school.

Stories about ancestors and gods formed another part of the Aztec oral tradition. The Aztecs told these stories to their children, passing them down from one generation

Aztec Calendar
This modern drawing shows the Aztec calendar with brightly painted colors.

to the next. After the Spanish conquered the Aztec Empire, these stories were written down. Much of what historians know about the Aztecs they learned from these written stories.

READING CHECK **Summarizing** What was one purpose of the Aztec oral tradition?

SUMMARY AND PREVIEW The Aztec Empire had a strict social structure, an influential religion, and strong scientific and artistic traditions. In the next section you will learn about another empire of the Americas—the Inca Empire—and the vast area that it included.

Section 2 Assessment

go.hrw.com
Online Quiz
KEYWORD: SQ7 CH15

Reviewing Ideas, Terms, and People **HSS** 7.7.2, 7.7.4, 7.7.5

1. **a. Describe** How was it decided when the Aztecs should plant crops or hold ceremonies?
   b. Rate Who do you think had the most difficult social role in Aztec society? Why?
2. **a. Identify** What did the Aztecs feed their gods?
   b. Explain Why did the Aztecs think human sacrifice was important?
3. **a. Identify** What might you find in an Aztec **codex**?
   b. Make Inferences Why do you think the Aztecs used so much stone in their art and building?
   c. Develop Make up a riddle like the Aztecs would have had in their oral tradition.

Critical Thinking

4. **Categorizing** Copy the graphic organizer on the right. Write the names of the different social groups in Aztec society in each of the empty boxes.

King

Slaves

FOCUS ON WRITING

5. **Describing Aztec Society** To which social class do you want the Aztec child in your dialogue to belong? Make a list of details about Aztec social structure, religion, and culture that he or she might describe to a friend.

The Inca Empire

If YOU were there...

You live in the Andes Mountains, where you raise llamas. You weave their wool into warm cloth. Last year, soldiers from the powerful Inca Empire took over your village and took your leaders away. Now you have new leaders—and they have totally different rules! They say you must all learn to speak a new language and send much of your woven cloth to the Inca ruler.

How do you feel about living in the Inca Empire?

> **BUILDING BACKGROUND** The Incas built their empire by taking over villages like the one in the paragraph you just read. They brought many changes to the villages they conquered.

The Rise of the Inca Empire

The Aztecs arose in Mesoamerica, in what is now Mexico. In South America another great empire arose. That empire belonged to the Incas. However, South America was the home of several civilizations before the Incas built their empire. These civilizations provided a foundation for the Incas. The Incas borrowed from the scientific and cultural achievements, such as farming techniques and craft-making skills, of these cultures.

What You Will Learn...

Main Ideas

1. The rise of the Inca Empire was due to conquest and the achievements of the Inca people.
2. Pizarro conquered the Incas and took control of the region.

The Big Idea

The Incas built a huge empire in South America, but they were conquered by the Spanish.

Key Terms and People

Pachacuti, *p. 423*
Quechua, *p. 424*
llamas, *p. 425*
Atahualpa, *p. 425*
Francisco Pizarro, *p. 425*

HSS 7.7.1 Study the locations, landforms, and climates of Mexico, Central America, and South America and their effects on Mayan, Aztec, and Incan economies, trade, and development of urban societies.

7.7.3 Explain how and where each empire arose and how the Aztec and Incan empires were defeated by the Spanish.

The Incas lived in a region of high plains and mountains.

Pre-Inca Civilizations

Around 900 BC, complex civilizations began to develop in what is now Peru. These included the Chavín (chah-VEEN) culture in the highlands, and the Nazca, Moche (MOH-chay), and Chimú (chee-MOO) cultures on the coast.

Each of these cultures learned to adapt to its environment. In doing so they made scientific advances. For example, in the steep mountains, people made terraces for farming. On the coast they developed irrigation systems so they could farm in the desert. As a result, farming could support large populations both in the highlands and on the coast.

These early cultures also built some of South America's first cities. In these cities people developed crafts such as textiles, pottery, and gold jewelry. Because the cities were also religious centers, religious symbols often appeared in the crafts. The influence of these early civilizations set the stage for the Inca civilization.

The Early Incas

The Incas began as a small tribe in the Andes. Their capital was Cuzco (KOO-skoh). In the mid-1400s a ruler named **Pachacuti** (pah-chah-KOO-tee) led the Incas to expand their territory. He gained territory through agreements with other tribes or conquest.

BIOGRAPHY

Pachacuti
Died 1471

Pachacuti became the Inca ruler in about 1438. Under his rule the Inca Empire began a period of great expansion. Pachacuti, whose name means "He who remakes the world," had the Inca capital at Cuzco rebuilt. He also established an official Inca religion.

The Inca Empire, 1530

Quito

Chan Chan

ANDES

SOUTH AMERICA

Sausa

Machu Picchu

Cuzco

Lake Titicaca

Nazca

Chuquiapo

Arequipa

Lake Poopó

PACIFIC OCEAN

Catarpe

ANDES

Tilcara

Copiapo

Talca

Maule River

ATLANTIC OCEAN

Inca Empire
Inca roads
Capital

0   150   300 Miles
0   150   300 Kilometers

GEOGRAPHY SKILLS   INTERPRETING MAPS

Place About how many miles did the Inca Empire stretch from north to south?

Preserving Food

Did you know that astronauts have something in common with the Incas? Both groups have made use of freeze-dried foods.

The Incas learned how to freeze-dry potatoes so they would last for a long time without spoiling. First, they left the potatoes on the ground overnight in the cold Andean weather to freeze. Then they stomped on the potatoes to squeeze out the water. Next, they soaked the potatoes in water for a few weeks. Finally, they dried them in the sun. The result was a very light potato that was easy to carry and could last for several years.

The Incas kept freeze-dried potatoes in storehouses in Cuzco until they needed them. The Incas' potatoes lasted a long time. They were also easy to prepare—just like the astronauts' food in space and the food in your pantry.

THE GRANGER COLLECTION, NEW YORK

ANALYSIS SKILL **ANALYZING INFORMATION**

How do you think the Incas' freeze-dried potatoes might be different from frozen potatoes available today?

Later Inca leaders continued to expand their territory. By the early 1500s the Inca Empire was huge, as the map on the previous page shows. It stretched from what is now northern Ecuador to central Chile and included coastal deserts, snowy mountains, fertile valleys, and thick forests.

Around 12 million people lived in the Inca Empire. To rule this empire, the Incas formed a strong central government.

Central Government and Language

The Incas didn't want the people they conquered to have too much power. So they made the leaders of conquered areas move out of their villages. Then they brought in new leaders who were loyal to the Inca government.

The Incas also made the children of conquered leaders travel to the capital to learn about Inca government and religion.

After awhile, the children went back to rule their villages, where they taught people the Inca way of life.

The Incas knew that to control their empire they had to communicate with the people. But the people spoke many different languages. To unify their empire, the Incas established an official language, **Quechua** (KE-chuh-wuh). All official business had to be done in that language.

Although the Inca had no written language, they kept records with cords called *quipus* (KEE-pooz). Knots in the cords represented numbers. Different colors stood for information about crops, land, and other important topics.

Economy

The Inca government also controlled the economy. Instead of paying taxes, Incas had to "pay" their government in labor.

This labor tax system was called the *mita* (MEE-tah). Under the *mita*, the government told each household what work to do.

Most Incas were farmers. They grew crops such as maize and peanuts in valleys where the climate was warm. In the cooler mountains they grew potatoes. In the highest mountains, people raised animals such as **llamas** (LAH-muhz), animals that are related to camels but native to South America, for meat and wool.

As part of the *mita*, people also had to work for the government. Farmers worked on government-owned farms in addition to their own farms. Villagers produced cloth and grain for the army. Other Incas worked in mines, served in the army, or built roads to pay their labor tax.

There were no merchants or markets in the Inca Empire. Instead, government officials would **distribute** goods collected through the *mita*. Leftover goods were stored in the capital for emergencies. But their well-organized government couldn't protect the Incas from a new threat—the Spanish.

READING CHECK **Summarizing** How did the Incas control government and language?

Pizarro Conquers the Incas

A civil war began in the Inca Empire around 1530. After the Inca ruler died his two sons, **Atahualpa** (ah-tah-WAHL-pah) and Huáscar (WAHS-kahr), fought to become the new ruler. Atahualpa won the war, but fierce fighting had weakened the Inca army.

The Capture of the King

On his way to be crowned, Atahualpa got news that a group of Spaniards had come to Peru. They were conquistadors led by **Francisco Pizarro**. Stories about the Spaniards amazed Atahualpa. One Inca reported:

> "They and their horses were supposed to nourish [feed] themselves on gold and silver . . . All day and all night the Spaniards talked to their books and papers . . . They were all dressed alike and talked together like brothers and ate at the same table."
>
> –Anonymous Inca, quoted in *Letter to a King* by Huamán Poma

After he had heard of the Spaniards' arrival, Atahualpa agreed to meet Pizarro. At that meeting, the Spaniards told Atahualpa to convert to Christianity. When he refused, they attacked. They captured Atahualpa and killed thousands of Inca soldiers.

ACADEMIC VOCABULARY

distribute to divide among a group of people

BIOGRAPHIES

Atahualpa
1502–1533

Atahualpa was the last Inca king. He was brave and popular with the Inca army, but he didn't rule for long. A Spanish friar offered Atahualpa a religious book to convince him he should accept Christianity. Atahualpa held the book to his ear and listened to it. When the book didn't speak, he threw it on the ground. The Spaniards used this as a reason to attack.

Drawing Inferences Why do you think Atahualpa refused to accept Christianity?

Francisco Pizarro
1475–1541

Francisco Pizarro organized expeditions to explore the west coast of South America. His first two trips were mostly unsuccessful. But on his third trip, Pizarro's luck changed. With only about 180 men, he conquered the Inca Empire, which had been weakened by disease and civil war. In 1535 Pizarro founded Lima, the capital of modern Peru.

Drawing Inferences Why do you think Lima, and not the Inca city of Cuzco, became Peru's capital?

The Capture of Atahualpa
Spaniard Francisco Pizarro kidnapped the Inca leader Atahualpa to defeat the Incas. This painting from the 1800s shows Pizarro leading the attack on the Inca ruler.

but in 1537 the Spaniards defeated the last of the Incas and gained control over the entire region.

The fall of the Inca Empire was similar to the fall of the Aztec Empire.

- Both empires had internal problems when the Spanish arrived.
- Cortés and Pizarro captured the leaders of each empire.
- Guns and horses gave the Spanish a great military advantage.
- Disease weakened native peoples.

After defeating both the Aztecs and Incas, the Spanish ruled their lands for about the next 300 years.

READING CHECK **Identifying Cause and Effect** What events led to the end of the Inca Empire?

Spanish Control

To win his freedom, Atahualpa asked his people to fill a room with gold and silver for Pizarro. The people rushed to bring jewelry, statues, and other objects. Melted down, the precious metals may have totaled 24 tons. However, the Spaniards killed Atahualpa anyway. Some Incas fought the Spaniards,

SUMMARY AND PREVIEW The Inca Empire's strong central government helped it control a huge area. But it could not survive the challenge posed by the Spanish. In the next section you will read about life and society in the Inca Empire at its height, before it was conquered by the Spanish.

Section 3 Assessment

go.hrw.com
Online Quiz
KEYWORD: SQ7 CH15

Reviewing Ideas, Terms, and People **HSS** 7.7.1, 7.7.3

1. **a. Identify** What were two things the central Inca government controlled?
   b. Explain How did pre-Inca civilizations adapt to their environment?
   c. Evaluate Do you think the *mita* system was a good government policy? Why or why not?
2. **a. Recall** When did the Spanish gain full control over the entire Inca region?
   b. Compare How was the end of the Inca Empire similar to the end of the Aztec Empire?
   c. Predict Predict what might have happened if **Atahualpa** had told **Pizarro** he accepted Christianity.

Critical Thinking

3. **Sequencing** Draw a time line like the one below. Use it to identify three key dates and events in the history of the Inca Empire.

FOCUS ON WRITING

4. **Thinking about the Inca Empire** Think about how you will describe the Inca Empire in your dialogue. Write down some notes about Inca language, government, food, and economy.

Inca Life and Society

If YOU were there...

You are an Inca noble. One day, you travel with the king and the army to take over new lands for the empire. There is a bloody battle, and you win a major victory. You want to make sure that later generations know about this important event, but your language has no written form.

How will you pass on your knowledge of history?

BUILDING BACKGROUND Certain people in the Inca Empire were responsible for making sure Inca history, legends, and customs got passed down to the next generation. To do this, they sang songs and wrote poems telling about everything from great battles to daily life.

Society and Daily Life

Inca society had two main social classes—an upper class and a lower class. The Incas from Cuzco made up the upper class. As they conquered new lands, the conquered people became Inca subjects and joined the lower class.

Daily Life for the Upper Class

The king, priests, and government officials made up the Inca upper class. While most noble men worked for the government, women from noble families had household duties such as cooking and making clothes. They also took care of children.

Sons of upper-class families went to school in Cuzco. They studied Quechua, religion, history, and law to prepare for lives as government or religious officials.

Upper-class families had many privileges. They lived in stone houses in Cuzco and wore the best clothes. They didn't have to pay the labor tax, and they often had servants. Still, as part of the Inca government, they had a duty to make sure that people in the empire had what they needed.

What You Will Learn...

Main Ideas

1. For the Incas, position in society affected daily life.
2. The Incas made great achievements in building, art, and oral literature.

The Big Idea

Many kinds of people made up Inca society in an empire known for grand architecture and complex oral literature.

Key Term
masonry, *p. 430*

HSS **7.7.2** Study the roles of people in each society, including class structures, family life, warfare, religious beliefs and practices, and slavery.

7.7.4 Describe the artistic and oral traditions and architecture in the three civilizations.

427

Daily Life for the Lower Class

Most Incas were farmers, artisans, or servants. There were no slaves in Inca society. Lower-class men and women farmed on government lands, served in the army, worked in mines, and built roads.

Parents taught their children how to work, so most children didn't go to school. But some carefully chosen young girls did go to school to learn weaving, cooking, and religion. Then they were sent to serve the king or work in the temple in Cuzco.

Lower-class Incas lived outside Cuzco in small houses. By law they had to wear plain clothes. Also, they couldn't own more goods than they needed.

History Close-up

Machu Picchu

Machu Picchu was a royal retreat for the Inca rulers. Built amid sacred mountain peaks, the city is an amazing engineering accomplishment. Its massive stone walls, steep staircases, and level fields were built so well that many remain today, more than 500 years later.

Scholars believe the Incas held festivals like this one in honor of the sun.

This narrow gate was the only entrance into Machu Picchu.

The Incas stored food in this warehouse.

Inca farmers grew corn, potatoes, and plants used for medicine in fields outside the city walls.

Religion

The Inca Empire had an official religion. When the Incas conquered new territories, they taught this religion to the conquered peoples. But the people could still worship their own gods, too. As a result, the many groups of people who made up the empire worshipped many different gods.

The sun god was important to Inca religion. As the sun set earlier each day in the winter, at Machu Picchu priests performed a ceremony to tie down the sun and keep it from disappearing completely. The Incas believed their kings were related to the sun god. As a result, the Incas thought their kings never really died.

This unique building had a bathroom, private garden, and guard area. Scholars think this is where the Inca ruler may have lived.

This canal built of rock brought water into the city.

ANALYSIS SKILL **ANALYZING VISUALS**

What features of Inca technology can you see in this illustration?

Inca Arts

Inca arts included beautiful textiles and gold and silver objects. While many gold and silver objects have been lost, some Inca textiles have survived for hundreds of years.

This llama is made of silver. Inca artisans made many silver offerings to the gods.

The Incas are famous for their textiles, which featured bright colors and detailed designs. Inca artists made cloth from cotton and from the wool of llamas.

In fact, priests brought mummies of former kings to many ceremonies. People gave these royal mummies food and gifts. Some Inca rulers even asked them for advice.

Inca ceremonies often included sacrifice. But unlike the Maya and the Aztecs, the Incas rarely sacrificed humans. They usually sacrificed llamas, cloth, or food.

Incas outside Cuzco worshipped their gods at local sacred places. The Incas believed certain mountaintops, rocks, and springs had magical powers. Incas performed sacrifices at these places as well as at the temple in Cuzco.

READING CHECK **Contrasting** How was daily life different for upper- and lower-class Incas?

Building, Art, and Oral Literature

The Incas had strong traditions of building, art, and storytelling. Many of their creations still exist today.

Building

The Incas are known for their massive buildings and forts made of huge, stone blocks. Workers cut the blocks so precisely that they didn't have to use cement to hold them together. Inca **masonry**, or stonework, was of such high quality that even today it is nearly impossible to fit a knife blade between the stones. In fact, many Inca buildings in Cuzco are still being used.

The Incas also built a system of very good roads in their empire. Two major highways that ran the length of the empire formed the basis of the system. Roads paved with stone crossed mountains and deserts. With these roads and rope bridges spanning rivers and canyons, the Incas connected all parts of the empire.

Art

The Incas produced works of art as well. Artisans made gold and silver jewelry and offerings to the gods. They even created a

Inca artisans also worked in gold. They made many beautiful objects such as this mask.

ANALYSIS SKILL ANALYZING VISUALS

What are some features of Inca art that you can see in these pictures?

life-sized field of corn out of gold and silver in a temple courtyard. Each cob, leaf, and stalk was individually crafted.

Incas also made some of the best textiles in the Americas. Archaeologists have found brightly colored Inca textiles that are still in excellent condition.

Oral Literature

While archaeologists have found many Inca artifacts, there are no written records about the empire produced before the Spanish conquest. Instead, Incas passed down stories and songs orally. Incas sang about daily life and military victories. Official "memorizers" learned long poems about Inca legends and history.

After the conquistadors came, some Incas learned how to speak and write in Spanish. They wrote about Inca legends and history. We know about the Incas from these records and from the stories that survive in the songs, dances, and religious practices of people in the region today.

READING CHECK Drawing Inferences How might the Inca road system have helped strengthen the empire?

SUMMARY AND PREVIEW The Aztec and Inca empires had some similarities in their rise and fall and in their culture. In the next chapter you will learn about the European explorations that caused the end of these two empires in the Americas.

---

go.hrw.com
Online Quiz
KEYWORD: SQ7 CH15

Section 4 Assessment

Reviewing Ideas, Terms, and People HSS 7.7.2, 7.7.4

1. **a. Identify** Who were members of the Inca upper class?
   b. Explain How were Inca government and religion related?
   c. Elaborate Why do you think Inca law outlined what clothes people of various classes could wear?
2. **a. Describe** What was impressive about Inca **masonry**?
   b. Draw Conclusions Were Inca oral traditions successful in preserving information? Why or why not?
   c. Predict Why do you think the Incas wanted to connect all parts of their empire with roads?

Critical Thinking

3. **Categorizing** Draw a chart like the one below. Use it to categorize different aspects of daily life among upper-class and lower-class Incas.

	Upper class	Lower class
Work		
School		
Clothing and shelter		
Religion		

FOCUS ON WRITING

4. **Describing Inca Society** From what social class is the Inca child in your dialogue? Make some notes about his or her daily life.

Inca Roads

Inca roads were more than just roads—they were engineering marvels. The Incas built roads across almost every kind of terrain imaginable: coasts, deserts, forests, grasslands, plains, and mountains. In doing so, they overcame the geography of their rugged empire.

Although the Incas had no wheeled vehicles, they relied on their roads for transportation, communication, and government administration. The roads symbolized the power of the Inca government.

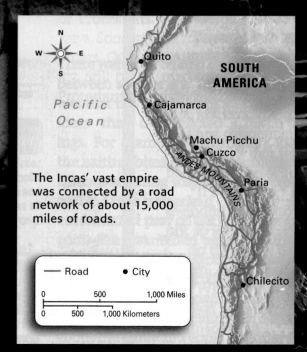

SOUTH AMERICA

Quito

Pacific Ocean

Cajamarca

Machu Picchu
Cuzco

ANDES MOUNTAINS

Paria

The Incas' vast empire was connected by a road network of about 15,000 miles of roads.

Chilecito

— Road   • City

0   500   1,000 Miles

0   500   1,000 Kilometers

Many roads were just three to six feet wide, but that was wide enough for people on foot and for llamas, which the Incas used as pack animals.

Inca engineers built rope bridges to cross the valleys of the Andes Mountains. Rope bridges could stretch more than 200 feet across high gorges.

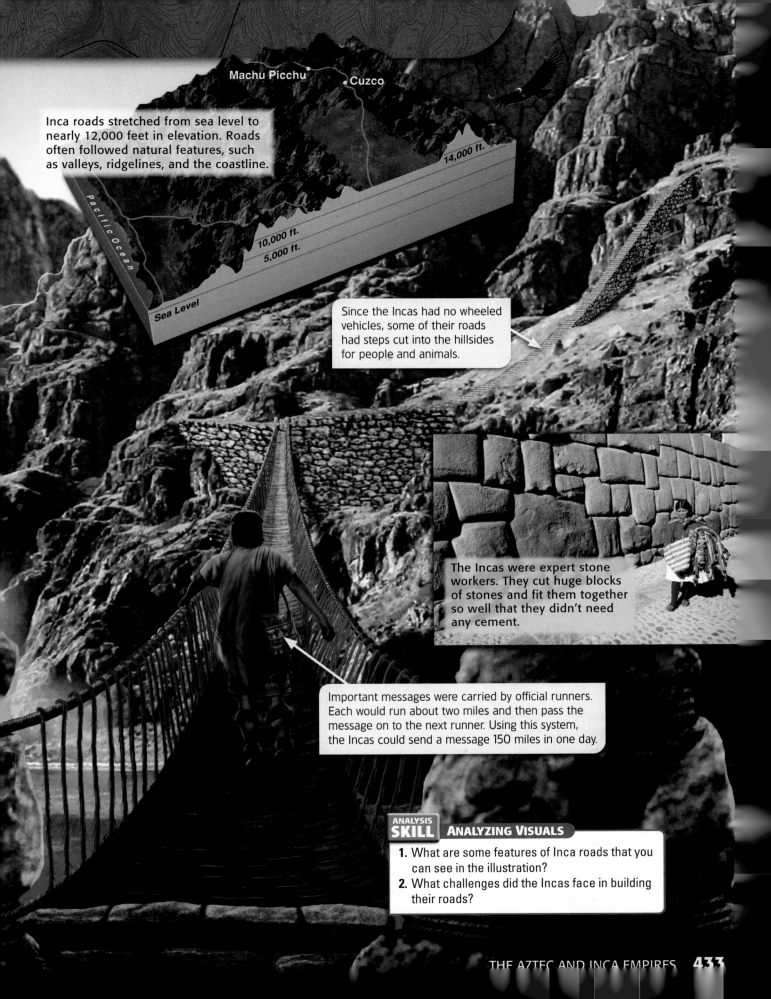

Machu Picchu · Cuzco

Inca roads stretched from sea level to nearly 12,000 feet in elevation. Roads often followed natural features, such as valleys, ridgelines, and the coastline.

14,000 ft.

10,000 ft.

5,000 ft.

Pacific Ocean

Sea Level

Since the Incas had no wheeled vehicles, some of their roads had steps cut into the hillsides for people and animals.

The Incas were expert stone workers. They cut huge blocks of stones and fit them together so well that they didn't need any cement.

Important messages were carried by official runners. Each would run about two miles and then pass the message on to the next runner. Using this system, the Incas could send a message 150 miles in one day.

ANALYSIS
SKILL **ANALYZING VISUALS**

1. What are some features of Inca roads that you can see in the illustration?
2. What challenges did the Incas face in building their roads?

Social Studies Skills

Analysis	Critical Thinking	Participation	Study

Interpreting Culture Maps

Understand the Skill

A culture map is a special type of political map. As you already know, political maps show human features of an area, such as boundaries, settlements, and roads. The human features on a culture map are cultural features, such as the languages spoken, major religions, or groups of people. Culture maps are one of several different types of political maps that historians often use. The ability to interpret them is an important skill for understanding history.

Learn the Skill

The guidelines for interpreting a culture map are similar to those for understanding any map.

❶ Use map basics. Read the title to identify the subject. Note the labels, legend, and scale. Pay particular attention to special symbols for cultural features. Be sure you understand what these symbols represent.

❷ Study the map as a whole. Note the location of the cultural symbols and features. Ask yourself how they relate to the rest of the map.

❸ Connect the information on the map to any written information on the subject.

Practice and Apply the Skill

Apply the guidelines to the map on this page. Use them to answer the questions here.

1. What makes this map a culture map?

2. Where did the Aztecs live?

3. What people lived to the north of the Aztecs?

4. What other peoples lived in the Lake Texcoco area?

5. What was the main culture in the town of Texcoco?

6. How does this map help you better understand the Aztec Empire?

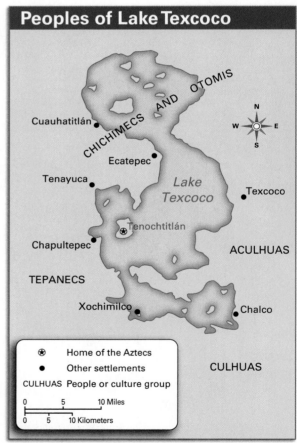

Peoples of Lake Texcoco

Visual Summary

Use the visual summary below to help you review the main ideas of the chapter.

QUICK FACTS

The Aztecs built a great empire from their capital at Tenochtitlán.

Spanish explorers led by Hernán Cortés conquered the Aztecs in 1521.

The Inca Empire stretched along the west coast of South America.

Francisco Pizarro and a group of Spanish explorers conquered the Incas in 1537.

Reviewing Vocabulary, Terms, and People

Match each numbered definition with the correct lettered vocabulary term.

a. codex   **g.** Francisco Pizarro

b. masonry   **h.** conquistadors

c. Moctezuma II   **i.** Hernán Cortés

d. Pachacuti   **j.** Quechua

e. causeways   **k.** Atahualpa

f. llamas

1. members of the camel family that Incas raised for wool

2. a type of ancient book

3. leader who expanded Inca Empire

4. raised paths across water or wet ground

5. led Spanish in defeat of Aztec Empire

6. Spanish soldiers who came to the Americas to explore new lands, search for gold, and spread their religion

7. stonework

8. Inca leader captured by the Spanish

9. official language of the Inca Empire

10. Aztec leader at the fall of the Aztec Empire

11. led Spanish in defeat of Inca Empire

Comprehension and Critical Thinking

SECTION 1 *(Pages 410–414)* **HSS** 7.7.1, 7.7.3

12. a Describe What was Tenochtitlán like? Where was it located?

b. Draw Conclusions What factor do you think played the biggest role in the Aztecs' defeat? Defend your answer.

c. Elaborate How did an Aztec religious belief play a role in the Spaniards' conquest of the Aztecs?

SECTION 2 *(Pages 416–421)* **HSS** 7.7.2, 7.7.4, 7.7.5

13. a. Identify What were the four basic classes of Aztec society?

b. Analyze What was the connection between warfare and Aztec religious ceremonies?

c. Elaborate How did Aztec art and architecture make use of natural materials?

SECTION 3 *(Pages 422–426)* **HSS** 7.7.1, 7.7.3

14. a. Recall Who was Pachacuti, and what did he accomplish?

b. Make Inferences What problems did the Incas overcome to rule their huge empire?

c. Predict What might have happened if Atahualpa and Huáscar had settled their argument peacefully?

SECTION 4 *(Pages 427–431)* **HSS** 7.7.2, 7.7.4

15. a. Describe What were some important features of Inca masonry? of the Inca road system?

b. Contrast How did daily life differ for the Inca upper class and for the Inca lower class?

c. Elaborate Why do scholars have to depend on archaeological evidence and documents written in Spanish for information on Inca civilization? How may our knowledge of Inca life have been affected?

Using the Internet

go.hrw.com
KEYWORD: SQ7 WH15

16. Activity: Making Diagrams In this chapter, you learned about the rise and fall of the Spanish, Aztec, and Inca empires. What you may not know is that the rise and fall of empires is a pattern that occurs again and again across history. Enter the activity keyword. Then create a diagram that shows the factors that cause empires to form as well as the factors that cause them to decline. What sort of diagram would best represent the forces in the rise and fall of empires?

Reviewing Themes

17. Politics What were the similarities between the rise of the Aztec Empire and the rise of the Inca Empire?

18. Science and Technology What methods did Aztec and Inca builders develop to overcome geographical challenges?

Reading Skills

Understanding Proposition and Support *For each sentence below, note in what ways you could support the proposition.*

19. The Aztecs had great skills in architecture and engineering.

20. The Incas had a highly structured government.

Social Studies Skills

21. Understanding Cultural Maps Look in the chapter at the maps of the Aztec and Inca empires. Why do you think the Aztec Empire didn't include all the land from Tula to Xoconocho? How would physical features have affected the Inca rulers' ability to rule their empire?

FOCUS ON WRITING

22. Writing a Lively Dialogue Review the notes you've taken about life in the Aztec and Inca empires. Think about what life would have been like for children in each place. Then write a dialogue in which the children describe and compare their lives.

To make your dialogue more interesting and lively, imagine what each child's personality is like. Use clear, sensory details to create a rich picture of each child's life. You may also want to describe the facial expressions each child might make while he or she is talking.

Standards Assessment

DIRECTIONS: Read each question, and write the letter of the best response.

1 Use the map to answer the following question.

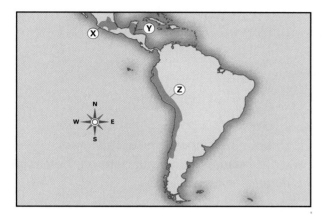

The Aztec and Inca empires are indicated on this map by

A X for the Inca and Y for the Aztec.

B Y for the Aztec and Z for the Inca.

C Y for the Inca and Z for the Aztec.

D X for the Aztec and Z for the Inca.

2 The following factors all helped the Spanish to conquer the Aztecs and Incas *except*

A European diseases.

B greater numbers of soldiers.

C superior weapons.

D existing problems within the empires.

3 Which statement *best* compares or contrasts agriculture in the Aztec and Inca empires?

A The Aztecs farmed on terraces and the Incas grew crops on *chinampas.*

B The Incas had to adapt to their environment while the Aztecs did not.

C Most people in both the Aztec and Inca empires were farmers.

D Both Aztecs and Incas raised llamas.

4 Aztec and Inca cultures differed in all of the following areas *except*

A in the worship of many different gods.

B in the practice of slavery.

C in trade within the empire.

D in the practice of human sacrifice.

5 Which people had a writing system *in addition to* a rich oral literature?

A both the Inca and the Aztec

B only the Inca

C only the Aztec

D neither the Inca nor the Aztec

Connecting with Past Learnings

6 Aztec warriors were highly honored members of society. Their status was *most* like that of warriors in which society that you studied in Grade 6?

A Chinese

B Athenian

C Sumerian

D Spartan

7 In your study of ancient history, you learned the Egyptians believed their ruler was related to the sun god. This is *most* like the beliefs of the

A Incas.

B Nazca.

C Aztecs.

D Maya.

Opinions about Historical Events

Even though history is mostly about facts, people can disagree about what those facts mean. When we disagree about the meaning of historical events, we often use persuasive arguments to convince others to agree with our opinion.

1. Prewrite

Stating Your Opinion

Persuasion begins with an opinion. Choose one of the topics suggested in the assignment, and write a statement of your opinion. Here is an example: *Malintzin was a traitor to her people.*

Building a Good Argument

In persuasion, an argument has nothing to do with anger or fighting. Instead, an argument is logical proof to support an opinion. Logical proof starts with **reasons**, which tell *why* you have an opinion. For each reason, you need **evidence**—facts, examples, or expert opinions.

> **Opinion:** *The Incas built the greatest early American empire.*
> **Reason:** *They established central control over the empire.*
> **Evidence:** *They created an official language, Quechua.* [fact]

Organizing Your Reasons

Organizing your reasons by **order of importance** can help you persuade your readers. Start with the least important reason and build to the most convincing one. Your readers will probably remember that reason.

2. Write

Here is a framework you can use to write your first draft.

Assignment

Write a persuasive essay supporting your opinion on one of the following topics:

- The Aztecs [or the Incas] built the most advanced early American empire.
- Hernán Cortés was [or was not] a villain.

TIP **Using Expert Opinions**

Experts are people who have researched and studied a particular topic. You can find their statements in this textbook or other books on the Aztecs or the Incas. Because these experts have studied the topic, their opinions are considered to be reliable. Readers are likely to find their opinions convincing.

ELA **Writing 7.2.4** Write persuasive compositions.

A Writer's Framework

Introduction	Body	Conclusion
■ Start with a question, a quotation, or a surprising fact. ■ State the topic and your opinion on it.	■ Include three reasons to support your opinion. ■ Support each reason with evidence. ■ Organize your reasons in order of importance, most important last.	■ Summarize your reasons. ■ Restate your opinion in different words. ■ Close by making a connection to a historical or current event.

3. Evaluate and Revise

Evaluating

Use these questions to discover ways to improve your first draft.

Evaluation Questions for a Persuasive Essay

- Does the introduction identify your topic and clearly state your opinion?
- Do you provide at least three reasons to support your opinion?
- Do you include facts, examples, or expert opinions to support each reason?
- Do you start a new paragraph with each reason?
- Does your conclusion restate your opinion in different words?
- Does your conclusion summarize your supporting reasons?
- Do you end by making a connection to another historical or current event?

> **TIP** **Fact v. Opinion** Knowing the difference between a fact and an opinion is important for both writers and readers of persuasive essays.
>
> - **Facts** are statements that can be proven true or false. *The Aztecs developed a calendar.*
> - **Opinions** are statements of personal belief and cannot be proven. *Tenochtitlán was a better city than any European city at the time.*

Revising

Look for sentences that begin with "There is," "There are," or "It is." These sentences have delayed or lost subjects that can weaken your writing. A **delayed subject** comes too late. A **lost subject** does not appear at all.

> **Delayed:** There are many historians who say that the Aztecs had a strong scientific tradition. (The subject is *historians*. Beginning the sentence with *There are* weakens its focus.)
>
> **Better:** Many historians say the Aztecs had a strong scientific tradition.
>
> **Lost:** It is believed that the Incas passed down stories orally. (The subject is lost, so we don't know *who* believes this.)
>
> **Better:** Archaeologists believe the Incas passed down stories orally.

4. Proofread and Publish

Proofreading

When you use expert opinions to support your opinion, you will probably include a direct quotation. Check to see whether you have enclosed any direct quotation in quotation marks.

Publishing

Get together with a group of students who have different opinions on the same topic. Make a list of all the reasons you have to support your opinion. Discuss the different opinions and then take a vote to see whether the discussion changed anyone's opinion about the topic.

● Practice and Apply

Use the steps and strategies in this workshop to write a persuasive essay.

The Early Modern World

What You Will Learn...

The world changed dramatically with the Age of Exploration. As European explorers sailed around the globe, they found new continents and began to see what the shape of the world was really like. In addition, new contacts between distant peoples and lands changed societies and economies around the world.

At the same time, European thinkers developed new ideas about government during a period known as the Enlightenment. These ideas led people to take up arms in revolutions and fight for their freedom.

In the next two chapters, you will learn how both European exploration and the Enlightenment helped shape the world we live in today.

Explore the Art

In this scene, young sailor Diego Bermúdez tends a sail on Columbus's first voyage to the Americas. Why might a young boy like Diego have joined Columbus on such a dangerous voyage?

The Age of Exploration

California Standards

History–Social Science

7.11 Students analyze political and economic change in the sixteenth, seventeenth, and eighteenth centuries (the Age of Exploration, the Enlightenment, and the Age of Reason).

Analysis Skills

HI 1 Explain central issues and problems from the past.

English–Language Arts

Speaking 7.1.4 Organize information to achieve particular purposes.

Reading 7.2.0 Students read and understand grade-level-appropriate material.

FOCUS ON SPEAKING

An Informative Report A teacher at an elementary school has asked you to create an informative report for fifth-graders about changes in Europe, Africa, Asia, and the Americas during the Age of Exploration. The teacher wants you to prepare a short speech and create a simple visual aid, such as a chart, to help teach her class.

CHAPTER EVENTS

WORLD EVENTS

1416 Henry the Navigator sets up his school of navigation.

1400

HOLT

History's Impact

▶ video series
Watch the video to understand the impact of the Columbian Exchange on Europe and America.

What You Will Learn...

In this chapter you will learn how European explorers first discovered the true size and shape of the world. This photo shows replicas of the ships Christopher Columbus used to sail to the Americas in 1492.

1488
Dias sails around the southern tip of Africa.

1492
Columbus arrives in the Americas.

1520
Magellan leads a voyage around the southern tip of South America.

1602
The Dutch East India Company is formed for trade between the Netherlands, Asia, and Africa.

| 1450 | 1500 | 1550 | 1600 | 1650 |

1443
The Korean writing system is developed.

c. 1500
Askia the Great rules Songhai.

c. 1647
Construction on the Taj Mahal is completed.

Reading Social Studies

by Kylene Beers

| Economics | Geography | Politics | Religion | Society and Culture | Science and Technology |

Focus on Themes In this chapter you will read about the European explorers who sailed to the Americas and the routes they followed to get there. You will learn how their explorations helped people understand the **geography** of the world. You will also learn how their explorations led to the discovery of new products and the creation of worldwide trade patterns. These patterns in time laid the foundation for a new **economic** system called capitalism.

Summarizing Historical Texts

Focus on Reading Summarizing is an important skill to have when you are reading a history book. Summarizing what you read can help you understand and remember it.

Summarizing A **summary** is a short restatement of the most important ideas in a text. The example below shows three steps used in writing a summary. First underline important details. Then write a short summary of each paragraph. Finally, combine these paragraph summaries into a short summary of the whole passage.

Additional reading support can be found in the

Inter active

Reader and Study Guide

An Italian sailor thought he could reach Asia by sailing west across the Atlantic. That sailor, Christopher Columbus, told his idea to the Spanish monarchs, Ferdinand and Isabella. He promised them great riches, new territory, and Catholic converts. It took Columbus several years to convince the king and queen, but Isabella eventually agreed to pay for his journey.

In August 1492 Columbus set sail with 88 men and three small ships, the *Niña*, the *Pinta*, and the *Santa María*. On October 12, 1492, he and his tired crew landed on a small island in the Bahamas. What was Columbus's mistake? He didn't realize another continent lay in front of him, and he believed he had reached Asia.

Summary of Paragraph 1
Christopher Columbus thought he could sail west to reach Asia. He convinced the queen of Spain to pay for his voyage.

Summary of Paragraph 2
Columbus set out in 1492 with three ships. He reached the Bahamas in October, but thought he was in Asia.

Combined Summary
In 1492, Christopher Columbus set out from Spain, heading for Asia. Instead he reached the Americas but thought he was in Asia.

You Try It!

The following passage is from the chapter you are about to read. As you read it, think about what details you would include in a summary of this passage.

Conquest of America

From Chapter 16 p. 450

When Spanish explorers arrived in the early 1500s, the Aztec Empire in Mexico and the Inca Empire in Peru were at the height of their power. Their buildings and the riches of their cities impressed the conquistadors. The Spanish saw these empires as good sources of gold and silver. They also wanted to convert the native peoples to Christianity.

Spanish explorers led by Cortés and Pizarro soon conquered the Aztecs and Incas. The Spanish had better weapons, and they also brought new diseases such as smallpox. Diseases killed possibly more than three-quarters of the native peoples, who had no immunity to the diseases. The Spanish soon ruled large parts of the Americas.

After reading the passage, answer the questions below.

1. What details from the first paragraph would you include in a summary? Write a summary statement for this paragraph.

2. What details from the second paragraph would you include in a summary? Write a summary statement for this paragraph.

3. Combine your two summaries into a single brief summary of the whole passage.

Key Terms and People

Chapter 16

Section 1
Henry the Navigator *(p. 448)*
Vasco da Gama *(p. 449)*
Christopher Columbus *(p. 449)*
Ferdinand Magellan *(p. 449)*
circumnavigate *(p. 449)*
Francis Drake *(p. 451)*
Spanish Armada *(p. 451)*

Section 2
Columbian Exchange *(p. 454)*
plantations *(p. 456)*
Bartolomé de las Casas *(p. 457)*
racism *(p. 457)*

Section 3
mercantilism *(p. 459)*
balance of trade *(p. 459)*
cottage industry *(p. 460)*
atlas *(p. 461)*
capitalism *(p. 463)*
market economy *(p. 463)*

Academic Vocabulary

Success in school is related to knowing academic vocabulary— the words that are frequently used in school assignments and discussions. In this chapter, you will learn the following academic words:

primary *(p. 455)*
acquire *(p. 460)*

As you read Chapter 16, decide which details of each paragraph you would include in a summary.

Great Voyages of Discovery

What You Will Learn...

Main Ideas

1. Europeans had a desire and opportunity to explore.
2. Portuguese and Spanish explorations led to discoveries of new trade routes, lands, and people.
3. English and French explorers found land in North America.
4. A new European worldview developed because of the discoveries.

The Big Idea

European explorers made discoveries that brought knowledge, wealth, and influence to their countries.

Key Terms and People

Henry the Navigator, *p. 448*
Vasco da Gama, *p. 449*
Christopher Columbus, *p. 449*
Ferdinand Magellan, *p. 449*
circumnavigate, *p. 449*
Francis Drake, *p. 451*
Spanish Armada, *p. 451*

HSS 7.11.1 Know the great voyages of discovery, the locations of the routes, and the influence of cartography in the development of a new European worldview.

If YOU were there...

Your uncle is a Portuguese ship captain who has just come back from a long sea voyage. He shows you a map of the new lands he has seen. He tells wonderful stories about strange plants and animals. You are studying to become a carpenter, but you wonder if you might like to be an explorer like your uncle instead.

How would you decide which career to choose?

BUILDING BACKGROUND A spirit of adventure swept across Europe in the 1400s. Improved maps showed new lands. Travelers' tales encouraged people to dream of finding riches and adventure.

Desire and Opportunity to Explore

An interest in discovery and exploration grew in Europe in the 1400s. Improvements in navigational tools, cartography, and shipbuilding allowed European sailors to go farther than they ever had before.

Reasons to Explore

Why did people set off to explore the world in the fifteenth century? First, they wanted Asian spices. Italy and Egypt controlled the trade routes to Asia, charging very high prices for spices. In fact, pepper cost more than gold. Many countries wanted to find a route to Asia so they could get spices without having to buy from Italian or Egyptian traders.

Religion gave explorers another reason to set sail. European Christians wanted to convert more people to their religion to counteract the spread of Islam in Europe, Africa, and Asia.

Simple curiosity was also an important motivation for exploration. Many people read stories of Marco Polo's travels and other explorers' adventures. They learned about new lands and creatures, and they became curious about the world.

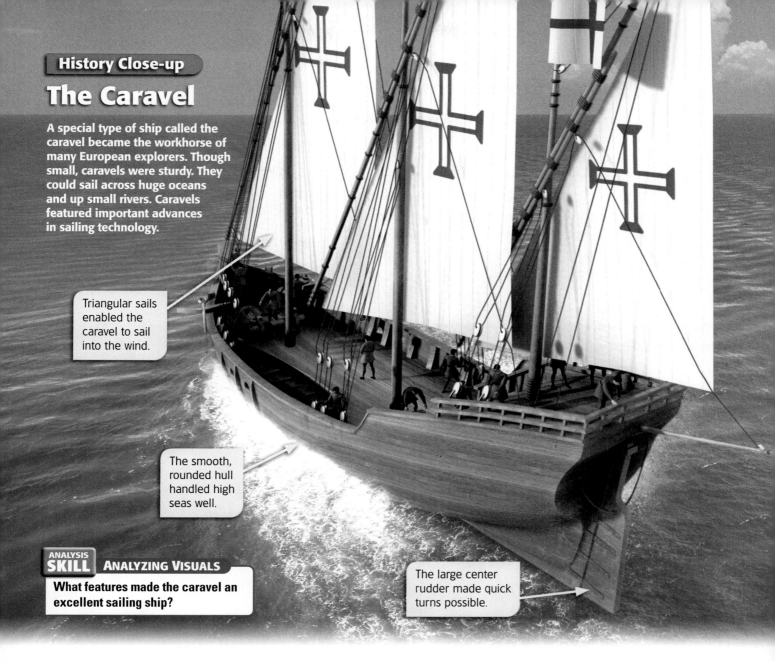

History Close-up
The Caravel

A special type of ship called the caravel became the workhorse of many European explorers. Though small, caravels were sturdy. They could sail across huge oceans and up small rivers. Caravels featured important advances in sailing technology.

Triangular sails enabled the caravel to sail into the wind.

The smooth, rounded hull handled high seas well.

ANALYSIS SKILL **ANALYZING VISUALS**

What features made the caravel an excellent sailing ship?

The large center rudder made quick turns possible.

Advances in Technology

Whatever their reasons for exploring, Europeans wouldn't have gotten very far without advances in technology. Sailors started using the astrolabe and the compass to find routes they could follow to reach faraway places and return safely home. More accurate maps allowed sailors to sail from one port to another without having to stay right along the coast. Before these advances, most sailors avoided the open sea out of fear they might not find their way back to land.

Other advances, mainly by the Portuguese, came in shipbuilding. They began building ships called caravels (KER-uh-velz). Caravels used triangular sails that, unlike traditional square sails, allowed ships to sail against the wind. By replacing oars on the ship's sides with rudders at the back of the ship, the Portuguese also improved the steering of ships. The new ships helped Portuguese sailors take the lead in exploring.

READING CHECK Analyzing What advances in technology aided exploration?

Portuguese and Spanish Explorations

A man who never went on any sea voyages was responsible for much of Portugal's success on the seas. Known as Prince **Henry the Navigator**, he built an observatory and a navigation school to teach sailors how to find their way. He also paid people to sail on voyages of exploration. Spanish sailors later followed the Portuguese example of exploration around the world.

Africa

Even with new technology, travel on the open sea remained dangerous and scary. One person described what happened to sailors on a voyage south.

"Those which survived could hardly be recognized as human. They had lost flesh and hair, the nails had gone from hands and feet . . . They spoke of heat so incredible that it was a marvel that ships and crews were not burnt."

–Anonymous sailor, quoted in Edward McNall Burns, et al., *World Civilizations*

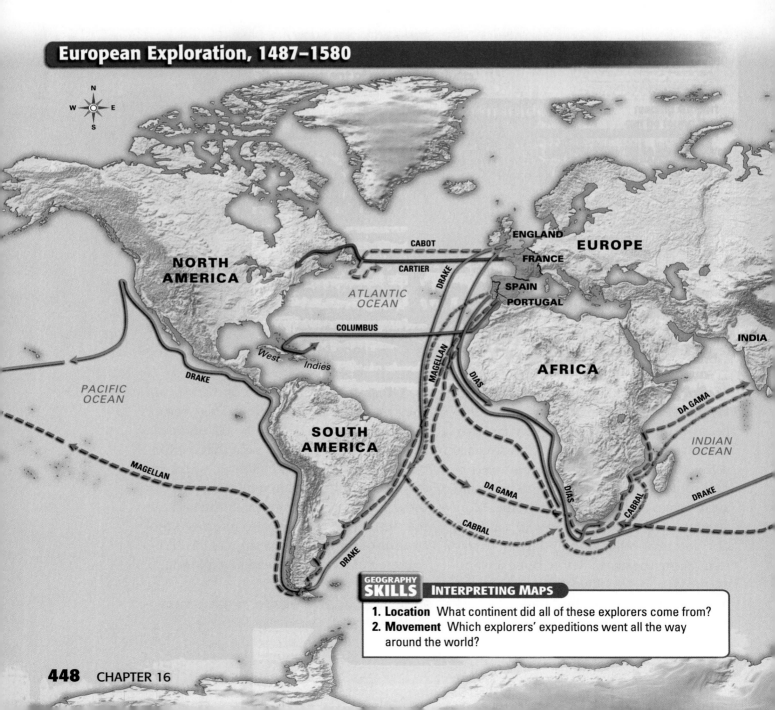

European Exploration, 1487–1580

GEOGRAPHY SKILLS **INTERPRETING MAPS**

1. **Location** What continent did all of these explorers come from?
2. **Movement** Which explorers' expeditions went all the way around the world?

In spite of the dangers, Portuguese explorers sailed south, setting up trading posts along the way.

In 1488 a ship led by Bartolomeu Dias succeeded in sailing around the southern tip of Africa. The crew, tired and afraid of the raging seas, forced Dias to turn back. However, they had found a way around Africa. **Vasco da Gama** sailed around Africa and landed on the west coast of India in 1498. A sea route to Asia had been found. See their routes on the map.

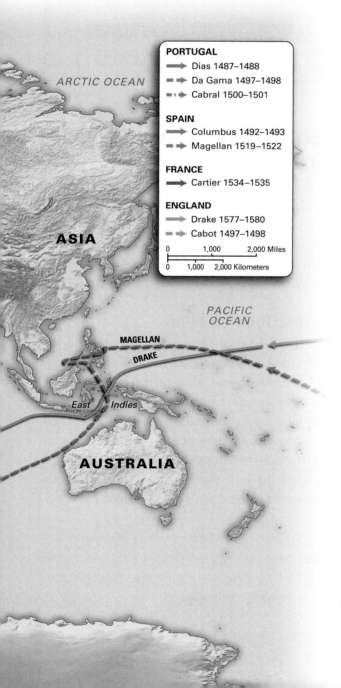

PORTUGAL
→ Dias 1487–1488
→ Da Gama 1497–1498
→ Cabral 1500–1501

SPAIN
→ Columbus 1492–1493
→ Magellan 1519–1522

FRANCE
→ Cartier 1534–1535

ENGLAND
→ Drake 1577–1580
→ Cabot 1497–1498

0   1,000   2,000 Miles
0 1,000 2,000 Kilometers

ARCTIC OCEAN

ASIA

PACIFIC OCEAN

MAGELLAN

DRAKE

East Indies

AUSTRALIA

A "New World"

Imagination, daring, and a few mistakes enabled Portuguese and Spanish sailors to discover the Americas. They thought these lands were a "new world."

An Italian sailor thought he could reach Asia by sailing west across the Atlantic. That sailor, **Christopher Columbus**, told his idea to the Spanish monarchs, Ferdinand and Isabella. He promised them great riches, new territory, and Catholic converts. It took Columbus several years to convince the king and queen, but Isabella eventually agreed to pay for his journey.

In August 1492 Columbus set sail with 88 men and three small ships, the *Niña*, the *Pinta*, and the *Santa María*. On October 12, 1492, he and his tired crew landed on a small island in the Bahamas. What was Columbus's mistake? He didn't realize another continent lay in front of him, and he believed he had reached Asia. At that time Europeans called Asia the Indies, so Columbus called the people who lived on the island Indians.

Columbus made three more journeys to America during his lifetime, never realizing that he had found a land unknown to Europeans. Columbus died still believing that he had reached Asia.

Another mistake enabled Portuguese explorer Pedro Cabral to discover South America. He tried to sail around Africa, but he sailed too far west, landing on the coast of what is now Brazil. In 1520 **Ferdinand Magellan** (muh-JEHL-uhn) led a voyage around the southern tip of South America. A Portuguese navigator sailing for Spain, Magellan daringly continued sailing into the Pacific even though his ships were dangerously low on food and fresh water. Although Magellan was killed before he made it back to Spain, the voyage he directed became the first to **circumnavigate**, or go all the way around, the globe.

FOCUS ON READING
What would you include in a summary of the information on this page?

LETTER
Columbus Describes America

After his first trip to the New World, Columbus wrote a letter to the king and queen of Spain describing what he found. In his letter, he tried to convince the monarchs that it was worth making other voyages to the New World.

Columbus used very positive language to describe the New World.

Spanish explorers had hoped to find gold, as well as spices, on their voyages.

“Española is a wonder. Its mountains and plains, and meadows, and fields, are so beautiful and rich for planting and sowing, and rearing cattle of all kinds, and for building towns and villages. The harbors on the coast, and the number and size and wholesomeness of the rivers, most of them bearing gold, surpass anything that would be believed by one who had not seen them.**”**

–Christopher Columbus, from
Selected Letters of Christopher Columbus,
translated by R. H. Major

ANALYSIS SKILL | ANALYZING PRIMARY SOURCES

Why do you think Columbus was so impressed with the features of the New World?

Conquest of America

When Spanish explorers arrived in America in the early 1500s, the Aztec Empire in Mexico and the Inca Empire in Peru were at the height of their power. Their buildings and the riches of their cities impressed the conquistadors. The Spanish saw these empires as good sources of gold and silver. They also wanted to convert the native peoples to Christianity.

Spanish explorers led by Cortés and Pizarro soon conquered the Aztecs and Incas. The Spanish had better weapons, and they also brought new diseases such as smallpox. Diseases killed possibly more than three-quarters of the native peoples, who had no immunity to the diseases. The Spanish soon ruled large parts of North and South America.

READING CHECK **Identifying Points of View**
Why did Europeans call the Americas a "new world"?

English and French in America

Like Spain and Portugal, England and France wanted to find a route to Asia to get spices. After Spain and Portugal explored and gained control of the southern routes, the English and French looked for a waterway through North America.

Exploring New Lands

In 1497 John Cabot, an Italian sailing for England, sailed west to the coast of Canada. Like Columbus, Cabot mistakenly thought he had reached Asia. In 1535 French explorer Jacques Cartier (zhahk kahr-tyay) sailed up the Saint Lawrence River into Canada. Although neither of these explorers found a route to Asia, they claimed land in North America for England and France.

Competing for Land and Wealth

Besides looking for a route to Asia, England hoped to find riches in the New World. But Spain controlled the gold and silver of the former Aztec and Inca empires. The English queen sent a sailor named **Francis Drake** to the Americas to steal gold and silver from Spanish ships called galleons. Drake became a rich and famous pirate.

Defeat of the Spanish Armada

The Spanish were furious with the English for these raids. In 1588 Spain sent 130 ships to attack England. This fleet, called the **Spanish Armada**, was part of Spain's large, experienced navy. But the English, with their faster ships and better guns, defeated the Armada. Returning from battle, more Spanish ships were lost in storms at sea. Fewer than half the Spanish ships ever returned to Spain.

The defeat of the Spanish Armada saved England from invasion. It also meant Spain no longer ruled the seas, and it allowed England to gain power.

READING CHECK **Making Generalizations** Why did France and England send explorers to North America?

A New European Worldview

The voyages of discovery changed the way Europeans thought of the world and their place in it. The explorations brought new knowledge about geography and proved some old beliefs wrong. For example, Europeans learned that ships didn't burn up crossing the equator and that the Americas were a separate landmass from Asia. Geographers made more accurate maps that reflected this new knowledge.

Improved mapmaking also helped shape a new European worldview. For the first time Europeans could see maps of the whole world. They saw new lands and possible trade routes. By controlling the trade routes and the resources in the new lands, they might gain great wealth. Voyages of

discovery brought the beginning of a new period in which Europeans would spread their influence around the world.

READING CHECK **Finding Main Ideas** How did cartography influence the development of a new European worldview?

SUMMARY AND PREVIEW European explorers sailed on voyages of discovery in the 1400s and 1500s. They found wealth, converts for Christianity, and new continents. In the next section you will read about the effects these discoveries had on Europe, Africa, the Americas, and Asia.

go.hrw.com
Online Quiz
KEYWORD: SQ7 HP16

Section 1 Assessment

Reviewing Ideas, Terms, and People HSS 7.11.1

1. **a. Describe** What were two improvements in shipbuilding that the Portuguese made?
   b. Explain Why were spices so expensive in Europe?
2. **a. Identify** Who directed the first voyage to **circumnavigate** the globe?
   b. Predict What might have happened if **Christopher Columbus** had decided to look to the east to find a route to Asia?
3. **a. Recall** Where did the English and French look for a route to Asia?
   b. Summarize How did the defeat of the **Spanish Armada** shift power in Europe?
4. **Explain** In what ways did the European worldview change in the 1400s and 1500s?

Critical Thinking

5. **Summarizing** Draw a chart like the one here. Use it to tell what each explorer discovered.

Explorer	Discovery

FOCUS ON SPEAKING

6. **Collecting Information** To begin noting information to include in your presentation, create a three-column chart. Label the first column "Africa," the second column "Asia," and the third column "The Americas." Look back through this section and note discoveries made by European explorers about each place.

Mapping New Worlds

During the Age of Exploration, Europeans began to learn more about the size and shape of the world. Sailors and explorers traveled to new lands and brought back new information about places. Then professional mapmakers used this knowledge to create maps. As explorers traveled farther, what had been blank areas on earlier maps disappeared, and people began to see how the world really was.

1536 This map from 1536 shows that the mapmaker was familiar with the coasts of Europe and Africa, but knew less about the Americas. In North America, for example, the coastline is not very accurate and the interior is completely blank.

Mapmakers never had all the information they needed to make their maps. They relied on many different sources of information, like explorers' accounts, earlier maps, and even legends.

Many early mapmakers illustrated their maps with legendary monsters like this one.

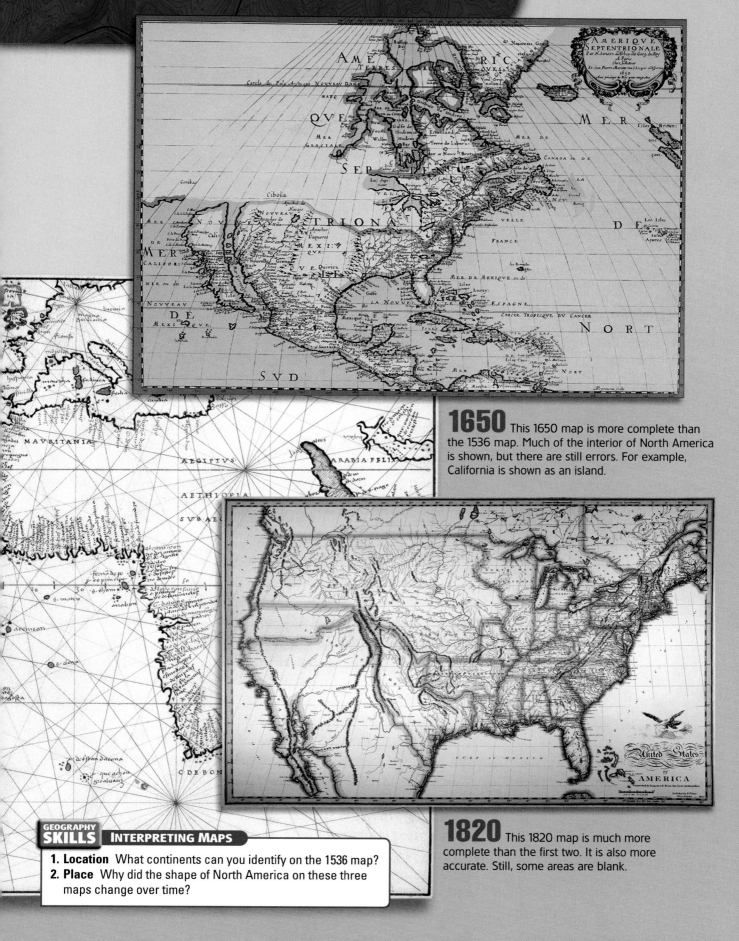

1650 This 1650 map is more complete than the 1536 map. Much of the interior of North America is shown, but there are still errors. For example, California is shown as an island.

1820 This 1820 map is much more complete than the first two. It is also more accurate. Still, some areas are blank.

1. Location What continents can you identify on the 1536 map?

2. Place Why did the shape of North America on these three maps change over time?

The Columbian Exchange

What You Will Learn...

Main Ideas

1. Plants and animals were exchanged among Europe, Asia, Africa, and the Americas.
2. Culture and technology changed as ideas were exchanged between Europe and the Americas.
3. Society and the economy changed in Europe and the Americas.

The Big Idea

The exchange of plants, animals, ideas, and technology between the Old World and the New World brought many changes all over the world.

Key Terms and People

Columbian Exchange, *p. 454*
plantations, *p. 456*
Bartolomé de las Casas, *p. 457*
racism, *p. 457*

HSS **7.11.2** Discuss the exchanges of plants, animals, technology, culture, and ideas among Europe, Africa, Asia, and the Americas in the fifteenth and sixteenth centuries and the major economic and social effects on each continent.

If **YOU** were there...

You live in a coastal town in Spain in the 1500s. This week, several ships have returned from the Americas, bringing silver for the royal court. But that's not all. The crew has also brought back some strange foods. One sailor offers you a round, red fruit. Natives in the Americas call it a "tomatl," he tells you. He dares you to taste it, but you are afraid it might be poisonous.

Will you taste the tomato? Why or why not?

BUILDING BACKGROUND New fruits and vegetables such as tomatoes and potatoes looked very strange to Europeans in the 1500s. But new foods were only one part of a much larger exchange of products and ideas that resulted from the voyages of discovery.

Plants and Animals

European explorers set out to find routes to Asia, but their discovery of new lands and new peoples had an effect they never imagined. The exchange of plants, animals, and ideas between the New World (the Americas) and the Old World (Europe) is known as the **Columbian Exchange**. It changed lives in Europe, Asia, Africa, and the Americas.

Old World Plants and Animals

One exchange to occur was the introduction of new plants to the Americas. When European explorers went to the Americas, they took seeds to plant crops. Bananas and sugarcane, originally from Asia, grew well in the warm, humid climate of some of the places where the Spanish and Portuguese settled. Europeans also planted oranges, onions, and lettuce.

Europeans also brought new animals to the Americas. Domesticated animals such as cows, goats, sheep, pigs, horses, and chickens all arrived in the New World with the Spanish.

The Columbian Exchange

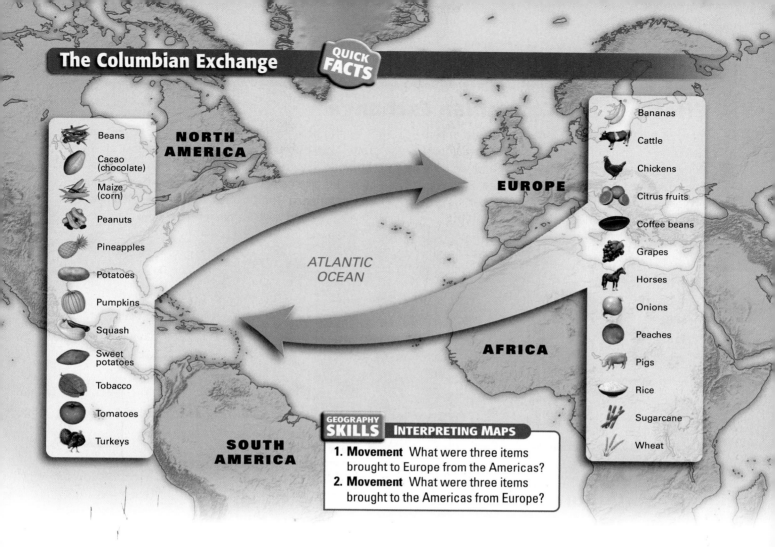

QUICK FACTS

Beans
Cacao (chocolate)
Maize (corn)
Peanuts
Pineapples
Potatoes
Pumpkins
Squash
Sweet potatoes
Tobacco
Tomatoes
Turkeys

NORTH AMERICA

EUROPE

ATLANTIC OCEAN

AFRICA

SOUTH AMERICA

Bananas
Cattle
Chickens
Citrus fruits
Coffee beans
Grapes
Horses
Onions
Peaches
Pigs
Rice
Sugarcane
Wheat

GEOGRAPHY SKILLS | **INTERPRETING MAPS**

1. **Movement** What were three items brought to Europe from the Americas?
2. **Movement** What were three items brought to the Americas from Europe?

Before the arrival of the Spanish, the people of the Americas didn't have many domesticated animals.

Even accidental exchanges occurred sometimes. Europeans unknowingly took some plants, animals, and diseases to the Americas. For example, rats hid on ships, and explorers carried germs for diseases such as measles and smallpox.

New World Plants and Animals

While Europeans introduced plants and animals to the New World, they also found plants and animals there they had never seen before. They took samples back to Europe as well as to Africa and Asia. This exchange of plants changed the eating habits of people around the world. For example, Europeans hadn't tried tomatoes until explorers brought them from the Americas. Now they are a **primary** ingredient in Italian food. Europeans also took back potatoes, beans, squash, avocados, pineapples, tobacco, and chili peppers. Even chocolate came from the Americas.

Europeans also carried New World products to other parts of the world. In this way, the Columbian Exchange affected Africa and Asia. Many plants from the Americas also grew well in West Africa and Asia. Sweet potatoes, peanuts, and tomatoes became staples in African cooking. American fruits such as pineapple became popular in India. In China, peanuts and maize became major crops.

READING CHECK **Identifying Cause and Effect**
What caused the Columbian Exchange?

ACADEMIC VOCABULARY

primary main, most important

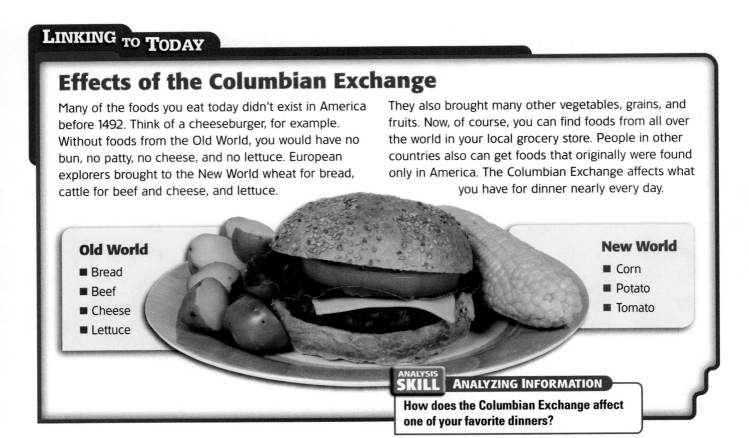

Effects of the Columbian Exchange

Many of the foods you eat today didn't exist in America before 1492. Think of a cheeseburger, for example. Without foods from the Old World, you would have no bun, no patty, no cheese, and no lettuce. European explorers brought to the New World wheat for bread, cattle for beef and cheese, and lettuce.

They also brought many other vegetables, grains, and fruits. Now, of course, you can find foods from all over the world in your local grocery store. People in other countries also can get foods that originally were found only in America. The Columbian Exchange affects what you have for dinner nearly every day.

Old World
- Bread
- Beef
- Cheese
- Lettuce

New World
- Corn
- Potato
- Tomato

ANALYSIS SKILL | **ANALYZING INFORMATION**

How does the Columbian Exchange affect one of your favorite dinners?

Culture and Technology

Along with plants and animals, Europeans introduced their ideas, culture, and technology to the places they explored. People in Asia, Africa, and the Americas all learned new ways of living and working.

Religion and Language

Some of the biggest cultural changes Europeans brought to places they conquered were in religion and language. Christians set out to convert people to their religion. Missionaries went to Asia and Africa, and they also worked to convert American Indians to Christianity. In some places, their religion blended with native traditions to create new kinds of religious practices.

In addition to spreading Christianity, missionaries ran schools. They taught their European languages such as Spanish, Portuguese, and Dutch, the language of the Netherlands.

THE IMPACT TODAY

People in many parts of Africa and the Americas still speak Spanish, Portuguese, French, or Dutch.

Technology

Besides religion and language, Europeans introduced new technologies. They took guns and steel to parts of Africa. In the Americas, they introduced guns and steel, as well as ways to use the wheel.

Europeans also introduced the idea of using animals as technology. They brought horses, which were good for transportation and for carrying heavy loads. Oxen could be used to plow fields. People also learned to make candles from cow fat.

European ideas also changed industries in the Americas. For example, animals were used to carry silver from mines. The introduction of sheep and sugarcane also created new industries. People began to make new kinds of textiles and to grow sugarcane on **plantations**, or large farms.

READING CHECK Summarizing How did European culture change life in the Americas?

Society and the Economy

As industries changed in some places, Europeans increased trade with Asia and the Americas. This change had huge social and economic effects, especially in Africa and the Americas.

Treatment of American Indians

Plantations and mines made money for Portugal and Spain. They also made some colonists in the Americas rich. But plantation agriculture and mining brought poor treatment of American Indians.

It took a lot of workers to run a plantation, so Spanish colonists forced American Indians to work on their land. Forced work, harsh treatment, or disease killed many American Indians. By the 1600s the Indian population had shrunk by more than 80 percent in some areas.

Some clergy in the Americas protested the terrible treatment of American Indians. A priest named **Bartolomé de las Casas** said that the Spanish should try to convert American Indians to Christianity by showing them love, gentleness, and kindness. The Spanish monarchs agreed, creating laws about the proper treatment of American Indians. However, the colonists did not always follow the laws.

Slavery and Society

Since forced labor and disease killed so many American Indians, las Casas and others suggested using enslaved Africans as workers. Africans had already developed immunities to European diseases. Soon, thousands of Africans were being shipped to the Americas as slave labor.

The mix of Africans, Europeans, and American Indians shaped the social order of the Americas. Europeans held the highest position in society. American Indians, Africans, and those of mixed background held the lowest positions. This social order was based on conquest and racism. **Racism** is the belief that some people are better than others because of racial traits, such as skin color. Both Africans and Indians had darker skin than Europeans did.

Europeans brought new ideas and technologies when they settled new lands. This illustration shows a scene in what is now New Mexico.

What evidence of technology can you see?

European manufactured goods, like this mirror, were new to the Americas.

Missions were built to help spread Christianity.

Europeans brought animals like oxen to pull carts.

Missions and settlements helped spread European languages.

© 1999 TAOS TIMELINE MURALS–GIOVANNA PAPONETTI

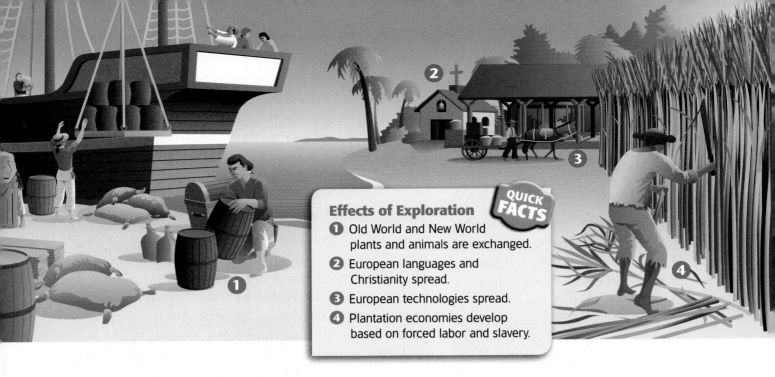

Effects of Exploration **QUICK FACTS**

❶ Old World and New World plants and animals are exchanged.

❷ European languages and Christianity spread.

❸ European technologies spread.

❹ Plantation economies develop based on forced labor and slavery.

Plantation agriculture and the use of slave labor continued in the Americas until the late 1800s. It continued to play a major role in the economies and societies of many countries of the Americas, Africa, and Europe for many years.

READING CHECK **Analyzing** How did the slave trade affect life in the Americas?

SUMMARY AND PREVIEW The voyages of discovery led to the Columbian Exchange. The Columbian Exchange brought new plants and animals, as well as social and economic changes, to Europe, Africa, Asia, and the Americas. In the next section you will read about more economic changes that developed in Europe.

Section 2 Assessment

go.hrw.com
Online Quiz
KEYWORD: SQ7 HP16

Reviewing Ideas, Terms, and People **HSS** 7.11.2

1. a. Recall Where did peanuts and maize become important crops?
b. Make Inferences Why was the exchange of plants and animals between the Old World and the New World called the **Columbian Exchange**?

2. a. Identify What were two technologies that Europeans introduced to the Americas?
b. Summarize How did contact with Europeans change life in the New World?

3. a. Define What is **racism**?
b. Analyze How was plantation agriculture related to **racism** in the Americas?
c. Evaluate Judge whether the ideas of **Bartolomé de las Casas** brought positive or negative changes to life in the Americas.

Critical Thinking

4. Summarizing Draw a diagram like the one here. Use it to show at least one each of

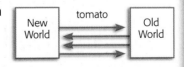

the plants, animals, cultural traits, and technologies that were exchanged between the Old World and the New World. You may draw more arrows if you need more.

FOCUS ON SPEAKING

5. Identifying Plants, Animals, and Technologies Add a column labeled "Europe" to your chart. In the appropriate columns of your chart, list the plants, animals, and technologies introduced in the various parts of the world by Europeans.

Origins of Capitalism

If YOU were there...

You are a merchant in Holland in the early 1700s. Your friends tell you about an exciting new business plan. Each of you will spend money on a ship that is sailing to the Indies to trade for spices. If the voyage is successful, you will all share in the money that it makes. But of course, there is always the danger that the ship will sink or be lost. Then you would lose everything.

Will you take a chance on this trading business?

BUILDING BACKGROUND The voyages of discovery influenced world economies. Nations used the natural resources of their colonies to make profits for themselves. This brought sweeping changes in patterns of world trade and shifted power among European nations.

A New Economy

The exchange of products between European countries and their colonies changed economic relations around the world. European countries saw their colonies as a way to get rich.

This new view of the colonies was part of an economic system called **mercantilism**—a system in which a government controls all economic activity in a country and its colonies to make the government stronger and richer. In the 1500s a country's strength was measured by how much gold and silver it had. Under mercantilism, then, governments did everything they could to get more of these precious metals. Mercantilism was the main economic policy in Europe between 1500 and 1800.

To stay rich, European countries tried to export more goods than they imported. The relationship of goods imported to goods exported is known as a country's **balance of trade**. The colonies played a key role in this balance of trade. Believing that colonies existed to help the ruling country, Europeans didn't let colonies trade with other countries. They didn't want their colonies' money going to other nations.

What You Will Learn...

Main Ideas

1. A new economic system called mercantilism emerged.
2. New trading patterns developed in the 1600s and 1700s.
3. Power in Europe shifted as a result of new trade routes, banking, and increased manufacturing.
4. Market economies changed business in Europe.

The Big Idea

Changes in international trading and marketing patterns influenced the development of a new economic system called capitalism.

Key Terms

mercantilism, *p. 459*
balance of trade, *p. 459*
cottage industry, *p. 460*
atlas, *p. 461*
capitalism, *p. 463*
market economy, *p. 463*

HSS 7.11.3 Examine the origins of modern capitalism; the influence of mercantilism and cottage industry; the elements and importance of a market economy in seventeenth-century Europe; the changing international trading and marketing patterns, including their locations on a world map; and the influence of explorers and map makers.

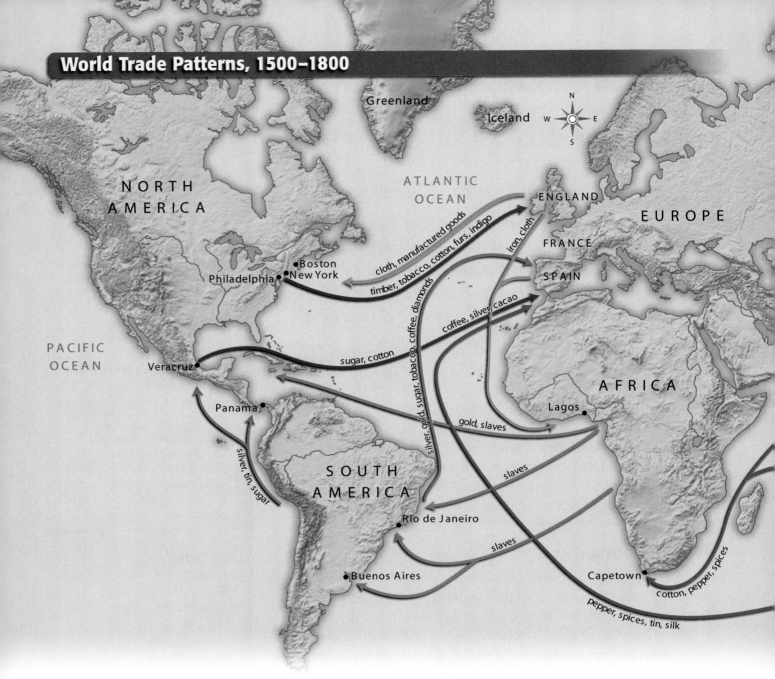

World Trade Patterns, 1500–1800

Greenland

Iceland

ATLANTIC OCEAN

NORTH AMERICA

ENGLAND

EUROPE

FRANCE

SPAIN

•Boston
Philadelphia• New York

cloth, manufactured goods

iron, cloth

timber, tobacco, cotton, furs, indigo

PACIFIC OCEAN

silver, gold, sugar, tobacco, coffee, diamonds

coffee, silver, cacao

Veracruz•

sugar, cotton

AFRICA

Panama•

Lagos •

silver, tin, sugar

gold, slaves

SOUTH AMERICA

slaves

Rio de Janeiro•

slaves

Capetown•

cotton, pepper, spices

•Buenos Aires

slaves

pepper, spices, tin, silk

ACADEMIC VOCABULARY

acquire to get

European countries used their colonies to **acquire** raw materials such as wood, furs, cotton, and dyes. This way they didn't have to buy raw materials from competing countries. In addition, they didn't allow their colonies to manufacture goods. That way they could take raw materials from their colonies and sell manufactured goods back to them. Manufactured goods were more valuable than raw materials were, so the colonies were good for the European countries' balance of trade.

Trade also created markets for manufactured goods. As a result, manufacturing in Europe—especially cottage industries—increased. **Cottage industry** was a system in which family members worked in their homes to make part of a product. A businessperson gave each family the materials it needed. The businessperson made money by selling the final product.

READING CHECK Evaluating Was mercantilism a good or bad policy for Europe? Why?

ASIA

Calcutta

Goa

East Indies

silk

INDIAN
OCEAN

GEOGRAPHY SKILLS | **INTERPRETING MAPS**

1. **Place** What were some goods taken from North America to Europe?
2. **Movement** What was taken from Africa to North and South America?

New Trading Patterns

Mercantilism created new trading patterns around the world. In the 1600s and 1700s trade routes connected Europe, Africa, Asia, and the Americas. Many of these routes linked European countries with their colonies. One major trading pattern involved the exchange of raw materials, manufactured products, and slaves among Europe, Africa, and the Americas. This particular trade network became known as the triangular trade.

The Atlantic slave trade was a major part of the trade network. The Portuguese, Dutch, and English all were active in the slave trade.

Slavery had been practiced in many places, including Africa, long before Europeans came. But the Atlantic slave trade was different in its size and its process. European traders crammed enslaved Africans on ships for the long voyage to the Americas. They chained people together, often without enough food or water. People got sick, and many died.

Between the late 1500s and early 1800s Europeans shipped millions of enslaved Africans to colonies in the New World. Most of these slaves were sent to South America and the Caribbean.

READING CHECK **Drawing Inferences** Why do you think trade among Europe, Africa, and the Americas was called triangular trade?

Power Shifts in Europe

Mercantilism was successful in Spain and Portugal, both of which had many wealthy colonies. But while they relied on their colonies for wealth, the northern European countries of England and the Netherlands developed new trade routes and banking industries. The new trade routes and banking, along with increased manufacturing, brought more wealth to England and the Netherlands and shifted the economic power in Europe.

Northern European Trade Routes

A book published in the late 1500s helped traders to find new wealth around the world. That important book was the first **atlas**, or collection of maps. Improved maps, made possible largely by the discoveries of explorers, encouraged traders to find new sources of wealth around the world.

Supply and Demand

Market economies are based on the idea of supply and demand. This idea states that people will produce goods that other people want. In Europe, market economies developed as populations grew and the world economy developed.

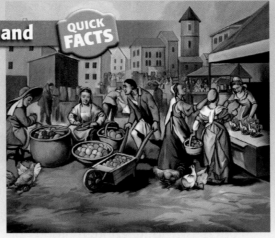

1 Population grew in Europe. With more people, there was a greater demand for goods.

2 Since people wanted more goods, companies worked to make, or supply, more goods.

England benefited from increased trade. New trading posts in India and China along with trade in North American colonies gave England access to huge markets and many resources.

The Netherlands also became a great trading power. Dutch merchants formed a company to trade directly with Asia. This company was the only one with the right to trade between the Netherlands, Asia, and Africa. The Dutch soon controlled many islands in East Asia, along with trading posts in India, Japan, and southern Africa.

Banking

Increased trade created a need for banks. Realizing this, the Dutch set up a bank. Jews were partly responsible for the growth of banking in the Netherlands. They migrated to the Netherlands in the late 1500s to escape religious persecution in other European countries. Because the Dutch government limited the work Jews could do, and because the Christian Church didn't allow Christians to lend money, many Jews entered the banking business. The Jews were so successful that English rulers invited them to England to help improve business there as well.

Banking improved business by making it easier for merchants to know they were receiving money of the proper value. Banks also loaned money to people who wanted to start new businesses. In doing so, banks contributed to economic growth.

READING CHECK Identifying Cause and Effect Why did power shift from Spain and Portugal to England and the Netherlands in the 1600s?

Market Economies

Economic growth and new wealth changed business in Europe. Because more people had wealth, they started buying more manufactured goods. The demand for goods increased.

There were several reasons for the increased demand for manufactured goods. First, Europe's population was growing—especially in the cities. More people meant a need for more goods. Second, farmers were growing food at lower costs. With lower expenses, people had more money to spend on manufactured goods. A third reason for increased demand was the addition of colonies, which had to get their manufactured goods from Europe.

3 Finally, the supply of goods met the demand for goods.

As the demand for goods rose, business-people realized they could make money by finding better ways to make manufactured goods. They wanted to increase the supply, or amount of goods offered, to meet the demand. This new way of doing business can be considered the beginning of a new economic system called capitalism. **Capitalism** is an economic system in which individuals and private businesses run most industries. Competition among these businesses affects how much goods cost.

Competition among different business-es is most successful in a market economy. In a **market economy**, individuals decide what goods and services they will buy. The government does not decide what people can buy or sell. A market economy works on a balance between supply and demand. If there is a great demand for a product, a seller will increase the supply in order to make more money.

The ability of individuals to control how they make and spend money is a benefit of a market economy and capitalism. In the 1800s capitalism would become the basis for most economic systems in the Western world.

READING CHECK **Summarizing** What is a market economy?

SUMMARY AND PREVIEW Discoveries and exchanges of goods and ideas around the world brought many changes, including new economic policies, such as mercantilism and capitalism. In the next chapter you will learn about political changes in Europe.

Section 3 Assessment

go.hrw.com
Online Quiz
KEYWORD: SQ7 HP16

Reviewing Ideas, Terms, and People **HSS** 7.11.3

1. **a. Describe** What was **cottage industry**?
   b. Explain How were colonies important to a country with the economic policy of **mercantilism**?
   c. Evaluate Was mercantilism a good policy for Europe's colonies? Why or why not?
2. **Identify** What countries were active in the slave trade?
3. **Summarize** Why did power shift to northern Europe?
4. **a. Identify** In what kind of economic system do individuals and private businesses run most industries?
   b. Explain How do supply and demand work in a **market economy**?

Critical Thinking

5. **Identifying Cause and Effect** Draw a diagram like the one here. Use it to show three other factors that contributed to the development of capitalism in England.

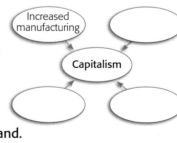

FOCUS ON SPEAKING

6. **Understanding Economics** Make note of changes to trade and economic systems brought about during the Age of Exploration.

from
Girl with a Pearl Earring

by Tracy Chevalier (1964–)

About the Reading *The 1999 novel* Girl with a Pearl Earring *is a work of historical fiction. It is set in the bustling city of Delft, in the Netherlands, during the 1660s. At this time, the Netherlands was one of the wealthiest, most powerful nations in the world. Nevertheless, many Dutch commoners struggled to pay high taxes. The main character of this novel is the teenaged daughter of one such commoner. To help support her family, Griet works as a maid to the family of a middle-class artist. The artist, Johannes Vermeer, was one of the greatest Dutch painters of his time.*

AS YOU READ Picture the city of Delft in your mind.

I had walked along that street all my life, but had never been so aware that my back was to my home. When I reached the end and turned out of sight of my family, though, it became a little easier to walk steadily and look around me. The morning was still cool, the sky a flat grey-white pulled close over Delft like a sheet, the summer sun not yet high enough to burn it away. The canal I walked along was a mirror of white light tinged with green. As the sun grew brighter the canal would darken to the color of moss.

Frans, Agnes, and I used to sit along that canal and throw things in ❶ —pebbles, sticks, once a broken tile—and imagine what they might touch on the bottom—not fish, but creatures from our imagination, with many eyes, scales, hands and fins. Frans thought up the most interesting monsters. Agnes was the most frightened. I always stopped the game, too inclined to see things as they were ❷ to be able to think up things that were not.

❸ There were a few boats on the canal, moving towards Market Square. It was not market day, however, when the canal was so full you couldn't see the water. One boat was carrying river fish for the stalls at Jeronymous Bridge. Another sat low on the water, loaded with bricks. The man poling the boat called out a greeting to me. I merely nodded and lowered my head so that the edge of my cap hid my face.

GUIDED READING

WORD HELP

inclined likely

❶ A major canal connected Delft to the cities of Rotterdam and The Hague.

What tells you that the canal was a central part of Griet's life?

❷ Griet claims that she is a realist—that she saw things "as they were."

What does this tell you about the description of the city that follows?

❸ *What details in this paragraph and the next suggest that Delft had a thriving economy?*

ELA Reading 7.3.3 Analyze characterization as delineated through a character's thoughts, words, speech patterns, and actions.

I crossed a bridge over the canal and turned into the open space of Market Square, even then busy with people criss-crossing it on their way to some task—buying meat at the Meat Hall, or bread at the baker's, taking wood to be weighed at the Weigh House. Children ran errands for their parents, apprentices for their masters, maids for their households. Horses and carts clattered across the stones. To my right was the Town Hall, with its gilded front and white marble faces gazing down from the keystones above the windows. To my left was the New Church, where I had been baptized sixteen years before. Its tall, narrow tower made me think of a stone birdcage. Father had taken us up it once. I would never forget the sight of Delft spread below us, each narrow brick house and steep red roof and green waterway and city gate marked forever in my mind, tiny and yet distinct. I asked my father then if every Dutch city looked like that, but he did not know. He had never visited any other city, not even The Hague, two hours away on foot.

I walked to the center of the square. There the stones had been laid to form an eight-pointed star set inside a circle. Each point aimed towards a different part of Delft. I thought of it as the very center of the town, and as the center of my life. Frans and Agnes and I had played in that star since we were old enough to run in the market. In our favorite game, one of us chose a point and one of us named a thing—a stork, a church, a wheelbarrow, a flower—and we ran in that direction looking for that thing. We had explored most of Delft that way.

One point, however, we had never followed. I had never gone to Papists' Corner, where the Catholics lived. The house where I was to work was just ten minutes from home, the time it took a pot of water to boil, but I had never passed by it.

❹ I knew no Catholics. There were not so many in Delft, and none in our street or in the shops we used. It was not that we avoided them, but they kept to themselves.

Girl with a Pearl Earring **(1665),**
by Johannes Vermeer

GUIDED READING

WORD HELP

apprentices people who work for or train under a master craftsman
gilded overlaid with a thin layer of gold
keystones the top center stones in an arch

❹ Most people in the Netherlands were Protestant.

How does Griet's description of Delft reflect what you learned about the Reformation?

CONNECTING LITERATURE TO HISTORY

1. **Analyzing** New trade routes and banking, along with increased manufacturing, brought wealth to England and the Netherlands. What details in this excerpt point to economic success of the Netherlands?

2. **Drawing Inferences** The Netherlands became a great trading power. What geographical feature of Delft—and, more broadly, the Netherlands—helped its merchants to succeed in trade?

Social Studies Skills

Analysis | Critical Thinking | Participation | Study

Identifying Central Issues

Understand the Skill

The circumstances that surround historical events can sometimes be complicated and difficult to understand. To accurately understand events, you must be able to identify the central issues involved. A *central issue* is the main topic of concern in a controversy, discussion, or event.

As you think about the central issues of events and problems in history, keep in mind that you need to consider the standards and values of the time. Thinking about the time in which people lived and the things that were important to them will help you understand central issues in history.

Learn the Skill

Use the following guidelines to identify the central issues as you read about historical events.

1 Identify the main subject of the information.

2 Determine the purpose of the information. Why has the information been provided? Sometimes knowing something about the author can help you determine his or her purpose in providing the information.

3 Find the strongest or most forceful statements in the information. These are often clues to the issues or ideas the writer thinks are the most central or important.

4 Think about values, concerns, ways of life, and major events that would have been important to the people of the times. Determine how the information might connect to those larger issues.

Practice and Apply the Skill

The following passage reports a discussion between a French explorer and some Algonquin Native Americans. The passage also gives clues to some larger central issues in relations between the French and the Native Americans in North America.

> *"* He [the Algonquin leader] communicated the plan to all the Algonquins, who were not greatly pleased with it, from fear that some accident might happen to the boy, which would cause us to make war on them ... I said that it was not acting like a brother or friend to refuse me what he [their leader] had promised, and what could result in nothing but good to them; taking the boy would be a means of increasing still more our friendship with them and forming one with their neighbors ... I replied that the boy would be able to adapt himself without difficulty to their manner of living and usual food, and that, if through sickness or the fortunes of war any harm should befall him, this would not interrupt my friendly feelings toward them ... But I said that if they treated him badly, and if any misfortune happened to him through their fault, I should in truth be displeased. *"*
>
> –Samuel de Champlain, from *Voyages of Samuel de Champlain, 1604–1618*, edited by W. L. Grant

Apply the guidelines to help you answer the following questions about the central issues of the dispute described in the passage.

1. What reason did the Indians give for not wanting to take the French boy?

2. What did Champlain say to convince them to cooperate?

3. What do you think is a larger central issue in relations between the French and the Native Americans?

Visual Summary

Use the visual summary below to help you review the main ideas of the chapter.

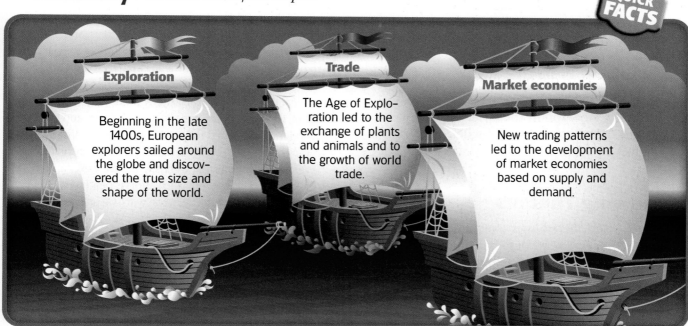

Exploration
Beginning in the late 1400s, European explorers sailed around the globe and discovered the true size and shape of the world.

Trade
The Age of Exploration led to the exchange of plants and animals and to the growth of world trade.

Market economies
New trading patterns led to the development of market economies based on supply and demand.

Reviewing Vocabulary, Terms, and People

*For each statement below, write **T** if it is true and **F** if it is false. If the statement is false, write the correct term that would make the sentence a true statement.*

1. **Christopher Columbus** led the first voyage to **circumnavigate** the globe.

2. The Spanish created large farms called **plantations** in the Americas.

3. The **Columbian Exchange** refers to the exchange of plants, animals, and ideas between the Old World and the New World.

4. An economic system in which the government controls all aspects of a country's economy to make it stronger is called **capitalism**.

5. In 1588 an English navy destroyed a fleet of Spanish ships called the **balance of trade**.

6. An **atlas** is a collection of maps.

7. The first person to reach India by sailing around Africa was **Bartolomé de las Casas**.

Comprehension and Critical Thinking

SECTION 1 *(Pages 446–451)* **HSS** **7.11.1**

8. **a. Recall** What did these people achieve: Vasco da Gama, Christopher Columbus, and Ferdinand Magellan?

   b. Draw Conclusions How did the astrolabe, the compass, and better maps affect travel by sea?

   c. Predict How might European history have been different if the Spanish Armada had defeated the English forces?

SECTION 2 *(Pages 454–458)* **HSS** **7.11.2**

9. **a. Identify** Name three plants and three animals that Europeans brought to the Americas. Name five plants that explorers took back to Europe from the Americas.

   b. Compare and Contrast What were some positive results of the Columbian Exchange? What were some negative results?

SECTION 2 (continued)

c. Elaborate How did diseases from Europe affect America—both in the short term and in the long term?

SECTION 3 *(Pages 459–463)* **HSS** 7.11.3

10. a. Identify Which countries became more wealthy and powerful by developing new trade routes and banking industries?

b. Analyze How did mercantilism eventually lead to the development of capitalism?

c. Predict How might the law of supply and demand affect an individual seller? How might it affect a buyer?

Reviewing Themes

11. Science and Technology How did improvements in technology help contribute to the beginning of the Age of Exploration?

12. Economics What led to the shift from mercantilism to capitalism?

Using the Internet
go.hrw.com
KEYWORD: SQ7 WH16

13. Activity: Understanding Technology in Exploration In this chapter you learned how accurate maps could not have been made without improved knowledge and technology. Enter the keyword above. Then research the Mars *Rover* and the Cassini-Huygens space probe, and create a PowerPoint presentation to display your research. Include information on technology that enables this kind of exploration, on how this changes the map of our solar system, and how it may change everyday life.

Reading Skills

Summarizing *Reread the text on p. 456. Use it to complete the following activities.*

14. Write a summary statement for each paragraph of the text.

15. Combine your paragraph summaries into a single summary statement for the whole text.

Social Studies Skills

Identifying Central Issues *The following passage comes from Christopher Columbus's journal. As you read it, think about the central issues in the discovery of the Americas. Then answer the questions that follow.*

"As I saw that they were very friendly to us, and perceived that they could be much more easily converted to our holy faith by gentle means than by force, I presented them with some red caps, and strings of beads to wear upon the neck, and many other trifles of small value, wherewith they were much delighted, and became wonderfully attached to us. Afterwards they came swimming to the boats, bringing parrots, balls of cotton thread, javelins, and many other things which they exchanged for articles we gave them, such as glass beads, and hawk's bells; which trade was carried on with the utmost good will . . . It appears to me, that the people . . . would be good servants and I am of opinion that they would very readily become Christians, as they appear to have no religion."

16. Why does Columbus give the people he meets in America gifts of caps and beads?

17. Why did the native people swim out to the Spaniards' boats?

18. What is the larger central issue in Columbus's first meeting with these people?

FOCUS ON SPEAKING

19. Creating Your Report Think back on what you've learned about the Age of Exploration. Plan the report that you will give to the fifth-grade students. Be sure to tell them about the new ideas, plants and animals, technologies, and economic systems that shaped the world during this time.

Make notes on 5–6 note cards to help you remember what you want to say in your report. Also, design a chart, graph, or other visual aid that will help in your presentation.

When you give your report, keep your audience in mind while you speak. Simplify or explain any vocabulary that a fifth-grader might not understand. Speak slowly and clearly so the students can understand what you are saying.

Standards Assessment

DIRECTIONS: Read each question, and write the letter of the best response.

1 Use the map to answer the following question.

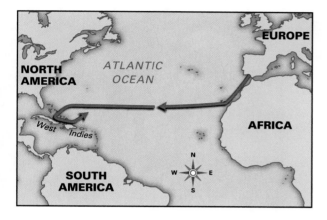

The route on the map indicates a voyage of exploration by

A John Cabot.

B Christopher Columbus.

C Vasco da Gama.

D Francis Drake.

2 Who was the first person to direct a voyage that went all the way around the world?

A Ferdinand Magellan

B Pedro Cabral

C Francis Drake

D Bartolomeu Dias

3 The Columbian Exchange is responsible for all of the following *except*

A the spread of disease from Europe to America.

B the introduction of the horse to Europe.

C the spread of American crops to Africa and Asia.

D the introduction of the wheel to America.

4 In the 1500s a nation's power depended *mainly* on

A the size of its army.

B its balance of trade.

C the number of colonies it founded.

D its wealth in gold and silver.

5 According to the policy of mercantilism, what was the *main* purpose of colonies?

A to be a source of slaves to work in the ruling country

B to provide a place where the ruling country could send undesirable people

C to help the ruling country have a favorable balance of trade

D to serve as bases from which the ruling country could launch attacks on enemies

Connecting with Past Learnings

6 In Grade 6 you learned that the Greeks were inspired by the explorations and adventures Homer reported in the *Odyssey*. What European explorer's adventures later similarly inspired other Europeans to explore?

A Genghis Khan

B Marco Polo

C Admiral Zheng He

D Mansa Musa

7 One result of the Columbian Exchange was the spread of Christianity. What other reason for Christianity's spread have you learned about this year?

A the Crusades

B the Spanish Inquisition

C the Reformation

D the Catholic Reformation

Enlightenment and Revolution

California Standards

History–Social Science

7.11 Students analyze political and economic change in the sixteenth, seventeenth, and eighteenth centuries (the Age of Exploration, the Enlightenment, and the Age of Reason).

Analysis Skills

HR 5 Detect different historical points of view on historical events.

HI 3 Explain the sources of historical continuity and how the combination of ideas and events explains the emergence of new patterns.

English–Language Arts

Writing 7.2.4 Write persuasive compositions.

Reading 7.2.4 Identify and trace the development of an author's argument, point of view, or perspective in text.

FOCUS ON WRITING

A Persuasive Article Imagine that you are a philosopher writing an article arguing for the ideas of the Enlightenment. How would you persuade people who don't agree with the new ideas? How will you change their minds? You will write a persuasive article in favor of Enlightenment ideas to be published in a pamphlet.

CHAPTER EVENTS

1642
Civil war begins in England.

1650

WORLD EVENTS

1647
Construction on the Taj Mahal is completed.

What You Will Learn...

In this chapter you will learn how ideas of the Enlightenment led to revolutions around the world. This photo shows a reenactment of one of these revolutions— the American Revolution.

1690
John Locke argues that government's power should be limited.

1759 Mary Wollstonecraft is born in London.

1776 The American colonies declare their independence.

1789 The French Revolution begins.

1700

1707
The Mughal Empire ends in India.

1750

1769 Spanish missionaries begin founding missions in California.

1780
Tupac Amaru leads a peasant revolt against Peru's colonial rulers.

1800

ENLIGHTENMENT AND REVOLUTION **471**

Reading Social Studies

by Kylene Beers

Focus on Themes This chapter will introduce you to the Enlightenment, an era of great **political** thinkers, writers, and activists. You will learn about some of these figures, among the most influential people in all of world history. In their ideas, you will see the roots of our modern government, a government brought about by bold statesmen who inspired a revolution. You will also see how similar revolutions changed **society and culture** in countries around the world.

Points of View in Historical Texts

Focus on Reading History is made up of issues, questions about what to do in a particular situation. Throughout history, people have looked at issues from all sides. Each person's view of the issue shaped what he or she thought should be done.

Identifying Points of View The way a person views an issue is called his or her point of view, or perspective. Points of view can be shaped by many factors, such as a person's background or political beliefs. When you read a historical document, figuring out the author's point of view can help you understand his or her opinions about an issue.

Additional reading support can be found in the

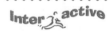

Interactive

Reader and Study Guide

Thomas Jefferson, from the Declaration of Independence

The history of the present King of Great Britain is a history of repeated injuries and usurpations, all having in direct object the establishment of a direct Tyranny over these States. To prove this, let Facts be submitted to a candid world.

He has refused his Assent to Laws, the most wholesome and necessary to the public good.

He has forbidden his Governors to pass Laws of immediate and pressing importance, unless suspended in their operation till his Assent should be obtained; and when so suspended, he has utterly neglected to attend to them.

Consider the author's background—Jefferson was a leader in the American colonies.

Look for emotional language—Words like *injuries* and *usurpations* make Jefferson's opinion clear.

Look at the evidence—Jefferson uses only examples of the king's flaws.

Put it all together to determine the author's point of view—Jefferson was opposed to the policies of the English king and wanted a change in government.

You Try It!

Read the following passage from this chapter. Then answer the questions that follow.

Rousseau

French thinker Jean-Jacques Rousseau criticized divine right. He believed in popular sovereignty—the idea that governments should express the will of the people. In The Social Contract, published in 1762, Rousseau declared, "Man is born free, but he is everywhere in chains." According to Rousseau, citizens submit to the authority of government to protect their own interests, entering into a "social contract." This contract gives the government the power to make and enforce laws as long as it serves the people. The government should give up that power if it is not serving the people.

From Chapter 17, p. 480

Think about the passage you have just read and then answer the questions below.

1. What do you think was Rousseau's point of view about France's government?

2. What words or phrases in this passage helped you identify his point of view?

3. How did Rousseau's own beliefs and ideas affect his point of view?

4. Do you think Rousseau's point of view was similar to or different from that of the king of France?

5. Who do you think would more likely share Rousseau's point of view: a wealthy French noble or a colonist planning a rebellion? Why do you think so?

Key Terms and People

Chapter 17

Section 1
Enlightenment *(p. 474)*
secular *(p. 475)*
Voltaire *(p. 476)*
salon *(p. 477)*
Mary Wollstonecraft *(p. 477)*

Section 2
John Locke *(p. 479)*
natural rights *(p. 480)*
Charles-Louis Montesquieu *(p. 480)*
Jean-Jacques Rousseau *(p. 480)*
popular sovereignty *(p. 480)*
Benjamin Franklin *(p. 481)*
Thomas Jefferson *(p. 481)*

Section 3
English Bill of Rights *(p. 485)*
Declaration of Independence *(p. 486)*
Declaration of the Rights of Man and of the Citizen *(p. 489)*

Academic Vocabulary

Success in school is related to knowing academic vocabulary—the words that are frequently used in school assignments and discussions. In this chapter, you will learn the following academic words:

contract *(p. 479)*
ideals *(p. 486)*

As you read Chapter 17, try to determine the points of view of the various figures you are studying.

Ideas of the Enlightenment

What You Will Learn...

Main Ideas

1. The Enlightenment was also called the Age of Reason.
2. The Enlightenment's roots can be traced back to earlier ideas.
3. New ideas came mainly from French and British thinkers.

The Big Idea

Enlightenment thinkers built on ideas from earlier movements to emphasize the importance of reason.

Key Terms and People

Enlightenment, *p. 474*
secular, *p. 475*
Voltaire, *p. 476*
salon, *p. 477*
Mary Wollstonecraft, *p. 477*

HSS **7.11.4** Explain how the main ideas of the Enlightenment can be traced back to such movements as the Renaissance, the Reformation, and the Scientific Revolution and to the Greeks, Romans, and Christianity.

If YOU were there...

You are a student in the early 1700s. It seems your teacher can pass or fail whomever he wants. You think the teacher should make his decisions about grades based on what a student has learned. You come up with a new idea—testing students so they can prove what they know. You think this idea will improve your grades as well as relations in your school.

Will you challenge the teacher's authority?

BUILDING BACKGROUND In the 1600s and 1700s, people like the student mentioned above began to question sources of authority in society—particularly those of religion and government. They thought that using reason and logic would lead to improvements in society. Their ideas spread quickly in Europe.

The Age of Reason

Discoveries made during the Scientific Revolution and on the voyages of discovery led to changes in Europe. A number of scholars were beginning to challenge long-held beliefs about science, religion, and government.

These new scholars relied on reason, or logical thought, instead of religious teachings to explain how the world worked. They believed human reason could be used to achieve three great goals—knowledge, freedom, and happiness—and that achieving these goals would improve society. The use of reason in guiding people's thoughts about philosophy, society, and politics defined a time period called the **Enlightenment**. Because of its emphasis on the use of reason, the Enlightenment was also known as the Age of Reason.

READING CHECK **Finding Main Ideas** How did the Enlightenment thinkers explain the world?

The Enlightenment's Roots

The main ideas of the Enlightenment had their roots in other eras. Enlightenment thinkers looked back to the Greeks, Romans, and the history of Christianity. The Renaissance, Reformation, and Scientific Revolution provided ideas also.

Greek and Roman Philosophers

Enlightenment thinkers used ideas from the ancient Greeks and Romans. Greek philosophers had observed an order and regularity in the natural world. Aristotle, for example, taught that people could use logic to discover new truths. Building on Greek ideas, Roman thinkers developed the concept of natural law, the idea that a law governed how the world operated.

With Greek and Roman beliefs as guidelines, Enlightenment thinkers began studying the world in a new way. They applied these beliefs not just to the natural world but also to the human world of society and government.

Christianity

The history of Christianity in Europe provides other clues about ideas that emerged in the Enlightenment. One theologian, Thomas Aquinas, had taught in the Middle Ages that faith paired with reason could explain the world. Although it was indebted to Aquinas, the Enlightenment was mostly a **secular,** or non-religious, movement. Enlightenment thinkers disagreed with the church's claims to authority and its intolerance toward non-Christian beliefs.

The Renaissance and Reformation

Other reactions to the Christian Church in Europe also influenced the ideas of the Enlightenment. For example, some Renaissance thinkers used Greek and Roman ideas to raise questions about established religious beliefs. These Renaissance thinkers were known as humanists.

Although most humanists were religious, they focused on human value and achievement rather than the glory of God.

The use of reason advanced science and technology, which in turn influenced the Enlightenment. Here, the Italian scientist Alessandro Volta explains a new invention, the battery.

Ideas of the Enlightenment
QUICK FACTS

- The ability to reason is what makes humans unique.

- Reason can be used to solve problems and improve people's lives.

- Reason can free people from ignorance, superstition, and unfair government.

- The natural world is governed by laws that can be discovered through reason.

- Like the natural world, human behavior is governed by natural laws.

- Governments should reflect natural laws and encourage education and debate.

Renaissance humanists believed people could improve their world by studying it and changing it. These ideas contributed to the Enlightenment idea of progress— the idea that humans were capable of improving their world.

Some Reformation ideas also reappeared during the Enlightenment. Like Martin Luther and other reformers, Enlightenment scholars questioned church authority. They found that religious beliefs didn't always fit in with what they learned from their logical study of the world.

The Scientific Revolution

The Scientific Revolution also influenced Enlightenment thinkers. Through experiments, scientists like Newton and Galileo had discovered that the world did not work exactly the way the church explained it. Using scientific methods of study, scientists discovered laws that governed the natural world. Enlightenment thinkers took the idea of natural laws one step further. They believed that natural laws must also govern human society and government.

READING CHECK Identifying Main Ideas
What were some movements that influenced the Enlightenment?

New Ideas

Enlightenment thinkers borrowed ideas from history to develop a new worldview. They believed the use of reason could improve society. To achieve this progress, they had to share their ideas with others.

French Philosophers

French philosophers popularized many Enlightenment ideas. One philosopher, **Voltaire** (vohl-TAYR), mocked government and religion in his writings. Instead of trusting God to improve human happiness, Voltaire believed humans could improve their own existence.

Having gotten in trouble for some of his writings, Voltaire also spoke out against censorship—removal of information considered harmful. He argued, "I [may] disapprove of what you say, but I will defend to the death your right to say it." His statement emphasized the Enlightenment goal of freedom of thought.

Enlightenment thinkers made an effort to share their thoughts with the public. Philosopher Denis Diderot (dee-DROH) edited a book called the *Encyclopedia*. This book included articles by more than 100 experts on science, technology, and history. The French king and the pope both banned the *Encyclopedia*.

In spite of censorship, Enlightenment ideas spread. One important place for the exchange of ideas was the **salon**, a social gathering held to discuss ideas. Women often hosted the salons. Most Enlightenment thinkers did not view women as equal to men. However, in hosting salons women could influence opinions.

British Writers

Women and men also began to publish their ideas in books, pamphlets, and newspaper articles. British writer **Mary Wollstonecraft**, for example, argued that women should have the same rights as men.

Enlightenment thinkers even applied their ideas of freedom and progress to economics. British writer Adam Smith believed economics was governed by natural laws. He argued that governments should not try to control the economy and that economic growth came when individuals were free to make their own choices. Like many Enlightenment thinkers, his ideas would have a lasting effect.

READING CHECK **Summarize** How did Enlightenment thinkers spread their ideas?

BIOGRAPHY

Voltaire
1694–1778

Voltaire is the pen name of the French philosopher and author François-Marie Arouet. He used his wit, intelligence, and sense of justice to poke fun at religious intolerance. Voltaire's skill and bold ideas made him a popular writer. In his writings he argued that the purpose of life is the pursuit of human happiness through progress in science and the arts.

Drawing Inferences Why did Voltaire poke fun at religious intolerance?

SUMMARY AND PREVIEW Scholars during the Enlightenment drew on ideas from previous eras. They proposed ideas about the importance of reason and progress. In the next section you will learn how the Enlightenment changed ideas about government.

Section 1 Assessment

go.hrw.com
Online Quiz
KEYWORD: SQ7 HP17

Reviewing Ideas, Terms, and People HSS 7.11.4

1. **a. Define** What was the **Enlightenment**?
   b. Explain What was the main goal of most Enlightenment thinkers?
2. **a. Define** What does it mean to say that the Enlightenment was a **secular** movement?
   b. Explain What was the connection between the discoveries of the Scientific Revolution and the Enlightenment?
   c. Elaborate How did the idea of natural law contribute to the Enlightenment?
3. **a. Describe** How did **Voltaire** feel about censorship?
   b. Explain What did Adam Smith contribute to Enlightenment ideas?

Critical Thinking

4. **Summarize** Draw a chart like this one. Use it to summarize the sources of Enlightenment ideas.

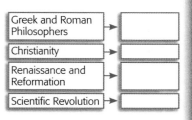

Greek and Roman Philosophers	→	
Christianity	→	
Renaissance and Reformation	→	
Scientific Revolution	→	

FOCUS ON WRITING

5. **Arguing for Enlightenment Ideas** Review the section for new ideas about science, religion, women's rights, and economics. How may these ideas help people? Write down what you could say in favor of Enlightenment ideas on these topics.

New Views on Government

What You Will Learn...

Main Ideas

1. The Enlightenment influenced some monarchies.
2. Enlightenment thinkers helped the growth of democratic ideas.
3. In America, the Enlightenment inspired a struggle for independence.

The Big Idea

Enlightenment ideas influenced the growth of democratic governments in Europe and America.

Key Terms and People

John Locke, *p. 479*
natural rights, *p. 480*
Charles-Louis Montesquieu, *p. 480*
Jean-Jacques Rousseau, *p. 480*
popular sovereignty, *p. 480*
Benjamin Franklin, *p. 481*
Thomas Jefferson, *p. 481*

HSS 7.11.5 Describe how democratic thought and institutions were influenced by Enlightenment thinkers (e.g., John Locke, Charles-Louis Montesquieu, American founders).

If **YOU** were there...

You are in a coffee house, discussing everything from politics to religion with friends. It is 1770. Suddenly, someone next to you questions the king's right to rule. Other people begin to agree with that person. As you listen to their logic, you wonder about other ways to run a government.

Would you support a government that didn't include a king or queen? Why or why not?

BUILDING BACKGROUND For centuries, Europe's monarchs had struggled with nobles and with church leaders for power. In England, Parliament limited the monarch's power. In some other countries, however, the kings and queens ruled without limits. The Enlightenment would change governments in Europe and in America.

Enlightenment Influence on Monarchies

In the 1600s and 1700s kings, queens, and emperors ruled Europe. (See the map.) Many of these monarchs believed that they ruled through divine right. That is, they thought that God had given them the right to rule as they chose. They also thought they shouldn't be limited by bodies such as England's parliament. King Louis XIV of France saw himself as the entire government. He declared, *"L'état, c'est moi!"* or "I am the state."

Although monarchs such as Louis XIV held the most power, other groups in society also had privileges. In France, for example, the nobles paid few taxes and held the highest positions in the army. The French clergy paid no taxes at all. However, most of the French people, the commoners, were poor, paid high taxes, and had no role in their government.

Outside of France, some monarchs began to change their ideas about how they ruled. They applied Enlightenment ideas to government. These rulers became known as enlightened despots.

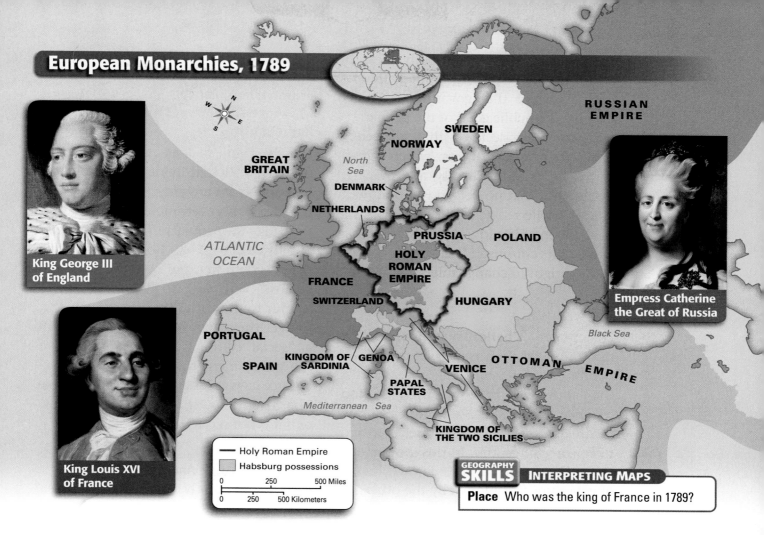

European Monarchies, 1789

King George III of England

King Louis XVI of France

Empress Catherine the Great of Russia

Holy Roman Empire

Habsburg possessions

0   250   500 Miles

0   250   500 Kilometers

GEOGRAPHY SKILLS **INTERPRETING MAPS**

Place Who was the king of France in 1789?

A despot is a ruler with absolute power. The enlightened despots tried to make life better for the commoners. They also thought they could make their countries stronger if the commoners were happier. Frederick II of Prussia was one such ruler. He approved reforms in law and education. Empress Catherine the Great of Russia was another enlightened despot. Her reforms gave the Russian nobility greater rights and powers.

Although the enlightened despots made some improvements in their countries, many Enlightenment thinkers looked for bigger changes. They began to consider the need for democracy.

READING CHECK **Contrasting** How do rule by divine right and rule by an enlightened despot differ?

Democratic Ideas

Some Enlightenment thinkers only challenged the idea of rule by divine right. Others went further. They developed some completely new ideas about how governments should work. Three of these thinkers—Locke, Montesquieu, and Rousseau—tried to identify the best possible form of government. The ideas of these Enlightenment thinkers contributed to the creation of modern democracy.

Locke

The English philosopher **John Locke** had a major influence on Enlightenment political thought. In 1690, he published *Two Treatises on Government*. In this work, Locke argued for government as a **contract** between the ruler and the people.

ACADEMIC VOCABULARY

contract a binding legal agreement

Because a contract bound both sides, the ruler's power would be limited. In fact, Locke thought that government existed only for the public good of the people.

Locke also declared that all people had certain **natural rights**, which included the rights to life, liberty, and property. He thought that no person was born with special privileges. According to Locke, the government should protect the natural rights of its citizens. If it didn't, the people had the right to change rulers.

Montesquieu

Frenchman **Charles-Louis Montesquieu** (mohn-te-SKYOO) was a member of the nobility. He built on Locke's ideas in *The Spirit of the Laws*, published in 1748. Montesquieu claimed that a government should be divided into separate branches to protect people's freedom. In this idea, known as the separation of powers, each branch of government is limited by the others. As a result, the separate branches must share power. None of them can control the government completely.

Rousseau

French thinker **Jean-Jacques Rousseau** (roo-SOH) criticized divine right. He believed in **popular sovereignty** (SAHV-ruhn-tee)—the idea that governments should express the will of the people. In *The Social Contract*, published in 1762, Rousseau declared, "Man is born free, but he is everywhere in chains." According to Rousseau, citizens submit to the authority of government to protect their own interests, entering into a "social contract." This contract gives the government the power to make and enforce laws as long as it serves the people. The government should give up that power if it is not serving the people.

READING CHECK **Analyzing** What idea appears in the works of both Locke and Rousseau?

Enlightenment Thinkers

The ideas of Locke, Montesquieu, and Rousseau contributed to the creation of modern democracy.

Who believed in separation of government powers?

THE GRANGER COLLECTION, NEW YORK

John Locke
1632–1704
- Government's power is limited.
- People have natural rights, such as life, liberty, and property.

Charles-Louis Montesquieu
1689–1755
- The powers of government should be separated into separate branches.

The Enlightenment in America

The ideas of these three philosophers spread throughout Europe. From Europe, they spread to the British colonists living in North America. Enlightenment ideas would have a big effect on America's history.

The British colonists already knew basic ideas about participation in government. Because they were British citizens, the colonists knew about Parliament and its control over the British monarch. When the British government began to chip away at what the colonists saw as their rights, the colonists fought back.

British Policy in North America

To learn more about this struggle, we must go back to the founding of the colonies. Other countries besides Britain settled and controlled land in North America. One of them was France.

Jean-Jacques Rousseau
1712–1778

■ **Governments should express the will of the people.**

■ **People enter into a social contract with their government, giving it the right to create and enforce laws.**

In North America the French and British had many disagreements. These conflicts led to war. Even though the British eventually defeated the French, years of fighting cost Britain a lot of money.

To raise funds, the British government created new taxes in the colonies. One tax added to the cost of molasses. Another new tax, called the Stamp Act, required colonists to pay more for newspapers, some legal documents, and other printed materials. People in England didn't have to pay these taxes. As a result, the colonists thought the taxes were unfair. The colonists wanted to be treated as British citizens. They wanted the same rights as Europeans.

Colonists' Views

Many colonial leaders were familiar with the ideas of the Enlightenment. Two leaders in particular—**Benjamin Franklin** and **Thomas Jefferson**—would apply those ideas to the colonists' complaints.

In 1766 philosopher and scientist Benjamin Franklin went to London. There he addressed the House of Commons in Parliament. He argued that the British government had no right to tax the colonists because they had no representative in Parliament. His argument against "taxation without representation" inspired riots against the tax in the colonies. The riots persuaded the British government to get rid of the Stamp Act.

Thomas Jefferson was a farmer, scientist, and scholar. He had been influenced by the Scientific Revolution. John Locke was another source of inspiration. In keeping with Locke's ideas, Jefferson believed that Britain had no right to govern or impose taxes on the colonies. He supported the idea of independence for the colonies. Jefferson also supported the separation of religious and political power. In this way, he reflected the Enlightenment's secular attitudes.

FOCUS ON READING

Why did the colonists' point of view on taxes differ from the view of the British government?

The Enlightenment Reaches America

1690 John Locke publishes *Two Treatises on Civil Government.*

1748 Montesquieu publishes *The Spirit of the Laws.*

1762 Rousseau publishes *The Social Contract.*

1690 | 1745 | 1755 | 1765 | 1775

1766 Benjamin Franklin argues against unfair tax policies in the American colonies.

1774 Thomas Jefferson argues that only voluntary loyalty to the king ties the American colonies to Great Britain.

THE GRANGER COLLECTION, NEW YORK

ANALYSIS SKILL **READING TIME LINES**

Who might have been influenced by Rousseau's writings?

Jefferson would later become president of the United States. His philosophies and achievements, based on Enlightenment ideas, helped to establish the democratic government and the rights we enjoy today in the United States.

READING CHECK **Finding Main Ideas** Why did some colonists want to be independent of Britain?

SUMMARY AND PREVIEW In the 1600s and 1700s some European monarchs thought they had a divine right to rule. As Enlightenment thinkers proposed new ways of thinking, people questioned the monarchs' rights. Democratic ideas spread. In the next section you will learn how these ideas changed governments in England, France, and America.

Section 2 Assessment

go.hrw.com
Online Quiz
KEYWORD: SQ7 HP17

Reviewing Ideas, Terms, and People HSS 7.11.5

1. **a. Define** What does divine right mean?
   b. Explain What did enlightened despots try to do?
2. **a. Define** What are **natural rights**?
   b. Explain What did Locke believe was the purpose of government?
   c. Elaborate Why would separation of powers protect people's freedoms?
3. **a. Describe** What role did **Benjamin Franklin** play in the American colonists' disagreement with the British government?
   b. Elaborate Why do you think many Americans consider **Thomas Jefferson** a hero?

Critical Thinking

4. **Identifying Cause and Effect** Draw a graphic organizer like the one shown. Use it to describe the effect of the British government's policies on its North American colonies.

British Policies

FOCUS ON WRITING

5. **Organizing Ideas about Government** Note ways Enlightenment ideas might improve government by making it more effective or fair. How would you present your arguments to someone who favors monarchy or rule by divine right?

John Locke

Would you risk arrest for your beliefs in people's rights?

When did he live? 1632–1704

Where did he live? England and the Netherlands

What did he do? Locke worked as a professor, physician, and government official. He wrote about the human mind, science, government, religion, and other topics.

Why is he important? Locke believed in the right of common people to think and worship as they pleased and to own property. He also had great faith in science and people's basic goodness. Not everyone liked his ideas. At one point Locke fled to Holland to avoid arrest by political enemies. Locke's ideas have inspired political reforms in the West for some 300 years.

Drawing Inferences Why do you think some people disliked Locke's ideas?

KEY IDEAS

" Men being, as has been said, by nature, all free, equal, and independent, no one can be . . . subjected to the political power of another, without his own consent. The only way whereby any one divests himself of his natural liberty . . . is by agreeing with other men to join and unite into a community. "

–John Locke, from *Second Treatise of Civil Government*

THE
W O R K S
OF
JOHN LOCKE, Esq;

In Three Volumes.

The CONTENTS of which follow in the next Leaf.

With Alphabetical Tables.

VOL. I.

The Fourth Edition.

LONDON,
Printed for Edmund Parker, at the Bible and Crown, in Lombard-Street; Edward Symon, against the Royal-Exchange, in Cornhill; Charles Hitch, at the Red-Lion, in Paternoster-Row; and John Pemberton, at the Golden-Buck, in Fleetstreet.

M. DCC. XL.

This book printed in 1740 is a collection of John Locke's writings.

The Age of Revolution

What You Will Learn...

Main Ideas

1. Revolution and reform changed the government of England.
2. Enlightenment ideas led to democracy in America.
3. The French Revolution caused major changes in France's government.

The Big Idea

Revolutions changed the governments of Britain, the American colonies, and France.

Key Terms

English Bill of Rights, *p. 485*
Declaration of Independence, *p. 486*
Declaration of the Rights of Man and of the Citizen, *p. 489*

HSS 7.11.6 Discuss how the principles in the Magna Carta were embodied in such documents as the English Bill of Rights and the American Declaration of Independence.

If YOU were there...

You live near Boston, Massachusetts. British soldiers have moved in and taken over your house. They say that the law allows them to take whatever they need. But your father doesn't want the soldiers living in your house and eating your food. What can he do to fight the king's laws?

Should your father disobey the king? Why or why not?

BUILDING BACKGROUND British soldiers in the North American colonies were just one sign that trouble was brewing. Ideas about the rights of the people were in conflict with ideas about the rights of monarchs. In England, the North American colonies, and France, this conflict led to violent revolutions.

Revolution and Reform in England

Enlightenment ideas inspired commoners to oppose monarchies that ruled without concern for the people's needs. However, the monarchs wouldn't give up their privileges. In England, Parliament forced the monarchy to change.

Trouble with Parliament

For many years, the English Parliament and the English monarchy had had an uneasy relationship. Parliament demanded that its rights and powers be respected. However, the monarchy stood for rule by divine right. The relationship between English monarchs and Parliament got worse.

The conflict led to a civil war in 1642. Representatives of Parliament led by Oliver Cromwell took over the country. The king, Charles I, was charged with various crimes and beheaded in 1649. Cromwell became a dictator. The years of his rule were troubled and violent.

George Washington led the colonial army to victory over the British in the American Revolution. In this 1851 copy of a famous painting, Washington is shown leading his troops across the Delaware River to attack British forces.

By 1660 many English people were tired of turmoil and wanted to restore the monarchy. They invited the dead king's son to return and rule England as Charles II. They made Charles promise to allow Parliament to keep the powers it had won in the civil war. These powers included the right to approve new taxes. Parliament was able to work with Charles II during most of his rule. However, when Charles died and his brother James became king, the trouble began again.

James II, an unpopular Catholic, tried to promote his religious beliefs in England, a Protestant country. As a result, Parliament invited the Protestant William of Orange, James's son-in-law, to invade England. When William and his wife, Mary, arrived in England in 1688, James and his family fled to France.

New Rights for the English People

Parliament offered the throne to William and Mary on one condition. They had to accept the **English Bill of Rights**, a document that listed rights for Parliament and the English people. This document, approved in 1689, drew on the principles of Magna Carta, which limited a ruler's power and recognized some rights for the people.

Magna Carta had been in place for hundreds of years, but the monarchs had not honored it. William and Mary agreed to honor Magna Carta. They also agreed that Parliament could pass laws and raise taxes. As a result, the monarchs ruled according to laws passed by Parliament. Divine right to rule had ended in England.

READING CHECK **Sequencing** What events led to the creation of the English Bill of Rights?

Democracy in America

Although the power of the monarchs was limited in England, some people in North America were not satisfied. Colonists there grew increasingly unhappy with both the king and Parliament.

A New Country

Some colonists disliked the laws and taxes that the British government had imposed. In addition, colonists were used to ruling themselves through their own assemblies, or congresses. They also believed that a faraway king and parliament could not understand life in America.

Many colonists protested British laws they thought were unfair. As conflict continued, colonial leaders met to resolve the crisis. At this meeting, called the First Continental Congress, the delegates decided to resist the British. Not all colonists wanted independence, but they did want to have fair laws and to feel safe. They created militias, or groups of armed men, to protect themselves from the British troops stationed in the colonies.

Fighting began in April of 1775 when a militia exchanged fire with British troops. In 1776 the colonial leaders gathered again. At that meeting, Thomas Jefferson wrote the **Declaration of Independence**, a document declaring the colonies' independence from British rule. Like Magna Carta, the Declaration stated people's rights to certain liberties. The Declaration begins with a sentence that also expresses Enlightenment **ideals**:

> "We hold these truths to be self-evident, that all men are created equal, that they are endowed by their Creator with certain unalienable Rights, that among these are Life, Liberty and the Pursuit of Happiness."
>
> –from the *Declaration of Independence*

In this passage, the word *unalienable* means "cannot be taken away." This wording shows the influence of John Locke's ideas

ACADEMIC VOCABULARY

ideals ideas or goals that people try to live up to

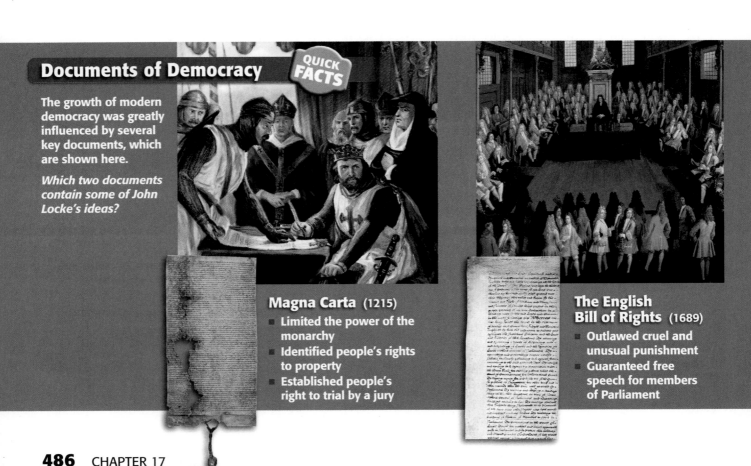

Documents of Democracy

QUICK FACTS

The growth of modern democracy was greatly influenced by several key documents, which are shown here.

Which two documents contain some of John Locke's ideas?

Magna Carta (1215)
- Limited the power of the monarchy
- Identified people's rights to property
- Established people's right to trial by a jury

The English Bill of Rights (1689)
- Outlawed cruel and unusual punishment
- Guaranteed free speech for members of Parliament

about natural rights. In addition, the Declaration of Independence said that people unhappy with their government had the right to change it. This statement builds on the ideas of Rousseau as well as Locke.

The Declaration of Independence was signed by representatives from all of the colonies. A new nation—the United States of America—was born.

A New Government

The British government finally agreed to end the fighting and recognize the United States. American leaders then met to form a new government. They wrote a set of rules called the Articles of Confederation. Under the Articles, the central government was weak. The Americans were afraid that a strong central government would be too much like a monarchy. However, the weak government didn't serve the needs of the people. A new government plan was needed.

Virginia farmer James Madison was a main author of the new plan—the Constitution. This document reflected the ideas of Montesquieu, who had proposed the separation of powers in 1748. In keeping with Montesquieu's idea, the Constitution divided power among three branches of government:

- The legislative branch, called Congress, would make laws.
- The executive branch, headed by the president, would enforce laws.
- The judicial branch, or court system, would interpret laws.

The Constitution did not address the rights of women or of slaves, and men without land couldn't vote. It did, however, guarantee the rights of most citizens.

READING CHECK **Finding Main Ideas** How were ideas of Enlightenment thinkers reflected in the American Revolution and the new American government?

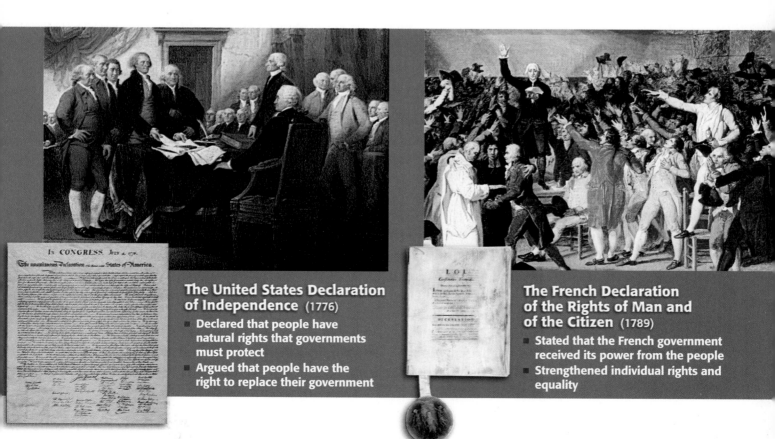

The United States Declaration of Independence (1776)
- Declared that people have natural rights that governments must protect
- Argued that people have the right to replace their government

The French Declaration of the Rights of Man and of the Citizen (1789)
- Stated that the French government received its power from the people
- Strengthened individual rights and equality

Women's March on Versailles
During the French Revolution, about 6,000 women marched to the palace at Versailles to demand bread from the king.

The French Revolution

As the Americans fought for and created a new nation, the French people paid close attention to events. They were inspired by the Americans to fight for their own rights.

An Unfair Society

The French king ruled over a society split into three groups called estates. The clergy were members of the First Estate and enjoyed many privileges. Nobles made up the Second Estate. They held important positions in the military, the government, and the courts.

Most French people belonged to the Third Estate. Included were peasants, craftworkers, and shopkeepers. The Third Estate paid the highest taxes but had few rights. Many members of the Third Estate were poor and hungry. They felt that the king didn't understand their problems. While the common people starved, King Louis XVI had fancy parties. His queen, Marie-Antoinette, spent huge amounts of money on clothes.

Meanwhile, the government was badly in debt. Louis XVI wanted to raise money by taxing the rich. To do so, in 1789 he called together members of the three estates.

The meeting did not go smoothly. Some members of the Third Estate were familiar with Enlightenment ideas. These members demanded a real voice in the meeting's decisions. Eventually, the Third Estate members formed a separate group called the National Assembly. This group demanded that the king accept a constitution limiting his powers.

Louis XVI refused to agree to such demands, angering the common people of Paris. Violence broke out on July 14, 1789. On that day a mob stormed a Paris prison, the Bastille. After forcing the guards to surrender, the mob took guns stored inside the building and freed the prisoners. The French Revolution had begun.

THE IMPACT TODAY
July 14, Bastille Day, is France's independence day.

Revolution and Change

After the Bastille fell, the revolution spread to the countryside. Peasants there were afraid that the king and nobles would crush the revolution. In events called the Great Fear, peasants took revenge on their noble landlords for years of poor treatment. In their rage and fear, the peasants burned country houses and monasteries.

Other leaders of the revolution were taking peaceful steps. The National Assembly wrote a constitution. It included some of the same ideas found in the writings of Enlightenment philosophers, the English Bill of Rights, and the Declaration of Independence. Called the **Declaration of the Rights of Man and of the Citizen**, this document guaranteed some freedoms for citizens and distributed the payment of taxes more fairly. Among the rights the Declaration supported were freedom of speech, of the press, and of religion. It also guaranteed that men could take part in the government.

Louis XVI was forced to accept the new laws, but new laws did not satisfy the revolution's leaders. In 1792 they ended the monarchy and created a republic. The next year, the leaders put Louis XVI on trial and executed him.

Facing unrest, in 1793 the new French government began to order trials of anyone who questioned its rule. In the period that followed, called the Reign of Terror, thousands of people were executed with the guillotine. This machine beheaded victims quickly with a heavy blade. The Reign of Terror ended when one of its main leaders, Maximilien Robespierre, was himself executed in July of 1794.

Although the Reign of Terror was a grim chapter in the story of the French Revolution, the revolution wasn't a failure. Eventually, France created a democratic government. Enlightenment ideas about freedom were powerful. Once they took hold, they would not go away. Many Europeans and Americans enjoy freedoms today thanks to Enlightenment ideas.

READING CHECK **Summarizing** What is the Declaration of the Rights of Man and of the Citizen?

SUMMARY AND PREVIEW Questions about divine right led to struggles between the English monarchy and Parliament. Enlightenment ideas inspired the American Revolution and led to democracy in the United States. The French also formed a republic. In the next chapter you will learn how Enlightenment ideas continue to influence world events.

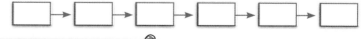

Section 3 Assessment

go.hrw.com
Online Quiz
KEYWORD: SQ7 HP17

Reviewing Ideas, Terms, and People HSS 7.11.6

1. **a.** Summarize What caused the conflict between the English monarchy and Parliament?
   b. Compare What was the connection between Magna Carta and the **English Bill of Rights**?
2. **a.** Identify What basic rights were listed in the **Declaration of Independence**?
   b. Explain How were Montesquieu's ideas reflected in the U.S. Constitution?
3. **a.** Describe How was French society organized before the French Revolution?
   b. Compare What did the Great Fear and the Reign of Terror have in common?

Critical Thinking

4. **Sequencing** Draw a graphic organizer like the one shown. Use it to describe the steps of the French Revolution.

☐→☐→☐→☐→☐→☐

FOCUS ON WRITING

5. **Exploring Changes in Government** Consider how Enlightenment ideas improved governments in England, the United States, and France. How would you answer someone who said that the Enlightenment caused only trouble?

Social Studies Skills

HSS **Analysis HI 3** Students explain the sources of historical continuity and how the combination of ideas and events explains the emergence of new patterns.

Analysis	Critical Thinking	Participation	Study

Continuity and Change in History

Understand the Skill

A well-known saying claims that "the more things change, the more they stay the same." Nowhere does this observation apply better than to the study of history. Any look back over the past will show many changes—nations expanding or shrinking, empires rising and falling, changes in leadership, and people on the move, to name just a few.

The reasons for change have not changed, however. The same general forces have driven the actions of people and nations across time. These forces are the "threads" that run through history and give it continuity, or connectedness. They are the "sameness" in a world of continuous change.

Learn the Skill

You can find the causes of all events of the past in one or more of these major forces or themes that connect all history.

1 **Cooperation and Conflict:** Throughout time, people and groups have worked together to achieve goals. They have also opposed others who stood in the way of their goals.

2 **Cultural Invention and Interaction:** The values and ideas expressed in peoples' art, literature, customs, and religion have enriched the world. But the spread of cultures and their contact with other cultures have produced conflict also.

3 **Geography and Environment:** Physical environment and natural resources have shaped how people live. Efforts to gain, protect, or make good use of land and resources have been major causes of cooperation and conflict in history.

4 **Science and Technology:** Technology, or the development and use of tools, has helped people make better use of their environment. Science has changed their knowledge of the world, and changed their lives, too.

5 **Economic Opportunity and Development:** From hunting and gathering to herding, farming, manufacturing, and trade, people have tried to make the most of their resources. The desire for a better life has also been a major reason people have moved from one place to another.

6 **The Impact of Individuals:** Political, religious, military, business, and other leaders have been a major influence in history. The actions of many ordinary people have also shaped history.

7 **Nationalism and Imperialism:** Nationalism is the desire of a people to have their own country. Imperialism is the wish to control other peoples. Both have existed through history.

8 **Political and Social Systems:** People have always been part of groups—families, villages, nations, or religious groups, for example. The groups to which people belong affect how they relate to people around them.

Practice and Apply the Skill

Check your understanding of the sources of continuity and change in history by answering the following questions.

1. How does the Enlightenment illustrate cultural invention and interaction in history?

2. What other forces in history were at work during the Enlightenment? Explain your answer.

Visual Summary

Use the visual summary below to help you review the main ideas of the chapter.

Enlightenment thinkers developed new ideas about government and society.

Enlightenment ideas helped inspire revolutions in America and Europe.

The Enlightenment

New governments created influential documents based on Enlightenment ideas that guaranteed people's rights and freedoms.

QUICK FACTS

Reviewing Vocabulary, Terms, and People

Match the words or names with their definitions or descriptions.

a. Enlightenment

b. English Bill of Rights

c. Voltaire

d. John Locke

e. natural rights

f. popular sovereignty

g. secular

h. Charles-Louis Montesquieu

i. Benjamin Franklin

1. non-religious

2. argued for the colonists' rights before Parliament

3. a period also known as the Age of Reason

4. proposed the separation of powers

5. document that William and Mary had to sign before they could rule

6. spoke out against censorship

7. the idea that governments should express the will of the people

8. included life, liberty, and property in Locke's view

9. argued against divine right in *Two Treatises on Civil Government*

Comprehension and Critical Thinking

SECTION 1 *(Pages 474–477)* **HSS** **7.11.4**

10. a. Identify What three goals did Enlightenment thinkers believe the use of reason could achieve?

b. Compare How was the influence of Greek and Roman ideas similar to the influence of the Scientific Revolution on the Enlightenment?

c. Elaborate Voltaire and others have argued against censorship. Is censorship ever acceptable? Explain your answer.

SECTION 2 (*Pages 478–482*) **HSS** **7.11.5**

11. a. Identify Who were two important leaders in the American colonies?

b. Compare and Contrast What ideas did Locke and Rousseau share? How did these ideas differ from most monarchs' ideas about government?

c. Elaborate Do you think things would have happened the same or differently in the colonies if colonial leaders had not been familiar with Enlightenment ideas? Explain your answer.

SECTION 3 (*Pages 484–489*) **HSS** **7.11.6**

12. a. Identify What event started the French Revolution?

b. Analyze What basic ideas are found in both the English Bill of Rights and Magna Carta?

c. Elaborate The way people interpret the Constitution has changed over the years. What do you think is a reason for this change?

Social Studies Skills

13. Understanding Continuity and Change in History The Enlightenment was a period of great change in Europe and America. However, it was also driven by some of the same forces that have driven the actions of people and nations across time. Choose one of the factors listed below that helped promote change during the Enlightenment. Write a sentence explaining how this factor influenced the Enlightenment. Then, choose one factor that shows historical continuity during the Enlightenment. Write a sentence explaining the influence of that factor on the Enlightenment.

Cooperation and Conflict	Economic Opportunity and Development
Cultural Invention and Interaction	Impact of Individuals
Geography and Environment	Nationalism and Imperialism
Science and Technology	Political and Social Systems

Reviewing Themes

14. Politics How did the English Bill of Rights and the Declaration of the Rights of Man and of the Citizen change the power of monarchs?

15. Society and Culture How would daily life have changed for a peasant after the French Revolution?

Using the Internet

16. Activity: Making a Collage The Age of Enlightenment was a time of religious, political, and economic change. Enlightenment thinkers such as John Locke, Benjamin Franklin, and Charles-Louis Montesquieu created ripples of change in democratic thought and institutions. Enter the activity keyword and learn more about these and other Enlightenment figures. Pick your favorite person and create a collage about his or her life and ideas.

Reading Skills

Understanding Points of View *Read the passage below and answer the questions that follow.*

> "From whatever side we approach our principle, we reach the same conclusion, that the social compact sets up among the citizens an equality of such a kind, that they all bind themselves to observe the same conditions and should therefore all enjoy the same rights."
>
> –Jean-Jacques Rousseau, from *The Social Contract*

17. What is Rousseau's point of view about rights?

18. Who might disagree with Rousseau?

FOCUS ON WRITING

19. Writing Your Article Use the work you have already done to write your persuasive article. In 3–4 sentences, introduce the ideas of the Enlightenment. In the next paragraph, discuss the benefits of these ideas to society and government. Conclude with a summary of your main points and a call to action—what you want readers of your article to do or think.

Standards Assessment

DIRECTIONS: Read each question, and write the letter of the best response.

1

> We hold these truths to be self-evident, that all men are created equal, that they are endowed by their Creator with certain unalienable Rights, that among these are Life, Liberty, and the pursuit of Happiness. That to secure these rights, Governments are instituted [organized] among Men, deriving [getting] their just powers from the consent of the governed, That whenever any Form of Government becomes destructive of these ends it is the Right of the People to alter or abolish it, and to institute new Government . . .
>
> —from *The Declaration of Independence*, 1776

This passage is based *mainly* on the ideas of which Enlightenment thinker?

A Voltaire

B John Locke

C Adam Smith

D Charles-Louis Montesquieu

2 The idea that a king's rule is limited is contained in which earlier document in English history?

A Magna Carta

B Ninety-Five Theses

C Proclamation of 1763

D The Declaration of Independence

3 The period of history known as the Enlightenment grew out of all of the following *except*

A the Renaissance.

B the ideas of the ancient Greeks.

C the Scientific Revolution.

D the writings of Confucius.

4 The U.S. Constitution divides the power to govern among the president, the Congress, and the courts. This approach to government is based on the ideas of which Enlightenment thinker?

A John Locke

B Denis Diderot

C Charles-Louis Montesquieu

D Mary Wollstonecraft

5 What view did the political thinkers of the Enlightenment share with the scientists of the Scientific Revolution?

A a belief in reason

B a belief in human rights

C a belief in divine right

D a belief in democracy

Connecting with Past Learnings

6 In Grade 6 you learned about the Greek philosopher Plato, who taught that society should be based on fairness and justice for all. Which European later *best* expressed Plato's idea?

A Oliver Cromwell

B Sir Isaac Newton

C Adam Smith

D Jean-Jacques Rousseau

7 You have learned about various forms of government. The Enlightenment idea that governments should express the will of the people was illustrated in ancient history by

A the Ten Commandments.

B the Roman Republic.

C the city-states of Mesopotamia.

D the teachings of the Buddha.

Cause and Effect in History

Assignment

Write a paper explaining one of the following topics:
(1) The effects of the Columbian exchange
(2) The causes of the French Revolution

"Why did it happen?" "What happened as a result?" Historians ask questions like these in order to study the causes and effects of historical events. In this way, they learn more about historical events and the links that form the chain between them.

TIP **Adding Facts and Details** For each cause or effect you identify, you need supporting facts and examples.

Example

Effect: New plants and animals introduced to Americas

■ European seeds

■ Bananas, sugarcane, onions

■ Domesticated animals

■ Cows, goats, sheep

1. Prewrite

Identifying Causes and Effects

A **cause** is an action or event that causes another event or situation to happen. An **effect** is what happens as a result of an event or situation. To understand historical events, we sometimes look at causes, sometimes look at effects, and sometimes look at both. For example, we could look at the causes behind Columbus's discovery of a new land, but we could also limit our discussion to the effects.

Collecting and Organizing Information

After choosing the topic you want to write about, gather information from the chapter in this textbook, an encyclopedia, or another library source. You can use graphic organizers like the ones below to organize your information:

ELA **Writing 7.2.0** Students write narrative, expository, and descriptive texts of at least 500–700 words.

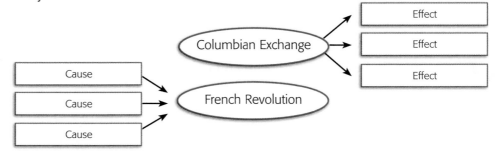

2. Write

You can use this framework to help you write your first draft.

A Writer's Framework

Introduction	Body	Conclusion
■ Briefly identify the event that you will discuss. [Columbian Exchange or French Revolution] ■ Identify at least three causes or effects you will discuss.	■ Explain the causes or effects one at a time, providing supporting facts and examples for each. ■ Present the causes or effects in order of importance, placing the most important point last.	■ Summarize your ideas about the causes or effects of the event.

3. Evaluate and Revise

Evaluating

Use the following questions to discover ways to improve your draft.

Evaluation Questions for an Explanation of Causes or Effects

- Does your introduction identify the event you are going to explain?
- Does your introduction identify the causes or effects you will discuss?
- Do you explain the causes or effects one at a time, using facts and examples to support each one?

- Do you present the causes or effects in order of importance? Do you discuss the most important cause or effect last?
- Does the conclusion summarize causes or effects and their importance?

Revising

Keep a sharp eye out for false cause-and-effect relationships. The fact that one event happened after another does not mean that the first event caused the second.

Historical events: Columbus sailed to America in 1492. John Cabot sailed to Canada in 1497.

False cause-and-effect relationship: Because Columbus sailed to America in 1492, John Cabot sailed to Canada in 1497. [Although Columbus's voyage happened before Cabot's discovery, it was not a cause.]

4. Proofread and Publish

Proofreading

As you proofread your paper, check to see whether you have unclear pronoun references. They occur when you have two different nouns or phrases the pronoun might refer to.

Unclear After the explorers conquered the native peoples, many of *them* died. [Does *them* refer to the explorers or the native peoples?]

Clear After the explorers conquered the native peoples, many of the native peoples died.

Publishing

With classmates who wrote about the same topic, create a booklet of essays to display in your classroom or in the school library.

● Practice and Apply

Use the steps and strategies outlined in this workshop to write an explanation of causes or effects.

TIP **Saving the Best for the Last** Why would you place the most important cause or effect at the end of your paper, rather than at the beginning? Think about your own experience. When you read something, what part do you remember best—the first or the last? When you hear a speech or your teacher presents a lesson, what sticks in your mind?

Most of the time, we remember what we heard last or read last. That is why it is often a good idea to "save the best for last."

TIP **Signaling Causes and Effects** Signal that you are about to discuss a cause or an effect with words and phrases like these:

- **Words and phrases that signal causes:** *because, due to, given that, since*

- **Words and phrases that signal effects:** *therefore, thus, consequently, so, as a result, for that reason*

Linking Past to Present

America and the World Today

The ideas that you have learned about in world history continued to shape the world after 1800. In particular, the rise of capitalism and the Enlightenment brought social, economic, and political changes to places throughout the world.

One place influenced by these key ideas was the United States of America. The United States was a young country in 1800. Upon gaining independence from Great Britain, citizens of the United States were eager to create a better society than they had known before. To improve their society, they formed a government based on the Enlightenment idea that citizens had a right to participate in government. They also created a market economy based on the ideas of capitalism.

Ideas from history continue to influence the world you live in today. We draw on the ideas of capitalism and the Enlightenment to advance science and technology, solve problems, and promote human rights in our society and in the world.

Capitalism

Capitalism developed in Europe in the 1600s. Today it is the basis for most countries' economic systems. Key features of capitalism are free trade, private investment, and the basic laws of supply and demand.

The United States and most other countries in the world have capitalist economies. People are free to buy and sell goods, and consumers often have a huge number of products from which to choose.

In the United States, capitalism drives economic policies on both small and large scales. For example, on a small scale, shopkeepers consider the law of supply and demand when determining how much to charge for their products. On a large scale, groups of countries often make free trade agreements with each other. For example, the North American Free Trade Agreement (NAFTA) is an agreement between the United States, Canada, and Mexico to eliminate taxes on goods traded among these three countries.

Capitalism has been responsible for economic growth around the world. Having proven to be a successful economic system, capitalism will continue to influence our society and the world in the future.

The Enlightenment

Just as capitalism has had a lasting impact on the world, so did the Enlightenment give rise to ideas that have influenced many countries. Enlightenment ideas have been especially influential in politics. The world's many democracies are built on these basic Enlightenment ideas:

- individual freedom
- free and fair elections
- the rights of citizens
- people's right to participate in their government
- government's responsibility to its citizens

The Enlightenment influenced and changed our ideas about government. This photo shows the California State Capitol in Sacramento.

In the United States, Enlightenment ideas continue to guide our political system. The government has a responsibility to its citizens to uphold their rights and to work to improve the country. Although different people have different opinions about what is best for the country, all citizens have the right and the responsibility to communicate their ideas to the government. For example, citizens over age 18 can influence the government by voting in elections. How else might you participate in your government?

Science and Technology

One idea that gave rise to the Enlightenment was the belief in the use of reason. The belief that people could use rational thought and the scientific method to explain the world began with the Scientific Revolution in the late 1500s. Today modern science and technology are built on the foundation of rational thought, and scientists around the world use the scientific method to increase their understanding of how the world works.

This increased understanding has led to major advances in science and technology in the last 200 years. For example, space exploration allows scientists to study our solar system and what lies beyond it. Scientists have sent satellites into space that enable people around the world to communicate in ways previously unimaginable. Also, in only a few decades, computers and the Internet have changed the ways we communicate with others and how we learn about the world.

There is value in studying the world just to gain knowledge, but scientists usually study the world in order to solve problems. For example, new and better medical techniques allow doctors to see injuries and heal diseases in the body without ever lifting a scalpel. Also, scientists have learned how to build stronger bridges and construct buildings to better withstand earthquakes. Researchers work to create new medicines to cure diseases and new types of car engines that don't pollute the air. These advancements and others in areas such as biology, genetics, and physics have had a remarkable impact on our world.

Scientists use technology to measure earthquakes. Here a scientist measures how much the ground moves at the site of a fault in the earth's crust.

Science and technology can help solve problems like traffic, which clogs highways like this one in Los Angeles.

Solving Problems

Although people's lives have been greatly improved by advancements in science and technology, problems still exist in our cities, in our country, and around the world. Using rational thinking, individuals, governments, private businesses, and cooperative associations study why problems exist and try to come up with solutions.

Some local problems may be solved by groups working together. For example, a city government and a private company may work together to widen roads or build a rail system to improve traffic in your town. Other problems, like poverty, exist worldwide. Private companies and government groups study the reasons for and the effects of this problem. Governments try to make policies to help reduce poverty. Individuals, along with local and international organizations, contribute their efforts and their money to help the poor. There will always be problems to solve, and the world will always need educated, rational thinkers.

Human Rights

Finally, an important issue around the world today is the issue of human rights. Building on ideas from the Enlightenment, many people agree on the basic right to live in freedom and dignity, and to have access to justice.

People from around the world encourage change in countries where human rights are not respected. National leaders can work to promote human rights everywhere. In addition, more than 190 countries are members of the United Nations (UN). The UN works to solve international economic, social, and humanitarian problems. It also strives to protect human rights. People involved in promoting human rights, along with scientists and other problem solvers, use ideas from world history to try to make the world today a better place. How will you contribute?

Nobel Peace Prize winners Nelson Mandela (top) of South Africa, Aung San Suu Kyi (middle) of Myanmar, and Shirin Ebadi (bottom) of Iran have all been recognized for their efforts to improve human rights and promote democracy.

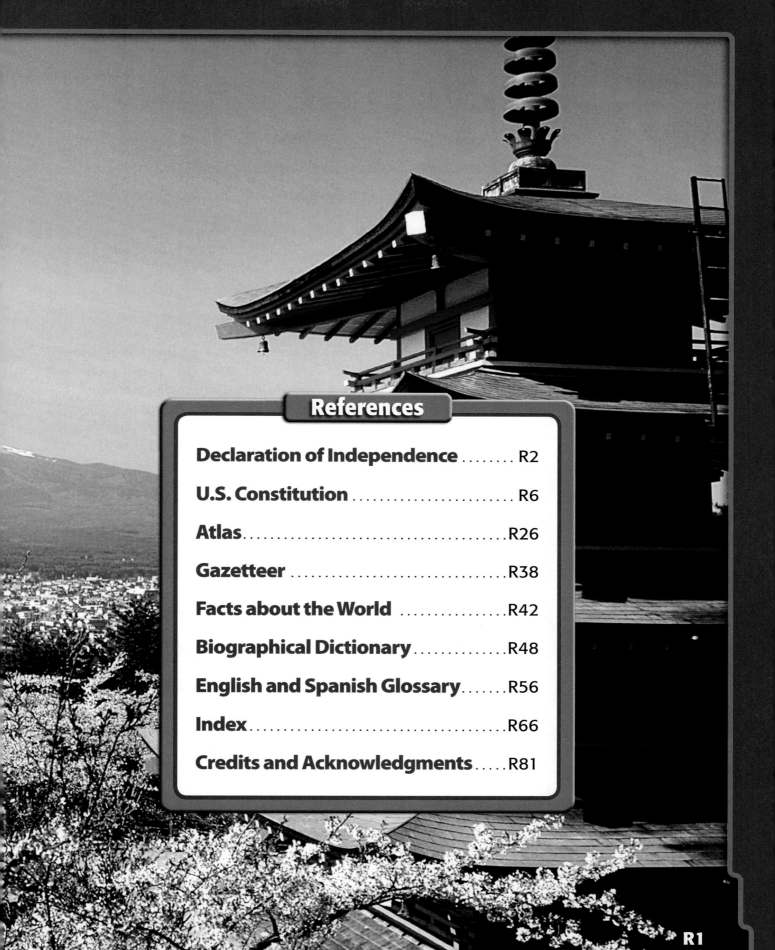

References

The Declaration of Independence

In Congress, July 4, 1776
The unanimous Declaration of the thirteen united States of America,

When in the Course of human events, it becomes necessary for one people to dissolve the political bands which have connected them with another, and to assume among the Powers of the earth, the separate and equal station to which the Laws of Nature and of Nature's God entitle them, a decent respect to the opinions of mankind requires that they should declare the causes which **impel** them to the separation.

We hold these truths to be self-evident, that all men are created equal, that they are **endowed** by their Creator with certain unalienable Rights, that among these are Life, Liberty, and the pursuit of Happiness. That to secure these rights, Governments are instituted among Men, deriving their just powers from the consent of the governed, That whenever any Form of Government becomes destructive of these ends, it is the Right of the People to alter or to abolish it, and to institute new Government, laying its foundation on such principles and organizing its powers in such form, as to them shall seem most likely to effect their Safety and Happiness. Prudence, indeed, will dictate that Governments long established should not be changed for light and transient causes; and accordingly all experience hath shown, that mankind are more disposed to suffer, while evils are sufferable, than to right themselves by abolishing the forms to which they are accustomed. But when a long train of abuses and **usurpations**, pursuing invariably the same Object **evinces** a design to reduce them under absolute **Despotism**, it is their right, it is their duty, to throw off such Government, and to provide new Guards for their future security.—Such has been the patient sufferance of these Colonies; and such is now the necessity which constrains them to alter their former Systems of Government. The history of the present King of Great Britain is a history of repeated injuries and usurpations, all having in direct object the establishment of an absolute **Tyranny** over these States. To prove this, let Facts be submitted to a **candid** world.

He has refused his Assent to Laws, the most wholesome and necessary for the public good.

He has forbidden his Governors to pass Laws of immediate and pressing importance, unless suspended in their operation till his Assent should be obtained; and when so suspended, he has utterly neglected to attend to them.

Vocabulary

impel force

endowed provided

usurpations wrongful seizures of power

evinces clearly displays

despotism unlimited power

tyranny oppressive power exerted by a government or ruler

candid fair

He has refused to pass other Laws for the accommodation of large districts of people, unless those people would **relinquish** the right of Representation in the Legislature, a right **inestimable** to them and **formidable** to tyrants only.

He has called together legislative bodies at places unusual, uncomfortable, and distant from the depository of their Public Records, for the sole purpose of fatiguing them into compliance with his measures.

He has dissolved Representative Houses repeatedly, for opposing with manly firmness his invasions on the rights of the people.

He has refused for a long time, after such dissolutions, to cause others to be elected; whereby the Legislative Powers, incapable of **Annihilation**, have returned to the People at large for their exercise; the State remaining in the mean time exposed to all the dangers of invasion from without, and **convulsions** within.

He has endeavored to prevent the population of these States; for that purpose obstructing the Laws of **Naturalization of Foreigners**; refusing to pass others to encourage their migration hither, and raising the conditions of new **Appropriations of Lands**.

He has obstructed the Administration of Justice, by refusing his Assent to Laws for establishing Judiciary Powers.

He has made Judges dependent on his Will alone, for the **tenure** of their offices, and the amount and payment of their salaries.

He has erected **a multitude of** New Offices, and sent hither swarms of Officers to harass our people, and eat out their substance.

He has kept among us, in times of peace, Standing Armies without the Consent of our legislature.

He has affected to render the Military independent of and superior to the Civil Power.

He has combined with others to subject us to a jurisdiction foreign to our constitution, and unacknowledged by our laws; giving his Assent to their Acts of pretended legislation:

For **quartering** large bodies of armed troops among us:

For protecting them, by a mock Trial, from Punishment for any Murders which they should commit on the Inhabitants of these States:

For cutting off our Trade with all parts of the world:

For imposing taxes on us without our Consent:

For depriving us in many cases, of the benefits of Trial by Jury:

Vocabulary

relinquish release, yield

inestimable priceless

formidable causing dread

annihilation destruction

convulsions violent disturbances

naturalization of foreigners the process by which foreign-born persons become citizens

appropriations of lands setting aside land for settlement

tenure term

a multitude of many

quartering lodging, housing

DECLARATION OF INDEPENDENCE

Vocabulary

arbitrary not based on law

render make

abdicated given up

foreign mercenaries soldiers hired to fight for a country not their own

perfidy violation of trust

insurrections rebellions

petitioned for redress asked formally for a correction of wrongs

unwarrantable jurisdiction unjustified authority

magnanimity generous spirit

conjured urgently called upon

consanguinity common ancestry

acquiesce consent to

For transporting us beyond Seas to be tried for pretended offences:

For abolishing the free System of English Laws in a neighboring Province, establishing therein an **Arbitrary** government, and enlarging its Boundaries so as to **render** it at once an example and fit instrument for introducing the same absolute rule into these Colonies:

For taking away our Charters, abolishing our most valuable Laws, and altering fundamentally the Forms of our Governments:

For suspending our own Legislature, and declaring themselves invested with Power to legislate for us in all cases whatsoever.

He has **abdicated** Government here, by declaring us out of his Protection and waging War against us.

He has plundered our seas, ravaged our Coasts, burnt our towns, and destroyed the lives of our people.

He is at this time transporting large armies of **foreign mercenaries** to complete the works of death, desolation and tyranny, already begun with circumstances of Cruelty & **perfidy** scarcely paralleled in the most barbarous ages, and totally unworthy the Head of a civilized nation.

He has constrained our fellow Citizens taken Captive on the high Seas to bear Arms against their Country, to become the executioners of their friends and Brethren, or to fall themselves by their Hands.

He has excited domestic **insurrections** amongst us, and has endeavored to bring on the inhabitants of our frontiers, the merciless Indian Savages, whose known rule of warfare, is an undistinguished destruction of all ages, sexes and conditions.

In every stage of these Oppressions We have **Petitioned for Redress** in the most humble terms: Our repeated Petitions have been answered only by repeated injury. A Prince, whose character is thus marked by every act which may define a Tyrant, is unfit to be the ruler of a free People.

Nor have We been wanting in attention to our British brethren. We have warned them from time to time of attempts by their legislature to extend an **unwarrantable jurisdiction** over us. We have reminded them of the circumstances of our emigration and settlement here. We have appealed to their native justice and **magnanimity**, and we have **conjured** them by the ties of our common kindred to disavow these usurpations, which, would inevitably interrupt our connections and correspondence. They too have been deaf to the voice of justice and of **consanguinity**. We must, therefore, **acquiesce** in the necessity, which denounces our Separation, and hold them, as we hold the rest of mankind, Enemies in War, in Peace Friends.

We, therefore, the Representatives of the united States of America, in General Congress, Assembled, appealing to the Supreme Judge of the world for the **rectitude** of our intentions, do, in the Name, and by Authority of the good People of these Colonies, solemnly publish and declare, That these United Colonies are, and of Right ought to be Free and Independent States; that they are Absolved from all Allegiance to the British Crown, and that all political connection between them and the State of Great Britain, is and ought to be totally dissolved; and that as Free and Independent States, they have full Power to levy War, conclude Peace, contract Alliances, establish Commerce, and to do all other Acts and Things which Independent States may of right do. And for the support of this Declaration, with a firm reliance on the Protection of Divine Providence, we mutually pledge to each other our Lives, our Fortunes and our sacred Honor.

John Hancock	Benjamin Harrison	Lewis Morris
Button Gwinnett	Thomas Nelson, Jr.	Richard Stockton
Lyman Hall	Francis Lightfoot Lee	John Witherspoon
George Walton	Carter Braxton	Francis Hopkinson
William Hooper	Robert Morris	John Hart
Joseph Hewes	Benjamin Rush	Abraham Clark
John Penn	Benjamin Franklin	Josiah Bartlett
Edward Rutledge	John Morton	William Whipple
Thomas Heyward, Jr.	George Clymer	Samuel Adams
Thomas Lynch, Jr.	James Smith	John Adams
Arthur Middleton	George Taylor	Robert Treat Paine
Samuel Chase	James Wilson	Elbridge Gerry
William Paca	George Ross	Stephen Hopkins
Thomas Stone	Caesar Rodney	William Ellery
Charles Carroll of Carrollton	George Read	Roger Sherman
George Wythe	Thomas McKean	Samuel Huntington
Richard Henry Lee	William Floyd	William Williams
Thomas Jefferson	Philip Livingston	Oliver Wolcott
	Francis Lewis	Matthew Thornton

The Constitution of the United States

Preamble

We the People of the United States, in Order to form a more perfect Union, establish Justice, insure domestic Tranquility, provide for the common defense, promote the general Welfare, and secure the Blessings of Liberty to ourselves and our Posterity, do ordain and establish this Constitution for the United States of America.

Article I The Legislature

Section 1. Congress

All legislative Powers herein granted shall be vested in a Congress of the United States, which shall consist of a Senate and House of Representatives.

Section 2. The House of Representatives

1. Elections The House of Representatives shall be composed of Members chosen every second Year by the People of the several States, and the Electors in each State shall have the Qualifications requisite for Electors of the most numerous Branch of the State Legislature.

2. Qualifications No Person shall be a Representative who shall not have attained to the Age of twenty five Years, and been seven Years a Citizen of the United States, and who shall not, when elected, be an Inhabitant of that State in which he shall be chosen.

3. Number of Representatives Representatives and direct Taxes shall be apportioned among the several States which may be included within this Union, according to their respective Numbers, ~~which shall be determined by adding to the whole Number of free Persons, including~~ **those bound to Service**[1] ~~for a Term of Years, and excluding Indians not taxed, three fifths of~~ **all other Persons**.[2] The actual **Enumeration**[3] shall be made within three Years after the first Meeting of the Congress of the United States, and within every subsequent Term of ten Years, in such Manner as they shall by Law direct. The Number of Representatives shall not exceed one for every

Note: The parts of the Constitution that have been lined through are no longer in force or no longer apply because of later amendments. The titles of the sections and articles are added for easier reference.

Legislative Branch

Article I explains how the legislative branch, called Congress, is organized. The chief purpose of the legislative branch is to make laws. Congress is made up of the Senate and the House of Representatives.

The House of Representatives

The number of members each state has in the House is based on the population of the individual state. In 1929 Congress permanently fixed the size of the House at 435 members.

Vocabulary

[1] **those bound to Service** indentured servants

[2] **all other Persons** slaves

[3] **Enumeration** census or official population count

thirty Thousand, but each State shall have at Least one Representative; and until such enumeration shall be made, the State of New Hampshire shall be entitled to choose three, Massachoosetts eight, Rhode-Island and Providence Plantations one, Connecticut five, New-York six, New Jersey four, Pennsylvania eight, Delaware one, Maryland six, Virginia ten, North Carolina five, South Carolina five, and Georgia three.

4. Vacancies When vacancies happen in the Representation from any State, the Executive Authority thereof shall issue Writs of Election to fill such Vacancies.

5. Officers and Impeachment The House of Representatives shall choose their Speaker and other Officers; and shall have the sole Power of impeachment.

Section 3. The Senate

1. Number of Senators The Senate of the United States shall be composed of two Senators from each State, chosen by the Legislature thereof, for six Years; and each Senator shall have one Vote.

2. Classifying Terms Immediately after they shall be assembled in Consequence of the first Election, they shall be divided as equally as may be into three Classes. The Seats of the Senators of the first Class shall be vacated at the Expiration of the second Year, of the second Class at the Expiration of the fourth Year, and of the third Class at the Expiration of the sixth Year, so that one third may be chosen every second Year; and if Vacancies happen by Resignation, or otherwise, during the Recess of the Legislature of any State, the Executive thereof may make temporary Appointments until the next Meeting of the Legislature, which shall then fill such Vacancies.

3. Qualifications No Person shall be a Senator who shall not have attained to the Age of thirty Years, and been nine Years a Citizen of the United States, and who shall not, when elected, be an Inhabitant of that State for which he shall be chosen.

4. Role of Vice-President The Vice President of the United States shall be President of the Senate, but shall have no Vote, unless they be equally divided.

5. Officers The Senate shall choose their other Officers, and also a President **pro tempore**,[4] in the Absence of the Vice President, or when he shall exercise the Office of President of the United States.

6. Impeachment Trials The Senate shall have the sole Power to try all **Impeachments**.[5] When sitting for that Purpose, they shall be on Oath or Affirmation. When the President of the United States is tried, the Chief Justice shall preside: And no Person shall be convicted without the Concurrence of two thirds of the Members present.

7. Punishment for Impeachment Judgment in Cases of Impeachment shall not extend further than to removal from Office, and disqualification to hold

The Vice President

The only duty that the Constitution assigns to the vice president is to preside over meetings of the Senate. Modern presidents have usually given their vice presidents more responsibilities.

Vocabulary

[4] **pro tempore** temporarily

[5] **Impeachments** official accusations of federal wrongdoing

and enjoy any Office of honor, Trust or Profit under the United States: but the Party convicted shall nevertheless be liable and subject to Indictment, Trial, Judgment and Punishment, according to Law.

Section 4. | Congressional Elections |

1. Regulations The Times, Places and Manner of holding Elections for Senators and Representatives, shall be prescribed in each State by the Legislature thereof; but the Congress may at any time by Law make or alter such Regulations, except as to the Places of choosing Senators.

2. Sessions ~~The Congress shall assemble at least once in every Year, and such Meeting shall be on the first Monday in December, unless they shall by Law appoint a different Day.~~

Section 5. | Rules/Procedures |

1. Quorum Each House shall be the Judge of the Elections, Returns and Qualifications of its own Members, and a Majority of each shall constitute a **Quorum**[6] to do Business; but a smaller Number may **adjourn**[7] from day to day, and may be authorized to compel the Attendance of absent Members, in such Manner, and under such Penalties as each House may provide.

2. Rules and Conduct Each House may determine the Rules of its Proceedings, punish its Members for disorderly Behaviour, and, with the Concurrence of two thirds, expel a Member.

3. Records Each House shall keep a Journal of its Proceedings, and from time to time publish the same, excepting such Parts as may in their Judgment require Secrecy; and the Yeas and Nays of the Members of either House on any question shall, at the Desire of one fifth of those Present, be entered on the Journal.

4. Adjournment Neither House, during the Session of Congress, shall, without the Consent of the other, adjourn for more than three days, nor to any other Place than that in which the two Houses shall be sitting.

Section 6. | Payment |

1. Salary The Senators and Representatives shall receive a Compensation for their Services, to be ascertained by Law, and paid out of the Treasury of the United States. They shall in all Cases, except Treason, Felony and Breach of the Peace, be privileged from Arrest during their Attendance at the Session of their respective Houses, and in going to and returning from the same; and for any Speech or Debate in either House, they shall not be questioned in any other Place.

2. Restrictions No Senator or Representative shall, during the Time for which he was elected, be appointed to any civil Office under the Authority of the United States, which shall have been created, or the **Emoluments**[8]

Vocabulary

[6] **Quorum** the minimum number of people needed to conduct business

[7] **adjourn** to stop indefinitely

[8] **Emoluments** salary

whereof shall have been increased during such time; and no Person holding any Office under the United States, shall be a Member of either House during his **Continuance**[9] in Office.

Section 7. | How a Bill Becomes a Law

1. Tax Bills All **Bills**[10] for raising Revenue shall originate in the House of Representatives; but the Senate may propose or concur with Amendments as on other Bills.

2. Lawmaking Every Bill which shall have passed the House of Representatives and the Senate, shall, before it become a Law, be presented to the President of the United States: If he approve he shall sign it, but if not he shall return it, with his Objections to that House in which it shall have originated, who shall enter the Objections at large on their Journal, and proceed to reconsider it. If after such Reconsideration two thirds of that House shall agree to pass the Bill, it shall be sent, together with the Objections, to the other House, by which it shall likewise be reconsidered, and if approved by two thirds of that House, it shall become a Law. But in all such Cases the Votes of both Houses shall be determined by yeas and Nays, and the Names of the Persons voting for and against the Bill shall be entered on the Journal of each House respectively. If any Bill shall not be returned by the President within ten Days (Sundays excepted) after it shall have been presented to him, the Same shall be a Law, in like Manner as if he had signed it, unless the Congress by their Adjournment prevent its Return, in which Case it shall not be a Law.

3. Role of the President Every Order, Resolution, or Vote to which the Concurrence of the Senate and House of Representatives may be necessary (except on a question of Adjournment) shall be presented to the President of the United States; and before the Same shall take Effect, shall be approved by him, or being disapproved by him, shall be repassed by two thirds of the Senate and House of Representatives, according to the Rules and Limitations prescribed in the Case of a Bill.

Section 8. | Powers Granted to Congress

1. Taxation The Congress shall have Power To lay and collect Taxes, **Duties**,[11] **Imposts**[12] and **Excises**,[13] to pay the Debts and provide for the common Defense and general Welfare of the United States; but all Duties, Imposts and Excises shall be uniform throughout the United States;

2. Credit To borrow Money on the credit of the United States;

3. Commerce To regulate Commerce with foreign Nations, and among the several States, and with the Indian Tribes;

4. Naturalization and Bankruptcy To establish an uniform **Rule of Naturalization**,[14] and uniform Laws on the subject of Bankruptcies throughout the United States;

Vocabulary

[9] **Continuance** term

[10] **Bills** proposed laws

[11] **Duties** tariffs

[12] **Imposts** taxes

[13] **Excises** internal taxes on the manufacture, sale, or consumption of a commodity

[14] **Rule of Naturalization** a law by which a foreign-born person becomes a citizen

Vocabulary

¹⁵ **Securities** bonds

¹⁶ **Letters of Marque and Reprisal** documents issued by governments allowing merchant ships to arm themselves and attack ships of an enemy nation

5. Money To coin Money, regulate the Value thereof, and of foreign Coin, and fix the Standard of Weights and Measures;

6. Counterfeiting To provide for the Punishment of counterfeiting the **Securities**¹⁵ and current Coin of the United States;

7. Post Office To establish Post Offices and post Roads;

8. Patents and Copyrights To promote the Progress of Science and useful Arts, by securing for limited Times to Authors and Inventors the exclusive Right to their respective Writings and Discoveries;

9. Courts To constitute Tribunals inferior to the supreme Court;

10. International Law To define and punish Piracies and Felonies committed on the high Seas, and Offences against the Law of Nations;

11. War To declare War, grant **Letters of Marque and Reprisal,**¹⁶ and make Rules concerning Captures on Land and Water;

12. Army To raise and support Armies, but no Appropriation of Money to that Use shall be for a longer Term than two Years;

13. Navy To provide and maintain a Navy;

14. Regulation of the Military To make Rules for the Government and Regulation of the land and naval Forces;

15. Militia To provide for calling forth the Militia to execute the Laws of the Union, suppress Insurrections and repel Invasions;

16. Regulation of the Militia To provide for organizing, arming, and disciplining, the Militia, and for governing such Part of them as may be employed in the Service of the United States, reserving to the States respectively, the Appointment of the Officers, and the Authority of training the Militia according to the discipline prescribed by Congress;

17. District of Columbia To exercise exclusive Legislation in all Cases whatsoever, over such District (not exceeding ten Miles square) as may, by Cession of particular States, and the Acceptance of Congress, become the Seat of the Government of the United States, and to exercise like Authority over all Places purchased by the Consent of the Legislature of the State in which the Same shall be, for the Erection of Forts, Magazines, Arsenals, dock-Yards, and other needful Buildings;—And

18. Necessary and Proper Clause To make all Laws which shall be necessary and proper for carrying into Execution the foregoing Powers, and all other Powers vested by this Constitution in the Government of the United States, or in any Department or Officer thereof.

Section 9. Powers Denied Congress

1. Slave Trade ~~The Migration or Importation of such Persons as any of the States now existing shall think proper to admit, shall not be prohibited~~

The Elastic Clause

The framers of the Constitution wanted a national government that was strong enough to be effective. This section lists the powers given to Congress. The last portion of Section 8 contains the so-called elastic clause.

~~by the Congress prior to the Year one thousand eight hundred and eight, but a Tax or duty may be imposed on such Importation, not exceeding ten dollars for each Person.~~

2. Habeas Corpus The Privilege of the **Writ of Habeas Corpus**[17] shall not be suspended, unless when in Cases of Rebellion or Invasion the public Safety may require it.

3. Illegal Punishment No **Bill of Attainder**[18] or **ex post facto Law**[19] shall be passed.

4. Direct Taxes No **Capitation**,[20] or other direct, Tax shall be laid, unless in Proportion to the Census or enumeration herein before directed to be taken.

5. Export Taxes No Tax or Duty shall be laid on Articles exported from any State.

6. No Favorites No Preference shall be given by any Regulation of Commerce or Revenue to the Ports of one State over those of another; nor shall Vessels bound to, or from, one State, be obliged to enter, clear, or pay Duties in another.

7. Public Money No Money shall be drawn from the Treasury, but in Consequence of Appropriations made by Law; and a regular Statement and Account of the Receipts and Expenditures of all public Money shall be published from time to time.

8. Titles of Nobility No Title of Nobility shall be granted by the United States: And no Person holding any Office of Profit or Trust under them, shall, without the Consent of the Congress, accept of any present, Emolument, Office, or Title, of any kind whatever, from any King, Prince, or foreign State.

Section 10. [Powers Denied the States]

1. Restrictions No State shall enter into any Treaty, Alliance, or Confederation; grant Letters of Marque and Reprisal; coin Money; emit Bills of Credit; make any Thing but gold and silver Coin a Tender in Payment of Debts; pass any Bill of Attainder, ex post facto Law, or Law impairing the Obligation of Contracts, or grant any Title of Nobility.

2. Import and Export Taxes No State shall, without the Consent of the Congress, lay any Imposts or Duties on Imports or Exports, except what may be absolutely necessary for executing it's inspection Laws: and the net Produce of all Duties and Imposts, laid by any State on Imports or Exports, shall be for the Use of the Treasury of the United States; and all such Laws shall be subject to the Revision and Control of the Congress.

3. Peacetime and War Restraints No State shall, without the Consent of Congress, lay any Duty of Tonnage, keep Troops, or Ships of War in time of Peace, enter into any Agreement or Compact with another State, or with a foreign Power, or engage in War, unless actually invaded, or in such imminent Danger as will not admit of delay.

Vocabulary

[17] **Writ of Habeas Corpus** a court order that requires the government to bring a prisoner to court and explain why he or she is being held

[18] **Bill of Attainder** a law declaring that a person is guilty of a particular crime

[19] **ex post facto Law** a law that is made effective prior to the date that it was passed and therefore punishes people for acts that were not illegal at the time

[20] **Capitation** a direct uniform tax imposed on each head, or person

Article II | The Executive

Section 1. | The Presidency

1. Terms of Office The executive Power shall be vested in a President of the United States of America. He shall hold his Office during the Term of four Years, and, together with the Vice President, chosen for the same Term, be elected, as follows:

2. Electoral College Each State shall appoint, in such Manner as the Legislature thereof may direct, a Number of Electors, equal to the whole Number of Senators and Representatives to which the State may be entitled in the Congress: but no Senator or Representative, or Person holding an Office of Trust or Profit under the United States, shall be appointed an Elector.

3. Former Method of Electing President The Electors shall meet in their respective States, and vote by Ballot for two Persons, of whom one at least shall not be an Inhabitant of the same State with themselves. And they shall make a List of all the Persons voted for, and of the Number of Votes for each; which List they shall sign and certify, and transmit sealed to the Seat of the Government of the United States, directed to the President of the Senate. The President of the Senate shall, in the Presence of the Senate and House of Representatives, open all the Certificates, and the Votes shall then be counted. The Person having the greatest Number of Votes shall be the President, if such Number be a Majority of the whole Number of Electors appointed; and if there be more than one who have such Majority, and have an equal Number of Votes, then the House of Representatives shall immediately choose by Ballot one of them for President; and if no Person have a Majority, then from the five highest on the List the said House shall in like Manner choose the President. But in choosing the President, the Votes shall be taken by States, the Representation from each State having one Vote; A quorum for this purpose shall consist of a Member or Members from two thirds of the States, and a Majority of all the States shall be necessary to a Choice. In every Case, after the Choice of the President, the Person having the greatest Number of Votes of the Electors shall be the Vice President. But if there should remain two or more who have equal Votes, the Senate shall choose from them by Ballot the Vice President.

4. Election Day The Congress may determine the Time of choosing the Electors, and the Day on which they shall give their Votes; which Day shall be the same throughout the United States.

5. Qualifications No Person except a natural born Citizen, or a Citizen of the United States, at the time of the Adoption of this Constitution, shall be eligible to the Office of President; neither shall any Person be eligible to

---

Executive Branch

The president is the chief of the executive branch. It is the job of the president to enforce the laws. The framers wanted the president's and vice president's terms of office and manner of selection to be different from those of members of Congress. They decided on four-year terms, but they had a difficult time agreeing on how to select the president and vice president. The framers finally set up an electoral system, which varies greatly from our electoral process today.

Presidential Elections

In 1845 Congress set the Tuesday following the first Monday in November of every fourth year as the general election date for selecting presidential electors.

---

that Office who shall not have attained to the Age of thirty five Years, and been fourteen Years a Resident within the United States.

6. Succession In Case of the Removal of the President from Office, or of his Death, Resignation, or Inability to discharge the Powers and Duties of the said Office, the Same shall devolve on the Vice President, and the Congress may by Law provide for the Case of Removal, Death, Resignation or Inability, both of the President and Vice President, declaring what Officer shall then act as President, and such Officer shall act accordingly, until the Disability be removed, or a President shall be elected.

7. Salary The President shall, at stated Times, receive for his Services, a Compensation, which shall neither be increased nor diminished during the Period for which he shall have been elected, and he shall not receive within that Period any other Emolument from the United States, or any of them.

8. Oath of Office Before he enter on the Execution of his Office, he shall take the following Oath or Affirmation:—"I do solemnly swear (or affirm) that I will faithfully execute the Office of President of the United States, and will to the best of my Ability, preserve, protect and defend the Constitution of the United States."

Section 2. Powers of Presidency

1. Military Powers The President shall be Commander in Chief of the Army and Navy of the United States, and of the Militia of the several States, when called into the actual Service of the United States; he may require the Opinion, in writing, of the principal Officer in each of the executive Departments, upon any Subject relating to the Duties of their respective Offices, and he shall have Power to grant **Reprieves**[21] and **Pardons**[22] for Offences against the United States, except in Cases of Impeachment.

2. Treaties and Appointments He shall have Power, by and with the Advice and Consent of the Senate, to make Treaties, provided two thirds of the Senators present concur; and he shall nominate, and by and with the Advice and Consent of the Senate, shall appoint Ambassadors, other public Ministers and Consuls, Judges of the supreme Court, and all other Officers of the United States, whose Appointments are not herein otherwise provided for, and which shall be established by Law: but the Congress may by Law vest the Appointment of such inferior Officers, as they think proper, in the President alone, in the Courts of Law, or in the Heads of Departments.

3. Vacancies The President shall have Power to fill up all Vacancies that may happen during the Recess of the Senate, by granting Commissions which shall expire at the End of their next Session.

Presidential Salary

In 1999 Congress voted to set future presidents' salaries at $400,000 per year. The president also receives an annual expense account. The president must pay taxes only on the salary.

Commander in Chief

Today the president is in charge of the army, navy, air force, marines, and coast guard. Only Congress, however, can decide if the United States will declare war.

Appointments

Most of the president's appointments to office must be approved by the Senate.

Vocabulary

[21] **Reprieves** delays of punishment

[22] **Pardons** releases from the legal penalties associated with a crime

The State of the Union

Every year the president presents to Congress a State of the Union message. In this message, the president introduces and explains a legislative plan for the coming year.

Judicial Branch

The Articles of Confederation did not set up a federal court system. One of the first points that the framers of the Constitution agreed upon was to set up a national judiciary. In the Judiciary Act of 1789, Congress provided for the establishment of lower courts, such as district courts, circuit courts of appeals, and various other federal courts. The judicial system provides a check on the legislative branch: It can declare a law unconstitutional.

Section 3. Presidential Duties

He shall from time to time give to the Congress Information of the State of the Union, and recommend to their Consideration such Measures as he shall judge necessary and expedient; he may, on extraordinary Occasions, convene both Houses, or either of them, and in Case of Disagreement between them, with Respect to the Time of Adjournment, he may adjourn them to such Time as he shall think proper; he shall receive Ambassadors and other public Ministers; he shall take Care that the Laws be faithfully executed, and shall Commission all the Officers of the United States.

Section 4. Impeachment

The President, Vice President and all civil Officers of the United States, shall be removed from Office on Impeachment for, and Conviction of, Treason, Bribery, or other high Crimes and Misdemeanors.

Article III   The Judiciary

Section 1. Federal Courts and Judges

The judicial Power of the United States shall be vested in one supreme Court, and in such inferior Courts as the Congress may from time to time ordain and establish. The Judges, both of the supreme and inferior Courts, shall hold their Offices during good Behavior, and shall, at stated Times, receive for their Services a Compensation, which shall not be diminished during their Continuance in Office.

Section 2. Authority of the Courts

1. General Authority The judicial Power shall extend to all Cases, in Law and Equity, arising under this Constitution, the Laws of the United States, and Treaties made, or which shall be made, under their Authority;—to all Cases affecting Ambassadors, other public Ministers and Consuls;—to all Cases of admiralty and maritime Jurisdiction;—to Controversies to which the United States shall be a Party;—to Controversies between two or more States —between a State and Citizens of another State; —between Citizens of different States;—between Citizens of the same State claiming Lands under Grants of different States, and between a State, or the Citizens thereof, and foreign States, Citizens or Subjects.

2. Supreme Authority In all Cases affecting Ambassadors, other public Ministers and Consuls, and those in which a State shall be Party, the supreme Court shall have original Jurisdiction. In all the other Cases before mentioned, the supreme Court shall have appellate Jurisdiction, both as to Law and Fact, with such Exceptions, and under such Regulations as the Congress shall make.

3. Trial by Jury The Trial of all Crimes, except in Cases of Impeachment, shall be by Jury; and such Trial shall be held in the State where the said Crimes shall have been committed; but when not committed within any State, the Trial shall be at such Place or Places as the Congress may by Law have directed.

Section 3. Treason

1. Definition Treason against the United States, shall consist only in levying War against them, or in adhering to their Enemies, giving them Aid and Comfort. No Person shall be convicted of Treason unless on the Testimony of two Witnesses to the same overt Act, or on Confession in open Court.

2. Punishment The Congress shall have Power to declare the Punishment of Treason, but no Attainder of Treason shall work **Corruption of Blood**,[23] or Forfeiture except during the Life of the Person attainted.

Vocabulary

[23] **Corruption of Blood** punishing the family of a person convicted of treason

Article IV Relations among States

Section 1. State Acts and Records

Full Faith and Credit shall be given in each State to the public Acts, Records, and judicial Proceedings of every other State. And the Congress may by general Laws prescribe the Manner in which such Acts, Records and Proceedings shall be proved, and the Effect thereof.

Section 2. Rights of Citizens

1. Citizenship The Citizens of each State shall be entitled to all Privileges and Immunities of Citizens in the several States.

2. Extradition A Person charged in any State with Treason, Felony, or other Crime, who shall flee from Justice, and be found in another State, shall on Demand of the executive Authority of the State from which he fled, be delivered up, to be removed to the State having Jurisdiction of the Crime.

3. Fugitive Slaves No Person held to Service or Labour in one State, under the Laws thereof, escaping into another, shall, in Consequence of any Law or Regulation therein, be discharged from such Service or Labour, but shall be delivered up on Claim of the Party to whom such Service or Labour may be due.

Section 3. New States

1. Admission New States may be admitted by the Congress into this Union; but no new State shall be formed or erected within the Jurisdiction of any other State; nor any State be formed by the Junction of two or more States, or Parts of States, without the Consent of the Legislatures of the States concerned as well as of the Congress.

The States

States must honor the laws, records, and court decisions of other states. A person cannot escape a legal obligation by moving from one state to another.

2. Congressional Authority The Congress shall have Power to dispose of and make all needful Rules and Regulations respecting the Territory or other Property belonging to the United States; and nothing in this Constitution shall be so construed as to Prejudice any Claims of the United States, or of any particular State.

Section 4. Guarantees to the States

The United States shall guarantee to every State in this Union a Republican Form of Government, and shall protect each of them against Invasion; and on Application of the Legislature, or of the Executive (when the Legislature cannot be convened), against domestic Violence.

Article V Amending the Constitution

The Congress, whenever two thirds of both Houses shall deem it necessary, shall propose Amendments to this Constitution, or, on the Application of the Legislatures of two thirds of the several States, shall call a Convention for proposing Amendments, which, in either Case, shall be valid to all Intents and Purposes, as Part of this Constitution, when ratified by the Legislatures of three fourths of the several States, or by Conventions in three fourths thereof, as the one or the other Mode of Ratification may be proposed by the Congress; Provided that ~~no Amendment which may be made prior to the Year One thousand eight hundred and eight shall in any Manner affect the first and fourth Clauses in the Ninth Section of the first Article; and~~ that no State, without its Consent, shall be deprived of its equal Suffrage in the Senate.

Article VI Supremacy of National Government

All Debts contracted and Engagements entered into, before the Adoption of this Constitution, shall be as valid against the United States under this Constitution, as under the Confederation.

This Constitution, and the Laws of the United States which shall be made in Pursuance thereof; and all Treaties made, or which shall be made, under the Authority of the United States, shall be the supreme Law of the Land; and the Judges in every State shall be bound thereby, any Thing in the Constitution or Laws of any State to the Contrary notwithstanding.

The Senators and Representatives before mentioned, and the Members of the several State Legislatures, and all executive and judicial Officers, both of the United States and of the several States, shall be bound by Oath or Affirmation, to support this Constitution; but no religious Test shall ever be required as a Qualification to any Office or public Trust under the United States.

National Supremacy

One of the biggest problems facing the delegates to the Constitutional Convention was the question of what would happen if a state law and a federal law conflicted. Which law would be followed? Who would decide? The second clause of Article VI answers those questions. When a federal law and a state law disagree, the federal law overrides the state law. The Constitution and other federal laws are the "supreme Law of the Land." This clause is often called the supremacy clause.

Article VII | Ratification

The Ratification of the Conventions of nine States, shall be sufficient for the Establishment of this Constitution between the States so ratifying the Same.

Done in Convention by the Unanimous Consent of the States present the Seventeenth Day of September in the Year of our Lord one thousand seven hundred and Eighty seven and of the Independence of the United States of America the Twelfth In witness whereof We have hereunto subscribed our Names,

George Washington—
President and deputy from Virginia

Delaware

George Read
Gunning Bedford Jr.
John Dickinson
Richard Bassett
Jacob Broom

Maryland

James McHenry
*Daniel of
  St. Thomas Jenifer*
Daniel Carroll

Virginia

John Blair
James Madison Jr.

North Carolina

William Blount
Richard Dobbs Spaight
Hugh Williamson

South Carolina

John Rutledge
*Charles Cotesworth
  Pinckney*
Charles Pinckney
Pierce Butler

Georgia

William Few
Abraham Baldwin

New Hampshire

John Langdon
Nicholas Gilman

Massachusetts

Nathaniel Gorham
Rufus King

Connecticut

William Samuel Johnson
Roger Sherman

New York

Alexander Hamilton

New Jersey

William Livingston
David Brearley
William Paterson
Jonathan Dayton

Pennsylvania

Benjamin Franklin
Thomas Mifflin
Robert Morris
George Clymer
Thomas FitzSimons
Jared Ingersoll
James Wilson
Gouverneur Morris

Attest:
*William Jackson,
Secretary*

Ratification

The Articles of Confederation called for all 13 states to approve any revision to the Articles. The Constitution required that 9 out of the 13 states would be needed to ratify the Constitution. The first state to ratify was Delaware, on December 7, 1787. Almost two-and-a-half years later, on May 29, 1790, Rhode Island became the last state to ratify the Constitution.

THE CONSTITUTION

Constitutional Amendments

Note: The first 10 amendments to the Constitution were ratified on December 15, 1791, and form what is known as the Bill of Rights.

Amendments 1–10. The Bill of Rights

Amendment I

Congress shall make no law respecting an establishment of religion, or prohibiting the free exercise thereof; or abridging the freedom of speech, or of the press; or the right of the people peaceably to assemble, and to petition the Government for a redress of grievances.

Amendment II

A well regulated Militia, being necessary to the security of a free State, the right of the people to keep and bear Arms, shall not be infringed.

Amendment III

No Soldier shall, in time of peace be **quartered**[24] in any house, without the consent of the Owner, nor in time of war, but in a manner to be prescribed by law.

Amendment IV

The right of the people to be secure in their persons, houses, papers, and effects, against unreasonable searches and seizures, shall not be violated, and no **Warrants**[25] shall issue, but upon probable cause, supported by Oath or affirmation, and particularly describing the place to be searched, and the persons or things to be seized.

Amendment V

No person shall be held to answer for a capital, or otherwise **infamous**[26] crime, unless on a presentment or **indictment**[27] of a Grand Jury, except in cases arising in the land or naval forces, or in the Militia, when in actual service in time of War or public danger; nor shall any person be subject for the same offence to be twice put in jeopardy of life or limb; nor shall be compelled in any criminal case to be a witness against himself, nor be deprived of life, liberty, or property, without due process of law; nor shall private property be taken for public use, without just compensation.

Amendment VI

In all criminal prosecutions, the accused shall enjoy the right to a speedy and public trial, by an impartial jury of the State and district wherein the crime shall have been committed, which district shall have been previously **ascertained**[28] by law, and to be informed of the nature and cause of the accusation; to be confronted with the witnesses against him; to have compulsory process for obtaining witnesses in his favor, and to have the Assistance of Counsel for his defence.

THE CONSTITUTION

Bill of Rights

One of the conditions set by several states for ratifying the Constitution was the inclusion of a bill of rights. Many people feared that a stronger central government might take away basic rights of the people that had been guaranteed in state constitutions.

Vocabulary

[24] **quartered** housed

[25] **Warrants** written orders authorizing a person to make an arrest, a seizure, or a search

[26] **infamous** disgraceful

[27] **indictment** the act of charging with a crime

[28] **ascertained** found out

Rights of the Accused

The Fifth, Sixth, and Seventh Amendments describe the procedures that courts must follow when trying people accused of crimes.

Trials

The Sixth Amendment makes several guarantees, including a prompt trial and a trial by a jury chosen from the state and district in which the crime was committed.

Amendment VII

In suits at common law, where the value in controversy shall exceed twenty dollars, the right of trial by jury shall be preserved, and no fact tried by a jury, shall be otherwise reexamined in any Court of the United States, than according to the rules of the common law.

Amendment VIII

Excessive bail shall not be required, nor excessive fines imposed, nor cruel and unusual punishments inflicted.

Amendment IX

The enumeration in the Constitution, of certain rights, shall not be construed to deny or disparage others retained by the people.

Amendment X

The powers not delegated to the United States by the Constitution, nor prohibited by it to the States, are reserved to the States respectively, or to the people.

Amendments 11–27

Amendment XI

Passed by Congress March 4, 1794. Ratified February 7, 1795.

The Judicial power of the United States shall not be **construed**[29] to extend to any suit in law or equity, commenced or prosecuted against one of the United States by Citizens of another State, or by Citizens or Subjects of any Foreign State.

Amendment XII

Passed by Congress December 9, 1803. Ratified June 15, 1804.

The Electors shall meet in their respective states and vote by ballot for President and Vice-President, one of whom, at least, shall not be an inhabitant of the same state with themselves; they shall name in their ballots the person voted for as President, and in distinct ballots the person voted for as Vice-President, and they shall make distinct lists of all persons voted for as President, and of all persons voted for as Vice-President, and of the number of votes for each, which lists they shall sign and certify, and transmit sealed to the seat of the government of the United States, directed to the President of the Senate;—the President of the Senate shall, in the presence of the Senate and House of Representatives, open all the certificates and the votes shall then be counted;—The person having the greatest number of votes for President, shall be the President, if such number be a majority of the whole number of Electors appointed; and if no person have such majority, then from the persons having the highest numbers not exceeding three on the list of those voted for as President, the House of Representatives shall choose immediately, by ballot, the President. But in choosing the

Vocabulary

[29] **construed** explained or interpreted

President and Vice President

The Twelfth Amendment changed the election procedure for president and vice president.

President, the votes shall be taken by states, the representation from each state having one vote; a quorum for this purpose shall consist of a member or members from two-thirds of the states, and a majority of all the states shall be necessary to a choice. ~~And if the House of Representatives shall not choose a President whenever the right of choice shall devolve upon them, before the fourth day of March next following, then the Vice-President shall act as President, as in case of the death or other constitutional disability of the President.~~—The person having the greatest number of votes as Vice-President, shall be the Vice-President, if such number be a majority of the whole number of Electors appointed, and if no person have a majority, then from the two highest numbers on the list, the Senate shall choose the Vice-President; a quorum for the purpose shall consist of two-thirds of the whole number of Senators, and a majority of the whole number shall be necessary to a choice. But no person constitutionally ineligible to the office of President shall be eligible to that of Vice-President of the United States.

Amendment XIII

Passed by Congress January 31, 1865. Ratified December 6, 1865.

1. Slavery Banned Neither slavery nor **involuntary servitude,**[30] except as a punishment for crime whereof the party shall have been duly convicted, shall exist within the United States, or any place subject to their jurisdiction.

2. Enforcement Congress shall have power to enforce this article by appropriate legislation.

Amendment XIV

Passed by Congress June 13, 1866. Ratified July 9, 1868.

1. Citizenship Defined All persons born or naturalized in the United States, and subject to the jurisdiction thereof, are citizens of the United States and of the State wherein they reside. No State shall make or enforce any law which shall abridge the privileges or immunities of citizens of the United States; nor shall any State deprive any person of life, liberty, or property, without due process of law; nor deny to any person within its jurisdiction the equal protection of the laws.

2. Voting Rights Representatives shall be apportioned among the several States according to their respective numbers, counting the whole number of persons in each State, ~~excluding Indians not taxed~~. But when the right to vote at any election for the choice of electors for President and Vice-President of the United States, Representatives in Congress, the Executive and Judicial officers of a State, or the members of the Legislature thereof, is denied to any of the ~~male~~ inhabitants of such State, ~~being twenty-one years of age~~, and citizens of the United States, or in any way abridged, except for participation in rebellion, or other crime, the basis of representation therein shall be reduced in the proportion which the number of such ~~male~~ citizens shall bear to the whole number of ~~male~~ citizens ~~twenty-one years of age~~ in such State.

Vocabulary

[30] **involuntary servitude** being forced to work against one's will

Abolishing Slavery

Although some slaves had been freed during the Civil War, slavery was not abolished until the Thirteenth Amendment took effect.

Protecting the Rights of Citizens

In 1833 the Supreme Court ruled that the Bill of Rights limited the federal government but not the state governments. This ruling was interpreted to mean that states were able to keep African Americans from becoming state citizens and keep the Bill of Rights from protecting them. The Fourteenth Amendment defines citizenship and prevents states from interfering in the rights of citizens of the United States.

3. Rebels Banned from Government No person shall be a Senator or Representative in Congress, or elector of President and Vice-President, or hold any office, civil or military, under the United States, or under any State, who, having previously taken an oath, as a member of Congress, or as an officer of the United States, or as a member of any State legislature, or as an executive or judicial officer of any State, to support the Constitution of the United States, shall have engaged in insurrection or rebellion against the same, or given aid or comfort to the enemies thereof. But Congress may by a vote of two-thirds of each House, remove such disability.

4. Payment of Debts The validity of the public debt of the United States, authorized by law, including debts incurred for payment of pensions and bounties for services in suppressing insurrection or rebellion, shall not be questioned. But neither the United States nor any State shall assume or pay any debt or obligation incurred in aid of insurrection or rebellion against the United States, or any claim for the loss or emancipation of any slave; but all such debts, obligations and claims shall be held illegal and void.

5. Enforcement The Congress shall have the power to enforce, by appropriate legislation, the provisions of this article.

Amendment XV

Passed by Congress February 26, 1869. Ratified February 3, 1870.

1. Voting Rights The right of citizens of the United States to vote shall not be denied or abridged by the United States or by any State on account of race, color, or previous condition of servitude.

2. Enforcement The Congress shall have the power to enforce this article by appropriate legislation.

Amendment XVI

Passed by Congress July 2, 1909. Ratified February 3, 1913.

The Congress shall have power to lay and collect taxes on incomes, from whatever source derived, without apportionment among the several States, and without regard to any census or enumeration.

Amendment XVII

Passed by Congress May 13, 1912. Ratified April 8, 1913.

1. Senators Elected by Citizens The Senate of the United States shall be composed of two Senators from each State, elected by the people thereof, for six years; and each Senator shall have one vote. The electors in each State shall have the qualifications requisite for electors of the most numerous branch of the State legislatures.

2. Vacancies When vacancies happen in the representation of any State in the Senate, the executive authority of such State shall issue writs of election to fill such vacancies: *Provided*, That the legislature of any State may

Prohibition

Although many people believed that the Eighteenth Amendment was good for the health and welfare of the American people, it was repealed 14 years later.

Women's Suffrage

Abigail Adams and others were disappointed that the Declaration of Independence and the Constitution did not specifically include women. It took many years and much campaigning before suffrage for women was finally achieved.

Taking Office

In the original Constitution, a newly elected president and Congress did not take office until March 4, which was four months after the November election. The officials who were leaving office were called lame ducks because they had little influence during those four months. The Twentieth Amendment changed the date that the new president and Congress take office. Members of Congress now take office during the first week of January, and the president takes office on January 20.

---

empower the executive thereof to make temporary appointments until the people fill the vacancies by election as the legislature may direct.

3. Future Elections This amendment shall not be so construed as to affect the election or term of any Senator chosen before it becomes valid as part of the Constitution.

Amendment XVIII

Passed by Congress December 18, 1917. Ratified January 16, 1919. Repealed by Amendment XXI.

1. Liquor Banned After one year from the ratification of this article the manufacture, sale, or transportation of intoxicating liquors within, the importation thereof into, or the exportation thereof from the United States and all territory subject to the jurisdiction thereof for beverage purposes is hereby prohibited.

2. Enforcement The Congress and the several States shall have concurrent power to enforce this article by appropriate legislation.

3. Ratification This article shall be inoperative unless it shall have been ratified as an amendment to the Constitution by the legislatures of the several States, as provided in the Constitution, within seven years from the date of the submission hereof to the States by the Congress.

Amendment XIX

Passed by Congress June 4, 1919. Ratified August 18, 1920.

1. Voting Rights The right of citizens of the United States to vote shall not be denied or abridged by the United States or by any State on account of sex.

2. Enforcement Congress shall have power to enforce this article by appropriate legislation.

Amendment XX

Passed by Congress March 2, 1932. Ratified January 23, 1933.

1. Presidential Terms The terms of the President and the Vice President shall end at noon on the 20th day of January, and the terms of Senators and Representatives at noon on the 3d day of January, of the years in which such terms would have ended if this article had not been ratified; and the terms of their successors shall then begin.

2. Meeting of Congress The Congress shall assemble at least once in every year, and such meeting shall begin at noon on the 3d day of January, unless they shall by law appoint a different day.

3. Succession of Vice President If, at the time fixed for the beginning of the term of the President, the President elect shall have died, the Vice President elect shall become President. If a President shall not have been chosen before the time fixed for the beginning of his term, or if the President elect shall have failed to qualify, then the Vice President elect shall act as President until a President shall have qualified; and the Congress may by law provide for the case wherein neither a President elect nor a Vice President shall have qualified, declaring who shall then act as President, or the manner in which one who is to act shall be selected, and such person shall act accordingly until a President or Vice President shall have qualified.

4. Succession by Vote of Congress The Congress may by law provide for the case of the death of any of the persons from whom the House of Representatives may choose a President whenever the right of choice shall have devolved upon them, and for the case of the death of any of the persons from whom the Senate may choose a Vice President whenever the right of choice shall have devolved upon them.

5. Ratification Sections 1 and 2 shall take effect on the 15th day of October following the ratification of this article.

6. Ratification This article shall be inoperative unless it shall have been ratified as an amendment to the Constitution by the legislatures of three-fourths of the several States within seven years from the date of its submission.

Amendment XXI

Passed by Congress February 20, 1933. Ratified December 5, 1933.

1. 18th Amendment Repealed The eighteenth article of amendment to the Constitution of the United States is hereby repealed.

2. Liquor Allowed by Law The transportation or importation into any State, Territory, or Possession of the United States for delivery or use therein of intoxicating liquors, in violation of the laws thereof, is hereby prohibited.

3. Ratification This article shall be inoperative unless it shall have been ratified as an amendment to the Constitution by conventions in the several States, as provided in the Constitution, within seven years from the date of the submission hereof to the States by the Congress.

Amendment XXII

Passed by Congress March 21, 1947. Ratified February 27, 1951.

1. Term Limits No person shall be elected to the office of the President more than twice, and no person who has held the office of President, or acted as President, for more than two years of a term to which some other person was elected President shall be elected to the office of President more than once. But this Article shall not apply to any person holding the office of President when this Article was proposed by Congress, and shall not prevent any person who may be holding the office of President, or acting as President, during the term within which this Article becomes operative from holding the office of President or acting as President during the remainder of such term.

2. Ratification ~~This article shall be inoperative unless it shall have been ratified as an amendment to the Constitution by the legislatures of three-fourths of the several States within seven years from the date of its submission to the States by the Congress.~~

Amendment XXIII

Passed by Congress June 16, 1960. Ratified March 29, 1961.

1. District of Columbia Represented The District constituting the seat of Government of the United States shall appoint in such manner as Congress may direct:

A number of electors of President and Vice President equal to the whole number of Senators and Representatives in Congress to which the District would be entitled if it were a State, but in no event more than the least populous State; they shall be in addition to those appointed by the States, but they shall be considered, for the purposes of the election of President and Vice President, to be electors appointed by a State; and they shall meet in the District and perform such duties as provided by the twelfth article of amendment.

2. Enforcement The Congress shall have power to enforce this article by appropriate legislation.

Amendment XXIV

Passed by Congress August 27, 1962. Ratified January 23, 1964.

1. Voting Rights The right of citizens of the United States to vote in any primary or other election for President or Vice President, for electors for President or Vice President, or for Senator or Representative in Congress, shall not be denied or abridged by the United States or any State by reason of failure to pay poll tax or other tax.

2. Enforcement The Congress shall have power to enforce this article by appropriate legislation.

Amendment XXV

Passed by Congress July 6, 1965. Ratified February 10, 1967.

1. Sucession of Vice President In case of the removal of the President from office or of his death or resignation, the Vice President shall become President.

2. Vacancy of Vice President Whenever there is a vacancy in the office of the Vice President, the President shall nominate a Vice President who shall take office upon confirmation by a majority vote of both Houses of Congress.

3. Written Declaration Whenever the President transmits to the President pro tempore of the Senate and the Speaker of the House of Representatives his written declaration that he is unable to discharge the powers and duties of his office, and until he transmits to them a written declara-

---

THE CONSTITUTION

Voting Rights

Until the ratification of the Twenty-third Amendment, the people of Washington, D.C., could not vote in presidential elections.

Presidential Disability

The illness of President Eisenhower in the 1950s and the assassination of President Kennedy in 1963 were the events behind the Twenty-fifth Amendment. The Constitution did not provide a clear-cut method for a vice president to take over for a disabled president or upon the death of a president. This amendment provides for filling the office of the vice president if a vacancy occurs, and it provides a way for the vice president—or someone else in the line of succession—to take over if the president is unable to perform the duties of that office.

tion to the contrary, such powers and duties shall be discharged by the Vice President as Acting President.

4. Removing the President Whenever the Vice President and a majority of either the principal officers of the executive departments or of such other body as Congress may by law provide, transmit to the President pro tempore of the Senate and the Speaker of the House of Representatives their written declaration that the President is unable to discharge the powers and duties of his office, the Vice President shall immediately assume the powers and duties of the office as Acting President.

Thereafter, when the President transmits to the President pro tempore of the Senate and the Speaker of the House of Representatives his written declaration that no inability exists, he shall resume the powers and duties of his office unless the Vice President and a majority of either the principal officers of the executive department or of such other body as Congress may by law provide, transmit within four days to the President pro tempore of the Senate and the Speaker of the House of Representatives their written declaration that the President is unable to discharge the powers and duties of his office. Thereupon Congress shall decide the issue, assembling within forty-eight hours for that purpose if not in session. If the Congress, within twenty-one days after receipt of the latter written declaration, or, if Congress is not in session, within twenty-one days after Congress is required to assemble, determines by two-thirds vote of both Houses that the President is unable to discharge the powers and duties of his office, the Vice President shall continue to discharge the same as Acting President; otherwise, the President shall resume the powers and duties of his office.

Amendment XXVI

Passed by Congress March 23, 1971. Ratified July 1, 1971.

1. Voting Rights The right of citizens of the United States, who are eighteen years of age or older, to vote shall not be denied or abridged by the United States or by any State on account of age.

2. Enforcement The Congress shall have power to enforce this article by appropriate legislation.

Amendment XXVII

Originally proposed September 25, 1789. Ratified May 7, 1992.

No law, varying the compensation for the services of the Senators and Representatives, shall take effect, until an election of representatives shall have intervened.

Expanded Suffrage

The Voting Rights Act of 1970 tried to set the voting age at 18. However, the Supreme Court ruled that the act set the voting age for national elections only, not for state or local elections. The Twenty-sixth Amendment gave 18-year-old citizens the right to vote in all elections.

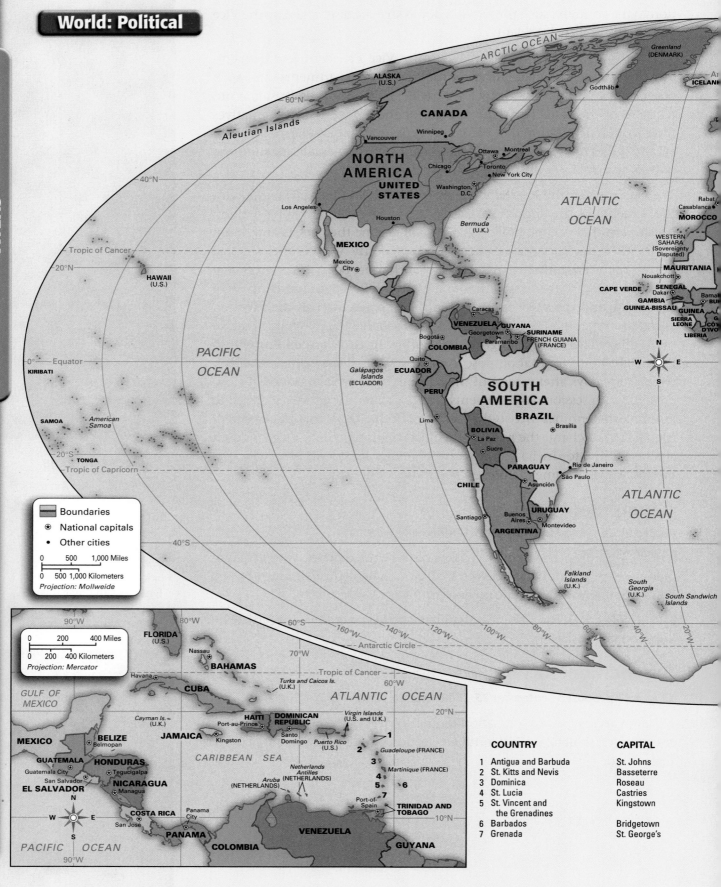

ATLAS

Boundaries
⊛ National capitals
• Other cities

| 0 | 500 | 1,000 Miles |
| 0 | 500 1,000 Kilometers | |

Projection: Mollweide

| 0 | 200 | 400 Miles |
| 0 | 200 | 400 Kilometers |

Projection: Mercator

COUNTRY	CAPITAL
1 Antigua and Barbuda	St. Johns
2 St. Kitts and Nevis	Basseterre
3 Dominica	Roseau
4 St. Lucia	Castries
5 St. Vincent and the Grenadines	Kingstown
6 Barbados	Bridgetown
7 Grenada	St. George's

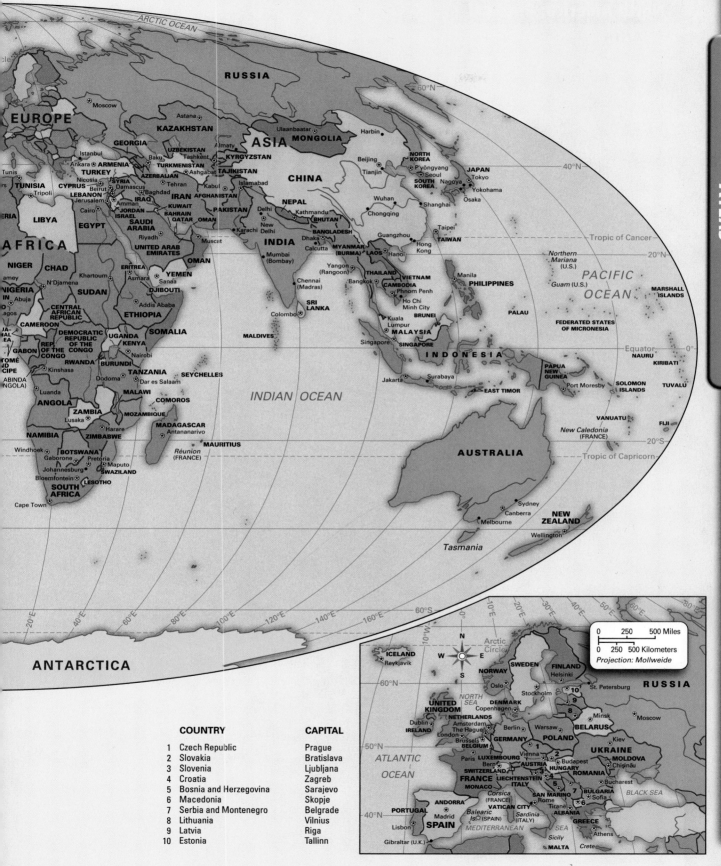

ARCTIC OCEAN

EUROPE

RUSSIA

KAZAKHSTAN

Moscow

Astana

ASIA

MONGOLIA

Ulaanbaatar

Harbin

60°N

GEORGIA

Istanbul

UZBEKISTAN

Almaty

KYRGYZSTAN

Beijing

NORTH KOREA

JAPAN

40°N

TURKEY

Ankara

ARMENIA

Baku

Tashkent

TAJIKISTAN

CHINA

Tianjin

P'yŏngyang

Seoul

SOUTH KOREA

Nagoya

Tokyo

Yokohama

TUNISIA

CYPRUS

Nicosia

AZERBAIJAN

Ashgabat

TURKMENISTAN

Osaka

Tunis

SYRIA

Damascus

Tehran

Kabul

Wuhan

Shanghai

LEBANON

Beirut

IRAQ

Baghdad

IRAN

Islamabad

AFGHANISTAN

Chongqing

Tripoli

Jerusalem

JORDAN

Amman

KUWAIT

PAKISTAN

NEPAL

Kathmandu

Guangzhou

Taipei

Tropic of Cancer

ISRAEL

Cairo

BAHRAIN

QATAR

Delhi

BHUTAN

Hong Kong

TAIWAN

20°N

LIBYA

EGYPT

SAUDI ARABIA

UNITED ARAB EMIRATES

New Delhi

Karachi

BANGLADESH

Dhaka

Calcutta

MYANMAR (BURMA)

LAOS

Hanoi

Northern Mariana (U.S.)

PACIFIC OCEAN

AFRICA

NIGER

CHAD

Khartoum

N'Djamena

ERITREA

Asmara

Sanaa

YEMEN

OMAN

Muscat

INDIA

Mumbai (Bombay)

Yangon (Rangoon)

THAILAND

Bangkok

VIETNAM

CAMBODIA

Phnom Penh

Manila

PHILIPPINES

Guam (U.S.)

MARSHALL ISLANDS

NIGERIA

Abuja

SUDAN

Addis Ababa

DJIBOUTI

ETHIOPIA

Chennai (Madras)

SRI LANKA

Ho Chi Minh City

BRUNEI

PALAU

FEDERATED STATES OF MICRONESIA

CAMEROON

CENTRAL AFRICAN REPUBLIC

DEMOCRATIC REPUBLIC OF THE CONGO

UGANDA

KENYA

Colombo

MALDIVES

MALAYSIA

Kuala Lumpur

GABON

REP. OF THE CONGO

Kinshasa

RWANDA

BURUNDI

Nairobi

Singapore

SINGAPORE

INDONESIA

Equator

NAURU

0°

SÃO TOMÉ AND PRÍNCIPE

CABINDA (ANGOLA)

Luanda

TANZANIA

Dodoma

Dar es Salaam

SEYCHELLES

Jakarta

Surabaya

PAPUA NEW GUINEA

Port Moresby

EAST TIMOR

SOLOMON ISLANDS

KIRIBATI

TUVALU

ANGOLA

ZAMBIA

Lusaka

MALAWI

MOZAMBIQUE

COMOROS

INDIAN OCEAN

VANUATU

New Caledonia (FRANCE)

FIJI

NAMIBIA

Windhoek

ZIMBABWE

Harare

BOTSWANA

Gaborone

Pretoria

MADAGASCAR

Antananarivo

MAURITIUS

Réunion (FRANCE)

AUSTRALIA

20°S

Tropic of Capricorn

Johannesburg

Bloemfontein

SWAZILAND

LESOTHO

Maputo

SOUTH AFRICA

Cape Town

Sydney

Canberra

Melbourne

NEW ZEALAND

Wellington

Tasmania

ANTARCTICA

20°E 40°E 60°E 80°E 100°E 120°E 140°E 160°E 60°S

COUNTRY	CAPITAL
1 Czech Republic	Prague
2 Slovakia	Bratislava
3 Slovenia	Ljubljana
4 Croatia	Zagreb
5 Bosnia and Herzegovina	Sarajevo
6 Macedonia	Skopje
7 Serbia and Montenegro	Belgrade
8 Lithuania	Vilnius
9 Latvia	Riga
10 Estonia	Tallinn

ICELAND

Reykjavik

Arctic Circle

NORWAY

SWEDEN

FINLAND

Helsinki

St. Petersburg

RUSSIA

0 250 500 Miles

0 250 500 Kilometers

Projection: Mollweide

NORTH SEA

DENMARK

Copenhagen

Oslo

Stockholm

10

UNITED KINGDOM

Dublin

IRELAND

Amsterdam

The Hague

NETHERLANDS

London

BELGIUM

Brussels

GERMANY

Berlin

Warsaw

POLAND

9

8

Minsk

BELARUS

Moscow

60°N

ATLANTIC OCEAN

50°N

Paris

LUXEMBOURG

FRANCE

Bern

SWITZERLAND

LIECHTENSTEIN

Vienna

1

AUSTRIA

2

Budapest

HUNGARY

ROMANIA

Kiev

UKRAINE

MOLDOVA

Chişinău

Bucharest

BLACK SEA

MONACO

ITALY

SAN MARINO

Rome

3

4

5

7

BULGARIA

Sofia

ANDORRA

Corsica (FRANCE)

VATICAN CITY

6

ALBANIA

Tirana

PORTUGAL

Madrid

Balearic Isl. (SPAIN)

Sardinia (ITALY)

GREECE

Athens

40°N

Lisbon

SPAIN

MEDITERRANEAN SEA

Sicily

Gibraltar (U.K.)

MALTA

Crete

-10°E 0° 10°E 20°E 30°E 40°E 50°E 60°E

ATLAS

North America: Physical

ASIA

EUROPE

ARCTIC OCEAN

+ North Pole

POLAR ICE PACK

Bering Strait

St. Lawrence Island

Bering Sea

Nunivak Island

Beaufort Sea

Queen Elizabeth Islands

Ellesmere Island

Greenland

BROOKS RANGE

Mt. McKinley 20,320 ft. (6,194 m)

ALASKA RANGE

Yukon River

Banks Island

Victoria Island

Baffin Bay

Baffin Island

Davis Strait

Denmark Strait

Cape Farewell

Kodiak Island

Gulf of Alaska

YUKON PLATEAU

Great Bear Lake

Arctic Circle

Alexander Archipelago

Queen Charlotte Islands

Mackenzie River

Great Slave Lake

Southampton Island

Hudson Strait

Labrador Sea

Vancouver Island

Peace River

Athabasca River

Lake Athabasca

Coats Island

Mansel Island

PACIFIC OCEAN

Mount Rainier 14,410 ft. (4,392 m)

COAST RANGE

CASCADE RANGE

Columbia River

Saskatchewan River

Nelson River

Lake Winnipeg

C A N A D I A N

S H I E L D

Hudson Bay

Anticosti Island

Prince Edward Island

Gulf of St. Lawrence

Cape Breton Island

Newfoundland

Cape Mendocino

Snake River

R O C K Y

G R E A T

Missouri River

St. Lawrence River

SIERRA NEVADA

CENTRAL VALLEY

Great Salt Lake

BLACK HILLS

Lake Superior

Lake Michigan

Lake Huron

Lake Ontario

A P P A L A C H I A N

M O U N T A I N S

Cape Cod

Long Island

ATLANTIC OCEAN

GREAT BASIN

DEATH VALLEY

Mount Whitney 14,494 ft. (4,419 m)

M O U N T A I N S

COLORADO PLATEAU

Platte River

P L A I N S

Colorado River

INTERIOR PLAINS

Ohio River

Cumberland R.

Tennessee River

PIEDMONT

Cape Hatteras

Bermuda

Guadalupe Island

RANGES

Gulf of California

BAJA CALIFORNIA

SIERRA MADRE OCCIDENTAL

Rio Grande

Red River

Arkansas River

Brazos River

Mississippi River

OZARK PLATEAU

ATLANTIC COASTAL PLAIN

GULF COASTAL PLAIN

FLORIDA PENINSULA

Cape Canaveral

Tropic of Cancer

SIERRA MADRE ORIENTAL

Gulf of Mexico

Florida Keys

Straits of Florida

Bahamas

Cuba

Greater Antilles

Jamaica

Hispaniola

Puerto Rico

Lesser Antilles

Popocatépetl 17,887 ft. (5,452 m)

YUCATÁN PENINSULA

Caribbean Sea

Trinidad

SIERRA MADRE DEL SUR

CENTRAL AMERICA

Lake Nicaragua

ISTHMUS OF PANAMA

SOUTH AMERICA

ELEVATION

Feet		Meters
13,120		4,000
6,560		2,000
1,640		500
656		200
(Sea level) 0		0 (Sea level)
Below sea level		Below sea level

Ice cap

0   300   600 Miles

0   300   600 Kilometers

Projection: Azimuthal Equal Area

N   W   E   S

0° Equator

North America: Political

ARCTIC OCEAN

ASIA

EUROPE

ICELAND

North Pole

ATLAS

Boundaries
⊛ **National capitals**
• **Other cities**

| 0 | 300 | 600 Miles |
| 0 | 300 | 600 Kilometers |

Projection: Azimuthal Equal Area

CANADA

UNITED STATES

MEXICO

PACIFIC OCEAN

ATLANTIC OCEAN

Greenland (DENMARK)

ALASKA (U.S.)
Anchorage
Juneau
Kodiak Island
Queen Charlotte Islands
Alexander Archipelago
Vancouver Island
Seattle
Portland
San Francisco
San Jose
Los Angeles
San Diego
Tijuana
Phoenix
Edmonton
Calgary
Vancouver
Winnipeg
Salt Lake City
Denver
Kansas City
Austin
San Antonio
Houston
Dallas
Memphis
New Orleans
Minneapolis
Milwaukee
Chicago
Indianapolis
St. Louis
Detroit
Cleveland
Columbus
Atlanta
Birmingham
Jacksonville
Norfolk
Washington, D.C.
Baltimore
Philadelphia
New York City
Boston
Ottawa
Toronto
Montreal
Quebec
Monterrey
Guadalajara
Mexico City
Puebla
Mérida
Belmopan
BELIZE
GUATEMALA
Guatemala City
San Salvador
EL SALVADOR
HONDURAS
Tegucigalpa
NICARAGUA
Managua
COSTA RICA
San José
PANAMA
Panama City
Havana
CUBA
JAMAICA
Kingston
HAITI
Port-au-Prince
DOMINICAN REPUBLIC
Santo Domingo
Nassau
THE BAHAMAS
Puerto Rico (U.S.)
San Juan
Miami
Florida Keys

Bering Strait
St. Lawrence Island
Nunivak Island
Bering Sea
Point Barrow
Beaufort Sea
Yukon River
Gulf of Alaska
Mackenzie River
Great Bear Lake
Great Slave Lake
Peace River
Banks Island
Victoria Island
Queen Elizabeth Islands
Ellesmere Island
Baffin Bay
Baffin Island
Southampton Island
Coats Island
Mansel Island
Hudson Bay
Hudson Strait
Davis Strait
Cape Farewell
Labrador Sea
Anticosti Island
Newfoundland
St. Pierre and Miquelon (FRANCE)
Cape Breton Island
Prince Edward Island
Gulf of St. Lawrence
Lake Winnipeg
Lake Superior
Lake Michigan
Lake Huron
Lake Erie
Lake Ontario
St. Lawrence R.
Cape Cod
Cape Hatteras
Cape Canaveral
Bermuda (U.K.)
Tropic of Cancer
Turks and Caicos Islands (U.K.)
ST. KITTS & NEVIS
ANTIGUA & BARBUDA
Guadeloupe (FRANCE)
DOMINICA
Martinique (FRANCE)
ST. LUCIA
BARBADOS
ST. VINCENT AND THE GRENADINES
GRENADA
TRINIDAD AND TOBAGO
Netherlands Antilles (NETHERLANDS)
Aruba (NETHERLANDS)
Virgin Is. (U.S., U.K.)
Cayman Is. (U.K.)
Caribbean Sea
Panama Canal
Gulf of Mexico
Straits of Florida
Gulf of California
Rio Grande
Balsas R.
Red River
Colorado River
Platte River
Missouri River
Mississippi River
Ohio R.
Snake River
Columbia River
Great Salt Lake
Cape Mendocino

SOUTH AMERICA

0° Equator

CENTRAL
AMERICA

Caribbean Sea

Panama
Canal

Gulf
of
Panama

Malpelo
Island

Mount Tolima
18,425 ft.
(5,616 m)

Margarita
Island

Tobago

Trinidad
Orinoco River
Delta

Lake
Maracaibo

Orinoco River

L L A N O S

Meta
River

GUIANA

Angel Falls

GUIANA
HIGHLANDS

Devil's Island
Cape Orange

Orinoco
River

ATLANTIC
OCEAN

Amazon
River Delta

Galápagos
Islands

Equator

Mount Chimborazo
20,561 ft.
(6,267 m)

Gulf of Guayaquil

Marañón River

Caquetá
River

Japurá
River

Rio Negro

Amazon
River

A M A Z O N
B A S I N

Amazon

River

Amazon
River

Equator 0°

Ucayali River

Juruá
River

River

Purus

Madeira

Tapajós
River

Xingu

River

Tocantins

River

Parnaíba

River

A N D E S

Mount Huascarán
22,205 ft.
(6,768 m)

Beni River

River

Mamoré

MATO GROSSO
PLATEAU

Araguaia

River

BRAZILIAN
HIGHLANDS

São Francisco

10°S

PACIFIC
OCEAN

Lake
Titicaca

Ancohuma Peak
20,958 ft.
(6,388 m)

River

Pilcomayo

Lake
Poopó

A T A C A M A   D E S E R T

A N D E S

C H A C O

Paraguay

River

BRAZILIAN
PLATEAU

Tropic of Capricorn

20°S

San Ambrosio
Island

San Félix Island

Salado

River

Paraná

Bermejo
River

Uruguay River

Tropic of Capricorn

Mount Aconcagua
22,834 ft.
(6,960 m)

Salado River

Juan Fernández
Islands

P A M P A S

Rio de la Plata

ATLANTIC
OCEAN

30°S

Colorado

River

Gulf of San Matías

Chiloé
Island

Chonos
Archipelago

P A T A G O N I A

Gulf of
San Jorge

Cape Tres Puntas

40°S

Bahía
Grande

Strait of
Magellan

Tierra del
Fuego

Falkland
Islands

South
Georgia
Islands

Cape Horn

50°S

ELEVATION

Feet		Meters
13,120		4,000
6,560		2,000
1,640		500
656		200
(Sea level) 0		0 (Sea level)
Below
sea level		Below
sea level

0   250   500 Miles

0   250   500 Kilometers

Projection: Azimuthal Equal Area

South America: Political

CENTRAL AMERICA

Caribbean Sea

Barranquilla
Cartagena

Caracas

VENEZUELA

Lake Maracaibo

Orinoco River

Medellín

Bogotá

COLOMBIA

Cali

Georgetown
Paramaribo

GUYANA

SURINAME

Cayenne
FRENCH GUIANA (FRANCE)

ATLANTIC OCEAN

Malpelo Island (COLOMBIA)

Quito

ECUADOR

Guayaquil

Río Negro

Amazon

Amazon River

Belém

Galápagos Islands (ECUADOR)

0° Equator

Equator 0°

PERU

Marañón River

Ucayali River

BRAZIL

Recife

Trujillo

Callao

Lima

Lake Titicaca

La Paz

Lake Poopó

BOLIVIA

Sucre

Arequipa

Brasília

São Francisco River

Salvador

Belo Horizonte

PACIFIC OCEAN

10°S

Paraguay River

PARAGUAY

Campinas

São Paulo

Rio de Janeiro

Tropic of Capricorn

20°S

Tropic of Capricorn

San Ambrosio Island (CHILE)

San Félix Island (CHILE)

Asunción

Curitiba

CHILE

Paraná River

Uruguay River

Pôrto Alegre

30°S

Juan Fernández Islands (CHILE)

Valparaíso
Santiago

Córdoba

Rosario

Buenos Aires

URUGUAY

Montevideo

ATLANTIC OCEAN

ARGENTINA

Río de la Plata

40°S

Boundaries
⊛ National capitals
• Other cities

0   250   500 Miles
0   250   500 Kilometers
Projection: Azimuthal Equal Area

Strait of Magellan

Falkland Islands (U.K.)

Tierra del Fuego

South Georgia Island (U.K.)

50°S

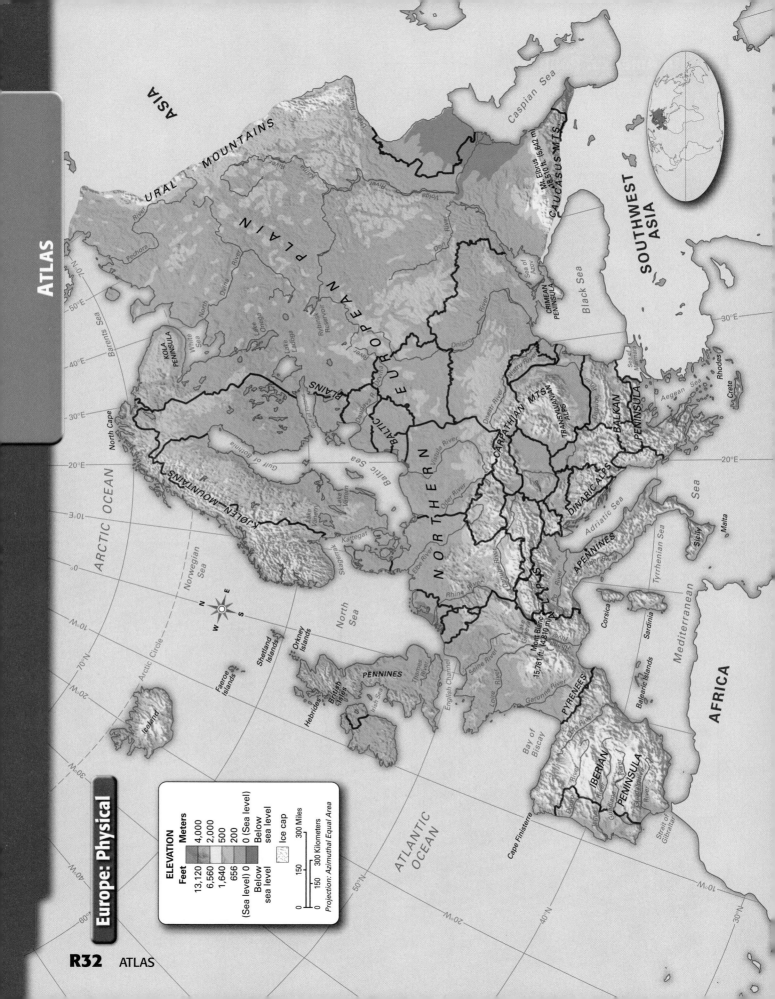

Europe: Physical

ELEVATION

Feet	Meters
13,120	4,000
6,560	2,000
1,640	500
656	200
(Sea level) 0	0 (Sea level)
Below sea level	Below sea level
	Ice cap

0   150   300 Miles

0   150   300 Kilometers

Projection: Azimuthal Equal Area

ASIA

URAL MOUNTAINS

NORTHERN EUROPEAN PLAIN

BALTIC PLAINS

Pechora River

North Dvina River

Kama River

Volga River

Don River

Ural River

Caspian Sea

Mt. Elbrus 18,510 ft. (5,642 m)

CAUCASUS MTS.

SOUTHWEST ASIA

Barents Sea

KOLA PENINSULA

White Sea

Lake Onega

Lake Ladoga

Rybinsk Reservoir

Dnieper River

Sea of Azov

CRIMEAN PENINSULA

Black Sea

30°E

North Cape

Gulf of Finland

Daugava R.

Dvina River

Vistula River

Dniester River

Nistru River

CARPATHIAN MTS.

TRANSYLVANIAN ALPS

BALKAN PENINSULA

Sea of Marmara

Aegean Sea

Rhodes

Crete

20°E

ARCTIC OCEAN

KJØLEN MOUNTAINS

Lake Vänern

Lake Vättern

Kattegat

Baltic Sea

Oder River

Elbe River

DINARIC ALPS

Adriatic Sea

APENNINES

Sea

Malta

Sicily

Norwegian Sea

Skagerrak

Rhine River

ALPS

Danube River

Mont Blanc 15,781 ft. (4,810 m)

Lake Geneva

Po River

Tiber River

Corsica

Sardinia

Tyrrhenian Sea

North Sea

Orkney Islands

Shetland Islands

Faeroe Islands

Iceland

Hebrides

British Isles

Irish Sea

PENNINES

Thames River

English Channel

Seine River

Loire River

Rhône River

Garonne River

PYRENEES

Ebro River

Bay of Biscay

Cape Finisterre

IBERIAN PENINSULA

Douro River

Tagus River

Guadiana River

Guadalquivir River

Strait of Gibraltar

Balearic Islands

Mediterranean Sea

AFRICA

ATLANTIC OCEAN

Arctic Circle

70°N

60°N

50°N

40°N

30°N

70°E

50°E

40°E

30°E

20°E

10°E

0°

10°W

20°W

30°W

40°W

N W E S

Europe: Political

Boundaries
⊛ National capitals
• Other cities

300 Miles
150
0
300 Kilometers
150
0

Projection: Azimuthal Equal Area

ASIA

URAL MOUNTAINS

Ural River

RUSSIA

Nizhny Novgorod

Volga River

Moscow

Caspian Sea

SOUTHWEST ASIA

Don River

Black Sea

Barents Sea

White Sea

North Cape

Gulf of Finland

St. Petersburg

FINLAND

Helsinki

ESTONIA
Tallinn

LATVIA
Riga

LITHUANIA
Vilnius

RUSSIA

BELARUS
Minsk

Kiev

UKRAINE

Dnipro River

MOLDOVA
Chişinău

ROMANIA
Bucharest

Danube River

BULGARIA
Sofia

Belgrade

SERBIA AND MONTENEGRO

Skopje

MACEDONIA

Athens

Aegean Sea

Rhodes

Crete

GREECE

Tiranë
ALBANIA

ARCTIC OCEAN

SWEDEN

Gulf of Bothnia

Baltic Sea

Stockholm

Göteborg

NORWAY

Oslo

Bergen

Warsaw

POLAND

Krakow

Berlin

Dresden

CZECH REPUBLIC
Prague

SLOVAKIA
Bratislava

Budapest

HUNGARY

Zagreb

CROATIA

Vienna

AUSTRIA

SLOVENIA
Ljubljana

BOSNIA AND HERZEGOVINA
Sarajevo

Adriatic Sea

SAN MARINO
San Marino

ITALY

Rome
VATICAN CITY

Naples

Corsica (FRANCE)

Sardinia (ITALY)

Sicily

MALTA
Valletta

Mediterranean Sea

DENMARK
Copenhagen

Hamburg

Elbe River

GERMANY

Cologne
Bonn

Luxembourg
LUXEMBOURG

Munich

LIECHTENSTEIN
Vaduz

SWITZERLAND
Bern

A L P S

Lake Geneva

Milan

Po River

MONACO
Monaco

THE NETHERLANDS
Amsterdam

The Hague

BELGIUM
Brussels

Paris

Seine River

FRANCE

Lyon

Rhône River

Marseille

North Sea

SCOTLAND
Edinburgh

UNITED KINGDOM

Liverpool

ENGLAND

WALES

London

Thames R.

NORTHERN IRELAND
Belfast

IRELAND
Dublin

British Isles

English Channel

Channel Islands (U.K.)

Loire River

Bay of Biscay

ANDORRA
Andorra la Vella

PYRENEES

Barcelona

Balearic Islands (SPAIN)

Valencia

Madrid

SPAIN

Tagus River

Seville

Gibraltar (U.K.)

Strait of Gibraltar

PORTUGAL

Lisbon

ICELAND
Reykjavik

Faeroe Islands (DENMARK)

Shetland Islands

Arctic Circle

ATLANTIC OCEAN

AFRICA

Danube River

Inn River

ATLAS

Asia: Physical

ATLAS

ELEVATION

Feet	Meters
13,120	4,000
6,560	2,000
1,640	500
656	200
0 (Sea level)	0 (Sea level)
Below sea level	Below sea level

Ice cap

750 Miles

0 250 500 750 Kilometers

Projection: Azimuthal Equal Area

EUROPE

AFRICA

AUSTRALIA

PACIFIC OCEAN

INDIAN OCEAN

S I B E R I A

HIMALAYAS

Mount Everest 29,035 ft. (8,850 m)

Mount Ararat 16,945 ft. (5,165 m)

Asia: Political

Boundaries
⊛ National capitals
• Other cities

0 250 500 750 Miles
0 250 500 750 Kilometers
Projection: Two-Point Equidistant

EUROPE

RUSSIA

MONGOLIA

CHINA

KAZAKHSTAN

UZBEKISTAN
TURKMENISTAN
KYRGYZSTAN
TAJIKISTAN
AFGHANISTAN
PAKISTAN

INDIA

NEPAL
BHUTAN
BANGLADESH
MYANMAR (BURMA)

IRAN
IRAQ
SAUDI ARABIA
YEMEN
OMAN
UNITED ARAB EMIRATES
QATAR
BAHRAIN
KUWAIT
JORDAN
ISRAEL
LEBANON
SYRIA
CYPRUS
TURKEY
GEORGIA
ARMENIA
AZERBAIJAN

JAPAN
NORTH KOREA
SOUTH KOREA
TAIWAN
PHILIPPINES
VIETNAM
LAOS
THAILAND
CAMBODIA
MALAYSIA
SINGAPORE
BRUNEI
INDONESIA
EAST TIMOR
SRI LANKA
MALDIVES

AUSTRALIA
AFRICA

PACIFIC OCEAN
INDIAN OCEAN

EUROPE

SOUTHWEST
ASIA

ATLAS

Azores

Madeira
Islands

Strait of
Gibralt

Canary
Islands

ATLAS MOUNTAINS

Mediterranean Sea

Gulf of
Sidra

Suez Canal

Persian Gulf

Tropic of Cancer

S A H A R A

QATTARA
DEPRESSION

Cape
Blanc

EL DJOUF

AHAGGAR
MOUNTAINS

AIR MTS.

TIBESTI
MOUNTAINS

LIBYAN DESERT

Nile River

Lake
Nasser

NUBIAN
DESERT

Red Sea

Cape Verde
Islands

Cape Verde

Senegal River

Niger River

S   A   H   E   L

S U D A N

Lake
Chad

CHAD
BASIN

Blue Nile

White Nile

Lake
Tana

Gulf of Aden

FOUTA
DJALLON

White Volta

Black Volta

Benue River

Lake
Volta

SUDAN
BASIN

ETHIOPIAN
HIGHLANDS

HORN OF AFRICA

SOMALI
PENINSULA

Cape
Palmas

Gulf of
Guinea

ADAMAWA
MTS.

Ubangi
River

Cape
Lopez

CONGO
BASIN

Congo
River

Lake
Albert

Lake
Edward

Lake
Turkana

RIFT VALLEY

Mount Kenya
17,058 ft.
(5,199 m)

Equator

Kasai River

Lake
Kivu

Lake
Victoria

SERENGETI
PLAIN

Mount Kilimanjaro
19,340 ft.
(5,895 m)

INDIAN
OCEAN

Ascension

ATLANTIC
OCEAN

MITUMBA

WESTERN RIFT VALLEY

Lake
Tanganyika

EASTERN RIFT VALLEY

MASAI
STEPPE

Zanzibar

Seychelles

Lake
Mweru

Lake
Rukwa

Cunene
River

Lake
Malawi
(Nyasa)

Cape Delgado

Comoro
Islands

ELEVATION

Feet		Meters
13.120		4,000
6,560		2,000
1,640		500
656		200
(Sea level) 0		0 (Sea level)
Below sea level		Below sea level

Lake
Kariba

Zambezi River

Okavango
Delta

Victoria
Falls

KALAHARI BASIN

NAMIB DESERT

Limpopo River

Madagascar

Mauritius

Réunion

0   250   500 Miles

0   250   500 Kilometers

Projection: Azimuthal Equal Area

Tropic of
Capricorn

KALAHARI
DESERT

Tropic of Capricorn

Mozambique Channel

Orange River

Vaal River

GREAT
KARROO

DRAKENSBERG
MOUNTAINS

Cape of
Good Hope

EUROPE

SOUTHWEST ASIA

Azores (PORTUGAL)

Madeira (PORTUGAL)

Strait of Gibraltar

Casablanca • Rabat

Algiers • Tunis

Mediterranean Sea

TUNISIA

Tripoli

Alexandria

Canary Islands (SPAIN)

MOROCCO

El Aaiún

WESTERN SAHARA (Claimed by Morocco)

Tropic of Cancer

ALGERIA

LIBYA

Giza • Cairo

Suez Canal

EGYPT

Nile River

Lake Nasser

Red Sea

MAURITANIA

Nouakchott

MALI

NIGER

CHAD

Khartoum

ERITREA

Asmara

Gulf of Aden

CAPE VERDE

Praia

SENEGAL

Dakar

GAMBIA

Banjul

Bissau

GUINEA-BISSAU

Bamako

Niger River

BURKINA FASO

Niamey

Lake Chad

N'Djamena

SUDAN

Blue Nile

White Nile

DJIBOUTI

Djibouti

GUINEA

Conakry

Freetown

SIERRA LEONE

Monrovia

LIBERIA

CÔTE D'IVOIRE

Yamoussoukro

Abidjan

Ouagadougou

GHANA

Accra

BENIN

TOGO

Lomé

Porto-Novo

NIGERIA

Abuja

Lagos

Gulf of Guinea

Malabo

EQUATORIAL GUINEA

SÃO TOMÉ AND PRÍNCIPE

São Tomé

CAMEROON

Yaoundé

CENTRAL AFRICAN REPUBLIC

Bangui

ETHIOPIA

Addis Ababa

SOMALIA

Mogadishu

0° Equator

REPUBLIC OF THE CONGO

Libreville

GABON

Brazzaville

CABINDA (ANGOLA)

Kinshasa

Congo River

Kisangani

DEMOCRATIC REPUBLIC OF THE CONGO

RWANDA

Kigali

Bujumbura

BURUNDI

UGANDA

Kampala

Lake Victoria

KENYA

Nairobi

Equator 0°

INDIAN OCEAN

SEYCHELLES

Victoria

ATLANTIC OCEAN

Luanda

TANZANIA

Dodoma

Lake Tanganyika

Dar es Salaam

Mombasa

Pemba

Zanzibar

St. Helena (U.K.)

ANGOLA

Lubumbashi

Lake Malawi (Nyasa)

COMOROS

Moroni

MALAWI

Lilongwe

ZAMBIA

Lusaka

Zambezi River

MOZAMBIQUE

MADAGASCAR

Antananarivo

MAURITIUS

Port Louis

Réunion (FRANCE)

Harare

ZIMBABWE

Bulawayo

NAMIBIA

Windhoek

BOTSWANA

Gaborone

Tropic of Capricorn

Boundaries

National capitals

Other cities

0   250   500 Miles

0   250   500 Kilometers

Projection: Azimuthal Equal Area

Pretoria

Johannesburg

Bloemfontein

Orange River

Maseru

LESOTHO

SWAZILAND

Mbabane

Maputo

SOUTH AFRICA

Cape Town

Gazetteer

GAZETTEER

A

Aachen (AH-kuhn) (51°N, 6°E) a city in Germany; it was the capital of Charlemagne's empire (p. 237)

Africa the second-largest continent (p. R36)

Alps a mountain range extending across south-central Europe (p. R32)

Amazon a large rain forest region in northern South America east of the Andes (p. R30)

Amazon River a river east of the Andes in South America; it flows through a rain forest and into the Atlantic Ocean (p. R30)

Andes Mountains a mountain range along the west coast of South America (p. R30)

Arabian Peninsula an arid region in southwest Asia; Islam developed in the Arabian Peninsula (p. 55)

Asia the world's largest continent, bounded by the Arctic, Pacific, and Indian oceans (p. R34)

Asia Minor a large peninsula in west Asia, between the Black Sea and the Mediterranean Sea, forming modern Turkey (p. 32)

Atlas Mountains a mountain range on the northwest coast of Africa (p. R36)

Aztec Empire an empire in what is now Mexico; it reached its height in the early 1500s (p. 411)

B

Baghdad (33°N, 44°E) a city in modern Iraq; it was the center of Islam from the mid-700s to 800s (p. 81)

Bahamas a group of islands in the Atlantic Ocean off of the southeastern coast of Florida; Christopher Columbus landed in the Bahamas on his first voyage to the Americas (p. R28)

Black Sea a sea between southeast Europe and Asia, north of Asia Minor (p. R32)

Brazil the largest country in South America (p. R31)

Byzantine Empire the eastern part of the Roman Empire that developed non-Roman influences (p. 37)

Byzantium (buh-ZAN-shuhm) an ancient Greek city in modern Turkey; Constantinople was built on its site (p. 25)

C

Canterbury (51°N, 1°E) a city near London, England; it was a popular pilgrimage destination during the Middle Ages and the subject of Chaucer's *The Canterbury Tales* (p. 270)

Chang'an see **Xi'an**

Chile a country in western South America; the Inca Empire stretched into central Chile (p. R31)

China a country in East Asia; a series of dynasties built China into a world power (p. R35)

Cluny (KLOO-nee) (46°N, 5°E) a town in France; a group of monks formed a religious order there in the early 900s (p. 271)

Congo River a river that flows through the plains of sub-Saharan Africa (p. R36)

Constantinople (KAHN-stant-uhn-oh-puhl) (41°N, 29°E) a city now called Istanbul located in modern Turkey; it was established as the capital of the Roman Empire and later became capital of the Byzantine Empire (p. 37)

Córdoba (KAWR-doh-bah) (38°N, 5°W) a city in southern Spain; it was the center of Muslim rule in Spain (p. 81)

Cuzco (KOO-skoh) (14°S, 72°W) a city in Peru; it was the capital of the Inca Empire (p. 423)

Delft (52°N, 4°E) a city in the Netherlands that was the setting for Tracy Chevalier's novel *Girl with a Pearl Earring* (p. 464)

Djenné a West African city that was the center of trade for gold, kola nuts and other mined goods during the Songhai Empire (p. 143)

Drakensburg Range a mountain range near the coast of southeast Africa (p. R36)

Edo (AY-doh) (36°N, 140°E) a city that became capital of Japan in 1603 under the Tokugawa shogunate; it is now called Tokyo (p. 199)

Egypt a country in northeast Africa and location of the mouth of the Nile River (p. R37)

Esfahan (es-fah-HAHN) (33°N, 52°E) a city in modern Iran; it was the capital of the Safavid Empire and considered one of the world's most magnificent cities during the 1600s (p. 91)

Española, or **Hispaniola** an island in the West Indies; it was visited by Christopher Columbus in 1492 and was the early center of Spanish rule in the Americas (p. R28)

Eurasia a large landmass that includes both Europe and Asia (p. 230)

Europe a continent of many peninsulas located between Asia and the Atlantic Ocean (p. R32)

Florence (44°N, 11°E) a city in Italy; ruled by the Medici family in the 1400s, it was a major center for culture and trade (p. 301)

Gao (GOW) (16°N, 0°W) a major trading city in Africa that was capital of the Songhai Empire (p. 143)

Gaul an ancient region in Western Europe, consisting mainly of parts of modern France and Belgium (p. 25)

Geneva (46°N, 6°E) a city in Switzerland; John Calvin hoped to make Geneva a model Christian city (p. 341)

Genoa (JIN-uh-wuh) (44°N, 10°E) a port city in Italy (p. 301)

Ghana (GAH-nuh) a West African country located between the Niger and Senegal Rivers; it was the site of a powerful empire established around 300 (p. 131)

Grand Canal a series of waterways linking major Chinese cities; the longest man-made waterway in the world (p. 167)

Heian (HAY-ahn) (35°N, 136°E) a city in Japan now called Kyoto; it was a cultural center and capital of Japan for many centuries (p. 199)

Honshu Japan's largest island (p. R34)

Inca Empire an empire in South America that stretched from what is now northern Ecuador to central Chile; it reached its height in the early 1500s (p. 423)

Indonesia an island country in Asia between the Indian Ocean and the Pacific Ocean (p. R35)

GAZETTEER

GAZETTEER

Japan a mountainous island country off the eastern coast of Asia near China and the Koreas (p. R35)

Jerusalem (32°N, 35°E) a city in Israel; as part of the Holy Land, Muslims and Christians fought to control it during the Crusades (p. 25)

K

Kaifeng (KY-fuhng) (35°N, 114°E) the capital of China during the Song dynasty (p. 172)

Korea a country in eastern Asia near China and Japan that influenced early Japanese culture; it is now divided into two countries called North Korea and South Korea (p. 199)

Koumbi Saleh (KOOM-bee SAHL-uh) a major trading city in the empire of Ghana (p. 131)

M

Malaysia a country in Southeast Asia between the Indian Ocean and the Pacific Ocean (p. R35)

Mali (MAH-lee) a West African country located on the Niger River; it was the location of an empire that reached its height around 1300 (p. 137)

Mecca (21°N, 40°E) an ancient city in Arabia and the birthplace of Muhammad (p. 55)

Medina (muh-DEE-nuh) (24°N, 40°E) a city in Arabia north of Mecca; people there were among the first to accept Islam (p. 55)

Mediterranean Sea a large sea surrounded by Europe, Africa, and Asia (p. R32, R34)

Mesoamerica a region that includes the southern part of modern Mexico and part of northern Central America; the first permanent farming settlements in the Americas developed in Mesoamerica (p. 385)

Milan (muh-LAHN) (45°N, 9°E) a city in Italy; it was a major trading center during the 1300s (p. 301)

Morocco a country in North Africa (p. R37)

N

Niger River a major river in West Africa (p. R36)

Normandy (49°N, 0°E) a region in northern France; it was home of William the Conqueror, who became king of England in 1066 (p. 244)

North America a large continent in the northern and western hemispheres, bordered on the west by the Pacific Ocean and on the east by the Atlantic Ocean (p. R28)

Northern European Plain a vast, flat land area that stretches from the Atlantic Ocean in the west to the Ural Mountains in the east (p. R32)

P

Palenque (pah-LENG-kay) (18°N, 92°W) an ancient Maya city in what is now southern Mexico (p. 391)

Palestine a region of southwest Asia that Christians and Muslims fought to control during the Crusades; it is known as the "Holy Land" of Judaism, Christianity, and Islam (p. 264, 267)

Roman Empire a large and powerful empire that included all land around the Mediterranean Sea; it reached its height around AD 117 (p. 25)

R

Rome (42°N, 13°E) a city in Italy near the Mediterranean Sea; it was the capital of the Roman Empire (p. 25)

Rub' al-Khali (ROOB ahl-KAH-lee) the world's largest sand desert; it covers most of the southern Arabian Peninsula (p. 55)

S

Sahara the world's largest desert, located in northern Africa (p. R36)

Scandinavia a large peninsula in northern Europe (p. 231)

Songhai (SAHNG-hy) a large and powerful empire in West Africa during the 1400s and 1500s (p. 143)

South America a large continent in the southern and western hemispheres, bordered on the west by the Pacific Ocean and on the east by the Atlantic Ocean (p. R30)

T

Tenochtitlán (tay-NAWCH-teet-LAHN) (19°N, 99°W) the capital of the Aztec Empire; Mexico City was built on the site of Tenochtitlán (p. 411)

Tikal (tee-KAHL) (17°N, 90°W) a major Maya city in modern Guatemala (p. 391)

Timbuktu (tim-buk-TOO) (17°N, 3°W) a city in West Africa that began as a camp for traders around AD 1100 and became a major center of culture and learning (p. 131)

Troy (40°N, 26°E) an ancient city in what is now Turkey; according to Greek legend and literature, it was the site of the Trojan War (p. 14)

Turkey a country occupying Asia Minor and a southeast portion of the Balkan Peninsula (p. R35)

U

Ural Mountains a mountain range that forms a natural boundary between Europe and Asia (p. R32)

V

Venice (45°N, 12°E) a city in Italy that was a major trading center during the 1300s (p. 301)

W

Wittenberg (VIT-uhn-berk) (52°N, 13°E) the city in Germany where Martin Luther nailed his Ninety-Five Theses to the door of a church (p. 341)

X

Xi'an (34°N, 109°E) the capital of China during the Tang dynasty (p. 167)

Z

Zambezi River a river that flows through southeastern Africa (p. R36)

Ancient Civilizations

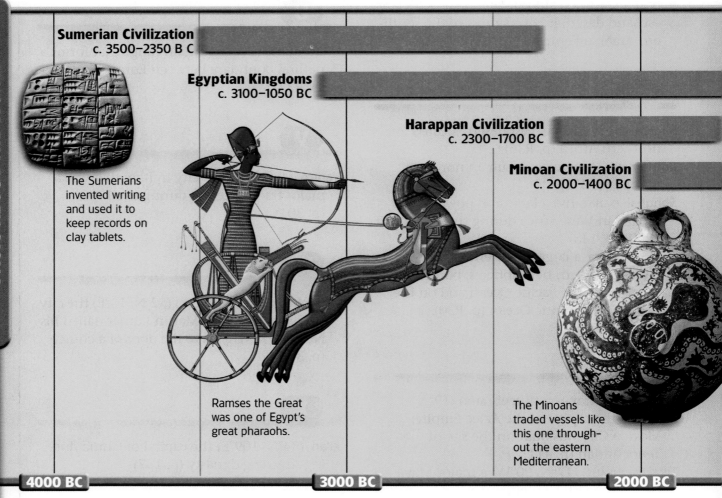

Sumerian Civilization
c. 3500–2350 B C

The Sumerians invented writing and used it to keep records on clay tablets.

Egyptian Kingdoms
c. 3100–1050 BC

Harappan Civilization
c. 2300–1700 BC

Minoan Civilization
c. 2000–1400 BC

Ramses the Great was one of Egypt's great pharaohs.

The Minoans traded vessels like this one through-out the eastern Mediterranean.

4000 BC　　3000 BC　　2000 BC

Important Dates

c. 4000–3000 BC The first cities are founded in Sumer.

c. 3500 BC The Sumerians invent writing.

c. 3500 BC Maize (corn) is domesticated in Mesoamerica.

c. 3200 BC The Sumerians invent the wheel.

c. 3100 BC Upper Egypt and Lower Egypt are united.

c. 2500 BC The Great Pyramid of Khufu is built in Egypt.

c. 2350 BC The first empire is created in Mesopotamia.

c. 1750 BC The earliest known set of written laws is issued by Hammurabi.

c. 1250 BC Hinduism begins to develop.

c. 1100 BC The Phoenicians create an alphabet.

c. 1050 BC Saul becomes the first King of Israel.

c. 500 BC Buddhism begins to develop.

c. 500 BC Athens becomes the world's first democracy.

c. 140 BC Confucianism becomes China's official government philosophy.

c. 100 BC The Silk Road connects China and Southwest Asia.

27 BC The Roman Empire begins.

c. AD 30 Christianity begins to develop.

c. AD 200 The Maya build large cities in Mesoamerica.

c. AD 320 The Gupta dynasty begins in India.

AD 476 The western Roman Empire falls.

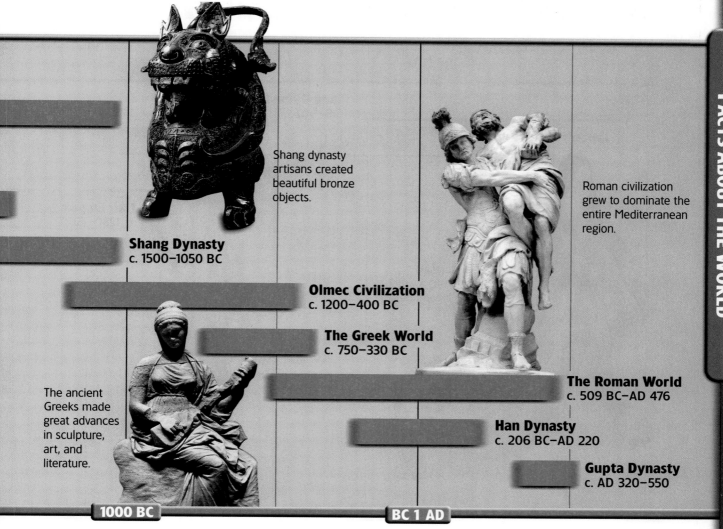

Shang dynasty artisans created beautiful bronze objects.

Roman civilization grew to dominate the entire Mediterranean region.

Shang Dynasty
c. 1500–1050 BC

Olmec Civilization
c. 1200–400 BC

The Greek World
c. 750–330 BC

The ancient Greeks made great advances in sculpture, art, and literature.

The Roman World
c. 509 BC–AD 476

Han Dynasty
c. 206 BC–AD 220

Gupta Dynasty
c. AD 320–550

1000 BC

BC 1 AD

Important People

Sargon (c. 2350 BC) was a king of Akkad, a land north of Sumer. He created a powerful army and used it to build the world's first empire.

Hammurabi (ruled c. 1792–1750 BC) founded the Babylonian Empire and issued the first known written code of laws.

Queen Hatshepsut (ruled c. 1503–1482 BC) was a ruler of Egypt who expanded trade routes.

Siddhartha Gautama (c. 563–483 BC) was an Indian prince who became known as the Buddha. His teachings became the foundation for Buddhism.

Confucius (c. 551–479 BC) was a Chinese philosopher and teacher. His teachings, known as Confucianism, became a major philosophy in China.

Alexander the Great (c. 356–323 BC) built one of the largest empires in the ancient world and spread Greek culture throughout his empire.

Pericles (c. 495–429 BC) was an Athenian orator and politician. During his 30-year rule, Athenian democracy reached its height.

Shi Huangdi (c. 259–210 BC), the first Qin emperor, united China for the first time and built what would become the Great Wall of China.

Augustus (c. 63 BC–AD 14) was Rome's first emperor. During his reign Rome entered the Pax Romana.

Jesus of Nazareth (c. AD 1–30) was one of the most influential people in history. His life and teachings were the basis for Christianity.

Medieval to Early Modern Times

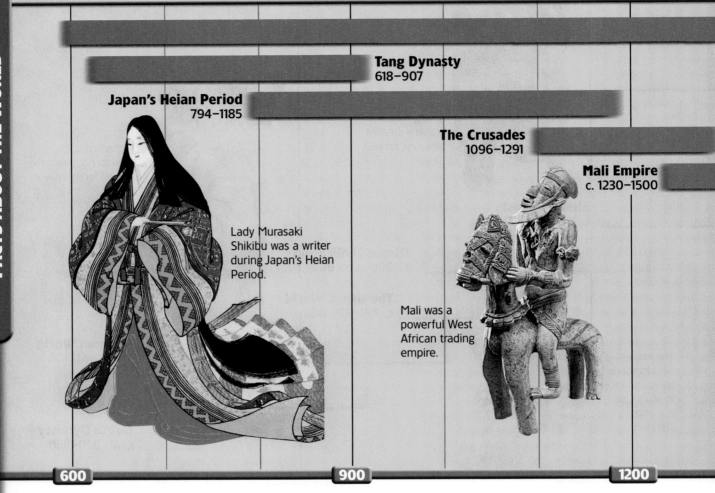

Tang Dynasty
618–907

Japan's Heian Period
794–1185

The Crusades
1096–1291

Mali Empire
c. 1230–1500

Lady Murasaki Shikibu was a writer during Japan's Heian Period.

Mali was a powerful West African trading empire.

600   900   1200

Important Dates

476 The western Roman Empire falls.

534 The Byzantine emperor Justinian creates a unified code of laws.

581 The Sui dynasty reunites China.

622 Muhammad leaves Mecca for Medina.

711 The Moors invade Spain.

800 Pope Leo III crowns Charlemagne Emperor of the Romans.

1066 William the Conqueror leads the Norman invasion of Britain.

1192 The first shogun takes power in Japan.

1215 A group of nobles forces King John to sign Magna Carta.

1324 Mansa Musa leaves Mali on a hajj to Mecca.

1347–1351 The Black Death strikes Europe.

1453 The Ottoman Turks capture Constantinople.

1492 Christopher Columbus sails to the Americas.

1517 Martin Luther posts his Ninety-Five Theses.

1521 Hernán Cortés conquers the Aztec Empire.

1537 Francisco Pizarro conquers the Inca Empire.

1545–1563 The Council of Trent meets to reform Catholic teachings.

1588 England defeats the Spanish Armada.

1633 Galileo is put on trial for promoting ideas that go against the Catholic Church.

1776 The American colonies declare independence from Great Britain.

1789 The French Revolution begins when a mob storms the Bastille in Paris.

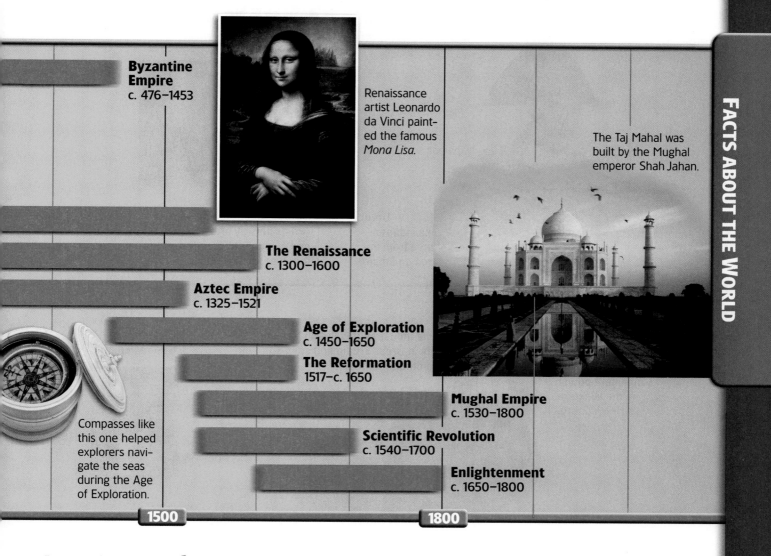

Byzantine Empire c. 476–1453

Renaissance artist Leonardo da Vinci painted the famous *Mona Lisa.*

The Taj Mahal was built by the Mughal emperor Shah Jahan.

The Renaissance c. 1300–1600

Aztec Empire c. 1325–1521

Age of Exploration c. 1450–1650

The Reformation 1517–c. 1650

Mughal Empire c. 1530–1800

Scientific Revolution c. 1540–1700

Enlightenment c. 1650–1800

Compasses like this one helped explorers navigate the seas during the Age of Exploration.

1500

1800

Important People

Muhammad (c. 570–632) was the founder of Islam. He spread Islam's teachings to the people of Arabia. His teachings make up the Qur'an.

Charlemagne (742–814) was a Frankish king who ruled most of what is now France and Germany. He helped promote Christianity in western Europe.

Lady Murasaki Shikibu (c. 1000) was a court lady during Japan's Heian Period. She wrote *The Tale of Genji,* considered by some to be the world's first novel.

Kublai Khan (1215–1294) was a Mongol ruler who completed the conquest of China and founded the Yuan dynasty.

Mansa Musa (c. 1300) was the ruler of the Mali Empire at the height of its wealth and power. He helped spread Islam throughout West Africa.

Johann Gutenberg (c. 1390–1468) was a German inventor who invented a method of printing with moveable type.

Christopher Columbus (1451–1506) was an Italian navigator who sailed to the Americas for Spain searching for a route to Asia.

Leonardo da Vinci (1452–1519) painted the *Mona Lisa,* one of the world's most admired paintings.

Sir Isaac Newton (1642–1727) was one of the most influential scientists in history. He proposed a law of gravity to explain the movement of objects.

The Modern World

Napoleon

1804
Politics
Napoleon is crowned emperor of France.

1829
Politics Greece wins independence from the Ottoman Empire.

1850s–1890
Society and Culture
Artists portray ordinary people and events realistically during the Realism movement.

1800

1823
Politics
The Monroe Doctrine makes the United States the dominant power in the Western Hemisphere.

1830s
Science and Technology
The Industrial Revolution transforms life in Great Britain and soon spreads to other countries.

1875

1871
Politics Otto von Bismarck founds the German Empire.

Otto von Bismarck

Events and People

Politics

1790s Toussaint-L' Ouverture successfully leads a rebellion of slaves against French rule in Haiti.

1811 Simon Bolívar helps Venezuela fight for its independence from Spain, influencing independence movements in Bolivia, Colombia, and Ecuador.

1837 Queen Victoria begins her 63-year reign in the United Kingdom.

1868 Tokugawa Keiki resigns as the last shogun of Japan.

1916 Jeanette Rankin becomes the first woman elected to the United States House of Representatives.

1933 Mohandas Gandhi begins a 21-day hunger strike as a non-violent protest against British rule in India.

1949 Mao Zedong transforms China into a Communist nation.

1994 Nelson Mandela is elected the first black president of South Africa after many years of struggling against apartheid.

Science and Technology

1856 Henry Bessemer develops a method for converting iron into steel.

1886 Josephine Cochran receives a patent for the first workable dishwasher.

1903 Orville and Wilbur Wright complete the first controlled aircraft flight.

Israeli flag

1948
Politics
The country of Israel is established.

1989
Politics Communist control collapses in Bulgaria, Czechoslovakia, East Germany, Hungary, Poland, and Romania.

1950

2025

1939–1945
Politics World War II is fought in Europe, North Africa, and Asia between the Axis powers and Allies.

1957
Science and Technology
The Soviet Union launches the satellite Sputnik 1, beginning the space race.

Sputnik 1

1983
Society and Culture The Internet becomes available to the general public.

2001
Politics Terrorists attack the World Trade Center in New York City and the Pentagon in Washington, D.C. on September 11, 2001.

1905 Albert Einstein introduces the theory of relativity.

1911 Marie Curie wins the Nobel Prize in chemistry for discovering several radioactive elements including radium.

1925 George Washington Carver publishes a book on how to find industrial uses for agricultural products.

1969 Neil Armstrong becomes the first person to walk on the moon.

1996 Ian Wilmut clones a mammal, Dolly the sheep.

Society and Culture

1824 Louis Braille introduces a reading system for the blind.

1848 Karl Marx and Friedrich Engels introduce *The Communist Manifesto*.

1880 Pyotr Ilyich Tchaikovsky pens the *1812 Overture* to commemorate Russia's victory over Napoleon in 1812.

1921 Pablo Picasso paints *The Three Musicians,* one of the most renowned cubist works.

1937 Zora Neale Hurston writes *Their Eyes Were Watching God.*

1997 J. K. Rowling publishes the first Harry Potter book.

2004 Lance Armstrong wins a record 6th Tour de France bicycle race.

Biographical Dictionary

A

'Abbas (1571–1629) Safavid leader, he took back land that had been lost to the Ottomans. He also made great contributions to the Safavid economy and culture. (p. 91)

Abu Bakr (uh-boo BAK-uhr) (c. 573–634) The first caliph, he ruled the Muslim world after Muhammad's death. (p. 80)

Akbar (1542–1605) Mughal emperor, he conquered new lands and worked to make the Mughal government stronger. He also began a tolerant religious policy that helped unify the empire (p. 92).

al-Idrisi (uhl-i-DREE-see) (1100–1165) Muslim geographer, he collected information from Arab travelers in order to write an accurate geography book. (p. 95)

Alighieri, Dante See Dante.

al-Khwarizmi (al-KWAHR-iz-mee) (c. 780–850) Muslim mathematician, he laid the foundation for modern algebra. (p. 96)

Aquinas, Thomas (uh-KWY-nuhs) (1225–1274) Dominican philosopher, he argued that rational thought could be used to support Christian belief. (p. 273)

Aristotle (384–322 BC) Greek philosopher, he wrote about astronomy, geography, and many other fields. His idea that people should observe the world carefully to draw logical conclusions helped shape science. (p. 355)

Askia the Great (c. 1443–1538) Songhai ruler, he overthrew Sunni Baru. His reign was the high point of Songhai culture. (p. 145)

Atahualpa (ah-tah-WAHL-pah) (1502–1533) The last Inca king, he was killed by Francisco Pizarro. (p. 425)

Attila (AT-uhl-uh) (c. 406–453) Leader of the Huns, he led invasions of Constantinople, Greece, Gaul, and northern Italy and was greatly feared by the Romans. (p. 33)

Augustus (63 BC–AD 14) First Roman emperor, he was originally named Octavian. He gained control of Rome after defeating Marc Antony in battle. As emperor, Augustus built many monuments and a new forum. (p. 25)

Avicenna (av-uh-SEN-uh) See Ibn-Sina.

B

Babur (BAH-boohr) (1483–1530) Indian emperor, he founded the Mughal Empire. (p. 92)

Bacon, Francis (1561–1626) English philosopher, he argued that science could be pursued in a systematic, logical fashion. His ideas helped develop the scientific method. (p. 364)

Benedict (c. 480–547) Italian saint and monk, he created a set of rules for monks to follow. (p. 236)

Botticelli, Sandro (bot-ti-CHEL-lee) (1445–1510) Italian Renaissance painter, he is famous for painting scenes from Roman myths. (p. 308)

Brahe, Tycho (TYOO-koh BRAH-huh) (1546–1601) Danish astronomer of the Scientific Revolution, he emphasized the importance of careful observation. (p. 360)

Brueghel, Pieter (BROY-guhl) (1525–1569) Belgian painter of the Northern Renaissance, he painted people in everyday activities. (p. 314)

Brunelleschi, Filippo (broo-nayl-LAYS-kee) (1377–1446) Italian Renaissance architect, he used mathematical formulas to design strong buildings. (p. 309)

Cabot, John (c. 1450–1499) Italian sailor who sailed for Henry VII of England, he reached the coast of Canada. (p. 450)

Cabral, Pedro (c. 1467–c. 1520) Portuguese sailor, he claimed Brazil for Portugal. (p. 449)

Calvin, John (1509–1564) Christian reformer, he taught about predestination, living good lives, and obeying God's laws. (p. 332)

Cartier, Jacques (zhahk kahr-tyay) (1491–1557) French explorer, he sailed up the Saint Lawrence River and claimed land in North America for France. (p. 450)

Cervantes, Miguel de (mee-GEL day ser-VAHN-tays) (1547–1616) Spanish writer, he wrote *Don Quixote*. (p. 316)

Charlemagne (SHAHR-luh-mayn) (742–814) King of the Franks, he was a brilliant warrior and strong leader. He was crowned Emperor of the Romans in 800. (pp. 237, 239)

Charles I (1600–1649) King of England, his conflict with Parliament caused the English Civil War. He was beheaded in 1649. (p. 484)

Charles II (1630–1685) King of England, he was the son of Charles I. He was asked by Parliament to rule England after the death of Oliver Cromwell. (p. 485)

Chaucer, Geoffrey (CHAW-suhr) (c. 1342–1400) Medieval English poet, he wrote *The Canterbury Tales*. (p. 270)

Clovis (c. 466–511) Frankish king, he built a huge kingdom in Gaul. (p. 33)

Columbus, Christopher (1451–1506) Italian sailor supported by the rulers of Spain, he reached the Americas in 1492. (pp. 449, 450)

Confucius (551–479 BC) Chinese philosopher, he emphasized ethical behavior for individuals and governments. (p. 177)

Constantine (KAHN-stuhn-teen) (c. 280–337) First Christian Roman emperor, he briefly reunited the two halves of the Roman Empire. He also moved Rome's capital to Constantinople. (p. 31)

Copernicus, Nicolaus (kih-PUHR-ni-kuhs) (1473–1543) Polish astronomer, his book *On the Revolution of the Celestial Spheres* helped begin the Scientific Revolution. (p. 359)

Cortés, Hernán (er-NAHN kawr-TAYS) (1485–1547) Spanish conquistador, he went to Mexico in search of gold and conquered the Aztec Empire. (p. 413)

Cromwell, Oliver (1599–1658) Leader of Parliament, he overthrew King Charles I in 1642 and became ruler of England. (p. 484)

Charlemagne

BIOGRAPHICAL DICTIONARY

da Gama, Vasco See Gama, Vasco da.

da Vinci, Leonardo See Leonardo da Vinci.

Dante (DAHN-tay) (1265–1321) Italian Renaissance poet, he wrote *The Divine Comedy* in the Italian language. (p. 306)

Descartes, René (ruh-NAY day-CART) (1596–1650) French philosopher, he believed that nothing should be accepted as true if it had not been proven. His ideas helped develop the scientific method. (p. 365)

Dias, Bartolomeu (c. 1450–1500) Portuguese explorer, he sailed around the southern tip of Africa. (p. 449)

Diderot, Denis (duh-NEE dee-DROH) (1713–1784) French Enlightenment philosopher, he edited a multi-volume book called the *Encyclopedia*. (p. 476)

Diocletian (dy-uh-KLEE-shuhn) (c. 245–c. 316) Roman emperor, he divided the Roman Empire into two halves. (p. 31)

Drake, Francis (c. 1540–1596) English sailor, he was sent to the Americas to steal gold and silver from Spanish ships. (p. 451)

Du Fu (712–770) One of China's greatest poets, he lived during the Tang dynasty. (p. 173)

Dürer, Albrecht (AWL-brekt DYUR-uhr) (1471–1528) German Renaissance artist, he is famous for his prints and woodcuts. (p. 315)

Eleanor of Aquitaine (c. 1122–1204) Queen of France and England, she was one of the most powerful women in Europe in the Middle Ages. (p. 246)

Erasmus, Desiderius (des-i-DEER-ee-uhs i-RAZ-mus) (1466–1536) Dutch priest, he published *In Praise of Folly* in which he criticized corrupt clergy. His criticisms helped inspire the Protestant Reformation. (p. 314)

Esma'il (is-mah-EEL) (1487–1524) Ruler of Persia, he founded the Safavid Empire. (p. 90)

Fatimah (c. 600–633) Muhammad's daughter, she holds a place of honor in the Islamic religion. (p. 65)

Ferdinand (1452–1516) King of Spain, he and his wife Isabella completed the Reconquista. They forced Jews in Spain to become Christian or leave and banned Islam. (p. 284)

Francis of Assisi (c. 1182–1226) Italian saint, he encouraged people to be kind to others and founded the Franciscan Order. (p. 272)

Franklin, Benjamin (1706–1790) American colonial leader, he argued that the British government had no right to tax the colonists because they had no representation in Parliament. (p. 481)

Eleanor of Aquitaine

G

Galilei, Galileo (gal-uh-LEE-oh gal-uh-LAY) (1564–1642) Italian scientist, he was the first scientist to routinely use experiments to test theories. He was placed on trial for supporting theories that contradicted Church teachings. (p. 361)

Gama, Vasco da (c. 1460–1524) Portuguese sailor, he sailed around Africa to reach India. (p. 449)

Genghis Khan (JENG-guhs kahn) (c. 1162–1227) Ruler of the Mongols, he led his people in attacks against China and against other parts of Asia. His name means "universal leader." (p. 180)

Gregory VII (1020–1085) A powerful medieval pope, he fought with Holy Roman Emperor Henry IV over the power to choose church officials. (p. 263)

Gutenberg, Johann (YOH-hahn GOO-tuhn-berk) (c. 1400–1468) German printer, he developed a printing press that used movable type. (p. 313)

H

Henry IV (1050–1106) Holy Roman Emperor, he fought against Pope Gregory VII over the power to choose church officials. (p. 263)

Henry VIII (1491–1547) King of England, he split with the Catholic Church and declared himself head of the Church of England, or Anglican Church. (p. 333)

Henry the Navigator (1394–1460) Prince of Portugal, he helped promote exploration by Portuguese sailors. (p. 448)

Holbein, Hans (HAWL-byn) (1497–1543) Swiss Renaissance painter, he is known largely for his portraits. (p. 315)

I

Ibn Battutah (1304–c. 1368) Muslim traveler and writer, he visited Africa, India, China, and Spain. (p. 95)

Ibn-Sina (980–1037) Muslim doctor, he wrote a book on medicine that was used throughout Europe until the 1600s. He is known in the West as Avicenna. (p. 96)

Ignatius of Loyola (ig-NAY-shuhs) (1491–1556) Spanish noble and saint, he founded the Society of Jesus, or the Jesuits. (p. 336)

Ieyasu, Tokugawa See Tokugawa Ieyasu.

Isabella (1451–1504) Queen of Castile in Spain, she helped complete the Reconquista. She and her husband banned Islam and forced all Jews in Spain to become Christian or leave. She also helped pay for the voyages of Christopher Columbus. (p. 284)

J

James II (1633–1701) King of England, he tried to re-introduce Roman Catholicism to England, a Protestant country. He was replaced as ruler by William and Mary. (p. 485)

Jefferson, Thomas (1743–1826) American colonial leader and author of the Declaration of Independence, he believed that Britain had no right to govern or impose taxes on the colonies. (p. 481)

Jesus (c. AD 1–c. 30) Founder of Christianity, he is considered the Savior by Christians and a prophet by Muslims. (p. 61)

Joan of Arc (c. 1412–1431) French peasant girl, she rallied the French troops during the Hundred Years' War. (p. 278)

Justinian (juh-STIN-ee-uhn) (c. 483–565) Emperor of the eastern Roman Empire, he organized all Roman laws into a legal system called Justinian's Code. He also reconquered much of the Mediterranean and built Hagia Sophia. (pp. 36, 41)

K

Kepler, Johannes (1571–1630) German astronomer, he proved that the planets orbit the sun. (p. 360)

Khadijah (ka-DEE-jah) (600s) Muhammad's wife, she was a successful trader. (p. 59)

Khayyám, Omar See Omar Khayyám.

Kublai Khan (KOO-bluh KAHN) (1215–1294) Mongol ruler, he completed the conquest of China and founded the Yuan dynasty. (p. 181, 187)

L

Las Casas, Bartolomé de (1474–1566) Spanish priest, he protested the terrible treatment of American Indians. He attempted to convert the Indians to Christianity. (p. 457)

Leeuwenhoek, Antoni van (ANT-uh-nee LAY-ven-hook) (1632–1723) Dutch scientist, he was the first person to use a microscope as a scientific instrument. (p. 363)

Leo Africanus (c. 1485–c. 1554) Muslim traveler, he wrote about his journeys in Africa. (p. 144)

Leonardo da Vinci (lay-oh-NAHR-doh dah VEEN-chee) (1452–1519) Genius of the Renaissance, he was a painter, sculptor, inventor, engineer, town planner, and mapmaker. (p. 308)

Li Bo (701–762) One of China's greatest poets, he lived during the Tang dynasty. (p. 173)

Li Qingzhao (ching-ZHOW) (1081–1141) China's greatest female poet, she lived during the Song dynasty. (p. 173)

Locke, John (1632–1704) English philosopher, he thought that government was a contract between the ruler and the people. (pp. 479, 483)

Louis XIV (1638–1715) French king, he believed that he ruled by divine right. (p. 478)

Louis XVI (1754–1793) French king at the time of the French Revolution, he refused to sign a constitution limiting his power. He was tried and later executed. (p. 488)

Luther, Martin (1483–1546) German priest credited with starting the Reformation, he nailed a list of complaints about the Catholic Church to a church door in Wittenberg, Germany. (p. 330)

M

Machiavelli, Niccolo (mahk-yah-VEL-lee) (1469–1527) Italian writer and politician, he wrote *The Prince* in which he advised leaders on how to rule. (p. 306)

Madison, James (1751–1836) American colonial leader, he was the primary author of the Constitution. (p. 487)

Magellan, Ferdinand (muh-JEL-uhn) (c. 1480–1521) Portuguese explorer who sailed for Spain, his crew was the first to circumnavigate the globe. (p. 449)

Maimonides (my-MAHN-uh-deez) (1135–1204) Jewish scholar, he tried to unite the work of Aristotle with Jewish ideas. (p. 356)

Malintzin (mah-LINT-suhn), or **Malinche** (c. 1501–1550) Native American guide and interpreter for the Spanish conquistadors, she helped Cortés in his conquest of the Aztecs. (pp. 414, 415)

Mansa Musa (MAHN-sah moo-SAH) (died c. 1332) Mali's greatest and most famous ruler, he was a devout Muslim. He made a famous pilgrimage to Mecca that helped spread Mali's fame. (pp. 138, 141)

Marie-Antoinette (1755–1793) French queen and wife of King Louis XVI, she lived extravagantly and was executed during the French Revolution. (p. 488)

BIOGRAPHICAL DICTIONARY

Medici, Cosimo de' (KOH-zee-moh day MED-i-chee) (1389–1464) Italian banker and leader of Florence, he wanted to make Florence the greatest city in the world. His actions helped bring about the Renaissance. (p. 302)

Mehmed II (1432–1481) Ottoman sultan, he defeated the Byzantine Empire in 1453. (p. 89)

Merici, Angela (may-REE-chee) (c. 1474–1540) Italian saint, she founded the Ursuline Order. (p. 336)

Michelangelo (mee-kay-LAHN-jay-loh) (1475–1564) Italian Renaissance artist, he designed buildings, wrote poetry, and created sculptures and paintings. (pp. 308, 311)

Moctezuma II (MAWK-tay-SOO-mah) (1466–1520) The last Aztec emperor, he was killed in the Spanish conquest led by Cortés. (p. 413)

Montesquieu, Charles-Louis (mohn-te-SKYOO) (1689–1755) French Enlightenment thinker, he believed that government should be divided into separate branches to protect people's freedom. (p. 480)

Muhammad (c. 570–632) Founder of Islam, he spread Islam's teachings to the people of Arabia. His teachings make up the Qu'ran. (p. 59)

Murasaki Shikibu (moohr-ah-sahk-ee shee-kee-boo) (c. 978–c. 1026) Japanese noble and writer, she wrote *The Tale of Genji*, the world's first known novel. (pp. 205, 209)

N, O

Newton, Sir Isaac (1642–1727) English scientist, he studied and simplified the work of earlier scientists. He identified four laws that explained how the physical world works. (p. 362)

Oda Nobunaga (ohd-ah noh-booh-nah-gah) (1534–1582) Japanese shogun, he fought to unify all of Japan. (p. 217)

Omar Khayyám (oh-mahr-ky-AHM) (c. 1048–c. 1131) Sufi poet, mathematician, and astonomer, he wrote *The Rubáiyát*. (p. 97)

P

Pacal (puh-KAHL) (603–683) Maya king, he had a temple built in the city of Palenque to record his achievements as a ruler. (p. 393)

Pachacuti (pah-chah-KOO-tee) (died 1471) Inca ruler, he greatly expanded the Incas' territory. (p. 423)

Patrick (400s) Christian saint, he converted the people of Ireland to Christianity. (p. 235)

Petrarch (PEH-trahrk) (1304–1374) Early Italian Renaissance scholar, he wrote about the importance of knowing history. (p. 310)

Pizarro, Francisco (1475–1541) Spanish conquistador, he conquered the Inca Empire. (p. 425)

Murasaki Shikibu

Polo, Marco (1254–1324) Italian trader, he traveled to China and later wrote about his trip. During his time in China he served as a government official in Kublai Khan's court. (p. 299)

Ptolemy (TAHL-uh-mee) (AD 100s) Ancient Greek astronomer and geographer, he studied the skies and made maps of the Mediterranean region. (p. 356)

Rabelais, François (FRAN-swah RAB-uh-lay) (1483–1553) French Renaissance writer, he poked fun at the ideas of the Middle Ages. (p. 316)

Richard I (1157–1199) King of England, he led Christian soldiers in the Third Crusade. He earned the respect of his enemies as well as Christian soldiers for his bravery and his fairness. (p. 266)

Robespierre, Maximilien (roh-bes-pyer) (1758–1794) A leader of the French Revolution, his execution ended the Reign of Terror. (p. 489)

Rousseau, Jean-Jacques (roo-SOH) (1712–1778) French philosopher, he believed in popular sovereignty and the social contract between citizens and their governments. (p. 480)

Saladin (1137–1193) Muslim general, he led the Muslim forces during the Third Crusade. (p. 266)

Schliemann, Heinrich (HYN-rik SHLEE-mahn) (1822–1890) Famous archaeologist, he discovered the location of Troy. (p. 14)

Shah Jahan (1592–1666) Ruler of the Mughal Empire, he built the Taj Mahal to honor his wife. (p. 93)

Shakespeare, William (1564–1616) English Renaissance writer and playwright, he is considered by many to be the greatest English writer of all time. (p. 317)

Shikibu, Murasaki See Murasaki Shikibu.

Shotoku (shoh-toh-koo) (573–621) Japanese regent, he was one of Japan's greatest leaders. He was influential in bringing Buddhism and Chinese ideas to Japan. (p. 202)

Smith, Adam (1723–1790) British economist, he argued that governments should not interfere in economic matters and that economic growth came when individuals were free to make their own choices. (p. 477)

Suleyman I (soo-lay-MAHN) (c. 1494–1566) Ottoman ruler, he governed the empire at its height. (p. 90)

Sundiata (soohn-JAHT-ah) (died 1255) Founder of the Empire of Mali, his reign is recorded in legends. (p. 136)

Sunni Ali (SOOH-nee ah-LEE) (died 1492) Emperor of Songhai, he conquered Mali and made Songhai into a powerful state. (p. 143)

Taizong (TY-tzong) (600–649) Chinese emperor of the Tang dynasty, he conquered much of Asia, reformed the military, and created codes of law. (p. 167)

Theodora (c. 500–548) Empress of the eastern Roman empire and Justinian's wife, she helped her husband rule. (pp. 37, 41)

Titian (TISH-uhn) (c. 1488–1576) Italian Renaissance painter, he painted many scenes from history. (p. 308)

Tokugawa Ieyasu (toh-koohg-ah-wuh ee-eyahs-ooh) (1543–1616) Japanese shogun, he unified all of Japan and began the Tokugawa shogunate. (p. 217)

Tunka Manin (TOOHN-kah MAH-nin) (ruled c. 1068) King of the Empire of Ghana, his kingdom was visited by Muslim writers. (p. 134)

Tyndale, William (TIN-duhl) (c. 1494–1536) English professor, he translated the Bible into English. He was later executed as a heretic. (p. 332)

BIOGRAPHICAL DICTIONARY

U

Urban II (c. 1035–1099) Medieval pope, he called on Christians to launch the First Crusade. (p. 264)

V

van Eyck, Jan (yahn vahn-YK) (1395–1441) Northern Renaissance artist, he was best known for his portraits. (p. 315)

Voltaire (vohl-TAYR) (1694–1778) French philosopher, he mocked government and religion in his writings. (pp. 476, 477)

W

William and Mary (1650–1702; 1662–1694) Rulers of England, they agreed to the English Bill of Rights, which limited their powers and recognized some rights for English citizens. (p. 485)

William the Conqueror (c. 1028–1087) Powerful French noble who conquered England, he brought feudalism to Britain. (p. 244)

Wollstonecraft, Mary (1759–1797) British writer, she argued that women should have the same rights as men. (p. 477)

Wu (625–705) Empress of China during the Tang dynasty, she ruled ruthlessly and brought prosperity to China. (p. 168)

X, Y, Z

Xavier, Francis (ZAYV-yuhr) (1506–1552) Jesuit priest and missionary, he introduced Catholicism to parts of India and Japan. (p. 338)

Yang Jian (yang jee-EN) (541–604) Chinese emperor, he reunified China after the Period of Disunion and established the Sui dynasty. (p. 167)

Voltaire

Zheng He (juhng HUH) (c. 1371–c. 1433) Chinese admiral during the Ming Dynasty, he led great voyages that spread China's fame throughout Asia. (p. 183)

Zhu Yuanzhang (JOO yoo-ahn-JAHNG) (1368–1398) Emperor of China and founder of the Ming dynasty, he led an army that overthrew the Mongols. (p. 182)

English and Spanish Glossary

MARK	AS IN	RESPELLING	EXAMPLE
a	alphabet	a	*AL-fuh-bet
ā	Asia	ay	AY-zhuh
ä	cart, top	ah	KAHRT, TAHP
e	let, ten	e	LET, TEN
ē	even, leaf	ee	EE-vuhn, LEEF
i	it, tip, British	i	IT, TIP, BRIT-ish
ī	site, buy, Ohio	y	SYT, BY, oh-HY-oh
	iris	eye	EYE-ris
k	card	k	KAHRD
ō	over, rainbow	oh	OH-vuhr, RAYN-boh
u̇	book, wood	ooh	BOOHK, WOOHD
ȯ	all, orchid	aw	AWL, AWR-kid
ȯi	foil, coin	oy	FOYL, KOYN
au̇	out	ow	OWT
ə	cup, butter	uh	KUHP, BUHT-uhr
ü	rule, food	oo	ROOL, FOOD
yü	few	yoo	FYOO
zh	vision	zh	VIZH-uhn

*A syllable printed in small capital letters receives heavier emphasis than the other syllable(s) in a word.

Phonetic Respelling and Pronunciation Guide

Many of the key terms in this textbook have been respelled to help you pronounce them. The letter combinations used in the respelling throughout the narrative are explained in the following phonetic respelling and pronunciation guide. The guide is adapted from *Merriam-Webster's Collegiate Dictionary, Eleventh Edition; Merriam-Webster's Biographical Dictionary;* and *Merriam-Webster's Geographical Dictionary.*

A

alchemy a forerunner of chemistry (p. 357)
alquimia precursora de la química (pág. 357)

animism the belief that bodies of water, animals, trees, and other natural objects have spirits (p. 117)
animismo creencia de que las masas de agua, los animales, los árboles y otros elementos naturales tienen espíritu (pág. 117)

aqueduct (A-kwuh-duhkt) a human-made channel that carries water from distant places (p. 26)
acueducto canal hecho por el ser humano que transporta agua desde lugares alejados (pág. 26)

archaeology (ahr-kee-AH-luh-jee) the study of the past based on materials people have left behind (p. 8)
arqueología estudio del pasado a través de los objetos que dejaron las personas tras desaparecer (pág. 8)

artifact an object created and used by humans (p. 8)
artefacto objeto creado y usado por los humanos (pág. 8)

atlas a collection of maps (p. 461)
atlas colección de mapas (pág. 461)

B

balance of trade the relationship of goods imported to goods exported (p. 459)
balanza comercial relación entre los bienes importados y los exportados (pág. 459)

barometer a scientific instrument that measures air pressure (p. 363)

barómetro instrumento científico que mide la presión atmosférica (pág. 363)

Black Death a deadly plague that swept through Europe between 1347 and 1351 (p. 279)

Peste Negra plaga mortal que azotó Europa entre 1347 y 1351 (pág. 279)

bureaucracy a body of unelected government officials (p. 178)

burocracia cuerpo de empleados no electos del gobierno (pág. 178)

Bushido (BOOH-shi-doh) the code of honor followed by the samurai in Japan (p. 214)

Bushido código de honor por el que se regían los samuráis en Japón (pág. 214)

Byzantine Empire the society that developed in the eastern Roman Empire after the fall of the western Roman Empire (p. 38)

Imperio bizantino sociedad que surgió en el Imperio romano de oriente tras la caída del Imperio romano de occidente (pág. 38)

C

caliph (KAY-luhf) a title that Muslims use for the highest leader of Islam (p. 80)

califa título que los musulmanes le dan al líder supremo del Islam (pág. 80)

calligraphy decorative writing (p. 98)

caligrafía escritura decorativa (pág. 98)

capitalism an economic system in which individuals and private businesses run most industries (p. 463)

capitalismo sistema económico en el que los individuos y las empresas privadas controlan la mayoría de las industrias (pág. 463)

caravan a group of traders that travel together (p. 56)

caravana grupo de comerciantes que viajan juntos (pág. 56)

Catholic Reformation the effort of the late 1500s and 1600s to reform the Catholic Church from within; also called the Counter-Reformation (p. 334)

Reforma católica iniciativa para reformar la Iglesia católica desde dentro que tuvo lugar a finales del siglo XVI y en el XVII; también conocida como Contrarreforma (pág. 334)

causeway a raised road across water or wet ground (p. 411)

carretera elevada carretera construida sobre agua o terreno pantanoso (pág. 411)

chivalry (SHIV-uhl-ree) the code of honorable behavior for medieval knights (p. 249)

caballería código de comportamiento y honor de los caballeros medievales (pág. 249)

Christian humanism the combination of humanist and religious ideas (p. 314)

humanismo cristiano combinación de ideas humanistas y religiosas (pág. 314)

circumnavigate to go all the way around (p. 449)

circunnavegar rodear por completo (pág. 449)

citizen a person who can participate in government (p. 25)

ciudadano persona que puede participar en el gobierno (pág. 25)

civil service service as a government official (p. 178)

administración pública servicio como empleado del gobierno (pág. 178)

clan an extended family (p. 200)

clan familia extensa (pág. 200)

clergy church officials (p. 269)

clero funcionarios de la Iglesia (pág. 269)

codex (KOH-deks) an ancient book of historical records (p. 420)

códice libro antiguo con documentos históricos (pág. 420)

Columbian Exchange the exchange of plants, animals, and ideas between the New World and the Old World (p. 454)
intercambio colombino intercambio de plantas, animales e ideas entre el Nuevo Mundo y el Viejo Mundo (pág. 454)

compass an instrument that uses the earth's magnetic field to indicate direction (p. 174)
brújula instrumento que utiliza el campo magnético de la Tierra para indicar la dirección (pág. 174)

congregation an assembly of people who belong to a church (p. 345)
fieles grupo de personas que pertenecen a una iglesia (pág. 345)

conquistadors (kahn-kees-tuh-DOHRS) Spanish soldiers in the Americas who explored new lands, searched for gold and silver, and tried to spread Christianity (p. 413)
conquistadores soldados españoles en América que exploraron nuevas tierras, buscaron oro y plata e intentaron difundir el cristianismo (pág. 413)

corruption the decay of people's values (p. 34)
corrupción decadencia de los valores de las personas (pág. 34)

cottage industry a system in which people work at home to make a product (p. 460)
industria artesanal sistema en el que las personas trabajan en casa para fabricar un producto (pág. 460)

court a group of nobles who live near and serve or advise a ruler (p. 204)
corte grupo de nobles que viven cerca de un gobernante y lo sirven o aconsejan (pág. 204)

Crusades a long series of wars between Christians and Muslims in Southwest Asia fought for control of the Holy Land from 1096 to 1291 (p. 264)
cruzadas larga sucesión de guerras entre cristianos y musulmanes en el sudoeste de Asia para conseguir el control de la Tierra Santa; tuvieron lugar entre el año 1096 y el año 1291 (pág. 264)

daimyo (DY-mee-oh) large landowners of feudal Japan (p. 212)
daimyo grandes propietarios de tierras del Japón feudal (pág. 212)

Declaration of Independence a document written in 1776 that declared the American colonies' independence from British rule (p. 486)
Declaración de Independencia documento redactado en 1776 que declaró la independencia de las colonias de Norteamérica del dominio británico (pág. 486)

Declaration of the Rights of Man and of the Citizen a document written in France in 1789 that guaranteed specific freedoms for French citizens (p. 489)
Declaración de los Derechos del Hombre y del Ciudadano documento redactado en Francia en 1789 que garantizaba libertades específicas para los ciudadanos franceses (pág. 489)

Edict of Nantes (NAHNT) a decree issued in 1598 by King Henry IV that granted religious freedom in most of France (p. 343)
edicto de Nantes decreto promulgado en 1598 por el rey Enrique IV que otorgaba libertad religiosa en la mayor parte de Francia (pág. 343)

English Bill of Rights a document approved in 1689 that listed rights for Parliament and the English people and drew on the principles of Magna Carta (p. 485)
Declaración de Derechos inglesa documento aprobado en 1689 que enumeraba los derechos del Parlamento y del pueblo de Inglaterra, inspirada en los principios de la Carta Magna (pág. 485)

Enlightenment a period during the 1600s and 1700s when reason was used to guide people's thoughts about society, politics, and philosophy (p. 474)

Ilustración período durante los siglos XVII y XVIII en el que la razón guiaba la opinión de las personas acerca de la sociedad, la política y la filosofía (pág. 474)

Eurasia the large landmass that includes both Europe and Asia (p. 230)

Eurasia gran masa continental que incluye a Europa y Asia (pág. 230)

excommunicate to cast out from the church (p. 261)

excomulgar expulsar de la Iglesia (pág. 261)

extended family a family group that includes the father, mother, children, and close relatives (p. 116)

familia extensa grupo familiar que incluye al padre, la madre, los hijos y los parientes cercanos (pág. 116)

F

federalism the sharing of power between local governments and a strong central government (p. 345)

federalismo sistema de distribución del poder entre los gobiernos locales y un gobierno central fuerte (pág. 345)

feudalism (FYOO-duh-lih-zuhm) the system of obligations that governed the relationships between lords and vassals in medieval Europe (p. 243)

feudalismo sistema de obligaciones que gobernaba las relaciones entre los señores feudales y los vasallos en la Europa medieval (pág. 243)

figurehead a person who appears to rule even though real power rests with someone else (p. 213)

títere persona que aparentemente gobierna aunque el poder real lo ostenta otra persona (pág. 213)

Five Pillars of Islam five acts of worship required of all Muslims (p. 68)

los cinco pilares del Islam cinco prácticas religiosas que los musulmanes tienen que observar (pág. 68)

fossil a part or imprint of something that was once alive (p. 8)

fósil parte o huella de un ser vivo ya desaparecido (pág. 8)

friar a member of a religious order who lived and worked among the public (p. 272)

fraile miembro de una orden religiosa que vivía y trabajaba entre la gente (pág. 272)

G

Grand Canal a canal linking northern and southern China (p. 167)

Gran Canal canal que conecta el norte y el sur de China (pág. 167)

griot a West African storyteller (p. 147)

griot narrador de relatos de África occidental (pág. 147)

gunpowder a mixture of powders used in guns and explosives (p. 174)

pólvora mezcla de polvos utilizada en armas de fuego y explosivos (pág. 174)

H

haiku a type of Japanese poem with three lines and 17 syllables that describes nature scenes (p. 250)

haiku tipo de poema japonés de tres líneas y 17 sílabas en el que se describen escenas de la naturaleza (pág. 250)

harem an area of an Ottoman household where women lived apart from men (p. 90)

harén zona de una casa otomana en la que las mujeres vivían separadas de los hombres (pág. 90)

ENGLISH AND SPANISH GLOSSARY

heresy (HER-uh-see) religious ideas that oppose accepted church teachings (p. 282)
herejía ideas religiosas que se oponen a la doctrina oficial de la Iglesia (pág. 282)

history the study of the past (p. 6)
historia el estudio del pasado (pág. 6)

Holy Land the region on the eastern shore of the Mediterranean Sea where Jesus lived, preached, and died (p. 264)
Tierra Santa región de la costa este del mar Mediterráneo en la que Jesús vivió, predicó y murió (pág. 264)

Huguenot (HYOO-guh-naht) a French Protestant (p. 342)
hugonote protestante francés (pág. 342)

humanism the study of history, literature, public speaking, and art that led to a new way of thinking in Europe in the late 1300s (p. 304)
humanismo estudio de la historia, la literatura, la oratoria y el arte que produjo una nueva forma de pensar en Europa a finales del siglo XIV (pág. 304)

Hundred Years' War a long conflict between England and France that lasted from 1337 to 1453 (p. 278)
Guerra de los Cien Años largo conflicto entre Inglaterra y Francia que tuvo lugar entre 1337 y 1453 (pág. 278)

hypothesis a solution a scientist proposes to solve a problem (p. 366)
hipótesis solución que un científico propone para resolver un problema (pág. 366)

indulgence a document given by the pope that excused a person from penalties for sins he or she had committed (p. 329)
indulgencia documento concedido por el Papa que perdonaba a una persona las penas por los pecados que hubiera cometido (pág. 329)

interest a fee that borrowers pay for the use of someone else's money (p. 302)
interés suma que las personas que toman dinero prestado pagan por el uso del dinero de otra persona (pág. 302)

Islam a religion based on the messages Muhammad is believed to have received from God (p. 60)
Islam religión basada en los mensajes que se cree que Mahoma recibió de Dios (pág. 60)

isolationism a policy of avoiding contact with other countries (p. 186)
aislacionismo política de evitar el contacto con otros países (pág. 186)

Janissary an Ottoman slave soldier (p. 88)
jenízaro soldado esclavo otomano (pág. 88)

Jesuits members of a Catholic religious order created to serve the pope and the church (p. 336)
jesuitas miembros de una orden religiosa católica creada para servir al Papa y a la Iglesia (pág. 336)

jihad (ji-HAHD) to make an effort or to struggle; has also been interpreted to mean holy war (p. 67)
yihad esforzarse o luchar; se ha interpretado también con el significado de guerra santa (pág. 67)

K

kente a hand-woven, brightly colored West African fabric (p. 151)
kente tela muy colorida, tejida a mano, característica de África occidental (pág. 151)

knight a warrior in medieval Europe who fought on horseback (p. 242)
caballero guerrero de la Europa medieval que luchaba a caballo (pág. 242)

llama (LAH-muh) an animal related to the camel that is native to South America (p. 425)

llama animal de la familia del camello, originario de Sudamérica (pág. 425)

M

Magna Carta a document signed in 1215 by King John of England that required the king to honor certain rights (p. 276)

Carta Magna documento firmado por el rey Juan de Inglaterra en 1215 que exigía que el rey respetara ciertos derechos (pág. 276)

maize (MAYZ) corn (p. 387)

maíz cereal también conocido como elote o choclo (pág. 387)

manor a large estate owned by a knight or lord (p. 245)

señorío gran finca perteneciente a un caballero o señor feudal (pág. 245)

market economy an economic system in which individuals decide what goods and services they will buy (p. 463)

economía de mercado sistema económico en el que los individuos deciden qué tipo de bienes y servicios desean comprar (pág. 463)

masonry stonework (p. 430)

mampostería obra de piedra (pág. 430)

medieval (mee-DEE-vuhl) referring to the Middle Ages (p. 234)

medieval relativo a la Edad Media (pág. 234)

mercantilism a system in which a government controls all economic activity in a country and its colonies to make the government stronger and richer (p. 459)

mercantilismo sistema en el que el gobierno controla toda la actividad económica de un país y sus colonias con el fin de hacerse más fuerte y más rico (pág. 459)

Mesoamerica a region that includes the southern part of what is now Mexico and parts of northern Central America (p. 384)

Mesoamérica región que incluye la zona sur del actual México y zonas del norte de Centroamérica (pág. 384)

Middle Ages a period that lasted from about 500 to 1500 in Europe (p. 234)

Edad Media nombre con el que se denomina el período que abarca aproximadamente desde el año 500 hasta el 1500 en Europa (pág. 234)

minaret a narrow tower from which Muslims are called to prayer (p. 97)

minarete torre fina desde la que se llama a la oración a los musulmanes (pág. 97)

monastery a community of monks (p. 236)

monasterio comunidad de monjes (pág.236)

monk a religious man who lived apart from society in an isolated community (p. 236)

monje religioso que vivía apartado de la sociedad en una comunidad aislada (pág. 236)

mosaic a picture made with pieces of colored stone or glass (p. 39)

mosaico dibujo hecho con trozos de piedra o cristal de colores (pág. 39)

mosque (MAHSK) a building for Muslim prayer (p. 63)

mezquita edificio musulmán para la oración (pág. 63)

Muslim a follower of Islam (p. 60)

musulmán seguidor del Islam (pág. 60)

N

natural law a law that people believed God had created to govern how the world operated (p. 274)

ley natural ley que las personas pensaban que Dios había creado para controlar el funcionamiento del mundo (pág. 274)

ENGLISH AND SPANISH GLOSSARY

natural rights the belief that developed during the Enlightenment that people had certain rights, such as the right to life, liberty, and property (p. 480)

derechos naturales creencia que se desarrolló durante la Ilustración de que las personas tenían ciertos derechos, como el derecho a la vida, a la libertad y a la propiedad (pág. 480)

oasis a wet, fertile area within a desert (p. 56)

oasis zona húmeda y fértil en un desierto (pág. 56)

observatory a building used to study astronomy (p. 398)

observatorio edificio que sirve para estudiar la astronomía (pág. 398)

obsidian a sharp, glasslike volcanic rock (p. 390)

obsidiana roca volcánica cortante y parecida al vidrio (pág. 390)

oral history a spoken record of past events (p. 147)

historia oral registro hablado de hechos ocurridos en el pasado (pág. 147)

Parliament (PAHR-luh-muhnt) the lawmaking body that governs England (p. 277)

Parlamento órgano legislador que gobierna Inglaterra (pág. 277)

patron a sponsor (p. 97)

mecenas patrocinador (pág. 97)

Period of Disunion the time of disorder that followed the collapse of the Han Dynasty in China (p. 166)

Período de Desunión época de desorden en la historia de China tras la caída de la dinastía Han; se extendió desde el 220 hasta el 589 (pág. 168)

perspective a method of showing a three-dimensional scene on a flat surface so that it looks real (p. 307)

perspectiva método para mostrar una escena de forma tridimensional en una superficie plana con el fin de que parezca real (pág. 307)

pilgrimage a journey to a sacred place (p. 62)

peregrinación viaje a un lugar sagrado (pág. 62)

plantation a large farm (p. 456)

plantación hacienda de grandes dimensiones (pág. 456)

Popol Vuh (poh-pohl voo) a book containing Maya legends and history (p. 399)

Popol Vuh libro que contiene las leyendas y la historia de los mayas (pág. 399)

popular sovereignty the Enlightenment idea that governments should express the will of the people (p. 480)

soberanía popular idea de la Ilustración que consiste en que los gobiernos deben expresar la voluntad del pueblo (pág. 480)

porcelain a thin, beautiful pottery invented in China (p. 173)

porcelana cerámica bella y delicada creada en China (pág. 173)

primary source a first-hand account of an event created by someone who took part in or witnessed the event (p. 7)

fuente primaria relato de un hecho por parte de alguien que participó o presenció el hecho (pág. 7)

Protestant a Christian who protested against the Catholic church (p. 331)

protestante cristiano que protestaba en contra de la Iglesia católica (pág. 331)

proverb a short saying of wisdom or truth (p. 148)

proverbio refrán breve que expresa sabiduría o una verdad (pág. 148)

purgatory in Catholic teaching, a place where souls went before they went to heaven (p. 329)

purgatorio en la enseñanza católica, lugar al que van las almas antes de pasar al cielo (pág. 329)

Q

Quechua (KE-chuh-wuh) the language of the Inca (p. 424)

quechua idioma de los incas (pág. 424)

Qur'an (kuh-RAN) the holy book of Islam (p. 60)

Corán libro sagrado del Islam (pág. 60)

R

racism the belief that some people are better than others because of racial traits, such as skin color (p. 457)

racismo creencia de que algunas personas son mejores que otras debido a los rasgos raciales, como el color de la piel (pág. 457)

rain forest a moist, densely wooded area that contains many different plants and animals (p. 114)

selva tropical zona húmeda y con muchos árboles que contiene muchas variedades de plantas y animales (pág. 114)

rationalist someone who looks at the world in a reasonable and logical way (p. 356)

racionalista alguien que entiende el mundo de manera lógica y razonable (pág. 356)

Reconquista (re-kahn-KEES-tuh) the effort of Christian kingdoms in northern Spain to retake land from the Moors during the Middle Ages (p. 283)

Reconquista esfuerzo de los reinos cristianos del norte de España por recuperar los territorios en posesión de los moros durante la Edad Media (pág. 283)

Reformation (re-fuhr-MAY-shuhn) a reform movement against the Roman Catholic Church that began in 1517; it resulted in the creation of Protestant churches (p. 328)

Reforma movimiento de reforma contra la Iglesia católica romana que comenzó en 1517; resultó en la creación de las iglesias protestantes (pág. 328)

regent a person who rules a country for someone who is unable to rule alone (p. 202)

regente persona que gobierna un país en lugar de alguien que no puede hacerlo por su cuenta (pág. 202)

religious order a group of people who dedicate their lives to religion and follow common rules (p. 272)

orden religiosa grupo de personas que dedican su vida a la religión y respetan una serie de normas comunes (pág. 272)

Renaissance (re-nuh-SAHNS) the period of "rebirth" and creativity that followed Europe's Middle Ages (p. 303)

Renacimiento período de "volver a nacer" y creatividad posterior a la Edad Media en Europa (pág. 303)

rift a long, deep valley formed by the movement of the earth's crust (p. 112)

fisura valle largo y profundo formado por el movimiento de la corteza terrestre (pág. 112)

S

Sahel (sah-HEL) a semiarid region in Africa just south of the Sahara that separates the desert from wetter areas (p. 114)

Sahel región semiárida de África, situada al sur del Sahara, que separa el desierto de otras zonas más húmedas (pág. 114)

salon a social gathering held to discuss ideas during the Enlightenment (p. 477)

tertulia reunión social para debatir ideas; se acostumbraban celebrar durante la Ilustración (pág. 477)

samurai (SA-muh-ry) a trained professional warrior in feudal Japan (p. 212)

samurai guerrero profesional del Japón feudal (pág. 212)

sand dune a hill of sand shaped by the wind (p. 56)

duna colina de arena modelada por el viento (pág. 56)

savannah an open grassland with scattered trees (p. 114)

sabana pradera abierta con árboles dispersos (pág. 114)

scholar-official an educated member of China's government who passed a series of written examinations (p. 178)

funcionario erudito miembro culto del gobierno de China que habia aprobado una serie de exámenes escritos (pág. 178)

science a particular way of gaining knowledge about the world (p. 355)

ciencia manera específica de adquirir conocimientos sobre el mundo (pág. 355)

scientific method a step-by-step method for performing experiments and other scientific research (p. 365)

método científico método detallado para realizar experimentos y otros tipos de |investigaciones científicas (pág. 365)

Scientific Revolution a series of events that led to the birth of modern science; it lasted from about 1540 to 1700 (p. 354)

Revolución científica serie de acontecimientos que condujeron al nacimiento de la ciencia moderna; se extendió desde alrededor del 1540 hasta el 1700 (pág. 354)

secondary source the information gathered by someone who did not take part in or witness an event (p. 7)

fuente secundaria información recopilada por alguien que no participó ni presenció un hecho (pág. 7)

secular non-religious (p. 475)

seglar no religioso, laico (pág. 475)

sedentary settled (p. 56)

sedentario establecido en un lugar (pág. 56)

serf a worker in medieval Europe who was tied to the land on which he or she lived (p. 245)

siervo trabajador de la Europa medieval que estaba atado al territorio en el que vivía (pág. 245)

Shia (SHEE-ah) a member of the second-largest branch of Islam (p. 90)

shia miembro de la segunda rama más importante del Islam (pág. 90)

Shinto the traditional religion of Japan (p. 200)

sintoísmo religión tradicional de Japón (pág. 200)

shogun a general who ruled Japan in the emperor's name (p. 213)

shogun general que gobernaba a Japón en nombre del emperador (pág. 213)

shrine a place at which people worship a saint or god (p. 62)

santuario lugar en el que las personas rinden culto a un santo o a un dios (pág. 62)

silent barter a process in which people exchange goods without contacting each other directly (p. 132)

trueque silencioso proceso mediante el que las personas intercambian bienes sin entrar en contacto directo (pág. 132)

social structure the way a society is organized (p. 10)

estructura social forma en que se organiza la sociedad (pág. 10)

society a community of people who share a common culture (p. 10)

sociedad comunidad de personas que comparten la misma cultura (pág. 10)

souk (SOOK) a market or bazaar in the Islamic world (p. 56)

zoco mercado o bazar del mundo islámico (pág. 56)

Spanish Armada a large fleet of Spanish ships that was defeated by England in 1588 (p. 451)

Armada española gran flota de barcos españoles que fue derrotada por Inglaterra en 1588 (pág. 451)

Spanish Inquisition an organization of priests in Spain that looked for and punished anyone suspected of secretly practicing their old religion (p. 284)

Inquisición española organización de sacerdotes en España que perseguía y castigaba a las personas sospechas de practicar su antigua religión (pág. 284)

sub-Saharan Africa Africa south of the Sahara (p. 112)

África subsahariana parte de África que queda al sur del Sahara (pág. 112)

Sufism (soo-fi-zuhm) a movement in Islam that taught people they can find God's love by having a personal relationship with God (p. 96)

sufismo movimiento perteneciente al Islam que enseñaba a las personas que pueden hallar el amor de Dios si establecen una relación personal con Él (pág. 96)

sultan an Ottoman ruler (p. 89)

sultán gobernante otomano (pág. 89)

Sunnah (sooH-nuh) a collection of writings about the way Muhammad lived that provides a model for Muslims to follow (p. 67)

Sunna conjunto de escritos sobre la vida de Mahoma que proporciona un modelo de comportamiento para los musulmanes (pág. 67)

Sunni a member of the largest branch of Islam (p. 90)

suní miembro de la rama más importante del Islam (pág. 90)

T

theory an explanation a scientist develops based on facts (p. 355)

teoría explicación que desarrolla un científico basándose en hechos (pág. 355)

Thirty Years' War a series of wars from 1618 to 1648 that involved many of the countries of Europe (p. 344)

Guerra de los Treinta Años sucesión de guerras desde 1618 a 1648 en la que participaron muchos de los países europeos (pág. 344)

tolerance acceptance (p. 83)

tolerancia aceptación (pág. 83)

topography the shape and elevation of land in a region (p. 230)

topografía forma y elevación del terreno en una región (pág. 230)

V

vassal a knight who promised to support a lord in exchange for land in medieval Europe (p. 243)

vasallo caballero de la Europa medieval que prometía apoyar a un señor feudal a cambio de tierras (pág. 243)

vernacular the common language of a people (p. 306)

lengua vernácula lengua común de un pueblo (pág. 306)

W

woodblock printing a form of printing in which an entire page is carved into a block of wood, covered with ink, and pressed to a piece of paper to create a printed page (p. 174)

xilogafia forma de impresión en la que una página completa se talla en una plancha de madera, se cubre de tinta y se presiona sobre un papel para crear la página impresa (pág. 174)

X, Y, Z

Zen a form of Buddhism that emphasizes meditation (p. 208)

zen forma del budismo que se basa en la meditación (pág. 208)

Index

INDEX

Rabelais, François, 316
racism, 457
rain forests, 114, 115p, 386
Ramadan fast, 68
Ramayana, 10
Raphael, 307, 307p
rationalism, 273, 498–99; and
democracy, 367f
rationalists, 356, 358
Reading Skills: Understanding Specialized Vocabulary,
4; Finding Main Ideas, 22;
Understanding Chronologi-
cal Order, 2; Understanding
Through Questioning, 78;
Understanding Fact and
Opinion, 128; Drawing
Conclusions, 164; Under-
standing Stereotypes and Bias,
196; Understanding Cause
and Effect Structure, 258;
Understanding the Roots of
Our Language, 296; Evaluating Web-Based Information,
326; Comparing and Con-
trasting, 352; Understanding
Texts by Setting a Purpose,
382; Understanding Propo-
sition and Support, 408;
Understanding Summarizing,
444; Understanding Points of
view, 472
Reading Social Studies, H12–H15
realism, 314, 315p
reason, 273, 367, 438, 474–77,
498–99
Reconquista, 283–84, 283m
Reformation: Enlightenment
thinking and, 476; in modern
times, 332f; results of, 344f;
trial of Galileo, 368; from
without, 328–31
regent, 202
Region, H1
Reign of Terror, 489
relative location, H1
religion: of Aztecs, 418–19;
Buddhism, 168–69, 201f,
203, 208; Catholic Reformation, 334–37; in China, 168;
conflict over in England, 485;
conflict with science, 368–69,
368p; Crusades, 264–68; divi-

sion and wars over, 340–44,
341m; effects of Columbian
Exchange, 456; effects of
Reformation, 340–45; Enlightenment thinking and, 476;
of Europe in Middle Ages,
234–38, 260–61, 262–63,
269–74, 282–85; human-
ism and, 304–5, 310, 314;
of Incas, 429–30; of Japan,
199, 200, 201f, 203, 208; of
Mali, 137–38, 140; of Maya,
396, 397; of medieval Europe
vs. Japan, 250; as motive for
exploration, 446; Protestant
Reformation, 328–31; Scientific Revolution and, 368–69;
similarities in different faiths,
60c; in Songhai Empire, 144;
sources of history of, 12;
unification of cultures, 83; of
West Africa, 117, 150, 151. See
also Buddhism; Christianity;
Islam; Judaism
religious orders, 272, 336
ren, 177
Renaissance, 303–10, 312–17,
475–76; art of 305c, 305p,
307p, 308p
Return of the Hunters (Brueghel the
Elder), 314p
revolution, 484–85
Rhine River, 233p
rice, 171, 171p
Richard I (king of England), 266,
266f
rifts, 112
Rig Veda, 10
rivers, H10p, 232–33; *See also*
Niger River
roads: of Incas, 430, 431m, 431p,
432, 432f–33f; in Mongol
China, 182; solving problems
of, 498p, 499
Robespierre, Maximillen, 489
Roland, 249
Roman Catholic Church: challenges to in Middle Ages, 282–85;
conflict with Protestants,
340–44; Crusades of, 264–68;
missionaries of, 338, 338m–
39m, 338p, 339p, 413; new
orders, 272, 336; Reformation, 328–31, 334–37, 336p,
368–69; science and, 368–69;
in Spain, 334–35

Roman Empire, 25m; after fall
of, 234; architecture of, 12,
20p–21p, 34p; beliefs and
values in, 13; building of, 24;
changing historical views of,
13–14; citizenship in, 25–26;
contributions to civilization,
26–28, 26f, 26p–27p; division of, 31, 31m; emperors of,
25; Enlightenment thinking
and, 475; fall of, 34–35, 35c;
influence of, 24; invasions of,
31–34, 32m; under Justinian,
36–37; legal system, 25–26;
problems of, 30–31; rebirth of
ideas of, 305; spread of Christianity in, 28m; time line of,
34f–35f; use of Silk Road, 299
Rome, 31, 32–33, 34–35, 35p, 36,
270
Romeo and Juliet (William
Shakespeare): excerpt from,
318f–19f
Rosetta Stone, 12
Rousseau, Jean-Jacques, 480,
481p, 487
route map, H9
Rubáiyát, The (Omar Khayyám),
97

S

Safavid Empire, 90–91, 91m
Sahara Desert, 114, 114p, 131
Sahel, 114
Saladin, 266, 267f, 267p
salon, 477
salt: mining of, 115; as motive
for war, 145; as trade item, 83,
119, 131–32, 132p, 143
samurai, 214p, 215f; knights vs.,
248, 249–50, 249p; life of,
212–15; society of, 213f
sand dunes, 56
Santa María (ship), 449
savannah, 114, 115p
Saxons, 32m, 33
scale, H6
Scandinavia, 232, 233p
Schliemann, Heinrich, 14, 14p
scholar-officials, 178–79, 179p,
186
science: acceptance of, 364–66;
achievements of Islamic

INDEX

Credits and Acknowledgments

Acknowledgments

For permission to reprint copyrighted material, grateful acknowledgment is made to the following sources:

Dutton Signet, a division of Penguin (USA) Group Inc.: From *Beowulf*, translated by Burton Raffel. Translation copyright © 1963, renewed copyright © 1991 by Burton Raffel.

Gracewing: From "The Clothing and Footwear of the Brethren" from *The Rule of Saint Benedict* by Saint Benedict, translated by Abbot Parry, OSB, and Esther de Waal. Translation copyright © 1988 by the Estate of Abbot Parry, OSB; introduction copyright © 1995 by Esther de Waal.

Grove Press, Inc.: "Very soon they die-" by Matsuo Basho, translated by Harold G. Henderson and "The breezes of spring" by Ki no Tomonori from *Anthology of Japanese Literature*, compiled and edited by Donald Keene. Copyright © 1955 by Grove Press.

The Hakluyt Society, London: From *The Travels of Ibn Battuta, A.D. 1325–1354*, 2nd ser., no. 110, edited by H. A. R. Gibb. Copyright © 1958 by The Hakluyt Society.

Alfred A. Knopf, a division of Random House, Inc.: From *The Tale of Genji* by Lady Murasaki Shikibu, translated by Edward G. Seidensticker. Copyright © 1976 by Edward G. Seidensticker.

Pearson Education Limited: From *Sundiata: An Epic of Old Mali* by D. T. Diane, translated by G. D. Pickett. Copyright © 1965 by Addison Wesley Longman Ltd.

Penguin Books, Ltd.: "Quiet Night Thoughts" by Li Po from *Li Po and Tu Fu*, translated by Arthur Cooper. Copyright © 1973 by Arthur Cooper. From "The Blood Clots" and "The Merciful" from *The Koran*, translated by N. J. Dawood. Copyright © 1956, 1959, 1966, 1968, 1974 by N. J. Dawood.

Plume, a division of Penguin Group (USA) Inc.: From *Girl with a Pearl Earring* by Tracy Chevalier. Copyright © 1999 by Tracy Chevalier.

Routledge, Ltd.: From *The Pillow-Book of Sei Shōnagon*, translated by Arthur Waley. Copyright 1928 by Arthur Waley.

Simon & Schuster Adult Publishing Group: From *Popol Vuh* by Dennis Tedlock. Copyright © 1985, 1996 by Dennis Tedlock.

Stanford University Press, www.sup.org.: From *The Tale of the Heike*, translated with an introduction, by Helen Craig McCullough. Copyright © 1988 by the Board of Trustees of the Leland Stanford Jr. University. All rights reserved.

Weidenfeld & Nicolson, Ltd.: Excerpt (Retitled "A Knight Speaks") by Rutebeuf from *The Medieval World: Europe 1100–1350* by Friedrich Heer, translated from the German by Janet Sondheimer. Copyright © 1961 by George Weidenfeld and Nicolson Ltd. English translation copyright © 1962 by George Weidenfeld and Nicolson Ltd.

Sources Cited:

Two African proverbs from "African Proverbs - A Collection of My Favorites" from *Princeton Online* web site, accessed October 20, 2004, at http://www.princetonol.com/groups/iad/lessons/middle/af-prov2.htm.

From "Al-Bakri" and "Al-'Umrari" from *Corpus of Early Arabic Sources for West African History*, translated by J. F. P. Hopkins, edited and annotated by N. Levtzion and J. F. P. Hopkins. Published by Cambridge University Press, Cambridge, United Kingdom, 1981.

Illustrations and Photo Credits

Front Matter: Page ins01, © Roger Viollet/Getty Images; ins03, © Roger Viollet/Getty Images; ins05, Copyright British Museum, London; ins06, Dept. of the Environment, London, UK,/Bridgeman Art Library; ins08, The Granger Collection, New York; ins09, Musee des Gobelins, Paris, France, Lauros/The Bridgeman Art Library; vi (l), Justin Kerr, K5174/Kerr Associates; vi (b) Chuck Nacke/Woodfin Camp & Associates; vii, Richard T. Nowitz/National Geographic Image Collection; viii- ix, ©Ali Kazuyoshi Nomachi/Pacific Press Service; ix (c), ©Ali Kazuyoshi Nomachi/Pacific Press Service; ix (r), Bibliotheque Nationale de Cartes et Plans, Paris, France/Bridgeman Art Library; x (b), Rossi Xavier /Gamma Press, Inc.; x (t), Dagli Orti (A)/The Art Archive; xi, PhotoDisc; xii, Dallas and John Heaton/Corbis; xiii (l), © Archivo Iconografico, S.A./CORBIS; xiii (r), Sakamoto Photo Research Laboratory/Corbis; xiv, Scala/Art Resource, NY; xv, Archivo Iconografico, S.A./Corbis; xvi, Ray Manley/SuperStock; xvii, AKG-Images; xviii, ©Justin Kerr, K1453/Kerr Associates; xix (t), Angelo Cavalli/SuperStock; (b), The Trustees Of The British Museum, London; xx, Image courtesy of NASA/Kennedy Space Center; xxi (l), The Granger Collection, New York; (r), Réunion des Musées Nationaux/Art Resource, NY; xxv, Archivo Iconografico, S.A./CORBIS; H11 (t) © Daily News Pix; (c) © Robert Maass/CORBIS; (bl) © Randy Wells/CORBIS; (br) © Glen Allison/Getty Images.

Unit One, Chapter 1: 2–3, Alexis Rosenfeld/Science Photo Library/Photo Researchers, Inc.; 7(tl), Ancient Art & Architecture Collection Ltd/ Topham/The Image Works/The Image Works, Inc.;7 (tr), Justin Kerr/Kerr Associates; 7(c), Pascal Goetgheluck/Science Photo Library/Photo Researchers, Inc.; 8, Chuck Nacke/Woodfin Camp & Associates; ; 9, O. Louis Mazzatenta/National Geographic Image Collection;11(cr), White Star S.R.L.; 11(tl), Douglas Mason/Woodfin Camp & Associates; 13, Gaillarde Raphael/Ministere de la Culture/Draclyo/Gamma Press, Inc.; 14(tl), Bettmann/Corbis; 14(t), Yann Arthus-Bertrand/ CORBIS; 19, Gianni Dagli Orti/Corbis; **Chapter 2:** 20–21, Richard T. Nowitz/National Geographic Image Collection; 20(br), AKG-Images; 21(cl), Bildarchiv Preussischer Kulturbesitz/Art Resource, NY; 21(cr), Haghia Sophia Istanbul/Dagli Orti/Art Archive; 24, SuperStock; 26(cr), PRISMA/Ancient Art & Architecture Collection Ltd.; 26(br), Joseph Sohm/The Image Works; 27 l, SEF/Art Resource, NY; 27(br), Andrew McKinney/Ambient Images; 27(cr), SIME s.a.s/eStock Photo; 29, Scala/Art Resource, NY; 34(tl), Scala/Art Resource, NY; 34(tr), Scala/Art Resource, NY; 35(tl), Erich Lessing/Art Resource, NY; 35(tc), Carolyn Brown/Image Bank/Getty Images; 41(br), Danny Lehman/CORBIS.

Unit Two, Chapter 3: 50–51, Ali Kazuyoshi Nomachi/Pacific Press Service; 50(br), Scala/Art Resource, NY; 51(cl), Fitzwilliam Museum, University of Cambridge, UK/Bridgeman Art Library; 51(bl), Bettmann/CORBIS; 51(br), RÇunion des MusÇes Nationaux/Art Resource, NY; 54(cl), Peter Ginter/Bilderberg/Peter Arnold, Inc.; 58, Sergio Pitamitz/Alamy Images; 60(tl), Topham/The Image Works, Inc.; 60(tc), AKG-Images; 60(tr), Art Directors & TRIP Photo Library; 60(c), Murat Ayranci/SuperStock; 62(bl), Fitzwilliam Museum, University of Cambridge, UK/Bridgeman Art Library; 64(t), Ali Kazuyoshi Nomachi/Pacific Press Service; 65(bl), Christine Osborne/CORBIS; 65(bc), John and Lisa Merrill/CORBIS; 67(tl), Ali Kazuyoshi Nomachi/Pacific Press Service; 71, Hazem Palace Damascus/Dagli Orti/The Art Archive; **Chapter 4:** 76–77, Peter Marlow/Magnum Photos; 77(c), Burt Silverman/National Geographic Image Collection; 77(bl), Bettmann/CORBIS; 77(bc), Army Museum Madrid/Dagli Orti/Art Archive; 83, Mary Evans Picture Library; 84(tr), Ian Dagnall/Alamy Images; 84(t), Vanni Archive/ CORBIS; 86(br), Kamran Jebreili/AP/Wide World Photos; 86(tr), EPA/Mike Nelson/AP/Wide World Photos; 87(tr), Vahed Salemi/AP/Wide World Photos; 87(cl), EPA/Mike Nelson/AP/Wide World Photos; 89, The Granger Collection, New York; 92, Hilarie Kavanagh/Stone/Getty Images; 94(bl), Bibliotheque Nationale de Cartes et Plans, Paris, France/Bridgeman Art Library; 94(br), R & S Michaud/Woodfin Camp & Associates; 95(br), The Granger Collection, New York; 96, R & S Michaud/Woodfin Camp & Associates; 97, Archivo Iconografico, S.A./Corbis; 98(tl), Helene Rogers/Art Directors & TRIP Photo Library; 98(tr), Art Directors & TRIP Photo Library; 98(cl), Robert Frerck/Odyssey/Chicago.

Unit Three, Chapter 5: 108–109, Rossi Xavier/ Gamma Press, Inc.; 108(cr), Andoni Canela/ ASA/Aurora Photos; 109(bc), Werner Forman/Art Resource, NY; 109(br), Erich Lessing/Art Resource, NY; 114(tr), Frans Lemmens/Photographer's Choice; 115(tl), Nicholas Parfitt/Stone/Getty Images; 115(tr), Gary Cook/Alamy Images; 117(tl), Robert Frerck/Odyssey/Chicago; 118, Colasanti/TravelSite; 120(cl, br), Dagli Orti (A)/ The Art Archive; 120(tr), Nik Wheeler/CORBIS; 120(bl), Aldo Tutino/Art Resource, NY; 121(cr), Reza; Webistan/CORBIS; 121(tr), HIP/Scala/Art Resource, NY; **Chapter 6:** 126–127, PhotoDisc; 126(br), Bob Burch/Index Stock Imagery; 127(cl), Erich Lessing/Art Resource, NY; 127(bc), Werner Forman/Art Resource, NY; 127(bl), The Art Archive; 127(br), Trustees of the British Museum, London; 131(tr), Dr. Roderick McIntosh; 132, John Elk III Photography; 133(cl), Carol Beckwith&Angela Fisher/HAGA/The Image Works, Inc.; 135, Steve McCurry/Magnum Photos; 137(tr), Private Collection, Credit: Heini Schneebeli/ Bridgeman Art Library; 141(br), The Granger Collection, New York; 143(cr), Trustees of The British Museum, London; 144, Sandro Vannini/ Corbis; 148, Pascal Meunier/Cosmos/Aurora Photos; 150(br), AFP/Getty Images; 150(bc), Reuters/Corbis; 151, Penny Tweedie/Corbis;153, The Newark Museum/Art Resource, NY.

Unit Four, Chapter 7: 162–163, Dallas and John Heaton/Corbis; 162(br), Art Directors & TRIP Photo Library;163(c), National Palace Museum, Taipei, Taiwan/Bridgeman Art Library; 163(cr), Freelance Consulting Services Pty Ltd/Corbis; 163(bc), Sekai Bunka Photo/Ancient Art & Architecture Collection, Ltd.;163(br), G K & Vikki Hart/PhotoDisc; 170(b), Keren Su/China Span; 171(cr), Keren Su/Corbis; 172(b), Carl & Ann Purcell/Corbis; 173(c), Ric Ergenbright/Corbis; 174(bl), Liu Liqun/Corbis; 174(cl), China Photo/ Reuters/Corbis; 174(tl), Paul Freeman/Private Collection/Bridgeman Art Library; 175(tr), Tom Stewart/CORBIS; 175(tc), Private Collection/ Bridgeman Art Library; 176, Traditionally attributed to: Yan Liben, Chinese, died in 673. Northern Qi Scholar's Collating Classic Texts (detail), Chinese, Northern Song dynasty, 11th century. Object place: China. Ink and color on silk. 27.6 x 114 cm (10 7/8 x 44 7/8 in.), Museum of Fine Arts, Boston; 178(tc), Snark/Art Resource, NY; 187(br), National Palace Museum, Taipei, Taiwan/Bridgeman Art Library; 188–189, Keren Su/CORBIS; 193, Peter Harholdt/CORBIS; **Chapter 8:** 194–195, Spectrum Colour Library; 194(br), Royalty Free/Corbis;195(cr), National Museum, Tokyo/A.K.G., Berlin/SuperStock;195 (bl), The Art Archive; 195(bc), Detail), Bibliotheque Nationale, Paris, France/Bridgeman Art Library; 195(br), Erich Lessing/Art Resource, NY; 200, Rijksmuseum voor Volkenkunde Leiden (Leyden)/Dagli Orti/Art Archive; 201(bl), Ronald Sheridan/Ancient Art & Architecture Collection, Ltd.; 201(bc), The Granger Collection, New York; 201(br), Royalty Free/CORBIS; 202(cr), Bettmann/ Corbis; 202(b), Kenneth Hamm/Photo Japan; 203, Art Directors & TRIP Photo Library; 205, (Detail) Musee des Beaux-Arts, Angers, France/ Giraudon/Bridgeman Art Library; 206, Archivo Iconografico, S.A./CORBIS; 207(c), Burstein

CREDITS AND ACKNOWLEDGMENTS

Collection/Corbis; 207(bl), Sakamoto Photo Research Laboratory/Corbis; 208, Catherine Karnow/Corbis; 209(br), Sekai Bunka Photo/ Ancient Art & Architecture Collection, Ltd.; 211, Private Collection/Dagli Orti/The Art Archive; 214(cl), Roger Viollet/Getty Images; 214(bc), Fitzwilliam Museum, University of Cambridge, UK/Bridgeman Art Library; 215(br), Gunshots/Art Archive; 215(bc), Kenneth Hamm/Photo Japan.

Unit Five, Chapter 9: 226–227, Robert Harding Picture Library; 226(br), The Crosiers/Gene Plaisted, OSC; 227(c), SuperStock; 227(bl), The Granger Collection, New York; 227(bc), Art Archive; 232, Vittoriano Rastelli/Corbis; 232(tl), Stephen Studd/Stone/Getty Images; 233(tr), Stefano Scata/Getty Images; 235, The Crosiers/Gene Plaisted, OSC; 238(tr), North Wind Picture Archives; 239(br), Scala/Art Resource, NY; 240, Snark/Art Resource, NY; 241, The Art Archive/Prehistoric Museum Moesgard Hojbjerg Denmark/Dagli Orti; 247, Bibliotheque Nationale, Paris, France/Bridgeman Art Library; 249(tl), Sakamoto Photo Research Library/Corbis; 249(tr), Alinari/Art Resource, NY; 250(br), Freer Gallery of Art, Smithsonian Institution, Washington D.C. Purchase, F1963.5/ Freer Gallery of Art and the Arthur M Sackler Gallery of Art/Smithsonian; **Chapter 10:** 256–257 Archiv Iconografico, S.A./Corbis; 256 (br), The British Museum/HIP/Topham/The Image Works, Inc.; 257(cl), The British Library/Topham-HIP/ The Image Works, Inc.; 257(cr), G K & Vikki Hart/PhotoDisc; 257(bc), ChinaStock; 261(b), Elio Ciol/CORBIS; 261(cr), Erich Lessing/Art Resource, NY; 262(tr), Hulton Archive/Getty Images; 262(tl), Hulton Archive/Getty Images; 265(t), Archivo Iconografico, S.A./CORBIS; 266, Mary Evans Picture Library; 267(tr), Galleria degli Uffizi Florence/Dagli Orti/Art Archive; 269, Ben Mangor/SuperStock; 273(tr), Archivo Iconografico, S.A./CORBIS; 273(c), Jim Cummins/ Corbis; 274(tl), Vanni/Art Resource, NY; 274(tr), Erich Lessing/Art Resource, NY; 275(tr), Gjon Mili//Time Life Pictures/Getty Images Editorial; 276, Ancient Art & Architecture Collection, Ltd.; 277(t), Dept. of the Environment, London, UK/ Bridgeman Art Library; 278(cl), Bettmann/Corbis; 278(tr), The Granger Collection, New York; 278 (c), Wolfgang Kaehler/Corbis; 285, Scala/Art Resource, NY.

Unit Six, Chapter 11: 294–295, Ray Manley/ SuperStock; 294(br), Giraudon/Art Resource, NY; 295(cl), North Wind Picture Archives; 295(cr), SuperStock; 295(bl), RÇunion des MusÇes Nationaux/Art Resource, NY; 295(br), Werner Forman/Art Resource, NY; 299(bl), The Granger Collection, New York; 299(tr), SuperStock; 300(b), Massimo Piacentino/ Sylvia Cordaiy Photo Library Ltd./Alamy Images; 300(cr), Ted Spiegel/Corbis; 301(cr), Yann Arthus-Bertrand/ CORBIS; 305(bl), Alinari/Art Resource, NY; 305(br), San Pietro in Vincoli, Rome, Italy/Mauro Magliani/SuperStock; 306(t), Erich Lessing/Art Resource, NY; 307(cr), Scala/Art Resource, NY; 307(bc), Scala/Art Resource, NY; 308(cl), The Granger Collection, New York; 308(tl), Bettmann/CORBIS; 308(t), Scala/Art Resource, NY; 308(cr), Gianni Dagli Orti/Corbis; 311(br), Scala/Art Resource, NY; 312(bl), The Bodleian Library, Oxford/Art Archive; 313(bl), The Granger Collection, New York; 314(b), Erich Lessing/Art Resource, NY; 315(cr), Scala/Art Resource, NY; 316, Bettmann/CORBIS; 317, National Portrait Gallery, London/SuperStock; 319, AKG-Images; **Chapter 12:** 324–325, James L. Amos/Corbis; 324(br), SEF/Art Resource, NY; 325(cl), Scala/Art

Resource, NY; 325(cr), AKG-Images; 325(bl), Dorling Kindersley Ltd. Picture Library; 325(br), G. Tortoli/Ancient Art & Architecture Collection, Ltd.; 329(tl, br), AKG-Images; 330(br), Scala/Art Resource, NY; 330(bl), AKG-Images; 332(tr), AP/Wide World Photos; 332(tc), Liaison/Getty Images; 335, Snark/Art Resource, NY; 336(tl), Scala/Art Resource, NY; 336(tc), Centro Mericiano Brescia / Dagli Orti/Art Archive; 336(tc), RÇunion des MusÇes Nationaux/Art Resource, NY; 337(tr), Archivo Iconografico, S.A./Corbis; 338(tr), David Muench/Corbis; 339(tc), Art Resource, NY; 339(cr), Museu do Caramulo, Portugal/Bridgeman Art Library; 342(bl), AKG-Images; 342(br), The Granger Collection, New York; 343(bl), Erich Lessing/Art Resource, NY; 343(tr), Erich Lessing/ Art Resource, NY; 344, Erich Lessing/Art Resource, NY; **Chapter 13:** 350–351, Bill Ross/Corbis; 350(cr), The Stocktrek Corp/Brand X Pictures/Alamy Images; 350(br), Fundacion Miguel Mujica Gallo, Museo do Oro del Peru; 351(cl), Royal Society, London, UK/Bridgeman Art Library; 351(cr), Galleria degli Uffizi Florence/ Dagli Orti (A)/Art Archive; 351(bl), Burstein Collection/CORBIS; 351(bc), Hilarie Kavanagh/Stone/Getty Images; 355, Erich Lessing/Art Resource, NY; 356(tr), The Granger Collection, New York; 357(tl), Rabatti- Domingie/akg-images; 357(tr), Biblioteca Nazionale Marciana Venice / Dagli Orti (A)/Art Archive; 358(bl), The Granger Collection, New York; 363, Science Museum, London/Topham-HIP/The Image Works, Inc.; 365(tl), Sotheby's/ akg-images; 365(tr), Erich Lessing/Art Resource, NY; 366, Sam Dudgeon/HRW; 368, RÇunion des MusÇes Nationaux/Art Resource, NY; 369(tl), Scala/Art Resource, NY.

Unit Seven, Chapter 14: 380–381, David Hiser/ Stone/Getty Images; 381(cl), Burke/Triolo Productions/Foodpix; 381(c), Erich Lessing/Art Resource, NY; 381(bl), Dagli Orti/Art Archive; 381(bc), Gianni Dagli Orti/Corbis; 387(tr), Stephanie Maze/Corbis; 388(cr), Richard Brunck./ Mary Ellen Deland Pohl, Ph.D.; 391(bl), Justin Kerr, K4809/Kerr Associates; 391(br), Erich Lessing/Art Resource, NY; 391(cr), Kimberly White/Reuters/Corbis; 393(cr), Scala/Art Resource, NY; 395(b), Justin Kerr, K4806/Kerr Associates; 396(b), Justin Kerr, K1453/Kerr Associates; 398(bl), Robert Frerck/Odyssey Productions, Chicago; 399(tr), The Trustees Of The British Museum, London; **Chapter 15:** 406–407, Angelo Cavalli/SuperStock; 406(cr), The Trustees Of The British Museum, London; 406(br), British Library/Art Archive; 407(cl), Werner Forman/ Art Resource, NY; 407(cr), Fundacion Miguel Mujica Gallo, Museo do Oro del Peru; 407(bc), Freer Gallery of Art, Smithsonian Institution, Washington D.C., Purchase F1932.28/Freer Gallery of Art and the Arthur M Sackler Gallery of Art/Smithsonian; 411(tr), Mexican National Museum, Mexico City 9–2256/D.Donne Bryant/ DDB Stock Photography; 413(br), Archivo Iconografico, S.A./Corbis; 413(bl), Academia BB AA S Fernando Madrid/Dagli Orti/Art Archive; 415(br), Bettmann/Corbis; 416(bl), The Granger Collection, New York; 416(br), Art Directors & TRIP Photo Library; 417(bl, bc), The Granger Collection, New York; 417(br), Bettmann/CORBIS; 418(bl), Antochiw Collection Mexico/Mireille Vautier/Art Archive; 418(bc), Bettmann/CORBIS; 418(bl), Biblioteca Medicea-Laurenziana, Florence, Italy/Bridgeman Art Library; 419(br), Banco Mexicano de Imagenes/ INAH/Bridgeman Art Library; 419(tr), Museo del Templo Mayor Mexico/Dagli Orti/Art Archive; 420(tl, cr), Trustees of the British Museum,

London; 421(tr), David Sanger Photography; 422(b, Robert Frerck/Odyssey/Chicago; 423(tr), New York Historical Society, New York/Bridgeman Art Library; 424(tc), The Granger Collection, New York; 424(tr), Sam Dudgeon/HRW; 425(bl), Museo Pedro de Osma Lima/Mireille Vautier/Art Archive; 425(br), MusÇe du ChÊteau de Versailles /Dagli Orti/Art Archive; 426, Victoria & Albert Museum, London/Art Resource, NY; 428, Robert Giusti/National Geographic Image Collection; 430(tl), American Museum of Natural History, New York/Bridgeman Art Library; 430(tr), Stuart Franklin/Magnum Photos; 431(tl), Museo del Banco Central del Ecuador-Quito. 0–19224/D. Donne Bryant/DDB Stock Photography; 433(cr), Kevin Schafer/CORBIS.

Unit Eight, Chapter 16: 442–443, Image courtesy of NASA/Kennedy Space Center; 442(br), National Maritime Museum; 443(bc), RÇunion des MusÇes Nationaux/Art Resource, NY; 443(bl), Werner Forman/Art Resource, NY; 443(br), Dave Jacobs/Index Stock Imagery; 450, SuperStock; 452–453, Royalty Free/CORBIS; 452(br), The Stapleton Collection/Bridgeman Art Library; 453(tr), Royalty Free/CORBIS; 453(br), The Granger Collection, New York; 456, Victoria Smith/HRW; 457, Giovanna Paponetti ; 465, Scala/Art Resource, NY; **Chapter 17:** 470–471, Phil Degginger/Alamy Images; 471(cl), Philip Mould, Historical Portraits Ltd, London, UK/Bridgeman Art Library; 471(c), Tate Gallery, London/Art Resource, NY; 471(cr), Explorer, Paris/SuperStock; 471(bl), Burstein Collection/CORBIS; 471(bc), David Muench/Corbis; 475, Scala/Art Resource, NY; 479(tl), National Portrait Gallery, London/ SuperStock; 479(cl), Alexander Burkatovski/ Corbis; 479(tr), Erich Lessing/Art Resource, NY; 480(l), The Granger Collection, New York; 480(r), Stefano Bianchetti/Corbis; 481, RÇunion des MusÇes Nationaux/Art Resource, NY; 482, The Granger Collection, New York; 483(bc), Archivo Iconografico, S.A./Corbis; 485, Metropolitan Museum of Art, New York/Bridgeman Art Library; 486(cl), Bettmann/CORBIS; 486(bl), Dept. of the Environment, London, UK/Bridgeman Art Library; 486(cr), The Granger Collection, New York; 486(br), Custody of the House of Lords Record Office/Parliamentary Archives; 487(cl), Bettmann/Corbis; 487(bl), Joseph Sohm; Visions of America/Corbis; 487(cr), RÇunion des MusÇes Nationaux/Art Resource, NY; 487(br), Document conservÇ au Centre historique des Archives nationales Ö Paris/Centre historique des Archives nationales (CHAN); 488, AKG-Images; **Chapter 18:** 496(cr), Panoramic Images; 497(tr), David Paul Morris/Getty Images; 498(b), Harvey Schwartz/ Index Stock Imagery 499(cr), David Longstreath/ AP/Wide World Photos; 499(br), Mary Altaffer/ AP/Wide World Photos.

Back Matter: Pages R0-R1, Spectrum Colour Library; R42 (l), Gianni Dagli Orti/Corbis; (c), ©HIP/Scala/ Art Resource, NY; (r), ©Scala/Art Resource, NY; R43 (t), ©Musée Cernuschi Paris / Dagli Orti/Art Archive; (b), ©National Archaeological Museum Athens / Dagli Orti/Art Archive; (r), ©Timothy McCarthy/Art Resource, NY; R44 (l), The Art Archive; (r), Private Collection, Credit: Heini Schneebeli/Bridgeman Art Library; R45 (t), Gianni Dagli Orti/Corbis; (bl), National Maritime Museum; (r), Hilarie Kavanagh/ Stone/Getty Images; R46 (tr), Snark/Art Resource, NY; (bl), Hulton-Deutsch Collection// CORBIS; (br), SuperStock; R47 (tl), HRW Photo Research Library; (tr), Robert Maas/CORBIS; (bl), Sovfoto/Eastfoto; (br), Beth A. Keiser/AP/Wide World Photos.

Staff Credits

The people who contributed to *Holt California Social Studies: World History, Medieval to Early Modern Times* are listed below. They represent editorial, design, intellectual property resources, production, emedia, and permissions.

Lissa B. Anderson, Melanie Baccus, Charles Becker, Jessica Bega, Ed Blake, Gillian Brody, Shirley Cantrell, Erin Cornett, Rose Degollado, Chase Edmond, Mescal Evler, Rhonda Fariss, Marsh Flournoy, Leanna Ford, Bob Fullilove, Matthew Gierhart, Janet Harrington, Rhonda Haynes, Rob Hrechko, Wilonda Ieans, Cathy Jenevein, Kadonna Knape, Cathy Kuhles, Debbie Lofland, Bob McClellan, Joe Melomo, Richard Metzger, Andrew Miles, Cynthia Munoz, Karl Pallmeyer, Chanda Pearmon, Jarred Prejean, Shelly Ramos, Désirée Reid, Curtis Riker, Marleis Roberts, Diana Rodriguez, Gene Rumann, Annette Saunders, Jenny Schaeffer, Kay Selke, Ken Shepardson, Michele Shukers, Chris Smith, Christine Stanford, Elaine Tate, Jeannie Taylor, Joni Wackwitz, Ken Whiteside